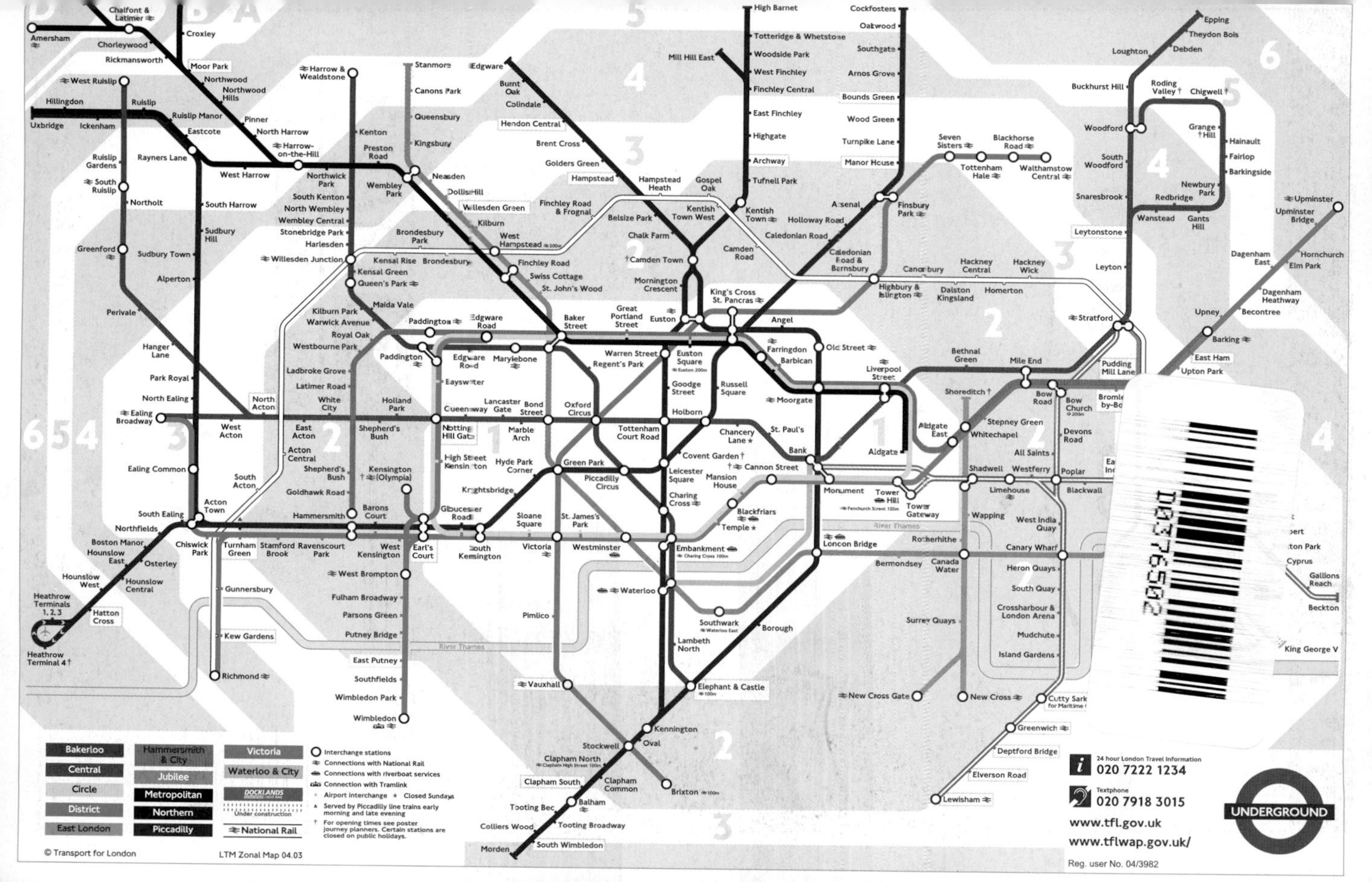
Amersham
Chalfont & Latimer
Chorleywood
Rickmansworth
Croxley
Moor Park
Northwood
Northwood Hills
Pinner
North Harrow
Harrow-on-the-Hill
West Ruislip
Hillingdon
Uxbridge
Ickenham
Ruislip
Ruislip Manor
Eastcote
Rayners Lane
Ruislip Gardens
South Ruislip
Northolt
Greenford
Perivale
Hanger Lane
Park Royal
North Ealing
Ealing Broadway
Ealing Common
West Harrow
South Harrow
Sudbury Hill
Sudbury Town
Alperton
Harrow & Wealdstone
Kenton
Preston Road
Northwick Park
South Kenton
North Wembley
Wembley Central
Stonebridge Park
Harlesden
Willesden Junction
Wembley Park
Stanmore
Canons Park
Queensbury
Kingsbury
Neasden
Dollis Hill
Willesden Green
Kilburn
West Hampstead
Brondesbury Park
Brondesbury
Kensal Rise
Kensal Green
Queen's Park
Maida Vale
Kilburn Park
Warwick Avenue
Royal Oak
Westbourne Park
Ladbroke Grove
Latimer Road
White City
North Acton
West Acton
East Acton
Acton Central
South Acton
Acton Town
South Ealing
Northfields
Boston Manor
Hounslow East
Osterley
Hounslow West
Hounslow Central
Hatton Cross
Heathrow Terminals 1, 2, 3
Heathrow Terminal 4
Chiswick Park
Turnham Green
Stamford Brook
Ravenscourt Park
Gunnersbury
Kew Gardens
Richmond
Edgware
Burnt Oak
Colindale
Hendon Central
Brent Cross
Golders Green
Hampstead
Finchley Road & Frognal
Belsize Park
Chalk Farm
Hampstead Heath
Gospel Oak
Kentish Town West
Camden Road
Camden Town
Mornington Crescent
Finchley Road
Swiss Cottage
St. John's Wood
Paddington
Edgware Road
Baker Street
Great Portland Street
Euston
Marylebone
Edgware Road
Bayswater
Queensway
Lancaster Gate
Notting Hill Gate
Holland Park
Shepherd's Bush
Shepherd's Bush
Kensington (Olympia)
Goldhawk Road
Hammersmith
Barons Court
West Kensington
Earl's Court
West Brompton
Fulham Broadway
Parsons Green
Putney Bridge
East Putney
Southfields
Wimbledon Park
Wimbledon
High Street Kensington
Gloucester Road
South Kensington
Knightsbridge
Hyde Park Corner
Marble Arch
Bond Street
Oxford Circus
Regent's Park
Warren Street
Euston Square
Goodge Street
Tottenham Court Road
Green Park
Piccadilly Circus
Sloane Square
Victoria
St. James's Park
Westminster
Pimlico
Vauxhall
Leicester Square
Covent Garden
Charing Cross
Embankment
Waterloo
Lambeth North
Southwark
Blackfriars
Temple
Mansion House
Cannon Street
Chancery Lane
Holborn
Russell Square
King's Cross St. Pancras
Angel
Farringdon
Barbican
Moorgate
St. Paul's
Bank
Old Street
Liverpool Street
Aldgate
Monument
Tower Hill
Tower Gateway
London Bridge
Borough
Elephant & Castle
Kennington
Oval
Stockwell
Brixton
Clapham North
Clapham Common
Clapham South
Balham
Tooting Bec
Tooting Broadway
Colliers Wood
South Wimbledon
Morden
High Barnet
Totteridge & Whetstone
Woodside Park
Mill Hill East
West Finchley
Finchley Central
East Finchley
Highgate
Archway
Tufnell Park
Kentish Town
Holloway Road
Caledonian Road
Caledonian Road & Barnsbury
Arsenal
Finsbury Park
Manor House
Turnpike Lane
Wood Green
Bounds Green
Arnos Grove
Southgate
Oakwood
Cockfosters
Seven Sisters
Tottenham Hale
Blackhorse Road
Walthamstow Central
Highbury & Islington
Canonbury
Dalston Kingsland
Hackney Central
Hackney Wick
Homerton
Bethnal Green
Mile End
Stratford
Shoreditch
Aldgate East
Whitechapel
Stepney Green
Shadwell
Wapping
Rotherhithe
Canada Water
Bermondsey
Surrey Quays
New Cross Gate
New Cross
Limehouse
Westferry
Poplar
All Saints
Devons Road
Bow Road
Bow Church
Pudding Mill Lane
West India Quay
Canary Wharf
Heron Quays
South Quay
Crossharbour & London Arena
Mudchute
Island Gardens
Cutty Sark for Maritime Greenwich
Greenwich
Deptford Bridge
Elverson Road
Lewisham
Blackwall
Cyprus
Gallions Reach
Beckton
King George V
Epping
Theydon Bois
Debden
Loughton
Buckhurst Hill
Roding Valley
Chigwell
Grange Hill
Hainault
Fairlop
Barkingside
Woodford
South Woodford
Snaresbrook
Newbury Park
Redbridge
Gants Hill
Wanstead
Leytonstone
Leyton
Upminster
Upminster Bridge
Hornchurch
Elm Park
Dagenham East
Dagenham Heathway
Becontree
Upney
Barking
East Ham
Upton Park
River Thames
Bakerloo
Central
Circle
District
East London
Hammersmith & City
Jubilee
Metropolitan
Northern
Piccadilly
Victoria
Waterloo & City
DOCKLANDS
Under construction
National Rail
Interchange stations
Connections with National Rail
Connections with riverboat services
Connection with Tramlink
Airport interchange
Closed Sundays
Served by Piccadilly line trains early morning and late evening
For opening times see poster journey planners. Certain stations are closed on public holidays.
© Transport for London
LTM Zonal Map 04.03
24 hour London Travel Information
020 7222 1234
Textphone
020 7918 3015
www.tfl.gov.uk
www.tflwap.gov.uk/
Reg. user No. 04/3982
UNDERGROUND
D0376502

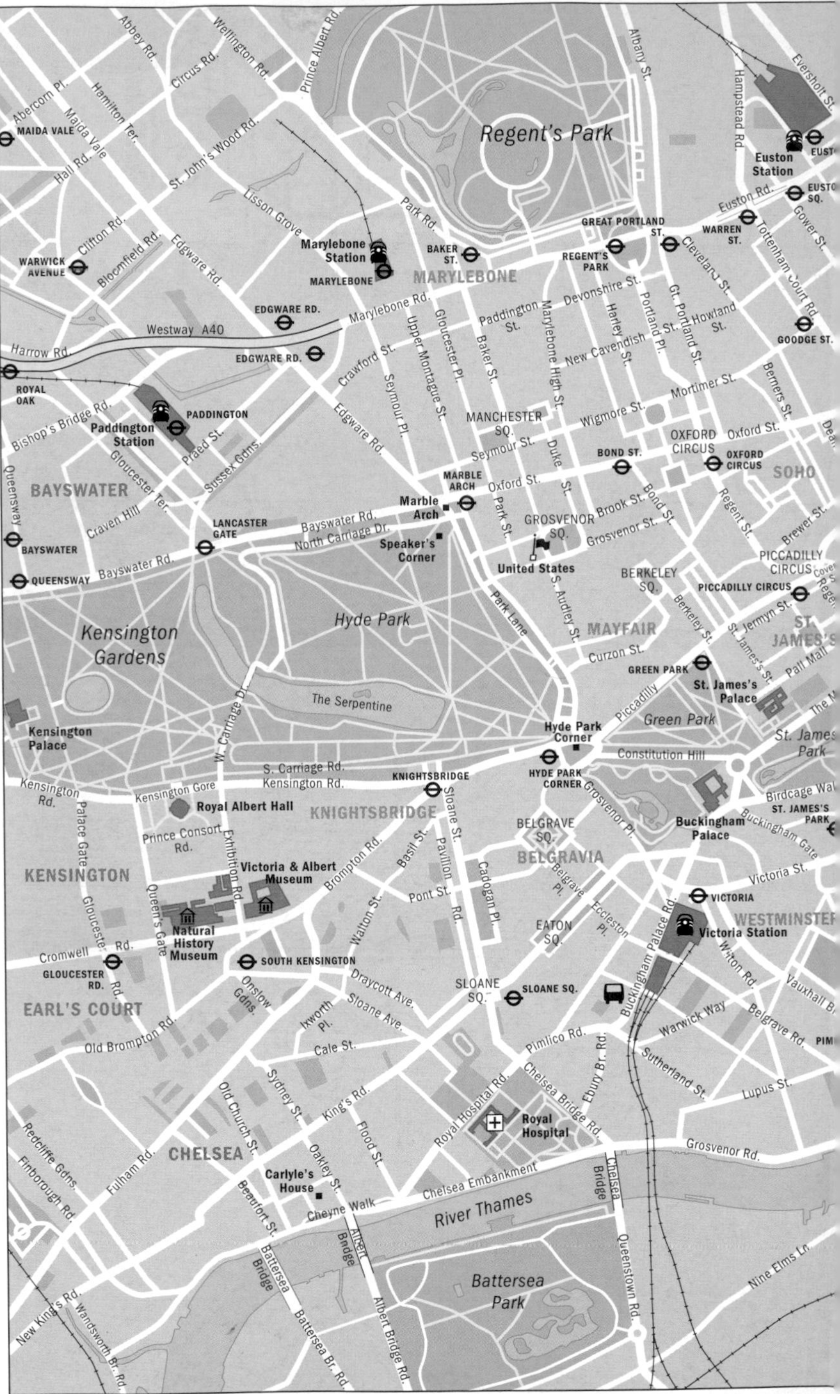

Abbey Rd.
Wellington Rd.
Prince Albert Rd.
Circus Rd.
Abercorn Pl.
Hamilton Ter.
Maida Vale
MAIDA VALE
Hall Rd.
St. John's Wood Rd.
Lisson Grove
Regent's Park
Albany St.
Hampstead Rd.
Eversholt St.
Euston Station
Euston Rd.
EUSTON SQ.
Gower St.
Park Rd.
Clifton Rd.
Bloomfield Rd.
Edgware Rd.
WARWICK AVENUE
Marylebone Station
MARYLEBONE
BAKER ST.
MARYLEBONE
GREAT PORTLAND ST.
REGENT'S PARK
WARREN ST.
Tottenham Court Rd.
Cleveland St.
Devonshire St.
EDGWARE RD.
Marylebone Rd.
Upper Montague St.
Gloucester Pl.
Paddington St.
Baker St.
Marylebone High St.
Harley St.
Portland Pl.
Gt. Portland St.
Howland St.
GOODGE ST.
Westway A40
Harrow Rd.
EDGWARE RD.
Crawford St.
Seymour Pl.
New Cavendish St.
ROYAL OAK
PADDINGTON
Paddington Station
Bishop's Bridge Rd.
Praed St.
Sussex Gdns.
Edgware Rd.
MANCHESTER SQ.
Wigmore St.
Mortimer St.
Berners St.
Seymour St.
Duke St.
BOND ST.
OXFORD CIRCUS
Oxford St.
OXFORD CIRCUS
SOHO
Queensway
Gloucester Ter.
BAYSWATER
Craven Hill
MARBLE ARCH
Oxford St.
Marble Arch
Park St.
GROSVENOR SQ.
Brook St.
Bond St.
Regent St.
Brewer St.
LANCASTER GATE
Bayswater Rd.
North Carriage Dr.
Speaker's Corner
Grosvenor St.
BAYSWATER
United States
BERKELEY SQ.
PICCADILLY CIRCUS
QUEENSWAY
Bayswater Rd.
PICCADILLY CIRCUS
Jermyn St.
Hyde Park
Park Lane
S. Audley St.
MAYFAIR
Berkeley St.
St. James's St.
ST. JAMES'S
Kensington Gardens
Curzon St.
GREEN PARK
Pall Mall
St. James's Palace
The Serpentine
Piccadilly
Green Park
W. Carriage Dr.
Hyde Park Corner
Kensington Palace
St. James's Park
Constitution Hill
HYDE PARK CORNER
S. Carriage Rd.
Kensington Rd.
KNIGHTSBRIDGE
Kensington Rd.
Kensington Gore
Royal Albert Hall
Sloane St.
Grosvenor Pl.
Birdcage Walk
ST. JAMES'S PARK
KNIGHTSBRIDGE
BELGRAVE SQ.
Buckingham Palace
Buckingham Gate
Palace Gate
Prince Consort Rd.
Basil St.
Pavilion Rd.
BELGRAVIA
KENSINGTON
Exhibition Rd.
Brompton Rd.
Victoria & Albert Museum
Belgrave Pl.
Victoria St.
Cadogan Pl.
Gloucester Rd.
Queen's Gate
Walton St.
Pont St.
Eccleston Pl.
VICTORIA
Natural History Museum
EATON SQ.
WESTMINSTER
Victoria Station
Cromwell Rd.
GLOUCESTER RD.
SOUTH KENSINGTON
Buckingham Palace Rd.
Wilton Rd.
Draycott Ave.
Vauxhall Br.
EARL'S COURT
Onslow Gdns.
Ixworth Pl.
Sloane Ave.
SLOANE SQ.
SLOANE SQ.
Warwick Way
Belgrave Rd.
Old Brompton Rd.
Cale St.
Pimlico Rd.
Ebury Br. Rd.
Sutherland St.
Sydney St.
Old Church St.
Chelsea Bridge Rd.
Lupus St.
King's Rd.
Royal Hospital Rd.
Royal Hospital
Flood St.
Oakley St.
Redcliffe Gdns.
Finborough Rd.
Fulham Rd.
CHELSEA
Grosvenor Rd.
Chelsea Embankment
Chelsea Bridge
Carlyle's House
Beaufort St.
Cheyne Walk
River Thames
Albert Bridge
Battersea Bridge
Queenstown Rd.
Nine Elms Ln.
Battersea Park
New King's Rd.
Wandsworth Br. Rd.
Battersea Br. Rd.
Albert Bridge Rd.

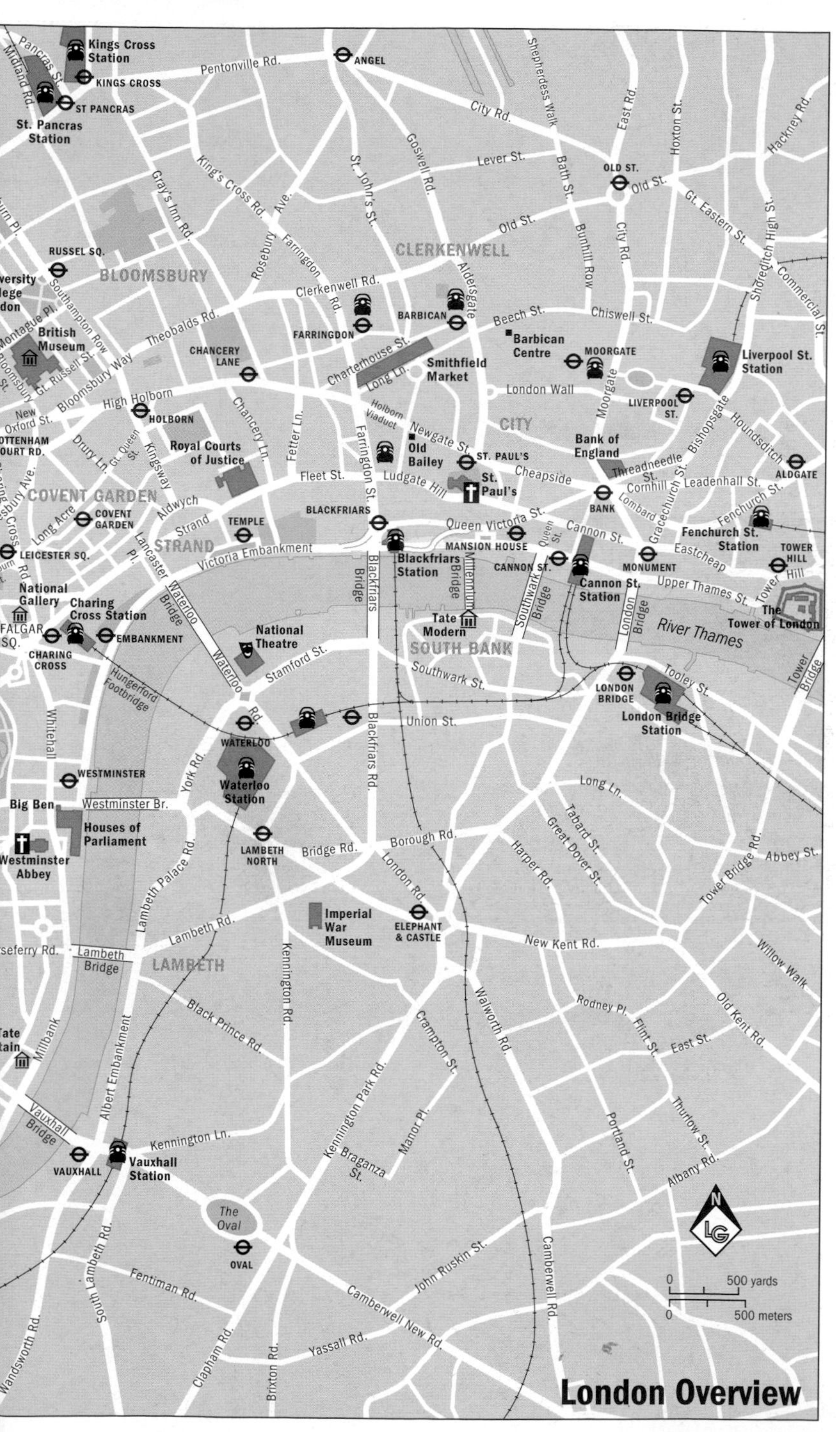

Kings Cross Station
KINGS CROSS
ST PANCRAS
St. Pancras Station
Pancras St.
Midland Rd.
Pentonville Rd.
ANGEL
City Rd.
Shepherdess Walk
East Rd.
Hoxton St.
Hackney Rd.
Goswell Rd.
St. John's St.
Lever St.
Bath St.
OLD ST.
Old St.
Gt. Eastern St.
King's Cross Rd.
Gray's Inn Rd.
Rosebury Ave.
Farringdon Rd.
CLERKENWELL
Bunhill Row
City Rd.
Shoreditch High St.
Commercial St.
RUSSEL SQ.
BLOOMSBURY
Southampton Row
Clerkenwell Rd.
Aldersgate
Chiswell St.
BARBICAN
FARRINGDON
Beech St.
Barbican Centre
Theobalds Rd.
Montague Pl.
British Museum
Bloomsbury St.
Gt. Russell St.
Bloomsbury Way
CHANCERY LANE
Charterhouse St.
Long Ln.
Smithfield Market
MOORGATE
Liverpool St. Station
London Wall
LIVERPOOL ST.
New Oxford St.
High Holborn
HOLBORN
TOTTENHAM COURT RD.
Drury Ln.
Gt. Queen St.
Kingsway
Royal Courts of Justice
Chancery Ln.
Fetter Ln.
Holborn Viaduct
Newgate St.
Old Bailey
ST. PAUL'S
CITY
Moorgate
Bank of England
Threadneedle St.
Bishopsgate
Houndsditch
ALDGATE
Farringdon St.
Fleet St.
Ludgate Hill
St. Paul's
Cheapside
Cornhill
Leadenhall St.
Fenchurch St.
COVENT GARDEN
Aldwych
Strand
BLACKFRIARS
BANK
Lombard St.
Gracechurch St.
Long Acre
COVENT GARDEN
TEMPLE
Queen Victoria St.
MANSION HOUSE
Queen St.
Cannon St.
Fenchurch St. Station
TOWER HILL
LEICESTER SQ.
STRAND
Lancaster Pl.
Victoria Embankment
Blackfriars Station
Blackfriars Bridge
Millennium Bridge
CANNON ST.
Cannon St. Station
MONUMENT
Eastcheap
Tower Hill
Upper Thames St.
National Gallery
Charing Cross Station
Waterloo Bridge
Southwark Bridge
London Bridge
The Tower of London
TRAFALGAR SQ.
EMBANKMENT
CHARING CROSS
National Theatre
Tate Modern
SOUTH BANK
River Thames
Tower Bridge
Hungerford Footbridge
Stamford St.
Waterloo Rd.
Southwark St.
LONDON BRIDGE
Tooley St.
London Bridge Station
Whitehall
WATERLOO
Union St.
Blackfriars Rd.
WESTMINSTER
York Rd.
Waterloo Station
Long Ln.
Big Ben
Westminster Br.
Tabard St.
Great Dover St.
Houses of Parliament
LAMBETH NORTH
Bridge Rd.
Borough Rd.
Harper Rd.
Tower Bridge Rd.
Abbey St.
Westminster Abbey
Lambeth Palace Rd.
London Rd.
Imperial War Museum
ELEPHANT & CASTLE
Lambeth Rd.
New Kent Rd.
Horseferry Rd.
Lambeth Bridge
LAMBETH
Kennington Rd.
Willow Walk
Black Prince Rd.
Rodney Pl.
Flint St.
Old Kent Rd.
Walworth Rd.
Crampton St.
East St.
Tate Britain
Millbank
Albert Embankment
Kennington Park Rd.
Manor Pl.
Thurlow St.
Portland St.
Vauxhall Bridge
Kennington Ln.
VAUXHALL
Vauxhall Station
Braganza St.
Albany Rd.
The Oval
OVAL
N
LG
South Lambeth Rd.
John Ruskin St.
Camberwell Rd.
0
500 yards
500 meters
Fentiman Rd.
Camberwell New Rd.
Wandsworth Rd.
Clapham Rd.
Brixton Rd.
Yassall Rd.
London Overview

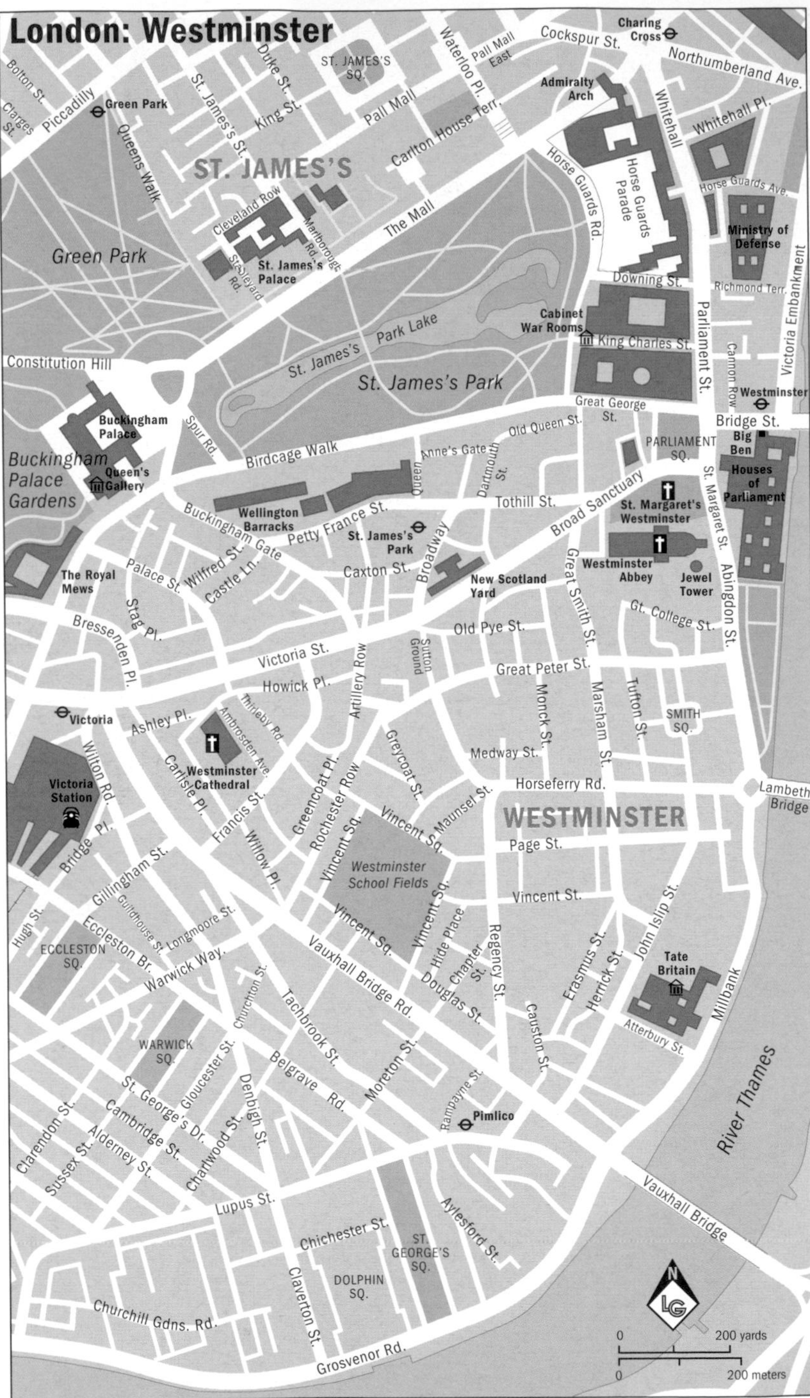
London: Westminster
Charing Cross
Cockspur St.
Northumberland Ave.
Pall Mall East
Waterloo Pl.
ST. JAMES'S SQ.
Duke St.
Bolton St.
Clarges St.
Piccadilly
Green Park
St. James's St.
King St.
Pall Mall
Carlton House Terr.
Admiralty Arch
Whitehall
Whitehall Pl.
Queens Walk
ST. JAMES'S
Cleveland Row
Marlborough Rd.
Stable Yard Rd.
St. James's Palace
The Mall
Horse Guards Rd.
Horse Guards Parade
Horse Guards Ave.
Ministry of Defense
Green Park
Downing St.
Richmond Terr.
Victoria Embankment
Parliament St.
Cabinet War Rooms
King Charles St.
St. James's Park Lake
Constitution Hill
St. James's Park
Cannon Row
Westminster
Great George St.
Bridge St.
Buckingham Palace
Spur Rd.
Old Queen St.
PARLIAMENT SQ.
Big Ben
Birdcage Walk
Queen Anne's Gate
Dartmouth St.
Buckingham Palace Gardens
Queen's Gallery
Houses of Parliament
Tothill St.
Broad Sanctuary
St. Margaret's Westminster
St. Margaret St.
Wellington Barracks
Buckingham Gate
Petty France St.
St. James's Park
Broadway
Westminster Abbey
Jewel Tower
Abingdon St.
The Royal Mews
Palace St.
Wilfred St.
Castle Ln.
Caxton St.
New Scotland Yard
Great Smith St.
Stag Pl.
Gt. College St.
Bressenden Pl.
Old Pye St.
Sutton Ground
Artillery Row
Victoria St.
Great Peter St.
Howick Pl.
Monck St.
Marsham St.
Tufton St.
Victoria
Ashley Pl.
Thirleby Rd.
Ambrosden Ave.
SMITH SQ.
Westminster Cathedral
Greycoat St.
Medway St.
Wilton Rd.
Carlisle Pl.
Horseferry Rd.
Lambeth Bridge
Victoria Station
Francis St.
Greencoat Pl.
Rochester Row
Mausel St.
Vincent Sq.
WESTMINSTER
Bridge Pl.
Willow Pl.
Page St.
Westminster School Fields
Gillingham St.
Vincent St.
Guildhouse St.
Hugh St.
Longmoore St.
Eccleston Br.
Hide Place
Chapter St.
Regency St.
John Islip St.
ECCLESTON SQ.
Warwick Way
Vauxhall Bridge Rd.
Douglas St.
Erasmus St.
Herrick St.
Tate Britain
Churchton St.
Tachbrook St.
Causton St.
Millbank
Atterbury St.
WARWICK SQ.
Moreton St.
River Thames
Gloucester St.
St. George's Dr.
Belgrave Rd.
Rampayne St.
Denbigh St.
Pimlico
Clarendon St.
Cambridge St.
Alderney St.
Sussex St.
Charlwood St.
Vauxhall Bridge
Lupus St.
Aylesford St.
Chichester St.
ST. GEORGE'S SQ.
DOLPHIN SQ.
Claverton St.
Churchill Gdns. Rd.
Grosvenor Rd.
N
LG
0
200 yards
0
200 meters

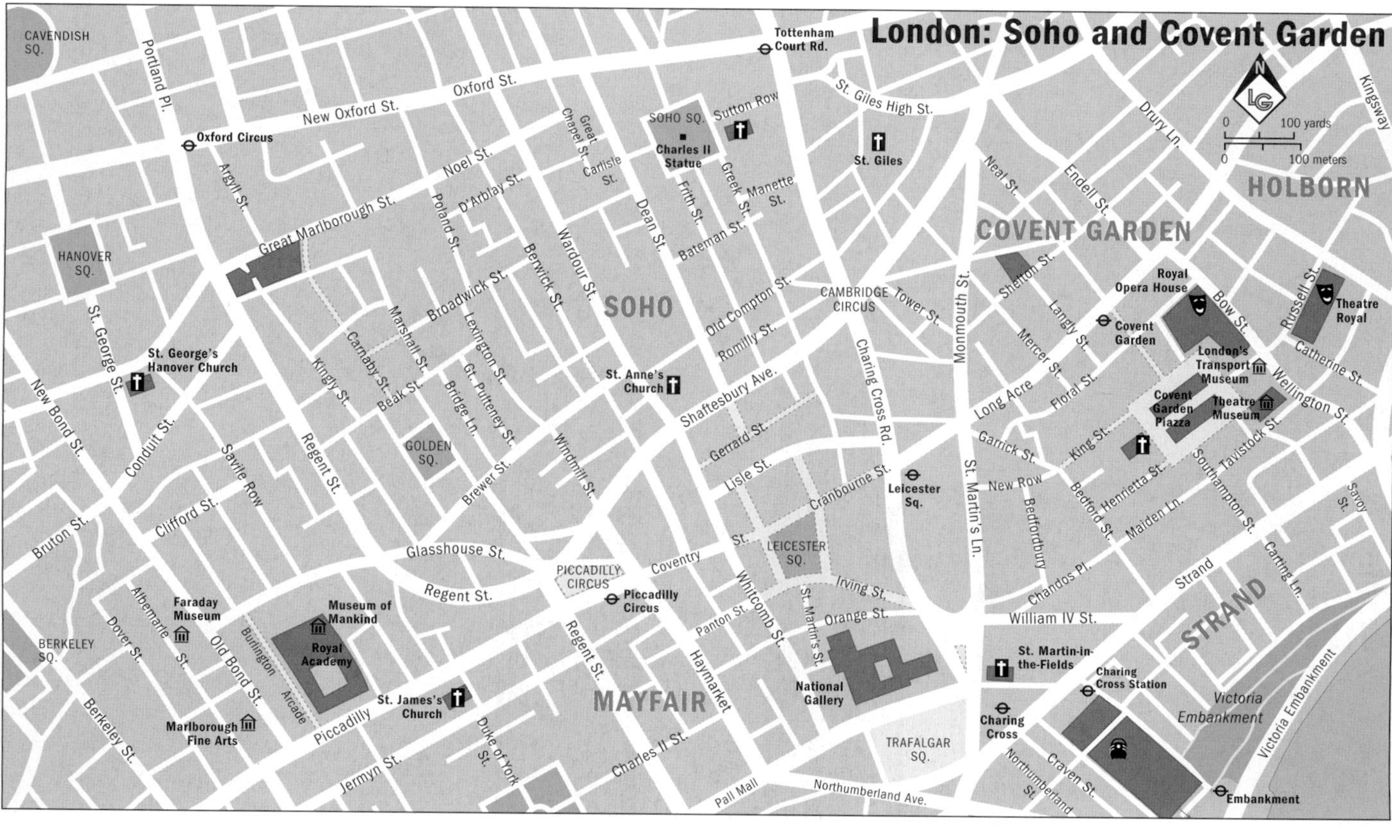
London: Soho and Covent Garden
0
100 yards
0
100 meters
HOLBORN
COVENT GARDEN
SOHO
MAYFAIR
STRAND
CAVENDISH SQ.
HANOVER SQ.
SOHO SQ.
GOLDEN SQ.
LEICESTER SQ.
BERKELEY SQ.
TRAFALGAR SQ.
PICCADILLY CIRCUS
CAMBRIDGE CIRCUS
Tottenham Court Rd.
Oxford Circus
Piccadilly Circus
Leicester Sq.
Covent Garden
Charing Cross
Charing Cross Station
Embankment
Charles II Statue
St. Giles
St. George's Hanover Church
St. Anne's Church
St. James's Church
St. Martin-in-the-Fields
Royal Opera House
Theatre Royal
London's Transport Museum
Theatre Museum
Covent Garden Piazza
National Gallery
Museum of Mankind
Royal Academy
Faraday Museum
Marlborough Fine Arts
Portland Pl.
Oxford St.
New Oxford St.
Argyll St.
Noel St.
Great Marlborough St.
Poland St.
D'Arblay St.
Great Chapel St.
Carlisle St.
Sutton Row
Greek St.
Manette St.
Frith St.
Dean St.
Bateman St.
Wardour St.
Berwick St.
Broadwick St.
Marshall St.
Carnaby St.
Kingly St.
Beak St.
Lexington St.
Gt. Pulteney St.
Bridge Ln.
Brewer St.
Windmill St.
Old Compton St.
Romilly St.
Shaftesbury Ave.
Gerrard St.
Lisle St.
Cranbourne St.
Charing Cross Rd.
Tower St.
Monmouth St.
St. Giles High St.
Neal St.
Endell St.
Drury Ln.
Kingsway
Shelton St.
Langly St.
Mercer St.
Floral St.
Long Acre
Bow St.
Russell St.
Catherine St.
Wellington St.
Garrick St.
King St.
New Row
Henrietta St.
Bedford St.
Southampton St.
Tavistock St.
Maiden Ln.
Bedfordbury
Chandos Pl.
St. Martin's Ln.
William IV St.
Strand
Carting Ln.
Savoy St.
Victoria Embankment
Craven St.
Northumberland St.
Northumberland Ave.
Pall Mall
Charles II St.
Haymarket
Whitcomb St.
Panton St.
Orange St.
Irving St.
St. Martin's St.
Coventry St.
Regent St.
Glasshouse St.
Piccadilly
Jermyn St.
Duke of York St.
Burlington Arcade
Old Bond St.
Albemarle St.
Dover St.
Berkeley St.
Bruton St.
Clifford St.
Savile Row
Conduit St.
New Bond St.
St. George St.

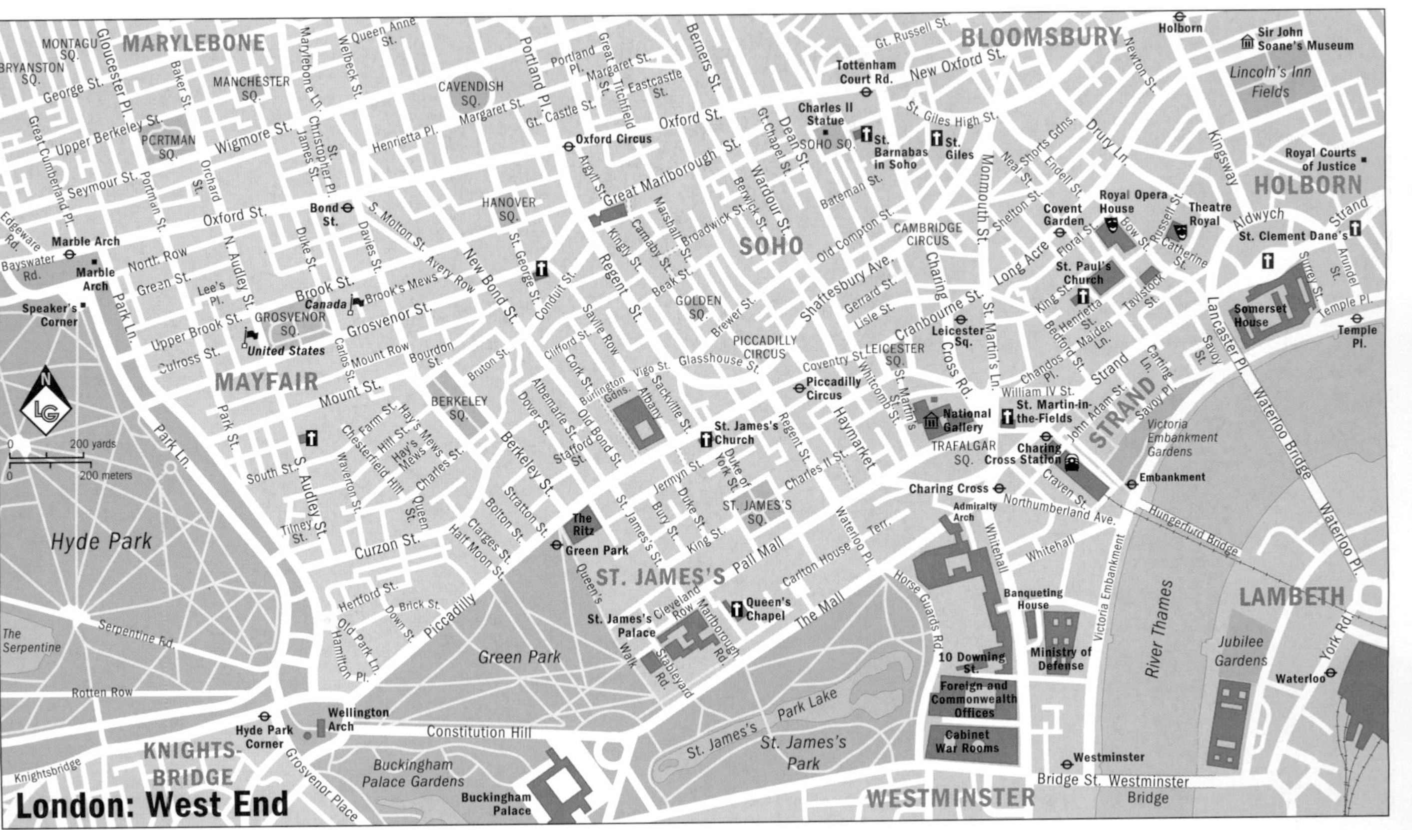

London: West End
MARYLEBONE
BLOOMSBURY
HOLBORN
SOHO
MAYFAIR
ST. JAMES'S
STRAND
LAMBETH
WESTMINSTER
KNIGHTS-BRIDGE
Hyde Park
Green Park
St. James's Park
River Thames
Lincoln's Inn Fields
Jubilee Gardens
Victoria Embankment Gardens
Buckingham Palace Gardens
The Serpentine
Sir John Soane's Museum
Royal Courts of Justice
St. Clement Dane's
Somerset House
Theatre Royal
Royal Opera House
St. Paul's Church
St. Martin-in-the-Fields
National Gallery
Charing Cross Station
Banqueting House
Ministry of Defense
10 Downing St.
Foreign and Commonwealth Offices
Cabinet War Rooms
Queen's Chapel
St. James's Palace
The Ritz
Buckingham Palace
Wellington Arch
Marble Arch
Speaker's Corner
Charles II Statue
St. Barnabas in Soho
St. Giles
St. James's Church
Albany
Canada
United States
Holborn
Tottenham Court Rd.
Oxford Circus
Bond St.
Hyde Park Corner
Green Park
Piccadilly Circus
Leicester Sq.
Covent Garden
Charing Cross
Embankment
Westminster
Waterloo
Temple Pl.
TRAFALGAR SQ.
LEICESTER SQ.
SOHO SQ.
GOLDEN SQ.
HANOVER SQ.
BERKELEY SQ.
GROSVENOR SQ.
CAVENDISH SQ.
MANCHESTER SQ.
PORTMAN SQ.
MONTAGU SQ.
BRYANSTON SQ.
ST. JAMES'S SQ.
CAMBRIDGE CIRCUS
PICCADILLY CIRCUS
Oxford St.
Regent St.
Piccadilly
Pall Mall
The Mall
Haymarket
Shaftesbury Ave.
Charing Cross Rd.
Strand
Kingsway
Aldwych
New Oxford St.
Long Acre
Whitehall
Constitution Hill
Park Ln.
New Bond St.
Old Bond St.
Victoria Embankment
Waterloo Bridge
Hungerford Bridge
Westminster Bridge
Serpentine Rd.
Rotten Row
200 yards
200 meters
0

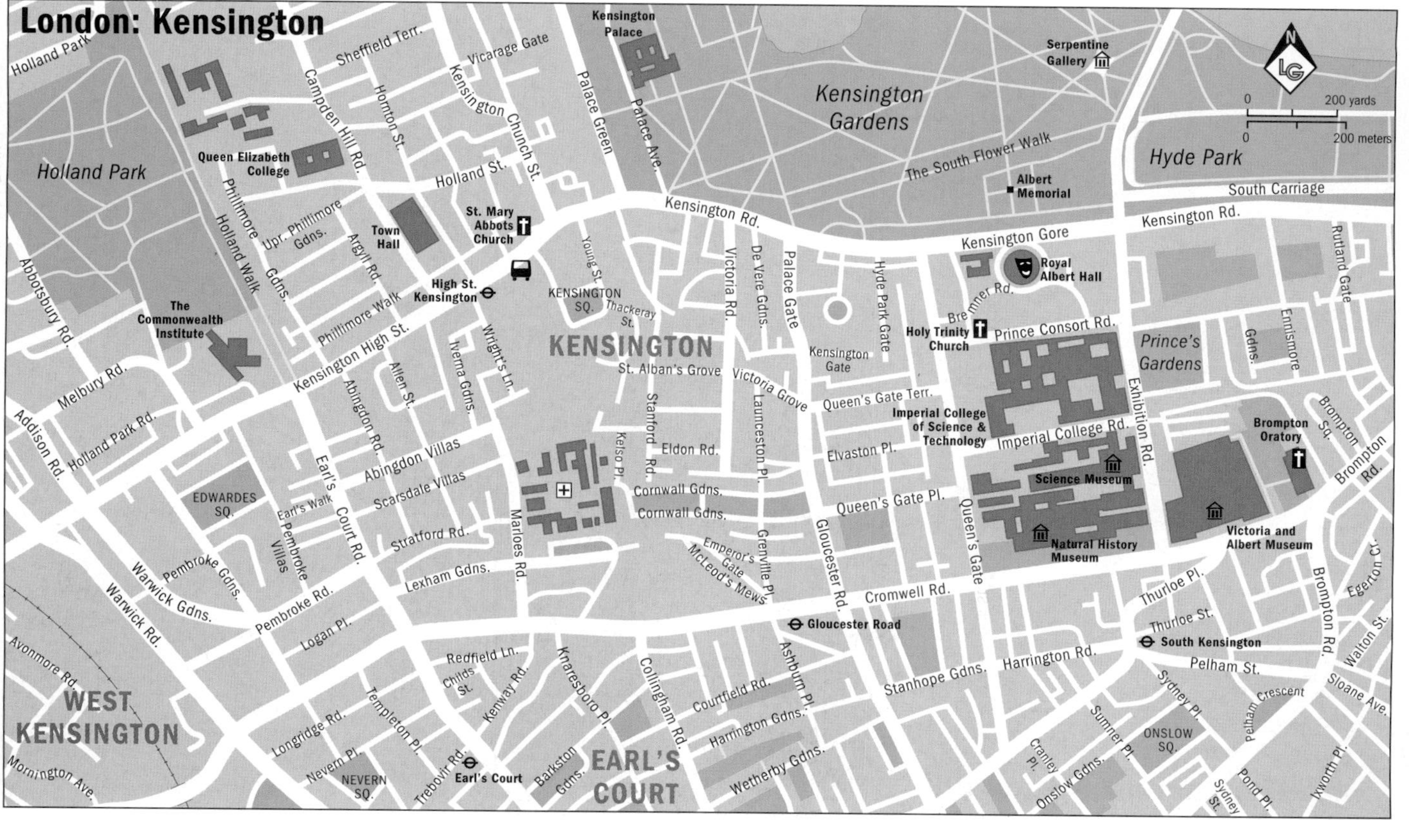

London: Kensington
N
LG
0
200 yards
0
200 meters
Holland Park
Holland Park
Holland Walk
Phillimore Gdns.
Upr. Phillimore Gdns.
Queen Elizabeth College
The Commonwealth Institute
Abbotsbury Rd.
Melbury Rd.
Addison Rd.
Holland Park Rd.
Sheffield Terr.
Campden Hill Rd.
Hornton St.
Vicarage Gate
Kensington Church St.
Holland St.
Town Hall
Argyll Rd.
Phillimore Walk
St. Mary Abbots Church
High St. Kensington
Kensington High St.
Allen St.
Iverna Gdns.
Wright's Ln.
Abingdon Rd.
Abingdon Villas
Scarsdale Villas
Earl's Court Rd.
Earl's Walk
Pembroke Villas
EDWARDES SQ.
Pembroke Gdns.
Warwick Gdns.
Warwick Rd.
Pembroke Rd.
Logan Pl.
Stratford Rd.
Lexham Gdns.
Marloes Rd.
Kensington Palace
Palace Green
Palace Ave.
Kensington Gardens
The South Flower Walk
Albert Memorial
Serpentine Gallery
Hyde Park
South Carriage
Kensington Rd.
Kensington Rd.
Kensington Gore
Young St.
KENSINGTON SQ.
Thackeray St.
KENSINGTON
St. Alban's Grove
Victoria Rd.
De Vere Gdns.
Palace Gate
Hyde Park Gate
Kensington Gate
Victoria Grove
Launceston Pl.
Stanford Rd.
Eldon Rd.
Kelso Pl.
Cornwall Gdns.
Cornwall Gdns.
Emperor's Gate
McLeod's Mews
Grenville Pl.
Gloucester Rd.
Queen's Gate Terr.
Elvaston Pl.
Queen's Gate Pl.
Queen's Gate
Royal Albert Hall
Bremner Rd.
Holy Trinity Church
Prince Consort Rd.
Imperial College of Science & Technology
Imperial College Rd.
Science Museum
Natural History Museum
Exhibition Rd.
Prince's Gardens
Gdns.
Ennismore
Rutland Gate
Brompton Sq.
Brompton Oratory
Brompton Rd.
Victoria and Albert Museum
Egerton Cr.
Brompton Rd.
Walton St.
Cromwell Rd.
Gloucester Road
Thurloe Pl.
Thurloe St.
South Kensington
Pelham St.
Sloane Ave.
Harrington Rd.
Stanhope Gdns.
Sydney Pl.
Pelham Crescent
Ixworth Pl.
Sumner Pl.
ONSLOW SQ.
Cranley Pl.
Onslow Gdns.
Sydney St.
Pond Pl.
Ashburn Pl.
Courtfield Rd.
Harrington Gdns.
Wetherby Gdns.
Collingham Rd.
Kenway Rd.
Knaresboro Pl.
Redfield Ln.
Childs St.
Barkston Gdns.
EARL'S COURT
Earl's Court
Trebovir Rd.
Templeton Pl.
Longridge Rd.
Nevern Pl.
NEVERN SQ.
Avonmore Rd.
WEST KENSINGTON
Mornington Ave.

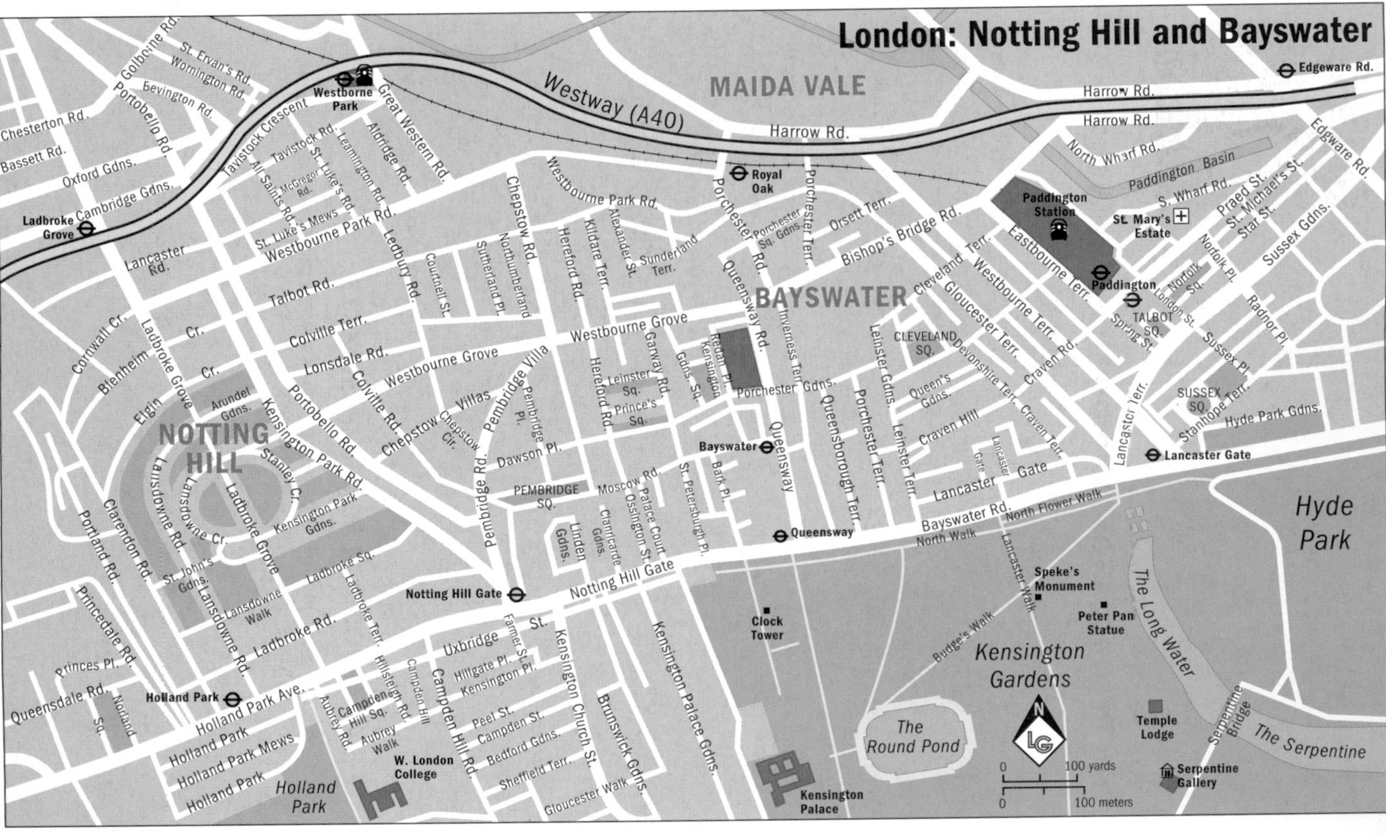
London: Notting Hill and Bayswater
MAIDA VALE
BAYSWATER
NOTTING HILL
Westway (A40)
Hyde Park
Kensington Gardens
Holland Park
The Long Water
The Serpentine
Serpentine Bridge
The Round Pond
Edgeware Rd.
Westbourne Park
Royal Oak
Ladbroke Grove
Paddington Station
Paddington
St. Mary's Estate
Lancaster Gate
Bayswater
Queensway
Notting Hill Gate
Holland Park
Speke's Monument
Peter Pan Statue
Clock Tower
Kensington Palace
Temple Lodge
Serpentine Gallery
W. London College
100 yards
100 meters
Harrow Rd.
Edgware Rd.
North Wharf Rd.
Paddington Basin
S. Wharf Rd.
Praed St.
St. Michael's St.
Star St.
Sussex Gdns.
Norfolk Pl.
Norfolk Sq.
London St.
Radnor Pl.
TALBOT SQ.
Spring St.
Sussex Pl.
SUSSEX SQ.
Stanhope Terr.
Hyde Park Gdns.
Lancaster Terr.
Eastbourne Terr.
Westbourne Terr.
Gloucester Terr.
Cleveland Terr.
Craven Rd.
Devonshire Terr.
Craven Terr.
CLEVELAND SQ.
Queen's Gdns.
Craven Hill
Lancaster Gate
Leinster Gdns.
Leinster Terr.
Porchester Terr.
Queensborough Terr.
Inverness Terr.
Porchester Gdns.
Queensway
Queensway Rd.
Porchester Rd.
Porchester Sq. Gdns.
Orsett Terr.
Bishop's Bridge Rd.
Bayswater Rd.
North Flower Walk
North Walk
Lancaster Walk
Budge's Walk
Redan Pl.
Kensington Gdns. Sq.
Garway Rd.
Leinster Sq.
Prince's Sq.
Hereford Rd.
Bark Pl.
St. Petersburgh Pl.
Moscow Rd.
Palace Court
Ossington St.
Clanricarde Gdns.
Linden Gdns.
PEMBRIDGE SQ.
Pembridge Rd.
Pembridge Villa
Pembridge Pl.
Dawson Pl.
Westbourne Grove
Kildare Terr.
Alexander St.
Sunderland Terr.
Westbourne Park Rd.
Chepstow Rd.
Northumberland
Sutherland Pl.
Courtnell St.
Ledbury Rd.
Great Western Rd.
Aldridge Rd.
Leamington Rd.
St. Luke's Rd.
Tavistock Rd.
Tavistock Crescent
McGregor Rd.
All Saints Rd.
St. Luke's Mews
Talbot Rd.
Colville Terr.
Lonsdale Rd.
Colville Rd.
Chepstow Villas
Chepstow Cir.
Portobello Rd.
Kensington Park Rd.
Kensington Park Gdns.
Stanley Cr.
Ladbroke Sq.
Ladbroke Grove
Ladbroke Terr.
Ladbroke Rd.
Lansdowne Cr.
Lansdowne Rd.
Lansdowne Walk
St. John's Gdns.
Arundel Gdns.
Elgin Cr.
Blenheim Cr.
Cornwall Cr.
Lancaster Rd.
Cambridge Gdns.
Oxford Gdns.
Bassett Rd.
Chesterton Rd.
Golborne Rd.
St. Ervan's Rd.
Wornington Rd.
Bevington Rd.
Clarendon Rd.
Portland Rd.
Princedale Rd.
Princes Pl.
Queensdale Rd.
Norland Sq.
Holland Park Ave.
Holland Park Mews
Notting Hill Gate
Uxbridge St.
Farmer St.
Hillgate Pl.
Kensington Pl.
Hillsleigh Rd.
Campden Hill
Campden Hill Sq.
Aubrey Rd.
Aubrey Walk
Campden Hill Rd.
Peel St.
Campden St.
Bedford Gdns.
Sheffield Terr.
Gloucester Walk
Kensington Church St.
Brunswick Gdns.
Kensington Palace Gdns.

■ THE RESOURCE FOR THE INDEPENDENT TRAVELER

"The guides are aimed not only at young budget travelers but at the indepedent traveler; a sort of streetwise cookbook for traveling alone."

—*The New York Times*

"Unbeatable; good sight-seeing advice; up-to-date info on restaurants, hotels, and inns; a commitment to money-saving travel; and a wry style that brightens nearly every page."

—*The Washington Post*

"Lighthearted and sophisticated, informative and fun to read. [Let's Go] helps the novice traveler navigate like a knowledgeable old hand."

—*Atlanta Journal-Constitution*

"A world-wise traveling companion—always ready with friendly advice and helpful hints, all sprinkled with a bit of wit."

—*The Philadelphia Inquirer*

■ THE BEST TRAVEL BARGAINS IN YOUR PRICE RANGE

"All the dirt, dirt cheap."

—*People*

"Anything you need to know about budget traveling is detailed in this book."

—*The Chicago Sun-Times*

"Let's Go follows the creed that you don't have to toss your life's savings to the wind to travel—unless you want to."

—*The Salt Lake Tribune*

■ REAL ADVICE FOR REAL EXPERIENCES

"The writers seem to have experienced every rooster-packed bus and lunar-surfaced mattress about which they write."

—*The New York Times*

"Value-packed, unbeatable, accurate, and comprehensive."

—*The Los Angeles Times*

"[Let's Go's] devoted updaters really walk the walk (and thumb the ride, and trek the trail). Learn how to fish, haggle, find work—anywhere."

—*Food & Wine*

LET'S GO PUBLICATIONS

TRAVEL GUIDES

Australia 8th edition
Austria & Switzerland 12th edition
Brazil 1st edition
Britain & Ireland 2005
California 10th edition
Central America 9th edition
Chile 2nd edition
China 5th edition
Costa Rica 2nd edition
Eastern Europe 2005
Ecuador 1st edition **NEW TITLE**
Egypt 2nd edition
Europe 2005
France 2005
Germany 12th edition
Greece 2005
Hawaii 3rd edition
India & Nepal 8th edition
Ireland 2005
Israel 4th edition
Italy 2005
Japan 1st edition
Mexico 20th edition
Middle East 4th edition
Peru 1st edition **NEW TITLE**
Puerto Rico 1st edition
South Africa 5th edition
Southeast Asia 9th edition
Spain & Portugal 2005
Thailand 2nd edition
Turkey 5th edition
USA 2005
Vietnam 1st edition **NEW TITLE**
Western Europe 2005

ROADTRIP GUIDE

Roadtripping USA **NEW TITLE**

ADVENTURE GUIDES

Alaska 1st edition
New Zealand **NEW TITLE**
Pacific Northwest **NEW TITLE**
Southwest USA 3rd edition

CITY GUIDES

Amsterdam 3rd edition
Barcelona 3rd edition
Boston 4th edition
London 2005
New York City 15th edition
Paris 13th edition
Rome 12th edition
San Francisco 4th edition
Washington, D.C. 13th edition

POCKET CITY GUIDES

Amsterdam
Berlin
Boston
Chicago
London
New York City
Paris
San Francisco
Venice
Washington, D.C.

LONDON 2005

Rabia Mir Editor

Researcher-Writers
Aviva Gilbert
Robert Hodgson

Nicholas Kephart Map Editor
Stef Levner Managing Editor

St. Martin's Press New York

HELPING LET'S GO. If you want to share your discoveries, suggestions, or corrections, please drop us a line. We read every piece of correspondence, whether a postcard, a 10-page email, or a coconut. **Address mail to:**

Let's Go: London
67 Mount Auburn Street
Cambridge, MA 02138
USA

Visit Let's Go at **http://www.letsgo.com,** or send email to:

feedback@letsgo.com
Subject: "Let's Go: London"

In addition to the invaluable travel advice our readers share with us, many are kind enough to offer their services as researchers or editors. Unfortunately, our charter enables us to employ only currently enrolled Harvard students.

Maps by David Lindroth copyright © 2005 by St. Martin's Press.

Let's Go: London Copyright © 2005 by Let's Go, Inc. All rights reserved. Printed in the United States of America. No part of this book may be used or reproduced in any manner whatsoever without written permission except in the case of brief quotations embodied in critical articles or reviews. Let's Go is available for purchase in bulk by institutions and authorized resellers. For information, address St. Martin's Press, 175 Fifth Avenue, New York, NY 10010, USA. www.stmartins.com.

Distributed outside the USA and Canada by Macmillan, an imprint of Pan Macmillan Ltd.
20 New Wharf Road, London N1 9RR
Basingstoke and Oxford
Associated companies throughout the world
www.panmacmillan.com

ISBN: 0-312-33553-9
EAN: 978-0312-33553-3
First edition
10 9 8 7 6 5 4 3 2 1

Let's Go: London is written by Let's Go Publications, 67 Mount Auburn Street, Cambridge, MA 02138, USA.

Let's Go® and the LG logo are trademarks of Let's Go, Inc.
Printed in the USA.

ADVERTISING DISCLAIMER. All advertisements appearing in Let's Go publications are sold by an independent agency not affiliated with the editorial production of the guides. Advertisers are never given preferential treatment, and the guides are researched, written, and published independent of advertising. Advertisements do not imply endorsement of products or services by Let's Go, and Let's Go does not vouch for the accuracy of information provided in advertisements.

If you are interested in purchasing advertising space in a Let's Go publication, contact: Let's Go Advertising Sales, 67 Mount Auburn St., Cambridge, MA 02138, USA.

ABOUT LET'S GO

GUIDES FOR THE INDEPENDENT TRAVELER

At Let's Go, we see every trip as the chance of a lifetime. If your dream is to grab a machete and forge through the jungles of Brazil, we can take you there. If you'd rather bask in the Riviera sun at a beachside cafe, we'll set you a table. We write for readers who know that there's more to travel than sharing double deckers with tourists and who believe that travel can change both themselves and the world—whether they plan to spend six days in London or six months in Latin America. We'll show you just how far your money can go, and prove that the greatest limitation on your adventures is not your wallet, but your imagination. After all, traveling close to the ground lets you interact more directly with the places and people you've gone to see, making for the most authentic experience.

BEYOND THE TOURIST EXPERIENCE

To help you gain a deeper connection with the places you travel, our researchers give you the heads-up on both world-renowned and off-the-beaten-track attractions, sights, and destinations. They engage with the local culture, writing features on regional cuisine, local festivals, and hot political issues. We've also opened our pages to respected writers and scholars to hear their takes on the countries and regions we cover, and asked travelers who have worked, studied, or volunteered abroad to contribute first-person accounts of their experiences. We've also increased our coverage of responsible travel and expanded each guide's Alternatives to Tourism chapter to share more ideas about how to give back to local communities and learn about the places you travel.

FORTY-FIVE YEARS OF WISDOM

Let's Go got its start in 1960, when a group of creative and well-traveled students compiled their experience and advice into a 20-page mimeographed pamphlet, which they gave to travelers on charter flights to Europe. Four and a half decades later, we've expanded to cover six continents and all kinds of travel—while retaining our founders' adventurous attitude toward the world. Our guides are still researched and written entirely by students on shoestring budgets, experienced travelers who know that train strikes, stolen luggage, food poisoning, and marriage proposals are all part of a day's work. This year, we're expanding our coverage of South America and Southeast Asia, with brand-new *Let's Go: Ecuador*, *Let's Go: Peru*, and *Let's Go: Vietnam*. Our adventure guide series is growing, too, with the addition of *Let's Go: Pacific Northwest Adventure* and *Let's Go: New Zealand Adventure*. And we're immensely excited about our new *Let's Go: Roadtripping USA*—two years, eight routes, and sixteen researchers and editors have put together a travel guide like none other.

THE LET'S GO COMMUNITY

More than just a travel guide company, Let's Go is a community. Our small staff comes together because of our shared passion for travel and our desire to help other travelers see the world. We love it when our readers become part of the Let's Go community as well—when you travel, drop us a postcard (67 Mt. Auburn St., Cambridge, MA 02138, USA) or send us an e-mail (feedback@letsgo.com) to tell us about your adventures and discoveries.

For more information, visit us online: www.letsgo.com.

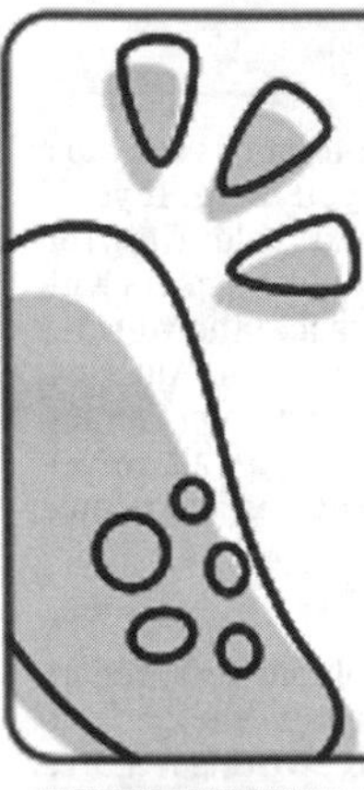

LONDON'S FREE TELEPHONE BOOKING SERVICE

You can now call **FREE** on **0800 LONDON** for London information and to book discounted rates for London hotels, theatre, airport transfers and sightseeing

Advisors available every day from 8am to midnight.
From outside the UK dial **+44 800 LONDON**

0800 LONDON - London's Free Telephone Booking Service

London Information Centre™
LEICESTER SQUARE

Free information and half price hotels. Every day.

Visit us in person in the centre of Leicester Square or call us on **020 729 22 333.**
From outside the UK call **+44 20 729 22 333**

London Information Centre, Leicester Square, London
Open every day from 8am to 11pm

The number one internet site for London offers essential information to help organise the perfect visit to London. Guaranteed lowest rates on London's leading hotels and information on 15,000 reviewed and quality assessed London products and services.

You can now also book over the phone on 0207 437 4370
From outside the UK call +44 207 437 4370

The #1 Internet Site for London™

Over 30 million customers served

CONTENTS

daytripping 299

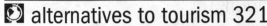

alternatives to tourism 321

service directory 335

index 340

map appendix 351

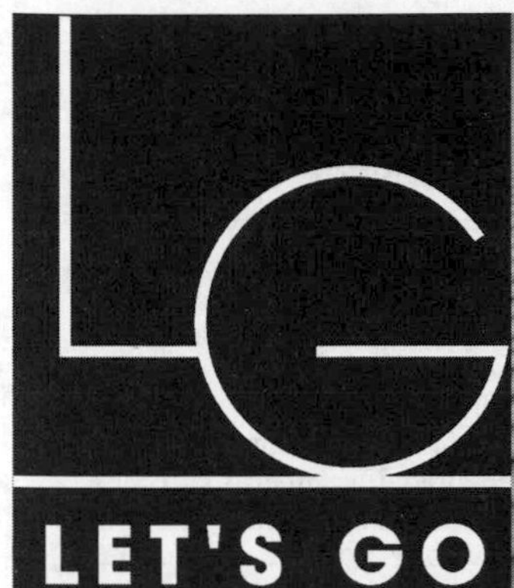

PROUDLY PRESENTS...

beyondtourism.com

explore a different path of experience

SEARCH for volunteer, work, and study abroad opportunities...

FIND LISTINGS FOR: Central & South America | OFFERING EXPERIENCE IN: Indigenous Issues | CONTAINING WORD(S)

LEARN about featured destinations, organizations, and issues from all over the world...

Take a Look

Au Pair Work in Western Europe

Community Service in North America

Environmentalism in Central and South American

Featured Articles

Featured Destination: Puerto Rico

Nepal: Children Workers in Nepal

Costa Rica: Asociación Salvemos Las Tortugas de Parismina

Australia: Bushcare Australia

Eastern Europe: Balkan Sunflowers

South Africa: Visions in Action

PLAN your next trip with Let's Go...

For travel books and advice, visit letsgo.com

RESEARCHER-WRITERS

Aviva Gilbert *The City of London, Notting Hill, South Bank, West End, Westminster, North London, East London, West London, Hampton.*

Born and bred in Berkeley, California. As a history and literature major Aviva appreciated the tales embedded in the streets of London. By day, nit-picky accommodations' research complemented her investigation of the ins and outs of Royal establishments. By night, the booty-shaking queen grooved with celebrities like Janet Jackson. Though she favored red wine before her expedition, she soon developed into a beer expert, pleasantly surprised by the strength of a British pint. Aviva always wants to be in twenty places at once and with her in-depth research, it looked like she was.

Robert Hodgson *Bayswater, Bloomsbury, Chelsea, Clerkenwell, Holborn, Kensington & Earl's Court, Knightsbridge & Belgravia, Marylebone & Regent's Park, West End, South London, Richmond.*

Professional, candid and sometimes prone to slapstick misfortunes, Bobby traveled from New England to England with the fantasy of meeting (and dissing) Margaret Thatcher. Though he didn't run into the Iron Lady, he was content with a Jackie Chan encounter and a few Molly Ringwald sightings. A seasoned stage performer at his university, Bobby was the theatrical king who revitalized our entertainment section—and his steadfast addiction to British Big Brother shed dazzling new light on the many pleasures of BBC TV. From the perplexity of London's transport system to the mélange of cuisines in the city, Bobby could find his way through all.

CONTRIBUTING WRITERS

Thomas Sleigh studied Political Science at Cambridge University (1997-2000). He was a Fulbright Scholar to Harvard University (2003-4), and now works in London.

Russell Graney spent June 2002 interning in London in the Marketing and Sales Department at Mulberry, Co. Ltd. He is now a student at Harvard College.

Laura Krug — *Editor,* Let's Go: Britain & Ireland 2005

Adrián Maldonado — *Associate Editor,* Let's Go: Britain & Ireland 2005

Patrick McKee — *Research Writer,* Let's Go: Britain & Ireland 2005

Brighton, Cambridge, Canterbury, Salisbury, Stonehenge, Windsor and Eton.

Kriston Keating — *Research Writer,* Let's Go: Britain & Ireland 2005

Bath, Oxford, Stratford-upon-Avon.

ACKNOWLEDGMENTS

Rabia THANKS: Aviva and Bobby, you were resplendent! You guys did a lot and did it with a smile. Your wit and humor rocked my LG world—couldn't have asked for more. Stef, you were my knight without the shining armour. Edits, scones, high-fives, advice, help and more help...owe you big time. Nick, thank you for putting up with my ever-changing mind and for dealing with the intricacy of West End. Now I know what a dream team means.

This time getting the names right: Maude, we were in this back-to-back and I really appreciate all your (haute!) support. Margot, for the edits and the laughs, *cheers* mate. Mapland stars, *shukran* for making the process enjoyable. Jeremy and Vicky—couldn't have done it without you. B&I for the help with daytrips: *merci*.

Both my Sarah's it was a long journey thank you for helping me make it. Roomies, Sauleh and Preppy, *shukria*. To everyone who were there with suggestions, help and hugs: *gracias*. Mama and Abu, you've always been there and you know how I feel. Don't worry I'm bringing "the book" home.

Nick THANKS: I would like to thank my liberal activist editor, her wayward views on Margaret Thatcher, her occasional but all too frequent outbursts, and her impeccable musical tastes. Both RWs for their unflinching attention to the labyrinth that are the London streets, and for the opportunity to eavesdrop on their macabre travel stories. Let me also thank my parents and my sisters for reminding me how much of a tan I am missing by not returning home to San Diego, and Tish for listening to my complaints all summer about wayward research writers. And the mapland air-conditioning.

Editor
Rabia Mir
Managing Editor
Stef Levner
Map Editor
Nick Kephart
Typesetter
Christine Yokoyama

Publishing Director
Emma Nothmann
Editor-in-Chief
Teresa Elsey
Production Manager
Adam R. Perlman
Cartography Manager
Elizabeth Halbert Peterson
Design Manager
Amelia Aos Showalter
Editorial Managers
Briana Cummings, Charlotte Douglas, Ella M. Steim, Joel August Steinhaus, Lauren Truesdell, Christina Zaroulis
Financial Manager
R. Kirkie Maswoswe
Marketing and Publicity Managers
Stef Levner, Leigh Pascavage
Personnel Manager
Jeremy Todd
Low-Season Manager
Clay H. Kaminsky
Production Associate
Victoria Esquivel-Korsiak
IT Director
Matthew DePetro
Web Manager
Rob Dubbin
Associate Web Manager
Patrick Swieskowski
Web Content Manager
Tor Krever
Research and Development Consultant
Jennifer O'Brien
Office Coordinators
Stephanie Brown, Elizabeth Peterson

Director of Advertising Sales
Elizabeth S. Sabin
Senior Advertising Associates
Jesse R. Loffler, Francisco A. Robles, Zoe M. Savitsky
Advertising Graphic Designer
Christa Lee-Chuvala

President
Ryan M. Geraghty
General Manager
Robert B. Rombauer
Assistant General Manager
Anne E. Chisholm

HOW TO USE THIS BOOK

COVERAGE LAYOUT. The book organizes the neighborhoods in an alphabetical order with the exception of north, south, east and west London. Therefore, two neighborhoods that would be farther apart in the alphabetical order might be geographically next to each other. Look at the London overview map to familiarize yourself with the city's layout and refer to map thumbnails throughout the book for location reminders.

TRANSPORTATION INFORMATION. The book mentions the nearest tube station to most establishments. When there is no Tube icon (⊖) it means that no Tube station is close to the listing, refer to your maps for guidance. Check the **Discover** section and the Night Bus map in the **Map Appendix** for information on bus routes.

PRICE DIVERSITY. For price diversity icons refer to p. xiii. We rank establishments in order of quality, and give the ☒ to the best establishments.

WHEN TO USE IT

TWO MONTHS BEFORE. Our book is filled with practical information to help you before you go. **Essentials** has advice about passports, plane tickets, insurance, and more. The **Accommodations** chapter can help you with booking a room from home.

TWO WEEKS BEFORE. Start thinking about your ideal trip. **Discover London** lists the city's top delights and also includes our **Walking Tours** (complete with maps), Let's Go Picks (the best and quirkiest that London has to offer), and the scoop on each of the city's neighborhoods. It also includes itineraries for seeing **London In One Week (Or Less), London for a day for £0** and our list of the top 25 reasons to visit London.

ON THE ROAD. When you reach London, you will spend most of your time in the following chapters: **Sights, Museums, Food, Pubs, Nightlife, Entertainment,** and **Shopping.** Don't miss our **Hidden Deal** and **Big Splurge** sidebars, which point you to some of the best ways to save (and to spend) your pounds—from cheap designer clothes to Indian massages. Learn about what's in the news and what's history, through **In the News** and **Local Legend.** In a **Local Story,** we even got a Queen's Guard to talk to us. When you feel like venturing outside the city, the **Daytripping** chapter will help: it provides a list of options for one-day and overnight trips away from London from elegant Hampton Court to charming Cambridge. The **Service Directory** contains a list of vital local services from where to find transport information, to how to contact your Embassy. Finally, remember to put down this guide once in a while and go exploring on your own; you'll be glad you did.

A NOTE TO OUR READERS. The information for this book was gathered by *Let's Go* researchers from May through August of 2004. Each listing is based on one researcher's opinion, formed during his or her visit at a particular time. Those traveling at other times may have different experiences since prices, dates, hours, and conditions are always subject to change. You are urged to check the facts presented in this book beforehand to avoid inconvenience and surprises.

1 2 3 4 5

PRICE RANGES >>LONDON

Our researchers list establishments in order of value from best to worst; our favorites are denoted by the Let's Go thumbs-up (☒). Since the best value is not always the cheapest price, we have incorporated a system of price ranges for quick reference. Our price ranges are based on a rough expectation of what you will spend. For **accommodations,** we base our price range off the cheapest price for which a single traveler can stay for one night. For **restaurants** and other dining establishments, we estimate the average amount that you will spend in that restaurant. The table below tells you what you will *typically* find in London at the corresponding price range; keep in mind that a particularly expensive ice cream stand may still only be marked a ❷, depending on what you will spend.

ACCOMMODATIONS	RANGE	WHAT YOU'RE *LIKELY* TO FIND
❶	under £20	Most dorm rooms, such as HI or other hostels or university dorm rooms. Expect bunk beds and a communal bath; you may have to provide or rent towels and sheets.
❷	£21-34	Upper-end hostels or small hotels. You may have a private bathroom, or there may be a sink in your room and communal shower in the hall.
❸	£35-49	A small room with a private bath. Should have decent amenities, such as phone and TV. Breakfast will probably be included in the price of the room.
❹	£50-74	Similar to 3, but may have more amenities or be in a more touristed area.
❺	above £75	Large hotels or upscale chains. If it's a 5 and it doesn't have the perks you want, you've paid too much.

FOOD	RANGE	WHAT YOU'RE *LIKELY* TO FIND
❶	under £5	Mostly street-corner stands, pizza places, or snack bars. Besides pub sandwiches, rarely a sit-down meal.
❷	£5-8	Sandwiches, pub grub, fish&chips, and cheap ethnic eateries. You may have the option of sitting down or getting take-out.
❸	£9-12	Mid-priced entrees. Fancier gastro-pubs and higher-quality ethnic food. Tip'll bump you up a couple dollars, since you'll probably have a waiter or waitress.
❹	£13-16	A somewhat fancy restaurant with a decent wine list or the very best gastro-pubs. Few restaurants in this range have a dress code, but most look down on t-shirt and jeans.
❺	above £16	Elegant setting and a long wine list. Trousers and dress shirts are usually expected. Don't order PB&J.

L805 GYU
97022

INSIDE

Discover London

London offers the visitor a bewildering array of choices: Leonardo at the National or Hirst at Tate Modern; tea at The Ritz or chilling in the Fridge; Rossini at the Royal Opera or Les Mis at the Queen's; Bond Street couture or Camden cutting-edge—you could spend your entire stay just deciding what to do and what to leave out. This chapter is designed to help put some method into the madness of visiting London.

London is often described as more a conglomeration of villages than a unified city. While this understates the civic pride Londoners take in their city as a whole, it is true that locals are strongly attached to their neighborhoods. Each area's heritage and traditions are still alive and evolving, from the City's 2000-year-old association with trade to Notting Hill's West Indian Carnival. Thanks to the feisty independence and diversity of each area, the London "buzz" is continually on the move—every few years a previously disregarded neighborhood explodes into cultural prominence. In the 60s Soho and Chelsea swung the world; the late 80s saw grunge rule the roost from Camden; and in the 90s the East End sprung Damien Hirst and the Britpack artists on the world. More recently, South London has come to prominence with the cultural rebirth of the South Bank and the thumping nightlife of a recharged Brixton.

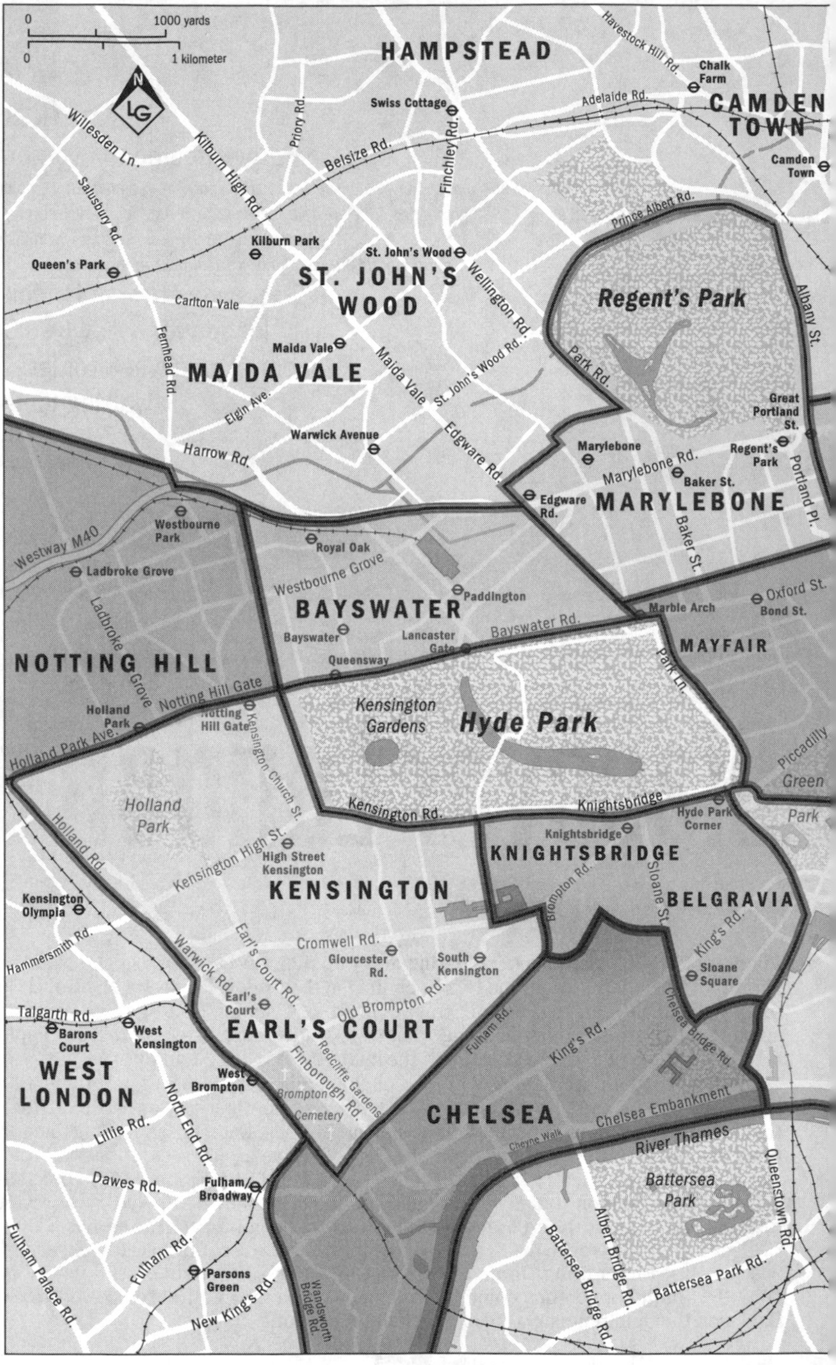

0 1000 yards
0 1 kilometer

HAMPSTEAD
Havestock Hill Rd.
Chalk Farm
CAMDEN TOWN
Adelaide Rd.
Swiss Cottage
Willesden Ln.
Kilburn High Rd.
Priory Rd.
Belsize Rd.
Finchley Rd.
Camden Town
Salusbury Rd.
Prince Albert Rd.
Kilburn Park
St. John's Wood
Queen's Park
ST. JOHN'S WOOD
Wellington Rd.
Regent's Park
Albany St.
Carlton Vale
Maida Vale
Fernhead Rd.
MAIDA VALE
Maida Vale
St. John's Wood Rd.
Park Rd.
Elgin Ave.
Great Portland St.
Warwick Avenue
Edgware Rd.
Marylebone
Regent's Park
Harrow Rd.
Marylebone Rd.
Baker St.
Portland Pl.
Edgware Rd.
MARYLEBONE
Westbourne Park
Westway M40
Royal Oak
Baker St.
Ladbroke Grove
Westbourne Grove
Paddington
Oxford St.
BAYSWATER
Marble Arch
Bond St.
Ladbroke Grove
Bayswater
Lancaster Gate
Bayswater Rd.
MAYFAIR
NOTTING HILL
Queensway
Park Ln.
Notting Hill Gate
Holland Park
Notting Hill Gate
Kensington Gardens
Hyde Park
Kensington Church St.
Holland Park Ave.
Piccadilly
Green Park
Holland Park
Kensington Rd.
Knightsbridge
Hyde Park Corner
Holland Rd.
Knightsbridge
KNIGHTSBRIDGE
Kensington High St.
High Street Kensington
Brompton Rd.
Sloane St.
KENSINGTON
BELGRAVIA
Kensington Olympia
King's Rd.
Hammersmith Rd.
Cromwell Rd.
Warwick Rd.
Earl's Court Rd.
Gloucester Rd.
South Kensington
Sloane Square
Earl's Court
Old Brompton Rd.
Chelsea Bridge Rd.
Talgarth Rd.
Barons Court
West Kensington
EARL'S COURT
Fulham Rd.
King's Rd.
Redcliffe Gardens
WEST LONDON
North End Rd.
West Brompton
Finborough Rd.
Brompton Cemetery
CHELSEA
Chelsea Embankment
Lillie Rd.
Cheyne Walk
River Thames
Dawes Rd.
Fulham Broadway
Battersea Park
Queenstown Rd.
Albert Bridge Rd.
Fulham Rd.
Battersea Bridge Rd.
Fulham Palace Rd.
Parsons Green
Battersea Park Rd.
New King's Rd.
Wandsworth Bridge Rd.

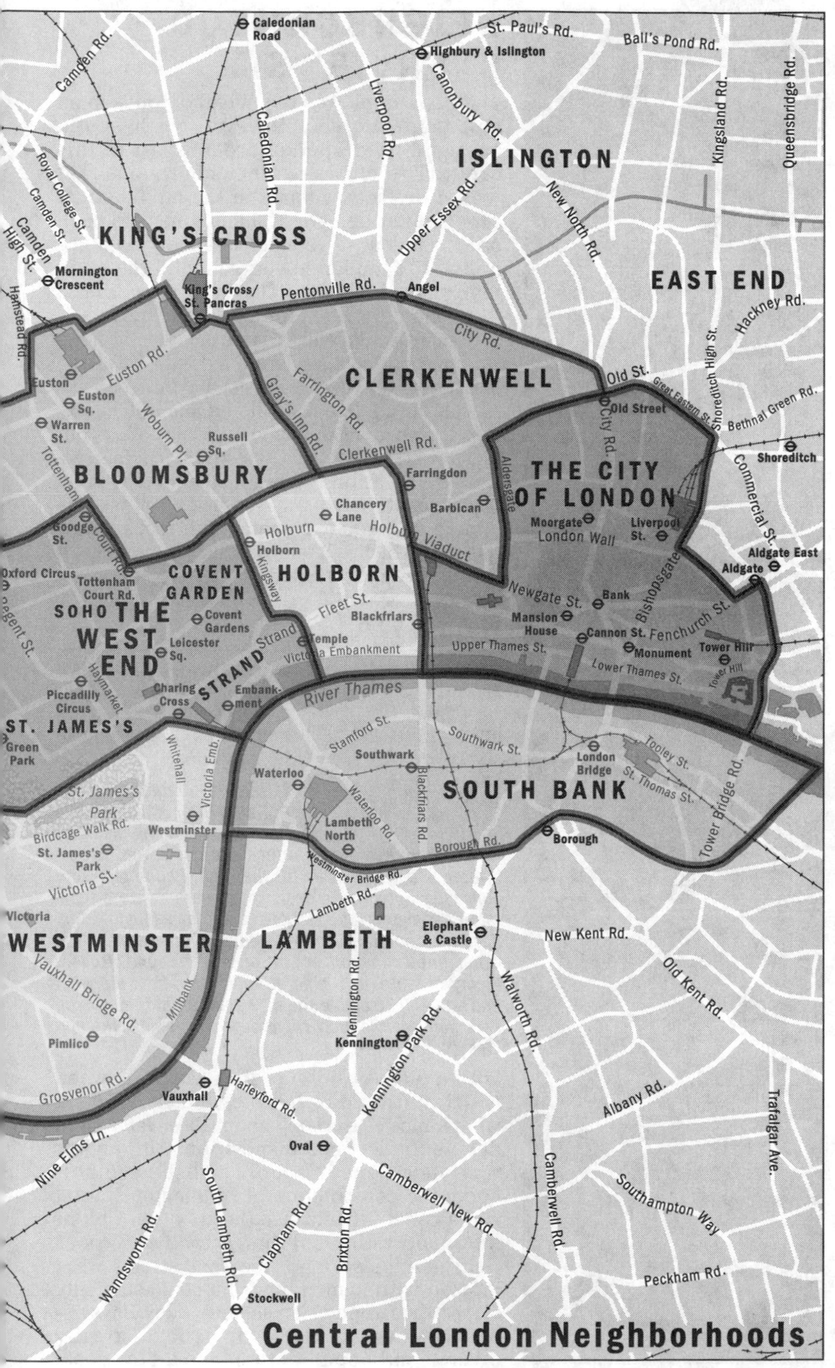

Central London Neighborhoods

Let's Go Picks

Best place to be trampled to death: The left side of a Tube escalator during rush hour.

Best place to buy an umbrella: Strike back with a quality fightin' brollie from **James Smith & Sons** (p. 255).

Best route to a heart attack: "Full English breakfast, please." Rinse. Repeat.

Best place to blow £1000: Sloane Street (p. 258), home to every posh chain imaginable.

Best place to get Blow for £1000: The drug dealers around **King's Cross** (p. 282).

Best meal for under £4: An 11" pizza from **ICCo.** (p. 166).

Best view/stairs ratio: Monument (p. 91), in The City, which provides an amazing view, plus a certificate of achievement for getting to the top.

Best place to ponder the meaning of life inside a fake pharmacy: Damien Hirst's art installation at **Tate Modern** (p. 137).

Best Chinese fish lips: Mr. Kong (p. 180) in Soho—they come with goose web.

Best place to buy a hookah: Edgware Road (p. 105), in "Marlebanon."

Best place to get a hooker: The alleys around **King's Cross** (p. 282).

Best James Bond villain named for a London architect: Goldfinger, named for the architect who ruined Ian Fleming's view with Two Willow Rd. (p. 122).

NEIGHBORHOOD OVERVIEWS

The book organizes the neighborhoods in an alphabetical order. However, north, south, east and west London are not part of this order. Therefore, two neighborhoods that would be farther apart in the alphabetical order might be geographically next to each other. Look at the London overview map (see p. 2-3) to familiarize yourself with the city's layout and refer to the map thumbnails throughout the book for location reminders.

Usually in all the listings we mention the nearest Tube station as underground is the way to go in London. However, keep in mind that the Tube closed during late night hours and it is important to know which bus to take back after your night out (see **Night Bus** map, p. 382). In this section we mention the main streets that most buses pass through. Once on that street you can look at very self-explanatory bus maps on the bus stop which will tell you which bus to take. If confused—ask somebody!

BAYSWATER

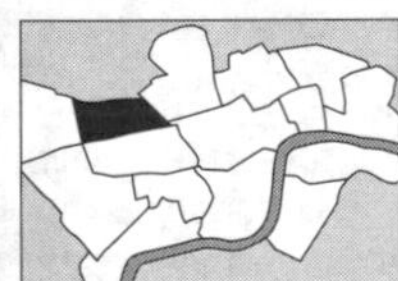

SEE MAP, p. 359

BAYSWATER QUICKFIND: Food, p. 164; pubs, p. 193; entertainment, p. 233; shopping, p. 254; accommodations, p. 279.

None too large, the longest stretch of walking you'll have to do is along pleasant fringes of Kensington Gardens and Hyde Park. Bayswater and Queensway for the west; Paddington and Lancaster Gate for the east. Note that there are 2 separate Paddington Tube stations: the Hammersmith & City line runs from tracks in the Paddington train station; the other lines run from a station underground. ***Buses:*** *Plenty of routes converge at Paddington from the West End and Knightsbridge The #12 and #94 run along Hyde Park from Marble Arch. Night buses: Bayswater Rd. and Westbourne Grove.*

With a plum position nestled snugly between Notting Hill, Marylebone, and Hyde Park, what's most surprising about Bayswater is its decidedly *un*-posh disposition. Although it was once London's most stylish neighborhood, the construction of Paddington station and a canal transformed the area into a bit of a transportation hub. Its attractive mass of Georgian houses and tree-lined streets were infused with immigrants who could suddenly afford the property costs, and today Bayswater has them to thank for its fantastically diverse and popular ethnic food. Low costs also provide the neighborhood with London's best and most convenient budget accommodations (travelers, take note). Close to everything and enduringly attractive, Bayswater is just beginning to be reexamined by ahead-of-the-curve Londoners; pre-re-gentrification, though, it remains alternately lively and quaint, with just the first hints of swank.

DON'T MISS...

Food: Cheap and tasty Caribbean food at Mr. Jerk; luscious Lebanese at Levantine; London's best in frozen goodness at La Bottega del Gelato.

Shopping: The Sunday Artists' Market along Bayswater Rd.; Whiteley's, the biggest shopping center in central London.

BLOOMSBURY

BLOOMSBURY QUICKFIND: Sights, p. 87; museums & galleries, p. 140; food, p. 166; pubs, p. 193; entertainment, p. 234; shopping, p. 255; accommodations, p. 282.

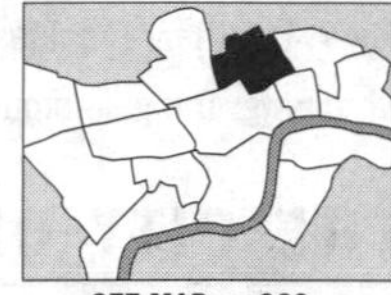
SEE MAP, p. 360

*Though fairly large, Bloomsbury is a pleasant district to walk around. A plethora of stations make Bloomsbury easy to get to from all over London: King's Cross is the system's biggest interchange, while Goodge St. and Russell Sq. are most central for the sights. **Buses:** Run mostly north-south, either between Warren St. and Tottenham Crt. Rd. stations (along Gower St. heading south, along Tottenham Crt. Rd. heading north), or between Euston and Holborn along Southampton Pl. Night buses: Tottenham Crt. Rd., Gower St., and New Oxford St.*

Home to dozens of universities, colleges, and specialist hospitals, not to mention both the British Museum and the British Library, Bloomsbury is London's undisputed intellectual powerhouse. In the early 20th century, the quiet squares and Georgian terraces resounded to the intellectual musings of the Bloomsbury Group, which included T.S. Eliot, E.M. Forster, and Virginia Woolf. Today, they house student halls and dozens of affordable accommodations. Bloomsbury offers everything you'd expect in an area dominated by students—bookstores, cheap food, and a million and one places to loaf about in the sun.

DON'T MISS...

Sights: The beautifully preserved treasures of the British Library; the bizarre preserved corpse of Jeremy Bentham.

Museums: Revisit childhood at the delightful Pollock's Toy Museum; revisit everything else at the recently revamped British Museum.

Food: Great fish 'n' chips at North Sea Fish Restaurant; Italian goodies at ICCo.

Pubs: Newman Arms's upstairs Pie Room, serves authentic British grub that is not only edible but tasty.

CHELSEA

CHELSEA QUICKFIND: Sights, p. 89; museums & galleries, p. 141; food, p. 167; entertainment, p. 234; shopping, p. 256.

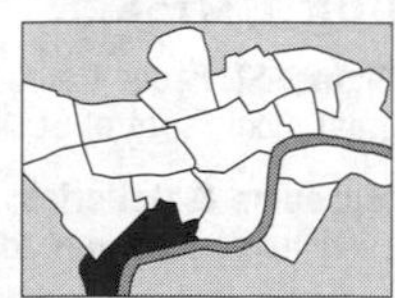
SEE MAP, p. 361

*In a borough where even the poorest resident drives a BMW, public transportation is a low priority–be prepared to walk. Sloane Sq., on Chelsea's eastern boundary, is the lone stop. **Buses:** Most run from Sloane Sq. down the King's Rd. on their way from Knightsbridge or Victoria. Night buses: Sloane Sq. and King's Rd.*

Chelsea has the cachet of Knightsbridge and Kensington without their stuffiness. In the 19th century, Cheyne Walk and surrounding streets hummed to the discussions of Edgar Allan Poe, George Eliot, Dante Gabriel Rossetti, Oscar Wilde, J.M.W. Turner, John Singer Sargent, and James MacNeill Whistler. The tone was a bit different in the 1960s and 70s, when King's Rd. was the launching point for miniskirts and punk rock. Stifled by a surfeit of wealth, today's Chelsea has little stomach for radicalism and it's still-artistic character has lost whatever bohemian edge might have lingered through the 80s. You'll find nothing more shocking than electric-blue frocks on the King's Rd., and local luminaries now include Hugh Grant, Liz Hurley, Britt Ekland, and a string of B-list celebrities and trust-fund kids known collectively as "Sloane Rangers." In any case, Chelsea manages to retain a little of its old-time glamour, helped along by the presence of numerous modeling agencies around Sloane Sq.

DON'T MISS...

Sights: The National Army Museum.

Entertainment: Royal Court Theatre; all that jazz at the 606 Club.

Food: Late, lazy breakfast at the Chelsea Bun and Buonasera.

Shopping: The glamorous vintage collection at Steinberg & Tolkien.

THE CITY OF LONDON

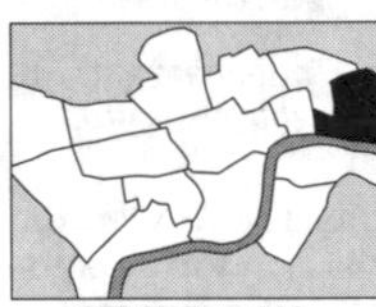

SEE MAP, p. 362

THE CITY OF LONDON QUICKFIND: Sights, p. 90; museums & galleries, p. 141; food, p. 168; pubs, p. 195; entertainment, p. 235.

Public transportation in the City is geared toward getting office workers around; within the compact City, walking is easiest. ***Rail:*** *Cannon St., Liverpool St., and Blackfriars, along with London Bridge across the river, provide service to commuters. Of the numerous Tube stations, Bank and St. Paul's are within easy reach of most sights; Tower Hill is useful for destinations farther east.* ***Buses:*** *Dozens of routes pass through the City: those from the West End and Holborn arrive along Ludgate Hill and Holborn Viaduct, while Liverpool St. station is the terminus for buses arriving from north London.*

The City is where London began—indeed, for most of its history, the City *was* London. The City's past sits uneasily with its present: to most Londoners its status as the most important financial center in Europe is an outlying irrelevance. A quarter of a million people work here during the day, but by night the City's population shrinks to a measly 8000, most of whom live in the 1970s towers of the luxury **Barbican Centre.** Not surprisingly, little happens here outside office hours. The majority of restaurants and pubs are aimed squarely at the millions of tourists who out number the pigeons at **St. Paul's Cathedral** and storm the **Tower of London.** London's two most famous sights, which look glorious seen from the water at **Tower Bridge** or from the air at the top of the **Monument.** For a less crowded, equally breathtaking view of the City, try standing on the **Millennium Bridge** facing St. Paul's at dusk. If you're a fan of Christopher Wren, the City is the place for you, with 24 of his churches squeezed between temples of commerce.

DON'T MISS...

Sights: St. Pauls' Cathedral and views from each gallery; the Tower early in the morning; the great picnic spot of St.Dunstan's in the east.

Museums & Galleries: Almost 2000 years of history at the fabulous Museum of London. Everything you'd want to about money at the Bank Museum.

Food: Hidden veggie delights at The Place Below.

Entertainment: Top plays and musical acts in the hard-to-navigate Barbican Centre.

CLERKENWELL

CLERKENWELL QUICKFIND: Sights, p. 95; museums & galleries, p. 143; food, p. 169; pubs, p. 196; nightlife, p. 210; entertainment, p. 235; accommodations, p. 285.

Walking is the best way to get around Clerkenwell. ⊖Everything is in walking distance of Farringdon; southern and eastern parts can be reached from Barbican and northern parts can be reached by Angel. ***Buses:*** *Routes on Clerkenwell Rd. and Roseberry Ave. Night buses: Roseberry Ave.*

SEE MAP, p. 363

Under the vamped-up guise of "Cityside"—a reference to its position on the boundaries of the City of London—Clerkenwell was the success story of the late 1990s. If it's no longer cutting-edge cool, that's a bonus: less attitude, more fun. With stylish restaurants, new-age bars, popular club venues, and a pub on every corner, this quiet neighborhood wakes up when the lights dim. Behind the industrial facade and the bustling nightlife, Clerkenwell harbors deep historical roots, and it is this coexistence of modernity and history that defines its character. Not the prettiest neighborhood to spend the day strolling in, though; once a distillery-filled ghetto district, its industrial facade and a strong hint of grime still remain.

DON'T MISS...

Pubs: Full English breakfast at Fox & Anchor; Mediterranean lunch at The Eagle; specialty ales at The Jerusalam Tavern.

Nightlife: Dancing at fabu megaclub Fabric; leisurely lounging at Fluid.

HOLBORN

HOLBORN QUICKFIND: Sights, p. 97; museums & galleries, p. 143; food, p. 170; pubs, p. 197; nightlife, p. 211; entertainment, p. 236; shopping, p. 257.

Holborn is easily walkable–compact and easy to navigate. ⊖Holborn, Farringdon, Chancery Ln. (closed Su), and Temple (closed Su). ***Buses:*** *High Holborn, Kinsway St. and Fleet St. Night buses: Theobalds Rd. Kinsway St. and Fleet St.*

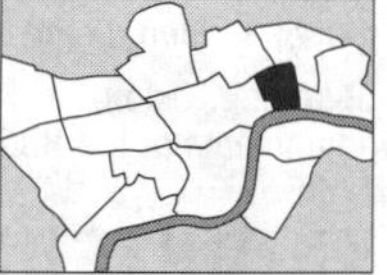

SEE MAP, p. 363

London's second-oldest area, Holborn was the first part of the city settled by Saxons—"Aldwych," on the western edge of Holborn, is Anglo-Saxon for "old port." Once a center of medieval monasticism, today Holborn is associated with two unholy professions: law and journalism. If you thought lawyers had it good at home, wait until you see the **Inns of Court,** colleges-*cum*-clubs for barristers that have been growing in wealth and power for centuries. East of the Inns, **Fleet Street** remains synonymous with the British press even though the newspapers have since moved on. After hours, the nightlife is restricted to Holborn's many historic pubs, whose past patrons include Sam Johnson and Samuel Pepys.

DON'T MISS...

Sights: St. Etheldreda's, a gem to rival the famous jewelry of Hatton Garden; labyrinthine gardens and halls of the Temple. The artistic splendor of Somerset House.

Museums & Galleries: Silver parrots and gold snuffboxes at the Gilbert Collection Galleries; genius run wild at the eclectic museum of Sir John Soane

Pubs: Ye Olde Mitre, probably the best pub in London; ale appreciation at Ye Olde Cheshire Cheese; Sweeny Todd's old haunts at the Old Bank of England.

KENSINGTON & EARL'S COURT

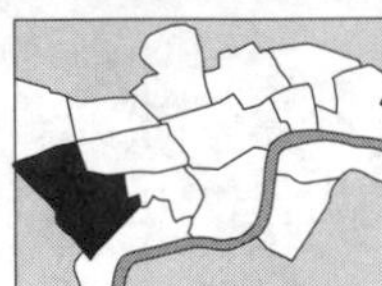

SEE MAP, pp. 364-365

KENSINGTON and EARL'S COURT QUICKFIND: Sights, p. 100; museums & galleries, p. 145; food, p. 171; pubs, p. 198; entertainment, p. 236; shopping, p. 257; accommodations, p. 286.

One of central London's larger neighborhoods, public transport is necessary to get around. ⊖Stations are helpfully named: High St. Kensington for the High St., South Kensington for the South Kensington museums, and Earl's Court for Earl's Court. ***Buses:*** *Numerous buses ply the High St. before climbing up Kensington Church St. to Notting Hill; to get to South Kensington take #49 or 70.*

The past stomping ground of Princess Diana, Kensington is characterized by two major divisions: the posh consumer mecca of **Kensington High Street** in the west and the awe-inspiring museums and colleges of **South Kensington's** "Albertopolis" in the east—no prizes for guessing which was Di's favorite. The presence of 2000 French schoolkids at the local *lycée* gives parts of South Kensington a distinctly continental feel, helped by numerous good, cheap restaurants. Both High St. and South Ken have a smattering of budget accommodations, but neither can compare with "Kangaroo Valley" in **Earl's Court** to the southwest. In the 1960s and 70s, Earl's Court was the sole preserve of Aussie backpackers and the gay population. Today others have caught on to its combination of cheap accommodations with good transport links.

DON'T MISS...

Sights: The big green of Hyde Park and Kensington Gardens; great, gilded Albert reigning over his South Ken legacies; the Royal Dress Collection in Kensington Palace.

Museums: Victoria & Albert tops most people's lists, but those with kids shouldn't ignore the Natural History and Science Museums nearby.

Food: Complex and contemplative Indian cuisine at Zaika; tea at the Palace in the Orangery; rooftop garden dining magic at Babylon.

Shopping: Oxford St. variety without Oxford St. crowds on Kensington High St.; sophisticated adornments at the British Hatter.

KNIGHTSBRIDGE & BELGRAVIA

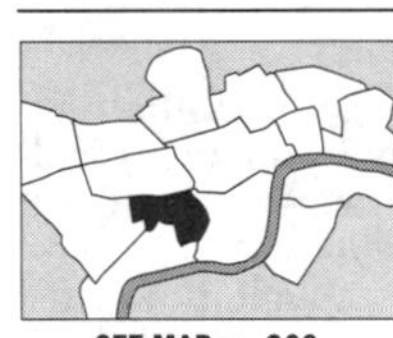

SEE MAP, p. 366

KNIGHTSBRIDGE & BELGRAVIA QUICKFIND: Sights, p. 102; food, p. 172; pubs, p. 198; shopping, p. 258; accommodations, p. 290.

Knightsbridge and Belgravia are both easy and pleasant to walk around. ⊖Knightsbridge station is near all the shops; most of the hotels in Belgravia are accessible from Victoria, while the north end, near the park, sits on top of Hyde Park Corner. ***Buses:*** *Numerous routes converge on Hyde Park Corner, Sloane St., and Brompton Rd. NIght buses: Hyde Park Corner and Knightsbridge.*

Knightsbridge and Belgravia are naturally both smug and wildly expensive. The location comes at such a price that even millionaire penthouse owners have sold their property to foreign embassies and consulates—the only people who can afford the land anymore. Not surprisingly, the primary draw for tourists is the window shopping. **Knightsbridge** is home to two of the biggest names in all of store-dom: famed department stores Harrods and Harvey Nichols exude an air of superiority. **Belgravia,** which occupies the region east of Sloane St., is an expanse of grand 19th-century mansions occupied by aforementioned millionaires and embassies.

DON'T MISS...

Sights: Apsley House, with a 25 ft. nude Napolean; a rare glimpse into Buckingham Palace gardens at the Wellington Arch.

Shopping: Harrods—you have to see it to believe it; Harvey Nichols, Diana's favorite department store; designer collections on Sloane St.; designer clothes for much less at Pandora.

Food: Opulence run amok at the swanky Lanesborough.

MARYLEBONE & REGENT'S PARK

MARYLEBONE & REGENT'S PARK QUICKFIND: Sights, p. 103; museums & galleries, p. 147; food, p. 173; entertainment, p. 237; accommodations, p. 291

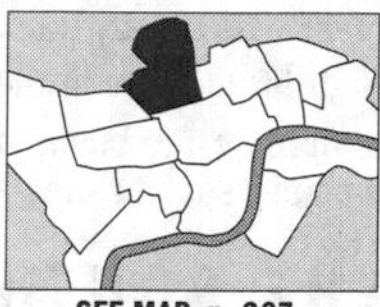
SEE MAP, p. 367

The main problem getting around Marylebone is crossing the vast and boring expanse in the middle. Baker St. is convenient for Marylebone's northern sights; Bond St. covers the south. Confusingly, there are 2 entirely separate Edgware Rd. stations; fortunately, they're not far apart. ***Buses:*** *The best way of getting across Marylebone. 10 bus routes link north and south via Baker St. (going south) and Gloucester Pl. (heading north), while 7 more ply Edgware Rd. Night buses: Along Marylebone Rd., Gloucester Pl., Baker St., Oxford St., and Edgeware Rd.*

Marylebone is defined by its borders. To the east, beautiful **Portland Place** is an architectural wonder. To the west, culturally eclectic **Edgware Road** boasts many Middle Eastern eateries, shops, and markets. To the south, the West End's **Oxford Street** is a shopaholic's paradise. Rounding out the northern border of Marylebone, **Regent's Park** is a giant and popular stretch of greenery surrounded by elegant Regency terraces. More than London's biggest football practice-ground, the park is home to a panoply of sights including the golden dome of the London Central Mosque, while nearby, Marylebone Rd. and Baker St. trap tourists with Madame Tussaud's and the Planetarium. Marylebone High St. drives a wedge of trendy shops, cafes, and restaurants on its way from Marylebone Rd. to Oxford St.

DON'T MISS...

Sights: A slow, leisurely walk through Regent's Park.

Museums: One of the world's finest private art collections with Britain's biggest array of armor at the Wallace Collection.

Food: A charming culinary experience at Mandalay; delicious Persian food at Patogh.

NOTTING HILL

NOTTING HILL QUICKFIND: Sights, p. 105; food, p. 174; pubs, p. 200; nightlife, p. 212; entertainment, p. 237; shopping, p. 259.

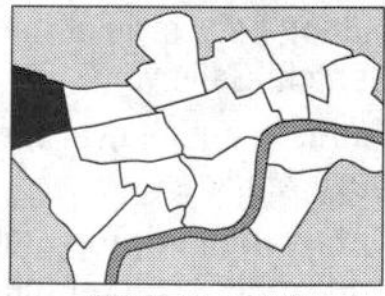
SEE MAP, p. 359

Getting to Notting Hill is easy, getting around slightly less so. Notting Hill Gate serves the south, while Ladbroke Grove deposits you close by Portobello Rd. The only problem with Ladbroke is the Tube line it serves means you'll have to transfer at least once. ***Buses:*** *#52 runs from Ladbroke Grove down to the Gate and Kensington Park Rd. From the West End, #12 and 94 will get you to Notting Hill Gate, while a plethora of buses make the trip up from High St. Kensington.*

For decades one of London's most vibrant, ethnically mixed neighborhoods, Notting Hill has become a victim of its own boho-chic trendiness (helped on by a certain movie). In some spots, the mix of bohemians, immigrants, and blue-collar workers that sustained its vitality is being displaced by an influx of yuppies, which explains some of the lofty prices. The northern portion of **Portobello Road** around the Westway, where the tenements and local markets lie, still retains much of its original character, but venture too far off Portobello Rd., and you'll be find a quiet neighborhood of indistinguishable two-family homes. Still, it's a lovely place to spend an afternoon, especially on market days. Annually during the final week in August, the whole neighborhood explodes with Caribbean color and sound during the **Notting Hill Carnival;** originally started by West Indian immigrants as a local street party, it has become a giant summer festival attended by over two million people.

DON'T MISS...

Food: Yummy, affordable pastries at Lisboa; greasy, delicious fish 'n' chips at George's; lazy breakfasts at Lazy Daisy Cafe.

Nightlife: Groove in The Market.

Shopping: The bustle of Portobello Market on a Friday or Saturday; your choice of environmentally sound caffeinated concoctions at Tea and Coffee Plant.

THE SOUTH BANK

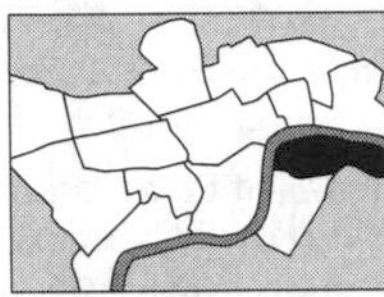
SEE MAP, pp. 368-369

THE SOUTH BANK QUICKFIND: Sights, p. 106; museums & galleries, p. 148; food, p. 176; pubs, p. 200; nightlife, p. 212; entertainment, p. 238; accommodations, p. 292.

Poorly served by public transportation, most South Bank attractions are best reached by walking along the river. The closest station to the South Bank Centre is across the river at Embankment; take the Hungerford foot bridge. Use Waterloo for inland attractions, Southwark for Bankside, and London Bridge for Borough and Butlers Wharf.

Close to the City, but exempt from its party-squelching laws, the South Bank has long been London's entertainment center. In Shakespeare's time it was renowned for its theaters, cock-fighting, bull-baiting, and gentlemanly diversions of less reputable forms. Dominated by wharves and warehouses in the 19th century, the devastation of WWII forced the South Bank to rebuild—an opportunity for the neighborhood to reassert its fun-loving heritage. Now, the **"Millennium Mile"** stretches from the twirling London Eye in the west to the swank restaurants of Butlers Wharf in the east, passing by the cultural powerhouses of the Festival Hall, Hayward Gallery, National Theatre, National Film Theatre, Tate Modern, and Shakespeare's Globe Theatre, as well as the quirky riverside shops and eateries of Gabriel's Wharf and the OXO Tower.

DON'T MISS...

Sights: London—all of it, as seen from the top of the London Eye; the Queen's Walk, with the Thames on one side and artistic distractions on the other.

Museums & Galleries: Tate Modern, the world's largest modern art museum; award-winning, cutting-edge style at the Design Museum; shocking and provocative Britart exhibits at the new Saatchi Gallery.

Food: Beautiful river views at the Cantina del Ponte; top Turkish treats at Tas; goodies at Borough Market.

Entertainment: Top drama at the National Theatre, the Old Vic, and the Globe; classical, jazz, and world music at the South Bank Centre; celluloid variety at the National Film Theater; a literally enormous cinematic experience at the BFI IMAX.

Nightlife: The world heavyweight champion of clubbing: The Ministry of Sound.

THE WEST END

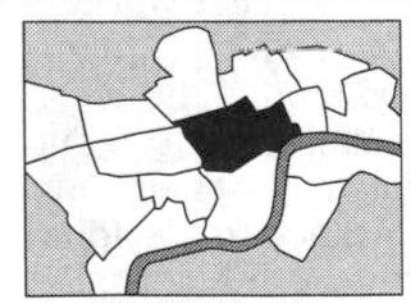
SEE MAP, p. 354

THE WEST END QUICKIND: Sights, p. 111; museums & galleries, p. 150; food, p. 177; pubs, p. 201; nightlife, p. 212; entertainment, p. 240; shopping, p. 261; accommodations, p. 292.

At the hub of London's transportation network, the West End is also surprisingly easy to walk. The Tube is best for getting in and out of the West End; it's not worth it for travelling 1 or 2 stops within the area. ***Buses:*** *The best way to get around. Many routes head from Trafalgar Sq. to the Strand, Piccadilly, and Charing Cross Rd.; more bus lines* *converge at Oxford Circus, from where they run south down Regent St. to Piccadilly Circus, west up Oxford St. to Marble Arch, and east to Tottenham Crt. Rd. Trafalgar Sq. is also the departure point for most of the Night Bus network.*

Whether it's shopping, eating, theatergoing, or clubbing, the West End is London's popular heartland, with a wider variety of activities than any other neighborhood in the city. This ill-defined district between royal Westminster and the financial powerhouse of the City was first settled by nobles wanting to be close to both; over time, the area became a patchwork of distinct communities. Wealthy Londoners still live in mansions in prestigious **Mayfair** and socialize in neighboring **St. James's** gentlemen's clubs. On the other side of Piccadilly Circus, young Londoners party in very different clubs—**Soho,** and around the very gay Old Compton St. is London's nightlife Nexus. **Oxford Street,** which forms Mayfair's northern boundary, has been London's premier shopping street for over 150 years—the weekend before Christmas, there's barely room to stand. The more fashion-conscious head to the boutiques of **Covent Garden,** southwest of Soho, along with crowds of tourists who just hang out in Inigo Jones's Piazza. South of Covent Garden, the **Strand** is mostly just a crowded thoroughfare that marks the way to majestic, pigeon-infested **Trafalgar Square,** a reminder of Britain's greater days.

DON'T MISS...

Sights: Soak in the atmosphere at St. James's; Oxford St. overload on Saturday; sunny Covent Garden Piazza; slinky Soho by night and gaudy Leicester Sq.

Museums & Galleries: Jazz hands and dramatic pauses are celebrated at the Theatre Museum; Tubes and trams at the Transport Museum.

Food: Top-notch Thai dishes at Busaba Eathai; some of London's best (and only) Mexican at Café Pacifico; a truly bazaar experience at Mô's Moroccan tea-room; the Piazza cafes of St. Christopher's Place.

Shopping: Funky clothes and shoes galore on Floral St. and Neal St., Covent Garden; top DJs' favorite record stores in Soho; window-shopping at the *couture* boutiques on Bond St.; Selfridges, London's favorite department store and bookstores galore on Charing Cross Rd.

Nightlife: Chilling on couches at Freud and AKA; the labyrinthine Heaven, Britain's most famous gay nightclub; drag queens of Madame Jojo's.

Entertainment: Sing-a-long *Sound of Music* in Leicester Sq.; jazz legends at Ronnie Scott's; the funniest funny-men at the Comedy Store.

WESTMINSTER

WESTMINSTER QUICKFIND: Sights, p. 116; museums & galleries, p. 152; food, p. 181; pubs, p. 202; entertainment, p. 244; accommodations, p. 293.

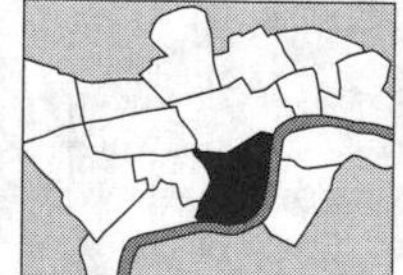
SEE MAP, p. 370

Getting here is not a problem. Victoria, to the west, doubles as a mainline ***train*** *station and the nearby London terminus for most long-distance coach services. ⊖Westminster deposits you near most sights; use St. James's Park for Buckingham Palace; use Pimlico for accommodations and Tate Britain. Charing Cross tube deposits you in Trafalgar Sq., it connecting Westminster and the West End.* ***Buses:*** *Numerous buses swirl around Parliament Sq. before being catapulted up Whitehall to Trafalagar Sq., down Victoria St. to Victoria, along the Embankment to Pimlico, and across the river into Lambeth.*

Westminster, with its postcard-friendly spires and lush parks, often feels like the heart of the old British Empire. It is, after all, home to both the Houses of Parliament and the Queen herself. But away from the towering elegance of Nelson's Column in Trafalgar Square, the bureaucracy of Whitehall, and the Gothic grandeur of the Abbey, Westminster is a surprisingly down-to-earth district—thousands of office workers make Victoria London's busiest Tube station. **Pimlico,** south of Victoria, is a quiet residential district with some of London's best B&Bs. Aside some notable exceptions, this is not the neighborhood for shoppers, clubbers, or foodies.

in recent news

Market Madness

London has a thriving population of street markets, ranging from a few stalls to many square blocks in size. Some have been around for years, others spontaneously pop up in parking lots for a few hours. Each has its own character, and there is something for everyone: from paper towel to Chinese food to Pakistani jewelry. Here are some tips for your expeditions:

Look out for one-time markets or day-specific one so you don't miss your chance at one-day a week sales.

Compare prices before buying. Just because the man at the streetside booth will sell at £30 doesn't mean the man 4 rows and 3 stalls back won't sell for £15.

Don't be afraid to bargain. This is not Harrods.

Don't even think about returning anything. Well, you can think about it but it's wishful thinking.

Unless you enjoy walking through seas of people try heading over **early**.

Market food is often greasy, cheap and *delicious*. Noodles, Indian food, crepes or fruit juice–take your pick but stay away from the meat.

Markets are a bad place to "window shop." The best stuff is rarely streetside. Serious or just curious, dive into the lines of stalls and head straight for the heart to get to the good stuff.

Still, with its proximity to Soho, the West End, Knightsbridge, and Chelsea, Westminster makes a great home base for any visit—and its sights are unbeatable.

DON'T MISS...

Sights: Nelson scowling from his pedestal above bustling Trafalgar Square; two duelling visions–the Gothic splendor of Westminster Abbey, and the neo-Byzantine grandeur of Westminster Cathedral; the Changing of the Guard at Buckingham Palace.

Museums & Galleries: The incomparable array of fine art at the National Gallery; the claustrophobic, secretive corridors and chambers of the Cabinet War Rooms.

Pubs: Ales at Sherlock Holmes.

NORTH LONDON

NORTH LONDON QUICKFIND: Sights, p. 120; museums & galleries, p. 153; food, p. 183; pubs, p. 203; nightlife, p. 218; entertainment, p. 244; shopping, p. 269; accommodations, p. 294.

Most individual neighborhoods are walkable, once you are there. Note that north of Euston you are in Zone 2, while Highgate and Golders Green are in Zone 3. You can always get off in Zone 2 and take a bus up. **Buses:** *Essential for getting to some out-of-the-way locations. Take advantage of the bus and local-area maps in Tube stations and at bus stops to help you find your way. Once you're in North London, buses are also the best way to get from one neighborhood to another.*

Green and prosperous, North London's inner suburbs are some of London's older outlying communities. **Hampstead** and **Highgate** were pleasant country retreats for centuries before urban sprawl engulfed them, and both still retain a distinct village atmosphere. Of the two, Hampstead is busier and more urbane, with a long line of intellectual associations from John Keats to Sigmund Freud. Closer to the center, **Camden Town** and **Islington** were grimy, working-class areas for most of the 19th and 20th centuries, but in the 1980s their stock shot up and both are now populated with wealthy liberals. Tony Blair lived in Islington before making the move to Downing St. However, during the weekend in Camden Town, you'd be hard-pressed to notice the yuppification. The gigantic street market is more popular than ever, attracting what looks like half the under-25 population of England every Sunday. In Islington the prosperity is more apparent: Upper St. has become one of London's top eating destinations, with over 100 restaurants within walking distance of Angel Tube. **Maida Vale** and **St. John's Wood** are wealthy residential northern extensions of Marylebone and Bayswater; particularly picturesque is **Little Venice,** at the confluence of three canals, while the most famous sight in these parts is the fairly unremarkable pedestrian crossing at **Abbey Road.**

DON'T MISS...

Sights: The wild and tangled Hampstead Heath; Kenwood House, a picture-perfect country mansion housing a great art collection; the hidden pastures of the Hill Garden; *Beatles* appreciation at Abbey Rd.

Food: Rolled-up goodness at La Creperie de Hampstead; affordable French elegance at Le Mercury; Carmelli's challah; super kebabs at Gallipoli.

Pubs: Everything a pub should be at Compton Arms; the delights of an enormous hot salt beef sandwich at the Wenlock Arms.

Shopping: Total weekend madness at Camden market; boutiques and antiques in Islington.

Nightlife: Out-of the way dance to trance at Canvas/The Cross; gay cabaret at the Black Cap; trendy Filthy McNasty's Whiskey Cafe.

Entertainment: Top-notch acts at Jazz Cafe; Tricycle's offbeat picks and flicks.

EAST LONDON

EAST LONDON QUICKFIND: Sights, p. 126; museums & galleries, p. 156; food, p. 187; pubs, p. 204; nightlife, p. 222; entertainment, p. 248; shopping, p. 271.

*Much of East London is surprisingly central; you're unlikely to get beyond Zone 2. The East End is well served by the Underground. Old St. is best for Hoxton/Shoreditch while Aldgate East and Liverpool St. are nearest Whitechapel sights. Farther east, the Tube swings away and the **DLR** takes over: these driverless trains (travelcards valid) will take you all the way down to Greenwich. **Buses:** Useful for getting from the City to the East End, but for distances farther east, the Tube and DLR are quicker.*

At Aldgate, the fabulous wealth of the City abruptly gives way to the historically impoverished **East End.** The divide is centuries-old: since both prevailing winds and the river current conspired to waft the pollution of the crowded City eastward, the rich fled to West London and the poor were grounded in the east. Cheap land together with proximity to the docks made the East End a natural site for immigration. Older residents still remember when this was a predominantly Jewish neighborhood, but today it's solidly Bangladeshi. **Brick Lane,** famed for its market and its restaurants, is now at the center of a new influx: independent artists and designers colonizing one of the last affordable areas in central London. East of Whitechapel, the East End remains poor until **Docklands.** Since the late 1980s, this vast man-made archipelago has been busy building itself up from an abandoned port into a mini-metropolis. Unfortunately, the construction has decimated the area's traditional communities and bulldozed much of its history—there's not much reason to get off the elevated DLR trains as they shuffle south toward **Greenwich.** Once the favorite residence of Elizabeth I, Greenwich is far removed from East London's present: steeped in history, it's a beautiful district with a wealth of sights.

DON'T MISS...

Sights: The Sunday market crawl—check out Spitalfields; hop on the DLR to Greenwich for a dose of suburbia and history.

Museums & Galleries: Promising newcomers and established talents at the spectacular Whitechapel Art Gallery; Shoho avant-garde work at the White Cube.

Food: Cruise bagel and balti joints along Brick Ln.

Nightlife: Herbal or Canteloupe to mix with the beautiful people; Vibe for low key nights on the town.

SOUTH LONDON

SOUTH LONDON QUICKFIND: Sights, p. 126; museums & galleries, p. 155; food, p. 186; nightlife, p. 222; entertainment, p. 247; shopping, p. 271.

*This area is largely bypassed by the **Tube;** overland **rail** makes up the difference, with service from Victoria, Waterloo, and London Bridge. **Buses:** From Brixton, the P4 will take you to all the Dulwich sights. 345 from South Ken., 333 from ELephant and Castle, 2 from Baker St. Night Buses: N2 from Victoria, N133 from Elephant and Castle and P5 goes from Brixton to all the Dulwich sites.*

Few divides are harder to bridge than that which separates South from North London. With a few exceptions (notably the South Bank), North Londoners regard everything south of the Thames as inherently disreputable, and South Londoners view their northern neighbors as insufferably pretentious. The truth is that South London's relatively recent development lacks a historical center to match that of the north, and can easily appear as a mess of Victorian railway suburbs. Yet this anonymity hides some of London's most dynamic neighborhoods. **Brixton** today is largely black, after a wave of West Indian immigrants during the 1940s and 50s that led to race riots in the 1980s and 1995. Despite long association with drug-soaked poverty, Brixton is home to some thumping nightlife: clubs are often open until 10am. Neighboring **Dulwich** couldn't be more different, a quiet and prosperous hilly village filled with golf greens and country clubs.

DON'T MISS...

Museums: Dulwich Picture Gallery, a fantastic collection of Old Masters.

Food: Top vegetarian food and fish in an atmospheric church crypt at Bug.

Nightlife: Grooving in the jam-packed Tongue&Groove; serious trance action at Fridge.

Entertainment: Headline rock, pop, and world acts at the famous Brixton Academy.

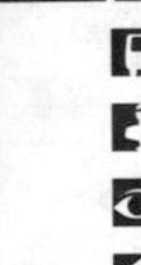

WEST LONDON

WEST LONDON QUICKFIND: Sights, p. 130; food, p. 188; entertainment, p. 248; shopping, p. 273; accommodations, p. 295.

*West London is huge, but most sights are easy to get to. If you've got the time, a **river boat** is the most relaxing way of getting to Kew. The District Line goes to most sights. **Buses:** Invaluable for getting to some of the more obscure sights and also an efficient way of getting between West London neighborhoods.*

West London stretches for miles along the Thames before petering out in the hills and vales of the Thames. The river changes tack so often and so sharply that it makes no sense to talk about the north or south bank, and communities have developed almost in isolation from their neighbors. **Shepherd's Bush,** one of these relatively autonomous districts, distinguishes itself with a number of well-known concert and theater venues, while **Hammersmith** bridges the gap between the shopping malls around the Tube station and the pleasant parks and pubs along the Thames. Historically, the western reaches of the Thames were fashionable spots for country retreats, and the river still winds through the grounds of stately homes and former palaces. The neighborhoods surrounding **Kew Gardens** and **Turnham Green/ Chiswick** are also full of pleasant shops and eateries.

DON'T MISS...

Sights: The lush gardens and lavish furnishings of Chiswick House; the even lusher Kew Gardens.

Food: All things French at Maison Blanc; vegetarian delights at the Gate.

Entertainment: Being part of a live studio audience at BBC Television Centre; a double bill pf international art flicks at Riverside Studios.

TOP 25 REASONS TO VISIT LONDON

25. Somerset House. This elegant manor is home to 3 top museums: The Gilbert Collection of Decorative Arts, The Hermitage Rooms, and the world-famous Courtaud Institute Galleries. See p. 144.

24. Oxford Street. London's shopping mecca, Oxford St. is always packed—on Saturdays, you can barely move. It's all worth it, though, with every major chain, countless bargain stalls, and tons of one-off boutiques offering the most stylish clothes and accessories you'll find anywhere in the world. See p. 261.

23. Regent's Park. London's most attractive and most popular park, boasting a wide range of landscapes from soccer-scarred fields to Italian-style formal gardens. See p. 103.

22. Bayswater. The culinary delights in this neighborhood are unbeatable. See p. 164.

21. The view from the Monument. From atop Christopher Wren's memorial to the Great Fire of 1666, you can see everything—and they even give you a certificate of achievement just for climbing up. See p. 91.

20. The Old Bank of England. One of London's very best pubs, with meat pies that will blow your mind. See p. 197.

19. Café Zagora. This is what London's multiculturalism is all about—a Moroccan-Lebanese restaurant staffed by Poles in Hogarth's old neighborhood. The decor is elegant, the food remarkable, and the service impeccable. See p. 189.

18. Fabric. As big and bold as a nightclub can get, Fabric's 3 dance floors can (and often do) hold up to 2000 dedicated clubbers. See p. 210.

17. Houses of Parliament. Neo-Gothicism's greatest architectural triumph, the Houses of Parliament bear their history and traditions with grace and stunning beauty. See p. 76.

16. Leicester Square and Picadilly Circus. The circus came to town—and forgot to leave. See p. 114

15. Zaika. An excellent Indian restaurant, Zaika wows with its innovative, intelligent colors and flavors. The service is excellent, and the decor is hip and comfortable. One bite, and you'll be hooked on "British" food forever. See p. 172.

14. The London Eye. The largest observational wheel in the world, the London Eye offers 360-degree views of all of London. Time your visit right, and you can look down on the Houses of Parliament and Buckingham Palace glowing in the sunset. See p. 106.

13. St. Paul's. Christopher Wren's masterpiece, the towering dome of St. Paul's dominates The City of London. See p. 80.

12. The British Museum. Imagine every museum you've ever been to, then multiply by 10. The British Museum has over 50,000 items, from the Rosetta Stone and endless mummies to African fetish dolls and tribal costumes. See p. 133.

11. Ye Olde Mitre. Hands-down our favorite pub in London, Ye Olde Mitre was built in 1546 by the Bishop of Ely. Its two dark rooms are incredibly cozy, the staff is friendly, and the bitters are excellent. See p. 197.

10. Shakespeare's Globe Theatre. You can take a tour to see behind-the-scenes, but for the full Globe experience, attend one of the many performances. See the excellent, innovative productions from the hard wooden benches, or commune with Elizabethan peasantry as a groundling. See p. 239.

9. The Tower of London. Arrive early in the morning to beat the crowds, and you'll be treated to one of London's most evocative sights. Home to a long and bloody past and a resplendent present—the Yeomen of the Guard and the Crown Jewels are guaranteed to impress. See p. 83.

8. The British Library Galleries. A stunning collection of books and manuscripts is on display in the new British Library building. Highlights include a Magna Carta, Joyce's handwritten *Finnegan's Wake,* and original handwritten Beatles lyrics. See p. 140.

7. Portobello Road Markets. Everything you've never wanted or needed, all in one place. Portobello Rd. has to be seen to be believed—come on a Saturday morning for the full effect; hundreds of thousands of people combing through everything from used clothes to antique china. See p. 259.

6. Brixton nightlife. Brixton is home to London's most exciting new club scene—not bad for a former slum. Clubs like Tongue&Groove and the Fridge are both hip and welcoming, filled with energetic, stylish young dancers. Many clubs and bars stay open all night so you can party until dawn. See p. 221.

5. The Victoria & Albert Museum. The largest museum of decorative arts in the world, the V&A is home to a 500-year-old Iranian carpet, a pair of 1990s latex hotpants, and just about everything in between. See p. 138.

4. Tea at Ritz. The quintessential English tea, Tea at Ritz offers visitors the ultimate in luxury and old-fashioned elegance. Feast on cucumber sandwiches, scones, and clotted cream—for a few hours you can live like royalty. See p. 163.

3. Westminster Abbey. In its thousand years, this beautiful building has seen countless kings crowned, celebrated, and buried. The Abbey is the resting place of Britain's greatest men and women, from royalty to poets and scientists. See p. 78.

2. The National Gallery. The National Gallery holds an incredible collection of art. The brand-new Sainsbury Wing is a treasure trove of medieval art while other rooms house Manet, Van Gogh, Rubens, Rembrandt, and two of only 34 Vermeers in the world. No matter what your taste in art, you'll never want to leave. See p. 135.

1. The Tate Modern. London is home to the world's most active and innovative modern art community, and this is where it shows. Tate Modern displays art of every stripe, from sculpture to installations to claymation; all is carefully curated and guaranteed to be both refreshing and challenging. See p. 137.

LONDON FOR A DAY ON £0

In a city of £100 jeans and £4 cappuccinos, sometimes it seems like nothing comes cheap. Well, *Let's Go* does, and if you're currently suffering from the got-no-money blues, we've got the perfect mood-elevator to brighten things up: London on £0.

A few conditions for the night before you begin so you don't pass out from hunger during this adventure. Stop by the nearest **Sainsbury's** or **Safeway** market and pick up cheap picnic fixin's. Also, if you don't have a weekly Travelcard already, you'll have to buy a day's bus or tube pass to get around.

First, spend your **morning** on a museum high (steel yourself against all the guilt-inducing "Donation" please; remember, you're on a mission!). Take your pick from some of the best and most exhilarating collections in the world. The **Tate Modern** would be our choice, but go with the **National Gallery** if you want breadth, the **Tate Britain** if you want, well, Britain, or the **Victoria and Albert Museum** if you want a decorative extravaganza. For the most non-British of cultural artifacts, head to the **British Museum.** Take **lunchtime** to picnic and stroll in a park. **Hyde Park** and **Kensington Gardens** would be the obvious choice. If it's Sunday, enjoy the loonies at Speaker's Corner. **Regent's Park**, of course, is actually prettier. For a smaller, thoroughly charming alternative, try **Lincoln's Inn Fields** or **Middle Temple Garden** in Holborn or **Holland Park** in Kensington. In the **early afternoon** browse one of London's famous street markets—no need to buy anything, the atmosphere is what you really want to see anyway. The best and biggest of the lot will be in **Camden Town.** If it's Saturday, though, **Portabello Market** might be even busier and more entertaining. Take **mid-afternoon** to try out one of the more specialized museums that the city has to offer. The **British Library Galleries** are fascinating, and not just for the bookish. The **Theatre Museum** in Covent Garden will be heaven for a West End fan. South Ken's **Natural History Museum** and **Science Museum** bring out the geek (and 10 year old) in all of us. The **National Portrait Gallery** is all about faces, and tiny **Sir John Soanes Museum** in Holborn offers an eclectic grab-bag of artifacts. **Early evening** is window-shopping time. Just seeing **Harrod's** and **Harvey Nichols** in Knightsbridge is a necessary London experience. Or you can browse **Oxford Street** and **Regent Street,** the center of consumer culture. **Kensington High Street** is a bit less crowded, and **Bond Street** is a bit more upmarket and swanky. At **night,** bust out the dinner picnic and relax with some free entertainment. The Piazza in **Covent Garden** is a good place to catch street performers and musicians, and summertime sees a number of free concerts in the city's parks; **Music on a Summer Evening** can be enjoyed from outside the ticketed area on Hampstead Heath, **Trafalgar Square** and **Victoria Park** also see big-screen broadcasts of Royal Opera and Royal Ballet performances. Finally, at **midnight,** your free day fully enjoyed and savored, recommence spending far too much money in this lovely city. Get thee to a bar!

LONDON IN ONE WEEK (OR LESS)

THREE DAYS

DAY 1: ROYAL WESTMINSTER

Begin your visit with our **Walking With Royalty** walking tour (p. 18). The tour takes you through all the major Westminster sights, from **Buckingham Palace** to **10 Downing Street** via the **National Gallery and Trafalgar Square.** After dinner, have a pint with the politicians at the **Red Lion** pub (p. 202).

DAY 2: TOWER AND SOUTH BANK

Take our **Millennium Mile** walking tour (p. 20) to experience the full range of London's appeal—begin at the **Tower of London,** visit **Tate Modern,** and finish with a spectacular vista from the **London Eye.** Cap off the day with a pint at one of the South Bank's historic and beautiful **pubs** (p. 200), or head farther south to **Brixton** for some serious clubbing (p. 221).

DAY 3: THE WEST END

The West End offers enough amusements to fill an entire week, let alone one day. Spend the morning hitting the boutiques on **Convent Garden** (p. 267) but don't miss **Hamley's** (p. 263), the toy store of the gods. Take tea at **The Ritz** (p. 163) and feel like an aristocrat for a few hours. In the evening, sample the jazz at **Ronnie Scott's** (p. 241) or head to **Strawberry Moons** (p. 214) for a night of booty-shaking.

FIVE DAYS

DAY 4: HOLBORN AND THE CITY

Begin your day at **St. Paul's Cathedral** (p. 80)—get there early to avoid the crowds—then head to the **Museum of London** (p. 141) for the inside scoop on London's history. Next, visit Holborn and see the **Temple** (p. 97), once the seat of the Knights Templar, or watch a trial at the **Royal Courts of Justice** (p. 98). A short walk will take you to **St Etheldreda's** (p. 98), a stunning medieval church, and to **Ye Olde Mitre** (p. 197), our favorite London pub. The nearby **Bleeding Heart Tavern** (p. 170) serves tasty English classics.

DAY 5: KENSINGTON

Spend the morning in Albertopolis: visit the **Victoria & Albert Museum** (p. 138), **The Natural History Museum,** or **The Science Museum** (p. 145). There's only time for one, as **Kensington High Street** beckons with its brilliant shopping (p. 257). Royals fans should visit **Kensington Palace** (p. 100), home of the Royal Dress Collection. The Palace is on the edge of **Hyde Park** (p. 86), which contains rolling hills, a pond, and even an art gallery. For dinner, head to **Zaika** (p. 172).

SEVEN DAYS

DAY 6: GO WEST, YOUNG MAN

Take a daytrip to **Richmond** (p. 302). **Richmond Park** has enough rolling fields and woods to fill the day, but be sure to visit the **aristocratic manors** in the area, especially **Ham House,** with its stunning grounds and gardens. The manors have their own amazing gardens, but none can match the **Royal Botanical Gardens, Kew** (p. 131), whose glass houses and gardens display flora from all over the world. **Café Zagora** (p. 189), on the way back to the city, and serves Moroccan-Lebanese food in an amazing atmosphere.

DAY 7: PUBS, CLUBS AND MANUSCRIPTS

Spend the morning in the **British Museum,** but don't linger too long or you may never leave. Walk up Gower St., past **University College London**—if you've the stomach for it, visit UCL founder **Jeremy Bentham,** whose embalmed corpse is still on display (p. 87). The **British Library Galleries** (p. 133) house a must-see collection of historical documents, from Magna Carta to the Beatles. At night, head to Clerkenwell or Islington for a **pub crawl** (p. 196), or to megaclub **Fabric** (p. 210) to dance the night away.

WESTMINSTER

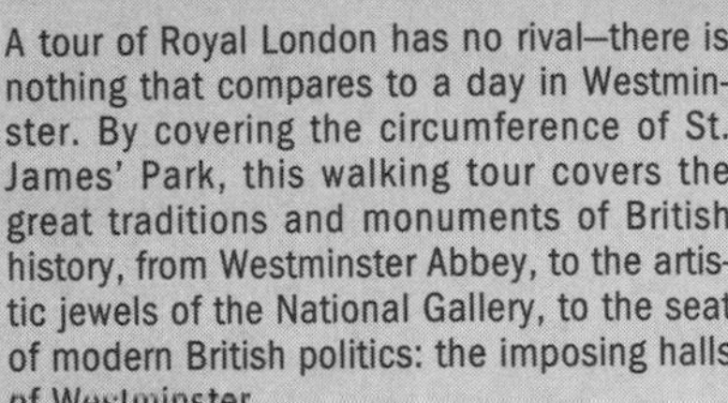

A tour of Royal London has no rival—there is nothing that compares to a day in Westminster. By covering the circumference of St. James' Park, this walking tour covers the great traditions and monuments of British history, from Westminster Abbey, to the artistic jewels of the National Gallery, to the seat of modern British politics: the imposing halls of Westminster.

Time: 7-9 hr.

Distance: 1.7 mi. (2.7km)

When To Go: Early morning

Start: Westminster Abbey

Finish: The Houses of Parliament

What To Bring: A snack & a picnic lunch

Call well ahead: Buckingham Palace.

1 WESTMINSTER ABBEY. Avoid the crowds by **arriving early** at medieval Westminster Abbey (p. 78). As a place for royal coronations and burials since 1065, the Abbey immortalizes past monarchs in the impressive Royal Tombs. Along with the departed literati and musicians in the Poet's Corner, the Abbey also shelters the remains of Winston Churchill. The Abbey has been the sight of royal coronations from the Middle Ages to the present—the Abbey will hold Prince Charles's coronation, should he become King of England. Explore the monastery and gardens, but limit yourself to approximately 1hr. before heading to Buckingham Palace. Either make the 15min. walk there or take the Tube from Westminster to St. James's Park.

2 BUCKINGHAM PALACE. First occupied by Queen Victoria in 1832, the Palace (p. 75) continues to house the Royal family. During August and September, the State Rooms, the Throne Room, the White Drawing room, the magnificent Galleries and the beautifully manicured Gardens are open for tours. *Call well ahead for tickets.* The **Changing of the Guard** outside Buckingham Palace takes place at 11:20am, though to gain an unobstructed view aim to arrive by 10:30am. *The Changing of the Guard takes place daily Apr.-Oct., every other day Nov.-Mar., provided the Queen is in residence, it is not raining too hard, and there are no pressing state functions.* After the Palace, take a stroll down the Mall, following the same annual route of the Queen on her way to open Parliament. To your right, **St. James's Park** (p. 119) offers a pleasant site for a snack. To your left is **St. James's Palace**. Approaching the end of the Mall pass through Admiralty Arch and into...

3 TRAFALGAR SQUARE. Designed by John Nash, London's largest square serves as a forum for public rallies and protest movements, not to mention controversial art. On December 31, the square hosts the City's largest New Year's Eve celebration (p. 116). All proceedings are soberly observed by statues of Lord Nelson (perched on his column), George IV, Charles I and George Washington. The eastern "Fourth Plinth" is reserved for rotating contemporary sculpture installations.

4 NATIONAL GALLERY. Considering the thousands of works on display, it's hard to believe that this gallery was founded with only 38 pictures. Depending on your interests, spend anywhere from 1hr. to the remainder of the day savoring European masterpieces dating from the Middle Ages to the close of the 18th century. The Gallery, organized chronologically into four wings, contains gems from the Italian Renaissance, the Dutch and Spanish Golden Ages and French Impressionism, along with rotating exhibitions on single artists. To use your time most efficiently, design your own tour at the electronic stations (p. 135). Hungry? The expensive restaurant atop the National Portrait Gallery offers spectacular views of the city. Tachbrook St. has a number of cheap establishments. Consider a having a picnic lunch at the feet of Trafalgar Square's bronze lions. After lunch, walk south along Whitehall, where you will pass a long stretch of imposing Ministry building facades (p. 117).

5 HORSEGUARDS. The Guards on the world's most popular postcard inspire giggles and distraction attempts from thousands of tourists per year. Because it's highly unlikely that any provocation will prompt a response, we saved you the trouble and interviewed one of the Queen's Life Guards (p. 118). Technically "the Queen's Guard" only refers to those at Buckingham Palace and St. James's Palace.

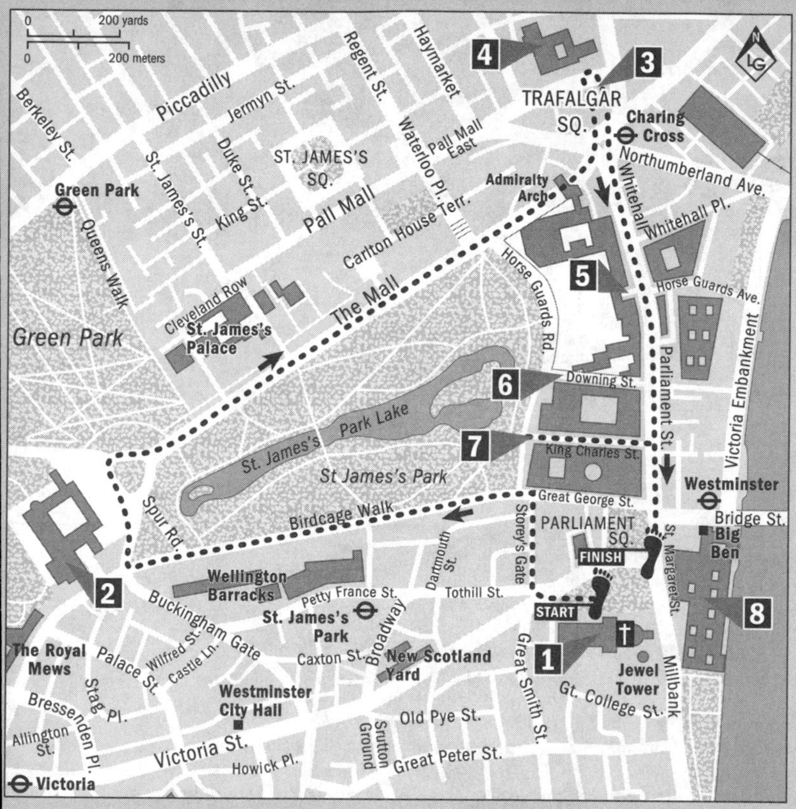

6 10 DOWNING STREET. Former residence of Churchill, Thatcher, and all the other British Prime Ministers, today 10 Downing St. is home to Gordon Brown, Chancellor of the Exchequer. Tony Blair's family is too big for No. 10 so he's now in No. 11 (p. 117). You won't be able to walk on Downing Street but you might see the Prime Minister going in or out of work.

7 CABINET WAR ROOMS. From 1938 to 1944, Winston Churchill ran the British war effort from these converted coal cellars (p. 152). The 19 rooms on show have been perfectly restored to their wartime appearance, right down to the paperclips. Highlights include "Churchill's personal loo," a small room containing the top-secret transatlantic hotline.

8 THE PALACE OF WESTMINSTER. Also known as **The Houses of Parliament** (p. 76). Contains both the House of Lords and the House of Commons, Westminster Palace has been at the heart of English governance since the 11th century. Crossing MPs can be spotted from the **New Palace Yard,** while the **Old Palace Yard** was formerly a site for executions. Look above to see famous **Clock Tower. Big Ben,** the 14-ton bell inside the clock, still chimes on the hour. To enter Parliament, either wait in line for the limited seats in the Stranger's Gallery, or pre-book a tour of the State Rooms. *Call ahead to arrange tours and find out about debate times.*

THE MILLENNIUM MILE: THE SOUTH BANK

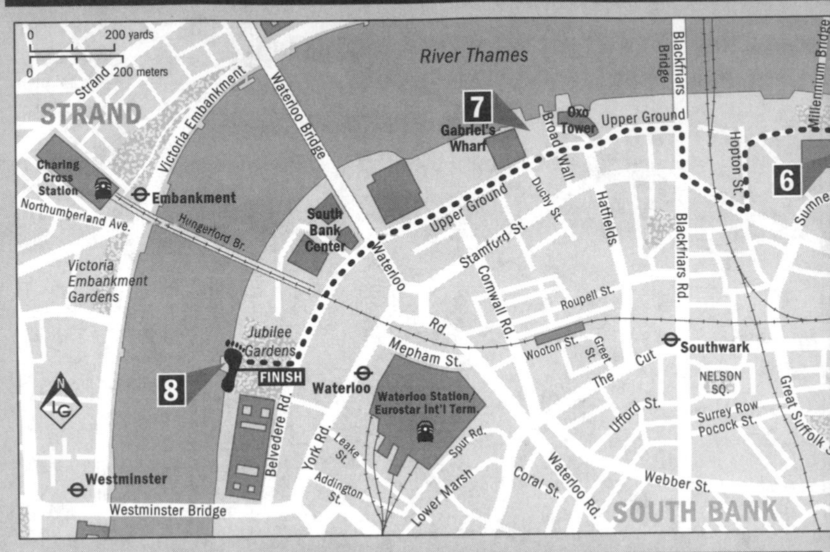

Distance: 2.5 mi. (4km)

When To Go: Start early morning

Start: ⊖Tower Hill

Finish: ⊖Westminster

Once a rather seedy neighborhood, the South Bank is now home to London's densest concentration of cultural centres. The Tate Modern is just one of the South Bank's artistic powerhouses. Shakespeare's Globe Theatre had its first season in 1997, and each subsequent season brings bolder and better interpretations of Will's works. Concert halls in the area host every type of music, and theatres present an unparalleled range of new works. Commercial Gabriel's Wharf thrives in the excitement of the area. Fantastic city views from Tate Modern, OXO Wharf and, of course, London Eye, in addition to the understated beauty of a walk along the Thames, are constant draws. Meanwhile, the highly acclaimed Jubilee Line Extension–which includes a revamped interior at London Bridge–has greatly facilitated transportation to the South Bank and helped to transform the area into the cultural haven it was originally intended to be.

1 TOWER OF LONDON. Begin your trek to the Tower **early** to avoid the crowds. Tours given by the Yeomen Warders meet every 90min. near the entrance. Listen as they expertly recount tales of royal conspiracy, treason, and murder. See the **White Tower,** once both fortress and residence of kings. Shiver at the executioner's stone on the tower green and pay your respects at the Chapel of St. Peter ad Vinculum, holding the remains of 3 queens. First get the dirt on the gemstones at **Martin Tower,** then wait in line to see the **Crown Jewels.** The jewels include such glittering lovelies as the First Star of Africa, the largest cut diamond in the world (p. 83).

2 TOWER BRIDGE. An engineering wonder that puts its plainer sibling, the London Bridge, to shame. Marvel at its beauty, but skip the Tower Bridge Experience. Or better yet, call ahead to inquire what times the Tower drawbridge is lifted (p. 91).

3 DESIGN MUSEUM. On Butler's Wharf, let the Design Museum introduce you to the latest innovations in contemporary design, from marketing to movements in haute couture. See what's to come in the forward-looking Review Gallery or hone in on individual designers and products in the Temporary Gallery. From the DM, walk along the **Queen's Walk.** To your left you will find the **HMS Belfast,** which was launched upon Normandy, France on D-Day, 1938.

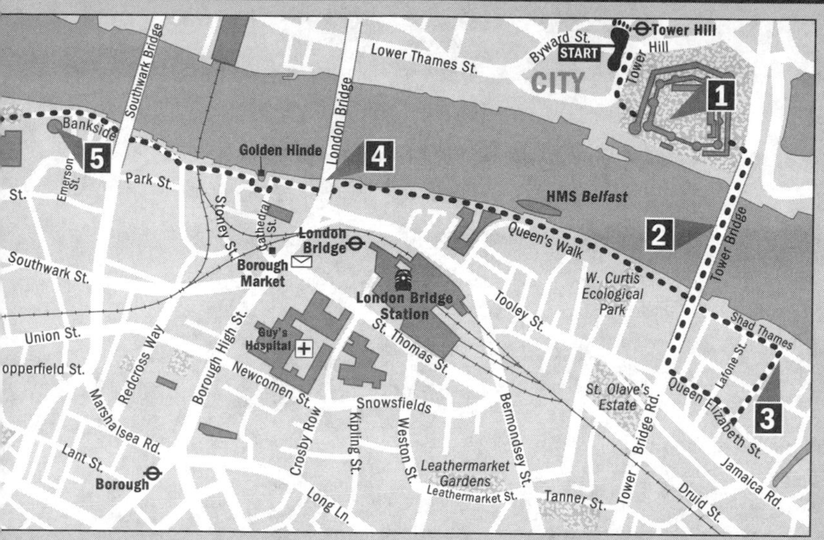

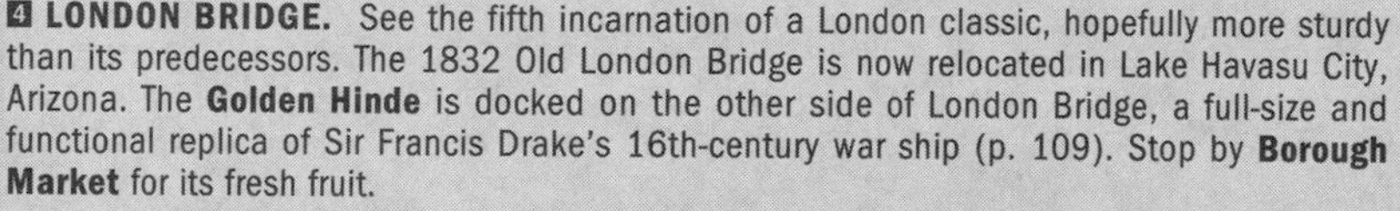

4 LONDON BRIDGE. See the fifth incarnation of a London classic, hopefully more sturdy than its predecessors. The 1832 Old London Bridge is now relocated in Lake Havasu City, Arizona. The **Golden Hinde** is docked on the other side of London Bridge, a full-size and functional replica of Sir Francis Drake's 16th-century war ship (p. 109). Stop by **Borough Market** for its fresh fruit.

5 SHAKESPEARE'S GLOBE THEATER. "I hope to see London once ere I die," says Shakespeare's Davy in *Henry IV, Part II.* In time, he may see it from the beautiful recreation of Will's most famous theater. Excellent exhibits reveal how Shakespearean actors dressed and the secrets of stage effects, and tell of the painstaking process of rebuilding of the theater almost 400 years after the original burned down (see p. 107). You might be able to catch a matinee performance if you time your visit right. *Call ahead for tour and show times.*

6 TATE MODERN. It's hard to imagine anything casting a shadow over the Globe Theatre, but the massive former Bankside Power Station does just that. One of the world's premier modern art museums, the Tate's arrangements promise a new conceptual spin on well-known favorites and works by emerging British artists. Be sure to catch one of the informative docent tours and don't forget to ogle the rotating installation in the Turbine Room.

7 GABRIEL'S WHARF. Check out the cafes, bars, and boutiques of colorful **Gabriel's Wharf.** If you missed the top floor of the Tate Modern, go to the public viewing gallery on the 8th floor of the **OXO Tower** Wharf (see p. 109). On your way to the London Eye stop by the **South Bank Centre**. Established as a primary cultural center in 1951, it now exhibits a range of music from Philharmonic extravaganzas to low-key jazz. You may even catch one of the free lunchtime or afternoon events (see p. 108). *Call ahead for dates and times.*

8 LONDON EYE. Once known as the Millennium Wheel; given its "like-named" siblings—the misbehaving "Bridge" and bloated ego of "Dome"—it's no surprise that it shed its Millennium maiden name at the first possible chance (p. 106). The London Eye has firmly established itself as one of London's top attractions, popular with locals and tourists alike. The Eye offers amazing 360° views from its glass pods. If you time it right, you can see all of London lit up in the sunset. *Book in advance to avoid the long queues but be sure to check the weather for the day.*

18:50
Poole
Page 2 of 2
Bournemouth
Branksome
Parkstone
Poole
18:47
Staines via Richmond
Vauxhall
Queenstown Road
Clapham Junction
Wandsworth Town
Putney, Barnes
Mortlake
North Sheen
Richmond
St Margarets
Twickenham
Whitton, Feltham
Ashford, Staines
18:45
8 26 36
Departures
BODY SHOP
JOURNEY

INSIDE

Essentials

PLANNING YOUR TRIP

ENTRANCE REQUIREMENTS

Passport (p. 25). Required of non-EU citizens.

Visa (p. 26). Most countries require a visa for entry while some need one if stay exceeds 90 days.

Work Permit (p. 26). Required of all foreigners planning to work in UK.

EMBASSIES AND CONSULATES

BRITISH CONSULAR SERVICES ABROAD

For up-to-date information on entry requirements and British consular services, check the Foreign Office website (www.fco.gov.uk).

For addresses of British embassies in countries not listed here, consult the **Foreign and Commonwealth Office** (☎020 7270 1500; www.fco.gov.uk) or your local telephone directory. Some large cities have a local British consulate that can handle most of the same functions as an embassy.

ENGLISH	AMERICAN
bank holiday	public holiday
barmy	insane, erratic; hot weather
bathroom	room containing a bathtub
bird (slang)	girl
biro	ballpoint pen
bit of alright (slang)	attractive (of girls)
bloke	guy
bobby (slang)	police officer
bonnet	car hood
brilliant (exclamation)	all purpose enthusiastic
bonkers	crazy
(car) boot	car trunk
braces	suspenders
brolly	umbrella
bum bag	fanny pack
busker	street musician
caravan	trailer, mobile home
cinema	movie theater ('theatre' is only live theater)
car park	parking lot
cheeky	mischievous
cheerio	goodbye
cheers	thanks
chemist	pharmacy
chuffed	happy
concessions	special discounts (for students, seniors, children etc.)
coach	inter-city bus
dicey, dodgy	sketchy
the dog's bollocks (slang)	the best
dosh, dough (slang)	money
durex	(common brand of) condom

Australia: British High Commission, Commonwealth Ave., Yarralumla, Canberra, ACT 2600 (☎02 6270 6666; www.uk.emb.gov.au). Open M-F 8:45am-5pm. **Consulates** also in Adelaide, Brisbane, Melbourne, Perth, and Sydney.

Canada: British High Commission, 80 Elgin St., Ottawa, ON K1P 5K7 (☎613-237-1530; www.britainincanada.org), or British Consulate-General, College Park, 777 Bay St., Suite 2800, Toronto, ON M5G 2G2 (☎416-593-1290). Both open M-F 8:30am-5pm. **Consulates** also in Calgary, Dartmouth, Montreal, Quebec City, St. John's, Vancouver and Winnipeg.

France: British Embassy, 35 Rue du Faubourg-St-Honoré, 75383 Paris CEDEX 08 (☎01 44 51 31 00; www.amb-grandebretagne.fr). Open M-F 9:30am-1pm and 2:30pm-6pm. Consulate-General, 18 bis rue d'Anjou, 75008 Paris (☎01 44 51 31 00).M,W-F 9:30am-12:30pm and 2:30pm-5pm, Tu 9:30am-4:30pm. Open **consulates** also in Bordeaux, Lille, Lyon, and Marseille.

Ireland: British Embassy, 29 Merrion Rd., Ballsbridge, Dublin 4 (☎01 205 3700; www.britishembassy.ie). Open M- F 9:30am -noon.

New Zealand: British High Commission, 44 Hill St., Thorndon, Wellington 1 (☎04 924 2888; www.britain.org.nz); mailing address P.O. Box 1812, Wellington. Open M-F 8:45am-5pm. Consulate-General, 17th fl., NZI House, 151 Queen St., Auckland 1 (☎09 303 2973); mailing address Private Bag 92014, Auckland 1.

US: British Embassy, 3100 Massachusetts Ave. NW, Washington, D.C. 20008 (☎202-588-6500; www.britainusa.com). Open M-F 9am-4pm. Consulate-General, 845 3rd Ave., New York, NY 10022 (☎212-745-0200). Open M-F 8-11:30am. **Consulates** also in Atlanta, Boston, Chicago, Dallas, Denver, Houston, Los Angeles, Miami, San Francisco and Seattle.

CONSULAR SERVICES IN LONDON

In case of emergency you can call the embassy or counsulate at any time. There is always a telephone line open 24 hr. for emergencies.

Australia: Australia House, Strand (☎7379 4334 or 7887 5776; www.australia.org.uk). ⊖Temple. Open M-F 9am-5pm; **consular** services 9:30am-3:30pm. In an emergency, dial ☎0500 890 165 toll-free to contact the Foreign Affairs Dept.'s Consulate Officer in Canberra.

Canada: MacDonald House, 1 Grosvenor Sq. (☎7258 6600; www.dfait-maeci.gc.ca/london). ⊖Bond St. or Charing Cross. Open M-F 8:30am-5pm.

Ireland: 17 Grosvenor Pl. (☎7235 2171). ⊖Hyde Park Corner. **Consular** services at Montpelier House, 106 Brompton Rd. (☎7225 7700). ⊖Knightsbridge. Open M-F 9:30am-4:30pm.

New Zealand: New Zealand House, 80 Haymarket (☎7930 8422; www.nzembassy.com). ⊖Piccadilly Circus. **Consular** services open M-F 9am-5pm.

United States: 24 Grosvenor Sq. (☎7499 9000; www.usembassy.org.uk). ⊖Bond St. or Marble Arch. Open M-F 8:30am-5:30pm; phones answered 8am-10pm.

TOURIST OFFICES

Tourist information tailored to visitors from specific countries can be found at www.visitbritain.com. For tourist information offices in London, see the ***Service Directory,*** *p. 339.*

London is represented abroad by the **British Tourist Authority** (BTA), and in the UK by the **London Tourist Board.** BTA offices abroad supply advance tickets to major attractions and travel passes as well as information on how to get to Britain, where to stay, and what to do. They also sell the **Great British Heritage Pass,** which grants entrance to almost 600 sights around Britain. (4 days £22, 7 days £35, 15 days £46, 1 month £60.) There are BTA offices in:

Australia, Level 2, 15 Blue Street, North Sydney, NSW 2060 (☎2 9021 4400).

Canada, 5915 Airport Rd., Suite 120, Mississauga, ONT L4V 1T1 (☎905-405-1840).

Ireland, 18-19 College Green, Dublin 2 (☎01 670 8000).

New Zealand, Level 17, 151 Queen St., Auckland 1 (☎09 303 1446).

United States, 7th fl., 551 Fifth Ave., New York, NY 10176-0799 (☎800-462-2748). Also Chicago (☎800-462-2748) and Los Angeles (☎310-470-2782).

DOCUMENTS AND FORMALITIES

PASSPORTS

REQUIREMENTS

Citizens of European Union countries only need a valid national identity card to enter UK; citizens of all other countries must be in possession of a valid passport and, if necessary, a visa (see below). Britain does not allow entrance if the holder's passport expires in under six months.

ENGLISH	AMERICAN
ensuite	with bathroom
fag (slang)	cigarette
fanny (obsolete)	vagina
first floor	second floor
fortnight	two weeks
full stop	period (punctuation)
geezer (slang)	guy
gob (vulgar)	mouth
grotty	grungy
high street	main street
to hire	to rent
holiday	vacation
hoover	vacuum cleaner
interval	intermission
jumper	sweater/ sweatshirt
knackered (slang)	tired, worn out
knickers	underwear ("Don't get your knickers in a twist)
knob (vulg.)	penis; awkward person
lavatory, loo	restroom
lay-by	roadside turnout
leader (press)	editorial
to let	to rent (property)
liberal (politics)	centre-right
lift	elevator
lorry	truck
mac (Macintosh)	raincoat
mad	crazy
mate	pal
mingin'	gross
motorway	highway
mobile	cellphone
naff (slang)	shabby, in poor taste
nappy	diaper

ENGLISH	AMERICAN
pants	underpants
petrol	gasoline
phone box, call box	telephone booth
take the piss, take the mickey (slang)	make fun
pissed	drunk
Paki (derog.)	racial slur for Pakistani or any South Asian.
plaster	generic Band-Aid
poof (vulgar)	gay person
prat (vulgar)	unpleasant person
to pull (slang)	to "score"
public school	prestigious private school
quid (slang)	pound (money)
queue	line
quay (pron. "key")	river bank
return ticket	round-trip ticket
to ring (up)	to telephone
roundabout	rotary intersection
rubber	eraser
to sack	to fire someone
self-catering	with kitchen
serviette	napkin
shag (slang)	sex, to have sex
single ticket	one-way ticket
snog (slang)	kiss
slag (vulgar)	bitch
sod it (vulgar)	forget it
suspenders	garters
subway	underpass
ta (slang)	thanks
takeaway	takeout
ta-ta (slang)	goodbye
thick	stupid
tights	pantyhose

NEW PASSPORTS

Citizens of Australia, Canada, Ireland, New Zealand, and the US can apply for a passport at some post offices and at any passport office or court of law.

PASSPORT MAINTENANCE

Photocopy the page of your passport with your photo, as well as your visas, traveler's check serial numbers, and any other important documents. Carry a set of copies in a safe place, apart from the originals, and leave another set at home.

If you lose your passport, notify the local police immediately and the nearest embassy or consulate of your home government. To expedite its replacement, you will need to know all information previously recorded and show ID and proof of citizenship. In some cases, a replacement may take weeks to process, and it may be valid only for a limited time. Any visas stamped in your old passport will be irretrievably lost. In an emergency, ask for immediate temporary traveling papers that permit you to re-enter your home country.

VISAS, INVITATIONS, AND WORK PERMITS

VISAS

Citizens of Australia, Canada, New Zealand, and the US do not require visas for visits of under six months. For a complete list of countries with visa-free travel to the UK, check http://ukvisas.gov.uk. Tourist visas can be obtained from the British consulates listed on p. 23.

WORK PERMITS

A visa or relevant permit is required by all non-EU citizens intending to **work** or **study** in the UK, or who intend to stay longer than 6 months for whatever reason. EU citizens staying over 3 months must apply for a residence permit after their arrival in the UK. For details of long-term visas and work, study, and residence permits, see **Alternatives to Tourism,** p. 329.

IDENTIFICATION

When travelling carry at least two forms of identification on your person, including at least one photo ID; a passport and a driver's license is usually adequate. Never carry all of your IDs together; split them up in case of theft or loss.

STUDENT, TEACHER, AND YOUTH IDENTIFICATION

The **International Student Identity Card (ISIC),** the most widely accepted form of student ID, provides access to a 24hr. emergency helpline, insurance benefits for US cardholders (see **Insurance,** p. 32), and discounts on everything from airfare to museum admission. Applicants must be full-time secondary or post-secondary school students at least 12 years of age. Due to the proliferation of fake ISICs, some services (particularly airlines) require additional proof of student identity.

The **International Teacher Identity Card (ITIC)** offers teachers the same insurance coverage as the ISIC and similar but limited discounts. For travelers who are under 26 but are not students, the **International Youth Travel Card (IYTC)** also offers many of the same benefits as the ISIC.

Each of these identity cards costs US$22 or equivalent. Many student travel agencies issue the cards. For a list of issuing agencies or more information, see the **International Student Travel Confederation (ISTC)** website (www.istc.org).

The **International Student Exchange Card (ISE)** is a similar identification card available to students, faculty, and youth aged 12 to 26. The card provides discounts, medical benefits, access to a 24hr. emergency helpline, and the ability to purchase student airfares. The card costs US$25; call US ☎800-255-8000 for more info, or visit www.isecard.com.

MONEY

CURRENCY AND EXCHANGE

The currency chart below is based on August 2004 exchange rates between the British pound (UK£) and Australian dollars (AUS$), Canadian dollars (CDN$), European Union euros (EUR€), New Zealand dollars (NZ$), and US dollars (US$). Check the currency converter on websites like www.xe.com or www.bloomberg.com or a major newspaper for the latest exchange rates.

As a general rule, it's cheaper to convert money in London than at home. While currency exchange will be available in your arrival airport, it's wise to bring enough foreign currency to last for the first 24 to 72 hr. of your trip.

When changing money abroad, try to go only to banks or bureaux de change that have at most a 5% margin between their buy and sell prices. Since you lose money with every transaction, **convert large sums** (unless the currency is depreciating rapidly), **but no more than you'll need.**

ENGLISH	AMERICAN
torch	flashlight
Tory	Conservative Party suppoter
trousers	pants
vest	undershirt
waistcoat	men's vest
wanker (vulgar)	idiot
way out	exit
wasted	very drunk
WC	restroom
wicked (slang)	cool
yob (slang)	uncultured person
zed	the letter Z

For translations regarding food, refer to the 'Menu Reader' on p. 164.

WRITTEN	PRONOUNCED
Berkeley	BAHK-lee
Berkshire	BAHK-sher
Birmingham	BERM-ing-um
Cholmondely	CHUM-lee
Derby	DAR-bee
Dulwich	DULL-ich
Edinburgh	ED-in-bur-ra
Featherstonehaw	FAN-shaw
Gloucester	GLOS-ter
Greenwich	GREN-ich
Grosvenor	GRO-vna
gaol	JAIL
Islington	IHZ-ling-tun
Leicester	LES-ter
Marylebone	MAR-lee-bun
Magdalen	MAUD-lin
quay	KEY
Norwich	NOR-ich
Salisbury	SAULS-bree
Southwark	SUTH-uk
Thames	TEMS
Worcester	WOO-ster

CURRENCY (£)		
	AUS$ = £0.40	£1 = AUS$2.45
	CDN$ = £0.41	£1= CDN$2.47
	EUR€ = £0.34	£1= EUR€1.50
	NZ$ = £0.54	£1= NZ$2.93
	US$ = £0.67	£1= US$1.84

If you use traveler's checks or bills, carry some in small denominations (the equivalent of US$50 or less) for times when you are forced to exchange money at disadvantageous rates. Bring a range of denominations since charges may be levied per check cashed. Store your money in a variety of forms; ideally, at any given time you will be carrying some cash, some traveler's checks, and an ATM and/or credit card.

TRAVELER'S CHECKS

Traveler's checks are one of the safest and least troublesome means of carrying funds. American Express and Visa are the most recognized brands. Many banks and agencies sell them for a small commission. Ask about refund hotlines and the location of refund centers when purchasing checks, and always carry emergency cash.

American Express: Checks available with commission at select banks, at all AmEx offices, and online (www.americanexpress.com; US residents only). American Express cardholders can also purchase checks by phone (☎888-269-6669). AAA offers commission-free checks to its members. Checks available in Australian, Canadian, euro, Japanese, British, and US currencies. For purchase locations or more information contact AmEx's service centers: in Australia ☎800 68 80 22; in New Zealand 0508 555 358; in the UK 0800 587 6023; in the US and Canada 800-221-7282; elsewhere, call the US collect at +1 801-964-6665.

Visa: Checks available (generally with commission) at banks worldwide. For the location of the nearest office, call Visa's service centers: in the UK ☎0800 51 58 84; in the US 800-227-6811; elsewhere, call the UK collect at +44 173 331 8949.

Travelex/Thomas Cook: In the US and Canada call ☎800-287-7362; in the UK call 0800 62 21 01; elsewhere call the UK collect at 44 1733 31 8950.

CREDIT, DEBIT, AND ATM CARDS

Cards accepted by establishments are abbreviated as follows: AmEx for American Express, MC for Mastercard, V for Visa. Discover and Diners Club are rarely accepted, and are not listed.

CREDIT CARDS. Try paying with a credit or debit card whenever possible—you'll get a much better exchange rate than for cash or travelers checks. Credit cards may also offer services such as insurance or emergency help, and are sometimes required to reserve hotel rooms or rental cars. **MasterCard** and **Visa** are most welcomed, and **Diners Club** and **Discover** are rarely accepted. Credit cards are useful for **cash advances,** which allow you to withdraw local currency from associated banks and ATMs abroad (see below). If you intend to use your credit card extensively in London, alert your card issuer before leaving; otherwise, they could block your card for "suspicious activity." If you will also be making cash advances through cash machines in London, you will need to ask your card issuer for a 4-digit PIN.

ATMS. If you have an **ATM card** (aka cash cards), chances are it will be able to withdraw money from UK ATMs; other ATM functions (including checking your balance, transferring funds, etc.) may not be accessible depending on what kind of ATM card you have. British machines only accept **4-digit PINs,** so if yours is longer, check with your bank to see if the first four digits will work in the UK or if you need a new code. UK cash machines do not have letters on the keypad, so be sure to memorize your PIN in numerical form. You'll get the same wholesale exchange rates as credit cards, but beware that many banks levy fees for withdrawing money abroad—up to US$5 per transaction. **Be sure to note your bank's phone number before you leave.**

DEBIT CARDS. Debit cards (aka 'switch' or 'solo' cards), are as convenient as credit cards but withdraw money directly from your bank account. A debit card can be used wherever its associated credit card company (usually Mastercard or Visa) is accepted. The two major international money networks are **Cirrus** (to locate ATMs US ☎800-424-7787; www.mastercard.com) and **Visa/PLUS** (to locate ATMs US ☎800-843-7587; www.visa.com). ATMs of major British banks (including Barclays, HSBC, Lloyds TSB, National Westminster, Royal Bank of Scotland) accept both networks.

CASH ADVANCES. In an emergency, you can also withdraw money from most cash machines and bank tellers with a credit card, up to your cash advance limit. There are often high transaction fees associated with foreign cash advances (up to US$10 plus 2-3%), plus cash advances are normally charged at higher interest rates than purchases, with no grace period for payment until interest kicks in, either.

ESSENTIAL INFORMATION

PIN CUSHION

To withdraw money from a cash machine (ATM) in Europe, you must have a four-digit Personal Identification Number (PIN). If your PIN is longer than four digits, ask your bank whether you can just use the first four, or whether you'll need a new one. Credit cards don't usually come with PINs, so if you intend to hit up ATMs in Europe with a credit card to get cash advances, call your credit card company before leaving and request one.

People with alphabetic, rather than numerical, PINs may also be thrown off by the lack of letters on European cash machines. The corresponding numbers to use are:

1=QZ
2=ABC
3=DEF
4=GHI
5=JKL
6=MNO
7=PRS
8=TUV
9=WXY

Note that if you mistakenly punch the wrong code into the machine three times, it will swallow your card for good.

GETTING MONEY FROM HOME

If you run out of money while traveling, the easiest and cheapest solution is to have someone back home make a deposit to your credit card or ATM card. Failing that, consider one of the following options. The online **International Money Transfer Consumer Guide** (http://international-money-transfer-consumer-guide.info) may also be of help.

WIRING MONEY

It is possible to arrange a bank money transfer, which means asking a bank back home to wire money to a bank in London. This is the cheapest way to transfer cash, but it's also the slowest, usually taking several days. Note that some banks may only release your funds in local currency, potentially sticking you with a poor exchange rate; inquire about this in advance. Money transfer services like Western Union are faster and more convenient than bank transfers—but also much pricier. Western Union has many locations worldwide: visit www.westernunion.com, or call in Australia ☎800 501 500, in Canada 800-235-0000, in the UK 0800 83 38 33, in the US 800-325-6000. To wire money within the US using a credit card (MasterCard, Visa), call ☎800-225-5227. Money transfer services are also available at American Express and Thomas Cook offices .

US STATE DEPARTMENT (US CITIZENS ONLY)

In serious emergencies only, the US State Department will forward money within hours to the nearest consular office, which will then disburse it according to instructions for a US$15 fee. If you wish to use this service, you must contact the Overseas Citizens Service division of the US State Department (☎317-472-2328; nights, Sundays, and holidays 202-647-4000).

COSTS

Budget travel in London is somewhat of an oxymoron, but the cost of your trip will vary considerably depending on how you travel and where you stay. Before you go spend some time calculating a reasonable per-day budget and stick to it. Based on the estimates below, you could get away with spending £35 (US$50) a day, sharing a cheap B&B room, buying food in supermarkets, only hitting the free sights, and staying home at night, but £50 (US$80) is a more reasonable minimum if you want to fully experience London.

Accommodations: Count on spending at least £25 per person per night in a dorm or a shared hotel room. For **longer stays**, you should be able to negotiate a discount.

Food: By shopping in supermarkets and eating frugally, you could get away with spending £8 per day; at restaurants you're unlikely to spend less than £15, even if you're careful.

Admissions charges: London's major museums (including the Tate Modern, the British Museum, and the National Gallery) are all free. Sights range from free to over £10, so ask yourself if you really need to see that wax model of Elvis.

Entertainment & Nightlife: Costs in London can really add up: club covers are rarely under £10, and a pint of beer is about £3. Theater and concert tickets range from £5 for student standbys at off-West End locations to over £20 for cheaper tickets to a well-known show.

Transport: At a bare minimum, 2 bus rides a day will cost £2; for any serious sightseeing you should invest in a Travelcard (see p. 41).

TIPPING AND BARGAINING

Tips in restaurants are often included in the bill (sometimes as a service charge). If gratuity is not included, you should tip your server about 15%. Taxi drivers should receive a 10-15% tip, and bellhops and chambermaids usually expect somewhere between £1-3. Never tip bartenders, even in pubs. If you're at an outdoor market, bargaining is sometimes acceptable. The only other places where you should haggle are the electronics shops along **Tottenham Court Road** (p. 255).

TAXES

Both Britain and Ireland have a 17.5% **Value Added Tax (VAT),** a sales tax applied to everything but food, books, medicine, and children's clothing. The tax is **included** in the amount indicated on the price tag—no extra expenses should be added at the register. The prices stated in *Let's Go* include VAT. Upon exiting Britain, non-EU citizens can reclaim VAT (minus an administrative fee) through the **Retail Export Scheme,** though the complex procedure is probably only worthwhile for large purchases. You can obtain refunds only for goods you take out of the country. Participating shops display a "Tax Free Shopping" sign and may have a purchase minimum of £50-100 before they offer refunds. To claim a refund, fill out the form you are given in the shop and present it with the goods and receipts at customs upon departure (look for the Tax Free Refund desk at the airport). At peak times, this process can take as long as an hour. You can receive your refund directly at most airports. To obtain the refund by check or credit card, send the form (stamped by customs) back in the envelope provided. You must leave the country within three months of your purchase in order to claim a refund and you must apply before leaving the UK.

PACKING

Pack lightly, lay out only what you absolutely need, then take half the clothes and twice the money. The Travelite FAQ (www.travelite.org) is a good resource for tips on traveling light.

Luggage: Be sure that you can carry your luggage up and down stairs, as steep staircases are unavoidable at most Tube stops and in many B&Bs and hostels.

Clothing: A rain jacket is essential year-round. Londoners generally dress conservatively and darkly—a pair of black trousers will help you blend in. Be sure to pack some semi-dressy trousers and shoes, especially if you plan to go clubbing: many clubs ban jeans and sneakers. Flip-flops are must haves for grubby hostel showers.

Converters and Adapters: In the UK, electricity is 240 volts AC, enough to fry any 110V North American appliance. Americans and Canadians should buy an adapter (which changes the shape of the plug; US$5) and a converter (which changes the voltage; US$20). An adapter without a convertor spells trouble; an exception is laptops which often contain internal power converters. New Zealanders and Australians won't need a converter, but will need an adapter to use anything electrical. For more on all things adaptable, check out http://kropla.com/electric.htm.

First-Aid Kit: For a basic first-aid kit, pack bandages, a pain reliever, antibiotic cream, a thermometer, a Swiss Army knife, tweezers, moleskin, decongestant, motion-sickness remedy, diarrhea or upset-stomach medication (Pepto Bismol or Imodium), an antihistamine, and sunscreen.

Toiletries: You'll easily find all the toiletries you need in London. However, they are likely to be more expensive than home. Contact lens solution is extremely expensive in London. Also bring your glasses and a copy of your perscription in case you need emergency replacements.

SAFETY AND HEALTH

Your country's embassy is usually your best resource when things go wrong.

DRUGS AND ALCOHOL

The legal **drinking age** in the UK is a complicated beast. Technically, it's legal for anyone to drink alcohol in private, but there are many regulations regarding who can buy or sell it. To buy alcohol in a **shop,** you have to be at least 18; it's illegal to buy alcohol on behalf of an underage person. Eighteen is also the normal drinking age in **bars** and **pubs,** but you can drink in a pub at 16 with food, or even at 14 in a **restaurant.** Enforcement is generally lax—you need to look *really* young before anyone will demand ID—but punishments are severe. **Smoking** is simpler—you have to be 16 or older.

Drugs are dealt with harshly and you could be jailed or deported if convicted. Be especially wary in nightclubs. If you need to take a drug for **medical reasons,** check that it is legal in the UK, and always carry a prescription or note from you doctor. **Cannabis** in U.K. is a Class C drug, meaning that carrying a small amount of marijuana is no longer an arrestable offense in most cases; possession of larger amounts risks your being treated as a dealer, for which penalties are far stiffer.

SPECIFIC CONCERNS

In case of ***emergency,*** *dial* ☎ ***999*** *free from any phone.*

VIOLENT CRIME. London is as safe a big city as you're likely to find. By American and even most European standards, violent crime is rare, and police rarely carry anything more deadly than a truncheon. While most of London's dodgier neighborhoods—Hackney, Tottenham, and parts of South and East London—are far off the tourist trail, you should take extra care after dark around **King's Cross,** the **East End,** and **Brixton.** Finally, never venture alone into parks after dark, and **never admit you're traveling alone.**

THEFT. When it comes to theft (especially pickpocketing or bag snatching), London's track record is worse than many major cities. Don't put a **wallet** in your back pocket, and don't keep all your valuables (money, important documents) in one place. If you carry a **handbag,** buy a sturdy one with a secure clasp and wear it crosswise with the clasp against you. Use a money belt and keep a small cash reserve (say £40) somewhere safe, like in a sock.

RACISM. London has traditionally prided itself on being an exceptionally tolerant city, but the great increase in immigration since the 1950s has taken its toll. While overall London is color-blind, in **South London,** tensions are worst between black immigrants and poor whites; there's also friction within the black community between West Indians and Africans. In **East London,** South Asians are on the receiving end. These trouble spots aside, races mix in London to a greater extent than in most cities. Among second-generation immigrants, there's little cultural distinction.

TERRORISM. The risk of injury from terrorism in London is minute—you're far more likely to be run over. More information on international and domestic terrorism and the UK's response is available from the Foreign and Commonwealth Office (☎7270 1500; www.fco.gov.uk), the Prime Minister's office website (www.pm.gov.uk), and the Metropolitan Police (☎7230 1212; www.met.police.uk).

The most important thing for travelers is to gather as much information as possible before leaving and to **keep in contact** while overseas. Depending on the circumstances at the time of your trip, you may want to register with your home embassy or consulate when you arrive. **Travel advisories** (below) lists offices to contact and websites to visit to get the most updated list of advisories for travelers.

TRAVEL ADVISORIES. The following government offices provide travel information and advisories:

Australian Department of Foreign Affairs and Trade: ☎13 00 555135; www.dfat.gov.au.
Canadian Department of Foreign Affairs and International Trade (DFAIT): In Canada and the US call ☎800-267-8376, elsewhere call ☎+1 613-944-4000; www.dfait-maeci.gc.ca. Ask for their free booklet, *Bon Voyage...But.*
New Zealand Ministry of Foreign Affairs: ☎04 439 8000; www.mft.govt.nz/travel/index.html.
US Department of State: ☎202-647-5225; http://travel.state.gov. For their booklet *A Safe Trip Abroad,* call ☎202-512-1800.

PRE-DEPARTURE HEALTH

In your **passport,** write the names of people you wish to be contacted in case of a medical emergency, and list any allergies or medical conditions. Matching a prescription to a foreign equivalent is not always safe or possible. If you take prescription drugs, consider carrying up-to-date prescriptions, or a note from your doctor stating the medication's trade name, manufacturer, chemical name, and dosage. While traveling, be sure to keep all medication with you in your carry-on luggage.

IMMUNIZATIONS AND PRECAUTIONS

Travelers over 2 years old should make sure that the following vaccines are up to date: MMR (for measles, mumps, and rubella); DTaP or Td (for diphtheria, tetanus, and pertussis); IPV (for polio); Hib (for *haemophilus* influenza B); and HepB (for Hepatitis B). For recommendations on immunizations and prophylaxis, consult the CDC (see below) in the US or the equivalent in your home country.

INSURANCE

Travel insurance covers four basic areas: medical/health problems, property loss, trip cancellation/interruption, and emergency evacuation. Though regular insurance policies may well extend to travel-related accidents. Prices for travel insurance purchased separately generally run about US$50 per week for full coverage, while trip cancellation/interruption may be purchased separately at a rate of US$3-5 per day depending on length of stay.

Medical insurance (especially university policies) often covers costs incurred abroad; check with your provider. **US Medicare** does not cover foreign travel. **Canadian** provincial health insurance plans increasingly do not cover foreign travel; check with the provincial Ministry of Health or Health Plan Headquarters for details. **Australians** traveling in the UK are entitled to many of the services that they would receive at home as part of the Reciprocal Health Care Agreement. **Homeowners' insurance** (or your family's coverage) often covers theft during travel and loss of travel documents (passport, plane ticket, railpass, etc.) up to US$500.

ISIC and **ITIC** (see p. 26) provide basic insurance benefits to US cardholders, including US$100 per day of in-hospital sickness for up to 60 days and US$5000 of accident-related medical reimbursement (see www.isicus.com for details). Cardholders have access to a toll-free 24hr. helpline for medical, legal, and financial emergencies overseas. **American Express** (US ☎800-528-4800) grants most cardholders automatic collision and theft insurance and ground travel accident coverage of US$100,000 on flight purchases made with the card.

INSURANCE PROVIDERS

STA (see p. 35) offers a range of plans that can supplement your basic coverage. Other private insurance providers in the US and Canada include: Access America (☎800-284-8300; www.acessamerica.com); Berkely Group (☎800-323-3149; www.berkely.com); Globalcare Travel Insurance (☎800-821-2488; www.globalcare-cocco.com); Travel Assistance International (☎800-821-2828; www.europ-assistance.com); and Travel Guard (☎800-826-4919; www.travelguard.com). Columbus Direct (☎020 7375 0011; www.columbusdirect.co.uk) operates in the UK and AFTA (☎02 9264 3299; www.afta.com.au) operates in Australia.

USEFUL ORGANIZATIONS AND PUBLICATIONS

The US **Center for Disease Control and Prevention** (**CDC;** ☎877-FYI-TRIP; www.cdc.gov/travel) maintains an international travelers' hotline and an informative website. The CDC's comprehensive booklet *Health Information for International Travel* (The Yellow Book), an annual rundown of disease, immunization, and general health advice, is free online or US$29-40 via the Public Health Foundation (☎877-252-1200; http://bookstore.phf.org). Consult the appropriate government agency of your home country for consular information sheets on health, entry requirements, and other issues for various countries (see the listings in the box on **Travel Advisories,** p. 32). For quick information on health and other travel warnings, call the **Overseas Citizens Services** (☎888-407-4747; M-F 8am-8pm; after-hours ☎202-647-4000; ☎317-472-2328 from overseas), or contact a passport agency, embassy, or consulate abroad. For information on medical evacuation services and travel insurance firms, see the US government's website at http://travel.state.gov/medical.html or the British Foreign and Commonwealth Office (www.fco.gov.uk). For general health info, contact the **American Red Cross** (☎800-564-1234; www.redcross.org).

STAYING HEALTHY

Common sense is the simplest prescription for good health while you travel. Drink lots of fluids to prevent dehydration and constipation, and wear sturdy, broken-in shoes and clean socks.

FOOD- AND WATER-BORNE DISEASES

Tap water throughout London is not completely safe, take appropriate precaution. Two recent diseases originating in British livestock have made international headlines. **Bovine spongiform encephalopathy (BSE),** better known as **mad cow disease,** is a chronic degenerative disease affecting the central nervous system of cattle. The human variety is called new variant Cruetzfeldt-Jakob disease (nvCJD), and both forms involve invariably fatal brain damage. Information on nvCJD is not conclusive, but the disease is thought to be caused by consuming infected beef. The risk is extremely small (around 1 case per 10 billion meat servings); regardless, travelers might consider avoiding beef and beef products while in the UK. Milk and dairy products are not believed to pose a risk.

The UK and Western Europe experienced a serious outbreak of **Foot and Mouth Disease (FMD)** in 2001. FMD is easily transmissible between cloven-hoofed animals (cows, pigs, sheep, goats, and deer), but does not pose a threat to humans, as it causes mild symptoms, if any. In January 2002, the UK regained **international FMD free status.** Nearly all restrictions on rural travel have been removed. Further information on these diseases is available through the CDC (www.cdc.gov/travel) and the British Department for Environment, Food & Rural Affairs (www.defra.gov.uk).

AIDS, HIV, & STDS

For detailed information on **Acquired Immune Deficiency Syndrome (AIDS)** in Britain, call the **US Centers for Disease Control's** 24hr. hotline at ☎800-342-2437, or contact the **Joint United Nations Programme on HIV/AIDS (UNAIDS),** 20, ave. Appia, CH-1211 Geneva 27, Switzerland (☎41 22 791 3666). Note that individuals who do not appear to be in good health may be required to undergo a medical exam, including an HIV test, prior to entry to the UK.

MEDICAL CARE ON THE ROAD

*In an **emergency**, dial ☎**999** free from any phone. For a list of Accident and Emergency rooms in London, see Service Directory, p.334.*

Medical care in the UK is either part of the government-run National Health Service or is privately administered: doctors and hospitals often work for both NHS and privately. EU citizens, citizens of many Commonwealth countries, and full-time students at British universities are eligible for free treatment from NHS. Many US health insurance plans (but not Medicare) will cover emergency treatment abroad in private clinics, but you may be asked to pay up front and then apply for a reimbursement to your insurer. If you're unsure whether you have medical coverage in the UK, it's best to play it safe and buy travel insurance (see p. 32) before you leave.

CHEMISTS (PHARMACIES). For minor ailments (light burns, blisters, coughs, and sneezes), you can try going to a chemist. **Boots** is the biggest chain. You'll find a trained pharmacist behind the prescription drugs counter. They'll either recommend medication, or advise you to see a doctor if they think it's serious. Note that chemists are rarely open late or on Sundays. Most hospitals have 24hr. pharmacies, but may only serve patients with prescriptions.

MEDICAL EMERGENCIES. In a life-threatening situation, call ☎**999** from any phone to request an ambulance. For less acute situations, most London hospitals run 24hr. **Accident and Emergency** (A&E) or **Casualty** wards. A list of A&E departments in London can be found in the **Service Directory,** see p. 337. If your condition isn't judged serious, be prepared to wait for hours, especially on Friday and Saturday nights.

If you are concerned about obtaining medical assistance while traveling, you may wish to employ special support services. The *MedPass* from **GlobalCare, Inc.,** 6875 Shiloh Rd. East, Alpharetta, GA 30005, USA (☎800-860-1111; fax 678-341-1800; www.globalcare.net), provides 24hr. international medical assistance, support, and medical evacuation resources. The **International Association for Medical Assistance to Travelers (IAMAT;** Canada ☎519-836-0102; US ☎716-754-4883; www.cybermall.co.nz/NZ/IAMAT) has free membership, and offers detailed info on immunization requirements and sanitation.

Those with medical conditions (such as diabetes, allergies to antibiotics, epilepsy, heart conditions) may want to obtain a **Medic Alert** membership (first year US$35, annually thereafter US$20), which includes a stainless steel ID tag, among other benefits, like a 24hr. collect-call number. Contact the Medic Alert Foundation, 2323 Colorado Ave, Turlock, CA 95382, USA (☎888-633-4298; outside US 209-668-3333; www.medicalert.org).

GETTING TO LONDON

BY PLANE

When it comes to airfare, a little effort can save you a bundle. If your plans are flexible enough to deal with the restrictions, courier fares are the cheapest. Tickets bought from consolidators and standby seating are also good deals, but last-minute specials, airfare wars, and charter flights often beat these fares. The key is to hunt around, to be flexible, and to ask persistently about discounts. Students, seniors, and those under 26 should never pay full price for a ticket.

AIRFARES

Airfares to London peak between June and mid-September, and again from early December to New Year. Fares are almost always much higher for trips that do not include a Saturday night. "Open return" tickets are normally pricier than fixing a return date when buying the ticket. Round-trip flights are the cheapest; "open-jaw" (arriving in and departing from different cities) tickets tend to be pricier. On commercial airlines, patching one-way flights together is the most expensive way to travel. However, many "budget" airlines charge independently for each segment. Depending on route and season, **fares** for roundtrip flights to London range: US$250-600 from eastern USA and Canada, US$300-800 from the west; AUS$1300-1800 from Australia and NZ$2000-3500 from New Zealand.

BUDGET AND STUDENT TRAVEL AGENCIES

While knowledgeable agents specializing in flights to London can make your life easy and help you save, they may not spend the time to find you the lowest possible fare—they get paid on commission. Travelers holding **ISIC** and **IYTC cards** (see p. 26) qualify for big discounts from student travel agencies. Most flights from budget agencies are on major airlines, but in peak season some may sell seats on less reliable chartered aircraft.

CTS Travel, 30 Rathbone Pl., London W1T 1GQ, UK (☎0207 209 0630; www.ctstravel.co.uk). A British student travel agency with offices in 39 countries including the US; Empire State Building, 350 Fifth Ave., Suite 7813, New York, NY 10118 (☎877-287-6665; www.ctstravelusa.com).

STA Travel, 5900 Wilshire Blvd., Ste. 900, Los Angeles, CA 90036, USA (24hr. reservations and info ☎800-781-4040; www.sta-travel.com). A student and youth travel organization with over 150 offices worldwide (check their website for a listing of all their offices), including US offices in Boston, Chicago, New York, San Francisco, Seattle, and Washington, D.C. Ticket booking, travel insurance, railpasses, and more. Walk-in offices are located throughout Australia (☎03 9349 4344), New Zealand (☎09 309 9723), and the UK (☎0870 1 600 599).

Travel CUTS (Canadian Universities Travel Services Limited), 187 College St., Toronto, ONT M5T 1P7 (☎416-979-2406; www.travelcuts.com). Offices across Canada and the US including Los Angeles, New York, Seattle, and San Francisco.

USIT, 19-21 Aston Quay, Dublin 2 (☎01 602 1777; www.usitworld.com), Ireland's leading student/budget travel agency, has 22 offices throughout Northern Ireland and the Republic of Ireland. Offers programs to work in North America.

Wasteels, Skoubogade 6, 1158 Copenhagen K. (☎3314 4633; www.wasteels.com). A huge chain with 180 locations across Europe. Wasteels sells BIJ tickets discounted 30-45% off regular fare, and 2nd-class international point-to-point train tickets with unlimited stopovers for those under 26 (sold only in Europe).

FLIGHT PLANNING ON THE INTERNET. The Internet may be the budget traveler's dream when it comes to finding and booking bargain fares, but the array of options can be overwhelming. Many airline sites offer special last-minute deals on the Web. Some good websites for these are www.cheapflights.com and www.travelpage.com.

STA (www.sta-travel.com) and **StudentUniverse** (www.studentuniverse.com) provide quotes on student tickets, while **Orbitz** (www.orbitz.com), **Expedia** (www.expedia.com), and **Travelocity** (www.travelocity.com) offer full travel services. **Priceline** (www.priceline.com) lets you specify a price, and obligates you to buy any ticket that meets or beats it; **Hotwire** (www.hotwire.com) offers bargain fares, but won't reveal the airline or flight times until you buy. Other sites that compile deals for you include www.bestfares.com, www.flights.com, www.lowestfare.com, www.onetravel.com, and www.travelzoo.com.

Increasingly, there are online tools available to help sift through multiple offers; **SideStep** (www.sidestep.com; download required) and **Booking Buddy** (www.bookingbuddy.com) let you enter your trip information once and search multiple sites.

An indispensable Internet resource is the **Air Traveler's Handbook** (www.faqs.org/faqs/travel/air/handbook), a comprehensive listing of links to everything you need to know before you board a plane.

COMMERCIAL AIRLINES

The commercial airlines' lowest regular offer is the **APEX** (Advance Purchase Excursion) fare, which provides confirmed reservations and allows "open-jaw" tickets. Generally, reservations must be made seven to 21 days ahead of departure, with 7-14 day minimum-stay and up to 90 day maximum-stay restrictions. These fares carry hefty cancellation and change penalties (fees rise in summer). Book peak-season APEX fares early. Use **Microsoft Expedia** (msn.expedia.com) or **Travelocity** (www.travelocity.com) to get an idea of the lowest published fares, then use the resources outlined here to try and beat those fares. Low-season fares should be appreciably cheaper than the **high-season** (mid-June to Sept.) ones listed here.

TRAVELING FROM NORTH AMERICA

Basic round-trip fares to London, US$300-800. Standard commercial carriers like **American** (☎800-433-7300; www.aa.com), **United** (800-538-2929; www.ual.com), and **Northwest** (800-447-4747; www.nwa.com) probably offer the most convenient flights, but they may not be the cheapest. Check **Lufthansa** (800-399-5838; cms.lufthansa.com), **British Airways** (800-247-9297; www.britishairways.com), **Air France** (800-237-2747; www.airfrance.us), and **Alitalia** (800-223-5730; www.alitaliausa.com) for cheap tickets from destinations throughout the US to all over Europe.

EUROPEAN DISCOUNT AIRLINES

Travelers from Ireland and the continent can take advantage of the numerous no-frills budget airlines criss-crossing Europe. By only taking direct bookings, flying between lesser-known airports and cutting back on free drinks, food, and sometimes baggage allowances, this new breed of carrier offers regular services at prices often lower than trains and ferries, let alone commercial airlines. In short it is the best thing that has happened to travelers recently. Also, these are an ideal way from London to other major European cities.

bmibaby: UK ☎0870 264 2229;www.bmibaby.com.

buzz: UK ☎0870 240 7070; www.buzzaway.com.

easyJet: UK ☎0871 750 0100; www.easyjet.com.

go: UK ☎0870 60 76 543, elsewhere call 44 1279 66 63 88; www.go-fly.com.

Ryanair: Ireland ☎0818 303 030, UK 087 246 00 00; www.ryanair.com.

TRAVELING FROM AUSTRALIA AND NEW ZEALAND

Air New Zealand: New Zealand ☎0800 73 70 00; www.airnz.co.nz. Auckland to London.

Qantas Air: Australia ☎13 11 31, New Zealand 0800 101 500; www.qantas.com.au. Flights from Australia and New Zealand to London for around AUS$2000.

Singapore Air: Australia ☎13 10 11, New Zealand 0800 808 909; www.singaporeair.com. Flies from Auckland, Sydney, Melbourne, and Perth to Western Europe.

Thai Airways: Australia ☎1300 65 19 60, New Zealand 09 377 38 86; www.thaiair.com. Flies from Auckland, Sydney, and Melbourne to Amsterdam, Frankfurt, and London.

AIR COURIER FLIGHTS

Those who travel light should consider courier flights. Couriers help transport cargo on international flights by using their checked luggage space for freight. Generally, couriers must travel with carry-ons only and deal with complex flight restrictions. Most flights are round-trip only, with short fixed-length stays (usually one week) and a limit of one ticket per issue. Many of these flights operate only out of major gateway cities, mostly in North America. Round-trip courier fares from the US to London run about US$200-500. Most flights leave from Los Angeles, Miami, New York, or San Francisco in the US; and from Montreal, Toronto, or Vancouver in Canada. Generally, you must be over 21 (in some cases 18). In summer, the most popular destinations usually require an advance reservation of about two weeks (you can usually book up to two months ahead). Super-discounted fares are common for "last-minute" flights (three to 14 days ahead).

STANDBY FLIGHTS

Traveling standby requires considerable flexibility in arrival and departure dates and cities. Companies dealing in standby flights sell vouchers rather than tickets, along with the promise to get you to your destination (or near your destination) within a certain window of time (typically 1-5 days). You call in before your specific window of time to hear your flight options and the probability that you will be able to board each flight. You can then decide which flights you want to try to make, show up at the appropriate airport at the appropriate time, present your voucher, and board if space is available. Vouchers can usually be bought for both one-way and round-trip travel. You may receive a monetary refund only if every available flight within your date range is full; if you opt not to take an available (but perhaps less convenient) flight, you can only get credit toward future travel. Carefully read agreements with any company offering standby flights as tricky fine print can leave you in the lurch, and it can be difficult to receive refunds. To check on a company's service record in the US, call the Better Business Bureau (☎703-276-0100).

TICKET CONSOLIDATORS

Ticket consolidators, or **"bucket shops,"** buy unsold tickets in bulk from commercial airlines and sell them at discounted rates. The best place to look is in the Sunday travel section of any major newspaper (such as *The New York Times*), where many bucket shops place tiny ads. Call quickly, as availability is typically extremely limited. Not all bucket shops are reliable, so insist on a receipt that gives full details of restrictions, refunds, and tickets, and pay by credit card (in spite of the 2-5% fee) so you can stop payment if you never receive your tickets. For more info, see www.travel-library.com/air-travel/consolidators.html.

BY CHUNNEL TUNNEL

Traversing 27 mi. under the sea, the Chunnel is fast and convenient, though it is the least scenic route from England to France.

BY TRAIN. Eurostar, Eurostar House, Waterloo Station, London SE1 8SE (UK ☎08705 186 186; www.eurostar.com), runs frequent trains between London and the continent. Ten to 28 trains per day run to 100 destinations including Paris (4hr., US$75-300, 2nd class), Disneyland Paris, Brussels, Lille, and Calais.

BY CAR. Eurotunnel (UK Customer relations, P.O. Box 2000, Folkestone, Kent CT18 8XY; www.eurotunnel.co.uk), shuttles cars and passengers between Kent and Nord-Pas-de-Calais. Return fares for vehicle and all passengers range from UK£283-317 with car. Book online or via phone.

GETTING INTO LONDON

THE AIRPORTS

HEATHROW

Location: Near Hounslow, West London, 15 mi. from Central London. ***Contact:*** *☎087 0000 0123; www.baa.co.uk/main/airports/heathrow.*

Heathrow is colossal, crowded, and chaotic—just what you'd expect from one of the world's busiest international airports. Airlines and destinations are divvied up among its four terminals as listed below, with a few exceptions—if in doubt, check with the airline.

Terminal 1: Domestic flights and British Airways's European destinations, except for flights to Amsterdam and Paris. Also British Airways flights to Tokyo, Hong Kong, Johannesburg, San Francisco, and Los Angles.

Terminal 2: All non-British Airways flights to Europe with the exception of Air Malta and KLM; British Airways flights to Basle.

Terminal 3: Intercontinental flights, except British Airways, Qantas, and Sri Lankan Airlines; British Airways flights to Miami.

Terminal 4: British Airways intercontinental flights (except Miami) and services to Amsterdam and Paris; Air Malta; KLM; Qantas; Sri Lankan Airlines; and any other flights that won't squeeze into terminals 1, 2, or 3.

TRANSPORTATION TO/FROM CENTRAL LONDON

In the book we use the tube icon (⊖) to represent underground stations.

UNDERGROUND. The cheapest and best way to get to London from Heathrow. Heathrow's two Tube stations form a loop on the end of the Piccadilly Line—trains stop first at **Heathrow Terminal 4** and then at **Heathrow Terminals 1, 2, 3** (both Zone 6) before swinging back towards central London. Note that stairs are an integral part of most Tube stations. *(☎0845 330 9880; www.thetube.com. 50-70min. from central London, every 4-5min. £3.80, under 16 £1.50.)*

TRAIN. The **Heathrow Express** provides a speedy but expensive connection from Heathrow to Paddington station. An added bonus is check-in facilities at Paddington. Ticket counters at Heathrow even accept foreign currency. *(☎0845 600 1515; www.heathrowexpress.co.uk. 15min., daily every 15min. 5:10am-11:40pm. Railpasses and Travelcards not valid. £13, return £25; child £6/£11.50; £2 extra if bought on the train. Ask about day returns and group specials. AmEx/MC/V.)*

BUS. The **Airbus A2** crawls from Heathrow to Russel Square, stopping off at various points on the way. *(☎0870 580 8080; www.nationalexpress.com. 1¼-1¾hr.; every 30-45min. 6am-8pm Heathrow-King's Cross. £10, return £15; ages 5-15 half price.)* **National Express**

(which operates Airbus) also runs coaches between Heathrow and Victoria Coach Station. *(Contact and prices as above. 40-80min., approx. every 20min. Operates daily 5:35am-9:35pm Heathrow-Victoria, 7:30am-11:30pm Victoria-Heathrow.)*

SHUTTLE. Hotelink runs shared shuttles from Heathrow to hotels in London. Book at least 48hr. ahead. *(☎01293 532 244; www.hotelink.co.uk. Operates daily 4am-6pm Heathrow-London, 4am-10pm London-Heathrow. £15.)*

TAXI. With metered fares to central London unlikely to be under £50, and journey times never under 1hr., you'd have to be rich and inane to take a **licensed taxicab** from Heathrow to London by yourself. A **minicab** is slightly cheaper and just as slow. You can have a contact in London (hotel and hostel owners will often oblige) book a minicab to meet you; expect to pay at least £25-30 including waiting, parking, and tip.

GATWICK

Location: *Sussex, 30 mi. south of London.* ***Contact:*** *☎0870 000 2468; www.baa.co.uk/main/airports/gatwick.*

Though Gatwick is much farther from London, numerous swift and affordable train services often make it easier to get to than Heathrow. Transport facilities are concentrated in the **South Terminal;** a futuristic free monorail shuttle connects the South Terminal to the newer **North Terminal,** which has better shops and restaurants.

TRANSPORTATION TO/FROM CENTRAL LONDON

TRAIN. Three train companies run between Gatwick and London, and they all charge different prices and tickets are non-transferable between services. The **Gatwick Express** non-stop service to Victoria station would like you to think it's the only train to London, but the cheaper **Connex** commuter trains run the same route just as frequently and takes just a few minutes longer. *(Gatwick Express: ☎0845 850 1530; www.gatwickexpress.co.uk. 30-35min., Departs Gatwick 4:30, 5am, then every 15min. until midnight. £12, return £23.50; ages 5-15 £6/£11.75. Connex: ☎0845 5748 4950; www.connex.co.uk. 35-45min., every 15-20min. 5am-midnight and every hr. midnight-5am. £9.80, return £20; ages 5-15 £4.90/£5.10.)* Additionally, **Thameslink** commuter trains head regularly to King's Cross, stopping in London Bridge and Blackfriars. Beware that Thameslink stations typically have lots of stairs. *(☎0845 748 4950; www.thameslink.co.uk. 50min., daily every 30min. £9.80.)*

BUSES, SHUTTLES, & TAXIS. Gatwick's distance from London makes road services slow and unpredictable. National Express's **Airbus A5** takes 1½ hr. to travel to Victoria bus station. *(Contact details and prices same as for Heathrow. Hourly 4:15am-9:15pm from Gatwick, 6am-11pm from Victoria.)* The **Hotelink** shuttle offers a pick-up service from Gatwick to London hotels. *(See Heathrow for details. Operates from Gatwick to hotels daily from 6am-10pm and from hotels to Gatwick from 5am-6pm. £18 per person.)* You should never take a **licensed taxi** from Gatwick to London; the trip will take over an hour and cost at least £90. **Minicabs** are cheaper (£30-£40) but still leave you at the mercy of traffic; plus, you'll have to have a contact in London arrange for pickup. If you have heavy bags, take the train to Victoria and catch a taxi from there.

STANSTED

Location: *Essex, 30 mi. north of London.* ***Contact:*** *☎0870 000 0303; www.baa.co.uk/main/airports/stansted.*

TRANSPORTATION TO/FROM CENTRAL LONDON

TRAINS. The train station is below the terminal building. The **Stansted Express** offers frequent service to Liverpool St. Station. *(☎0845 748 4950; www.stanstedexpress.co.uk. 45min., M-Sa every 15-30min. 5:30am–midnight. £13.80, return £24.)*

BUS. The **Airbus A6/A7** runs every 30min. to Victoria station, 24hr. The A6 goes via the West End, the A7 via The City. *(Contact and prices same as for Heathrow. 1¼-1¾hr.)*

LUTON

Location: *Bedfordshire, 32 mi. north of London.* **Contact:** *☎0158 240 5100; www.london-luton.co.uk.*

Luton serves mostly charter flights and no-frills budget airlines.

TRANSPORTATION TO/FROM CENTRAL LONDON

The **Thameslink** train line that links Gatwick to King's Cross also continues north to Luton. *(Contact as for Gatwick. 30-40min.; every 30min. M-Sa 3:20am-1am, Su less frequently 6am-11:15pm. Single £10.40.)* **Green Line 757 buses** link Luton to the West End and Victoria. *(☎0870 608 7261; www.greenline.co.uk. 1-1¾hr.; 3 per hr. 8am-6pm, 2 per hr. 6-11pm, 1 per hr. 11pm-8am. Single £9, return £12; ages 5-15 £5.50/£8.)*

LONDON CITY AIRPORT

Location: *Docklands, East London.* **Contact:** *☎7646 0088; www.londoncityairport.com.*

Built over the former Royal Docks, it was once the heart of London's trading empire. Today, the main export is pin-striped business men.

TRANSPORTATION TO/FROM CENTRAL LONDON

Every 10min., **shuttles** make the 30min. run to Liverpool St. via Canary Wharf, or the 5min. run to Canning Town. *(To and from Liverpool St. via Canary Wharf: M-F 6:50am-9:20pm, Sa 6:50am-1:10pm, Su 11am-9:20pm; £3.50 to Canary Wharf, £6 to Liverpool St. To and from Canning Town: M-F 6am-10:30pm, Sa 6am-1pm, Su 10am-10:20pm; £3.)* Bus **#69** also runs to Canning Town, while the **#473** stops at Silvertown rail station. *(Both approx. every 10min., 6am-midnight, £1)*

TRAIN STATIONS

London's nine mainline stations date from the Victorian era, when each railway company had its own London terminus. After being unified for most of the 20th century, the 1990s saw the railways broken up and privatized again. Corporate loyalty means that some station staff are unwilling to tell you about rival services. For impartial advice, call **National Rail Enquiries.** *(24hr. ☎0845 748 4950.)* All London terminals are well served by bus and Tube services.

BUS STATIONS

Victoria Coach Station, Buckingham Palace Rd., is the hub of Britain's long-distance bus network. **National Express** is the largest operator of intercity services. *(☎0870 580 8080; www.nationalexpress.com.)* International services are dominated by **Eurolines,** which offers regular links to all major European cities. *(☎0870 514 3219; www.eurolines.co.uk.)* Much of the area around London is served by **Green Line** coaches, which leave from the Eccleston Bridge mall behind Victoria station. Purchase tickets from the driver. *(☎0870 608 7261; www.greenline.co.uk. ⊖Victoria.)*

GETTING AROUND LONDON

It's hard not to find a Londoner who wouldn't complain about the transportation (and of course the weather). Whether it's overcrowding on the Tube or British Rail delays, nothing is more deeply ingrained in the London psyche than the idea that its transport infrastructure is falling to pieces. For all this, London's transport system remains one of the world's best; there's hardly a spot in the city not served by frequent Tubes, buses, or trains. If occasionally there is a 20min. wait for a bus, or an overcrowded Tube, that's just part of the fun—and an opportunity to appreciate the fact that, when it comes to politeness under pressure (and avoiding bodily contact),

Londoners are first-rate. Oddly, what shocks visitors the most about London transportation seems least important to locals: the expense. Count on spending approximately £5 per day on public transportation.

BY PUBLIC TRANSPORTATION

Transport for London. 24hr. info, including route advice ☎7222 1234; www.tfl.gov.uk. Current delays and route changes ☎7222 1200.

Local gripes aside, London's public transport is remarkably efficient—and it's getting better. London's Mayor, Ken Livingstone, is the man who first introduced Travelcards in the 1980s, and scarcely a week goes by without new talk about making travel in London easier and cheaper. New fares are generally introduced in January.

ZONES

The public-transport network is divided into a series of concentric zones; ticket prices depend on the zones passed during a journey. To confuse matters, there are two different zoning systems. The **Tube, rail,** and **Docklands Light Railway (DLR)** network operates on a system of six zones, with Zone 1 being the most central. The **Buses** reduce this to four zones. Bus Zones 1, 2, and 3 are the same as for the Tube, and Tube Zones 4, 5, and 6 are bus Zone 4. **Almost everything of interest to visitors is in Zones 1 and 2.**

TRAVEL PASSES

All passes expire at 4:30am the day after the printed expiration date.

London's public transportation is the best way to get around the city, and you're almost bound to save money by investing in one of London's range of travel passes. Passes work on the Zone system (see above). Note that a Zone 1-4 pass will cover all bus routes in London, but Tube and other services only up to the Tube Zone 4 boundary. Passes can be purchased at Tube, DLR, and commuter rail stations. Avoid **ticket touts** hawking second-hand One-Day Travelcards, LT Cards, and Bus Passes; you might save a few pounds, but there's no guarantee the ticket will work. More importantly, it's illegal and penalties are stiff.

All children below the age of 5 can travel for free. Children from ages of 5-10 can travel for free on buses and pay half price on the train and tube. Ages 11-15 half priced fares. To qualify for child fares, especially teenagers **aged 14-15** must display a **child-rate Photocard** when purchasing tickets and traveling on public transportation. To qualify for student fares, full-time students at London universities must obtain a **Student Photocard.** These can be obtained free of charge from any Tube station on presentation of proof of age, and a passport-sized photo.

DAY TRAVELCARDS. Valid for bus, Tube, DLR, and commuter rail services for one day. There are 2 types of Day Travelcards: **Peak** cards (valid from midnight), **Off-Peak** cards (valid from midnight Sa-Sun, but from 9:30am M-F). Both Peak and Off-Peak Travelcards are valid until 4:30am the morning after the printed expiration date. **Fare:** Zones 1-2 Peak £5.30, Off-Peak £4.30; Zones 1-4 £7.30/£4.70; Zones 1-6 £11.10/£5.40. Child: Peak, half the adult fare; Off-Peak Zones 1-6 £2.

LT CARDS. LT Cards are just like Peak Day Travelcards except they're not valid on the commuter rail. The only type available to adults is for all 6 zones, which means you're only likely to use one when heading to or from Heathrow, and in this case it's cheaper than a Peak Day Travelcard. Zones 1-6 £8.20; child: £3.50.

CARNET. A book of 10 singles, for a Tube journey starting and finishing in Zone 1 only; cannot be used as extensions, nor can you purchase extensions for them. Each ticket must be validated at the station before you use it; failure to do so counts as fare evasion. Cheaper than buying individual singles, but unless you plan to do a lot of walking, a Travelcard is definitely better. £15; child: £5.

FAMILY TRAVELCARDS. For 1-2 adults and 1-4 children traveling together. When the only child is under 5, a child fare must be paid; otherwise under-5s go free. Each member must hold a Family Travelcard and must travel together. Validity as for Day Travelcards Off-Peak. Zones 1-2 £2.80, 1-4 £3.10, 1-6 £3.60, 2-6 £2.50; child 80p.

WEEKEND TRAVELCARDS. Valid 2 consecutive days Sa, Su and public holidays (e.g, Easter Sunday and Easter Monday). Zones 1-2 £6.40, 1-4 £7, 1-6 £8.10, 2-6 £5.70; child Zones 1-6 £3.

SEASON TICKETS. Weekly, monthly, and annual Travelcards can be bought at any time and are valid for 7 days, 1 month, or 1 year. respectively from the date of purchase. Matching **Photocard** required, free from Tube stations with an ID photo. **Rate:** Zone 1 only £17 weekly, £65.30 monthly, 1-2 £20.20/£77.60, 1-3 £23.80/£91.40; child: Zone 1 £7/£26.90, 1-2 8.20/31.50, 1-3 £11/£42.30.

BUS PASSES. Since Tube passes include access to the bus, buy a bus pass only if you won't be using the Tube. **One Day Bus Pass:** £2.50 all Zones. Child £1. **Weekly Bus Passes** £9.50 all Zones; child £4. Longer periods available.

THE UNDERGROUND

*24hr. ☎7222 1234; www.thetube.com. Free **Maps** of the Underground network are available at Tube stations and Transport for London info centers.*

Universally known as "the Tube," the Underground provides a fast and convenient way of getting around London. Within Zone 1, use the Tube only for longer journeys; adjacent stations are so close together that walking or taking a bus makes more sense. If you use the Tube frequently (and chances are you will), a **Travelcard** will save you money.

NAVIGATING THE SYSTEM. Color-coding makes navigating the 12 lines a breeze. **Platforms** are labeled by line name and general direction. If traveling on one of the lines that splits into two or more branches, check platform indicators or the front of the train. Unless you want to be run down by a commuter in full stride, **stand to the right** on escalators.

HOURS OF OPERATION. The Tube runs daily from approximately 5:30am to midnight, giving clubbers that extra incentive to party till dawn. The exact time of the first and last train from each station should be posted in the ticket hall; check if you think you'll be taking the Tube any time after 11:30pm. Trains run less frequently early mornings, late nights, and Sundays.

TICKETS. You can buy tickets from ticket counters or machines in all stations. Tickets must be bought at the start of a journey and are valid only for the day of purchase (including return tickets, but excluding carnets). **Keep your ticket for the entire journey;** it will be checked on the way out and may be checked at any time. There's a £10 **on-the-spot fine** for traveling without a valid ticket.

BUSES

*www.tfl.gov.uk/buses. For 24hr. travel info, use the Transport for London info line (☎7222 1234). **Helpful bus maps are available at most Tube stations and at Transport for London info centers.** Within the book we mention main streets through which the majority of the buses run for each neighborhood.*

Only tourists use the Tube for short trips in central London—chances are you'll spend half as long walking underground as it would take to get to your destination. If it's only a couple of Tube stops, or if it involves more than one change, a bus will likely get there faster. Excellent signage makes the bus system easy to use even for those with no local knowledge. Most stops display a map of local routes and nearby stops together with a key to help you find the bus and stop you need faster than you can say "mind the gap." If you're not sure where to get off, ask the driver or conductor.

Buses run approximately 5:30am to midnight; a reduced network of **Night Buses** (see below) fills in the gap. During the day, double-deckers generally run every 10-15min., while single-decker hoppers should come every 5-8min., though it's not uncommon to wait for 30min. only for 3 buses to show up in a row.

BUS STOPS. Officially bus stops come in two varieties, regular and request. Supposedly buses must stop at regular stops (red logo on white background), but only pull up at request stops (white on red) if someone rings the bell, or someone at the bus stop indicates to the driver with an outstretched arm. In reality, it's safest to ring/indicate at all stops. On the older, open-platform "Routemaster" buses, you're free to hop on and off whenever you like.

BUS TICKETS. Show your pass or buy a ticket from the driver as you board. Older buses still use conductors, who make the rounds between stops to collect fares. Despite the "exact change" warnings posted on buses, drivers and conductors usually give change, though a £5 note will elicit grumbles and anything larger risks refusal. Keep your ticket until you get off the bus, or you face a £5 on-the-spot fine. For **Prices,** see **"Fares Please!"** p. 44.

NIGHT BUSES. When honest folk are in bed, London's Night Buses come out to ferry party-goers home. Night Bus route numbers are prefixed with an N; they typically operate the same route as their daytime equivalents, but occasionally start and finish at different points. Many routes start from Trafalgar Sq. Most Night Buses operate every 30min. or 60min. midnight-5:30am.

DOCKLANDS LIGHT RAILWAY

Customer service ☎7363 9700 (open 8:30am-5:30pm M-F). Docklands travel hotline ☎7918 4000 (24hr.). www.tfl.gov.uk/dlr. Open M-Sa 5:30am-12:30am, and Su 7:30am-11:30pm.

The toy-like driverless cabs of this elevated railway provide a vital link in the transport network of East London. Obvious physical differences aside, the network is basically an extension of the Tube, with the same tickets and pricing structure; within the validity of a given ticket, you can transfer from Tube to DLR at no charge. Those combining Greenwich and Docklands in one day should enquire about **Rail and Sail** tickets.

SUBURBAN RAILWAYS

24hr. schedule and fare info ☎0845 748 4950; www.railtrack.co.uk.

In the suburbs, London's commuter rail network is almost as extensive as the Tube. In much of South and East London, this is the only option. Services are run by a range of companies: **Thameslink** heads north-south from Clerkenwell and The City of London; **Silverlink** runs east-west from Docklands to Richmond via Islington and Hampstead; and **WAGN** trains run from Liverpool St. to Hackney. Trains can dramatically cut journey times thanks to direct cross-town links—Silverlink takes 25min. from Hampstead to Kew, versus an hour by Tube. Trains run less frequently than the Tube—generally every 20-30min.—but service often continues later into the night. For journeys combining rail travel with Tube and DLR, you can buy a single ticket valid for the entire trip. Travelcards are also valid on most suburban rail services, though not on intercity lines that happen to make a few local stops.

COMMUTER BOATS

24hr. travel Transport for London (TfL) info line ☎7222 1234; www.tfl.gov.uk/river. Maps available at piers and TfL Travel Info Centres.

London's most important transport artery for most of its history, for the last century the Thames has been little used except for pleasure cruises. Nevertheless, a small number of regularly scheduled commuter boats are once more plying the river. There are 3 routes in operation: **Chelsea Harbour to Embankment via Cadogan**

ESSENTIAL INFORMATION

FARES PLEASE!

TUBE AND DLR FARES

Ticket prices on the London Underground depend on two factors: how many zones traveled and whether you traveled through Zone 1.

For journeys **including Zone 1,** prices are as follows (ages 5-15 given in parentheses):

Zone 1 only: £2 (60p)
1-2: £2.20 (80p)
1-3: £2.50 (£1)
1-4: £3 (£1.20)
1-5: £3.50 (£1.40)
1-6: £3.80 (£1.50)

The **Carnet** offers 10 tickets for travel in Zone 1 for £15 for adults and £5 for 5-15 year olds. Unlike other Tube tickets, Carnet tickets are valid for a year, not just on the day of purchase.

Outside Zone 1, prices are:

any 1 zone: £1.10 (40p)
2 zones: £1.50 (60p)
3 zones: £1.90 (80p)
4 zones: £2.20 (£1)
5 zones: £2.40 (£1)

BUS FARES

All tickets are good for traveling across the London bus network. Adults £1, children ages 11-15 years 40p, under 11 free.

NIGHT-BUS FARES

Same as day bus fares. Note that One Day and Family Travelcards, LT cards, and Bus Passes are valid only for journeys starting before 4:30am of the following day.

All the above ticket prices are valid until at least January 2005. For updated prices check www.tfl.gov.uk

(near Tate Britain), operated by Riverside Launches *(☎7352 5888; M-F 6:30am to 10:30pm; £4, return £8)*; **Savoy to Masthouse Terrace via Canary Wharf** operated by Thames Clippers *(☎7977 6892. M-F 6:55-9:10am and 2:50-7:40pm, occasionally through the weekend; £2.25-3.85, return £3.40-6.10, children half fare)*; and **Hilton Docklands to Canary Wharf,** also by Thames Clippers *(daily 6:30am-8:30pm; £2.25, return £3.40; ages 5-15 90p/£1.70)*. This ride takes about 3min. and we can't think of any use for it. See the TfL website for detailed timetables of departure times for all boats. Holders of a valid **Travelcard** receive one-third off most boat fares.

BY TAXI

LICENSED TAXICABS

Charges: First 390 yd./1¼min. £2, then £1.80 per mi. or 40p per min. until fare reaches £12.40, then 20p per 124yd./½min., more on Sa-Su, public holidays, and M-F 8pm-6am; 40p per additional passenger, 10p per item of luggage, pick-up minimum £2 extra. The meter is running upon arrival and can be up to £3.80 extra. Lost Property: 200 Baker St. (☎7918 2000). Baker St. Open M-F 9am-4pm.

"Black cabs" are very expensive as driving a London taxi is skilled work. Your driver has studied for years to pass a rigorous exam called "The Knowledge" to prove he knows the name of every street in central London and how to get there by the shortest possible route. When considering the expense, remember that all is relative—four people in a cab can be cheaper than the Tube fare over shorter distances.

Black cabs are specially designed for London's narrow streets and can turn on a sixpence—don't be afraid to hail one on the other side of the road. Available cabs are indicated by the blue "for hire" light by the driver and the orange "taxi" sign on the roof; frantic waving and a loud cry of "TAXI!" should do the trick. Taxis are obliged to take passengers anywhere in central London, even just one block, but longer journeys (excluding Heathrow airport) are at their discretion—it's best to negotiate a fare in advance if you're going outside the city. Basically, it costs £2 when you get in the taxi but from then it depends on traffic, direction, and distance. An approximate cost per hour to central London is £25-30, however, there is no flat rate. In any case, a **10% tip** is expected. It's possible to order a licensed cab by phone (see **Service Directory,** p. 339, for numbers), but most people book cheaper minicabs (see below).

MINICABS

*For listings of minicab services, see **Service Directory,** p. 338.*

Anyone with a car and a driving license can set themselves up as a "minicab" company—while only licensed cabs can ply the streets for hire, there are no regulations concerning pre-arranged pickups. As a result, competition is fierce and prices are lower than licensed cabs—but unless you know a reliable company, ordering a minicab is something of a crapshoot, though there's rarely any danger involved (not counting the often hair-raising driving). However, be especially careful with the dodgy drivers that turn up outside nightclubs at closing time. Note down a number before you go out and call from the club, or arrange to be picked-up in advance. Always agree on a price with the driver before getting in; some firms now have standardized price lists.

BY CAR

*For listings of car-rental firms in London, see the **Service Directory,** p. 336.*

You'd be crazy to drive in central London. Unless you have a secret parking spot, leave it to professionals. Various thoroughfares are off-limits to private vehicles during the week, on-street parking is almost non-existent, and off-street parking hideously expensive—not to mention the labyrinthine one-way streets and psychotic van drivers. Cars are only really useful for trips to the outer suburbs and for daytrips, though extensive rail and bus networks can get you most everywhere without a car.

The driving age in the UK is 17, though almost no one will rent cars to those under 23. It may be cheapest to organize car rental before you leave from one of the major international companies, most of which offer online booking.

BY FOOT

Too few visitors to London see any more of the city than the brief sprint from Tube station to sight and back—a pity as London is a great walking city. You can best appreciate London's various neighborhoods by spending some time walking around. Wherever you go, keep a lookout for the **blue plaques** that adorn the former residences of the great, the good, and the honorably obscure. Since London does not have a neat grid system, a good map is key to successful walking. A useful first purchase for travelers in London is the pocket-sized **London A-Z** (Geographer's A-Z Map Company, £5.95), available at most newsstands. Every Londoner owns one, and if you combine it with the maps in this book, you'll never (well, rarely) go wrong.

As in any big city, it's best to use caution when on foot. While London enjoys a remarkably low level of violent crime, **theft** is an increasing problem; be on the alert for pickpockets by day, and move in groups at night. Stick to busy, well-lit thoroughfares, especially in unfamiliar areas, and stay away from open spaces after dark. For more information, see **Crime,** p. 31. A far bigger menace to most foreigners than crime, though, is the fact that Britons drive on the left. Remember to **look right when crossing the road** and be very cautious—traffic is fast and unforgiving. Always use crosswalks and **never jaywalk.**

BY BIKE

*For a listing of bicycle and scooter rental shops in London, see **Service Directory,** p. 335. For more information check www.londonbicycle.com/links.htm.*

Biking in London is not for the faint of heart and can be dangerous if done outside a park. A strong motorists' lobby fights against any proposal to give an inch of the crowded streets over to cycle lanes, while bus drivers take delight in scaring the living daylights out of bikers who seek refuge in bus lanes. Always wear a helmet when riding; you'll probably want a face mask, too.

U.K. Phone Home

While in London, the baffling array of telephonic options is enough to make frustrated dialers wonder why they ever decided to move beyond that trusty old stalwart, the message in a bottle. Coin-operated payphones are expensive, and while calling cards can be cheaper, they don't allow for receiving calls. The most convenient phone system, of course, is the one that travels with you. For those who decide that a mobile phone is a must, then, there are a number of options; and a few of them might actually *save* you some money. Ideal situations depend, of course, on the length of your stay and what you plan to use the phone for.

Using your current phone. Most of the world—England included—operates mobiles with "GSM." If your phone is "world-capable" (check with the provider), you can call up your wireless company and ask for "international roaming" capabilities. The charges are steep, usually US$1.20-1.70/min. A clever way to save a bundle is to tell the phone company that you'll be out of the country for a while and you'd like to get a local service while you're gone—most will oblige and "unlock" your current phone so that you can buy a cheap pay-as-you-go phone chip in London and simply slip it into your current instrument. This done, you'll receive a local number and unlimited free incoming calls.

Aside from a brief period in the 1960s, **motor scooters** have never been as fashionable in London as they are in the rest of Europe—maybe it's the weather. Undeniably fun and fast, they're also dangerous and unstable, especially in the wet. Expect no mercy from London drivers, either. A driving license is sufficient to drive a 50cc moped; for 100cc you need to have taken Compulsory Basic Training (a government-approved course in handling 2-wheelers); for over 500cc you need a special motorcycle licence.

London Bicycle Tour Company, 1a Gabriel's Wharf, 56 Upper Ground (☎ 7928 6838; www.londonbicycle.com). ⊖Waterloo. Organizes bicycle tours of the city. Also rents bikes and roller skates. Open daily Apr.- Oct. 10am -6pm; call ahead Nov.-Mar.

London Cycling Campaign, 30 Great Guildford St. #228 (☎7928 7220; www.lcc.org.uk), ceaselessly works to improve the cyclists' lot in London. They also sell a series of maps detailing cycle routes in London and organize group rides. Open M-F 10am-5pm.

KEEPING IN TOUCH

BY MAIL

Royal Mail *☎0845 774 0740; www.royalmail.co.uk. See the leaflet "All you need to know," available at Post Offices, for details of all domestic and international rates.*

Britain's post is perhaps the best in the world. Mail a letter at 5pm and it will arrive by 10am the next day almost anywhere in the UK.

SENDING MAIL WITHIN THE UK

Collection times are posted on each postbox. **First Class** mail is delivered the next day (except Sunday), while **Second Class** takes up to three days. *(Rates: 1st class 28p up to 60g, 2nd class 20p, upto 750g weight maximum.)*

SENDING MAIL ABROAD

The Royal Mail divides the outside world into three price bands: Europe, World Zone 1, and World Zone 2. World Zone 1 includes North and South America, the Middle East, Africa, South and Southeast Asia. World Zone 2 is everything else. **Customs labels** are required for packets and parcels being sent outside the EU.

AIRMAIL. Letters should get to their destination country within 2 days for Western Europe, 3 for Eastern Europe, and 4 for everywhere else; the ultimate delivery time is dependent on the receiving mail system. All airmail should bear an "airmail" sticker (available at post offices) or have "PAR AVION—AIR MAIL" clearly marked in the upper-left-hand corner. (*To Europe 40p up to 20g, 57p 20-40g; to World Zones 1 and 2 43p for postcards, 27p up to 10g, 68p 10-20g.)*

SURFACE MAIL. surface mail is best for parcels: it's not available for letters within Europe, nor is it much cheaper than airmail for letters to the rest of the world. Delivery times are 2 weeks to Western Europe, 4 to Eastern Europe, and 8 weeks elsewhere. (*World Zone 1&2: 39p up to 20g, 66p 20-60g. 64p for small packet anywhere up to 100g, rising in stages to £2.11 for 450g.)*

RECEIVING MAIL IN LONDON

Two morning deliveries are made per day M-F, and one on Sa. To ensure speedy delivery, make sure mail bears the full **post code,** consisting of the 2-5 initial characters of the postal district (e.g. W1 in the West End, or WC2 for Holborn), followed by a space and then a number and two more letters that define the street.

POSTE RESTANTE. If you don't have a mailing address in London, you can still receive mail via Poste Restante (General Delivery). Mail is stored free of charge for two weeks from within the UK and one month from abroad (some post offices only hold up to five items). To find the address of a participating post office, call the Post Office counter service at ☎084 5722 3344. Mail to Poste Restante should be addressed as follows:

POSTE RESTANTE,
[Post office name],
[Post office street address],
LONDON [Post office postcode],
UNITED KINGDOM
Hold for: [Name of Recipient].

BY TELEPHONE

LONDON PHONE NUMBERS

London's phone code is ***020;*** *within this area all numbers are 8 digits long.* ***Note that all telephone numbers given in this book are in area code 020 unless otherwise specified.*** *For other common codes and useful numbers, see the* ***Phone Facts*** *sidebar.*

London's phone codes have changed four times in the last 16 years, so you may encounter some out-of-date numbers while in London. Here's the low-down on how to convert

Buying a phone. If you plan on staying in Europe for a month or more and don't have a world-capable phone, it might be wise decision to buy a European model when you arrive. You can do a bit of comparison shopping at the multitudes of phone stores on every London high street, but most likely the cheapest phone you'll find will run about £40 and will come with a pre-paid £5 airtime balance. You can then choose which service you'd like (all offer simple pay-as-you-phone plans) based on how much each charges for airtime—most Brits use Virgin, and you'll probably find that it's the cheapest option. Receiving calls is always free, and connection rates are generally about 15p per call (and 5p/min. after the 5th minute).

Renting a phone. Hassle-free, phone rental is actually abundant and easy; the trouble is, it's generally quite pricey as well. Costs vary, but generally expect to pay US$40-50 per week or US$80 per month as a base, with airtime fees added for each call made. The one scenario for which this could be ideal is if you need to *receive* lots of calls while you're in London. As always, incoming calls don't incur any costs, so if you're spending a week during which you'll have someone calling you frequently or for long periods of time, this might just be your best option. The London-based Rent-a-Mobile offers bargain £1 per day rental charges, with a £7 delivery fee. (www.rent-mobile-phone.com), while www.intouchglobal.com and www.roadpost.com have options for longer trips.

ESSENTIAL INFORMATION

PHONE FACTS

USEFUL NUMBERS

Emergency: 999

Operator: ☎100. Free.

Reverse-charge (collect): ☎155. Expensive (but not for you).

Directory enquiries: ☎118500 for UK enquiries anytime (40p to connect and 15per minute). www.bt.com for free UK directory enquiries.

International enquiries: ☎118505 (£1.50 to connect and a minimum call charge of £1.50).

Country codes

For an international line, dial ☎00 plus:

Australia: 61
Canada: 1
France: 33
Ireland: 353
Italy: 39
New Zealand: 64
South Africa: 27
USA: 1

Drop any leading zero from the local area code.

OTHER UK CODES

Aside from 020, there are a few other UK phone codes you should watch out for:

0800 and **0808** numbers are free.

0845 numbers are charged at the local rate.

0870 numbers are charged at the national (long-distance) rate.

Numbers starting with **09** are premium rate, charging £1-£1.50 per min. or more.

Numbers starting with **07** are mobile phones, costing around 30p per minute to call from a land line (more from a payphone).

from the old numbers to the new ones: starting in the late 1980s, London had two phone codes, **071** and **081;** in the 90s this was changed to **0171** and **0181.** To convert these old 7-digit numbers to the new 8-digit number, just prefix 7 (if it was an 0171 number) or 8 (for 0181) to the start of the old number.

CALLING FROM LONDON

To call abroad from a UK phone, dial the **international access code** (00), the **country code,** the **area code** less any leading zero, and finally the **local number.** Thus to call the Dublin number (01) 234 5678, dial 00 353 1 2345678 (353 is the Ireland country code). A number of country codes are given in **Phone Facts,** see p. 48. Most international calls are cheaper M-F 6pm-8am and Sa-Su; calls to Australia and New Zealand are cheaper 2:30-7:30pm and midnight-7am.

To make a local call, simply dial the number without the area code. For a long-distance call, you must first dial the 3- to 5-digit area code, including the initial zero. In foreign publications and some websites, the zero is sometimes omitted when the number is quoted with the UK country code (e.g. a London number may be given as 44 20 rather than 020). Call rates vary depending on the distance, the time of day, and the telephone company used. Rates are highest M-F from 9am to 6 or 7pm, somewhat lower on weekday evenings, and lowest on weekends.

PAYPHONES & REVERSE-CHARGE (COLLECT) CALLS. The majority of payphones are operated by BT (formerly British Telecom), recognizable by the red and blue piper logo. Phones typically accept phonecards, coins, and credit cards. **Payphones** are an expensive way to phone abroad. Still, that's nothing compared to the coronary implications of a **reverse-charge** international call—save them for people you really don't like. *(Reverse-charge operator ☎155.)*

If you're paying by cash, the minimum deposit is 20p. The **dial tone** is a continuous purring sound; a repeated double-purr means the line is **ringing.** Once you hang up, your remaining phonecard credit is rounded down to the nearest 10p. Payphones do *not* give change—if you use 22p from a 50p coin, the remaining 28p is gone once you put the receiver down. If you want to make another call, transfer remaining credit by pushing the "follow-on call" button. Note that **freephone (☎0800 and 0808)** and **emergency** calls **(☎999)** can be made free from any phone without inserting a card or coins.

One final word of warning: the party who initiates the call always pays, even when calling a cell phone—this means that you're charged a cell-phone rate (sometimes as high as 30 per min.) when you call someone's mobile phone. This, in addition to the connection charge and the fact that **you pay for ring-time** means that calling cell phones can be quite expensive. One solution when calling friends: call the cell phone and quickly ask them to call you back, as payphones accept incoming calls.

Other companies besides BT operate payphones in central London. To use these, you'll either need the company's special phonecard, or you can often use cash or a credit card. More common are private payphones, often installed in hostels and pubs. Since the owner can set his own rates on these money-gobbling devices, you'll probably save money by heading outside.

PREPAID CALLING CARDS. Probably the cheapest way to call long-distance, prepaid calling cards are sold in newsagents and post offices. Be sure to check **rates** and **connection charges** before you buy. If you're planning to make one long call, go for the card with the cheapest rate; for lots of short calls, look for a low connection charge. Before settling on a calling card plan, be sure to research your options in order to pick the one that best fits both your needs and your destination.

BILLED CALLING CARDS. These calling cards must be set up in your home country before you leave: contact your telephone provider. In the USA, AT&T, MCI and Sprint all offer their own versions. From the UK, simply dial the free access number and your account code: you'll then be able to either make a direct-dial call home, or reach an operator who'll make the connection for you. Once a month, the bill will be sent home—make sure someone's around to pay it! The disadvantages of these cards is that rates are usually high, and they're only good for calling their home country—you can make calls to other countries, but you'll be charged the rate for calling home *plus* the rate from home to the other country.

TIME DIFFERENCES

UK is at **Greenwich Mean Time (GMT).** New York (USA) is 5 hours behind, Vancouver (CAN) and San Francisco (USA) are 8 hours behind, Sydney (AUS) is 10 hours ahead, and Aukland (NZ) is 11 hours ahead.

BY EMAIL AND INTERNET

Although more people are getting connected at home and on the move, the number of cybercafes is burgeoning—scarcely a major street in London is without a dedicated Internet shop, or at least a regular cafe with a couple of terminals. *Let's Go* notes when Internet facilities are available in accommodations. One innovation is the BT Multi phone, a souped-up payphone that also offers slow and expensive Internet access via a touch screen and keyboard. Multi.phones are very expensive (from 50p for 5min.), and can be found in Tube stations, hotels, museums and a few hostels.

EXPENSIVE INTERNET. Don't use the Internet in the phone-booths. They are ridiculously expensive and eat your coins and are very very slow.

SPECIFIC CONCERNS

TRAVELING ALONE

There are many benefits to traveling alone, including greater independence. On the other hand, any solo traveler is more vulnerable target of harassment and street theft. As a lone traveler, try not to stand out as a tourist, and be especially careful in deserted areas. If questioned, never admit that you are traveling alone. Maintain regular contact with someone at home who knows your itinerary. For more tips, pick up *Traveling Solo* by Eleanor Berman (Globe Pequot Press, US$18), visit www.travelaloneandloveit.com, or subscribe to **Connecting: Solo Travel Network,** 689 Park Rd., Unit 6, Gibsons, BC V0N 1V7, Canada (☎604-886-9099; www.cstn.org; membership US$28-45).

WOMEN TRAVELERS

*Resources for women in London are listed in the **Service Directory,** p. 339.*

For a city like London, women need little additional general caution. Most hostels offer female-only rooms or will make one up on request; you should also be sure in any hostel or hotel that your door locks properly from the inside. If a hostel has communal showers, check them out before booking. By choosing centrally located accommodations, you'll help avoid solitary late-night treks and Tube rides. Look as if you know where you're going and approach older women or couples for directions if you're lost or uncomfortable. Always carry extra money for a phone call, bus, or taxi just in case, and memorize or write down the number of a local taxi firm before going out.

The best answer to verbal harassment is no answer at all. The extremely persistent can sometimes be dissuaded by a firm, loud, and very public "Go away!" Don't hesitate to seek out a police officer or a passerby if you are being harassed. Mace and pepper sprays are illegal throughout the UK.

GLBT TRAVELERS

Soho, particularly around Old Compton St., is London's gay nexus, though gay bars and pubs can be found throughout the city; *Let's Go* has included numerous rainbow-toting cafes, bars, and nightclubs in neighborhood listings. Newspaper resources include *The Pink Paper* (free) available from newsagents; *Gay Times* (£3) which covers political issues; and *Diva* (£2.25), a monthly lesbian lifestyle magazine with an excellent mix of features and good listings. *Boyz* (www.boyz.co.uk) is the main gay listings and lifestyle magazine for London (free from gay bars and clubs), while www.gingerbeer.co.uk offers the lesbian lowdown. Listed below are contact organizations, mail-order bookstores, and publishers that offer materials addressing some specific concerns. **Out and About** (www.planetout.com) offers a bi-weekly newsletter addressing travel concerns and a comprehensive site addressing gay travel concerns. The online newspaper **365gay.com** also has a travel section (www.365gay.com/travel/travelchannel.htm). To avoid hassle at airports, transgendered travelers should make sure that all of their travel documents consistently report the same gender.

Gay's the Word, 66 Marchmont St., London WC1N 1AB, UK (☎44 20 7278 7654; www.gaystheword.co.uk). The largest gay and lesbian bookshop in the UK, with both fiction and nonfiction titles. Mail-order service available.

Giovanni's Room, 1145 Pine St., Philadelphia, PA 19107, USA (☎215-923-2960; www.queerbooks.com). An international lesbian/feminist and gay bookstore with mail-order service (carries many of the publications listed below).

International Lesbian and Gay Association (ILGA), 81 rue Marché-au-Charbon, B-1000 Brussels, Belgium (☎32 2 502 2471; www.ilga.org). Provides political information, such as homosexuality laws of individual countries.

British Tourist Authority (US ☎800-462-2748); devotes a portion of its American site (www.travelbritain.org) to gay and lesbian travel information and publishes the guide *Britain: Inside & Out.* Visit www.gaybritain.org.

FURTHER READING: GAY, LESBIAN, BISEXUAL AND TRANSGENDER.

Spartacus 2003-2004: International Gay Guide. Bruno Gmunder Verlag (US$33).

Damron Men's Travel Guide, Damron Road Atlas, Damron Accommodations Guide, Damron City Guide, and *Damron Women's Traveller.* Damron Travel Guides (US$11-19). For info call ☎800-462-6654 or visit www.damron.com.

Ferrari Guides' Gay Travel A to Z, Ferrari Guides' Men's Travel in Your Pocket, Ferrari Guides' Women's Travel in Your Pocket, and *Ferrari Guides' Inn Places.* Ferrari Publications (US$16-20). Purchase online at www.amazon.com.

The Gay Vacation Guide: The Best Trips and How to Plan Them, Mark Chesnut. Kensington Books (US$15).

Transgender London: London and the Third Sex, by Claudia Andrei, Glitter Books (US$17.95).

TRAVELERS WITH DISABILITIES

Resources for disabled travelers in London are listed in the ***Service Directory,*** *p. 337. Within the book the "wheelchair accessible" note appears with every establishment that has disabled access.*

Traveling by public transport in London with a disability is difficult. The only fully wheelchair-accessible transportation system is the **Docklands Light Railway.** Only 40 out of 275 Tube stations are stair-free; accessible stations are marked on Tube maps with a wheelchair icon. Call ☎084 5330 9880 for help in planning a wheelchair accessible journey within London. For general tips, check www.mossresource.org and click on the "travel destinations: London" link.

Wheelchair-friendly "kneeling buses" are being introduced on many routes, while most newer buses incorporate features to make them easier to use for the elderly and disabled. Transport for London Access & Mobility (☎020 7941 4600) can provide information on public transportation within the city. You can call this number and they will tell you how to make the specific route you desire to undetake. For those who wish to rent cars, some major **car rental** agencies (Hertz, Avis, and National), as well as local agencies, such as Wheelchair Travel in Surrey (☎0148 323 3640), can provide and deliver hand-controlled cars. The National Rail website (www.nationalrail.co.uk) provides general information for travelers with disabilities as well as assistance phone numbers for individual rail companies. *Artsline* (www.artsline.org.uk) provides advice on the accessibility of London arts and entertainment events. Those with disabilities should inform airlines and hotels of their disabilities when making reservations. When in doubt, call ahead to restaurants, museums, and other facilities to find out if they are wheelchair-accessible.

The London Tourist Board's *London For All* leaflet, available at London Visitor's Centers (see p. 339), includes information on disabled access in London. *Access in London,* by Gordon Couch (Quiller Press; US$12) is an in-depth guide to accommodations, transport, and general accessibility in London.

USEFUL ORGANIZATIONS

Access Abroad, www.umabroad.umn.edu/access. A website devoted to making study abroad available to students with disabilities. The site is maintained by Disability Services Research and Training, University of Minnesota, University Gateway, Ste. 180, 200 Oak St. SE, Minneapolis, MN 55455, USA (☎612 624 6884).

Flying Wheels, 143 W. Bridge St., PO Box 382, Owatonna, MN 55060, USA (☎507 451 5005; www.flyingwheelstravel.com). Specializes in escorted trips to Europe for people with physical disabilities and plans custom trips worldwide.

The Guided Tour Inc., 7900 Old York Rd., #114B, Elkins Park, PA 19027, USA (☎800 783 5841; www.guidedtour.com). Organizes travel programs in London for persons with developmental and physical challenges in London.

MINORITY TRAVELERS

Minority travelers in London should have no problems—London's as multiracial and tolerant as cities come. The **Commission for Racial Equality (CRE),** St. Dunstan's House, 201-211 Borough High St., London SE1 1GZ (☎7939 0000; www.cre.gov.uk), offers a wide variety of publications on diversity and race relations and can provide advice to minority travelers who encounter harassment or discrimination.

DIETARY CONCERNS

In a country battered by foot-and-mouth disease and besieged by mad cows, it's not surprising that one in five Brits under age 25 is vegetarian. Almost all restaurants offer a range of vegetarian dishes. *Let's Go* notes restaurants with good vegetarian selections. For more information about vegetarian travel, contact **The Vegetarian Society of the UK** (☎0161 925 2000; www.vegsoc.org). South Indian **bhel poori** and **Thai-Chinese Buddhist** buffets are increasingly popular with budgetarians of all dietary persuasions for their cheap, filling, and wholesome

Will your phone work overseas?
Most cell phones won't!
Call Now!
Don't put up with:
• Exorbitant Roaming Charges
• Expensive Hotel Phones
• Inability to call friends and family
Call overseas for the cost of a local call!
• No Roaming Charges
• Free Incoming Calls
• Worldwide Wireless Coverage
• Local & Global Roaming SIM Cards
$99 & up
Call: 1-800-872-7626
intouchsmartcards.com
InTouch SmartCards
Mention this ad and receive a FREE calling card!

fare, including plenty for vegans. The travel section of the The Vegetarian Resource Group's website (www.vrg.org/travel) has a comprehensive list of organizations and websites that are geared toward helping vegetarians and vegans traveling abroad. For more information, visit your local bookstore or health food store, and consult *The Vegetarian Traveler: Where to Stay if You're Vegetarian, Vegan and Environmentally Sensitive*, by Jed and Susan Civic (Larson Publications; US$16). Vegetarians will also find numerous resources on the web; try www.vegdining.com, www.happycow.net, and www.vegetariansabroad.com, for starters.

Bhel poori and Buddhist restaurants are also a boon to **kosher** travelers, since they offer religiously exacting standards and a complete absence of meat products. Jews with a taste for meat, or who prefer to eat in rabbinically certified establishments, will spend most of their mealtimes in the enclaves of North London, particularly **Golders Green** (see p. 183). For more information, check out the *Jewish Travel Guide*, edited by Michael Zaidner (Vallentine Mitchell; US$18). Travelers who eat **halal** will have little trouble eating well in London, as long as they have a good appetite for North Indian, Turkish, and Middle-Eastern food. Marylebone and Bayswater have the highest concentration of Lebanese restaurants and Islington the most Turkish. Indian restaurants are fairly ubiquitous (though not all are *halal*), and the **East End** is known for its large Bangladeshi community. Travelers looking for halal restaurants may find www.zabihah.com a useful resource.

OTHER RESOURCES

Let's Go tries to cover all aspects of budget travel, but we can't put *everything* in our guides. *London A-Z* (£5) and *Time Out Weekly* (£2.35) are publications that you will find helpful during your stay in London.

HELPFUL WEBSITES

London Tourist Board: www.londontouristboard.com. Info for visitors, including addresses of London Visitor Centers.

LondonTown: www.londontown.com. Tourist info, special offers, maps, listings, and resources for travelers with special needs.

Visit Britain: www.visitbritain.com. The British Tourist Association website. Lots of useful info about visiting Britain and London.

Transport For London: www.tfl.gov.uk. Comprehensive info on public transportation in London, including ticket prices and current service reports.

London Theatre Guide: www.londontheatre.co.uk. Reviews, listings, tickets, chatrooms, and theater seating plans.

WWW.LETSGO.COM Our freshly redesigned website features extensive content from our guides; community forums where travelers can connect with each other and ask questions or advice—as well as share stories and tips; and expanded resources to help you plan your trip. Visit us soon to browse by destination, find information about ordering our titles, and sign up for our e-newsletter!

INSIDE

Life and Times

LONDON THROUGH THE AGES

ROMANS TO NORMANS (AD 43-1042)

LONDON BRIDGE, TAKE I. In AD 43, **Aulus Plautius** landed in Kent with 40,000 battle-hardened Romans and marched north until he found his way barred by the Thames. Pausing here to await the Emperor Claudius, Aulus busied his troops with the building of a bridge. Situated at the lowest navigable point on the river, and soon the center of an excellent network of Roman roads, the crossing naturally became a trade focal point. Merchants set up on the north bank of the river: London—or rather, Londinium—was born. By the end of the 2nd century London could boast a forum four times the size of Trafalgar Sq. and a population of 45,000 drawn from all over the Empire.

A NEW BEGINNING. In the mid-5th century, Anglos and Saxons overran southern Britain and began ethnically cleansing their new home of its Celtic inhabitants. In 604, on a mission from Rome, St. Augustine converted the local king and consecrated the first Bishop of London, Mellitus. In the same year, work started on the first **St. Paul's Cathedral.** The City of London's higgledy-piggledy street plan can be traced to this era: turning the orderly Roman city inside-out, the new inhabitants built their houses on the solid surface of the old Roman roads.

LONDON BRIDGE, TAKE II. London's prosperity brought unwelcome attention: 9th-century **Vikings** made the transition from raiders to conquerors. In 871, the Danes occupied London; it took **Alfred the Great** 15 years to retake it. Even so, Danes still controlled half of England (the "Danelaw"), and intermittent war continued for over a century. In 1013, London came under Danish rule once more when **King Æthelred the Unready** (an Old English pun—his name means "Well-advised the ill-advised") fled to Normandy. This time London was reconquered with the help of a 19-year-old Norwegian, Olaf, who hitched ropes between his fleet and the bridge supports and rowed away. The supports gave way, the Danes fell into the Thames, and the song "London Bridge is Falling Down" was born. Even so, when Æthelred died in 1016 the kingdom passed (peacefully) to a Dane, **Canute,** who made London the capital of an empire encompassing present day England, Denmark, and Norway.

THE MIDDLE AGES (1042-1485)

CONQUEST. Canute's successors held on to England until 1042, when Æthelred's son **St. Edward the Confessor** became king. London owes its status as a capital to Edward, who wanted to live near his favorite new church, the West Minster; **Westminster** has been home to the English government ever since. Edward's death in 1066 set the scene for the most famous battle in English history. **William of Normandy** claimed that Edward (who grew up in Normandy and was half-Norman) had promised him the throne; **Harold,** Earl of Wessex, disagreed. The difference was resolved on October 14th, at Hastings. By sunset Harold was dead, and William had a new kingdom. The Norman monarchs tried to awe their new capital into submission with the construction of the **Tower of London** (see p. 83) and the now-vanished Baynard and Montfichet castles.

INCORPORATION. Desperate for money to finance their wars, Norman kings made numerous concessions to London. London was incorporated in 1191, granting the city a measure of self-governance and independence from the crown: the first Mayor, **Henry FitzAilwyn,** was elected in 1193. His present-day successor, the Lord Mayor, still presides over the 680 acres of the City of London; even today, the Queen may not enter the City without the mayor's permission.

A CENTURY OF HORRORS. For the largest European city (north of the Alps), the 14th century was a time of calamity. In 1348, plague arrived, borne by rats carried on ships from the continent. The resulting **Black Death** claimed the lives of 30,000 people—perhaps half the city's total population. Thousands more died in the later outbreaks of 1361, 1369, and 1375. In 1381 came the **Peasants' Revolt.** Incensed by a new poll tax, 60,000 men marched on London, destroyed the Savoy palace, and burned legal records in the **The Temple** (see p. 97). After the peasants occupied the Tower, the 14-year-old **Richard II** agreed to meet their leader **Wat Tyler** at Smithfield. During a heated discussion, the Mayor of London killed Tyler with a dagger; Richard rode calmly forward and informed the peasants that he would grant all their demands if only they would return peacefully to their homes. Incredibly, the crowd believed him. As soon as he was safe, Richard had the ringleaders executed and withdrew his promises of better conditions.

A THORNY PROBLEM. The year 1387 saw the birth of **Henry V,** England's first ruler since the Conquest to speak English as his first language. While Henry V proved to be one of England's most capable kings, his son **Henry VI** led England into the quagmire known as the **Wars of the Roses.** As told by Shakespeare, in **Middle Temple Garden** (see p. 98) the warring parties plucked the red and white roses that would serve as their emblems. Tired of Henry's dithering, London's merchants gave full backing to the financially astute **Edward IV,** whose shared interest in business led them to overlook his equally shared interest in their wives. In 1476, Under Edward's patronage **William Caxton** set up a printing press in Westminster; after his death, his aptly named assistant Wyknyn de Worde moved the presses to **Fleet Street** (see p. 97), the start of what would be the heart of the British printing industry until the 1980s.

FLUX IN THE REGENCY (1485-1685)

THE TUDOR AGE. In the next century, London's population would quadruple to 200,000, mostly through immigration from rural areas hit hard by agricultural changes and by **Henry VIII's** dissolution of the monasteries in 1536. Many of the new arrivals found employment on Henry's numerous building projects, including palaces at **Hampton Court** (see p. 299), **Whitehall** (p. 117), and **St. James's** (p. 112); others built the equally luxurious houses that soon lined the Strand between the City and Westminster. The sumptuousness of the court can be seen in the portraits of Henry's court artist, the German Hans Holbein.

Henry's only son, **Edward VI,** reigned only six years before dying in 1553 at the age of 15. He was succeeded by his Catholic sister **Mary I,** who earned her nickname "Bloody Mary" for her campaign against the Anglican church established by her father—though in reality, Henry VIII and Elizabeth both led far bloodier religious persecutions.

ELIZABETH'S LONDON. Elizabeth I, daughter of Henry VIII and Anne Boleyn, inherited none of her father's marital woes—indeed, her refusal to marry earned her the title "The Virgin Queen"(how true this title was is yet another scandal!). Under Elizabeth's reign, explorers Sir Francis Drake and Walter Raleigh expanded the English Empire's horizons, while dramatists such as **William Shakespeare, Christopher Marlowe,** and **Ben Jonson** expanded its literary horizons. At first, plays were performed in the courtyards of London inns, with audiences packed into the galleries. The city authorities soon sent the actors packing over the river to Southwark, where **James Burbage** had constructed London's first custom-built playhouse named The Theatre, which was later renamed **The Globe** (see p. 107).

A SCOTTISH KING. Elizabeth's refusal to take a husband led to her cousin, James VI of Scotland, inheriting the throne to become **James I** of England. If London loved Elizabeth, it only tolerated James. Closing himself up in Whitehall, James replied to the people's desire to see his face with the retort "then I will pull down my breeches and they shall also see my arse." Nevertheless, James was not wholly uncaring of the fate of Londoners: he gave his backing to an ambitious project to supply London with fresh drinking water via hollowed-out wooden pipes from a new reservoir in Clerkenwell. Such improvements were all the more necessary as London continued its unchecked expansion: the city was increasingly spilling beyond the walls and into the future **West End**—which was preferred since prevailing winds carried the stench and pollution of the growing metropolis eastward.

WAR AND REGICIDE. James's autocratic tendencies meant that his passing, in 1625, was little mourned. Affairs did not improve under his son, **Charles I.** Beset by military defeat abroad, religious dissent at home, and tensions between Charles I and the House of Commons degenerated into the 1642 **Civil War**. The Civil War was basically an armed conflict between the Parliamentarians and Royalists (supporters of the monarchy). London's support for Parliament sealed the king's fate: without the city's money and manpower, his chance of victory was slim. The king was tried for treason in Westminster Hall, spent his last night in **St. James's Palace** (p. 112), before his execution on the lawn of Banqueting House on January 25, 1649. Oliver Cromwell was elected to the Parliament as the Lord Protector of the Commonwealth of England (1653-58).

Though Cromwell's firm hand restored the health of the Puritan-dominated **Commonwealth,** Parliament proved to be as repressive and unpopular as the king it replaced. Not content with simply outlawing theater and most other forms of entertainment, it went as far as banning music in churches and even, in 1652, to abolish Christmas—Cromwell accused the holiday of being a Catholic superstition.

A TUMULTUOUS DECADE. The Commonwealth didn't last long. In 1660, **Charles II** returned from exile in Holland to a rapturous welcome. Among those accompanying him on his return was **Samuel Pepys** (PEEPS), whose diary of 1660s London provides an invaluable account of this tumultuous time. The happy-go-lucky atmosphere of the Restoration's early years died in the **Great Plague** of 1665, in which more than 75,000 Londoners perished. Worse disaster was to follow: early in the morning of September 2, 1666, fire broke out in a bakery on Pudding Ln. When the **Great Fire** was finally extinguished, 80% of London lay in ruins, including 80 churches, 13,000 homes, St. Paul's, the Guildhall, and virtually every other building of note save the Tower.

In the face of this devastating double blow, **Christopher Wren** submitted a daring plan to rebuild London on a rational basis, with wide boulevards and sweeping vistas. His grand scheme floundered in the face of opposition from existing landowners, and in the end Wren had to settle for the commission to rebuild **St. Paul's Cathedral** (see p. 80) and 51 lesser churches. The fire itself was commemorated by Wren's simple **Monument** (see p. 91), a 202 ft. high column situated 202 ft. from the spot where the fire broke out. As London rebuilt, some former refugees discovered that they preferred life beyond the city limits. In the latter part of the century speculators threw up numerous handsome squares and terraces in the West End; **Downing Street** (see p. 19) was the brainchild of George Downing, a Massachusetts native, and—appropriately enough—consummate political fixer.

THE ENLIGHTENED CITY (1685-1783)

A GLORIOUS REVOLUTION. Under the leadership of the Dutch **William and Mary,** London gradually supplanted Amsterdam as the linchpin of international trade, an achievement greatly aided by the 1964 founding of the **Bank of England** (see p. 94) on the model of the Bank of Amsterdam. Other future financial behemoths had less obvious beginnings: **Lloyd's of London** (see p. 95) the world's oldest insurance market, started out as Edward Lloyd's coffee shop, where captains congregated to exchange shipping gossip.

PARLIAMENT SUPREME. On the accession of William, Parliament fixed the line of succession to ensure that no Catholic would ever sit on the throne again. The upshot was that in 1714 the crown passed to a German prince who spoke no English, **George I,** who was the former the Elector of Hanover. By this time, however, most of the business of government was handled by the man who invented for himself the role of Prime Minister, **Robert Walpole.** During Walpole's 20 years at the top, writers such as **Jonathan Swift, Alexander Pope,** and **Henry Fielding** wrote articles criticizing Walpole, while **John Gay's** wildly popular *Beggar's Opera* (1728) simultaneously satirized government corruption and the current fad for Italian operas. Walpole and the King were far more comfortable with the music of **George Frederick Handel,** who had followed George I from Hanover. Handel is best remembered for his English-language oratorios such as the *Messiah* (1741), and his later music is recognized as quintessentially English.

JOHNSON'S LONDON. When **George III** came to the throne in 1760, Britain had its first English-speaking king in 70 years. Although George is best remembered for losing America and going mad, between these two calamities the capable hands of **Pitt the Younger** (only 24 when he became Prime Minister in 1783) restored Britain to robust financial health. Meanwhile, London added an intellectual sheen to its mercantile character. The **British Museum** opened its doors in 1759, and the city eagerly followed the well-publicized doings of **Samuel Johnson,** famed wit and author of the charmingly idiosyncratic *Dictionary* (1755). Together with his good friend and painter **Sir Joshua Reynolds,** Johnson founded **The Club** in 1764, an exclusive institution whose members included historian **Edward Gibbon,** economist **Adam Smith,** and writer **James Boswell.** Later Boswell wrote *Life of Johnson* providing an unforgettable portrait of the great man and his era. Reynolds was also the prime mover behind the 1768 foundation of the **Royal Academy of Arts** (see p. 150), whose early members included royal favorite painters like Thomas Gainsborough.

A MODERN CITY. In the latter part of the 18th century, London began to take on many of the characteristics of the present-day city. As the focus of life shifted westwards, **Oxford Street** became the capital's main shopping artery, tempting customers with new-fangled ideas such as window displays and fixed prices. In 1750, London Bridge—until then the sole crossing over the Thames—acquired a neighbor, **Westminster Bridge,** which in 1802 inspired poet **William Wordsworth's** tribute to the beauty of the sleeping city, *Composed upon Westminster Bridge.*

With the trappings of a modern city, London also acquired modern problems, not least among them a massive increase in crime. Much of this could be attributed to the widening gulf between rich and poor, but there was another cause: cheap liquor. **Gin,** invented in Holland in the 17th century, was so cheap and plentiful that by the 1730s consumption had risen to an average of two pints per week for every man, woman, and child in the city—memorably illustrated in **William Hogarth's** allegorical prints, *Gin Lane* and *Beer Street.* In 1751 Parliament passed the Gin Act, imposing government regulation of the sale of alcohol; as a result, mortality rates dropped dramatically. In the same year magistrate and novelist **Henry Fielding,** together with his brother John, established the **Bow Street Runners,** a band of volunteer "thieftakers" which evolved into the Metropolitan Police. Even so, crime was still prevalent enough that in the 1770s the Prime Minister, the Lord Mayor, and even the Prince of Wales were all robbed in broad daylight.

FROM REGENCY TO EMPIRE (1783-1901)

BREAKING DOWN AND BUILDING UP. There could be no mistaking the Prince of Wales (the future **George IV**) for his staid father. From the moment he turned 21 in 1783, the Prince announced himself through flamboyant opposition to his father's ministers and an utter disregard for convention. When, after overcoming an earlier bout in 1788 (subject of the play and film, *The Madness of King George III*), the king descended into permanent insanity in 1811, the heir to the throne assumed power as the **Prince Regent.**

Unpopular as a wastrel ruler concerned more with his appearance than the state of the country, the Regent's obsession with self-aggrandizement nevertheless brought important benefits to London. Inspired by the changes wrought by Napoleon in Paris, he dreamt of creating a grand processional way leading from Marylebone Park to his residence at Carlton House. **John Nash** was the architect chosen to transform this vision into reality: the result was some of London's best-loved architecture. From the grand

AD 43 Romans bridge the Thames at Londinium

60 Boudicca's rebellion

604 St. Augustine in London

871 Vikings occupy London

1066 Norman Conquest

1176-1209 Construction of Old London Bridge

1189 Incorporation of the city

1269 Westminster Abbey rebuilt and reconsecrated

1348 Black Death kills 30,000–almost half the city

1381 Peasants' Revolt

1455-1485 Wars of the Roses

1485-1603 Tudor dynasty

1599 Globe Theatre opens

1603-1649 and **1660-1688** House of Stuart

1605 Gunpowder Plot against James I and Parliament fails

1649 Charles I beheaded and Commonwealth declared

1666 Great Fire destroys city

1675-1710 Rebuilding of St. Paul's Cathedral under Wren

1688-9 Glorious Revolution

1714 House of Hanover takes power with George I

1759 British Museum opens

1837-1901 Queen Victoria

1858 The Great Stink

1863 Metropolitan line opens, the first underground railway

1888 Jack the Ripper

1915 German bombs bring WWI to London

1940 The Blitz devastates the City and the East End

1953 Elizabeth II crowned

2000 Ken Livingstone, first democratic Mayor of London elected.

Nash Terraces surrounding the renamed and remodeled **Regent's Park** (see p. 103), to the great sweep of **Regent's Street** leading up to **Piccadilly Circus** (see p. 112), from where the Haymarket would complete the journey to Carlton House. Alas, all this work was in vain: when the Prince Regent finally became **George IV** in 1820 (five years before the completion of Piccadilly Circus). He abruptly ordered Carlton House demolished, and commissioned Nash to remodel **Buckingham Palace** (see p. 75) for his future residence.

It was the age of the dandy and the aesthete. Fashion was changed forever when **Beau Brummel,** the king's confidant and self-appointed arbiter of taste, did away with gold braid and lace, and made black the new pink. **Romanticism** announced itself in the works of **Lord Byron** and **John Keats;** the London these men occupied can still be seen in the masterful landscapes of **John Constable** and **J.M.W. Turner.**

TRACKS AND ARCHITECTS. If the Regency gave London a new face, the Victorian age supplied the skeleton. By the time the 18-year-old **Queen Victoria** ascended to the throne in 1837, London was already at the heart of the largest Empire the world had ever seen, and the city's population increased by almost a million for every decade of Victoria's 64-year reign. Expansion was driven by the new factories of steam-powered manufacturing, so it was made possible by steam-powered transportation. London's first **railway** opened in 1836, connecting London Bridge to the then-distant suburb of Greenwich; by 1876 there were 10 railway companies connecting London to the rest of Britain, each with its own terminal and tracks. Pressure on the capital's roads was relieved in 1863 with the inauguration of the **Metropolitan Line,** the world's first underground railway. Together with horse-drawn trams, the railways made commuting possible for the first time: once-rural villages such as Islington and Hampstead were rapidly engulfed by the voracious city.

Victorian architects reacted to the rush of modernization with a return to the distant past. **Neo-Gothic** architecture was all the rage, as can be seen in **Charles Barry's** enormous and ornate **Houses of Parliament** (see p. 76). A similar sensibility motivated painter-poet **Dante Gabriel Rossetti,** who founded the influential **Pre-Raphaelite Brotherhood** and unleashed on the unsuspecting public a wave of stylized medieval pastiche and dark-lipped maidens. The general anti-modern feeling of the age was best captured by designer and poet **William Morris,** who founded the **Arts and Crafts** movement in the belief that the Industrial Revolution had destroyed notions of taste and craftsmanship.

FROM LABOR TO LABOUR. Many Victorian artistic movements were deeply influenced by the work of visionary poet and artist **William Blake,** who as early as 1804 had written about the "dark satanic mills" spawned by the Industrial Revolution. Working and living conditions for the majority of the capital's inhabitants were appalling, with health care and sanitation almost non-existent. **Child labor** was unregulated until 1886, **cholera** raged until the **Great Stink** of 1858 forced Parliament to reform the city's sewers, and air pollution was such that in 1879 the capital was shrouded in smog for the entire winter. Another human tragedy struck in 1888, when police searched in vain for **Jack the Ripper,** a serial killer who killed women prostitutes in or near London's Whitechapel District.

This was the London that inspired **Charles Dickens** to write such urban masterpieces as *Oliver Twist* (1837-1839), and saw **Karl Marx** lead the proto-communist First International, founded in London in 1864. Even so, it was not until the last third of the century that significant progress was made: in 1867, the **Reform Bill** extended the vote to most of London's working men and in 1870 the **Education Act** provided schooling for all. Organized labor also made headway: in 1889, Marx's daughter Eleanor led gas workers in a strike which won recognition for the 8-hour day, while in 1893 the working classes found a political voice with the establishment of the **Independent Labour Party.**

THE 20TH CENTURY

SOCIAL COMMENTARY AND SHOPPING. Although Edward VII did not succeed his mother until 1901, Victorian morality had already begun to crumble during the "naughty nineties," when two Irish-born adopted Londoners, taboo-breaking **George Bernard Shaw** and flamboyant **Oscar Wilde,** thrilled theatergoers and shocked the authorities. **Emmeline Pankhurst** started the Woman's Social and Political Union to win the vote for women, a struggle that lasted until 1928. The stunts pulled off by her and her suffragettes were meat and drink to the new tabloid press, which had been born with the launching of the **Daily Mail** in 1896 and rapidly became London's main source of news.

King George II

The changes wrought on London by steam in the previous century were completed by the advance of electricity and petroleum power; by the outbreak of the First World War in 1914, London was recognizably the same city it is today. Red double-decker buses and clean, electrically powered Underground trains delivered Londoners to new department stores such as **Selfridges** (opened 1909) and **Harrods,** which moved to its present site in 1905. Numerous **West End** theatres and cinemas became the epicenter of the London entertainment scene, while brand new telephone booths all over town took care of getting in touch with friends before any show.

Buckingham Palace

ON THE AIR. Londoners greeted the outset of **World War I** in 1914 with jubilant confidence, and recruiting stations were besieged by eager young men. The horror of modern warfare was soon brought home, when in 1915 the first German air raid on London killed 39. As the boom brought on by the wartime economy came to an end, London began to feel the pain: unemployment rose and in 1926 the 10-day **General Strike** brought the nation to a standstill amid fears of revolution. In the end, though, the main beneficiary of the strike was the radio. The paralysis of Fleet St. during the strike made the nation dependent on the new **BBC** (British Broadcasting Corporation) for news.

Dickens House

THE INTELLECTS OF THE TIME. While **George Orwell** took the conscious decision to share in the people's plight (his experiences living with the East End poor are chronicled in *Down and Out in Paris and London*), others chose to argue from positions of comfort. Such were the members of the intellectual circle known as the **Bloomsbury Group.** So-called because it met in Bloomsbury, the group was less a school of thought than a group of extremely talented friends. Those associated with the group included novelists **Virginia Woolf** and **E.M. Forster,** and economist **John Maynard Keynes;** the fringes of the group were populated with no-less extraordinary intellects, including philosopher **Bertrand Russell,** writer **Aldous Huxley,** and poet **T.S. Eliot.**

LONDON DEFIANT. Oswald Mosley who had served in the House of Commons (1918-31) successively as a Conservative, an Independent and a Labourite, founded the British Union of Fascists in 1932. London was deponent to fascism with Mosley's and his followers' hostile demonstrations in the Jewish section of eastern London.

When **World War II** broke out in 1939, London was ill-prepared: the thousands of gas-masks issued in expectation of German chemical attacks were useless against the incendiary devices of **The Blitz.** Starting on September 7th, 1940, London suffered 57 days of consecutive bombing; regular raids continued until 1941. In 1944, a new rain of death started with the advent of V-1 and V-2 missiles. By the end of the war, London had suffered destruction on a scale unseen since the Great Fire. If the all-night vigils of volunteer firefighters had saved St. Paul's, the same could not be said for the House of Commons, Buckingham Palace, or most of the East End. Over 130,000 houses had been damaged beyond repair, and a third of the City of London flattened.

THE THATCHER YEARS. Home to thousands of European exiles and American troops during the war, London transformed itself from hide-bound capital of empire to cosmopolitan city of the world. **Carnaby Street** and the **King's Road** became the twin foci of a London peopled by hipsters and bohemians. Local boys the **Rolling Stones** battled for supremacy with the **Beatles,** who set up in **Abbey Road** in 1964, and **The Who** chronicled the fights between scooter-riding "mods" and quiff-toting "rockers." Somewhat belatedly, in 1966 *Time* magazine announced that London "swings, it is the scene."

Swinging London died with the oil shocks of the 1970s. Unemployment rose as conflict between unions and the government resulted in the three-day week in 1974 and the **winter of discontent** five years later. In 1979 Britons elected their first female Prime Minister, **Margaret Thatcher,** the "Iron Lady." A polarizing figure in British politics even today, Thatcher's program of economic liberalization combined with a return to "Victorian values" in everyday life brought her into direct conflict with the overwhelmingly Labour-dominated **Greater London Council** and its charismatic leader "Red" **Ken Livingstone.** Thatcher's solution was to abolish the GLC, depriving London of its sole unified administrative structure and devolving power to the 33 boroughs. Thatcher's monetarist program called for deregulation, tax cuts, greater use of supply side policies, and a rigorous control of the money supply in order to keep inflation low. Upon entering office, income tax was cut immediately and offset by an increase in VAT, representing an important shift from direct to indirect taxation. However, the tax rate in the top-earning bracket was cut significantly more than in the medium-earning bracket, leading critics to highlight a preference for the rich.

Under Mrs. Thatcher Britain became the pioneer in the global wave of privatization. However, with growing tensions with union leaders and with the introduction of the "Polls Tax," riots broke out in 1990. Unease amongst the Conservative MPs sparked deep divisions within the party, and the problems continued to mount. These divisions were highlighted towards the late 1980s when the question of Britain's economic and political relationship with Europe arose. Mrs. Thatcher rejected any form of political and economic integration with Europe, which struck the wrong note with many of her colleagues.

In November 1990, following a high-profile resignation from the Hose of Commons Leader Geoffrey Howe, former cabinet Michael Heseltine stood against the prime minister in the Conservative Party leadership ballot. Barely surviving the first round and persuaded that a second attempt would result in a humiliating defeat, Margaret Thatcher "retired" on November 22, 1990. Her other major contribution to London was the redevelopment of **Docklands** and the Docklands Light Railway.

INTO THE FUTURE. The lackluster John Major replaced Mrs. Thatcher. Real change, though, would have to wait for 1997 and the election of another charismatic reformer. The Rt. Hon. Anthony Charles Lynton "Tony" Blair was elected as Prime Minister in 1997 bringing the Labour party into government after 18 consecutive years of Conservative Rule. Blair's stated priorities on coming into office were "education, education, education." In his second term, he extended his list to include other public services like the National Health Service. However, like many Western leaders, since September 11, 2001 his agenda has been dominated by foreign affairs. Critics to the left of the Labour Party feel that he has compromised its founders' socialist principles.

The new government poured millions into a plan to make London the "Capital of the Millennium." The much-vaunted "river of fire" merely fizzled, and thousands of VIP guests had to wait for hours outside the **Millennium Dome.** Other projects have had more success. Gilbert Scott's 1930s Bankside power station reopened in 2000 as the world's largest modern art museum, the **Tate Modern** (see p. 137). If Norman Foster's reputation suffered when his **Millennium Bridge,** was closed for safety reasons after just three days, it recovered with his ambitious reworking of the **Great Court** (see p. 133), of the British Museum.

On the political front, London regained a unified voice with the election of maverick Ken Livingstone as its first-ever **directly elected mayor** in 2000. Relationships with Westminster soured even before Ken took office, during a bitter primary campaign when Tony Blair tried to prevent the highly popular Livingstone from winning the Labour Party nomination. Undaunted, Ken stood as an independent and won by a landslide. Livingston was re-elected for his second term on June 10, 2004. Britain today stands at a place juggling its relations between its trans-Atlantic and European friends (see p. 71).

THE LIVING CITY

THE CITY TODAY

SIZE

London is a city of 7 million people—down from its pre-war peak of almost 9 million, but still the largest city in Europe, especially if you include the further 3 million living just outside

Ethnic London

While ethnic "ghettos" are rare in London, most communities have a neighborhood focus, where members can find the sights, smells, and sounds (if not the sunshine) of their former homeland.

South Asians, London's largest ethnic group, are also the most fragmented. Sikhs from **Punjab** congregate in Ealing, the **East End** is the center of the **Bengali** community, and **Pakistanis** prefer **Walthamstow.**

London's **black** population is divided into two main groups: those of **Caribbean** origin, whose cultural focus is in **Brixton,** and 160,000 **Africans,** mostly West African in origin, who tend to settle in **West London.**

Though few of London's ethnic **Chinese** actually live there, they still pack **Soho's** Chinatown on weekends to shop and eat—though today they are often outnumbered by tourists.

From oil-rich Saudis to Lebanese refugees, **Arabs** come together over kebabs and strong coffee on **Edgware Road.**

Many other ethnic groups are harder to spot. The majority of the strong **Jewish** community lead secular lives, though you'll still see plenty of *yamulkas* in **Golders Green.** A large number of **Cypriot Greeks** gather in numerous *tavernas* around **Camden Town.** London's largest foreign-born community is also its least visible—you won't find any **Irish** neighborhoods, but there's good *craic* in any number of Irish pubs around the city.

the boundaries of **Greater London** (so called to distinguish it from the historic square mile of the City of London). Even so, London's enormous size—over 30 mi. wide east-west, covering some 650 sq. mi.—has less to do with its population than with the English aversion to apartments: the majority of homes are single-family houses, each with its own patch of garden. Add to this an aversion to city-wide planning and a strong sense of community, and you're left with a sprawling, messy metropolis of proudly distinct neighborhoods.

ETHNIC COMPOSITION

Today, one in three Londoners belongs to an ethnic minority, a figure that will rise to 40% in 5 years. London's origins as a trading center and port mean that it has always been home to a number of small foreign communities. The first large-scale immigration occurred in the 17th century, as religious wars sent Protestants from all over Europe seeking refuge in England: 1685 saw the arrival of 30,000 French **Huguenots.** A new wave of persecutions in the 19th century brought 20,000 Russian and Polish **Jews,** many of whom were cheated into believing they had arrived in America. With the rise of fascism in the 1930s the population swelled with fleeing Germans and Austrians. After WWII, communism sent hundreds of thousands of Central and Eastern Europeans spilling into England, including 250,000 Polish refugees. The post-war collapse of the British Empire brought a new type of immigrant: rather than fleeing persecution, these were people who had been brought up in the British system and had been taught to think of Britain as their "mother country"—or at least a source of economic opportunity unheard of at home. If the 250,000 **Irish** and 60,000 **Chinese** in London tended towards the latter, the former was true for many of London's 300,000 **West Indians** and 500,000 **Asians** (in Britain, "Asian" always refers to someone of Indian, Pakistani, or Bangladeshi origin). More recently, political upheaval in Britain's former colonies has sent a new wave of refugees to London, including some 160,000 **West Africans.**

CULTURE

LITERATURE

English literature flourished under the reign of Elizabeth I and London produced many reputable literates. **Edmund Spencer's** glorification of England and Elizabeth I in *The Faerie Queene* earned him a favor at court while **John Donne** wrote metaphysical poetry and penned erotic verse on the side. Playwright **Christopher Marlowe** lost his life in a pub brawl, but not before he produced plays of temptation and damnation, such as *Tamburlaine* (c.1587). A giant of the Elizabethan era, **William Shakepeare** continues to loom over the entirety of English literature.

The Puritans in London in the late 16th and early 17th centuries produced a huge volume of beautiful literature, including **John Milton's** epic *Paradise Lost* (1667) and **John Bunyan's** allegorical *Pilgrim's Progress* (1678). In 1719, **Daniel Defoe** inaugurated the era of the English novel with his popular island-bound *Robinson Crusoe.* In the Victorian period, poverty and social change spawned the sentimental novels of **Charles Dickens;** *Oliver Twist* (1838) and *David Copperfield* (1849) draw on the bleakness of his childhood in Portmouth and portray the harsh living conditions of working-class Londoners. Partly in reaction to the rationalism of the preceding century, the Romantic movement of the early 1800s found its greatest expression in verse and poems such as *Lyrical Ballads* by **William Wordsworth** began to color London's poetic scene.

"On or about December 1910," wrote **Virginia Woolf,** "human nature changed." Woolf, a key member of the Bloomsbury Group, was among the ground-breaking practitioners of Modernism (1910-1930). One of Modernism's poetic champions was **T.S. Eliot,** who grew up in Missouri, USA but became the "Pope of Russell Square."

Fascism and the horrors of WWII motivated musings on the nature of evil, while the ravenous totalitarian state of **George Orwell's** *1984* (1949) strove to strip the world of memories and words of meaning. Nostalgia pervades the poems of **John Betjeman,** while an angry working-class found mouthpieces in Kingsley Aims and postcolonial voices like **Salman Rushdie.**

Today, a nomination for the annual **Booker Prize,** Britain's most prestigious award for literature, brings instant best-seller status. London's home-grown literature has a tendency toward the tradition of satire and dry humor started by Jonathan Swift and Samuel Johnson in the 18th century. **Julian Barnes's** *Letters from London* (1995)—a collection of *New Yorker* pieces about life in the capital—provides outsiders with an insider perspective. **Dorris Lessing's** *London Observed* (1993) chronicles London through the eyes of an outsider-turned-insider, and **Martin Amis's** murder mystery *London Fields* (1991) turns the city inside-out. More recently, fictional diaries have been all the rage: **Helen Fielding** charts the trials and tribulations of being young, single, and insecure in the wildly popular *Bridget Jones's Diary* (1999) and its sequel, *The Edge of Reason* (2001), while **Sue Townsend**—whose *Secret Diary of Adrian Mole, aged 13 3/4* was a hit with teenagers in 1989—has followed her hapless protagonist into premature middle age with *Adrian Mole: the Cappuccino Years* (2000). A couple of years into the millennium the hapless protagonist has given way to a mischievous wizard and **J.K. Rowling's** Harry Potter has smashed every children's book sales record known to man.

MUSIC

In the middle ages, traveling minstrels sang narrative folk ballads in the courts of the rich. During the Renaissance, London's ears were tuned to cathedral anthems, psalms and madrigals. **Henry Purcell** (1659-1695) in the Baroque period created instrumental music for Shakespeare's plays and London's first opera, *Dido and Aeneas*. Today's audiences are familiar with the operettas of W.S. Gilbert (1836-1911) and Arthur Sullivan (1842-1900); the pair were rumored to hate each other, but produced gems such as *The Mikado* and *The Pirates of Penzance*.

The central role London has played on the world music scene since the 1960s needs little introduction. The **Beatles** may have started in Liverpool, but they hotfooted it down to London as soon as possible, where the **Rolling Stones** soon joined battle over the hearts and minds of

University College

East London Mosque

Stock Exchange

NO WORK ALL PLAY

Wicket Nation

Footy madness is a phenomenon London visitors have come to expect and can usually understand to some degree—there aren't too many nations in which soccer/football isn't at least familiar. But what about that other national pastime—the one with the funny white uniforms and pancake flat bats? Just how does **cricket** work, and will you ever be able to understand what the TV and newspaper reporters keep going on about? Herewith, an (abridged) outline of the most endearingly British of competitive sports:

The sides: 11 players on each team (each "side").

The competition: Cricket matches vary in length. Most important are the international **tests;** they last for 5 days (with play spanning about 8-10 hours each day!). While the one-day matches last for...well, one day.

The setup: In the middle of the oval-shaped **cricket grounds** is a rectangular area; a **wicket** pokes out of the ground at each end of the rectangle, and two offensive **batsmen** (from the same side) each take an end. A **bowler** for the side playing defense will be pitching the ball to the batsman opposite

teenagers everywhere. The scooter-riding **Mod** movement abhorred American-influenced rock'n'roll, preferring introspective ballads by **The Kinks** and **The Who,** who soon expanded into "Rock Operas" such as *Quadrophenia* (1973). This new genre of musical theater had been pioneered five years earlier, when composer **Andrew Lloyd Webber** and lyricist **Tim Rice** wrote *Joseph and the Amazing Technicolor Dreamcoat* for a high-school production. Despite such revolutionary beginnings, the duo soon descended into polished populism: Lloyd Webber went on to write such crowd-pleasers as *Starlight Express* and *Phantom of the Opera*, and Rice's collaboration with Walt Disney on films such as *Aladdin* and *The Lion King* won him three Oscars. Just when it seemed that London music had reached an artistic dead-end, it roared back to life in the hands of the **Sex Pistols,** created by Malcolm McLaren to drum up publicity for his King's Rd. boutique, "Sex."

In the late 1980s the focus of British music swung north to Manchester, before landing back down with a bump in the mid-1990s as groups like Blur and Pulp fought it out with Manchester-boys-come-south **Oasis.** Meanwhile, musical standards reached a new low with the carefully crafted appeal of the **Spice Girls**. Another nineties phenomenon was the explosive growth of electronic music, born of the rave craze that started in Britain in the late 1980s: bands like **Prodigy, Portishead, Massive Attack,** and the **Chemical Brothers** provide the high-octane power for serious dancing in the capital's mega-clubs. London is also responsible for some of the giants of synthesizer age like **George Michael** while songs like *Candle in the Wind* by **Elton John** became a legend in the music world.

CONTEMPORARY ART

If there's one thing the varied strands of contemporary London art have in common, it's an uncanny ability to unnerve. London's earliest proponents of the stomach-churning school were figurative: the late **Francis Bacon** (1909-1992), who ghoulishly reworked Velazquez's portrait of Innocent X in his *Screaming Popes* series; and **Lucien Freud** (b. 1922), Sigmund's grandson, whose oddly unrealistic "realist" nudes continue to break new ground in portraiture. In the 1960s, the eye-strain inducing abstractions of "Op-Art" created by **Bridget Riley** (b. 1931) sent aspirin sales soaring. After going underground in the 1980s, the London art scene re-exploded on the national conscious in 1995 when **Damien Hirst** won

Britain's most prestigious artistic accolade, the **Turner Prize.** Other recent works to have provoked a storm include brothers **Jake and Dinos Chapman's** sculptures of toy figures engaged in highly unnatural activities and **Rachel Whiteread's** *House*, a concrete cast of the inside of a London townhouse. With the turn of the century it seems that shock art may have had its day. A sober piece by video artist **Steve MacQueen** beat **Tracey Emin's** unmade bed (complete with used condoms) to the 1999 Turner, and the 2000 prize went to **Wolfgang Tillmans,** a German-born but London-based photographer, over **Glenn Brown's** reproduction of a sci-fi bookjacket.

FILM

The British film industry began as an extension of the stage. British films of the early 1900s tended to be technologically crude; many were nothing more than recordings of stage plays, often with the same sets and actors. American companies moved in during the mid-20s, and home production withered.

Alexander Korda spearheaded a minor resurgence in the 1930s. Korda founded London Films and turned it into one of the finest studios in the world. London Films produced a slew of great flicks, including *Things to Come*, *The Scarlet Pimpernel*, and *The Private Life of Henry VIII*, a brilliant and successful film that made Charles Laughton a star. A post-WWII boom saw British studios expand, only to slump in the 1960s with the rise of television. While the major studios shrivelled, independent production expanded with the aid of American expats like John Houston and Stanley Kubrick. A lack of government support has left the industry high and dry but movies like *Trainspotting* still manage to make the international scene. Actors like **Hugh Grant** and **Cloin Firth** in movies like *Love Actually* continue to win hearts both inside and outside London, while *Bend it like Beckham* gave everybody a taste of "real" football.

SPORT

Londoners have always been sports mad. Medieval Londoner William FitzStephen described **football** (soccer) games being played in the 12th century, and football is still the capital's prime diversion. From August until May, thousands turn out every weekend to see top London teams: **Arsenal, Chelsea, West Ham,** and **Tottenham Hotspur** ("Spurs" for short). Football

him (with a **wicketkeeper** ready to catch it behind). The nine other players on defense spread themselves out, ready to chase down any hits.

Scoring and winning: The batsmen use several different types of swing ("different **strokes**") to hit the ball anywhere on the grounds, and a **run** is scored each time the two batsmen are able to run and switch positions after one man has hit the ball (hundreds of runs are scored in each match). A batsman is **out** if the bowler manages to hit a wicket with his pitch ("a wicket is **taken**"), if his hit is caught on the fly, or if a wicket is taken while batsmen are running. A side's **inning** is over after 10 of their 11 batsmen have gotten out, and the two sides switch. Within the innings, **overs** divide every 6 consecutive at-bats, and a new bowler will throw the next 6 to the batsman at the opposite end of the grounds. In a one-day match each side bats for 50 overs each unless all their batsmen are out.

Confused? We didn't even mention the intricate details yet, but at the very least, armed with your new knowledge, you can begin to make sense of England's enduring wicket madness. And maybe you will understand why they are so happy when they win the Ashes....that is if they ever do.

is very much a lads game—beer and rude songs are essential parts of the ritual—but violence is more publicized than prevalent; you'll often see fathers and their young sons (dressed, naturally, in full team "strip" and matching scarf) cheering on their team from the terraces.

Rugby is the other main winter sport, though it's far less popular in London than in the North. Divided into two slightly-differing species, Rugby Union and Rugby League, Union rules the roost in London: **Wasps, Harlequins,** and **Saracens** are the top London teams. More than football, though, Rugby is a game of international rivalries: even those with no team affiliation follow the ups and downs of England at the international matches at **Twickenham.**

In spring, when the rugby fields are little more than expanses of mud, attention turns to **cricket.** A game, according to one anonymous commenter, "which the English have invented in order to give themselves some conception of eternity," cricket is the ideal way to spend long summer days. "Test matches" last up to five days with lunch and tea breaks. **Middlesex** and **Surrey** are the main London teams; their grounds at **Lords** and the **Oval** respectively, are also used to host international test matches in which England traditionally loses abysmally. Anything else would be "just not cricket," as they say.

Ironically, the sport which gives London the most international attention is the one Londoners care the least about. Although it has a long and distinguished history in the city (Henry VIII was a keen player in his youth), **tennis**—seen as a snob's game—is something most Londoners tune into during the **Wimbledon** fortnight, then promptly tune out again. More democratic is the **London Marathon,** held every April, which sees over 30,000 runners complete the grueling 26-mile course from Greenwich, in southeast London, to the final stretch just outside Buckingham Palace.

THE MEDIA

PRINT MEDIA

NEWSPAPERS

Although circulation has been dropping in the UK for the last 40 years, newspapers still wield enough power to make and break governments. *The Sun* used to be the most popular and most sensational of the mass-market **tabloids** that dominated the British newspaper market. Today, however, *The News of the World* reigns (mainly because of its coverage of the Beckham marital crises). The *Daily Mail* tries to bridge the intellectual gap between the tabloids and the unmanageable pages of broadsheets. *The Times* has gone downmarket under the ownership of Rupert Murdoch (who also owns *The Sun)* and arch-rival *The Daily Telegraph* (dubbed 'Torygraph') and *Financial Times*, are unmistakably right-wing. Leaning to the left are *The Independent* and *The Guardian*. Daily papers usually share their name with an overgrown **Sunday** double; *The Guardian* and *The Sun* are exceptions: their Sunday equivalents are *The Observer* and *The News of the World*, respectively. London's best **local daily,** the tabloid-format but marginally more intelligent *Evening Standard* is published in several editions throughout the day. The *Standard* was joined in 1999 by the daily *Metro*, free in Tube stations M-F (though they're usually all gone by 9am).

MAGAZINES

News magazines are generally published weekly and provide a more in-depth examination of issues than the papers, often with a strong political slant. *The Economist* is the most respected and apolitical of the bunch; political hacks get their kicks from the New Labour *New Statesman* and the Tory *Spectator*. For a less reverent approach, *Private Eye* walks a fine line between hilarity and libel.

Lifestyle magazines are the biggest sellers. The UK editions of women's mags such as *Cosmopolitan* tend to be more forthright than their US counterparts, while men's equivalents *FHM* and *Loaded* leave little to the imagination. Pure **style** magazines range from the ad-laden pages of British *Vogue* to the object-oriented stark recommendations of *i-D* and *Wallpaper*. **Music** mags such as *Melody Maker* and *New Musical Express* carry details of gigs, and **clubbing** reviews *Mixmag* and *Jockey Slut* give the biz on hot nightspots. Still, the Londoner's bible is *Time Out* (W), worth every penny of its £2.35 cover price.

BROADCAST MEDIA

Whether on radio or TV, British broadcasting has a strong national identity. While there's no denying the influence from across the Atlantic, it's largely limited to pop music and the occasional show. The most popular British programs are about as far from showbiz glamour as possible: the number one soap, *Eastenders*, follows the working-class lives of people in East London; ridiculously long-running radio rival *The Archers* does the same for struggling farmers. As for comedy, the renowned British sense of humor has resulted in some of the world's funniest and least-exportable. Lately, British television has had a wide worldwide impact—*Survivor*, *Who Wants to be a Millionaire*, and *The Weakest Link* were all British. Despite the popularity of reality TV, we have to thank the British media for comic classics like *Monty Python's Flying Circus* and *Mr. Bean* which are old but forever gold.

British television's self-image as the best in the world is buckling under the same commercial pressures found in the rest of the Western world, but there's still a large variety of shows to be found on the telly's five broadcast channels. This is largely because every television-set owner in Britain is required to purchase an annual "TV license," the proceeds of which go directly to the BBC—in return, the BBC is not allowed to run advertisements. (Although it's publicly funded, the BBC is independent of the Government.) This guarantees money for serious programming, alongside an obligation to satisfy the people who foot the bill—including the lower-income groups that advertisers normally scorn. The publicly-funded **BBC 1** remains more popular than its commercial rivals, and its presence results in an unavoidable upwards pressure on its main commercial rival **ITV.** The BBC's "cultural" channel, **BBC 2,** has a commercial counterpart in **Channel 4;** both mix in-depth news, documentaries, and ground-breaking dramas with test-runs of comedies which, if successful, often transfer to their more populist siblings. Finally, **Channel 5,** launched in the late 1990s, has yet to carve itself a British following.

ON THE AIR

Pop/Indie/Rock

BBC radio 1 (97-99FM)
Capital Radio (chart rock, 95.8FM)
XFM (alternative rock, 104.9FM)
Kiss (dance music, 100FM)

Adult Rock

Virgin (105.8FM/ 1215AM)
Heart (106.2FM)

Easy listening

BBC radio 2 (89.2FM)
Magic (105.4FM)
Capital Gold (1548AM)

Classic

BBC Radio 3 (91.3FM)
Classic FM (100.9FM)

Other Music

Jazz FM (102.2FM)
Mean Country 1035 (country 1035AM)
FLR (soul and R&B, 107.3FM)

Ethnic/Minority

Spectrum International Radio (news and music, 558AM)
BBC Asian network (630AM)

News

BBC Radio 4 (93.5FM/720AM/198LW)
News DIrect (97.3FM)

Sports

BBC Radio 5 Live (909AM/693AM)

Talk/Local

BBC London Live (94.9FM)
Thames (107.8FM)
LBC (1152AM)

2005 HOLIDAYS AND FESTIVALS

Winter	
Dec. 25	Christmas
Dec. 26	Boxing Day
Dec. 31	New Year's Eve
Jan. 1	New Year's Day
Feb. 9	Chinese New Year
Spring	
Mar. 17	St. Patrick's Day
Mar.	Oxford and Cambridge Boat Race (www.theboatrace.org)
Mar. 25	Good Friday
Mar 28	Easter Monday
Apr. 17	London Marathon
May	Museums and Galleries Month
Last week of May	FA Cup Final (www.thefa.com)
May 2 and 30	May Day Bank Holidays
May 24-27	Chelsea Flower Show (www.rhs.org.uk)
Summer	
June 1- Aug. 31	Royal Academy Summer Exhibition (www.royalacademy.org)
June	Trooping the Color (www.royal.gov.uk)
June 20-July 3	Wimbledon Lawn Tennis Championships (www.wimbeldon.org)
June 29-July 3	Henley Royal Regatta (www.hrr.co.uk)
July -Sept.	BBC "Proms" (www.bbc.co.uk/proms)
Aug. 12-14	Brecon Jazz Festival (www.breconjazz.co.uk)
Aug. 28-29	Notting Hill Carnival
Aug. 29	Summer Bank Holiday
Sept. 1-3	CAMRA Beer Festival (www.camra.org.uk)
Autumn	
Late Sept.	London Open House (www.londonopenhouse.org)
Early-Mid Nov.	State Opening of Parliament (www.parliament.uk)
Early-Mid. Nov.	London Film Festival (www.lff.org.uk)
Nov. 5	Bonfire Night
Nov. 12	Lord Mayor's Show (www.lordmayorsshow.org)
Nov. 13	Remembrance Sunday

UK AND USA: FRIENDS WITH BENEFITS?

Bob Kagan wrote that Americans are from Venus and Europeans from Mars. From the late 1990s onwards, popular opinion in Britain has suggested that it must choose between its "special relationship" with the United States and its role as a central part of the European Union. Yet this is a false dichotomy. Britain must draw upon its shared history with the United States and geopolitical proximity to the EU to plot a careful course between them, acting as both power broker and keystone.

British-US links stretch back to the landing of the Mayflower in Plymouth Massachusetts in 1620 and have been marked by many highs and lows. The War of Independence (American Revolution) was the nadir, and Britain's occasional support for Confederate forces in the Civil War helped keep realtions sour for a further hundred years. Imposing coastal defences on the Eastern seaboard, many manned through the 19th-century, betray the suspicion with which the US regarded its once master across the Atlantic. Yet with so many shared ideologies, family links, and cross-Atlantic business capital and financing, the relationship was bound to improve. Most vital to this was US support for Britain in both World Wars. Since 1945 the relationship could hardly have been better: a shared nuclear programme in the 1950s escalated the UK to nuclear-power status, and joint military actions through NATO membership and bi-lateral arrangements have made the relationship closer still.

Personalities have helped bring the US and Britain closer. Prime Minister Harold Macmillan and President Kennedy were said to get along well, despite their age difference. The young President, in 1963, confided in the older statesman that he got bad headaches if he went too long without a woman, to which Macmillan replied that he would rather have the headaches. Some differences, then, remained! Thatcher and Reagan got along famously, with the Prime Minister backing the President in his drive to end the Cold War, and receiving diplomatic and logistical support in the Falklands War in 1982. Most recently, Prime Minister Tony Blair struck up an extremely close relationship with President Clinton, his ideological soulmate, both pursuing the new politics of the "Third Way" together. Of considerable surprise to many in his left-wing Party, Blair has formed a very close relationship with President Bush, with whom he shares few political beliefs. The "special relationship" therefore, has been catalyzed by good personal friendships between leaders, and has transcended party boundaries.

Britain's uneasy role in the EU can be traced back through hundreds of years to the realist tradition of international relations, which has pitted nations against one another in a constantly shifting game of diplomacy and war. The result of this was that by the start of the 20th-century almost no single state in Europe trusted another—Britain's self-perception as a superior nation, bolstered by a huge Empire and Commonwealth, was summed up in a headline in *The Times of London* concerning the thick fog that hung over the English Channel between Britain and France: "Fog on the Channel: continent cut off." Yet the horrors of war have, above all else, molded British relations with Europe. The two World Wars have left a deep scar in the psyche of older Britons, and almost every school child is brought up learning about 1930s Nazi aggression. Politically, Britain has been a late-comer to European politics. French President De Gaulle, who sheltered during WWII in Dolphin Square on the banks of the river Thames, rather ungratefully twice vetoed British membership to the European Economic Community due to the fear that they might be a "Trojan Horse" for American political interests. Since joining in 1975 Britain has been a reluctant member of the EU. Extremely anti-European PM Margaret Thatcher riled many EU states by demanding a rebate for the British financial contribution to the organization, and made a series of hostile speeches throughout the 1980s. Since then, Britain has negotiated opt-outs from binding Europe-wide legislation, and since 1997, despite having its most pro-EU Prime Minister yet in Tony Blair, Britain has not joined the Single European Currency. Inside Britain the debate rages as to whether membership of the EU is good for Britain, and fringe political parties regularly raise the issue of complete withdrawal from the Union, a line which has even been encouraged by some MPs from the main opposition Conservative Party.

Recently the war in Iraq was has driven a wedge between Europe and US, with Britain choosing to side with the US rather than the EU. Tony Blair was forced to play the "honest broker" between deeply opposed American and European Administrations.

After Kagan made his Mars and Venus comments, German Foreign Minister Joschka Fischer responded that Europeans are the "children of Mars," and being born to the God of War—forged in two World Wars—makes them more critical of war than American counterparts. Despite these differences, and perhaps because of them, Britain will remain a critical friend to both the US and Europe. The idea that Britain must somehow choose between the two is false.

Thomas Sleigh studided Political Science at Cambridge University from 1997 to 2000. He was a Fulbright Scholar to Harvard University (2003-4) where he taught a class on American Foreign Policy. He now works in London.

INSIDE

Sights

The sights in London are unbeatable—you're guaranteed to find far too many sights of interest than you have time for. If you're looking for traces of London's Roman past, the City of London is the place to be. Medieval buildings are rare in London, but the few that remain are remarkable. The Tower of London gets a lot of attention, but don't miss The Temple and St. Etheldreda's, both in Holborn, and the medieval churches of Clerkenwell. There's no shortage of Renaissance buildings, since practically the entire city was rebuilt after the Great Fire of 1666. Architect Christopher Wren built dozens of churches throughout London after the fire. The highest concentration of Wren churches can be found in the City of London, alongside his masterpiece St. Paul's. Be sure to stop by Picadilly Circus, the bright lights and non-stop motion epitomizes the Central area. If you're a Royal buff, Westminster can't be beat—let our **Westminster** walking tour (p. 18) guide you through Royal London, from Westminster Abbey to Buckingham Palace. For the best of modern London, take our **Millennium Mile** walking tour (p. 20), which takes you from the Tower of London, past London bridge and Shakespeare's Globe Theatre, to the Tate Modern and the London Eye. If it all gets to be too much, try leaving Central London for a day—the grand manors of West London and the maritime past of East London are just a Tube ride away. Some of the best of London's sights are hidden in little courtyards and alleyways, even in the busy neighborhoods. Be sure to give yourself some time to wander.

ORGANIZED TOURS

Although it may sound hackneyed, a good city tour has its advantages: it offers a quick overview of London's major sights and historic neighborhoods, and while few venture off the beaten path, you can see where you're going, unlike point-to-point excursions by Tube. However, don't make the mistake of thinking a city tour will give you time to see everything properly—just because your tour has stops at every important sight, it doesn't follow that you'll be able to see it all in a day. If you decide to take a tour, use it as a preview, a helpful starting point in planning rest of your stay. For a cheaper deal see sidebar, *In the Red Bus #14*, p. 75.

THE BUS IS YOUR FRIEND. Tube-happy tourists usually ignore London's bus fleet. Try to take advantage of this convenient form of transportation. For starters, skip the expensive taxi fare home by taking a night bus after a late night out. In daylight, even a long walk from a tube station can be shortened by hopping the right line and day, week, and month Tube passes are good across the entire London bus network.

BUS TOURS

The classic London tour is on an open-top double-decker bus—and in good weather, it's undoubtedly the best way to get an overview of the city. However, if you're booking in advance, you might prefer to insure against rain and choose a bus with a roof upstairs, since you'll see little from street level. Most operators run hop-on, hop-off services. Be sure to check schedules and how long tickets are valid before purchasing. Tickets are sold at hotels and by agencies all over London, many agencies have hawkers on the street. Be careful though—travelers have reported overpaying for tickets and being misled about concessionary and child fares by untrustworthy middlemen. In any case, you can usually buy tickets on the bus.

The Big Bus Company, 48 Buckingham Palace Rd. (☎ 7233 9533; www.bigbus.co.uk). ⊖Victoria. Choice of live commentary in English or recorded in 8 languages. Multiple routes, with buses every 5-15min. 1hr. walking tours and mini Thames cruise included. Also books fast-track entry tickets to many attractions. Tickets valid 24hr. from first use. £18, children £9.

London Duck Tours, County Hall (☎ 7928 3132; www.frogtours.com). ⊖Waterloo or Westminster. Duck Tours operates a fleet of amphibious vehicles that follow a 70min. non-stop road tour with a splash into the Thames for a 30min. cruise. Tours depart County Hall, opposite the London Eye. £17.50, concessions £14, children £12, family £50.

Original London Sightseeing Tour (☎ 8877 1722; www.theoriginaltour.com). 4 different routes, with buses every 20min. Also books fast-track entry tickets to many attractions. Tickets valid 24hr. £17, under-16 £8.50; online booking £1 off.

WALKING TOURS

For a more ground-level, in-depth account, try a walking tour led by a guide. A good bet if you want to know a lot about one area. Tours usually focus on a specific aspect of a neighborhood's past, often taking in parts of London most visitors never see. Prebooking is occasionally required and an umbrella is a good idea.

Original London Walks (☎ 7624 3978; recorded info 7624 9255; www.walks.com). The biggest walking-tour company, *with the most variety*. Weekly program (12-16 walks per day), from "The Beatles Magical Mystery Tour" to nighttime "Jack the Ripper's Haunts" and guided visits to larger museums. Most walks last 2hr. £6, concessions £4, under-16 free.

Streets of London (☎ 07812 501 418; www.thestreetsoflondon.com). 2hr. tours (2-4 walks per day) concentrating on the City of London and Clerkenwell. £5, concessions £4.

ALTERNATIVE TOURS

BY BIKE. Organized bicycle tours let you cover plenty of ground while still taking you to places double-decker buses can't go. Make sure to take one that is far from the main roads, unless you want to be gripping the handlebars in fear. The **London**

Bicycle Tour Company has been operating bike tours for eight years. The pace is leisurely, and tours are designed to keep contact with road traffic to a minimum; prices include bike hire, helmet, and comprehensive insurance. The *Royal West* tour takes you along the South Bank, Chelsea, Kensington, and the West End, while the *East Tour* encompasses the City, Docklands, and the East End. The shorter *Middle London* tour takes in The City and Covent Garden. *(Tours start from the LBTC store, 1a Gabriel's Wharf. ☎ 7928 6838; www.londonbicycle.com. ⊖ Waterloo or Southwark. Call for exact times, specific tours, and booking. Royal Tours 9 mi., 3½hr. Middle London 6 mi., 3hr. Book in advance. £16.)*

BY BOAT. A trip on the Thames provides an alternative overview of London—for centuries, the river was London's main highway. Pick up the *River Thames Boat Service Guide* at Tube stations for comprehensive details of all London's different river services; for commuter services, see p. 43, for trips upriver to Hampton Court, see p. 299, and for services to Greenwich. **Catamaran Cruises** operates a non-stop sightseeing cruise with recorded commentary, leaving year-round from Waterloo Pier and from Embankment Pier. *(☎ 7987 1185. Fare: £7.50, concessions £5.80, children £5.50.)* **Bateaux London** operates the luxury river Thames restaurant cruise brand of Catamaran Cruises. *(☎ 7925 2215; www.bateauxlondon.com.)*

MAJOR ATTRACTIONS

BUCKINGHAM PALACE

WESTMINSTER QUICKFIND: Discover, p. 11; sights, p. 116; museums & galleries, p. 152; food, p. 181; pubs, p. 202, entertainment, p. 244; accommodations, p. 293

***Location:** At the end of the Mall, between Westminster, Belgravia, and Mayfair. ⊖ St. James's Park, Victoria, Green Park, or Hyde Park Corner. **Contact:** ☎ 7839 1377; www.royal.gov.uk.*

Originally built for the Dukes of Buckingham, Buckingham House was acquired by George III for his new wife Queen Charlotte in 1761. Charlotte gave birth to 14 of her 15 children at Buckingham House. George IV, the next sovereign, decided it wasn't nearly big enough to be a royal residence, and commissioned John Nash to expand the existing building to a palace status. Neither George IV nor his successor William IV ever lived in the Palace because when the 1834 fire left Parliament without a home, William offered Buckingham. Three years later, however, Queen Victoria moved in. It's been the

the hidden deal

In The Red Bus #14

If you balk at the cost of an organized tour, take a regular bus and save pounds. An all-day bus pass costs just £2.50 (£1 for children). Yes, you'll miss the commentary but you can get on and off according to your own schedule. Plus, you'll be riding the *genuine* Double Deckers.

The #14 route:

South Kensington: Welcome to Albertopolis, arguably the greatest concentration and finest collaboration of museums in the world (see p. 146 and p. 145).

Knightsbridge: Home of highbrow Harrods and Haughty Harvey Nick's (see p. 258).

Hyde Park Corner: The First Royal Park and bastion of free speech at Speaker's Corner on Sunday (see **p. 86**).

Piccadilly Circus: Eros, neon signs and plenty of tourists (see **p. 114**).

Leicester Square: In case you still haven't decided which West End show to see—or you want to see another (see **p. 114** and **p. 227**)!

Tottenham Court Road: Intersects Oxford Street for the hard core shoppers (see **p. 261** and **p. 254**).

royal residence ever since. The structure was too small for Victoria's rapidly growing family; a solution was found by removing Nash's Marble Arch (which now stands just north at Marble Arch) and building a 4th wall to enclose the courtyard.

THE STATE ROOMS. The Palace opens to visitors every August and September while the Royals are off sunning themselves. Advance booking is recommended; for handicapped visitors it is required. Don't expect to find any insights into the Queen's personal life—the State Rooms are the only rooms on view, and they are used only for formal occasions, such as entertaining visiting heads of state. Fortunately, they are also the most sumptuous in the Palace. Look for the secret door concealed in one of the **White Drawing Room's** mirrors, through which the Royals enter the state apartments. After ascending the grand staircase, you can tour the chromatically labeled drawing rooms, bedecked in white, blue, and green. You also see the **Throne Room,** and the domed and glittering **Music Room.** The **Galleries** display many of the finest pieces in the Royal Collection, including works by Rembrandt, Rubens, Poussin, and Canaletto, as well as extremely rare Gobelins tapestries. Liz has graciously allowed commoners into the **Gardens,** home to rare flowers and birds—keep off the grass! *(Enter on Buckingham Palace Rd. For tickets ☎ 7766 7300; www.royal.gov.uk; or the Ticket Office, Green Park. Open daily early Aug.- late Sept. 9:30am-4:15pm. Adults £12.95, concessions £11, under 17 £6.50, under-5 free, family of 5 £30.)*

CHANGING OF THE GUARD. The Palace is protected by a detachment of Foot Guards in full dress uniform, bearskin hats and all. "Changing of the Guard" refers not to replacing the sentries, but to the exchanging of guard duty between different Guards regiments. When they meet at the central gates of the palace, the officers of the regiments touch hands, symbolically exchanging keys, et voilà, the guard is officially changed. Often musical troops provide an accompanying soundtrack. To witness the spectacle, show up well before 11:30am and stand directly in front of the palace in view of the morning guards, or use the steps of the Victoria Memorial as a vantage point. Mid-week days are the least crowded. To get a better close-up of the guards, watch along the routes of the troops prior to their arrival at the palace (10:40am-11:25am) between St. James's Palace and the Victoria Memorial or along Birdcage Walk. *(Daily Apr.-Oct., every other day Nov.-Mar., provided the Queen is in residence, it's not raining hard, and there are no pressing state functions. Call ☎ 7766 7300 to hear about any interruptions. Free.)*

THE HOUSES OF PARLIAMENT

WESTMINSTER QUICKFIND: Discover, p. 11; sights, p. 116; museums & galleries, p. 152; food, p. 181; pubs, p. 202, entertainment, p. 244; accommodations,p. 293.

Location: *Parliament Sq, in Westminster. Enter at St. Stephen's Gate, between Old and New Palace Yards. ⊖Westminster.* ***Contact:*** *Commons Info Office ☎ 7219 4272; www.parliament.uk. Lords Info Office ☎ 7219 3107; www.lords.uk. Debates: Both houses are open to all while Parliament is in session (Oct.-July M-W); afternoon waits can be over 2hr. M-Th after 6pm and F are least busy, but there may be an early adjournment. Ask the security guards when they expect the queue to move most quickly. Tickets required for Prime Minister's Question Time (W noon), for tickets write to your MP; non-residents contact your embassy. Commons usually in session M-W 2:30-9:30pm, Th 11:30am-7:30pm, F 9:30am-3pm. Lords usually sits M-W from 2:30pm, Th 3pm, occasionally F 11:30am; closing times vary.* ***Tours:*** *British residents: Tours held year-round M-W 9:30am-noon and F 2:30-5:30pm; contact your MP to book. Overseas visitors: Oct.-July, tours F 3:30-5:30pm. Non-residents must apply in writing at least 4 weeks ahead to: Parliamentary Education Unit, Norman Shaw Building, SW1A 2TT (☎ 7219 2105; edunit@parliament.uk). Summer tours: Open to all Aug.-Sept. M-Sa 9:15am-4:30pm. Reserve through Firstcall (☎ 0870 906 3773). £7, concessions £5, under 5 free.*

The Palace of Westminster, the buildings in which Parliament (the House of Lords and House of Commons) sits since the 11th century, after Edward the Confessor established his court on the grounds here. William the Conqueror greatly extended the walls, most notably with the addition of Westminster Hall in 1099. The massive fire of 1834 eliminated all except Westminster Hall (see below) and everything that you see today has been added in the 19th and 20th centuries. The rebuilding started in 1835 under the joint command of classicist Charles Barry and Gothic champion Augustus Pugin, and the resulting clash of temperaments created a masterful combination of both styles of architecture. The exterior is mostly Gothic, and the interior rooms and halls have a classic dimension. Access to the Palace has been restricted since a bomb killed an MP in 1979, but visitors can see some of the inside on the way to the galleries. Few tourists are able to take part in one of the immensely popular tours, but don't despair; debates are open to all while the Houses are in session.

BIG BEN & VICTORIA TOWER. The Clock Tower standing guard on the northern side of the building is famously nicknamed **Big Ben.** "Big Ben" strictly refers only to a 14-ton bell, and not even the one in the clock tower (the authentic Ben is inside). Ben was named after the robustly proportioned Sir Benjamin Hall, who served as Commissioner of Works when the bell was cast and hung in 1858. The nickname stuck to the Tower even after the bell was removed. At 98.5m, the southern Victoria Tower is 2m taller than its northern brother. Designed to hold the parliamentary archives, the tower holds copies of every Act of Parliament passed since 1497. A flag flown from the top indicates that Parliament is in session; when the Queen is in the building a special Royal banner is flown instead of the Union flag.

WESTMINSTER HALL. Behind the scowling statue of Oliver Cromwell squats this massive unadorned chamber, the sole survivor of the 1834 fire. While its exterior sits fin the Clock Tower's shadow, it stuns from within. The magnificent hammerbeam roof, constructed in 1394, is considered to be one of the finest timber roofs ever made. Originally the setting for medieval feasts and markets, it was converted into law courts when Henry VIII decamped to Whitehall. It also once had a secret entrance into the House of Commons. The hall almost burned in an air raid in 1941. Today it's used for public ceremonies, the lying-in-state of monarchs, and occasional exhibitions.

DEBATING CHAMBERS. Visitors to the debating chambers must first pass through **St. Stephen's Hall,** which stands on the site of St. Stephen's Chapel. In 1550 St. Stephen's became the meeting place of the House of Commons; members would sit in the quire stalls facing each other, a tradition that continues till today. The Commons have since moved on, but four brass markers still show where the Speaker's Chair used to stand. At the end of the hall, the octagonal **Central Lobby** marks the separation of the two houses, with the Commons to the north and the Lords to the south. The lobby is the best example of the gothic/classical coexistence: the walls have ornate mosaics from 1870 depicting the Kingdom's patron saints while the gothic archways hold stone sculptures of monarchs perched over the doors. There is access to the **House of Lords** via the Peers' Lobby, which smug MPs have bedecked with scenes of Charles I's downfall. The ostentatious chamber itself is dominated by the sovereign's Throne of State under an elaborate gold gilt canopy—only when the golden throne is occupied can the Commons and the Lords gather together. The Lord Chancellor presides over the Peers from the **Woolsack,** a red cushion the size of a VW Beetle. Next to him rests the almost 6 ft. gold **Mace,** which is brought in to open the House each morning. The lords themselves face each other from their red leather benches arranged around the room. In contrast with the Lords, the beautiful but restrained **House of Commons** has simple green-backed benches under an intricate but comparatively plain, wooden roof. This is not entirely due to the difference in class—the Commons was destroyed by bombs in 1941, and rebuilding took place during a time of post-war austerity.

The Speaker sits at the center-rear of the chamber, from where he keeps order in the room. The government MPs sit to his right and the opposition to his left. However, with room for only 437 out of 635 MPs, things can get hectic when all are present. The front benches are reserved for government ministers and their opposition "shadows;" the Prime Minister and the Leader of the Opposition face off across their dispatch boxes. The commons chamber is very much a debating chamber; the arguments can get heated

St. Paul's

Tower Bridge

Trafalgar Square

and very lively. While most debates are sparsely attended, it's worth visiting just to hear the witty barbs flung across the room. You can get a schedule of what is being debated when you enter.

WESTMINSTER ABBEY

WESTMINSTER QUICKFIND: Discover, p. 11; sights, p. 116; museums & galleries, p. 152; food, p. 181; pubs, p. 202, entertainment, p. 244; accommodations, p. 116.

Location: *Parliament Sq., in Westminster. Access Old Monastery, Cloister, and Garden from Dean's Yard, behind the Abbey. Westminster.* ***Contact:*** *Abbey ☎7654 4900; Chapter House 7222 5152; www.westminster-abbey.org.* ***Open:*** *Abbey: M-Tu and Th-F 9:30am-3:45pm, W 9:30am-3:45pm and 6-7pm, Sa 9:30am-1:45pm, Su open for services only. Museum: Daily 10am-4pm. Chapter House: Daily 10am-4pm. Cloisters: Daily 8am-6pm. Garden Apr.-Sept. Tu-Th 10am-6pm, Oct.-Mar. daily 10am-4pm. Audioguides: Available M-F 9:30am-3pm, Sa 9:30am-1pm. £2.* ***Tours:*** *90min. M-F 10, 11am, 2, 3pm; Sa 10, 11am; Apr.-Oct. also M-F 10:30am and 2:30pm. £3, includes Old Monastery.* ***Admission:*** *Abbey and Museum: £6, concessions and ages 11-15 £4, under-11 free, family of 4 £12. Services free. Cloisters & Garden: Free. No photography. Partially wheelchair accessible.*

Originally founded as a Benedictine monastery, Westminster Abbey has evolved to become a house of kings and queens both living and dead. On December 28, 1065, Saint Edward the Confessor, last Saxon King of England, was buried in the Abbey in his still-unfinished Abbey church of the West Monastery. Almost exactly a year later, on Christmas day, the Abbey saw the coronation of William the Conqueror, first Norman king. Thus even before it was completed, the Abbey's twin traditions as the birthplace and final resting place of royalty had been established. Almost nothing remains of St. Edward's Abbey: Henry III's 13th-century Gothic reworking created most of the grand structure you see today. In 1540, Henry VIII dissolved the monasteries, expelling the monks and adopting control of the Abbey. Fortunately, Henry's respect for his royal forebears outweighed his vindictiveness against Catholicism, so Westminster escaped destruction and desecration. Much of the monastic artwork had been lost over time, but the structure and the vaulted Gothic architecture are beautifully preserved. The Abbey became a "Royal Peculiar," under the direct control of Henry VIII. Under this ambiguous status, the Abbey has evolved into a center of ceremony for the nation. Every crowned ruler since 1066 has been coronated here, and

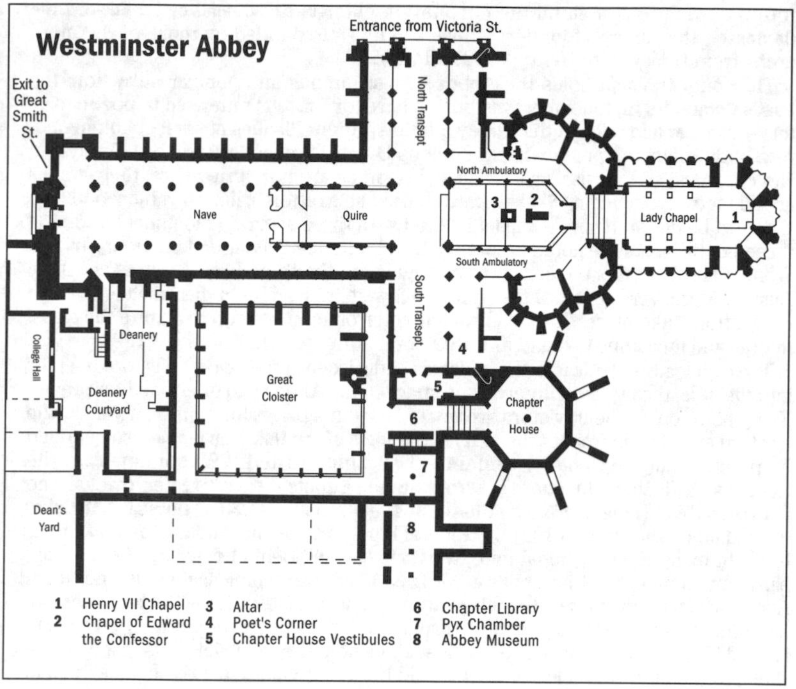

Westminster Abbey

Entrance from Victoria St.
Exit to Great Smith St.
North Transept
North Ambulatory
Nave
Quire
Lady Chapel
South Ambulatory
South Transept
Deanery
College Hall
Deanery Courtyard
Great Cloister
Chapter House
Dean's Yard

1 Henry VII Chapel
2 Chapel of Edward the Confessor
3 Altar
4 Poet's Corner
5 Chapter House Vestibules
6 Chapter Library
7 Pyx Chamber
8 Abbey Museum

many married here. The Abbey is also a place for Royal funerals. The varied uses and styles in the Abbey have combined to make an intriguing and often strange mix of statues, tombs, and plaques.

INSIDE THE ABBEY

Due to the Abbey's status as a tourist mecca, visitors are obliged to follow a set route. Upon entering through the **Great North Door** visitors are thrust into a strange assortment of larger-than-life statues of 18th and 19th-century politicians. Victorian Prime Ministers Disraeli and Gladstone could not stand each other in life, but in death their figures stand close together. The narrow **North Ambulatory** leads past a four chapels to the left; each shaped differently and hold assorted monuments to dearly departed Brits. This walk is also the only chance to see the monolithic, but simple tombs of Edward I and Henry III. Continuing on, you reach a side cove where **Elizabeth I** shares a gilded tomb with her Catholic half-sister and rival **Bloody Mary.** You'll come out into the **Henry VII Chapel**—one of the most intricate gothic cielings in the world. The fan vaulting is far more detailed and much lighter than typical gothic architecture. A magnifying mirror on the ground allows for a closer look. There are also stalls of the Knights of the Order of Bath; look at the plaques on the back of the stalls to see the owner's name (now, many foreign presidents). At the end, **Henry VII** lies in his enclosed, mammoth tomb in front of the **Royal Airforce Chapel,** on the spot where Oliver Cromwell lay for three years before he was removed and hanged posthumously. Most of the royals rest in this part of the Abbey. Along the south side of the chapel the ornate tomb of **Mary, Queen of Scots** distracts visitors from the plainer floor graves of Charles II, William III, Mary II, and Queen Anne.

On exiting the chapel, you can't miss the **Coronation Chair,** built for Edward I and used since 1308. The shelf below the seat was made to house the Scottish Stone of Scone, which Edward brought south after conquest in 1296—the Stone was finally returned to Scotland in 1996, with the promise of being returned for future coronations. Behind the coronation chair is the **Chapel of St. Edward the Confessor,** the Abbey's founder, whose tomb is surrounded by those of the monarchs from Henry III to Henry V (1272-1422).

The south transept holds the Abbey's most famous and popular attraction: the **Poet's Corner.** Its first member was buried here for reasons unrelated to poetic mastery—**Chaucer** had a job in the Abbey administration. Plaques at his feet commemorate both poets and prose writers such as Dylan Thomas, Alfred Lord Tennyson, Henry James, and Lewis Carroll. These honorees are not buried here; their graves are all far away, including **Shakespeare** (buried in Stratford); nor do you need to be a writer to be honored here—**Handel** is feted with three separate monuments. Joining these poetic ranks are noted actors such as Laurence Olivier and Sir Henry Irving. Women are feted too: the corner pays homage to the three Brontë sisters and Jane Austen. At the very center of the Abbey, a few stairs lead up to the **Sanctuary,** where coronations take place. Cordons prevent you from climbing up to admire the glass, marble and limestone Cosmati mosaic floor, dating from 1268.

The trail leads outside into the cloisters and gardens (see below). Visitors re-enter into the **nave,** the largest uninterrupted space in the Abbey and often used for prayer. Every hour, on the hour, vistors are invited to join a priest for a brief prayer. At the western end (just in front of the exit) is the **Tomb of the Unknown Warrior,** surrounded by poppies and bearing the remains of an unidentified WWI soldier from the trenches of Flanders. In letters set from molten bullets it says "greater love hath no man than this." Hanging from a column by the tomb is the **US Congressional Medal of Honor,** laid on the grave in 1921 by General Pershing. Just beyond the tomb is a marble floor memorial to national hero, **Winston Churchill.** Behind the stone, on the wall, hangs a monument to Churchill's great friend **FDR.** Stretching eastwards, the North Aisle starts with memorials to 20th-century Prime Ministers. **Isaac Newton's** massive monument, set into the left-hand Quire screen, presides over a tide of physicists around his grave in the nave itself, while adjacent in the aisle biologists rest near the shockingly simple floor-memorial of would-be pastor **Charles Darwin.** Just beyond, in the shadow of the Quire, is the resting place of the Abbey's organists. As you exit look behind you and above to see the 10 statues of international 20th-century Christian martyrs perched over the exit gate, including **Martin Luther King, Jr.**

OLD MONASTERY, CLOISTERS & GARDENS

Formerly a major monastery, the Abbey complex still stretches far beyond the church itself including both gardens and other structues. Note that all the sights below are accessible through the Dean's Yard entrance behind the Abbey, without going through the building. A door off the east cloister leads to the octagonal **Chapter House,** the original meeting place of the House of Commons, whose 13th-century tiled floor is the best-preserved in Europe. The faded but still exquisite frescoes of the *Book of Revelations* around the walls date from this period, as do the sculpture and floor tiles. Next door, the lackluster **Abbey Museum** is housed in the Norman undercroft. The highlight of the collection is the array of fully dressed medieval royal **funeral effigies,** undergarments and all. The **Great Cloisters** hold yet more tombs and commemorative plaques; a passageway running off the southeastern corner leads to the idyllic flowering **Little Cloister** courtyard, from where another passage leads to the 900-year-old **College Gardens,** which are kept in immaculate condition by the very dedicated groundskeeper.

ST. PAUL'S CATHEDRAL

THE CITY OF LONDON QUICKFIND: Discover, p. 6, sights, p. 90; museums & galleries, p. 152, food, p. 168; pubs, p. 195.

Location: *St. Paul's Churchyard, The City of London.* ***Contact:*** *☎ 7246 8348; www.stpauls.co.uk. St. Paul's.* ***Open:*** *M-Sa 8:30am-4:30pm, last admission 4pm; open for worship daily 7:15am-6pm; dome and galleries open M-Sa 9:30am-4pm. Audioguide available in many languages 10am-3:30pm; £3.50, concessions £3.* ***Tours:*** *Supertour 90min. M-F 11, 11:30am, 1:30, 2pm. £2.50, concessions*

£2, children £1 English only. Special Triforium tour M-F 11:30am and 2:30pm, book in advance. £5 per person. Audioguide available in many languages 10am-3:30pm; £3.50, concessions £3. Evensong: The cathedral choir sings evensong M-Sa at 5pm. Arrive at 4:50pm to be admitted to seats in the Quire. 45min., free. ***Admission:*** *£7 concessions £6, children £3; worshippers free. Group of 10 or more 50p discounts per ticket. Partially wheelchair accessible.*

Majestic St. Paul's remains a cornerstone of London's architectural and historical legacy, as well as an obvious tourist magnet. Currently, there is construction being done on both the inside and outside of the Cathedral; it is expected to be finished by 2005. Sir Christopher Wren's masterpiece is the fifth cathedral to occupy the site; the original was built in 604 AD. Incredibly, Wren's is not the largest of the five: the fourth, "Old St. Paul's," begun in 1087, bore Europe's tallest spire. By 1666, when the Great Fire swept it away, Old St. Paul's was already ripe for replacement. In fact, Wren had been asked to submit a restoration plan in 1663. It wasn't until 1668, however, that actual construction began. Church and architect were at loggerheads from the start: when the bishops finally approved his *third* design, Wren started building. Sneakily, Sir Wren had persuaded the king to let him make "necessary alterations" as work progressed, and the building that emerged in 1708 bore a close resemblance to Wren's second "Great Model" design, the architect's favorite. After the Great Fire, the cathedral only just survived another: on December 29, 1940, St. Paul's was again in flames. German firebombs landed on the cathedral and were put out by the volunteer St. Paul's Fire Watch. The Watch broke up after the war, but lives on in its present incarnation as The Friend's of St. Paul's organization.

INTERIOR. The entrance leads to the nave, the largest space in the cathedral. The enormous memorial to the Duke of Wellington completely fills one of the arches; 13,000 Englishmen crowded the church for his funeral, today the number is limited to 2500. Note that, unlike medieval churches, the Duke isn't actually buried in the cathedral floor—his and all the other graves are all downstairs in the crypt. The nave leads to the second-tallest freestanding dome in Europe (after St. Peter's in the Vatican), which seems even larger from inside, its height extended by the false perspective of the paintings on the inner surface. A restoration project will obstruct the full effect of the perfect dome until mid-2005. The **Galleries,** however, will remain open (see below). The north transept functions as the **baptistry,** with the white marble font whose lid is so heavy machinery is needed to lift it. The third version of William Holman Hunt's ethereal *The Light of the World* hangs opposite the font. The south transept holds the larger-than-life **Nelson Memorial,** hailing Britain's most famous naval hero. The stalls in the **Quire** narrowly escaped a bomb, but the old altar did not. It was replaced by the current marble **High Altar,** above which looms the fiery ceiling mosaic of *Christ Seated in Majesty.* The altar itself bears a dedication to the Commonwealth dead of both World Wars, while immediately behind it is the **American Memorial Chapel,** in honor of the 28,000 US soldiers based in Britain who died during WWII. The chapel area is a testament to the alliance between the US and UK during that war. The north quire aisle holds Henry Moore's *Mother and Child,* one of the church's best pieces of sculpture. The south quire aisle contains one of the only statues to survive from Old St. Paul's: a swaddled tomb effigy of **John Donne,** Dean of the Cathedral and famous poet. The monument to Donne almost didn't make it; burn marks can be seen at its base.

SCALING THE HEIGHTS. St. Paul's dome is built in three parts: an inner brick dome, visible from the inside of the cathedral; an outer timber structure; and between the two, a brick cone that carries the weight of the lantern on top. The first stop is the narrow **Whispering Gallery,** reached by 259 shallow wooden steps. None of the galleries are wheelchair accessible, and the first climb is the only one that isn't steep, narrow or slightly strenuous. Circling the base of the inner dome, the Whispering Gallery is a perfect resounding chamber: whisper into the wall, and your friend on the other side will hear you—or theoretically they could if everyone else weren't trying the same thing. Instead, admire the scenes from the life of St. Paul painted on the canopy. The gallery is the only opportunity to look down on the nave from the inside; the other two galleries are strictly for panoramics. From here, the

St. Paul's Cathedral

SELECTED MONUMENTS AND TOMBS

1 Earl Kitchener
2 Lord Leighton
3 General Gordon
4 Duke of Wellington
5 Sir Joshua Reynolds
6 Dr. Samuel Johnson
7 General Abercromby
8 Sir John Moore
9 Lord Nelson
10 J.M.W. Turner
11 Admiral Collingwood
12 Admiral Earl Howe
13 John Howard
14 John Donne

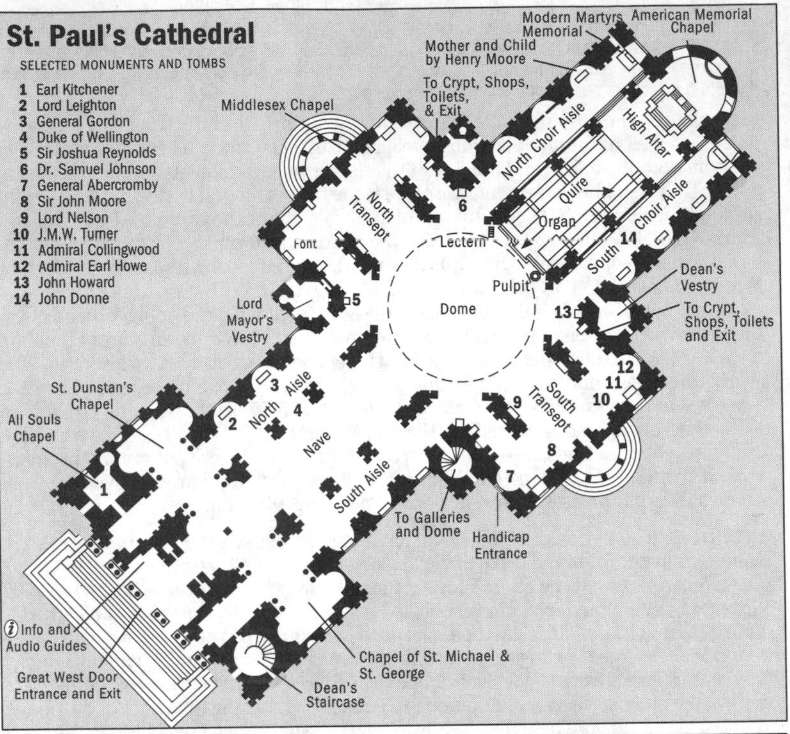

Modern Martyrs Memorial
American Memorial Chapel
Mother and Child by Henry Moore
To Crypt, Shops, Toilets, & Exit
Middlesex Chapel
North Choir Aisle
High Altar
Quire
Organ
North Transept
Font
Lectern
Pulpit
South Choir Aisle
Dean's Vestry
To Crypt, Shops, Toilets and Exit
Lord Mayor's Vestry
Dome
St. Dunstan's Chapel
All Souls Chapel
North Aisle
Nave
South Aisle
South Transept
To Galleries and Dome
Handicap Entrance
Info and Audio Guides
Great West Door Entrance and Exit
Chapel of St. Michael & St. George
Dean's Staircase

The Tower

1 Crown Jewels
2 Chapel Royal of St. Peter and Vincula
3 Beauchamp Tower
4 Queen's House
5 Bell Tower
6 Bloody Tower
7 Wakefield Tower
8 Lanthorn Tower
9 Cradle Tower
10 Well Tower
11 Develin Tower
12 Salt Tower
13 Broad Arrow Tower
14 Constable Tower
15 Martin Tower
16 Brick Tower
17 Bowyer Tower
18 Flint Tower
19 Devereux Tower
20 Brass Mount
21 Legge's Mount
22 Traitors' Gate
23 Byward Tower
24 Middle Tower
25 St. Thomas' Tower
26 Entrance
27 Exits

Moat
Outer Ward
Fusiliers' Museum
Parade
Scaffold Site
White Tower
Hospital
Tower Green
Wardrobe Tower
Armories
Outer Ward
Moat
Tower Wharf

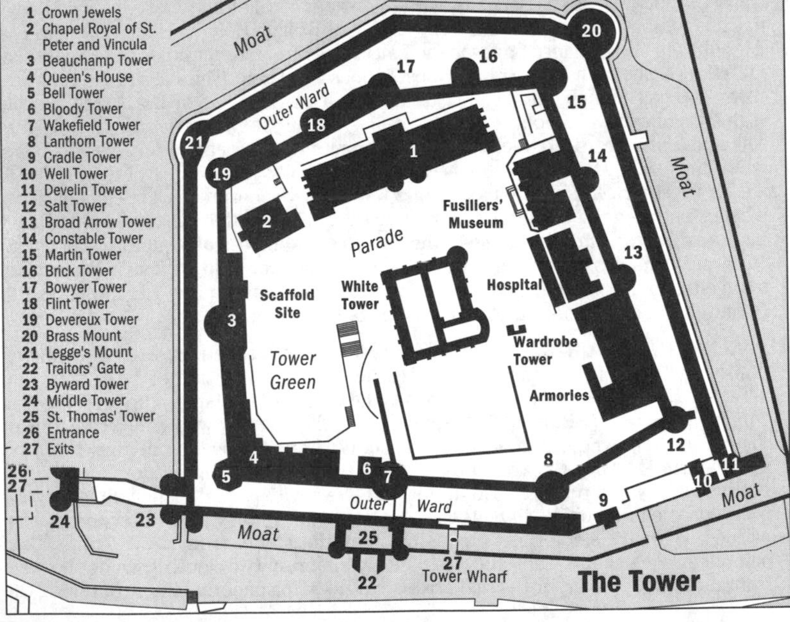

Don't be left out...

Get your TRAVEL on.

The International Student Identity Card

$22 is ALL it takes to SAVE $100's at home and abroad!

save in the U.S. or worldwide

International Student Identity Card
Carte d'étudiant internationale / Carné internacional de estudiante
STUDENT
Studies at / Étudiant à / Est. de Enseñanza
University of California, Berkeley
Name / Nom / Nombre
Debbie Lee
Born / Né(e) le / Nacido/a el
04/29/1982
Validity / Validité / Validez
09/2004 - 12/31/2005
ISIC

Student savings in more than **7,000 locations** across the US & **100 countries worldwide-** *something no other card can offer!*

- /2 Price Admission
- Reduced Rates
- Accommodations
- Entertainment
- Communications
- Internet

visit www.myISIC.com to find out about discounts and the benefits of carrying your ISIC.

SIC

Call or visit ISIC online to purchase your card today:

www.myISIC.com (800) 474.8214

eTravel

exploration
education
excitement
experience

Good to go.

STA TRAVEL
www.statravel.com

CST #1017560-40
(800) 351.3214

WE'VE BEEN PLANNING ONE TRIP FOR 25 YEARS. YOURS.

STUDENT TRAVEL & BEYOND

adventurous can climb another 119 steps to the Stone Gallery (warning: some parts have a circa five foot clearance). The Stone Gallery is outside the cathedral at the base of the outer dome. The heavy stone balustrade, not to mention taller modern buildings, puts you within the skyline and not above it, so take a deep breath and persevere up the final 152 dizzying steps to the Golden Gallery at the base of the lantern. The view from the top is impressive, though an equally grand vista can be had for fewer steps from the top of the Monument (see p. 91).

PLUMBING THE DEPTHS. The mosaic-floored crypt is bright and surprisingly welcoming; the sheer number of memorials, however, makes finding individual graves a bit difficult. On hand volunteers, though who have maps of all the headstones. The free "Key to the Crypt" brochure from the information desk is indispensable. The crypt is packed wall-to-wall with plaques and tombs of great Britons (and the occasional foreigner). Nelson commands pride of place, with radiating galleries filled with gravestones and tributes honoring other military heroes, from Epstein's bust of T.E. Lawrence (of Arabia) to a plaque commemorating the casualties of the Gulf War. Florence Nightingale is also honored here. The neighboring chamber contains Wellington's massive tomb, its stark simplicity in contrast to the ornate monument upstairs. The rear of the crypt, now the chapel of the "most excellent Order of the British Empire," bears the graves of artists, including Sir William Blake, J.M.W. Turner, and Henry Moore. They are crowded around the starkly simple black slab concealing the body of Sir Christopher Wren. Inscribed on the wall above is his famous epitaph: *Lector, si monumentum requiris circumspice* ("Reader, if you seek his monument, look around"). Also in the crypt are St. Paul's various incarnations and the treasury, with a glittering collection of silver and gold plates, cups, and robes, including the Bishop of London's Jubilee cape and a silk robe with 73 churches and St. Paul's Cathedral embroidered upon it in gold. A memorial to the late Queen Mother has been added to the new Golden Jubilee Display.

THE TOWER OF LONDON

THE CITY OF LONDON QUICKFIND: Discover, p. 6; sights p. 90; museums & galleries p. 90; food p. 168; pubs, p. 195.

Location: *Tower Hill, next to Tower Bridge, in the The City of London, within easy reach of the The South Bank and the East End.* ***Contact:*** *☎0870 756 6060, ticket sales ☎0870 756 7070 www.hrp.org.uk or www.tower-of-london.org.uk. ⊖Tower Hill or DLR: Tower Gateway.* ***Open:*** *Mar.-Oct. M 10am-6pm, Tu-Sa 9am-6pm, Su 10am-6pm; buildings close at 5:45pm, last ticket sold 5pm and last entry 5:30pm; Nov.-Feb. all closing times 1hr. earlier, and on M opens at 10am.* ***Tours:*** *Yeoman Warder Tours: Meet near entrance. 1hr., every 90min. M 10am-3:30pm, Tu-Sa 9:30am-3:30pm, Su 10am-3:30pm. Tower Green: Open only by Yeoman tours or after 4:30pm or for daily services. Audioguides £3.* ***Admission:*** *£13.50, concessions £10.50, ages 5-15 £9; under 5 free, family of 5 £37.50. Tickets also sold at Tube stations or by phone; buy them in advance, as queues at the door are horrendous.*

The Tower of London, one of the most deservedly popular attractions in the city, has served as palace, prison, royal mint, and living museum over the past 900 years. The turrets and towers are impressive not only for their appearance but for their integral role in England's history. William the Conqueror's wooden structure of 1067 was replaced in 1078 by a stone fortress that over the next 20 years would grow into the White Tower. Richard the Lionheart began the construction of additional defenses in 1189, and further work was done by Henry III and Edwards I, II and III. The tower has remained essentially unchanged since medieval times. The whole castle used to be surrounded by a broad moat, but severe contamination led to its draining in 1843; it has since sprouted lawns enjoyed by the Yeomen Warders. These "Beefeaters"—whose nickname may be a reference to their daily allowance of meat in former times— still guard the fortress, dressed in their distinctive blue everyday uniforms or elaborate red ceremonial uniforms. To be eligible for Beefeaterhood, a candidate must have at least 22 years of service in the armed forces, as well as a strong appetite for flash photography and an inherent love for tourists. All this history and tradi-

tion notwithstanding, with 2.5 million visitors a year, the Tower very much feels like a medieval theme park—complete with gift shops and costumed performers. To make the most of your visit, buy tickets in advance and **arrive as early as possible**—before the school buses unload. It becomes difficult to appreciate the Tower with all the crowds milling about: show up at 9am on a M-Th morning, and you'll have the run of the place. Happily for visitors, the fortress is divided into seven more-or-less self-contained areas, which can be visited in any order. An enjoyable and popular way to get a feel for the Tower is to join one of the animated and fairly theatrical **Yeoman Warders' Tours** (see above), which will fill you in on the history and legends associated with the Tower. Be careful of the infamous ravens though—they bite!

WESTERN ENTRANCE & WATER LANE. Historically, the main overland entrance to the Tower was over a double system of drawbridges via the mini-fortress where the ticket offices now stand. **Lion Tower,** of which only the foundations remain, was the first line of defense, followed by **Middle Tower,** where today tickets are collected and bags searched. Years ago, a third drawbridge existed here over the once-working moat. After passing over the ex-moat, you enter the **Outer Ward** (created by Edward I's 13th century expansion) through **Byward Tower.** Byward tower was once the private royal entrance. To enter after closing time, one still needs a top-secret password. The password, which is known only by the Yeoman and other high-ranking officials, has been changed daily since 1327. Just beyond Byward Tower, the massive **Bell Tower** dates from 1190; the curfew bell has been rung nightly for over 500 years. The stretch of the Outer Ward along the Thames is **Water Lane,** which until the 16th century was adjacent to the river. The partially submerged and heavily barred **Traitor's Gate** was built by Edward I but is now associated with the many famous prisoners who passed through it, such as Queen Anne Boleyn. The gate gets its name from the multitude of treason suspects who arrived through it, although it was primarily used to receive supplies from ships traveling the Thames.

MEDIEVAL PALACE. In this sequence of rooms, archaeologists have attempted to recreate the look and feel of the Tower during the reign of Edward I (1275-1279). The self-guided tour starts at **St. Thomas's Tower,** a half-timbered set of rooms above the Traitor's Gate. The rooms start out bare and are progressively filled with 13th-century decor and furniture. The court, with a gilded, reconstructed throne, is the highlight of the walk, as well as a small but extraordinary (if only because of their advanced age) collection of 13th-century artifacts in the final room.

WALL WALK. The Wall Walk is a series of eight towers that run along the eastern wall constructed by Henry III in the mid-13th century. The wall is entered via Salt Tower, originally used to house guests and then adapted into a prison. Its long service as a prison is witnessed by the fascinating and still-legible inscriptions scratched by inmates, including religious messages from persecuted Catholics and an elaborate astrological table carved by a convicted sorcerer. Unsurprisingly, the tower may be haunted, dogs allegedly refuse to enter it. At the end of the walk is Martin Tower. The Martin Tower traces the history of the British Crown and is now home to a fascinating collection of retired crowns—sans gemstones which have been recycled into the current models. There are also models of some of the more famous jewels, including the fist-sized Cullinan diamond, at 3106 carats, the largest ever found, as well as a display on diamond cutting and a glittering pile of 12,314 DeBeers diamonds, the number in George IV's coronation crown.

JEWEL HOUSE. Be sure to visit Martin Tower before seeing the crown jewels—Jewel House has almost no documentation, and the jewels are much more interesting once you know some stories behind them. The crown jewels have been held in the Tower for centuries and moved only during times of war. The Jewel Treasury is located in Waterloo Barracks on the north side of the Tower and the long queue is a miracle of crowd management. Tourists file past room after room of rope barriers while video projections show larger-than-life depictions of Queen Elizabeth II's coronation and 3D rotating images of the jewels in action. Finally, visitors are ushered into the vault, past two-foot-thick steel doors, and onto moving walkways that takes them past the crowns and ensure that no awestruck gazers hold up the queue. Not to worry though, viewers can ride the walkways multiple time. Most of the items on display come from the spectacular Coronation regalia. With the exception of the Coronation Spoon, everything dates from after 1660, since Cromwell melted down the original booty. While the eye is naturally drawn to the **Imperial State Crown,** home to the Stuart Sapphire along with 16 other sapphires, 2876 diamonds, 273 pearls, 11 emeralds, and five rubies, don't miss the **Sceptre with the Cross,** topped with the First Star of Africa, the largest quality cut diamond in the world. Look for the **Queen Mother's Crown,** which contains the Koh-I-Noor diamond; legend claims the diamond will bring luck only to women. Wealth like this is rarely on public display; be careful not to hit your head on the glass as you go in for one more incredulous look. That would be embarrassing.

WHITE TOWER. This tower is the centerpiece of the current fortress, it was the original "Tower of London." Originally a royal residence, the Conqueror's castle has also served as a wardrobe, storehouse, records office, mint, armory, and prison. The tour involves plenty of the requisite winding staircases; a much-shortened basement tour is available for those who cannot climb stairs. The path charted for visitors winds up three floors and then down; docents are on hand for confused sightseers. The walk starts with the first-floor **Chapel of St. John the Evangelist.** Remarkable for its quietly stunning simplicity, this 11th-century Norman chapel has Roman undertones and is one of the oldest and most beautiful spaces in the Tower. The spacious hall next door was most likely the royal **bedchamber** and the larger room next door would have been his **Great Hall.** Today it houses an impressive collection of armor and weapons from the royal collection. Don't miss Henry VIII's corset, without which he couldn't fit into his tournament armor. The not-so-petite king had armor made to fit his shapely stomach, and two layers of metal plates were needed to accommodate his generous size. Also be sure to see the miniature suits of armor designed for young nobles. Sometimes there are special exhibits on the top floor, a recent one featured histories of many Tower prisoners. The visit passes through endless displays of swords, cannons, pistols, and muskets on the second floor, before dropping to the basement for the final leg. This trails through the historic misrepresentation of the **Spanish Armory**—torture instruments that were displayed in the 17th century as being captured from the Spanish Armada (1588), but were actually from the Tower's own armory. Finally, you exit via the basement past a display telling how the Victorians "restored" the Tower to their ideal of a medieval fortress, demolishing many of its historic parts along the way.

TOWER GREEN. The lovely grassy western side of the **Inner Ward,** site of the Tower's most famous executions, was reserved for the private beheading of very important guests. Queens, of course, were not expected to stoop so low as to meet an executioner in public. Today, a plaque marks the site of the medieval scaffold and it is surrounded by a suite of houses that have been home to Tower officials for centuries. The Tudor **Queen's House** (which will become the King's House when Charles ascends the throne) is now occupied by the Governor of the Tower. Nearby, the **Beauchamp Tower** was usually reserved for high-class "guests," many of whom carved intricate inscriptions into the walls during their detention. On the north of Tower Green is the **Chapel Royal of St. Peter ad Vincula** last resting place of many Tower Green unfortunates. Originally just another City church, by the 13th century it found itself within the Tower walls. Three queens of England—Anne Boleyn, Catherine Howard, and Lady Jane Grey—are buried here, as well as Catholic saints Thomas More and John Fisher. Across the green is **Bloody Tower,** formerly Garden Tower. The tower got its new name after popularization by another famous Englishman, Shakespeare. It is the site where Richard III allegedly imprisoned and murdered his young nephews, Richard, age 9, and Edward V, the 12-year-old rightful heir to the throne. In 1674, the bones of two children were unearthed beneath a nearby staircase and subsequently interred in Westminster Abbey. There is still no proof, however, of Richard's guilt. Inside, the tower has been restored to its appearance in the early 17th century, when it housed erstwhile adventurer and treason suspect Sir Walter Raleigh. A replica of Raleigh's bedchamber and study fill the inside of the Bloody Tower, where Raleigh studied for 13 years in confinement.

OUTSIDE THE TOWER. The Tower's jurisdiction extends beyond its walls into the surrounding area, known as the **Liberty of the Tower.** Directly outside the walls is **Tower Hill,** the traditional site for public beheadings. The last execution was that of 80-year-old Lord Lovat, leader of the Jacobite rebellion, in 1747. Between the Tower and the Thames, the **Wharf** offers a view of Tower Bridge and Southwark. Ceremonial salutes are fired from the river bank here on royal birthdays and during state visits. After the hectic pace inside the Tower Walls the walk along the cobbled wharf is delightful.

CEREMONY OF THE KEYS. As the oldest continuously occupied castle in Europe, the Tower has a wealth of traditions, many of which can be seen and appreciated by travelers. One of the most popular is the Ceremony of the Keys. This nightly locking-up ritual has been performed every night without fail for over 700 years. At precisely 9:53pm, the Chief Warder locks the outer gates of the Tower before presenting the keys to the Governor amid much marching and salutation. *(For tickets, write 2 months in advance with the full name of those attending, a choice of at least 3 dates, and a stamped addressed envelope or international response coupon to: Ceremony of the Keys, Waterloo Block, HM Tower of London, EC3N 4AB. Free.)*

STEP ASIDE PLEASE. Nothing irks busy Londoners more than a clueless tourist who fails to recognize that there is a strict etiquette involved in Underground escalator relations. If you're not walking stand to the *right*.

HYDE PARK & KENSINGTON GARDENS

KENSINGTON & EARL'S COURT QUICKFIND: Discover, p. 8; sights, p. 100; museums & galleries, p. 145; food, p. 171; pubs, p. 198; entertainment, p. 236; shopping, p. 257; accommodations, p. 286.

***Location:** Framed by Kensington Rd., Knightsbridge, Park Ln., and Bayswater Rd.; bordered by Knightsbridge, Kensington, Bayswater, Marylebone, and Mayfair. **Contact:** ☎7298 2100; www.royalparks.org. Queensway, Lancaster Gate, Marble Arch, Hyde Park Corner, or High St. Kensington. **Open:** Hyde Park daily 5am-midnight, Kensington Gdns. dawn-dusk. "Liberty Drive" rides are accessible for seniors and the disabled; call ☎077 6749 8096. A full program of music, performance, and children's activities takes place during the summer; see park noticeboards for details. **Admission:** Free.*

Surrounded by London's wealthiest neighborhoods, Hyde Park has served as the model for city parks around the world, including Central Park in New York and Paris's Bois de Boulogne. Henry VIII stole the land from Westminster Abbey in 1536, and James I opened it to the public in 1637—the first royal park to be so opened.During an outbreak of the plague, terrified inhabitants of the city once set up camp here for a year in an attempt at quarantine. It's still the largest public space in central London, and the expansive grounds are popular with tourists and locals alike-- warm days attract swarms of pasty sunbathing Londoners. **Kensington Gardens,** contiguous with Hyde Park and originally part of it, was created in the late 17th century when William and Mary set up in Kensington Palace.

THE SERPENTINE. Officially known as the "Long Water West of the Serpentine Bridge," and that's just what it is. The long, snaking, 41-acre Serpentine was created in 1730 as decoration, but today it's actually used quite a bit: dog-paddling tourists and rowers have made it London's busiest swimming hole. Nowhere near the water, it's namesake **Serpentine Gallery** displays contemporary art (open daily 10am-6pm, free). *(Boating ☎7262 1330. Open Apr.-Aug. daily 10am-5pm (6pm in fine weather). £4 per person for 30min., £6 per hr.; children £1/£2. Deposit may be required. Swimming: At the Lido, south shore. ☎7706 3422. Open June-early Sept. daily 10am-5:30pm. £3.50, seniors £2, children 60p, family £7.50.)*

OTHER PARK SIGHTS. Running south of the Serpentine, the dirt horse track **Rotten Row** stretches westward from Hyde Park Corner. The name is a corruption of Route du Roi or "King's Road," as this was the royal route from Kensington Palace to Whitehall. At the southern end of Hyde Park and into Kensington Gardens clusters a group of statues: **Diana fountain** (the goddess, not the princess); the "family of man"; a likeness of **Lord Byron;** tiny **Peter Pan**, and a fig-leafed **Achilles** dedicated to Wellington. Recently, a fountain has been built across the park as a tribute to Diana, the princess. At the northeastern corner of the park, near Marble Arch, you can see free speech in action as proselytizers, politicos, and flat-out crazies dispense the fruits of their knowledge to bemused tourists at **Speaker's Corner** on Sundays.

Looking rather displaced by itself, **Marble Arch** was originally intended to be the front entrance to Buckingham Palace, but palace extensions and new roadways cut left Nash's 1828 monument off, leaving it stranded forlornly on a traffic roundabout. The arch now stands close to the former site of the Tyburn gallows, London's main execution site until 1783. *(Near the intersection of Park Ln., Oxford St., Edgware Rd., and Bayswater Rd. ⊖Marble Arch.)*

SIGHTS BY NEIGHBORHOOD

BLOOMSBURY

BLOOMSBURY QUICKFIND: Discover, p. 5; museums & galleries, p. 140; food, p. 166; pubs, p. 193; entertainment, p. 234; shopping, p. 255; accommodations, p. 282.

SEE MAP, p. 360

First settled in the 18th century, Bloomsbury acquired its intellectual character as it is home to both the British Museum and University College—London's first university. This reputation was bolstered in the early 20th century as Gordon Sq. rang with the philosophizing and womanizing of the famed Bloomsbury Group (see **Life & Times**, p. 61). Nowadays the student landscape is liberally dotted with tourist accommodations, though the area's high concentration of academic and artistic institutions maintains its cerebral air. The scads of leafy green squares and gardens are perfect for philosophical contemplation (or intellectual dozing, if you like).

ACADEMIA

⊖Warren St., Goodge St., and Tottenham Crt. Rd. stations serve the northern, central, and southern ends of Gower St., respectively.

Prime pilgrimage for the devoutly brainy— this strip of land along Gower Street and immediately to its east is London's academic heartland. The well-kept streets of this district are lined with world-renowned institutions such as University College, London (UCL) and the Royal Academy of Dramatic Art (RADA). On the other side of UCL from Gower St., **Gordon Square** was home to much of the Bloomsbury Group, while farther down Gower St., handsome **Bedford Square** is the only London square to retain all its original Georgian buildings

UNIVERSITY COLLEGE LONDON. Established in 1828 to provide an education to those excluded from Oxford and Cambridge, UCL was the first in Britain to ignore "race, creed, and politics" in admissions and, later, the first to allow women to sit for degrees. A key advisor during the first days of the college, social philosopher **Jeremy Bentham** still watches over his old haunts—his body has sat on display in the South Cloister since 1850. Less dramatic, but certainly more lively, the quiet squares and greens of the grounds make for good people-watching. At the southern end of Malet Street, the sight of UCL's massive central administrative building, **Senate House**, would quash the spirits of any student radical; during WWII it housed the BBC propaganda unit. George Orwell, who was employed by this so-called "Ministry of Information," used his experience there as the model for the Ministry of Truth in *1984*. *(Main entrance on Gower St. South Cloister entrance through the courtyard. Quadrangle gates close at midnight; access to Jeremy Bentham ends at 6pm. Free. Wheelchair accessible.)*

ST. PANCRAS & EUSTON ROAD

King's Cross St. Pancras unless otherwise specified.

The opening of the British Library in 1998 has rejuvenated this neighborhood, which was barely considered part of Bloomsbury until recently. Still, signs of its gritty past linger in the busy, dirty urban bustle of its downmarket streets. Travelers should be **careful** while walking alone near King's Cross Station after dark.

BRITISH LIBRARY. Castigated during its long construction by traditionalists for being too modern and by modernists for being too traditional, the new British Library building (opened 1998) now impresses all doubters with its stunning interior. The heart of the library is underground, with 12 million books on 200 mi. of shelving; the above-ground brick building is home to cavernous reading rooms and an engrossing **museum** (see p. 140). Displayed in a glass cube toward the rear of the building, the 65,000 volumes of the King's Library were collected by George III and bequeathed to the nation in 1823 by his less bookish son, George IV. The sunken Piazza out front offers a series of free concerts and events, although the integrated restaurant, cafés, and coffee bars are overpriced. *(96 Euston Rd. ☎7412 7332; www.bl.uk. All public spaces open M 9:30am-6pm, Tu 9:30am-8pm, W-F 9:30am-6pm, Sa 9:30am-5pm, Su 11am-5pm. Audioguides £3.50, concessions £2.50. Tours of public areas M, W, F, Sa 3pm, and Sa 10:30am; £6, concessions £4.50. Tours including one of the reading rooms Tu 6:30pm, Su and Bank Holidays 11:30am and 3pm; £7, students and concessions £5.50. Reservations recommended for all tours. Library free. Wheelchair accessible.)*

ST. PANCRAS STATION. Most visitors assume that the low concourse west of Midland Rd. is a railway station, and the soaring Gothic spires to the east the British Library. In fact, the opposite is true: this Victorian extravaganza is the facade of St. Pancras Station, whose massive 1868 train shed was once the largest undivided indoor area in the world. Ongoing construction means that views of the exterior will occasionally be obstructed by scaffolding. *(Euston Rd.)*

OTHER BLOOMSBURY SIGHTS

CORAM'S FIELDS. One of the most delightful spots in London, 7 acres of old Foundling Hospital grounds live on as a spectacular (and free) children's park. Kids of all ages will love the petting zoo and paddling pond, not to mention the special under-5 toilets; older kids will relish the hi-tech playgrounds. *(93 Guilford St. ☎7833 0198. Open daily 9am-dusk. No adults admitted without children. Free.)*

ST. GEORGE'S BLOOMSBURY. Time, the Blitz, and general disrepair have taken their toll on the facade of this 1730 Hawksmoor church, but a £1 million restoration project should bring it back to its former glory. The interior offers an unusual flat ceiling undecorated except for a central plaster rose. (Anthony Trollope was baptized before the gilded mahogany altar, also the setting of Dickens's *Bloomsbury Christening*.) The church's most unusual feature is its stepped spire, based on the ancient Mausoleum of Halikarnassos (one of the seven Wonders of the Ancient World—partly on display at the British Museum) and topped by a statue of George I. The restoration will also reintroduce the magnificent 10 ft. lions and unicorns that originally stood at George's feet. *(Bloomsbury Way. ☎7405 3044; www.stgeorgesbloomsbury.org.uk. Russell Square. The church hopes to be open for worship by Christmas 2004, but regular hours likely won't be set until spring 2005; call or check the website for hours.)*

CHELSEA

CHELSEA QUICKFIND: Discover, p. 5; museums & galleries, p. 141; food, p. 167; pubs, p. 195; entertainment, p. 234; shopping, p. 256.

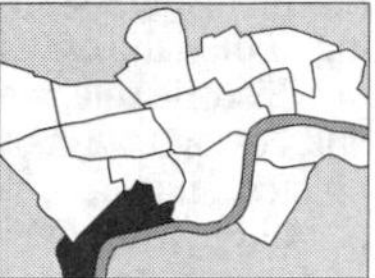

SEE MAP, p. 361

The only Tube station in Chelsea is Sloane Sq.; from here buses #11, 19, 22, 211, and 319 serve King's Rd.

As wealthy as neighboring Belgravia and Kensington, Chelsea boasts a riverside location and a strong artistic heritage. Henry VIII's right-hand man (and later victim) Saint Thomas More was the first big-name resident in the 16th century, but it was in the 19th century that the neighborhood acquired its reputation as an artistic hothouse with the founding of the famous Chelsea Arts Club. **Cheyne** (CHAIN-ee) **Walk** was home to J.M.W. Turner, George Eliot, Dante Gabriel Rossetti, and more recently Mick Jagger (at no. 48). Oscar Wilde, John Singer Sargent, and James McNeill Whistler lived on **Tite Street,** while Mark Twain, Henry James, and T.S. Eliot were also Chelsea residents at various times. The latest artist-in-residence is none other than Damien Hirst, who recently purchased a large houseboat moored near Cheyne Walk. Oddly enough, Chelsea's only other distinguishing aspect is military: the Chelsea Barracks, the Royal Hospital, and the National Army Museum all happen to be stationed in this bohemian paradise.

THE ROYAL HOSPITAL

***Location:** Two entrance gates on Royal Hospital Rd. **Contact:** ☎7881 5246 **Open:** Museum, Great Hall, and Chapel: M-Sa 10am-noon and 2-4pm, Su 2-4pm. (Museum closed on Su Oct.-Mar.) Grounds: Nov.-Mar. M-Sa 10am-4:30pm, Su 2-4:30pm; Apr. closes 7:30pm; Sept. 7pm; summer 8:30pm. Ranelagh Gardens have the same hours as the Grounds, but closed 12:45-2pm. **Admission:** Free. Wheelchair accessible.*

A monument, a garden park, and a retirement home—every day is veterans' day at this military complex. The environs of the Royal Hospital are home to the **Chelsea Pensioners,** who totter around the grounds as they have done since 1692. That's when Charles II established the place as a retirement home for army veterans ("hospital" meaning a place of shelter), and the entrance criteria have barely changed since: 20 years of distinguished service or a disability incurred while in service. The Hospital remains a military institution, with pensioners arranged in companies under the command of a retired officer; until 1805 they carried guns and acted as guards, but today they run the post office and museum. The graceful layout is a hallmark of Christopher Wren's design, and the beautifully smooth lawns are broken only by the gilded statue of Charles II in the central **Figure Court.** Between this central court and the street, doors lead to the airy **chapel** and **Great Hall,** where pensioners dine surrounded by an engraved list of every battle fought by the British. Off the west court, a small **museum** details the history and everyday hospital life and pensioners, along with a room of glittering medals, all bequeathed by their former owners.

Just west of the central court, the once-ritzy **Ranelagh Gardens** are now a quiet oasis free of high society—except during the week of the **Chelsea Flower Show,** late May 2005, when the braying masses of the Royal Horticultural Society descend en masse. *(www.rhs.org.uk. Tickets to the show must be purchased well in advance.)*

OTHER CHELSEA SIGHTS

SLOANE SQUARE AND KING'S ROAD. Sloane Square takes its name from British Museum founder Sir Hans Sloane (1660-1753), who spearheaded the neighborhood's transformation from a sleepy backwater to fashionable suburb. Until 1829, King's Road, stretching southwest from Sloane Sq., served as a private royal route from Hampton Court to Whitehall; more recently, though, it's been known as a breeding ground for nobility of the pop and fashion realm. In the 1960s Mary Quant launched the miniskirt on an unsuspecting world from King's Rd.; two decades later punk rock's most famous spokesmen, the Sex Pistols, were started as a publicity stunt for Malcolm McLaren's boutique at the World's End, 430 King's Rd.

CHELSEA PHYSIC GARDEN. Founded in 1673 to provide medicinal herbs to locals, the Physic Garden remains a carefully ordered living repository of useful, rare, or just plain interesting plants, ranging from opium poppies to leeks. (Those caught trying to filch the opiates will be giggled at, then arrested.) It has also played an important historic role, serving as the staging post from which tea was introduced to India and cotton to America. Today, the garden is a colorful, quiet place for wandering, picnics, and teas; you can purchase a wide array of flora on display. Tea served from 2-4:45pm, until 5:45pm on Su.*(66 Royal Hospital Rd. Entrance on Swan Walk. ☎7352 5646; www.chelseaphysicgarden.co.uk. Open early Apr.-Oct. W noon-5pm, Su 2-6pm; M-F noon-5pm during Chelsea Flower Show (late May) and Chelsea Festival (mid-June). £5, students and under 16 £3. Call ahead for wheelchair access.)*

CARLYLE'S HOUSE. In his time, the "Sage of Chelsea" Thomas Carlyle was the most famous writer and historian in England—at his death in 1881, admirers purchased his house and preserved it as a national monument. The house and garden in which he entertained Dickens, Tennyson, and Ruskin are more or less as they were during his life. *(24 Cheyne Row. ☎7352 7087. Open Apr.-Oct. W-F 2-5pm, Sa-Su 11am-5pm, last admission 4:30pm. £3.90, under 16 £1.80.)*

CHELSEA OLD CHURCH. This Saxon church had to be restored after WWII and the quiet, unspectacular interior won't do much for the lay observer. It is historically appealing, though, and fortunately, the bombs spared the southern chapel, where Saint Thomas More worshipped in the 16th century. Also, Henry VIII is reported to have married Jane Seymour here before the official wedding took place. Just down the street is Crosby Hall, a 15th-century hall that was More's residence in Bishopsgate before being moved, stone by stone, to its present position in 1910. *(2 Old Church St. ☎7795 1019; www.domini.org/chelsea-old-church. Open Tu-F 2-5pm and Su 1:30-5:30pm. Services Su 8am, 11am, 12:15pm, 6pm.)*

FREE INTERNET. Feeling disconnected? Feeling poor? Consider stopping by the nearest library and signing up for a free half hour of internet. It's available for non-members; all you need is a name.

THE CITY OF LONDON

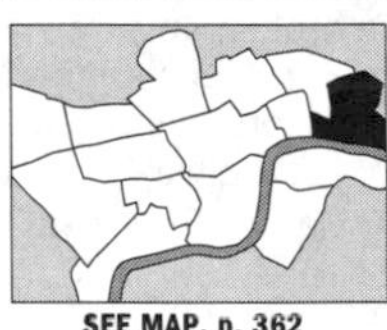

SEE MAP, p. 362

THE CITY OF LONDON QUICKFIND: Discover, p. 6; museums & galleries, p. 141; food, p. 168; pubs, p. 195; entertainment, p. 235. For ***St. Paul's Cathedral****, see p. 80. For The* ***Tower of London****, see p. 83.*

The ***City of London Information Centre,*** *St. Paul's Churchyard (☎7332 1456); ⊖St. Paul's. Open Apr.-Sept. daily 9:30am-5pm; Oct.-Mar. M-F 9:30am-5pm, Sa 9:30am-12:30pm. Offers leaflets and maps, provides information on current sights and shows, and gives info on traditional municipal events such as, held each year on the second Sa of Nov.*

The City of London (usually shortened to "the City") is the oldest part of London. As its name suggests, for most of its 2000 years this *was* London, all other districts being merely outlying villages. The most interesting sights, sounds and smells are located within walking distance of each other in what is conveniently called the **"Square Mile."** Today, archaeology is pulling London's history out of the ground, and the ancient Roman roots of the City are becoming ever more visible. The City strikes a strange balance between tradition and modernity; 400 year old churches share sidewalks with modern office buildings.The daytime population of the area is a steady flow of business people rushing about the streets. Above it all rises the dome of **St. Paul's** (p. 80) and the battlements of the **Tower of London** (p. 83). The 39 churches that have survived the fires and wars and the labyrinthine alleyways are almost the only reminders of the time when this was the beating heart of London. If sightseeing in the City, make the most of the morning and lunchtime—you'll have trouble finding anything open after 6pm. Since actual hours at City sights often change based on private events or the whims of a church vector, it's best to call in advance. Fortunately, the City packs enough into its small area that alternative sights are never far off, and with centuries to cover, there's always something to see.

ALL HALLOWS-BY-THE-TOWER

Location: Byward St. **Contact:** ☎ 7481 2928. www.allhallowsbythetower.org.uk ⊖Tower Hill. **Open:** Church 9am -6pm daily; crypt and museum M-Sa 11am-4pm, Su 1-4pm.

Nearly hidden by City redevelopment projects, All Hallows bears its longevity with pride. Just inside the entrance on the left stands the oldest part of the church, a Saxon arch dating from AD 675. The main chapel has three parts, the right and left transepts date from the 13th and 14th centuries respectively and the central ceiling from the 20th. The undercroft museum is home to a diverse collection of Roman and Saxon artifacts, medieval art, and church record books from the time of the plague; it is well worth a look. The main area displays wood from the Cutty Sark and porcelain from the Spanish Armada, as well as Sir Francis Drake's coat of arms. Samuel Pepys witnessed the spread of the Great Fire from its tower, while American associations include John Quincy Adams (married here, his wife lived in the parish) and William Penn (baptized here in 1644). The spectacular Lady Chapel is home to a magnificent altarpiece dating from 1500 and has been restored to look much as it did when it was built in 1489. The stark cement arches and barred windows of the nave, rebuilt after the Blitz, give this church a mysterious and impressive dignity.

MONUMENT

Location: Monument St. **Contact:** ☎ 7626 2717. ⊖Monument. **Open:** Daily 9:30am-5pm; last admission 4:40pm. **Admission:** £2, children £1.

The only non-ecclesiastical Wren building in the City, the Monument was built to commemorate the devastating Great Fire of 1666. Finished in 1677, the 202 ft.-tall column stands exactly that distance from the bakery on Pudding Ln. where fire first broke out. A white Doric column, the colossal Monument can only be scaled by climbing the very narrow spiral staircase inside. The climb brings you close to the copper urn of flames that caps the pillar, a mythic reminder of the Fire. The enclosed platform at the top, however, offers one of the best views of London, especially of the Tower Bridge. As the inscription on the outside says, the fire "rushed devastating through every quarter with astonishing swiftness and worse." In 1681, a small addition was made: "but Popish frenzy, which wrought such horrors, is not yet quenched." This bit of rabid anti-Catholicism was removed in 1830. The bravery required in making the steep climb is rewarded with a certificate of completion on the way out, the best souvenir. (*The Monument and the Tower Bridge Exhibition (see below) offer joint admission for £6.50, concessions £4.50, children £3.50.*)

TOWER BRIDGE

Location: Entrance to the Tower Bridge Exhibition is through the west side (upriver) of the North Tower. **Contact:** ☎ 7940 3985, lifting schedule ☎ 7940 3984; www.towerbridge.org.uk. ⊖Tower Hill or London Bridge. **Open:** Daily 10am-6pm; last entry 5:30pm. **Admission:** £5.50, concessions £4.25, ages 5-16 £3. Wheelchair accessible.

When TV and movie directors want to say "London," nine times out of ten they settle for a shot of Tower Bridge, which helps explain why tourists often mistake it for its plainer sibling, London Bridge. A relatively new bridge (1894), its impressive stature and bright blue suspension cables connect the banks of the Thames and rise above the many other bridges in the area. A marvel of engineering, the steam-powered lifting mechanism remained in use from 1894 until 1973, when electric motors took over. Though clippers no longer sail into London very often, there's still enough large river traffic for the bridge to be lifted around 1000 times per year, in the summer five or six times per day. Call to find out the schedule, or check the signs posted at each entrance. Historians and technophiles will appreciate the **Tower Bridge Exhibition,** which combines scenic 140 ft high glass-enclosed walkways with videos presenting a bell-and-whistle history of the bridge. If you're a fan of cheesy animatronics and oversized machinery, don't miss the Engine Room where dummies crank the original steam engines and mine coal amidst a soundtrack of—what else—an early 20th century engine room.

GUILDHALL YARD

***Location:** Off Gresham St. ⊖St. Paul's, Moorgate or Bank. Wheelchair accessible.*

Since the founding of the Corporation of London in 1193, the City has been governed from this site. The open stone courtyard is usually empty and feels strangely removed from the bustle of the City. The centerpiece of the yard is the Guildhall itself, on the north side of the Yard. As the name suggests, this is where the representatives of the City's 102 guilds, from the Fletchers (arrow-makers) to the Information Technologists meet under the aegis of the Lord Mayor whose offices occupy another Guildhall building. Excavations in the 1990s revealed the remains of a Roman amphitheater below the Yard; its ruins are on display in the Guildhall Art Gallery on the Yard's eastern side.

GUILDHALL. The towering Gothic hall dates from 1440, though after repeated remodeling in the 17th and 18th centuries—not to mention almost complete reconstruction following the Great Fire and the Blitz—little of the original remains. Still, the hall maintains its style and skeleton; there are statues and gargoyles inside to preserve the Gothic image. The stained-glass windows bear the names of all Mayors and Lord Mayors of the Corporation, past and present—the builders foresaw the City's longevity, as there's room for about 700 more. On either side of the wooden Minstrel's Gallery are 9 ft. statues of Apocalyptic giants Gog and Magog, as well as handcrafted wooden balconies and a monument to the ever-popular Duke of Wellington. Flags of each of the Twelve Great Liveries (the fishmonger's is particularly colorful) line the walls. The hall has seen numerous trials, including those of Lady Jane Grey and Archbishop Cranmer. These days it hosts banquets and, every fourth Thursday, public meetings of the **Court of Common Council.** These are presided over by the Lord Mayor, bedecked in traditional robes and followed by a sword-wielding entourage. These meetings are open to the public, and begin at 1pm—no cameras and no wandering around the hall. Downstairs there is a crypt, open only by guided tour. Guildhall is more often than not closed for events, but arrive early and you might be able to pop in for a look. It's worth it. *(Enter the Guildhall through the low, modern annex. Occasional tours offered–call ☎ 7606 3030, ext. 1463 for information; other inquiries 7606 3030. Open May-Sept. daily 10am-5pm, Sept. weekends are open-house; Oct.-Apr. closed Su. Last admission 4:30pm. Free.)*

OTHER GUILDHALL YARD SIGHTS. To the right of the Guildhall is the brand-new **Guildhall Art Gallery** (see p. 142), built with the express purpose of being a permanent companion to the Guildhall—it really should be called a museum. The **Guildhall Library,** in the 1970s annex and accessed via Aldermanbury or the Yard, specializes in the history of London and is open to all. Its unparalleled collection of microfilm and books is a must for any serious history scholars, and the friendly librarians make the experience all the more pleasurable. It houses the **Guildhall Clockmaker's Museum** (p. 143) as well. *(Entrance on Aldermanbury. ☎ 7332 1854. Library open to the public M-Sa 9:30am-5pm. Free.)*

THE BARBICAN

***Location:** Between London Wall, Beech St., Aldersgate, and Moorgate. ⊖Barbican or Moorgate. Wheelchair accessible.*

After WWII, the Corporation of London decided to redevelop this bomb-flattened 35-acre plot in the north of the City (the site of the ancient Roman barbican or "fort") as a textbook piece of integrated development. Construction took 20 years, starting in 1962, and the result bears the hallmarks of its time: 40-story tower blocks and masses of grey concrete, linked by an intricate system of overhead walkways and open spaces. The center of Barbican is the distinctive P-shaped entertainment complex; there are also 18 residential buildings. The incorporation of lakes, waterfalls and gardens into the overall design, as well as the rows of flowers on apartment balconies, make the scene surprisingly pleasant and very un-industrial. Notoriously difficult to navigate, the Barbican recently underwent a multi-million-pound renovation simplifying the layout and improving its status and accessibility as an entertainment venue. New art gallery space and other functional changes have added space for even more displays of the arts.

BARBICAN CENTRE. Smack in the center of the Barbican is, logically enough, the Barbican Centre, a powerhouse of the arts. Described at its 1982 opening as "the City's gift to the nation," the complex houses a concert hall, two theaters, a small cinema, three art galleries, and numerous bars and eateries—if you can find them. The Centre can be hard to get around; staircases are long and elevators can be unreliable. Some patience and a good look at the directory should solve almost all problems. The **Lakeside Terrace** is a large piazza overlooking the water with picnic tables, sculpture, and sunken fountains flowing over waterfalls into a giant rectangular lake, opposite the stout 16th-century church of St. Giles Cripplegate. Skip the pricey cafes by the water and bring a picnic lunch. Most surreal and uniquely exotic is the level-3 **Conservatory,** a literal concrete jungle—tropical plants burst forth on multiple levels amid ventilation ducts and pipes from the center below. *(Main entrance on Silk St. From ⊖Moorgate or Barbican, follow the yellow painted lines. ☎7638 8891; www.barbican.org.uk. Open M-Sa 9am-11pm, Su 10am-11pm. Conservatory open Su noon-5pm. Free.)*

OTHER BARBICAN SIGHTS. Just behind St. Giles is a well-preserved section of **London Wall,** the city wall built by the Romans and maintained into the Middle Ages. Next to the Barbican Centre, overlooking the lake, is the distinctive and distinguished **Guildhall School of Music**—on hot days you can often hear students practicing. At the complex's southwestern corner is the **Museum of London** (see p. 141).

ST. MARY-LE-BOW

Location: *Cheapside, by Bow Ln. Access to the crypt via stairs in the west courtyard.* ***Contact:*** *☎7248 5139. www.stmarylebow.co.uk ⊖St. Paul's or Mansion House.* ***Open:*** *M-W 7:30am-6pm, Th 7:30am-6:30pm, F 7:30am-4pm.* ***Concerts:*** *Occasional Th 1:05pm, free.*

Another Wren creation, St. Mary's is most famous for its Great Bell, which from 1334 to 1874 rang the City curfew and wake-up call daily. In order to be a *true* Cockney, you must have been born within earshot of the bells. The gardens and the dark tower contrast with the gaudy modern interior. Gold-lined columns and a huge hanging crucifix dominate the room which also

Big Ben

Queen Anne

Westminster Abbey

contains the starkly simple altar and soundboard. The church had to be rebuilt almost completely after the Blitz, but the small 11th-century crypt, whose "bows" (arches) gave the church its epithet, survived. Since the 12th century, it has hosted the ecclesiastical Court of Arches, where the Archbishop of Canterbury swears in bishops. Today, the court shares space with **The Place Below** restaurant (see p. 169).

BANK OF ENGLAND

Location: *Threadneedle St. ⊖Bank.*

Government financial difficulties led to the founding of the "Old Lady of Threadneedle Street" in 1694, as a way of raising money without raising taxes—the bank's Scottish and British creditors supplied £1.2 million, and the national debt was born. The 8 ft. thick, windowless outer wall, enclosing four acres including a spacious and sunny courtyard, is the only remnant of Sir John Soane's 1788 building. Above it rises the current 1925 edifice. The decadent lobby is lovely, but you can **only enter on business.** Top-hatted guards in pink tailsuits will direct those who wander into the main entrance to the **Bank of England Museum,** around the corner on St. Bartholomew Ln. (see p. 142).

LOWER THAMES STREET

Location: *Just north of the Thames between London Bridge and the Tower. ⊖Monument. Wheelchair accessible.*

So busy that it must be crossed by overhead walkways, Lower Thames St. passes a number of interesting sights. At **London Bridge** it splits from Upper Thames St., more interesting for its history than its current bland incarnation. Close to the spot of the original Roman bridge, the first stone bridge across the Thames stood here from 1176 until 1832. Over the course of those years the bridge was widened, un-widened and fortified time and again with mixed results. The bridge may have survived until today had not 18th-century "improvements" fatally weakened the structure. Its replacement lasted until 1973, when a wealthy American bought it for £1.03 million and shipped it to Arizona, where it still rests. While underwhelming, the bridge does offer nice views of the river and Tower Bridge. A few steps up Lower Thames, **St. Magnus-the-Martyr** pays homage to its Roman namesake within the gold-tipped columns and fragrant wood typical of city churches. *(☎7623 8022. Open Tu-F 10am-4pm, Su 10am-1pm. Wheelchair accessible.)*

OTHER CITY OF LONDON SIGHTS

TEMPLE OF MITHRAS. Not as glorious as it sounds, the Temple of Mithras dwells incongruously in the shadow of the Temple Court. The ruins are the foundation of a building devoted to Mithras, an Eastern god popular among the Roman army who built the temple in the late 2nd century. The foundations, floor, and 2 ft. of wall were discovered during construction work in 1954 and shifted up 18 ft. to current street level. The ruins have been well preserved, complete with nubs of former columns. The **Museum of London** (see p. 141) displays artifacts unearthed during the excavation. *(On Queen Victoria St. ⊖Mansion or House or Bank.)*

ST. STEPHEN WALBROOK. On the site of a 7th-century Saxon church, St. Stephen (built 1672-79) was Wren's personal favorite and most architecturally perfect church. The unexpected simplicity and openness of the interior complements Henry Moore's stark freeform altar, dedicated in 1987. The church mixes classic columns and lines with Moore's ultra-modern circular structure. Honorary phones, donated by British Telecom, commemorate current rector Chad Varah, who founded the Samaritans—a crises hotline—here in 1953. It's still in operation now as a national crisis line. (*39 Walbrook. ☎7283 4444. ⊖Bank or Cannon St. Open M-F 9am-4pm; F 12:30pm for 1hr. organ concert. Wheelchair accessible.)*

ST. MARY WOOLNOTH. The only City church untouched by the Blitz, St. Mary's confirms the talent of Wren's pupil Nicholas Hawksmoor; this is his only City church. Early weekday mornings find the pews sprinkled with businessmen looking for some calm. The lack of lower windows is due to the lack of open space around the site at the time of its building (1716-27). Even so, the domed design and the semicircular windows up top fill the small church with light. The remarkable altarpiece and oak soundboard are particularly lovely. *(Junction of King William and Lombard Sts. ☎ 7626 9701. Open M-F 9:30am-4:30pm.)*

OTHER LOCAL SIGHTS. The most famous modern structure in the City is **Lloyd's of London.** What looks like a towering post-modern factory is actually the home of the world's largest insurance market, built in 1986. With raw metal ducts, lifts, and chutes on the outside, it wears its heart (or at least its internal organs) on its sleeve. *(Leadenhall St. ⊖Bank. Wheelchair accessible.)* Only the tower and outer walls remains of Wren's **St. Dunstan-in-the-East.** The blitzed, mossy ruins have been converted into a stunning garden that is now a peaceful picnic spot. Vines cover the gothic-style walls and a bubbling fountain surrounded by benches makes it an oasis in the City. *(St. Dunstan's Hill. ⊖Monument or Tower Hill. Wheelchair accessible.)* When rebuilding **St. Margaret Lothbury** in 1689, Wren was obliged to follow the lines of the former church, despite its north wall being shorter than its south; the result is a roof that's charmingly off-kilter. The sumptuous carved-wood screen was saved from other, now-demolished, City churches. An abundance of stained glass makes St. Margaret's unique. *(Lothbury. ☎ 7606 8330; www.stml.org.uk. ⊖Bank. Open M-F 8am-4:30pm; occasional concerts with guest musicians Th 1:10pm.. Wheelchair accessible.)*

CLERKENWELL

CLERKENWELL QUICKFIND: Discover, p. 7; museums & galleries, p. 143; food, p. 169; pubs, p. 196; nightlife, p. 210; entertainment, p. 235; accommodations, p. 285.

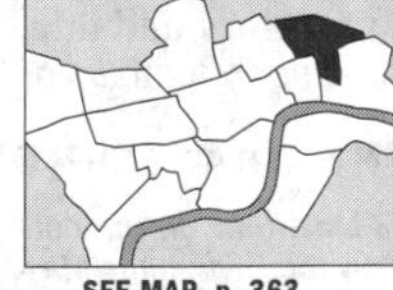

SEE MAP, p. 363

All sights are closest to ⊖Farringdon unless otherwise stated.

The rise and fall (and rise) of currently-hip Clerkenwell coincides, appropriately enough, with the fluctuating role that alcohol has played in the local economy. A monastic hamlet when it was first founded in the 12th century, an influx of brewers and distilleries about 600 years later brought a slew of liquor-centric jobs to the area. The population boomed a bit too strongly, though, and, Clerkenwell soon became the notorious slum detailed in Charles Dicken's *Oliver Twist.* The area was heavily damaged during WWII and then due to the fire in the 1980s and 90s. Today, it's less chic than before but definitely more fun, with a lively population of young bars and nightclubs. However, it does lack stroll-friendly prettiness or cleanliness and is best enjoyed for its indoor pleasures.

CLERKENWELL GREEN

Not very green at all—actually just a wider-than-normal street—Clerkenwell Green boasts a few venerable historical associations. Wat Tyler rallied the Peasants' Revolt here in 1381, and Lenin published the Bolshevik newspaper *Iskra* from no. 37a, the Green's oldest building (1737). It now houses the **Marx Memorial Library.** *(☎ 7253 1485. Open M-Th 1-2pm, book in advance for large groups. Closed Aug.)* Across from this revolutionary hotbed, the **Old Sessions House** (1782) was formerly the courthouse for the county of Middlesex—note the Middlesex arms on the portico. Reputedly haunted, it's now the enigmatic London Masonic Centre. *(Closed to the public.)* Overall, though, there's not too much to see on the Green. The friendly staff of **The 3 Things Coffee Room** *(53 Clerkenwell Close, by St. James' Church. ☎ 7251 6311. Open M-Sa 11am-6pm. MC/V);* cheerfully embraces those smart enough to visit. It offers a wealth of information and leaflets on the area, including a free guide to the Clerkenwell Historic Trail, which tours sights both fascinating and deservedly obscure. (Tip: skip everything north of Bowling Green Ln.) The shop also sells novelty wares by local artisans, as well as organic ice cream for £1.20.

ST. JOHN'S SQUARE

Bisected by the busy Clerkenwell Rd., St. John's Square occupies the site of the 12th-century **Priory of St. John,** former seat of the Knights Hospitallers. The Hospitallers (in full, the Order of the Hospital of St. John of Jerusalem) were founded in 1113 during the First Crusade to simultaneously tend the sick and fight heathens. What remains of their London seat is now in the hands of the British Order of St. John. Unaffiliated with the original order—which still exists, based in the Vatican—this Protestant organization founded their Ambulance Brigade in 1887 to provide first-aid service to the public.

ST. JOHN'S GATE. Built in 1504 as the main entrance to the priory, this stone gateway now arches grandly over the entrance to St. John's Sq. The small ground-floor museum mixes artifacts relating to the original priory and Knights Hospitallers with a hi-tech *Time to Care* room detailing the order's modern-day exploits in bringing band-aids to the masses. A history-laden and uninteresting 500th anniversary room was added in 2004. Join a tour to see the upstairs council chamber and the priory church (see below) which is otherwise closed to the public. *(St. John's Ln. ☎ 7324 4070; www.sja.org.uk/history. Open M-F 10am-5pm, Sa 10am-4pm. Tours Tu and F-Sa 11am and 2:30pm; tours by donation, call for group bookings. Museum free; donation requested.)*

PRIORY OF ST. JOHN. On the other side of Clerkenwell Rd. from the gate, cobblestones in St. John's Sq. mark the position of an original Norman church. The current building, dates to the 16th century, lies at the end of a pleasant cloister garden. Two panels of the 1480 Weston Triptych stand on their original altar, but the real treasure of the church is the crypt, a survivor from the original 12th-century priory and one of London's few remaining pieces of Norman architecture. *(Open only for tours of St. John's Gate, unless by special arrangement, see above.)*

THE CHARTERHOUSE

Location: *On the north side of Charterhouse Sq.* ***Contact:*** *☎ 7251 5002. ⊖Barbican.* ***Open:*** *Only for 1½hr. tours May-Aug. W 2:15pm. Book months in advance. Free; donation requested. Limited wheelchair access.*

Originally a 14th-century Carthusian monastery, the Charterhouse and its walls were built around the communal grave of thousands of victims of the 1349 Black Death. In 1611, the corpses got some new company when **Thomas Sutton** bought the property and established a foundation for the education of 40 boys and the care of 80 impoverished old men. Charterhouse School rapidly established itself as one of the most prestigious (and expensive) schools in England, but in 1872 moved to Surrey, leaving the complex to the (still penniless) pensioners. The weekly tour,, guides you through the grounds and into some of the buildings, including the Duke of Norfolk's Great Hall and the chapel with Sutton's ornate tomb. If you miss the tour you can admire the main gate, the same wooden door to which Henry VIII nailed the severed hands of the last Catholic monks.

ST. BARTHOLOMEW THE GREAT

Location: *Little Britain, off West Smithfield.* ***Contact:*** *☎ 7606 5171. ⊖Barbican.* ***Open:*** *Tu-F 8:30am-5pm, Sa 10:30am-1:30pm, Su 8:30am-1pm and 2:30-8pm. Free; recommended donation £3.*

Enter through a 13th-century arch, cunningly disguised as a Tudor house, to reach this gem of a Norman church. The peaceful, elevated courtyard provides a close view of its unique and eccentric exterior. Inside, the current neck-stretching nave was just the chancel of the original 12th-century church, which formerly reached all the way to the street. Hogarth was baptized in the 15th-century font, and at one time Benjamin Franklin worked at a printer's in the Lady Chapel. The tomb near the central altar is the resting place of **Rahere,** who in 1123 founded both the church and the neighboring **St. Bartholomew's Hospital,** just across Little Britain, was reconstructed in the 18th century and which is London's oldest as well as one of its largest. Within the hospital walls are the 16th-century church of **St. Bartholomew the Less** and a small **museum** on the hospital history (see p. 143).

HOLBORN

HOLBORN QUICKFIND: Discover, p. 7; museums & galleries, p. 143; food, p. 170; pubs, p. 197; nightlife, p. 211; entertainment, p. 236; shopping, p. 257; accommodations, p. 286.

Holborn native Sam Johnson once advised, "You must not be content with seeing Holborn's great streets and squares, but must survey the innumerable little lanes and courts." The delights of Holborn are found in the unexpected, jewel-like gardens hidden by sprawling offices. Extraordinary historic facades appear haphazardly among modern establishments, accompanied by the supremely strollable grounds of the district's **Inns of Court.** None of Holborn could be considered a tourist trap; but those who leave the main drag of High Holborn and Fleet Streets will be richly rewarded with the gothic splendor of **St. Etheldreda's,** the implausible collections of **Somerset House,** and the chance to observe thousands of lawyers in their natural habitat.

SOMERSET HOUSE. Somerset House was London's first purpose-built office block. Originally home to the Royal Academy, the Royal Society, and the Navy Board, the elegant neoclassical courtyard long induced a shiver of distaste in Londoners as the headquarters of the Inland Revenue. While the taxman still presides over the west and east wings, most of the building houses three art museums, the **Courtauld Institute Galleries,** the **Gilbert Collection of Decorative Art,** and **The Hermitage Rooms** (see p. 144). On sunny days, they face some competition from the spectacular view afforded by the **River Terrace** and its attractive but pricey outdoor cafe. From December to January, the central **Fountain Courtyard** is iced over to make an open-air rink, while in the summer months frolicking toddlers splash through the cool fountain jets. Thursday evenings from mid-June to mid-July also bring classical music concerts. *(Strand, just east of Waterloo Bridge. ☎7845 4600, events ☎7845 4670; www.somerset-house.org.uk. ⊖Charing Cross or Temple. Open daily 10am-6pm. Courtyard open daily 7:30am-11pm. 45min. tours of the building Sa 1:30 and 3:45pm. £2.75. Wheelchair accessible.)*

FLEET STREET

***Location:** Fleet St. is the continuation of the Strand between Temple Bar and Ludgate Circus. Note that Fleet St. is numbered up one side and down the other. ⊖Temple.*

Named for the (now underground) tributary that flows from Hampstead to the Thames, Fleet St. became synonymous with the London press in the 19th century, when it housed all of the major dailies. "Fleet Street" is still used to describe London-based newspapers, the famous facades, such as the *Daily Telegraph's* startling Greek and Egyptian Revival building and the *Daily Express*'s manse of chrome and black glass. After a standoff with the printers in 1986, Rupert Murdoch moved all his papers (including *The Times*) to Wapping, Docklands and initiated a mass exodus. Today, Fleet St. is home to some extraordinary churches, coffee shops, and photocopying stores Fleet Street's last nod to the printing process.

THE TEMPLE

***Location:** Between Essex St. and Temple Ave. (see map); church courtyard off Middle Temple Lane. ⊖Temple or Blackfriars. **Admission:** Free.*

The Temple is a complex of buildings that derives its name from the crusading Order of the Knights Templar (that's right, recently of *The Da Vinci Code* fame by Dan Brown) who embraced this site as their English seat in 1185. Today, the Temple houses legal and parliamentary offices, but its charming network of gardens and its medieval church remain open to the enterprising visitor. Make sure to check out the gabled Tudor **Inner Temple Gateway,** between 16 and 17 Fleet St., the 1681 fountain of Fountain Court, featured in Dickens's *Martin Chizzlewit,* and **Elm Court,** tucked behind the church, a tiny yet exquisite garden ringed by massive stone structures.

TEMPLE CHURCH. Temple Church is one of the finest surviving medieval round churches and London's first Gothic church, completed in 1185 on the model of Jerusalem's Church of the Holy Sepulchre. Stained-glass windows, towering ceilings, an original Norman doorway, and ten armored effigies complete the impressive interior, although much of it was rebuilt after WWII bombings. Adjoining the round church is a rectangular Gothic choir, built in 1240, with an altar screen by Wren (1682). The church hosts frequent recitals and musical services, including weekly organ recitals. *(☎ 7353 3470. Hours vary depending on the week's services and are posted outside the door of the church for the coming week. Organ recitals W 1:15-1:45pm; no services Aug.-Sept.)*

MIDDLE TEMPLE. The Middle Temple largely escaped the destruction of World War II and retains fine examples of 16th- and 17th-century architecture. In Middle Temple Hall (closed to the public), Elizabeth I saw Shakespeare act in the premiere of *Twelfth Night*, and his *Henry VI* points to Middle Temple Garden as the origin of the red and white flowers that served as emblems throughout the War of the Roses. (Open May-Sept. M-F noon-3pm.)

ELY PLACE

***Location:** From the Tube, walk east along High Holborn onto Charterhouse St., then make an immediate left through the gates. ⊖Chancery Ln.*

Step through the gates separating Ely Place from Holborn Circus, and you're no longer in London. In the 13th century, the Bishop of Ely built a palace here (later appropriated by Henry VIII). Though the palace is long gone, by a constitutional quirk the street remains outside the jurisdiction of local government (and police). Next to Ely Place, **Hatton Garden** (actually a street) is the center of Britain's gem trade, with dozens of diamond merchants.

ST. ETHELDREDA'S. The mid-13th-century Church of St. Etheldreda is the last remaining vestige of the Bishop of Ely's palace. St. Etheldreda's is now the only pre-Reformation Catholic church in the city, bought back from the Church of England in 1874 after centuries of rotating landlords (one bold but shortlived tenant tried to convert the building into a brewery in the mid-1700s). Inside, the surprisingly high ceiling swallows up the bustle of the streets, creating an island of calm in the midst of Holborn Circus. The self-described "ancient rector" is happy to hold forth on the history of Ely Place. And, creepily, the crypt houses a cafe. (*Open M-F noon-2:30pm*) serving light lunches. *(In Ely Place. ☎ 7405 1061. Church open daily 7:30am-7pm. Free.)*

ROYAL COURTS OF JUSTICE

***Location:** Where the Strand becomes Fleet St.; rear entrance on Carey St. **Contact:** ☎ 7947 6000. ⊖Temple or Chancery Ln. **Open:** M-F 9am-4:30pm; cases are heard 10am-1pm and 2-3:30pm. Be prepared to go through a metal detector security checkpoint when you enter. Cameras are not permitted inside the building; 50p to check them at the door. **Admission:** Free. Wheelchair accessible.*

This massive neo-Gothic structure, designed in 1874 by G. E. Street, holds its own amongst the distinguished facades of Fleet St. Inside are 88 courtrooms, chambers for judges and court staff, and cells for defendants. On slow court days, the real star here is the architecture; exterior views from Carey St. are spectacular, and the Great Hall features Europe's largest mosaic floor. Skip the uninspired display of legal costume and the insipid video tour (at the top of the stairs at the rear of the Great Hall); instead, watch the real thing. The back bench of every courtroom is open to the public during trials, unless the courtroom door says "In Chambers." The noticeboards beside the Enquiry Desk in the Great Hall display a list of cases being tried, or ask the Press Association office if there's anything particularly lurid that day.

ST. CLEMENT DANES. Legend places this church over the tomb of Harold Harefoot, a Danish warlord who settled here in the 9th century. Its fame with Londoners derives from its opening role in the famous nursery rhyme (*Oranges and Lemons say the bells of St. Clement's*—and they still do, daily, at 9am, noon, 3, and 6pm). In 1719, Gibbs replaced Wren's tower with a slimmer spire, and in 1941, the interior was gutted by firebombs. Restored inside to white-and-gold modernity, it's now the official church of the Royal Air Force. The church houses the RAF regimental standards and a small tribute to the American airmen who died in WWII (left of the inner doors). The quiet, simple crypt houses an eerie collection of 17th-century funerary monuments. **Warning: take care exiting** since traffic drives right through the cobblestoned square. *(At the eastern junction of Aldwych and Strand. ☎7242 8282. ⊖Temple. Open M-F 9am-4pm, Sa-Su 9:30am-3:30pm.)*

GRAY'S INN. With an appropriately colored facade on Gray's Inn Rd., Gray's Inn does not inspire joy from the outside—Dickens dubbed it "that stronghold of melancholy"—but inside, it's actually quite pleasant. Though the **Hall** (on the left as you pass through the Gray's Inn Rd. entrance) is closed to the public, its small chapel, with original 16th-century stained glass, is open weekdays. Don't come for the chapel, which is tiny and unremarkably modern. The main attraction is this picnic-perfect garden area. Francis Bacon maintained chambers here and purportedly designed these **Walks,** the largest and loveliest of any Inn. *(Between Theobald's Rd., Jockey's Fields, High Holborn, and Gray's Inn Rd.; the entrances along Gray's Inn Rd. are not marked—look for the "Private Road" signs. ⊖Chancery Ln. or Holborn. Chapel open M-F 10am-6pm. Gardens open M-F noon-2:30pm.)*

ST. BRIDE'S CHURCH. The unusual spire of Wren's 1675 church is the most imitated piece of architecture in the world: perhaps taking his cue from the church's name, a local baker used it as the model for the first multi-tiered wedding cake. Dubbed "the printers' cathedral" in 1531 when Wyken de Worde set up his press here, it has long been closely associated with nearby newspapermen. More literary associations include Pepys, baptized here, and Milton, who lived in the churchyard, which is today a popular lunchtime destination. Although the modern interior is disappointing, its underbelly is not: the crypt, closed in 1853 following a cholera epidemic, reopened in 1952 as a museum. Eclectic displays include the baker's wife's wedding dress, and bonnet, as well as the remains of a Roman pavement and ditch from about AD 180. This is the eighth church that has been built on this site, making it a place for Christian worship for 1500 years. *(St. Bride's Ave., just off Fleet St. ☎7427 0133; www.stbrides.com. ⊖Blackfriars. Open daily 8am-4:45pm. Lunchtime concerts. Free.)*

ST. DUNSTAN-IN-THE-WEST. An early-Victorian neo-Gothic church crammed between Fleet St. facades, St. Dunstan is most notable for its 1641 clock, whose bells are struck every 15min. by a pair of hammer-wielding muscle-men representing the mythical giant guardians of Lon-

The Mall

Tower of London

Chinatown Gate

don, Gog and Magog. The statue of Elizabeth I adorning the porch was saved from the 16th-century Lud Gate that stood nearby. The church today is a model of ecumenical worship—seven separate and lavish chapels house seven different faiths. While inside, note the elaborate wooden altar screen of the Eastern Orthodox chapel and take a peek at the plaque in memory of "The Honest Solicitor," that rarest inhabitant of Fleet St. *(186a Fleet St. ☎7405 1929; www.stdunstaninthewest.org. ⊖Temple or Chancery Ln. Open Tu 11am-3pm. Free.)*

LINCOLN'S INN

Location: *Between Lincoln's Inn Fields and Chancery Ln. ⊖Chancery Ln. or Holborn.* **Open:** *Chapel M-F noon-2:30pm.* **Admission:** *Free.*

Just to the east of **Lincoln's Inn Fields,** home to Sir John Soane's Museum and the Royal College of Surgeons (see p. 144), sprawl the grounds of Lincoln's Inn. John Donne, St. Thomas More, Walpole, Gladstone, and Disraeli are only a few of the Inn's illustrious former occupants. Since most of the Inn buildings are closed to the public, stroll between the beautiful buildings of **New Square** and picnic in its popular gardens. The **Chapel,** whose foundation stone was laid in 1620 by John Donne, sits above a unique open undercroft—once a popular spot for abandoning babies who would then be brought up in the Inn under the surname Lincoln.

KENSINGTON AND EARL'S COURT

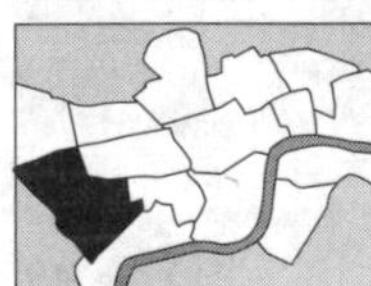

SEE MAP, pp. 364-365

KENSINGTON AND EARL'S COURT QUICKFIND: Discover, p. 8; museums & galleries, p. 145; food, p. 171; pubs, p. 198; entertainment, p. 236; shopping, p. 257; accommodations, p. 286.

Nobody took much notice of Kensington before 1689, but when the newly crowned William III and Mary II decided to move into Kensington Palace high society soon followed. In 1851, the gigantic Great Exhibition brought in enough money to finance the museums and colleges of South Kensington, converting it from a quiet residential suburb to an arts and sciences powerhouse; South Ken remains quiet and intellectual, while the north and west are distinctly posh. Blending into the neighborhood's southwestern corner, **Earl's Court** is a grimier district, full of character. It has also never shaken off its reputation as "Kangaroo Valley," earned in the 1960s and 1970s for its popularity with Australian expats.

KENSINGTON PALACE

Location: *Western edge of Kensington Gardens; enter through the park.* **Contact:** *☎0870 752 7777; www.hrp.org.uk. ⊖High St. Kensington or Queensway.* **Open:** *Daily Mar.-Oct. 10am-6pm; Nov.-Feb. 10am-5pm; last admission 1hr. before closing.* **Admission:** *£10.80, concessions £8.20, age 5-15 £7, family of 5 £32; all £1 discount online. Combo passes with Tower of London or Hampton Court available. Wheelchair accessible. MC/V.*

In 1689, William and Mary commissioned Christopher Wren to remodel Nottingham House into a palace. Kensington remained a principal royal residence until George III decamped to Kew in 1760, but it is still in use—Princess Diana was the most famous recent inhabitant. The palace tour includes the Hanoverian **State Apartments,** with *trompe l'oeil* by William Kent, but they are rather underwhelming. More impressive and more fun is the **Royal Ceremonial Dress Collection,** a magnificent spread of beautifully tailored and embroidered garments. For flashy decadence, look no further than the permanent display of Diana's evening gowns (why yes, that is the 1985 blue silk number in which she famously shimmied alongside John Travolta). For royal-utilitarian-chic, turn to the "Queen's Working Wardrobe" (through July 2005). Nothing is labeled, so you must submit to the audio tour. Those who love gowns, royals, or both, will be in heaven; others should skip it and instead wander through the palace **grounds,** set apart from the rest of Kensington Gardens and free. The gardens encompass Vanbrugh's grand 1704 **Orangery,** built for Queen Anne's dinner parties and now a popular setting for afternoon tea.

"ALBERTOPOLIS"

***Location:** Roughly bounded by Hyde Park to the north, Exhibition Rd. to the east, Cromwell Rd. to the south, and Queen's Gate to the west. ⊖South Kensington or High St. Kensington unless stated otherwise.*

Not to be outdone by self-congratulatory exhibitions of French arts and industry in Paris, Prince Albert, Queen Victoria's husband, proposed to hold a bigger and better "Exhibition of All Nations" in London. The Great Exhibition opened on May 1, 1851, in Hyde Park, housed in the Crystal Palace—a gigantic iron-and-glass structure 1848 ft. long, 408 ft. wide, and tall enough to enclose mature trees. By the time the exhibition was dismantled a year later, six million people had passed through it—as many as saw the Millennium Dome in 2000—and the organizers were left with a £200,000 profit. At Albert's suggestion, the money was used to buy 86 acres of land in South Kensington and found institutions promoting British arts and sciences. Even he would be surprised at how his dream has blossomed; today on this land stand not only the quartet of the **Royal Albert Hall, Victoria & Albert Museum** (p. 138), **Science Museum** (p. 145), and **Natural History Museum** (p. 146), but also the **Royal College of Music,** the **Royal College of Art,** and the **Imperial College of Science and Technology,** all world-renowned institutions in their fields. He might also be surprised to learn that "Albertopolis" is alternatively known as "Coleville" after Sir Henry Cole, the man who actually implemented all of Albert's ideas after the Prince's untimely 1861 death.

ALBERT MEMORIAL. Nightmarish or fairy-tale, depending on your opinion of Victorian High Gothic. George Gilbert Scott's 1868 canopy recently saw sunlight after a 10-year, £11.2 million restoration project. Queen Victoria, so famously devastated by her dear husband's death, decided to immortalize him in gigantic and gold-plated detail. At Albert's blindingly gilded feet, friezes represent the Four Industries, the Four Sciences, and the Four Continents, themes seemingly chosen more for their symmetry than their accuracy. *(☎7495 0916. Kensington Gore, on the edge of Kensington Gardens, just north of Royal Albert Hall. Tours Su 2 and 3pm; 45min. £3.50, concessions £3. The site itself is free. Wheelchair accessible.)*

ROYAL ALBERT HALL. In contrast to the ornate Albert Memorial across the street, the classical Royal Albert Hall is one of the more restrained pieces of Victorian architecture (as Queen Victoria once put it: "It looks like the British Constitution."), though there's nothing restrained about its size. Intended as an all-purpose venue, guests at the 1871 opening immediately noticed one shortcoming of the elliptical design—a booming echo that made it next to useless for musical concerts. Acoustic scientists finally solved the problem in 1968, installing dozens of discs suspended in a haphazard fashion from the dome. The hall has hosted Britain's first full-length indoor marathon, the first public display of electric lighting, and the world premiere of *Hiawatha.* It remains a versatile venue holding everything from boxing to rock concerts, but it's best known as the seat of the Proms classical-music concerts (see p. 236). Cirque du Soleil will hold their acrobatic spectacle *Dralion* here through January 2005. *(☎7589 8212; www.royalalberthall.com. Kensington Gore, just south of Kensington Gardens and the Albert Memorial. Box office at Door 12; open daily 9am-9pm.)*

OTHER KENSINGTON SIGHTS

HOLLAND PARK. Smaller and less touristed than Kensington Gardens, Holland Park probably makes for a better picnic spot or quiet stroll than its famous cousin. Set off from Kensington High St. and full of shady paths, the grounds also offer open fields, popular soccer pitches, tennis courts, Japanese gardens, cafes, and an open-air opera venue (at the Holland Park Theatre, see p. 236). Just up the street at 99 Kensington High St., take an elevator to some more greenery at the famous Rooftop Gardens, a bizarre and dazzling few acres that offer great views of the whole neighborhood. *(Bordered by Kensington High St., Holland Walk, and Abbotsbury Rd. Enter at Commonwealth Institute. ☎7471 9813; www.rbk.gov.uk/ParksnandGardens. ⊖High St. Kensington. Open daily dawn-dusk. Free.)*

LEIGHTON HOUSE. The home of painter Lord Fredric Leighton (1830-1896) is a perfect example of all that is endearing and ridiculous in Victorian tastes. Inspired by his trips to the Middle East, Leighton's home combines oriental pastiche, neoclassicism, and English homeliness. The centerpiece is the Arab Hall, a Moorish extravaganza of tilework and mosaic complete with fountain and carpets—the walls bear one of Europe's best collections of medieval Arabian tile. The other rooms contain works by Leighton and his contemporaries, including Millais, Tintoretto, and Edward Burne-Jones. Good for a quick peek, but unless you're already a fan you'll likely be disappointed. *(12 Holland Park Rd. ☎7602 3316; www.rbkc.gov.uk/leightonhousemuseum. ⊖High St. Kensington. Open M and W-Su 11am-5:30pm. Adults £3, concessions £1, family £6. 50min. tours W-Th 2:30pm, £3. 50min. audioguide, £3. MC/V £5 min.)*

KNIGHTSBRIDGE & BELGRAVIA

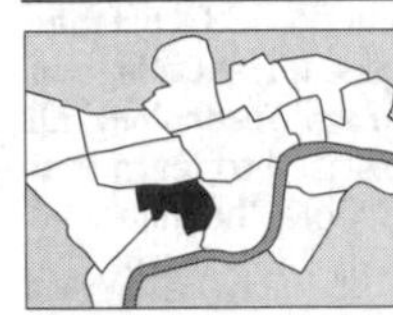

SEE MAP, p. 366

KNIGHTSBRIDGE & BELGRAVIA QUICKFIND: Discover, p. 8; food, p. 172; pubs, p. 198; nightlife, p. 211; shopping, p. 258; accommodations, p. 290.

Currently home to London's most expensive stores, it's hard to imagine that in the 18th century **Knightsbridge** was a racy district known for its taverns and highwaymen, taking advantage of the area's position just outside The City's jurisdiction. Gentrification has merely pushed the highway robbery indoors—just take a look at the price tags in Harrods and Harvey Nichols.

Squeezed between Knightsbridge, Chelsea, and Westminster, the wedge-shaped district of **Belgravia,** like Mayfair and Kensington before it, was catapulted to respectability by the presence of royalty. When George IV decided to make Buckingham Palace his official residence in the 1820s, developers were quick to build suitably grand buildings for aristocratic hangers-on nearby. **Belgrave Square,** the setting for *My Fair Lady*, is the most impressive of the set-pieces, now so expensive that the aristocracy has had to sell out to foreign governments. The primary reason most travelers come here is to get their passports replaced.

APSLEY HOUSE

Location: *Hyde Park Corner.* ***Contact:*** *☎7499 5676; www.english-heritage.org.uk/london. ⊖Hyde Park Corner.* ***Open:*** *Tu-Su 10am-5pm (Apr.-Oct.), 10am-4pm (Nov.-Mar.).* ***Admission:*** *£4.50, students concessions £3, children 5-18 £2.30, under-5 free. Joint ticket w/Wellington Arch £6/4.20/3/free. Free audio guide. Wheelchair accessible. MC/V.*

Named for Baron Apsley, the house later known as "No. 1, London" was bought in 1817 by the Duke of Wellington, whose heirs still occupy a modest suite of rooms on the top floor. The opulent house itself warrants a visit but most come for Wellington's fine art collection, much of which was given by the crowned heads of Europe following the Battle of Waterloo. Most of the old masters hang in the **Waterloo Gallery,** where the Duke held his annual Waterloo banquet around the stupendous silver centerpiece donated by the Portuguese government (now displayed in the dining room). X-ray analysis revealed that the famous Goya portrait of Wellington on horseback—the model for a thousand pub signs—was originally of Napoleon's brother Joseph Bonaparte. (Wellington himself didn't enjoy it for different reasons: he felt he looked "too heavy.") The Duke had great respect for his diminutive rival, Napolean, and a massive nude statue of the great Emperor in the main staircase proves that height is immaterial when you can be immortalized as a 25-ft. Roman god. In the basement gallery are caricatures from Wellington's later political career—his nickname "the Iron Duke" comes not from his steadfastness in battle, but from the metal shutters he put up on his windows to protect himself from stone-throwing reformers. Take the free audio guide so you don't miss the interesting history.

WELLINGTON ARCH

Location: *Hyde Park Corner.* ***Contact:*** *☎7930 2726; www.english-heritage.org.uk/london. ⊖Hyde Park Corner.* ***Open:*** *Apr.-Oct. W-Su 10am-5pm; Nov.-Mar. W-Su 10am-4pm.* ***Admission:*** *£3, concessions £2.30, children (ages 5-16) £1.50. Joint tickets w/Apsley House (see above). Wheelchair accessible. MC/V.*

Standing at the center of London's most infamous traffic intersection, the Wellington Arch was long ignored by tourists and Londoners alike. All that changed in April 2001, when the completion of a long restoration project revealed the interior to the public for the first time. Built in 1825, the "Green Park Arch" was meant to form part of a processional route to London, part of George IV's scheme to beautify the city. Intense uglification followed shortly, though, when the newly re-christened "Wellington Arch" was encumbered by an embarrassingly large statue of the Duke. The government immediately ordered the statue's removal, but desisted when Wellington threatened to resign from the army. The figure was finally replaced in 1912 by the even bigger (though less offensive) Quadriga of Peace. For a brief period in the last century, the Arch was home to London's smallest police station. Inside the arch, exhibitions on the building's history and the changing nature of war memorials play second fiddle to the two spectacular viewing platforms.

BROMPTON ORATORY

Location: *Thurloe Pl., Brompton Rd.* ***Contact:*** *☎7808 0900. ⊖South Kensington or Knightsbridge.* ***Open:*** *Daily 6:30am-8pm (M closes 7pm), except during frequent short services. Solemn Mass Su 11am.* ***Admission:*** *Free. Call for wheelchair access.*

On entering this church, properly called the Oratory of St. Philip Neri, you are transported to a world of ornate Baroque flourishes and lofty domes. London's second-largest Catholic church, the Oratory was built from 1874-1884 and was deliberately designed with a nave wider than St. Paul's. One of the altars was considered by the KGB to be the best dead-drop in London—until 1985, agents left microfilm and other documents behind a statue for other agents to retrieve. The church lives up to its reputation for music during its **Solemn Masses,** sung in Latin.

MARYLEBONE & REGENT'S PARK

MARYLEBONE & REGENT'S PARK QUICKFIND: Discover, p. 9; museums & galleries, p. 147; food, p. 173; pubs, p. 199; entertainment, p. 237; accommodations, p. 291.

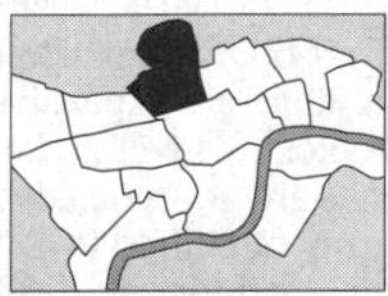

SEE MAP, p. 367

London's most beautiful park, plus a fictional sleuth and some vaguely creepy wax idols make up this neighborhood. There's a sheen of lunatic diversity evident in Marylebone's more notable attractions, and its character is appropriately scattered. Along the northern edge of the area lie the unavoidably touristy bits, with **Madame Tussaud's** and the entrance to **Regent's Park** drawing crowds to their **Baker Street** environs. To the west, **Edgware Road** is the center of London's large Lebanese community. A few Oxford Street-like attractions line the southernmost edge, and smack down in the middle of its residential Georgian heart lies the unbeatable Wallace Collection. This wide swath of fine 18th-century architecture has been home to famous residents, including Elizabeth Barrett, John Milton, and John Stuart Mill. The area's most famous resident is undoubtedly Sherlock Holmes, who called **221b Baker Street** home. No. 221 is actually the headquarters of the Abbey National bank (there was never a 221b), but, unsurprisingly, the Baker St. area has more than its share of Holmes-related tourist traps.

REGENT'S PARK

Location: *500 acres of gardens stretching north from Marylebone Rd. to Camden Town.* ***Contact:*** *☎7486 7905; police ☎7935 1259. ⊖Baker St., Regent's Park, Great Portland St., or Camden Town.* ***Open:*** *Daily 7am-dusk.* ***Admission:*** *Free.*

As the most attractive and popular park in London, Regent's Park has a wide range of landscapes from soccer-scarred fields to Italian-style formal gardens. However, it's all very different from the plans John Nash had in mind when he set out to redevelop the hunting ground and farmlands of Marylebone Park in the early 1800s. Nash's vision was a secluded paradise of wealthy villas hidden among exclusive, private gardens; fortunately for us commonfolk, Parliament intervened in 1811 and opened the space to all.

Most of the park's top attractions and activities lie along its **Inner Circle,** an exclusive-sounding road that separates the regal, flower-filled **Queen Mary's Gardens** from the rest of the park. Within the Gardens, the **Rose Garden** stands out and the well-muscled **Triton Fountain** boasts one sexy manfish; while the northwest quadrant is occupied by a fantastic **Open-Air Theatre** (see p. 237). Arching around Inner Circle is the **Boating Lake,** though boaters are confined to the central portion—the northern waters are reserved for massive amounts of duck love as the waterfowl breeding center for all London parks. You can rent a rowboat for use on the main lake; children can enjoy themselves on pedalos in the tiny **Children's Boating Lake.** *(Open Apr.-Sept. 10:30am-5pm, later Jul.-Aug. Rowboats £4.50 for 30min., £6 per 1hr.; under 14 £3/£4; £5 deposit. Discounts before 1pm; under 16 with adult only. Pedalos £3 per 20min. MC/V.)* Of the 40 villas planned by Nash, eight were built, and only two remain. After decades of housing charities, hospitals, and learned societies, **The Holme** and **St. John's Lodge** have returned to their intended function as private residences for the unimaginably rich. On the northern edge of Inner Circle, the formal **St. John's Lodge Gardens**—a blaze of lavender entered through an easy-to-miss gate near the Royal Parks office—look like something straight out of *The Secret Garden* and remain open to the public. Other buildings in the park include the **London Central Mosque** west of Boating Lake; the large red-brick complex of **Regent's College;** to the south of Inner Circle, and neo-Georgian **Winfield House,** the residence of the US ambassador, set within the park's western edge. And if you're looking for a rewarding climb, the impressive views of **Primrose Hill** lie just north of Regent's Park proper.

LONDON ZOO

Location: *Main gate on Outer Circle, Regent's Park.* ***Contact:*** *☎7722 3333; www.londonzoo.com. ⊖Camden Town plus 12min. walk guided by signs, or short ride on Bus #274 from Camden Town station. Or a 15min. walk through Regent's Park.* ***Open:*** *Daily Apr.-Oct. 10am-5:30p; Nov.-Mar. 10am-4pm. Last admission 1hr. before closing.* ***Admission:*** *£13, concessions £11, ages 3-16 £9.75, family of 4 £41. Wheelchair accessible. AmEx/MC/V.*

First opened in 1826, the London Zoo can be alternately great and frustrating; most exhibits are expansive and completely modern, but a few outdated bars-and-cement enclosures will make the softer hearts in the crowd cringe. The very earliest buildings are now considered too small to house animals, and instead test parents with an array of stuffed toys at exorbitant prices. Perennial favorites include the itch-inducing corridors of **BUGS!** and the jungle-gym spotted **Primate** house, but the big news here is reptilian: in June 2004, the brand-new **Komodo Dragon** exhibit bared its (impressive) fangs for the first time. For cuddlier fun head to the **Penguin Pool,** where the fat little birds waddle around on sleek structures designed by the avant-garde firm Tecton in 1934. If the cool, white architecture and clean lines are straight out of the *Bauhaus*, the spiral slide is pure Fisher Price. Pick up a *Daily Events* leaflet to catch all the free special displays and keeper talks.

MADAME TUSSAUD'S AND THE LONDON PLANETARIUM

Location: *Marylebone Rd.* ***Contact:*** *☎0870 400 3000; www.madame-tussauds.com. ⊖Baker St.* ***Open:*** *M-F 9:30am-5:30pm, Sa-Su 9am-6pm; during Jul.-Aug. daily 9am-6pm. Planetarium shows start every 30min.* ***Admission:*** *All tickets sold at both Madame Tussaud's and the Planetarium, valid for both. Prices depend on day of the week, entrance time, and season. £11-22, under 16 £6-17, concessions £9-18; option to include "Chamber Live" exhibit adds £3. Advance booking (by phone or online) £1 extra; groups (10+) approx. £1.50 less per person. Wheelchair accessible. AmEx/MC/V.*

Together, Madame Tussaud's and the London Planetarium constitute London's third-largest tourist attraction, and by far its most undeserving round-the-block queue. Unless you enjoy spending hours waiting outside and paying exorbitant prices, make sure to book ahead, get together with at least nine fellow-sufferers to use the group entrance, or hit during off-peak hours (late afternoon). The Planetarium and Madame T's are internally connected and can be visited in either order. But unless you've got a wealthy backer or a strong wax fetish, our best advice is to avoid going in the first place.

MADAME TUSSAUD'S. An indisputably unique 90min. experience, dodging the flash trajectories of your camera-happy covisitors and wondering how Michael Jackson can look so real while poor Liz Taylor gets made up in brothel-appropriate cosmetic confusion. No question, there's something innately fascinating about the eerie wax lookalikes on display, and ogling the best of them makes for a fun photo-op or two, but you'll spend more time being jostled around the crowded space than enjoying the effigies. It all concludes with **The Spirit of London,** an odd taxi-coaster ride through the city's history (it was built on bad animatronics and overlapping sound-bytes, apparently).

THE LONDON PLANETARIUM. Nothing wildly flashy nor densely scientific. This 20min. breeze through our solar system (and beyond) manages to avoid winningly-*both* Disneyworld corn and science class snoozyness. The overhead picture is snazzy enough to draw even the most earthbound passenger off the ground for a few moments. Don't expect to learn much or be blown away, but do cap off your waxy misadventure with this relaxing diversion.

PORTLAND PLACE

Oxford Circus or Regent's Park.

Perhaps the handsomest street in London (when constructed it was at least the widest), Portland Pl. was first laid out by Robert and James Adam in the 18th century. Its attraction today lies in the great variety of architectural styles on display. Design buffs will enjoy it, although others might not be overly dazzled. The street is a natural home for the **Royal Institute of British Architects** (RIBA), whose 1932 home is the most imposing building on Portland Pl.—particularly at night, when the facade is lit an eerie blue. Parts of the building are open to the public, including three exhibition galleries, an impressive architecture bookshop, and a small cafe/restaurant. *(66 Portland Pl. ☎ 7307 3888; www.architecture.com. Open Tu 10am-8pm, W-F 10am-5pm, Sa 10am-1:30pm. Free. Wheelchair accessible.)* Guarding the entrance to Portland Pl. from Regent St., the curved facade of the **Broadcasting Center** is instantly recognizable to all Britons as the symbol of the BBC (and still their main center for radio production). On the facade is Eric Gill's sculpture of Shakespeare's *Prospero* and *Ariel*, together with the BBC motto, "Nation shall speak peace unto nation." Renovated in 1975 and with a modern interior there is not much to see in **All Souls Langham Place,** originally designed by John Nash. *(☎ 7580 3522; www.allsouls.org. Open M-Sa 9:30am-6pm, Su 9am-9pm.)*

EDGWARE ROAD

Marble Arch or Edgware Rd.

Once part of a major Roman route out of London, Edgware Rd. is now the center of London's large Lebanese community, though it is popular with Middle Easterners of all nationalities. Lined with countless restaurants, shops, and grocery markets, Edgware Rd. is full of affordable hidden gems and fantastic food. From Marble Arch to Marylebone Rd., middle-aged men converse in Arabic over strong coffee and *hookahs* while veiled women visit English businesses signposted in Arabic.

NOTTING HILL

NOTTING HILL QUICKFIND: Discover, p. 9; food, p. 174; pubs, p. 200; nightlife, p. 212; entertainment, p. 237; shopping, p. 259; accommodations, p. 292.

SEE MAP, p. 359

Notting Hill has its best bits outside, and is ideal for a nice stroll. At the south, **Notting Hill Gate** is a relatively nondescript road of 1950s facades, and has a good range of shops and bars and is less posh than the rest of the neighborhood. To the north, **Portobello Road** houses a strong West Indian community, characterized by the reggae-heavy record stores and market stalls selling Caribbean foods. Intersecting Portobello Rd. north of the Westway, **Golborne Road** has its own colorful street scene, with Moroccan and Portuguese shops and cafes. Fans of Modernist architect Erno Goldfinger (see **Two Willow Road,** p. 122) will love the famous utilitarian high-rise **Trellick Tower** at the end of Golborne Rd. If you plan to visit Notting Hill, try to do so on Friday or Saturday, when the world-famous **Portobello Market** (see p. 259) is held. It spreads from Golborne Rd. all the way down Portobello Rd. and the surrounding streets, almost to Notting Hill Gate itself.

KIOSKS. Get tourist information from new computer kiosks on street corners. They offer BBC news, free outgoing e-mail, maps, and weather reports.

THE SOUTH BANK

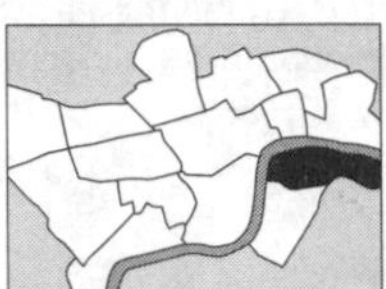

SEE MAP, pp. 368-369

THE SOUTH BANK QUICKFIND: Discover, p. 10; museums & galleries, p. 148; food, p. 176; pubs, p. 200; nightlife, p. 212; entertainment, p. 238; accommodations, p. 292.

During the Middle Ages, the South Bank was outside the jurisdiction of the City authorities, and thus, all manner of illicit attractions sprouted in "the Borough" at the southern end of London Bridge. Bankside soon became the city's entertainment center; citizens had to navigate the frozen Thames in the winter. After the Civil War, the South Bank's fortunes turned to the sea, as wharves groaned under the weight of cargoes from across the Empire. By the time shipping moved elsewhere in the late 1950s, the seeds of regeneration had been sown. From the 1951 Festival of Britain sprang the Royal Festival Hall, the nucleus of the South Bank Centre and heart of the new South Bank. The National Theatre followed 20 years later, and development has continued at such a pace that the South Bank is now once more the heart of the London art scene, with a visitor-friendly but decidedly untouristy conglomeration of art galleries, theatre, and music halls.

LONDON EYE

Location: *Jubilee Gardens, between County Hall and the Festival Hall.* ⊖*Waterloo.* ***Contact:*** *☎0870 444 5544; www.ba-londoneye.com.* ***Open:*** *Daily late May to mid-Sept. 9:30am-10pm; Apr. to late May and late Sept. 10:30am-8pm; Jan.-Mar. and Oct.-Dec. 10:30am-7pm. Open daily 8:30am-6:30pm. Tickets: Buy tickets from box office at the corner of County Hall before joining the queue at the Eye; advance booking recommended but check the weather. £11.50, concessions £9, under 16 £5.75. Wheelchair accessible.*

London's most recent poster-attraction. Also known as the Millennium Wheel, at 135m (430 ft.) the British Airways London Eye is the biggest observational wheel in the world, taller than St. Paul's Cathedral and visible from miles around. The lines are millennium-long, don't come in the middle of the day, you'll be there forever. The price is a bit steep, but to get the broadest view of the city, pay up and realize how huge London actually is. The ellipsoid glass "pods" give uninterrupted views from the top of each 30min. revolution: on clear days you can see Windsor in the west, though eastward views are blocked by skyscrapers farther down the river. Try to come at sunset when the backdrop is lovely too, otherwise you might find yourself high above in a sea of grey. In-flight guides are available in County Hall (£2.50). You can rent a private pod, call for details.

TATE MODERN AND THE MILLENNIUM BRIDGE

Location: *Queen's Walk, Bankside.* ⊖*Southwark, Blackfriars, or St. Paul's (across the bridge). Wheelchair accessible.*

Coupled together on Bankside are the overwhelming hit and the underwhelming miss of London's millennial celebrations. **Tate Modern** (see p. 137), created from the shell of former power station, is the modern art beacon of recent years, as visually arresting as its contents are thought-provoking. Built to link Tate to the City—with a proposed grand walkway stretching from Tate to St. Paul's—the **Millennium Bridge** outdid the Dome for underachievement, both visually and structurally. It was completed six months too late for the Y2K festivities, and closed for structural work soon after. It's open now, a futuristic walkway across the Thames. Though not particularly stunning, it is popular and practical, not only because it links two key neighborhoods, but because it's for pedestrians only: you can now enjoy the views mid-river without car-horns and careening buses.

SHAKESPEARE'S GLOBE THEATRE

Location: *Bankside, close to Bankside pier.* ***Contact:*** *☎7902 1500; www.shakespeares-globe.org. ⊖Southwark or London Bridge.* ***Open:*** *Daily May-Sept. 9am-noon (exhibit and tours) and 1-4pm (exhibit only), Oct.-Apr. 10am-5pm.* ***Tours:*** *Run daily every 30min. May-Sept. 9am-noon and Oct.-Apr 10am-5pm; 10am-noon when there's a matinee.* ***Admission:*** *Oct-Apr. £8, concessions £6.50, ages 5-15 £5.50, family of 5 £24, May-Sept. each 50p more. Wheelchair accessible. For info on performances,* *see p. 239.*

This incarnation of the Globe is faithful to the original, thatch roof and all. The original burned down in 1613 after a 14-year run as the Bard's preferred playhouse. Today's reconstruction had its first full season in 1997, and now stands as the cornerstone of the International Shakespeare Globe Centre. The informative exhibit inside covers the history of both and includes displays on costumes and customs of the theatre, and info on other prominent playwrights of the era. There's also an interactive display where you get to trade lines with recorded Globe actors. Try to arrive in time for a tour of the theater itself; it's no fun to learn all about it and then not see the real thing. Tours that run during a matinee skip the Globe, but are the *only* way to gain admission to the neighboring **Rose Theatre,** where both Shakespeare and Christopher Marlowe performed.

SOUTHWARK CATHEDRAL

Location: *Montague Close.* ***Contact:*** *☎7367 6700; www.dswark.org. ⊖London Bridge.* ***Open:*** *Daily 8am-6pm. Audioguide: £5, concessions £4, ages 5-15 £2.50. Photography: Camera permit £1.50; video permit £5.* ***Admission:*** *Free; £3.50 suggested donation. There is a group charge, and groups are asked to book in advance. Wheelchair accessible.*

A site of worship since 606, the cathedral has undergone numerous transformations in the last 1400 years. The majestic main chapel, once the entire church, is full of historical connections. Shakespeare's brother Edmond is buried here, and a rare stained glass window depicts charac-

the BIG $plurge

Two Views For Two

Forget the fancy restaurant dinners and walks on the beach. For a different kind of romantic evening, reserve a "Cupid's Capsule" just for two on the **London Eye,** and whisk your significant other 135m into the air. What could be more charming than cuddling up in your private glass pod as you slowly ascend to the top of the Eye and revel in the spectacular 360-degree birds-eye views?

After returning to the ground, continue the evening of sightseeing with a leisurely **champagne cruise** on the Silver Bonito boat. The boat departs from the pier at the Eye. St. Paul's, the Houses of Parliament, the Tower of London, the Globe Theatre, and the Tate Modern are all visible from the boat. The cruise includes live commentary, sundeck seating, and covers in case of rain. On a clear night, you can watch the sun set.

The **London Eye and River Cruise Experience** package guarantees fast-track entry (no long lines!) to the London Eye, followed by a 45-minute champagne cruise, souvenir guidebook and single-use flash camera (£50). Book on www.ba-londoneye.com, ☎870 500 0600, or in person at County Hall ticket office.

the local story

Going Global

The first (Shakepeare's) Globe burnt down in 1613 as a result of some sound effects gone wrong. The attic above the stage served as a "orchestra pit," where various sound effects were created. On that fateful day in 1613 a small canon was set off in the attic gallery as the sound was required for the play, *Henry VIII*. Unfortunately the staff perhaps didn't think about the large thick ring of straw that made up the roof. It caught quick fire and the rest is history.

The groundlings (commoners) would have the standing room area right in front of the stage (still do). They'd pay 1 penny to come see the show, and that was around a tenth of their weekly salary. We can only guess as to the lack of comfort in the pit: the alleged capacity was close to three thousand. And bathroom services were unheard of, largely because exiting the theatre would mean that not only would you lose your spot, but you might have to pay again. So groundlings relieved themselves on the spot. Lovely. The higher classes who purchased seats were allowed to use the stairwells as restrooms, a luxury the common man could only dream of. So while you enjoy the show today appreciate the modern WCs.

ters from Shakespearean plays. In the rear of the nave there are four smaller chapels, the northernmost Chapel of St. Andrew is specifically dedicated to those living with and dying from HIV and AIDS. In 2001 a new conference center and cafe were opened on the grounds, by Nelson Mandela, as part of the millennium celebrations. Near the centre, the **archaeological gallery** is actually a small excavation by the cathedral wall, revealing a 1st-century Roman road along with Saxon, Norman, and 18th-century remains. Various treasures from the cathedral's facelifts are on display; don't miss the medieval wooden decorations, including a scary one of the devil swallowing Judas. Next to the 13th-century **north transept,** the **Harvard chapel,** complete with stained-glass Veritas shield, commemorates John Harvard, who was baptized here in his parish church in 1607.

HMS BELFAST

i ***Location:*** *At the end of Morgans Ln. off Tooley St., also accessible via the Queen's Walk.* ***Contact:*** *☎ 7940 6300; www.iwm.org.uk. ⊖London Bridge.* ***Open:*** *Daily Mar.-Oct. 10am-6pm, Nov.-Feb. 10am-5pm. Last admission 45min. before closing.* ***Admission:*** *£7, concessions £5, under 16 free.*

This enormous cruiser was one of the most powerful ships in the world when launched in 1938. The *Belfast* led the landing at Normandy on D-Day and supported UN forces in Korea before graciously retiring in 1965. In 1971 she went on display as part of the Imperial War Museum and still holds her regal floating spot on the Thames, boasting a prodigious mid-river view. Children will love clambering over the decks and aiming the 40mm anti-aircraft guns at dive-bombing seagulls. A climb down the narrow steps shows the inner-workings of the carrier. You can tour the kitchens and operations room, where waxworks and sound recordings recreate the sinking of the German battleship *Scharnhorst* in 1943. The steep staircases and ladders from deck to deck add to the realism of it all, but make exploring the boat a physical challenge; on-deck benches are pleasant resting spots.

THE SOUTH BANK CENTRE

i ***Location:*** *On the riverbank between Hungerford and Waterloo Bridges; road access from Belvedere Rd. and Upper Ground. ⊖Waterloo or Embankment (across the Hungerford foot bridge).* *See also: For Festival Hall, Purcell Room, Queen Elizabeth Hall, and National Film Theatre, p. 238; for Hayward Gallery, p. 150*

With riverside state-of-the art buildings, this symphony of concrete is Britain's premier performance center. Its nucleus is the **Royal Festival Hall,** a piece of 1950s architecture that will begin a massive improvement scheme in 2005. The gigantic lobby—whose stepped ceiling is actually the underside of the concert hall—often hosts free events, from photo exhibits to jazz concerts. Near the Festival Hall, the **Purcell Room** and **Queen Elizabeth Hall** cater to intimate audiences and smaller concerts, while just behind it, **Hayward Gallery** shelters excellent shows of modern art. On the embankment beneath Waterloo Bridge, the **National Film Theatre** offers global cinematic fare, while past the bridge looms the **National Theatre.** This sleek modern theater operates, join a 1hr. backstage tour. *(☎7452 3000; www.nationaltheatre.org.uk. Tours M-Sa 10:15am, 12:15pm and 5:15pm. £5, concessions £4.25.)*

GABRIEL'S WHARF AND OXO TOWER

Location: *Between Upper Ground and the Thames. ⊖Blackfriars, Southwark, or Waterloo. Wheelchair accessible.*

The most colorful and least kitschy new additions to the South Bank are a result of the dedicated efforts of the Coin Street Community Builders (CSCB), a non-profit development company which has established the area as a model of integrated, affordable living. **Gabriel's Wharf** is a craftsy market-like area where little shops stretch from the water down into the surrounding streets. A few steps away is the Art Deco **OXO Tower,** built by a company that once supplied instant beef-stock to the entire British Empire. OXO Tower is famous for its clever subversion of rules prohibiting advertising on buildings, the windows subtly spell out "OXO." The Tower is now enveloped in the brick mass of the **OXO Tower Wharf,** another Coin Street development. Full of tiny boutiques and workshops run by some of London's innovative young designers. A free public viewing gallery on the eighth floor allows for prime views over the South Bank area, and connects to a bar and restaurant.

OTHER SOUTH BANK SIGHTS

VINOPOLIS. This Dionysian Disneyland bills itself as a *City of Wine*. The enterprise offers patrons an interactive (yes, that means samples) tour of the world's wine regions, starting with France and working eastward. European grapes hog the limelight, but there are also displays on less-well-known vini-cultural centers, like India, Thailand and Chile. In a liquor-y partnership, Bombay Sapphire gin cocktails are served in a futuristic blue bar. If you feel a tad too amateurish, a wine tasting lesson can be had for a mere £2. A truly extravagant production, the Vinopolis experience can be time-consuming—but with five tastings (from a choice of dozens) included in the price, by the end of the tour you'll be happy to have abided. *(1 Bank End, at the end of Clink St. ☎7940 8301; www.vinopolis.co.uk. ⊖London Bridge. Open M noon-9pm, Tu-Su noon-6pm. Last admission 2hr. before closing. £12.50, seniors £11.50, under 16 free but no wine; book of 5 extra tasting vouchers £2.50. Wheelchair accessible.)*

OLD OPERATING THEATRE AND HERB GARRET. Tucked into the loft of a 19th-century church is the oldest restored operating theater in the world. No doubt highly dramatic in the days before anesthesia, the surgeon's chair and restraining straps await their next patient. A fearsome array of saws and knives substantiates the exhibition on surgical history, accompanied by plenty of amputation illustrations. The neighboring **herb garret** smells heavenly; it was used by the hospital apothecary to prepare medicines. A 1718 cure for venereal disease instructs the practitioner to "take gardensnails, cleansed and bruised 6 gallons..." The multitude of frightful medical instruments, such as a trepanning drill, used to relieve headaches by boring a hole in the skull, attest to the beauty of modern medicine. *(9a St. Thomas's St. ☎7955 4791; www.thegarret.org.uk. ⊖London Bridge. Open daily 10:30am-5pm. Closed Dec. 12-Jan. 5. £4.25, concessions £3.25, children £2.50, family £11.)*

GOLDEN HINDE. This boat is a full-sized replica of Sir Francis Drake's famed world-circling vessel. The replica has outsailed the original since its launch in 1973, clocking up over 140,000 miles, rounding the globe twice, and starring in films from *Swashbuckler* to *Shogun*. Its lavish exterior leads to bare inside space, visitors can roam

the BIG $plurge

So Many Bottles, So Little Time

Vinopolis–the City of Wine–more like a universe. The masterminds have created a tour of the world following the all-important thread of viticulture. This tour starts with news on wine from Roman times, before heading to France: Bordeaux and then Rhone. You follow pictures, videos and grapes, until coming to Burgundy and then everyone's favorite, Champagne. You then arrive at Tasting Table 1. The spread of bottles are there for your choosing, ask one of the pros to pour you a taste. And another. Off again to Portugal, Germany, Chile, Argentina, and California. Table 2 comes out of nowhere, but everyone's fine with that, because it means more wine. Another taste and off you go again to far-away lands. You can also take a 30 minute wine-tasting class (£2), where you will learn to swish, gurgle and spit, minus the dentist.

The basic package includes 5 tastes, a Sapphire Gin Cocktail, and the tour (£12.50). However, we recommend the Ultimate Package (£20), which would satisfy even the heartiest drinkers.

1 Bank End, at the end of Clink St. ☎7940 8301; www.vinopolis.co.uk. ⊖London Bridge. Open M noon-9pm, Tu-Su noon-6pm. Last admission 2hr. before closing.

the deck and the sparsely-furnished rooms, but after ducking beneath the low ceilings in the gloomy innards of the ship, you'll be left wondering not only how Drake's crew managed it for a few months, but why you're paying for the privilege. *(St. Mary Overie's Dock, Cathedral St. ☎0870 011 8700. ⊖London Bridge. Open daily 9am-5:30pm. £3.50, concessions £3, children £2.50, family £10.)*

HAY'S GALLERIA. Glass-topped, and lined with uninspiring stores and restaurants, **Hay's Galleria** was once Hay's Wharf, one of the busiest docks in London and frequented by clippers such as the Cutty Sark (see p. 129). It was built as a storage space for teas; now, you can get an overpriced cup of your own from one of the many cafes in the space. Full of independent prints, some on loan from the Tate, the independent **Hay's Gallery** presents more compelling browsing than the stores around it. *(London Bridge City, off Tooley St. ☎7940 7770. ⊖London Bridge. Wheelchair accessible.)*

BUTLERS WHARF. Just east of Tower Bridge, Butlers Wharf is still criss-crossed by overhead walkways originally intended for cargo transport. The narrow cobbled streets contrast with the walking paths along the water. During the 1970s Butlers Wharf became home to London's largest artists' colonies. The party ended in 1980, when developers moved in: today, the wharf is lined with various shops and restaurants taking advantage of the fantastic views, including Cantina del Ponte (see p. 176).

LONDON AQUARIUM. As aquariums go, this is a small fish in a big sea, although it's the only one around. The main attractions are two three-story ocean tanks—one holds Atlantic fish, the other Pacific fish, including sharks. They're most impressive because of their size (the tanks not the sharks). Children can pet rays and fish at the two petting tanks if they don't mind getting wet all the way up to the shoulder. *(☎7967 8000; www.londonaquarium.co.uk. Open daily 10am-6pm, last admission 5pm. £8.75, concessions £6.50, under 14 £5.25, family of 4 £25. Wheelchair accessible.)*

DALÍ UNIVERSE. The posters scream, "500 works of art." This tells you all you need to know about this "gallery": it's quantity over quality. The entrance is a bizarre, blacked out tunnel with cut-out images of Salvador and Dalían quotations contrived to make the artist seem fabulously crazy. Almost all the works in this collection are multiple-run prints, castings, or reproductions. There are a few paintings. Only real Dalí enthusiasts will find it worth it, a smaller but better set of Dalís are free viewing in the Tate Modern (see p. 137). But if those famous melting watches and lithographs are your thing, spend on. Can't miss: one of Dali's custom designed sofas shaped like Mae West's lips, although you can't sit on it. *(☎7620 2720; www.daliuniverse.com. Open daily 10am-5:30pm. £12.50, concessions £11. Wheelchair accessible. AmEx/MC/V.)*

LONDON DUNGEON. The most effective instrument of torture here is the unbelievably long queue, although the fake urine smell inside is a close second. The dark, winding and slightly mildew-y inside offers imitations of various London horrors, from the Great Fire to Jack the Ripper. Face-painted employees help you along the self-guided descent through the dungeons. A Wicked Women gallery accuses Anne Boleyn of witchcraft; in "Judgement Day," visitors are convicted, sentenced, and hauled off to be executed for being gullible enough to spend money on this grisly themepark. To take part in the macabre experience, arrive when it opens or buy tickets in advance. *(28-34 Tooley St. ☎0207 403 7224; www.thedungeons.com. ⊖London Bridge. Open daily summer 9:30am-7:30pm; winter 10am-5:30pm £13.95, concessions £11.25, children £9.95. Groups over 20 get in the still slow fast-track line.)*

THE WEST END

OXFORD STREET & REGENT STREET

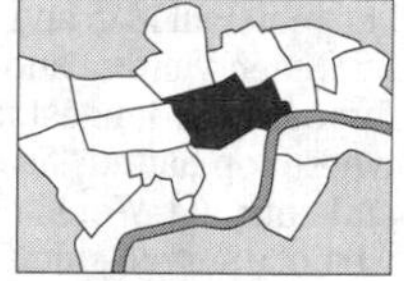

SEE MAP, p. 354

OXFORD STREET & REGENT STREET QUICKFIND: Discover, p. 10; museums & galleries, p. 150; food, p. 177; pubs, p. 201; nightlife, p. 212; entertainment, p. 240; shopping, p. 261; accommodations, p. 292.

OXFORD CIRCUS AND ENVIRONS

⊖Oxford Circus

Oscar Wilde famously quipped that **Oxford Street** is "all street and no Oxford"; there's precious little of beauty or historic interest on London's biggest commercial thoroughfare (so named because it follows the path of an ancient Roman road that leads to Oxford). Still, if you're intent on a photo-op with end-to-end double-decker buses, it's the place to be. **Regent Street** is more upmarket, as well as more imposing, even though none of Nash's original Regency arcades have survived. For some reason, **Oxford Circus** is one of London's most visited landmarks, although it's actually just a busy junction where Regent St. and Oxford St. cross. At Christmas, the crowds are so crazy that police control the crosswalks.

CARNABY STREET. In the 1960s, Carnaby St. was the center of Swinging London, a hotbed of sex, fashion, and youth culture. Since then, it's spent 30 years as a lurid tourist trap, with little more than postcards and Tube t-shirts. With a recent influx of big-name boutiques and a smattering of hot cafes and restaurants, though, it looks as though Carnaby could start to swing again. During the early evenings, a large after-five crowd of yuppies and shoppers lingers around Carnaby St. pubs and bars.

MAYFAIR & ST. JAMES'S

MAYFAIR & ST. JAMES'S QUICKFIND: Discover, p. 10; museums & galleries, p. 111; food, p. 178; pubs, p. 201; entertainment, p. 240; shopping, p. 264; accommodations, p. 292.

The average tourist doesn't linger in pricey, solemnly superior Mayfair and St. James's—many would-be sights, such as St. James's Palace and the gentlemen's clubs, are strictly out-of-bounds to all but aristocrats. Meanwhile, haughty sales people and outrageous prices do their best to keep window shoppers on the streets. On the other hand, the combination of wealth and conservatism make the area one of the few in London to retain its historic atmosphere, and this, together with its parks and art galleries, makes Mayfair well worth a few hours' stroll. Gaze at the riches you'll never possess, then head over to Soho and drink your cares away.

PICCADILLY

Piccadilly Circus or Green Park. For details of **Piccadilly Circus,** *see Soho, p. 113.*

Frilly ruffs were big business in the 16th century—one tailor made enough money from manufacturing these "piccadills" to build himself a fancy mansion called, aptly enough, 'Pickadill House'. The name stuck, though the house and the tailoring industry are long gone. Piccadilly is no longer the preferred address of gentlemen, but as home to the Ritz, Fortnum and Mason, and the Royal Academy, it's still very posh.

BURLINGTON HOUSE. Piccadilly's only surviving aristocratic mansion, Burlington House was built in 1665, though its current neo-Renaissance appearance dates from an 1870 remodeling. The Earls of Burlington have long since departed, but the house still has an aristocratic grandeur about it, thanks to its sheer size and peaceful open courtyard. Today, Burlington House is home to the **Royal Academy of Art** (see p. 134), as well as two other regal societies: the Royal Society of Chemistry and the Royal Astronomical Society.

19TH-CENTURY ARCADES. A number of early covered passageways lined with glass-fronted boutiques; in their 19th-century way are scattered around Piccadilly. They could be considered one of the first shopping malls. Today, the arcades make for a picturesque but anachronistic shopping experience. The oldest is the **Royal Opera Arcade,** between Pall Mall and Charles II St.; the most prestigious is the **Royal Arcade,** patronized by Queen Victoria and home of palace *chocolatiers* Charbonnel and Walker. The most famous, and longest, is the **Burlington Arcade,** next to Burlington House (see above) where top-hatted "beadles" enforce the original 1819 laws banning whistling, singing, and hurrying. Would-be shoppers note: these and the other more famous arcades have a bit of a stuffed-shirt feel; they're filled with upmarket (read: rather dull) clothing shops and jewelry boutiques. Shops inside keep their own hours, but most are open M-Sa about 10am-7pm, Su noon-5pm.

ST. JAMES'S CHURCH PICCADILLY. William Blake was baptized in this building, whose exterior is now darkened from the soot of London's mills. The current structure is largely a post-war reconstruction of what Wren considered his best parish church; the original wooden flowers, garlands, and cherubs by master carver Grinling Gibbons escaped the Blitz. The churchyard is home to a tourist-oriented craft market and, bizarrely enough, a *Café Nero*. *(Enter at 197 Piccadilly or on Jermyn St. ☎7734 4511; www.st-james-piccadilly.org. Church open M-Sa 9am-6:30pm, Su 1-4:30pm. Market open Tu-Sa 10am-6pm. Cafe open M-Sa 8am-7pm, Su 10am-7pm.)*

ST. JAMES'S

Piccadilly Circus or Green Park.

Ever since Henry VIII chose St. James's Palace to be the residence of the royal court—foreign ambassadors to Britain are still officially called "Ambassadors to the Court of St. James"—this has been London's most aristocratic address. Current occupants include Prince Charles; the late Queen Mum lived in neighboring Clarence House. Nearby **Pall Mall** is lined with exclusive **gentlemen's clubs,** steadfast bastions of wealth, tradition, and male privilege (most do not admit women); more can be found on **St. James's St.** For us commoners, this is an area to be seen primarily from the outside.

ST. JAMES'S PALACE. Built in 1536 over the remains of a leper hospital. St. James's is London's only remaining purpose-built palace (Buckingham Palace was a rough-and-ready conversion of a Duke's house). The massive gateway on St. James's St. is one of the few surviving parts of the original edifice; outside, a pair of bearskin-hatted guards stomp and turn in perfect unison. As the official home of the Crown, royal proclamations are issued every Friday from the balcony in the interior Friary Court, which is also where the accession of a new monarch is first announced. Unless your name starts with HRH (or ends with Parker-Bowles), the only part of the Palace you're likely to get into is the **Chapel Royal,** open for Sunday services from

October to Easter at 8:30 and 11:30am. From Easter to July, services are held in the Inigo Jones's **Queen's Chapel,** across Marlborough Rd. from the Palace, which was built in the 17th century for the marriage of Prince Charles I.

CARLTON HOUSE TERRACE & WATERLOO PLACE. Sweeping down from Piccadilly Circus, Regent St. comes to an abrupt halt at Waterloo Pl., with steps leading down to the Mall. Regent St. was built to be a triumphal route leading to the Prince Regent's residence at Carlton House, but by the time it was finished, the Prince (now George IV) had moved on to Buckingham Palace and had his old house pulled down. The aging royal architect, John Nash, was recommissioned to knock up something quickly on the site; the result was **Carlton House Terrace,** a pair of imposing classical buildings that dominate the northern side of the Mall. On **Waterloo Place,** between the two buildings, the statue of Duke of Wellington is dwarfed by a vast column topped by his boss, the "Grand Old" Duke of York, who docked the pay of his men in order to pay for the monument. The column's great height led many of the Duke's contemporaries to joke that he should climb it in order to flee his equally imposing debts.

OTHER MAYFAIR SIGHTS

SHEPHERD MARKET. This pedestrian area just north of Green Park occupies the site of the original **May Fair** that gave the neighborhood its name. A 17th-century version of Camden Market, the infamously raucous fair was closed down in 1706. Later in the century, Edward Shepherd developed the area as a market. Today the 18th-century buildings house tiny restaurants, shops, and pubs. *(⊖Hyde Park Corner or Green Park.)*

BOND STREET & SAVILE ROW. The oldest and most prestigious shops, art dealers, and auction houses in the city are found on these streets. **Old Bond Street,** the Piccadilly end of the street, is dominated by art and jewelry dealers, including home-grown luxury megastore Asprey and Gerrard, which stocks essentials such as leather Scrabble boards with gold inlay. Versace and Ralph Lauren aside, most of the designer boutiques are found along devastatingly highbrow **New Bond Street,** nearer to Oxford St. *(⊖Bond St. or Green Park. Note that Bond St. Tube is not on Bond St.; exit right onto Oxford St., then take the 2nd right onto New Bond St.)* **Savile Row,** running parallel to Bond St., is synonymous with elegant and expensive tailoring. The Beatles performed their last live gig on the roof of no. 3, during the filming of *Let It Be*. *(⊖Piccadilly Circus.)*

GROSVENOR SQUARE. One of the largest squares in central London, Grosvenor Sq. has gradually evolved into a North American diplomatic enclave, alongside its more popular role as a warm-weather picnic spot. John Adams lived at no. 9 while serving as the first US ambassador to England in 1785. A century and a half later, Eisenhower established his wartime headquarters at no. 20; memory of his stay persists in the area's nickname, "Eisenhowerplatz." The **US Embassy** faces the unassuming **Canadian High Commission** across the square. If you're not picnicking or meeting an ambassador, there's not much to see here. *(⊖Bond St. or Marble Arch.)*

SOHO

SOHO QUICKFIND: Discover, p. 10; museums & galleries, p. 150; food, p. 178; pubs, p. 201; nightlife, p. 214; entertainment, p. 240; shopping, p. 265; accommodations, p. 292.

A rainbow-hued extravaganza of trendy bars, cafes and restauraunts with a lingering hint of sex, drugs, and prostitution, Soho has a history of welcoming all colors and creeds to its streets. Early settlers included French Huguenots fleeing persecution in the 17th century. Today, a concentration of gay-owned restaurants and bars has turned **Old Compton Street** into the heart of gay London. Soho could also be considered the heart of London's theater and clubbing scenes. William Blake and Daniel Defoe lived on **Broadwick Street,** and a blue plaque above Quo Vadis restaurant at **28 Dean Street** marks the two-room flat where Karl Marx lived with his wife, maid, and five children while writing *Das Kapital*.

PICCADILLY CIRCUS

Piccadilly Circus.

Gaudy, brash, and world-famous. Four of the West End's major arteries (Piccadilly, Regent St., Shaftesbury Ave., and the Haymarket) merge and swirl around Piccadilly Circus. Tourist and pigeon-ridden (the flocking patterns of the two are amazingly similar), the square is flanked by the music triumvirate of HMV, Virgin Megastore, and Tower Records London. In the middle of all the glitz and neon stands the Gilbert's famous **Statue of Eros.** Dedicated to the Victorian philanthropist Lord Shaftesbury, Eros was actually meant to be an "Angel of Christian Charity," but the aluminum figure has never been known as such. The archer originally pointed his bow and arrow down Shaftesbury Ave. Recent restoration work has put his aim significantly off.

LEICESTER SQUARE

Leicester Sq. or Piccadilly Circus.

The circus came to town—and forgot to leave. Amusements at this entertainment hub range from London's largest cinemas to the **Swiss Centre** glockenspiel, whose renditions of anything from pop songs to Beethoven's Moonlight Sonata are enough to make even the tone-deaf cringe. *(Rings M-F at noon, 6, 7, 8pm; Sa and Su noon, 2, 4, 5, 6, 7, 8pm.)* After this you can get a henna tattoo, sit for a caricature, or humor the rants of innumerable street preachers. People-watching in this perpetual pedestrian traffic jam might just be a calorie-burning exercise. In the summer, a small funfair invades the square, adding to the hectic atmosphere.

CHINATOWN. It wasn't until the 1950s that immigrants from Hong Kong started moving en masse to these few blocks just north of Leicester Sq. Pedestrianized **Gerrard Street,** with scroll-worked dragon gates and pagoda-capped phone booths, is the self-proclaimed center of this tiny slice of Canton. Grittier **Lisle Street,** one block to the south, has more authenticity and cause less claustrophobia with numerous specialty markets, bookshops, and craft stores to complement all that food. Chinatown is most exciting during the Mid-Autumn Festival at the end of September, and the raucous Chinese New Year Festival in February; see **Festivals** p. 70. *(Between Leicester Sq., Shaftesbury Ave. and Charing Cross Rd.)*

SOHO SQUARE

Tottenham Crt. Rd. Park open daily 10am-dusk.

First laid out in 1681, Soho Sq. is a rather scruffy patch of green popular with picnickers. Its removed location makes the square more hospitable and less trafficked than its big brother, Leicester. If you're lucky, you might bump into Paul McCartney, whose business HQ is at no. 1 (MPL Communications)—crane your neck for a view of his first-floor office. Two monuments to Soho's cosmopolitan past border the square: London's only **French Protestant Church,** founded in 1550, and **St. Patrick's Catholic Church,** long the focal point of Soho's Irish and Italian communities. At the center of it all, the strange-looking mock-Tudor building in the middle is actually a Victorian garden shed that was never removed.

COVENT GARDEN

COVENT GARDEN QUICKFIND: Discover, p. 10; museums & galleries, p. 150; food, p. 180; nightlife, p. 216; entertainment, p. 240; shopping, p. 267; accommodations, p. 292.

Covent Garden.

The name is misleading: come to shop or to stroll, but don't come looking for greenery. One of the few parts of London popular with locals and tourists alike, Covent Garden retains a charm even as its shops become more mainstream. On the very spot where Samuel Pepys saw the first Punch and Judy show in England 350 years ago, street performers still entertain the hordes who flock here summer and winter, rain or shine. It's hard to imagine that for centuries this was London's main vegetable market (begun in medieval times, when it was just another "convent garden"); only in 1974 did the traders transfer to more spacious premises south of the river.

ROYAL OPERA HOUSE. Home to the prestigious **Royal Opera, Royal Ballet,** and **ROH Orchestra.** The Piazza's boutique-lined colonnade is now the rear of the ROH's rehearsal studios and workshops. The public can wander the ornate lobby of the original 1858 theater and preview shows on the giant projector screen, except before performances. The enormous, glass-roofed **Floral Hall** is also open to the public. From Floral Hall, take the escalator to reach the **terrace** overlooking the Piazza, where you can see the London Eye slowly turning in the distance. Verdi's *La Traviata* and Puccini's *Madama Butterfly* are two of the many shows that will be hosted in 2005. *(Enter on Bow St. or through the northeast of the Piazza. ☎ 7304 4000; www.royaloperahouse.org. 75min. backstage tours M-Sa 10:30am, 12:30pm, and 2:30pm; reservations essential. Open M-Sa 10am-3:30pm; box office M-Sa 10am-8pm. Tours £8, concessions £7.* *For performances, see p. 245.* *Wheelchair accessible. AmEx/MC/V.)*

ST. PAUL'S. Not to be confused with St. Paul's Cathedral, this 1633 Inigo Jones church is now the sole remnant of the original square. Shortage of funds explains its simplicity: the Earl of Bedford instructed the architect to make it "not much better than a barn." Known as "the actors' church" for its long association with nearby theaters, the interior is festooned with plaques commemorating the achievements of Boris Karloff, Vivien Leigh, and Charlie Chaplin. Musical lovers take note: Gilbert (one half of song-writing team Gilbert and Sullivan) was baptised here, and George Bernard Shaw set the opening of *Pygmalion* (later to be turned into *My Fair Lady)* under St. Paul's front portico. To enter the church, you must first pass through the peaceful **churchyard,** whose award-winning gardens provide a welcome shelter from the bustle of the surrounding streets. *(On Covent Garden Piazza; enter via the Piazza, King St., Henrietta St. or Bedford St. ☎ 7836 5221; www.spcg.org. Open M-F 8:30am-4:30pm, Sun. 11am morning services.)*

THEATRE ROYAL, DRURY LANE. Charles II met Nell Gwynn here in 1655, and 8 years later the Theatre Royal was founded. Even though the current building dates from only 1812, this is the oldest of London's surviving theaters and remains one of the most popular. In August 2004, the Mel Brooks' Broadway smash *The Producers* settled in for what promises to be a lengthy run. Join one of the actor-led backstage tours and you'll discover gems of Drury Lane lore, like the corpse and dagger found bricked up in the Royal's wall in the 19th century. *(Entrance on Catherine St. ☎ 7850 8791, box office 0870 890 1109, tours 7240 5357. Tours M-Tu and Th-F 2:15 and 4:45pm; W and Sa 10:15am and noon. £8.50, concessions £6.50. Wheelchair accessible. MC/V.)*

SEVEN DIALS. This radial configuration of six streets is a rare surviving example of 16th-century town planning. Thomas Neale commissioned the central pillar in 1694, with one sundial facing each street; the seventh dial is the column itself. The original column was pulled down in 1773 to rid the area of the "undesirables" who congregated around it. A replica, erected in 1989, attracts all types, including those just trying to avoid the oncoming traffic. It also tells the correct time to within 10 seconds—if you can figure out how to read it. *(Intersection of Monmouth, Earlham, and Mercer St.)*

THE STRAND

Charing Cross

Simply known as "Strand," this busy road is perhaps the oldest in London, predating the Romans. It was originally a riverside track, shifting watercourses and Victorian engineering left it high and dry; yet as the main thoroughfare between Westminster and the City, it remains as busy as ever. The only reminder of the many episcopal and aristocratic palaces that once made it London's top address are in nearby street names: Villiers St. recalls George Villiers, Duke of Buckingham, while Essex St. honors Elizabeth I's favorite, Robert Devereux, Earl of Essex. It's most attractive features are the dazzling **Savoy** complex, the art-deco fabulousness of the **Adelphi Theatre,** and, farther east, the museumified riches of **Somerset House** (see **Sights**, Holborn, p. 97).

CHARING CROSS. The tiered Gothic monument standing outside the Charing Cross station and Thistle Hotel was the last of the 14 crosses erected by Edward I in 1290 to mark the passage of his wife's funeral cortege (the cross itself is actually named for her: it's called "Eleanor's Cross"). Though many will tell you that "Charing" is a corruption of *chère reine*, French for "dear Queen," the word actually comes from the Old English *ceiring*, meaning a bend in the river. The original was destroyed by Cromwell in 1647, and the current monument is a 19th-century replica. To complete the deception, it's not even in the right place—the original stood on the spot now occupied by Charles I's statue in Trafalgar Square.

THE SAVOY. Considered the "fairest manor in all England," John of Gaunt's great Palace of Savoy was destroyed by rampaging peasants in 1381. Five hundred years later, the D'Oyly Carte Opera Company took its chances and moved into the new **Savoy Theatre,** the first in the world to be lit entirely by electricity. Managed by César Ritz, it was every bit as decadent as the Palace that once stood on the site. Don't be afraid to wander into the Savoy's grand foyer, second only to the Ritz in popularity for afternoon tea (see p. 182). Be careful as you cross the Savoy **driveway**—this short, narrow road is the only street in the UK where people drive on the right. *(On the south side of the Strand.)*

CLEOPATRA'S NEEDLE. The oldest monument in London, this Egyptian obelisk was first erected at Heliopolis in 1475 BC, making it some 1400 years older than Cleo herself. The Turkish Viceroy of Egypt presented it to Britain in 1819 in recognition of their help in booting Napoleon out of Africa, but it wasn't shipped out until 1877. The ship sank en route, but a salvage operation recovered the obelisk. It was finally re-erected in 1879. Underneath the foundation is a Victorian time-capsule containing a railway guide, numerous Bibles, and pictures of the 12 prettiest British women of the day—no asps, though. The scars at the needle's base and on the (Victorian) sphinx to its right were left by the first-ever bomb raid on London, by German zeppelins in 1917. *(North bank of the Thames between Hungerford and Waterloo Bridges.)*

WESTMINSTER

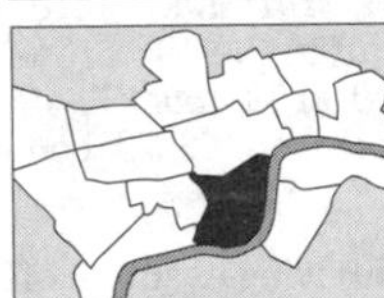
SEE MAP, p. 370

WESTMINSTER QUICKFIND: Discover, p. 11; museums & galleries, p. 152; food, p. 181; pubs, p. 202; entertainment, p. 244; accommodations, p. 293. For Buckingham Palace, see p. 75. For The Houses of Parliament, see p. 76. For Westminster Abbey, see p. 78.

TRAFALGAR SQUARE

Charing Cross or Leicester Sq. Wheelchair accessible.

John Nash first suggested laying out this square in 1820, but it took almost 50 years for London's largest traffic roundabout to take on its current appearance. The Nelson column only arrived in 1843, the larger-than-life lions at the base in 1868. The bronze beasts don't look very fierce because sculptor Sir Edmund Landseer's model died during the sittings, forcing him to work from a decomposing animal. Far scarier are the lègions of pigeons dive-bombing the square—enough to make a Hitchcock fan quake.

Trafalgar Sq. has traditionally been a focus for public rallies and protest movements, from the Chartist rallies of 1848 to the anti-apartheid vigils held outside South Africa House on the square's east side, in the early 90s. It's currently a gathering place for Londoners, whether it's to enjoy the sun or to meet before going out for the evening. Joyful congregations amass here on **New Year's Eve** to ring in midnight with the chimes of Big Ben; it's also tradition to break the ice in the frozen fountains before the clock strikes 12. Every December since the end of WWII, the square has hosted a giant **Christmas Tree,** provided by Norway as thanks for British assistance against the Nazis.

NELSON'S COLUMN. Not until the 1830s was it proposed to dedicate the square to England's 1805 defeat of Napoleon's navy at Trafalgar—considered to be the nation's greatest naval victory—and the battle that killed Lord Nelson. The fluted 51m granite column was erected in 1839. Due to pigeon detritus covering the statue, it was given a good cleaning as part of Mayor Livingstone's beautification project and now sparkles again. The four relief panels at the column's base were cast from captured French and Spanish cannons and commemorate Nelson's victories at Cape St. Vincent, Copenhagen, the Nile, and Trafalgar.

OTHER STATUES. Nelson is not the only national hero to watch over the square; to prove that the English are not sore losers, **George Washington** keeps watch from a horse just in front of the National Gallery (see p. 135). On leaving England, Washington vowed never to set foot on English soil again, and true to his word, the small plot of soil underneath his statue was specially brought over from the United States. The statue of **George IV** in the northeastern corner was originally intended to top the **Marble Arch** (see p. 75). The eastern "Fourth Plinth" was supposed to hold a sculpture of William IV, but due to funding problems it was never sculpted. From 1999-2003 commissioned modern pieces occupied the space, but it is now once again vacant. To the south of the square, a rare equestrian monument to **Charles I** stands on the site of the original Charing Cross (see below). The statue escaped Cromwell's wrath with the aid of one John Rivett, who bought it "for scrap" and did a roaring trade in souvenirs supposedly made from the figure. It was, in fact, hidden and later sold at a tidy profit to Charles II who re-erected it in 1633.

ST. MARTIN-IN-THE-FIELDS. The fourth church to stand here, James Gibbs's 1726 creation is instantly recognizable: the rectangular portico building supporting a soaring steeple made it the model for countless Georgian churches in Ireland and America. The front of the church sports Corinthian columns and George I's coat of arms. He was the church's first warden, and it's still the Queen's parish church; look for the royal box above and to the left of the altar. Handel and Mozart both performed here, and the church hosts frequent concerts (see p. 244). In order to support the cost of keeping the church open, there is a tourist-oriented **daily market** outside as well as a surprisingly extensive and delicious **cafe,** bookshop, and art gallery in the Crypt. The popular **London Brass Rubbing Centre** also is housed in undercroft, where you can create charcoal and pastel impressions of medieval brass plates to take home. *(St. Martin's Ln., northeast corner of Trafalgar Sq.; crypt entrance on Duncannon St. ⊖Leicester Sq. or Charing Cross. ☎7766 1100; www.stmartin-in-the-fields.org. Market open daily 11am-7pm. Brass rubbing £2.90-15. Open M-Sa 10am-6pm, Su noon-6pm. Tours offered Th. 11:30. Free.)*

WHITEHALL

***Location:** Between Trafalgar Sq. and Parliament Sq. ⊖Westminster, Embankment, or Charing Cross. Wheelchair accessible.*

Whitehall refers to the stretch connecting Trafalgar Sq. with Parliament Sq. and is synonymous with the British civil service. From 1532 until a devastating fire in 1698, it was the home of the monarchy and one of the grandest palaces in Europe, of which very little remains. Towards the northern end of Whitehall, **Great Scotland Yard** marks the former HQ of the Metropolitan Police. The front entrance (and commemorative plaque—there's not much to see) is one block south, at 3-8 Whitehall Pl. Nearer Parliament Sq., where Whitehall changes name to Parliament St.; heavily guarded steel gates mark the entrance to **Downing Street.** In 1735, no. 10 was made the official residence of the First Lord of the Treasury, a position that soon became permanently identified with the Prime Minister. The Chancellor of the Exchequer traditionally resides at no. 11, the Parliamentary Chief Whip at no. 12. Tony Blair's family, however, is too big for no. 10, so he's swapped with Gordon Brown next door. The street is closed to visitors, but if you wait long enough you might get a wave from the PM going to or coming from work. Outside the entrance to Downing St., in the middle of Whitehall, Edward Lutyen's **Cenotaph** (1919) stands, a tall and proud commemoration

the local story

Queen's Life Guard

Corporal of Horse Simon Knowles, in his 18th year at The Queen's Guard.

Q: What sort of training did you undergo?

A: In addition to a year of basic military camp, which involves mainly training on tanks and armored cars, I was also trained as a gunner and radio operator. Then I joined the service regiment at 18 years of age.

Q: So it's not all glamour?

A: Not at all, that's a common misconception. After armored training, we go through mounted training on horseback in Windsor for 6 months where we learn the tools of horseback riding, beginning with bareback training. The final month is spent in London training in full state uniform.

Q: Do the horses ever act up?

A: Yes, but it's natural. During the Queen's Jubilee Parade, with 3 million people lining the Mall, to expect any animal to be fully relaxed is absurd. The horses rely on the rider. If the guard is riding the horses confidently and strongly, the horse will settle down.

Q: Your uniforms look pretty heavy. Are they comfortable?

to the dead of WWI. Many of the islands in the middle of the road hold statues honoring monarchs and military heroes, a testament to the avenue's identity as the center of civil service.

HORSE GUARDS. The most photographed men in the area, the Queen's horse guards, hold court in the center of Whitehall. Two mounted soldiers of the Household Cavalry, in shining breastplates and plumed helmets, guard a shortcut to The Mall and St. James's Park. While anyone can walk through, only those with a special ivory pass issued by the Queen may drive past the gates. The guard changes M-F 11am, Sa-Su10am, with a dismount for inspection daily at 4pm—a 200 year tradition, broken only by WWII. Beyond the neoclassical building is the pebbly expanse of **Horse Guards Parade,** where the Queen ceremonially sizes up her troops during the Trooping of the Colour on the 2nd Saturday in June.

PARLIAMENT SQUARE

Westminster. Wheelchair accessible.

Laid out in 1750, Parliament Sq. rapidly became the focal point for opposition to the government due to its spacious gathering grounds and proximity to the lawmakers. Today, a continuous stream of heavy traffic is the demonstrator's best audience—with no pedestrian crossings it's hard to get to the square alive. No matter, protesters employ eye-catching placards that encourage drivers to honk their horns in protest. Those who make it across will find statues of Parliamentary greats as well as a huge cast of honest Abe Lincoln across the road behind the square. Standing opposite the **Houses of Parliament** (see **Sights** p. 76). South of the square rises **Westminster Abbey** (see **Sights** p. 78).

ST. MARGARET'S WESTMINSTER. Literally in Westminster Abbey's shadow, St. Margaret's is surprisingly full of light. This church enjoys a strange status: as a part of the Royal Peculiar it is not under the jurisdiction of the diocese of England or even the archbishop of Canterbury. It was built for local residents by Abbey monks sick of having to share their own church with laymen, and has been beautifully restored in the past few years. Since 1614, it's been the official worshipping place of the House of Commons—the first few pews are cordoned off for the Speaker, Black Rod, and other dignitaries. The gothic columns and arches support a decidedly un-gothic ceiling with lots of bright windows. The **Milton Window** (1888), in the back above the North Aisle, shows the poet (married here in 1608) dictating *Paradise Lost* to his daughters.

Stained glass images from the book fill the surrounding panels; his daughters and wife are buried here. Lining the South Aisle, the modern and geometric grey-hued 1966 **Piper Windows** replace those destroyed in WWII. Beautiful and beautifully restored, Margaret's is worth a visit. *(Parliament Sq. ⊖Westminster. ☎7654 4840. Open M-F 9:30am-3:45pm, Sa 9:30am-1:45pm, Su 2-5pm. Hours subject to change, call first. Free. Wheelchair accessible.)*

WESTMINSTER CATHEDRAL

Location: *Cathedral Piazza, off Victoria St. ⊖Victoria.* ***Contact:*** *☎7798 9055; www.westminstercathedral.org.uk.* ***Open:*** *Daily 8am-7pm.* ***Bell Tower:*** *Open Mar.-Nov daily 9am-12:30pm and 1pm-5pm, Dec.-Feb. Tu-Sa 9am-12:30pm. £3, concessions £1.50, family £7.* ***Admission:*** *Free, suggested donation £2.*

Following Henry VIII's divorce from the Catholic church, London's Catholic community remained without a cathedral until 1884 when the Church purchased a derelict prison on what used to be a monastery site. The neo-Byzantine church looks somewhat like a fortress, and is now one of London's great religious landmarks. Construction began in 1895, but the architect's plan outran available funds; by 1903, when work stopped, the interior remained unfinished. The result, however, is extraordinary. The four blackened brick domes still await mosaic inlay and contrast dramatically with the swirling green and white marble of the lower walls. The front altar is covered with a ornate marble canopy, called a baldachino; above that a 10m cross is suspended. The brightness of the mosaics contrasts with the coliseum style marble arches and balconies all made of marble. A lift, well worth the minimal fee, carries visitors up the striped 273 ft. **bell tower** for an all-encompassing view of Westminster, the river, and Kensington.

OTHER WESTMINSTER SIGHTS

ST. JAMES'S PARK & GREEN PARK. The streets leading-up to Buckingham Palace are flanked by two sprawling expanses of greenery: St. James's Park and St. James's Palace by Henry VIII. The latter being the more beautiful of the two. In the middle of the space is the placid St. James's Park Lake where you can catch glimpses of the pelicans that call it home—the lake and the grassy area surrounding it is an official waterfowl preserve. Across the Mall, the lush **Green Park** is the creation of Charles II; it connects Westminster and St. James. "Constitution Hill" refers not to the king's interest in political theory, but to his daily exercises. Sit on one of the lawn chairs scattered enticingly around

A: They're not comfortable at all. They were designed way back in Queen Victoria's time, and the leather trousers and boots are very solid. The uniform weighs about 3 stone [approx. 45lbs.] in all.

Q: How do you overcome the itches, sneezes, and bees?

A: Inherent discipline is instilled in every British soldier during training. We know not to move a muscle while on parade no matter what the provocation or distraction—unless, of course, it is a security matter. But our helmets are akin to wearing a boiling kettle on your head, so to relieve the pressure sometimes we use the back of our sword blade to ease the back of the helmet forward.

Q: How do you make the time pass while on duty?

A: The days are long. At Whitehall the shift system is derived on inspection in Barracks. Smarter men work on horseback in the boxes in shifts from 10am-4pm; less smart men work on foot from 7am-8pm. Some guys count the number of buses that drive past. Unofficially, there are lots of pretty girls around here, and we are allowed to move our eyeballs.

Q: What has been your funniest distraction attempt?

A: One day a taxi pulled up, and out hopped 4 playboy bunnies, who then posed for a photo shoot right in front of us. You could call that a distraction if you like.

both parks, and an attendant will magically materialize and demand money. Alternatively, act like a local and bring a blanket for a picnic, at no charge. *(The Mall. Open daily 5am-midnight. Lawn chairs available Apr.-Sept. 10am-6pm; June-Aug. 10am-10pm. £1.50 for 4hr, student deal: £25 for the season. Summer walks in the park, Th noon, 1 hr. long. Book in advance by calling ☎ 7930 1793.)*

THE ROYAL MEWS. The Mews wears many hats: it acts as a museum, stable, riding school and a working carriage house. The main attraction is the Queen's collection of coaches, including the cinderella-like "Glass Coach" used to carry royal brides, including Diana, to their weddings and the State Coaches of Australia, Ireland and Scotland. The biggest draw is the four-ton **Gold State Coach,** which can occasionally be seen tooling around the streets in the early morning on practice runs for major events. The attendant guarding the coach is himself a goldmine of royal information, full of tips on when and where to catch glimpses of their Royal Highnesses. Visitors can meet the carriage horses themselves, each named personally by the Queen. Each horse has undergone years of training to withstand the distractions of crowds, street traffic, and gun salutes. You can also see pictures of the Queen herself, in her more vigorous days, riding her black Canadian stallion *Burmese* at the Trooping of the Colour. Note that horses and carriages are liable to be absent without notice, and opening hours are subject to change. *(Buckingham Palace Rd. ⊖St. James's Park or Victoria. ☎ 7766 7302. Open daily Apr.-July and Sept. 11am-4pm, last admission 3:15pm; Aug.-Sept., 10am-5pm, last admission 4:15pm. £5.50, seniors £4.50, under 17 £3, family £14. Wheelchair accessible.)*

VICTORIA TOWER GARDENS. South of the Palace of Westminster and overlooking the Thames, the open lawn and magnificent backdrop make the gardens a favorite spot for MPs, tourists, professionals and TV crews running political features. For similar reasons, it's a first-rate picnic venue. Check out the superb cast of Rodin's Burghers of Calais and the memorial to suffragette Emmeline Pankhurst, which stands just inside the northwest gate. On the opposite side from the Palace, a small neo-Gothic and strangely pastel gazebo commemorates the abolition of slavery on British territory in 1834. *(On Millbank. ⊖Westminster. Open daily until dusk. Wheelchair accessible.)*

ST. JOHN'S, SMITH SQUARE. Four assertive corner towers distinguish this unusual example of English Baroque. Dickens once described it as "some petrified monster on its back with its legs in the air." The church is nicknamed "Queen Anne's Footstool" after the story that when the architect, Thomas Archer, asked the impatient Queen's advice, she upended her footstool and told him "like that." The church stood ruined for years following a bomb hit in 1941, reopening as a concert hall in 1969. *(Smith Sq. ⊖Westminster or St. James's Park. ☎ 7222 1061; www.sjss.org.uk. For concert info, see* p. 244.*)*

NORTH LONDON

NORTH LONDON QUICKFIND: Discover, p. 12; museums & galleries, p. 153; food, p. 183; pubs, p. 203; nightlife, p. 218; entertainment, p. 244; shopping, p. 269; accommodations, p. 294.

CAMDEN TOWN

As north London becomes increasingly affluent, those in search of a slice of tawdriness (or a good deal) come to Camden Town. The central Camden area, between Camden Town and Chalk Farm has thrown off attempts at gentrification thanks to the numerous **Street Markets,** now among London's most popular attractions.

CAMDEN HIGH STREET & CAMDEN MARKET

⊖Camden Town or Chalk Farm. See Shopping, p. 270. Wheelchair accessible.

Thanks to its markets, Camden Town turns into a sea of people every weekend. The stores on **Camden High Street,** to the right as you get off the Tube, distinguish themselves with elaborate facades, giant shoes, masks, and other brightly colored papier-mâché objects protruding from the walls above storefronts. If you want to shop, come on a weekday, when the stores are open and the crowds are gone. Come on a Friday and you might catch the weekend markets open too. The most pleasant is **Camden Lock Market,** which is spread out over a series of buildings around an open courtyard facing the canal. You can find plenty of unique and artistic market wares among millions of useless "curios" at **Stables Market.** The cheaper **Camden Market** and **Camden Canal Market,** filled with the requisite tacky trinkets and clubwear, are the most crowded.

REGENT'S CANAL

Location: *The Camden Lock Market (Camden Town) is the best place to catch boats.*

Regent's Canal is part of the Grand Union Canal, and was the main artery for bringing goods to London from the north in the days before railways. The canal today has little practical use, but a boat ride along its length can be relaxing and scenic. The still-functioning Camden Lock sits where Camden High St. crosses the canal; the courtyard nearby is now filled with all the eateries of the Camden Lock Market. Watch water buses being raised and lowered through the locks while you chow down. Passenger boats leave from here and head west to where the post-industrial landscape gives way first to Victorian houses and then to Regent's Park, the largest manicured park in the North. The canal actually passes through the middle of London Zoo on the way to Little Venice, though the banks are too high to afford a view of any wildlife. Little Venice also has boat tours, as well as floating restaurants and the **Puppet Theatre Barge.** The **London Waterbus Company** leaves from the Camden Lock Market (see p. 270) and makes the 90min. trip to Little Venice, with a stop at the Zoo. You can also board at Little Venice. *(☎7482 2660. Apr.-Oct. daily departures every hr. 10, 11am, noon, 1:15, 2, 3, 4 and 5pm; Nov.-Mar. Sa-Su every hr. 11am-4pm. Single £5.20, children and seniors £3.40; return £6.60/ £4.30. Single to Zoo, including admission, from Camden £14/£10.20, from Little Venice £14.50/£10.70.)*

HAMPSTEAD & HIGHGATE

HAMPSTEAD VILLAGE

Hampstead.

KEATS HOUSE. In this house, the great Romantic poet John Keats produced some of his last and finest work, fell in love with Fanny Brawne—his next-door neighbor's daughter—and coughed up his first drops of consumptive

the local story

Watch Your Head

Tower Green witnessed many beheadings in medieval England. While most were eventless there were of course instances that scandalized the growing English beheading industry.

Queen Anne Boleyn, the first Queen to die on the oak scaffold, was such a case. Queen Anne had been tried and convicted of witchcraft and incest on the sworn testimony of witnesses. She was 36. She was beheaded in 1536 at the request of her ex-husband King Henry VII, but was offered a chance to beg for her life. Instead of begging to be saved, however, she asked that the King search for an expert executioner, a certified professional and the King obliged. He had men search the city and the countryside, all through the country. When none could be located in the kingdom Henry was forced to look across the water to France, where professional axe-wielders were aplenty. An expert executioner's skill came at a price: twenty-eight pounds, ten shillings and six pence. This exorbitant pricetag put a huge dent in the King's treasury, but well a promise is a promise.

On the day of her execution the Queen met the Frenchman for the first and last time. His excellent reputation was well deserved: Queen Anne Boleyn's eyes were still moving side to side after the event.

blood, all between 1818 and 1820. The gardens are lovely, as is the house itself, though unfortunately, little of the original furnishing remains. The current space is a sparse recreation of its 1820 appearance, special only because of its literary inhabitant. Inside the house, copies of Keats's poems lie scattered about the well-kept rooms, together with Keats memorabilia and informative biographical displays. *(Keat's Grove. ☎7435 2062; www.keatshouse.org.uk. Open Apr.-Nov. Tu-Su noon-5pm; Nov.-Mar. Tu-Su noon-4pm. £3, concessions £1.50, under 16 free. Ticket valid for 1 yr. of unlimited visits. Partially wheelchair accessible.)*

FENTON HOUSE. Dating from 1686, this was one of the first houses built in Hampstead. First built by a master bricklayer, the house was owned by the Fenton family and other aristocrats until 1952. The first two floors of the house are home to a delicate collection of china, porcelain, and needlework, as well as a remarkable collection of early keyboard and stringed instruments that continues on the upper floors. These 17th- and 18th-century instruments are still played in the parlor during summertime concerts. The sprawling French garden provides a picturesque stroll and a prime relaxation spot, as well as an intricate flower garden, orchard, greenhouse, and beehive. On the last Sunday in September the house hosts Apple Day, with tastings, products and pies from the orchard. *(Hampstead Grove. ☎7435 3471. Open Apr.-Oct. W-F 2-5pm, Sa-Su 11am-5pm; Mar. Sa-Su 2-5pm, Closed Nov-Feb. £4.60, children £2.30, family £11.50. Joint ticket with 2 Willow Rd. (see below) £6.40. Garden only £1.Baroque Concerts May-Au.g, every other Th; £14, students £12.50. Apple Day £2, under 16 free. Partially wheelchair accessible.)*

TWO WILLOW ROAD. Looking like an unimposing 1950s-style mini-block, Two Willow Road was actually built in 1939 as the avant-garde home of architect Erno Goldfinger. Ian Fleming hated it so much, he named a James Bond villain after Goldfinger. It stands apart from the quaint Victorian facades that line the rest of the street; a masterpiece of modernist living, designed by Goldfinger down to the last teaspoon. The incredible use of space means that secret cabinets and doors pop up everywhere. Goldfinger and his wife were major Surrealist art collectors. With clothes still in their dry-cleaning plastic sheaves, everything looks as if the family had just popped out to raid Fort Knox. Family photos on the mantelpiece sit next to works of art by Max Ernst, Marchel Duchamp, and Goldfinger's wife, Ursula Blackwell. A pre-war gem for architecture buffs. *(15min. walk from ⊖Hampstead. ☎7435 6166. Open Apr.-Oct. Th-Sa noon-5pm. Timed ticket and 1hr. guided tours available at noon, 1 and 2pm. £4.50, children £2.25, family £11; joint ticket with Fenton House £6.40.)*

HAMPSTEAD HEATH

Train: Hampstead Heath. ⊖Hampstead. Bus # 210. **Open:** *24hr.* **Be careful after dark.** *Wheelchair accessible.*

Hampstead Heath is one of the last remaining traditional commons in England, open to all since at least 1312 thanks to the pluckiness of local residents, who, in the 19th century, successfully fought off attempts to develop it. Since Parliament declared in 1871 that the Heath should remain "forever open, un-enclosed, and un-built-upon"; it has since grown from 336 to 804 acres. Don't plan on covering it all—the Heath's gargantuan size makes that impossible, but do try and see a few of the gardens and of course the Kenwood Estate. Unlike so many other London parks, the Heath is not comprised of manicured gardens and paths, but wild, spontaneous growth tumbling over rolling pastures and forested groves. Feel free to picnic, but look out for the rabbits and foxes that dart around. The dirt paths through the Heath are not well signed and are as random as the surrounding vegetation. For that reason, it's best not to wander alone. On public holidays in spring and summer, **funfairs** are held at South End Green and on the south side of Spaniards Rd.

HILL GARDEN. Unless you're looking for this lovely secret garden, you're unlikely to find it. There are a few paths down from North End Way, but you may have to poke through the forest a bit if you miss the signed path. You'll know you're there when you see the exquisite, raised pergola (Italian arched walkway) guarding the gardens. The flower-encrusted walkway passes over the former kitchen gardens of Lord Leverhulme's mansion. The walkway was built as a way to go from the mansion of Lord Leverhulme (founder of Lever Soap) to his pleasure gardens without walking through an ancient right-of-way that still passes under the pergola. The summer sunsets here are particularly magnificent. *(Off Inverforth Close off North End Way. Open daily 8:30am to 1hr. before sunset.)*

KENWOOD HOUSE. A far contrast from the wild forests of the rest of the heath, this picture-perfect English country estate and its sprawling grounds are beautifully groomed and have their own lawns, ponds, and resident jackrabbits. The most impressive entrance sits at the head of the pasture, off Hampstead Ln. Alternatively, come up through the **Kenwood forest** to the south, past the estate's pond to the grandiose cream-stuccoed facade is revealed. On summer nights the pasture becomes an amphitheater for concerts on a bandstand across the pond. Edward Guinness, the first Earl of Iveagh purchased the home in 1922 not for living in, but to house his spectacular collection of Old Master paintings (see p. 153) that is now on display in the beautifully restored rooms. *(Road access from Hampstead Ln. Walk from Hampstead or Highgate or take bus #210 from ⊖Archway or Golders Green (Zone 3) or from points on North End Way or Spaniard's Rd. ☎8348 1286. Grounds open daily Apr.-Oct. 8am-8:30pm, Oct.-Mar. 8am-4:45pm. Wheelchair accessible.)*

PARLIAMENT HILL. Legend claims that Guy Fawkes and his accomplices planned to watch their destruction of Parliament from the top of this hill in 1605 (see p. 57). The hike to the top yields a panorama stretching to Westminster and beyond. At the foot of the hill, a series of ponds marks the final gasp of the River Westbourne before it vanishes under concrete on its way to the Thames. The brave can swim for free in the waters of the sex-segregated **bathing ponds.** *(The southeastern part of the Heath. Rail: Gospel Oak or Hampstead Heath.)*

GOLDERS GREEN

⊖Golders Green (Zone 3).

This little corner of North London is the center of Britain's Jewish community, although recent years have seen it diluted by other micro-communities. **Golders Green Road** is the axis around which life revolves; turn right from the station, and a few blocks down you'll start to see specialized shops, excellent kosher restaurants and Hebrew bookstores. Golders Hill Park—a western extension of Hampstead Heath—is at the heart of the area. Come on a Thursday or a Friday morning to experience the streets in full bloom. This is the best place to get kosher food in London, and there are numerous Halal restaurants on the main drag as well.

GOLDERS GREEN CREMATORIUM. Though visiting a crematorium may seem grim, don't let the neo-Romanesque chapel buildings scare you. Behind them lie several acres of picturesque, beautifully maintained gardens. Rosebush groves fill the northern side. Paths wander through leafy groves, water gardens, and open lawns, providing a fitting and peaceful memorial sanctuary. Each flower serves as a living grave for an individual and bears the names of the departed who were sprinkled there. Luminaries who ended up here include T.S. Eliot, H.G. Wells, Peter Sellers, Bram Stoker, Anna Pavlova, and five prime ministers. Don't expect to find them, they're not celebrated in any museum-like style. Sigmund Freud's ashes, in his favorite Greek vase, are locked in the Ernest George Columbarium; ask an attendant to let you in on weekdays. Benches scattered among the flowers and trees make for good resting spots. *(From ⊖Golders Green (Zone 3), turn right out of the exit, then right onto Finchley Rd. and follow it under the bridge then continue for 5min. before turning right on Hoope Ln. ☎8455 2374. Grounds open daily summer 9am-6pm, winter 9am-4pm; Chapel and Hall of Memory daily 9am-4pm. Free. Wheelchair accessible.)*

NO WORK ALL PLAY

Cricket Clubbing

Cricket enjoys a great deal of popularity in England, and the **Lord's Cricket Club** serves as the central UK hub of the sport. Club members, mostly elderly cricket loving men, are allowed in for free, but for the lowly commoner this isn't an option.

The first hurdle is membership. The venue has space for 30,000 fans, but the club membership has maxed out at 17,000, and will not grow larger. Don't despair, there are four ways to become a member. First, you can sign on as a player and play approximately 12 games, and if you're good enough you can join. Good luck. Second, if you're already good enough and famous and for some reason not a member you may be invited to join. Third, you can become Prime Minister. The PM gets a membership. Good luck again. And finally, you can go the good old fashioned way and sign up.

There's just one problem in signing up, however, and that's the wait. Since the club isn't growing, a member must die before a new one can join. Morbid, yes, but you can't have the member's room be too crowded now. This means that the large majority of the members are elderly. A *large*

ST. JOHN'S WOOD & MAIDA VALE

LORD'S CRICKET GROUND. The most famous cricket ground in England, Lord's is home to the local Marylebone Cricket Club (MCC) and host to most of London's international matches. To see the **Lord's Museum,** home to the **Ashes Urn** as well as all the cricket-related memorabilia you could ever want, attend a match or take a 100min. tour led by a senior club member. Included in the tours are the MCC members' Long Room, the ground, stands, and the architecturally striking though controversial media center. On game days, tours after 10am skip the Long Room and media center, though visitors get a discount on game tickets as compensation (no tours during international Test matches). Games take place on most days in summer. MCC games are £10 (students £4.50), but tickets to the rare international test matches are £45 and difficult to get. *(Enter at Grace Gate, on St. John's Wood Rd. ☎7432 1066; www.lords.org.uk. ⊖St. John's Wood plus 10min. walk. Tours daily noon and 2pm, Apr.-Sept. also 10am. Tours £7, concessions £5.50, under 16 £4.50, family £20. Wheelchair accessible.)*

ABBEY ROAD. Abbey Rd. itself is a long thoroughfare stretching from St. John's Wood to Kilburn; it's residential and tree-lined. Most people are only interested in the famous **zebra crossing** at its start, where it merges with Grove End Rd. The best way to stop traffic: a photo-op crossing the street a la John, Paul, George and Ringo. Stop to read the adulatory graffiti on the nearby street signs and walls, fans have come from all over the world. Next to the crossing, the **Abbey Road Studios** (3 Abbey Rd.), where the Beatles made most of their recordings, is closed to the public, but still in business. *(⊖St. John's Wood. Wheelchair accessible.)*

ST. PANCRAS OLD CHURCH

St. Pancras Rd. ☎7424 0724; www.stpancrasoldchurch.org.uk. Prayer services M-F 9am; Mass Su-M 9:30am, Tu 7pm. Free. Wheelchair accessible.

The oldest parish in Britain, the first church on this site was reputedly founded by Roman legionaries in 314 for early Christian worship. The present building dates from the 13th century though—some of the Norman masonry is visible on the north wall of the nave, if you manage to make it inside. The church is now a rather desolate spot, hard to get into except for services. If you do get a peek, don't miss the 6th-century altar stone that is rumored to have belonged to

St. Augustine of Canterbury. The large and lovely churchyard belies its macabre history. In the churchyard is Sir John Soanes's mausoleum and the **Hardy Tree,** designed by a young Thomas Hardy long before he became a writer. It features hundreds of tightly clustered headstones which seem to spring from the roots of a weeping ash.

SOUTH LONDON

SOUTH LONDON QUICKFIND: Discover, p. 14, museums & galleries, p. 155; food, p. 186; nightlife, p. 221; entertainment, p. 247; shopping, p. 271.

Initially, **Brixton** was just another South London railway suburb—actually a rather prosperous one, as the once-grand houses along Electric Ave. and Electric Ln. (the first streets in South London with electric lighting) testify. A poor, working-class area by the turn of the century, Brixton's greatest upheaval came after WWII. A steady stream of Caribbean immigrants starting in 1948 made Brixton the heart of London's West Indian community, and simmering racial tensions erupted with major riots in 1981, 1985, and 1995. Today, though, Brixton is quickly becoming a fashionable area for young artists and students, fueling the rise of an impressive club scene. A stroll through the area highlights the odd uniqueness of a town in flux: Afro-Caribbean markets, trendy new cafes, and increasing numbers of high street chain stores share street space. You can see the best of old Brixton early in the day, when **Brixton Market** is in full swing, and the best of new Brixton late at night, as young Brixtonians pile out of work and into the clubs and bars. *(⊖Brixton.)*

A short bus or train ride from Brixton, **Dulwich** could hardly offer a greater contrast; not much has changed in this old-money mecca in about four centuries. South London's snobbiest suburb, Dulwich bumbled along as an unremarkable country village until 1605, when Elizabethan heartthrob Edward Alleyn (played by Ben Affleck in *Shakespeare in Love*) bought the local manor—wealth and sprawling manors soon followed. His legacy lives on in the College of God's Gift, established according to his will for the education of 12 poor children. The original **Old College** buildings, including the chapel where Alleyn is buried, still stand close to Dulwich Picture Gallery (see p. 155). **Dulwich College,** now with 1600 very wealthy pupils, has since moved south to a palatial 19th-century site on College Rd. The college still profits from its private stretch of College Rd., south of the Common: its **toll gate** is the last in London. *(Rail: North or West Dulwich.)*

majority. The good news is that around 300 members die each year. So according to Lord's calculations, the waiting list is only 20 years long. Good luck staying alive long enough to join.

You face another membership hurdle if you're a woman. The club began accepting membership applications from women only three years ago, lagging behind the Melbourne Club (UKs biggest rivals), who invited women in a decade ago. Fair is fair, claims the Club, so women are on the 20 year list too, although 58 are active players. So good luck to the ladies.

Assuming you're lucky or an expert player and manage to join the club, don't jeopardize your spot by dressing down. Respectable outfits are required at all times. This is necessary, of course, due to the rigorous schedule of the club member. Upon mid-morning arrival, the match begins. Then of course, a break for lunch. Then more play, and then another break for tea. Don't spill—you don't want to wait another twenty years.

BROCKWELL PARK AND LIDO. This massive stretch of rolling and occasionally ill-maintained grass, is perfect for joggers and unleashed dogs, is actually rather picturesque once you walk past the bits of graffiti at the entrance. Along with tennis courts, a children's park, miles of walking paths, a dilapidated basketball court, and a BMX track, the park has refreshment rooms at its summit, which provide lovely views of London landmarks. *(www.brockwellpark.com. Between Tulse Hill and Dulwich Rd.; from ⊖Brixton, turn left, bear left at the fork onto Effra Rd., walk about 12min. then turn left again onto Brixton Water Ln., which has an unassuming entrance to the park a block and a half down on the right. Open daily 7:30am-dusk.)* The eastern edge of the park (to the left as you enter), off Dulwich Rd., holds the popular **Brockwell Lido,** a 1930s outdoor swimming pool often described as "London's beach." *(☎7274 3088; www.thelido.co.uk. Open May-Sept. M-F 6:45am-6pm, sometimes till 8pm depending on the weather; Sa-Su noon-6pm. £5, concessions £4, children £3. Morning £2.50/£2/£2. Wheelchair accessible.)*

EAST LONDON

EAST LONDON QUICKFIND: Discover, p. 13; museums & galleries, p. 156; food, p. 187; pubs, p. 204; nightlife, p. 222; entertainment, p. 248; shopping, p. 271.

WHITECHAPEL AND THE EAST END

Although the boroughs of the East End and the City are neighbors on the map, the two areas could not be more different. The border is as clear as it was when Aldgate and Bishopsgate were actual gates in the wall separating the City from the poorer quarters to the east. The oldest part of the East End, **Whitechapel,** is home of London's largest Bangladeshi community, as evidenced by the minaret of the **East London Mosque.** *(45 Fieldgate St., off Whitechapel. ⊖Aldgate East.)* Years ago the East was also home to the nucleus of London's sizable Jewish community—the old **Bevis Marks Synagogue** (Bevis Marks Rd.) is the largest of the area synagogues, and tiny synagogues are nestled into alleyways all over Whitechapel. Cheap rents have also drawn independent designers and artists. The best reason to visit the East End, though, is for its **restaurants and markets,** where shoppers congregate to search for bargains on Petticoat Lane, organic goods and crafts in cultural Spitalfields, and delicious dinners in any one of the competing Brick Lane eateries.

SPITALFIELDS MARKET. What was once one of London's main vegetable markets, Spitalfields has matured to be the creative market in the area. It was almost closed due to commercial development, but thanks to strong local opposition, one half of the enormous market hall was saved. Within the walls there is an unbeatable array of new designer clothes, crafts, antiques, and jewelry. Even more tempting are the many gourmet food stalls and cafes, selling everything from homemade truffles to Mongolian stir fry; organic food is available Friday through Sunday. *(Commercial St. ☎7377 1496. ⊖Liverpool St. Wheelchair accessible.)*

CHRIST CHURCH SPITALFIELDS. Christ Church is Wren's pupil, Nicholas Hawksmoor's largest church. It once stood proudly above its surroundings; with the area's growth, the size is less striking, but the stone facade is still impressive. Alas, this 1729 building is in a sorry state; derelict since 1957, it is only now slowly being restored to its former glory. A £7 million renovation project has been underway since 2001; and is still not complete. Doors are occasionally opened for services, but currently the area is more of a construction site. Call the Friends of the Church for more info and any opening hours. *(Commercial St., opposite Spitalfields market. ⊖Liverpool St. ☎7859 3035.)*

BRICK LANE. In the epicenter of Bangladeshi Britain, even the signs are written in Bengali. The lower half of Brick Ln., once noted for its Sunday market, now is an endless stretch of phenomenal curry houses. Towards its upper end, Brick Ln. has also become the hub of the East End's creative commercial renaissance. Hip boutiques speckle both sides of the street; the former **Truman Brewery,** spreads out on both sides of Brick Ln., and is now occupied by design and media consultants, sleek stores, and a cafe-bar-club trio that is one of East London's hottest nightspots. *Shoreditch (open only at rush hr.), Aldgate, Aldgate East, or Liverpool St.*

HOXTON & SHOREDITCH

Old St.; the center of the "Shoho scene" spreads either side of Old St. between the junction with Great Eastern St. and Kingsland Rd./Shoreditch High St.

While still sticking to its industrial roots, if only superficially, **"Shoho,"** has become one of London's trendiest districts. In the old days, struggling artists such as Damien Hirst and Tracey Emin saw potential in the neighborhood's dirt-cheap property and vacant warehouses, and Hoxton became the focus of an underground art scene. Eventually, word got around that this was the cool place to be, bringing an influx of artists from all over the world, followed by graphic and web designers. Many of the real artists have since fled, but the region still clings to its hip, dingy past: stop by before lunchtime—when most people are still sleeping off the night before—to get the full "deserted slum" experience or better yet around midnight when the neighborhood is out on the town.

DOCKLANDS

Skyscrapers, stores, and secretaries populate the busy Docklands area, which provides a stark antidote to the churches-and-monuments attitude of its more tourist-oriented neighbors. Until the 1960s, this man-made archipelago was the commercial heart of the British Empire, before ocean shipping began its descent toward being obsolete. The London Docklands Development Corporation (LDDC) was founded to revitalize the region (as large as metropolitan Paris) in 1981. Since then, Docklands has become one of the largest commercial developments in Europe—a mix of hi-tech office buildings, countless shops and restaurant and suburban-style housing. It's all linked by the slow but dependable trains of the Docklands Light Railway (DLR). Today, the area sits comfortably in its status as a temple to consumerism.

CANARY WHARF. At 800 ft., the glass panelled, pyramid-topped tower of **One Canada Square,** is Britain's tallest building. In the past two years it has been joined by almost equally tall companions—HSBC and Citigroup, whose logos can be seen from miles away. The area surrounding the tower, including the parks, malls, and restaurants, is commonly called Canary Wharf. The real draw here, besides the architecture, are the vast **Canada Place** and **Cabot Square** malls under and around the tower. The newest addition, the **Jubilee Place** shopping center sits a mere 2min. walk away across the plaza. Together the three contain close to 200 different shops, restaurants, and banks. The dockside plaza is predictably lined with upscale corporate restaurants and bars, although on a nice day they are a lovely place for a drink or a bite. It's worth standing in front of the map for a minute to get your bearings. *(/DLR: Canary Wharf or DLR: Heron Quays. Wheelchair accessible.)*

GREENWICH

DLR: Cutty Sark unless stated otherwise. The Greenwich Tourist Information Centre, Pepys House, 2 Cutty Sark Gdns. (☎0870 608 2000), offers all the usual services as well as a slick exhibition local history. Guided walking tours leave the center daily at 12:15pm for the town and Observatory and 2:15pm for the Royal Naval College. (£4, concessions £3, under 14 free.). Open daily 10am-5pm. Wheelchair accessible.

Maritime Greenwich, as it's officially known, has played many different roles over the last few centuries. It was first built as a Royal Palace, but the site's most notable fame comes from its maritime heritage. After the Royal family vacated the premises, Greenwich became home to the Royal Navy, and it served that role till 1997. Connected to this is Greenwich's other claim to fame, the Prime Meridian.

the local story

Taxidermy 101

Jeremy Bentham: noted scholar, gentleman, activist, and philosopher. Born 1748. Died 1832. Pickled 1833. That's right, the man credited with inventing British Utilitarianism—"the greatest happiness for the greatest number"—achieved his own great happiness by willing his taxidermied corpse to the college that he helped to establish. Nattily dressed, the eerie "Auto-Icon" sits at the end of University College London's South Cloister.

Centuries of lore have built up around the creepy cadaver since its grand debut nearly 2 centuries ago. A mix-up at the morgue left Bentham's actual head a tad banged up, so it was initially propped on his lap while a wax replacement sat atop the shoulders. However, the original went missing, and rumor points to some rascals at rival King's College who supposedly got in a jolly game of football before hiding it. Other sources contest that the original head is still kept in the UCL vaults somewhere, and the entire body is reunited for a few exclusive dinner parties every year with some of the world's top academics. Most amusing, though, is the report that the Auto-Icon regularly attends meetings of the College Council. As the story goes, Bentham is wheeled into his place among the members of the council, and in the minutes it's duly recorded: *Jeremy Bentham—present but not voting.*

The Royal Observatory, at the site of the line, was originally founded to produce accurate star-charts for navigation. This history of time-keeping led to Greenwich being chosen as the site of Britain's most famous white elephant, the **Millennium Dome.** Situated some way from the historic sights in World Heritage Site Greenwich, it's soon to enter into a new incarnation as a 26,000-seat stadium. Greenwich's relaxed pace and interesting (and largely free) sights and museums, makes it a more than pleasant place to spend a day.

RIVER TRIPS. Many people choose to make the **boat** trip (1hr.) from Westminster or Tower Hill; boats also run to the Thames Barrier. Travelcard holders get 33% off riverboat fares. **City Cruises** operates from Westminster Pier to Greenwich via the Tower of London. *(☎ 7740 0400; www.citycruises.com. Mar.-Nov. daily. Schedule changes constantly;* ***call for schedules.*** *Adult return £8.20, all-day "rover" ticket £8.70; child £4.10/£4.35; family cover of 5, £23.)* **Thames River Service** boats, run by the London Transport Service, also head from Westminster Pier to Greenwich via Embankment and Tower Hill, with some boats going to the Thames Barrier as well. *(☎ 7930 4097. Apr.-Oct. daily every 30min., 10am-5pm; June-Aug. until 7pm. Same prices as above.)* There is also a return service from Greenwich directly to the Thames Barrier. *(Practical information same as above. Adult return £5.60, child £2.80, student/senior £4.40, family £14.20. Wheelchair accessible. AmEx/MC/V.)*

ROYAL OBSERVATORY GREENWICH

Location: *At the top of Greenwich Park, a short but moderately steep climb from the National Maritime Museum; for an easier walk, take The Avenue from St. Mary's Gate at the top of King William Walk. There is also a tram that leave from the back of the Museum every 30min. on the hr.* ***Contact:*** *☎ 8312 6565; www.rog.nmm.ac.uk.* ***Open:*** *Daily 10am 5pm; last admission 4:30pm.* ***Admission:*** *Free. Partially wheelchair accessible.*

The climb to the peak of Greenwich Park is not for the lazy, but the view proves to be well worth the trek; you can see all of the Docklands and Westminster on a clear day. The peak is home to the unexciting **Royal Observatory,** housed in a pleasant Wren building. Charles II founded this site in 1675, along with the post of Astronomer Royal, accelerating the quest to solve the problem of determining longitude. Even though longitude was eventually solved without reference to the stars, Greenwich still plays an important role as marker of hemispheres. The **Prime Meridian** is the axis along which the astronomers' telescopes swung. The meridian is marked by a red LED strip in the courtyard that is photographed billions of times daily. Play the hemisphere hopping game "now I'm east, now I'm west," before ducking into **Flamsteed House,** a Wren creation "for the Observator's habitation and little for pompe." It now houses a few galleries of old astronomical equipment. Next to the Meridian Building's telescope display, walk around back and climb the **Observatory Dome,** cunningly disguised as a freakishly large rust-colored onion, to see the cleverly named 28-inch Telescope, constructed in 1893. It's still the 7th-largest refracting lens in the world, and although it was retired in 1971, it's still fully functional.

CUTTY SARK

King William Walk, by Greenwich Pier. ***Contact:*** *☎8858 2698; www.cuttysark.org.uk.* ***Open:*** *Daily 10am-5pm.* ***Admission:*** *£4.25, under 16 and concessions £3.25, family £10.50. Discounts for groups.*

Last of the great tea clippers, even land-lubbers will appreciate the Cutty Sark's long lean lines. Built in 1869, she was the fastest ship of her time, making the round-trip from China in only 120 days, carrying over a million pounds of tea. Retired from the sea in the 1930s, the deck and cabins have been partially restored to their 19th-century prime (complete with animatronic sailors). The hold houses an exhibition on the ship's history and a fascinating collection of figureheads. The upper deck has the officer's quarters, a far cry in comfort from those of the crew. Close by is the **Gypsy Moth,** the cozy 54 ft. craft in which 64-year-old Francis Chichester sailed solo around the globe in 1966. Though he didn't achieve his goal of matching the Cutty Sark's speed, he set numerous solo-sailing records during his 226 days afloat and was knighted on his return.

ROYAL NAVAL COLLEGE

Location: *King William Walk.* ***Contact:*** *☎8269 4791; www.greenwichfoundation.org.uk.* ***Open:*** *Daily 10am-5pm, Su chapel 12:30-5pm.* ***Admission:*** *Free.*

On the site of Henry VIII's Palace of Placentia—where both he and his daughters Mary and Elizabeth I were born—the Royal Naval College was built in 1696 as the Royal Hospital for Seamen, a naval retirement home along the same lines as the army's Royal Hospital in Chelsea (see p. 89). However, the strict regime proved unpopular with former seamen, and in 1873 it was converted into the Royal Naval College. In 1998, the Navy packed its bags and the newly formed University of Greenwich blew in, along with the famed **Trinity College of Music.** Visitors are free to wander the grandiose buildings and expansive grounds of Christopher Wren's campus. Make sure to check out the extravagant **Painted Hall,** which took Sir James Thornhill 19 years to complete. The colorful **Chapel** mixes Georgian and Rococco styles. The campus also has a Queen Mary bar and King William restaurant, should you want refreshments in regal surroundings (below the chapel and painted hall respectively).

OTHER GREENWICH SIGHTS

GREENWICH PARK. A former royal hunting ground, Greenwich Park is home to recreation and relaxation as young people and families come out in droves to sunbathe, strike up football games, and picnic. There's an interesting jumble of sights scattered around its hills too. The remains of a first-century Roman settlement and Saxon tumuli (burial mounds) are down the hill from the observatory. On the east side of the park is the **Queen Elizabeth Oak,** a rather grand title for a big dead log; for centuries before collapsing, the tree marked the spot where Henry VIII frolicked with an 11-fingered Anne Boleyn. Thankfully, a new oak was planted in the spot as a replacement in 1992. The garden in the southeast corner of the park combines English garden and fairy tale, complete with a deer park. The **Children's Boating Pool** just behind the museum gives children a chance to unleash pent-up sea-faring energy. The best itinerary is a pre-crowd early start at the observatory, then a consultation with the map plotting all the park's treasures, and then a leisurely walk down the hillwith stops at interesting ones. *(Park open daily 7am-dusk.)*

THAMES BARRIER. Around the next bend in the Thames from Greenwich stands the world's largest and strangest movable flood barrier, the reason that London no longer enjoys the ebb and flow of the tides. Constructed during the 1970s and (over) hyped as "the 8th wonder of the world," the barrier spans 520m and consists of 10 separate movable steel gates. When raised, the main gates stand as high as a five-story building. Nobody's allowed onto the barrier of course, but you can see it from the Thames Barrier Info Centre, which houses a video and history display. At the cafe you can see the massive gates in all their glory. *(Take the Thames River Services boat from Greenwich, or hop on the #188 or #177 buses from the center of town. ☎8305 4188. Open daily 10:30am-4:30pm. £1, children 50p, concessions 75p.)*

WEST LONDON

WEST LONDON QUICKFIND: Discover, p. 14; food, p. 188; entertainment, p. 248; shopping, p. 273; accommodations, p. 295.

*Confusingly, Shepherd's Bush and Hammersmith (both Zone 2) each have 2 entirely separate Tube stations. In **Shepherd's Bush,** the Central Line station is at the west end of the Green, while the Hammersmith and City Line is far west of the Green on Uxbridge Rd. ⊖Goldhawk Rd. is also convenient. Both **Hammersmith** stations are close to each other, but the Piccadilly and District Lines are more convenient for the bus station.*

SHEPHERD'S BUSH AND HAMMERSMITH

BBC TELEVISION CENTRE. This vast media complex is shaped like a giant question mark. Its sprawling buildings north of Shepherd's Bush is ground zero for British entertainment. The BBC is always looking for people to be part of studio audiences (see p. 249); for a more in-depth experience, take a fun 1½-2hr. backstage tour of the center. *(Wood Ln. ☎8743 8000; www.bbc.co.uk. ⊖White City. Tours M-Sa 10am, 10:20am, 1:15, 1:30, 3:30 and 3:45pm. Minimum age 10. Booking required, ☎0870 603 0304; no tickets sold at the door. £8, seniors £7, students and children £6. MC/V.)*

FARTHER WEST

CHISWICK

For sights, use ⊖Hammersmith then bus #190 or ⊖Turnham Green and bus #E3. The walk from ⊖Turnham Green can be confusing. Head south to Chiswick High Rd. Turn left, walk a couple blocks then turn right onto Chiswick Ln.; follow this until you hit Great West Rd., which is a major highway and cannot be crossed. Chiswick Ln. turns to the right, follow this until you come to the subway near the overpass. The subway is T-shaped—follow the signs for Chiswick House.

CHISWICK HOUSE. Faux-Italy in the middle of London. Both Chiswick House and its gardens were created by Richard Boyle, 3rd Lord Burlington (1694-1753), the first of many Englishmen to try to recreate Italy's hills in his backyard. Based on Palladio's Villa La Rotonda in Rome, the house's palatial airy design is packed with Italian details. Chiswick house was meant to be Burlington's entertaining home, and it's credited with kick-starting the English aristocracy's obsession with Palladian architecture. The beautiful **gardens** were as innovative as the home; laid out by William Kent, they were the first example of the naturalistic design that came to be known as the 18th-century English style—which is ironic, given its essentially Italian roots. The grounds today are act as a park, with a pond, open grassy areas, statues, and lots of winding woodsy trails. *(Between the Great West Rd. and the Great Chertsey Rd. ☎8995*

0508. House open Apr.-Oct. W-F and Su 10am-5pm, Sa 10am-2pm; Nov.-Mar. Pre-booked tours only. House £3.70, concessions £2.80, children £1.90. Gardens open daily 8am-dusk. Free. Frequently closes early for functions, ***call ahead.****)*

ROYAL BOTANICAL GARDENS, KEW

Location: *Kew, on the south bank of the Thames. The main entrance and visitors center is at Victoria Gate, nearest the Tube.* ***Contact:*** *☎8332 5000, 24hr. recorded information ☎8332 5655; www.kew.org. Kew Gardens (Zone 3).* ***Tours:*** *Start at Victoria Gate visitors center. 1hr. walking tours daily 11am and 2pm; free. "Explorer" hop-on-hop-off shuttle makes 35min. rounds of the gardens; 1st shuttle departs daily 11am, last 3:35pm. £3.50, children £1. "Discovery" 1hr. buggy tours for mobility impaired M-F 11am and 2pm; booking required, free.* ***Open:*** *Apr.-Aug. M-F 9:30am-6:30pm, Sa-Su 9:30am-7:30pm; Sept.-Oct. daily 9:30am-6pm; Nov.-Jan. daily 9:30am-4:15pm; Feb.-Mar. daily 9:30am-5:30pm. Last admission 30min. before closing. Glasshouses close 5:30pm Feb.-Oct., 3:45pm Nov.-Jan.* ***Admission:*** *£7.50, "late entry" (from 45min. before the glasshouses close) £5:50; concessions £5:50; under 16 free with adult.*

In the summer of 2003, UNESCO announced that the Royal Botanical Gardens as a World Heritage Site—a privilege shared by many of the historic sights in London. The 250-year-old Royal Botanical Gardens extends in a 300 acres swath along the Thames, and has a quiet green English placidity. Kew is also a leading center for botany thanks to its collection of thousands of flowers, fruits, trees, and vegetables from across the globe. It currently houses some 30,000 living species, and about 7 million pressed varieties.

The three **conservatories** are at the center of the collection. The steamy Victorian **Palm House** boasts Encephalartos Altensteinii, "The Oldest Pot Plant In The World," which is not at all what it sounds like. The **Princess of Wales Conservatory,** opened in 1987 by Diana but named for Augusta (the mother of George III), has a larger area under glass than any other, thanks to its innovative pyramid-like structure. Inside there are 10 different climate zones, from rainforest to desert, including two entirely devoted to orchids. The steamy **Temperate House** has a fabulous global display of flora—the various sections of the building tour around the world, at least in terms of plant life. The 20m-tall, 158 year old Jubaea Chilensis palm is the world's largest indoor plant, and it's still growing.

Outside the controlled environment of the houses, the gardens have all sorts of hidden treasures. The **Japanese Gateway and Garden** sits next to a giant **pagoda** and brings eastern flora to the park. There are also the native **Lilacs, Azaleas,** and a **Rhododendron Dell.** Be sure to visit the **Rock Garden** and the **Rose Pergola.** Out-of-season visitors will not be disappointed—the **Woodland Glade** is renowned for displays of autumn color. There's also a **lake** in the center of the Gardens. Close to the Thames in the northern part of the gardens, **Kew Palace** (closed for renovations until 2006) is a modest red-brick affair used by Royalty on Garden visits. On the hill behind and to the right of the palace, 17th-century medicinal plants flourish in the stunning **Queen's Garden;** small placards label one that cures back pain "caused by overmuch use of women." At the opposite end of the gardens, **Queen Charlotte's Cottage** is a faux-rustic building given by George III to his wife as a picnic site. Younger visitors will welcome the opportunity to **Be a Badger!**—a human-sized reconstruction of a badger's den, complete with tunnels, nests, and foodstores. A cafe, restaurant, and tea house are on-site, tucked amid the trees.

INSIDE

Museums and Galleries

Centuries as the capital of an empire upon which the sun never set, together with a decidedly English penchant for collecting, have endowed London with a spectacular set of museums. Art lovers, history buffs, and amateur ethnologists will not know which way to turn when they arrive. And there's even better news for museum lovers—after a decade which saw many museums shed their free admission to become some of the capital's most expensive attractions, admission to all major collections is now free indefinitely in celebration of the Queen's Golden Jubilee. However, note that almost all charge extra for temporary exhibitions—often so popular that tickets must be booked in advance.

MAJOR COLLECTIONS

BRITISH MUSEUM

BLOOMSBURY QUICKFIND: Discover, p. 5; sights, p. 87; museums & galleries, p. 140; food, p. 166; pubs, p. 193, shopping, p. 255; accommodations, p. 282.

Location: *Great Russell St.* ***Contact:*** *☎ 7323 8000; www.thebritishmuseum.ac.uk. ⊖Tottenham Crt. Rd., Russell Square, or Holborn.* ***Tours:*** *Free tours start 12:30pm at the Enlightenment Desk. Highlights Tour (90min.): daily 10:30am, 1, 3pm. Advanced booking recommended. £8, concessions £5. Other tours: Various other themed tours run throughout the week; check website or info desk for details.*

Audioguide £3.50. ***Open:*** *Great Court Su-W 9am-6pm Th-Sa 9am-11pm (9pm in winter). Galleries daily 10am-5:30pm, selected galleries have extended hours Th-F.* ***Admission:*** *Free; £3 suggested donation. Temporary exhibitions around £5, concessions £3.50. Wheelchair accessible. MC/V.*

The funny thing about the British Museum is that there's almost nothing British in it. Founded in 1753 as the personal collection of Sir Hans Sloane, in 1824 work started on the current neoclassical building, which took another 30 years to construct. With 50,000 items, the magnificent collection is somewhat undermined by a chaotic layout and poor labeling (especially in the less popular galleries), while staff shortages mean that even famous galleries are frequently and randomly closed to the public. If you've got your heart set on a particular exhibit, call ahead to check. To avoid getting lost, take one of the free tours, or purchase the color map available at the entrance (£2). Overall, the experience is an odd combination of Victorian-era exoticization of the foreign and more modern, PC multicultural reverence.

GREAT COURT. This is the largest covered square in Europe. Used as the British Library book stacks for the past 150 years, the courtyard is still dominated by a gigantic **Reading Room.** The blue chairs and desks, set inside a towering dome of books, have shouldered the weight of research by Marx, Lenin, and Trotsky, as well as almost every major British writer and intellectual.

WEST GALLERIES. From the main entrance, the large double doors to the left of the Reading Room lead to the Museum's most popular wing. The star of the **Egyptian Sculpture** rooms is the **Rosetta Stone,** whose trilingual inscriptions (in Greek, Heterotic, and Hieroglyphic) made the deciphering of ancient Egyptian possible. *(Room 4.)* Less iconic, but enduringly huge are the monumental friezes and reliefs of the Assyrian, Hittite, and other **Ancient Near Eastern** civilizations. *(Rooms 6-10, ground floor; the southern end of room 4 leads into room 6.)* Most famous of the massive array of **Greek sculpture** on show are the **Elgin Marbles,** statues from the Parthenon carved under the direction of Athens's greatest sculptor, Phidias. *(Room 18.)* Equally impressive are the almost perfectly preserved **Bassae Friezes,** displaying scenes from the battle between Perseus and the Amazons. *(Room 16, upstairs from 17.)* Other Hellenic highlights include remnants of two of the seven Wonders of the Ancient World, the **Temple of Artemis** at Ephesus and the **Mausoleum of Halikarnassos.** *(Rooms 21-22.)* Upstairs, the **Portland Vase** presides over **Roman** ceramics and housewares. When discovered in 1582, the vase had already been broken and replaced. In 1845, it was shattered by a drunken museum-goer. When it was put back together, 37 small chips were left over. Since then, the vase has been reconstructed twice, with more leftover chips being reincorporated each time—don't touch! *(Room 70.)*

NORTH GALLERIES. Revenge of the mummy: just when you thought you'd nailed Ancient Egypt, along come another 6 galleries. Full of painted wooden sarcophagi and bandaged mummies in various states of disrepair. *(Rooms 61-66, upper floor.)* Another highlight, the newer **African Galleries** are perhaps the best-presented in the museum, with a fabulous collection accompanied by soft chanting, video displays, and abundant documentation. *(Room 25, lower floor.)* More overflow from the West wing continues the Near Eastern theme. Musical instruments and board games from the world's first city, **Ur,** show that leisure time is a historical constant. *(Rooms 51-59.)* Nearby, the **Americas** collection is dominated by **Mexico**, which features some extraordinary Aztec artifacts. *(Rooms 26-27.)* Just off the Montague Pl. entrance is a fine collection of **Islamic art.** *(Room 34.)* Immediately above it the largest room in the museum is dedicated to the art of **China, South Asia,** and **Southeast Asia,** with some particularly fine Hindu sculpture. *(Room 33.)* Upstairs, the highlight of the **Korean** display is a sarangbang house built on-site. *(Room 67.)* A teahouse, meanwhile, is the centerpiece of the **Japanese** galleries. *(Rooms 92-94.)*

SOUTH & EAST GALLERIES. The upper level of the museum's southeast corner is dedicated to ancient and medieval **Europe,** including most of the museum's British artifacts. A highlight of the collection is the treasure excavated from the

Sutton Hoo Burial Ship; the magnificent inlaid helmet is the most famous example of Anglo-Saxon craftsmanship. Along with the ship is the Mildenhall Treasure, a trove of brilliantly preserved Roman artifacts. *(Room 41.)* Next door are the enigmatic and beautiful **Lewis Chessmen,** an 800-year-old Scandinavian chess set mysteriously abandoned on Scotland's Outer Hebrides. *(Room 42.)* Collectors and enthusiasts will also enjoy the comprehensive **Clock Gallery** *(Room 44)* and **Money Gallery** *(Room 68).*

HIGHLIGHTS IN A HURRY: Gape at the grandness of the **Great Court,** then hit the closely-packed stars of the **Egypt/Greece wing** (the Rosetta Stone, the Elgin Marbles, the Bassae Friezes, and the various Wonders of the Ancient World). Sweep through the moldy **sarcophagi** rooms in the North wing on your way to Africa, and finish up just in time at the delightful **Clock Gallery.**

NATIONAL GALLERY

WESTMINSTER QUICKFIND: Discover, p. 11; sights, p. 116; museums & galleries, p. 140; food, p. 181; pubs, p. 202; entertainment, p. 244; accommodations, p. 293.

***Location:** Main entrance on north side of Trafalgar Sq. ⊖Charing Cross or Leicester Square. **Contact:** ☎7747 2885; www.nationalgallery.org.uk. **Open:** M-Tu and Th-Su 10am-6pm, W 10am-9pm. Special exhibitions in the Sainsbury Wing occasionally open until 10pm. **Tours:** Start at Sainsbury Wing info desk. 1hr. gallery tours daily 11:30am and 2:30pm, W also 6:30pm; free. Audtioguides free, £4 suggested donation. **Admission:** Free; some temporary exhibitions £5-7, seniors £4-5, students and ages 12-18 £2-3. Wheelchair accessible at Sainsbury Wing on Pall Mall East.*

The National Gallery was founded by an Act of Parliament in 1824, with 38 pictures displayed in a townhouse; over the years it's grown to hold the burgeoning collection. Numerous additions have been made, the most recent (and controversial) being the massive modern Sainsbury Wing—Prince Charles described it as "a monstrous carbuncle on the face of a much-loved and elegant friend." The Sainsbury Wing holds almost all of the museum's large exhibitions as well as the restaurants and lecture halls. If you're pressed for time, which would be a shame, head to the **Micro Gallery** in the Sainsbury Wing, where you can design and print out a personalized tour of the paintings you want to see.

SAINSBURY WING. The rooms of the gallery's newest extension house its oldest, most fragile paintings, dating from 1260 to 1510. Most of the works on display are religious ones, with very few exceptions. The most famous of the devotional medieval paintings on display is the *Wilton Diptych*, a 14th-century altarpiece made by an unknown artist for (and featuring) Richard II (Room 53). The **early Renaissance** collection features Botticelli's *Venus and Mars*, an early plea to make love not war, and Piero della Francesca's ultra-famous *Baptism of Christ* (Rooms 58 and 66). One of the museum's most interesting works, the *Leonardo Cartoon* is a detailed preparatory drawing by Leonardo da Vinci for a never-executed painting. Other Leonardos on display include his second *Virgin on the Rocks* (Room 51). One of the finest of the Sainsbury Wing's offerings, however, is Van Eyck's 1434 masterpiece, the *Arnolfini Portrait*, hanging austerely in Room 56.

WEST WING. With paintings from 1510 to 1600, the West Wing is dominated by the Italian **High Renaissance,** both Roman and Venetian, and the first flowering of German and Flemish art. As you move through the rooms, the religious motifs give way to domestic and rural themes. Room 4 has Holbein's *The Ambassadors* with its optical illusion and subversive hidden messages, while exquisite paintings by Moroni line the walls of room 6. In Room 8, the artists of Rome and Florence are shown together; Parmigianino's nudes are a highlight. Rooms 9 and 10 focus on northern Italy, with the latter dominated by Titian. Rooms 11 and 12, featuring early Flemish works, hold some stunning Gossaerts and Beukalaer's domestic/religous scenes.

the local story

Blood-y Good Try

The Queen can rest easy tonight knowing that the crown jewels are safe, but past monarchs haven't been so lucky. In 1671 Charles II assigned his right-hand man, Sir Gilbert Talbot, the task of jewel guarding. Sir Talbot wasn't particularly fond of Tower life so he passed the task down the chain of command until it rested in the hands of his less-than-capable servant, Edward. Enter: Colonel Thomas Blood.

"Colonel" Blood, as he demanded to be called, was not a colonel at all, he was an ordinary man who was extraordinarily cunning and who took advantage of less extraordinary people, like humble Edward. One night Blood gathered a posse and headed to the Tower where his men paid Edward a surprise "visit." They greedily stuffed jewels down their trousers before escaping towards the wharf. Edward's son come home unexpectedly and, finding the jewels missing, gathered a posse of his own and chased the men to the docks, where they where caught. Strangely, though, King Charles II pardoned Blood and his men. Even more strangely, the king was so impressed with Blood's ravishing bravado that he gave Blood a seat on the royal court! Conspiracy theorists wonder if Charles conspired to rob himself. Clearly it pays to be bad.

NORTH WING. The North Wing spans the **17th century,** with an exceptional display of Flemish and Spanish Renaissance works spread over 17 rooms. The twin Vermeers in Room 16 are 2 of only 34 in the world; they tell the tale of a maiden's romantic love. Room 23 boasts no fewer than 18 Rembrandts, including his comparative Self Portrait at age 34 and Self Portrait at age 63, painted the year he died. Room 29 is dominated by Rubens's *Massacre of the Innocents* and his *Samson and Delilah,* along with dozens of his other works. Velàzquez's super-sensuous and at the time highly controversial *The Toilet of Venus* is at odds with the rest of his mostly religious output on show in room 30. Other Spanish masters Murillo and Zurbaran also have works hanging in the room.

EAST WING. Home to paintings from 1700 to 1900, is the most crowded, housing the most famous works and the Impressionist galleries. The focus is primarily on room 45, which features one of Van Gogh's *Sunflowers* which he hung in the guest room for his good friend Paul Gauguin, who also has paintings displayed nearby. Pissarro's landscapes and Cézanne's *Bathers* also are displayed. Room 44 contains a brilliant set of paintings by Seurat as well as work by Manet, Monet, and Renoir. A reminder that there was art on this side of the Channel too, Room 34 flies the flag with portraits by Reynolds and Gainsborough, as well as six luminescent Turners, ranging from the stormy realism of *Dutch Boats in a Gale* to the proto-Impressionist blur of *Margate from the Sea.* Room 46 has the striking Portrait of Angel de Soto by Picasso and Degas's masterpiece *The Ballet Dancers.*

TATE BRITAIN

WESTMINSTER QUICKFIND: Discover, p. 11; sights, p. 116; museums & galleries, p. 152; food, p. 181; pubs, p. 202.

Location: *Millbank, near Vauxhall Bridge, in Westminster.* *Pimlico.* ***Contact:*** *☎ 7887 8008; www.tate.org.uk.* ***Tours:*** *M-F: Art from 1500-1800 11am, 1800-1900 noon, Turner 2pm, 1900-2002 3pm. Sa-Su tours of 1500-2004 at noon and 3pm; all free. Audioguide £3, concessions £2.50. Lunchtime Lectures W or Th, Sa 1pm and Su 2:30pm. Regular events include: Gallery Talks, W-F lunchtime; Painting of the Month, M 1:15pm and Sa 2:30pm; Friday Lectures, F 1pm; Slide Lectures, Sa 1pm and Su 2:30pm.* ***Open:*** *Daily 10am-5:50pm, last admission 5pm.* ***Admission:*** *Free; special exhibitions £3-9.50. Wheelchair access via Clore Wing.*

Tate Britain now houses an excellent collection of British art including foreign artists working in Britain and Brits working abroad from 1500 to the present. There are four Tate Galleries in England; this the original Tate, opened in 1897 to house Sir Henry Tate's collection of "modern" British art. It was expanded to include the famed British painter's J.M.W. Turner bequest of 282 oils and 19,000 watercolors. The museum can feel like one big tribute to Turner. The **Clure Gallery** continues to display Turner's prolific collection of hazy British landscapes. The bulk of the museum consists of the **Tate Centenary Development,** rotating exhibits which loosely trace the chronology of art in Britain from 1500 to 2004. The rooms are organized through themed subdivisions such as "British Art & Asia" or "Art and Victorian Society." These galleries feature the fervent work of William Blake, as well as the paintings by the Pre-Raphaelites John Everett Millais, John Singer Sargent and Frederic Lord Leighton. Additional artists on display are John Constable, William Hogarth, Richard Long, Ben Nicholson, and David Hockney. Other beloved works include Henry Moore's incredible *Recumbent Figure* sculpture and John Singer Sargent's colorful Victorian portraits. The bulk of modern British art is absent, having been transferred to the Tate Modern at Bankside in 1999 (see below), but that doesn't means that what remains here is static or stodgy; Mark Boyle's fiberglass, lifesize recreation of a street curb is *tres avant garde.* The annual **Turner Prize** for contemporary art is still held here annually. Four contemporary British artists are nominated for the £30,000 prize; their shortlisted works go on show from late October to early January.

TATE MODERN

SOUTH BANK QUICKFIND: Discover, p. 10; sights, p. 106; museums & galleries, p. 137; food, p. 176; pubs, p. 200; nightlife p. 212; entertainment p. 238; accommodations p. 292.

Location: *Bankside, on the South Bank; main entrance; secondary entrance on Queen's Walk. From Southwark tube, turn left up Union then left on Great Suffolk, then left on Holland.* ⊖*Southwark or Blackfriars.* ***Contact:*** *☎ 7887 8000; www.tate.org.uk.* ***Tours:*** *Meet on the gallery concourses; free. History/Memory/Society noon, level 5; Nude/Body/Action 11am, level 5; Landscape/Matter/Environment 3pm, level 3; Still Life/Object/Real Life 2pm, level 3. Audioguide: 5 types: highlights, collection, architecture, children's tour, and the visually impaired tour, £2. Talks M-F 1pm. Meet at concourse on appropriate level; free.* ***Open:*** *Su-Th 10am-6pm, F-Sa 10am-10pm.* ***Admission:*** *Free. Wheelchair accessible on Holland St.*

Since opening in May 2000, Tate Modern has been credited with single-handedly reversing the long-term decline in museum-going numbers in Britain. Indeed, the curatorial scheme and the impressive collection have made Tate Modern controversial and popular. The largest modern art museum in the world (until New York's MOMA re-opens in 2005), its most striking aspect is Sir Giles Gilbert Scott's mammoth building, formerly the Bankside power station. What looks from the distance to be a huge factory with a towering smoke stack is actually the museum. The seventh floor has unblemished views of the Thames and north and south of London. The ground floor **Turbine Hall** is now an open, immense atrium that dwarfs the installations. A full one-third of the gallery space, all of level 4, is dedicated to temporary exhibits. Rest areas around the galleries provide chairs, books, and recorded commentary by artists, intellectuals, and celebrities.

Tate has been criticized for its groundbreaking controversial curatorial method. The museum groups works according to themes and subthemes such as "Still life/Object/Real Life" and then "Subversive Objects." In doing this the Tate has turned itself into a work of conceptual art—as many carefully chosen words are used to explain the logic behind each room's collection as are dedicated to the meaning behind the works themselves. Within this framework, however, curators have begun arranging more works by period and artist; but officially, everything is still organized according to four themes: **Still Life/Object/Real Life** and **Landscape/Matter/Environment** on level 3, and **Nude/Action/Body** and **History/Memory/Society** on level 5. This arrangement brings out some interesting contrasts:

successes include the nascent geometry of Cézanne's *Still Life with Water Jug* juxtaposed with Howard Hodgkin's splotchy *Dinner at Smith Square* in the "Art of the Everyday" room of the Still Life/Object/Real Life; Matisse's *Notre Dame* hangs next to CW Nevinson's harsh *Soul of the Soulless City*, in Landscape/Matter/Environment. In other rooms, the purported theme is only a substitute for a more conventional arrangement: in Landscape/Matter/Environment, the "Inner Worlds" room might as well be called "Surrealism," with painting and sculpture by Dalí, Miró and Dorothea Tanning. Magritte's wonderful *Reckless Sleeper* hangs here. One great positive that emerges from the strange thematic arrangement is the way in which viewers are exposed to many types of art and art of varied fame. It's now impossible to see the Tate's more famous pieces, which include Picasso's *Nude Woman with Necklace*, without also confronting challenging and invigorating works by less well-known contemporary artists.

Special exhibits in 2004/05 include "Time After Time" (Oct.6-Jan.2), "The Unilever series: Bruce Nauman in Turbine Hall" (Oct.12-Mar.28), and a Robert Frank show (Oct.27-Jan.30).

VICTORIA & ALBERT MUSEUM

KENSINGTON AND EARL'S COUT QUICKFIND: Discover, p. 8; sights, p. 106; museums & galleries, p. 137; food, p. 171; pubs, p. 198, entertainment, p. 236; shopping, p. 257; accommodations, p. 286.

Location: *Main entrance on Cromwell Rd., wheelchair-accessible on Exhibition Rd.* ***Contact:*** *☎7942 2000; www.vam.ac.uk. South Kensington.* ***Open:*** *Daily 10am-5:45pm, plus W and last F of month until 10pm.* ***Tours:*** *Meet at rear of main entrance; free. Introductory tours: Daily 10:30, 11:30am, 1:30pm, 3:30pm; W also 4:30pm. Focus tours: Daily 12:30, 2:30pm. Subjects change every 6 weeks. Talks and events meet at rear of main entrance. Gallery talks daily 1pm, 45-60min., free. Late View Events: Talks, tours, and live music W from 6:30pm; last F of month also features live performances, guest DJs, late-night exhibition openings, bar, and food.* ***Admission:*** *Free; additional charge for some special exhibitions. Wheelchair accessible.*

When the V&A was founded in 1852 as the Museum of Manufactures to encourage excellence in art and design, the original curators were deluged with objects from around the globe. Today, as the largest museum of decorative (and not so decorative) arts in the world, the V&A rivals the British Museum for the sheer size and diversity of its holdings—befit an institution dedicated to displaying "the fine and applied arts of all countries, all styles, all periods." Unlike the British Museum, the V&A's documentation is consistently excellent and thorough. Its 5 million sq. meters of galleries house the best collection of **Italian Renaissance sculpture** outside Italy, the largest array of **Indian art** outside India, and a gallery of fashion from the 16th century to the latest designers. And interactive displays, hi-tech touchpoints, and engaging activities ensure that the goodies won't become boring. Staff shortages can lead to the temporary closure of less-popular galleries without notice; it's best to call ahead on the day of your visit if you want to see a specific gallery. If you really want to see something in a cordoned-off gallery, try asking politely at the main entrance info desk: they may be convinced to send someone along to give you a private viewing. Themed itineraries available at the desk can help streamline your visit, and **Family Trail** cards suggested routes through the museum with kids.

BRITISH GALLERIES. The subject of a £31m refit, the vast British Galleries sprawl over three floors of reconstructed rooms documenting the progression of British taste and fashion from 1500-1900. From clothing to furniture to innumerable fascinating gadgets, exhibits all begin with the question "Who led taste" (the answer, of course, someone British).

DRESS COLLECTION. Don't expect to find everyday clothing in the V&A's world-famous costume collection: nothing but the finest haute couture through and through. Men's suits and women's gowns are displayed on mannequins, with panels describing the major designers of the 20th century, from John-Paul Gaultier to Issey

Miyake. The full exhibit is closed for renovations until January 2005; until then, a partial "Fashion Exhibit" will remain on display.

EUROPE. The ground-floor European collections are staggering in their breadth. A museum highlight is the **Raphael Gallery,** hung with eight massive cartoons (preliminary paintings) for tapestries commissioned by Leo X in 1515 to hang in the Sistine Chapel. The **Sculpture Gallery,** home to Canova's *Three Graces* (1814-17) and voluptuous *Sleeping Nymph* (1820-24), is not to be confused with the **Cast Courts.** If you only see one thing in the museum, make it this marvelous display of plaster reproductions of the world's great sculptural masterpieces, from Trajan's *Column* to Michelangelo's *David.* The **Medieval Treasury** houses some extraordinary enamels and vestments, including the beautiful *Clare Chasuble of 1272.* Rooms devoted to **Nothern Europe** display the fruits of the Late Middle Ages, including several Dürers.

ASIAN GALLERIES. If the choice of objects in the V&A's Asian collections seems to rely on national clichés (Indian temple carvings, Chinese porcelain), the objects themselves remain largely spectacular. Number one to see here is **Tippoo's Tiger,** the graphically fascinating 1799 model of a tiger eating a man— complete with organ sounds and crunching noises. The Turkish and Egyptian ceramics of the **Islamic Art** collection are overshadowed by the gigantic Ardabil carpet, woven in Iran in 1539 and containing an estimated 30 million knots. In addition to the requisite swords, armor, and paintings, the excellent **Japanese** gallery displays an array of contemporary ceramic sculpture and kimonos.

UPPER FLOORS. The upper levels are arranged by material, with specialist galleries devoted to everything from musical instruments to stained glass. In the **textile** collection, where you can try on kimonos and tweed jackets, long cabinets contain pull-out drawers with swatches of thousands of different fabrics. Turnstiles and solid steel doors protect the contents of the opulent **Jewelry** gallery. Two exceptions to the material-y themed galleries are the **Leighton** gallery, with a fresco by the eponymous Victorian painter, and the sprawling **20th-century** collections, a trippy highlight. Here, arranged by period and style, are illustration and design classics from Salvador Dalí's 1936 sofa modeled on Mae West's lips to a pair of 1990s latex hotpants.

HENRY COLE WING. The 6-level Henry Cole wing is home to the V&A's collection of **British paintings,** including some 350 works by Consta-

NO WORK ALL PLAY

Royal Birthday Party

Not everyone celebrates a birthday with a parade, but if you're the Queen of England, you do. Queen Elizabeth II's birthday actually falls on April 21st, but as the weather conditions are more favorable in summer, the celebration occurs on the 2nd Saturday of June. The party begins with a procession from Buckingham Palace to the Horse Guard's Parade. The household division of the Royal army marches out followed by footguards, house cavalry and mounted guards in ceremonial dress. Her Majesty the Queen comes last, riding in an open carriage with the princes and princess on horseback.

After the processional, the group rides to the Parade arena where the Queen conducts a ceremonial inspection of the troops. And by inspection, we mean she watches them ride around the arena. There, the Color is "Trooped." Nobles and Brits wise enough to write ahead in February are seated inside the arena, while visitors find themselves in a pack full of camera wielding amateurs straining for a view. After the trooping, the Queen rides back to the palace where a gun salute and a royal air force fly-over seal the deal. The spectators miss out on any birthday cake, but watching the army parade is a close second.

ble and numerous Turners. Also here is a display of **Rodin** bronzes, donated by the artist in 1914, and the "world's greatest collection" of **miniature portraits,** including Holbein's *Anne of Cleves*. In the library-like **print room,** anyone can ask to see original works from the prodigious collection *(Print room open Tu-F 10am-4:30pm, Sa 10am-1pm and 2-4:30pm).*

HIGHLIGHTS IN A HURRY: Make a tour of the cloth-tastic **Dress Collection** before heading over to see **Tippoo's Tiger,** the **Cast Courts,** and the sparkling **jewelry** collection. Finish up with a retro mindbend through the **20th Century** galleries.

MUSEUMS BY NEIGHBORHOOD

BLOOMSBURY

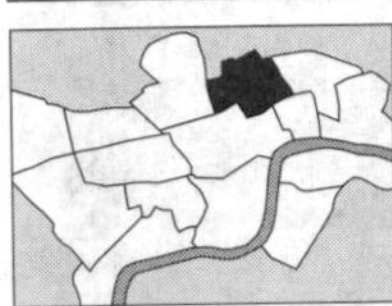

SEE MAP, p. 360

BLOOMSBURY QUICKFIND: Discover, p. 5; sights, p. 87; food, p. 166; pubs, p. 193; entertainment, p. 234; shopping, p. 255; accommodations, p. 282. For the British Museum, see p. 133.

BRITISH LIBRARY GALLERIES

Location: *96 Euston Rd.* ⊖*King's Cross St. Pancras.* ***Contact:*** ☎*7412 7332; www.bl.uk.* ***Open:*** *M and W-F 9:30am-6pm, Tu 9:30am-8pm, Sa 9:30am-5pm, Su 11am-5pm.* ***Tours*** *see British Library p. 88. Audioguides, £3.50, concessions £2.50.* ***Admission:*** *Library free. Wheelchair accessible.*

Housed within the British Library (see p. 88) is an appropriately stunning display of books, manuscripts, and related artifacts from around the world and throughout the ages. Displays are arranged by theme, and a rundown of highlights reads like some fantastic list of the most precious pages imaginable. Grab a **free map** at the main info desk, then enter the dark and lovely gallery: the **Literature** corner includes Shakespeare's first folio, as well as Lewis Carrol's hand-drawn first copy of *Alice in Wonderland*, personally donated by the author's young muse. The Lindisfarne *Gospels*, history's best-surviving Anglo-Saxon gospel and perhaps the most beautiful item on display, is part of the **Illuminated Manuscripts** section. **Music** showcases handwritten treats, from Handel's *Messiah* to an entire area devoted to the Beatles. Check out the original copy of the *Magna Carta* in **Historical Documents,** the fascinating pages of Leonardo da Vinci's notebook in **Science,** and the 4th century *Codex Sinaiticus* in **Bibles**— this Greek document is the earliest manuscript of the complete New Testament. Witness the **Dawn of Printing,** European-style, with one of 50 known original Gutenberg Bibles (1454), then see how Eastern printers had perfected the technique 700 years earlier on the *Million Charms of Empress Shôtoku*. In **Sacred Texts,** go for Sultan Baybar's ornate 1304 *Qur'an*. All through the gallery, sound archive jukeboxes allow visitors to hear snippets of the texts and music on display, and to the rear of the exhibition, the **Turning the Page** computer enables anyone to (electronically) peruse the ancient tomes. There is also an elaborate temporary exhibition space at the front of the museum; from Nov. 5, 2004 - Apr. 10, 2005, *Writer in the Garden* will explore the complex relationship between writers and the nature that inspires them, while May 20 - Oct. 23, 2005, will pay tribute to Hans Christian Andersen. Downstairs, the **Workshop of Sounds and Images** is aimed at a younger audience, with interactive displays charting the history of recording, from parchment to TV.

OTHER PERMANENT COLLECTIONS

POLLOCK'S TOY MUSEUM. A maze of tiny rooms and passageways congested with antique play things of high kitsch value. It's neither comprehensive nor remotely interactive, but the atmosphere of old-time creakiness goes well with the glass-framed treasures on display. Highlights include the oldest known teddy bear (*Eric*, "born" 1905), "Saucy Frauleins" who expose themselves at the tug of a string, and a room of elaborately furnished dollhouses that Barbie would kill for. None of the toys on display can be touched, limiting the museum's appeal for children; however, curious grownups will appreciate the detailed labels and informative asides. It all leads back to Pollock's own old-fashioned toy shop by the entrance, with traditional playthings at good modern prices. *(1 Scala St., entrance on Whitfield St. ☎ 7636 3452; www.pollockstoymuseum.com ⊖Goodge St. Open M-Sa 10am-5pm; last admission 4:30pm. £3, concessions and under 18 £1.50. AmEx/MC/V.)*

PERCIVAL DAVID FOUNDATION OF CHINESE ART. Heaven for lovers of Chinese porcelain, dull for others. This Georgian townhouse, part of the **School of Oriental and African Studies** (SOAS), boasts the finest collection of china outside of, well, China. On the ground floor temporary exhibitions, often using pieces from the 1700-item collection to illustrate trends and themes in Chinese art. The 1st floor houses superb early examples of imperial porcelain, including 13 pieces of extremely rare Ru wares collected by Sir Percival himself. The 2nd floor features later examples of blue-and-white Ming and painted Qing work. *(53 Gordon Sq. ☎ 7387 3909; www.pdfmuseum.org.uk. ⊖Euston Square or Euston. Open M-F 10:30am-5pm. Free. Wheelchair accessible.)*

EXHIBITION SPACES

Brunei Gallery, 10 Thornhaugh St., opposite the main SOAS entrance (☎ 7898 4915; www.soas.ac.uk/gallery). ⊖Russell Square. Also affiliated with SOAS (see above), this beautiful 3-floor space is devoted to carefully and elaborately crafted exhibitions of African and Asian art and culture. As its patron is the Sultan of Brunei, you'd expect nothing less. Highlights of the 2004-2005 season include exhibits on Sudan, Cameroonian photography, and Indian painting. Open M-F 10:30am-5pm when exhibitions are on; visit website or call for schedule. Free. Wheelchair accessible.

CHELSEA

CHELSEA QUICKFIND: Discover, p. 5; sights, p. 89; food, p. 167; pubs, p. 195; entertainment, p. 234; shopping, p. 256; accommodations, p. 285.

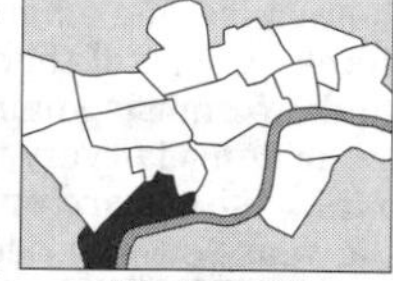

SEE MAP, p. 361

The only Tube station in Chelsea is Sloane Sq.; from here buses #11, 19, 22, 211, and 319 run down the King's Rd.

NATIONAL ARMY MUSEUM. Five floors of comprehensive, newly-renovated exhibits. If you're not in a militaristic mindset when you get here, this museum will certainly get you into one—weapons point at visitors at every turn. Starting with the battle of Agincourt in 1415 and running all the way to "The Modern Army," the chronological displays use life-size recreations, videos, dioramas, and memorabilia to recreate combat though the ages. The wax figures occasionally border on the ridiculous, but engaging interactive opportunities abound: feel the weight of a cannonball or hopscotch through the chronology of a battle. The brand-new Special Exhibit wing will house a Crimean War retrospective through March 2005. Naturally, there's also a permanent Waterloo display, complete with the skeleton of Napoleon's favorite horse, Marengo. *(Royal Hospital Rd. ☎ 7730 0717; www.national-army-museum.ac.uk. Open daily 10am-5:30pm. Free. Wheelchair accessible.)*

THE CITY OF LONDON

THE CITY OF LONDON QUICKFIND: Discover, p. 6; sights, p. 90; food, p. 168; pubs, p. 195; entertainment, p. 235.

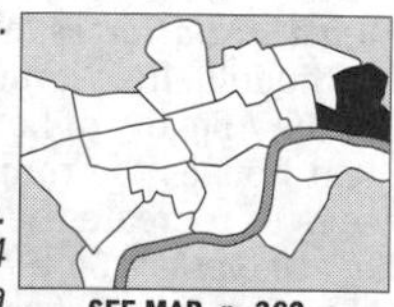

SEE MAP, p. 362

MUSEUM OF LONDON

Location: *London Wall; enter through the Barbican or from Aldersgate. Wheelchair users take elevator at Aldersgate entrance.* ***Contact:*** *☎ 087 0444 3852; www.museumoflondon.org.uk. ⊖Bank or Barbican.* ***Open:*** *M-Sa 10am-5:50pm, Su noon-5:50pm; last admission 5:30pm. Audioguides £2. Frequent demonstrations, talks, and guided walks; free-£10.* ***Admission:*** *Free. Wheelchair accessible.*

A visit to the Museum of London is the best and most enjoyable way to learn about London's history. Located in the southwest corner of the Barbican complex (see **Sights,** p. 92), the Museum of London resembles an industrial fortress from the outside. The City has built an overpass to access the museum from the Aldersgate side; the traffic there is impassable. Once inside, the engrossing collection traces the history of London from its Roman foundations to the present day, cleverly incorporating architectural history, such as the adjacent ruins of the ancient city walls. There's quite a bit to see, thankfully the museum is easy to move through. The **London Before London** display is a little excessive (the Ice Age was a pretty dull time for the city), but the museum quickly heats up. The **Roman** galleries are particularly impressive, with a reconstructed dining room built over an original mosaic floor and a large collection of artifacts and sculptures. The Anglo-Saxon and Medieval collections are small but excellent, including shields from the Norman invasion and an outstanding exhibit on Henry VIII's break from Catholicism. Best of all, a period-specific soundtrack accompanies each exhibit. Equally impressive are the 19th- and 20th-century displays, particularly the exhibit on poverty in the East End. The museum is worth a visit for the **Cheapside Hoard** alone, a 17th-century goldsmith's bounty uncovered in 1912, or for the **Lord Mayor's State Coach,** built in 1757 and dripping with gold carvings. Must-sees include the jewel-rich **Cheapside hoard, Duke Wellington's Hat and Boots,** a fun recreation of a **Victorian marketplace** and the **State Coach** which is still used on special occasions.

OTHER PERMANENT COLLECTIONS

BANK OF ENGLAND MUSEUM. Housed within the Bank itself (see **Sights** p. 94), this out of the ordinary museum traces the history from the Bank's foundation (1694) to the present day. The first gallery houses temporary exhibits and one Italian-style architecture of the bank. Waxworks man a recreation of Sir John Soane's original Stock Office, while a display of banknotes includes a handwritten one from 1697 for the sum of £22—the ease of forgery and the annoyance of exchanging odd sums led to the introduction of standard printed notes. A central theme in the exhibit is the evolution of paper currency over gold: an amusing pair of wax investors stage a mock debate regarding the issue in the **Rotunda** every five minutes. At the center of the room is a pyramid of gold bars; visitors are encouraged to try to pick one up. Different mini-displays showcase such varied things as the Bank's official silver and German firebomb casings. The whole experience culminates in a cheesy set of interactive screens in **The Bank Today** section, providing a helpful primer on everything from supply and demand to the ins and outs of international finance. An economics lesson and a wax museum in one, it's probably a lot more fun than the Bank itself.

Skip the first galleries and head straight to the Rotunda to check out the mini-cases and admire some gold, also stop by the Bank Today on the way out. *(Bartholomew Ln. ☎7601 5545; www.bankofengland.co.uk. ⊖Bank. Open M-F 10am-5pm. Free. Wheelchair accessible.)*

GUILDHALL ART GALLERY. This incredibly decadent new gallery would be much more aptly titled "museum." It's devoted to displaying the City's art collection. Breeze over the aging portraits of forgotten Lord Mayors and head downstairs immediately to the basement galleries, which hold a fine collection of Victorian and Pre-Raphaelite art include works by Stevens, Poynter, Rossetti, and Millais. The first floor Copley Gallery showcases John Singleton Copley's massive, *The Defeat of the Floating Batteries*, commissioned by the government for popular appreciation. To get the full effect it must be seen from the third floor balcony. While upstairs check out the Allegory of London, seated with Athene, Pallas, Peace and Plenty. The basement houses the ruins of a Roman amphitheater in a bizarre hi-tech gallery that seeks to recreate the gladiatorial experience in neon-green wire frames. *(Guildhall Yard, off Gresham St. ☎7332 3700; www.guildhall-art-gallery.org.uk. ⊖Moorgate, or Bank. Open M-Sa 10am-5pm, last admission 4:30pm; Su noon-4pm, last admission 3:45pm. Free all day F and Sa-Th after 3:30pm; otherwise £2.50, concessions £1, under 16 free. Wheelchair accessible.)*

THE CLOCKMAKERS' MUSEUM. A one-room museum measuring the 500-year history of clockmakers through clocks, watches, chronometers, and sundials. The display includes a watch belonging to Mary Queen of Scots and the one worn by Sir Edmund Hillary when he climbed Everest. Impressive old grandfather clocks share space with pocketwatches; the keeper of the clocks comes in weekly to wind them all by hand. *(Enter through Guildhall Library on Aldermanbury. ☎7606 3030; www.clockmakers.org. ⊖St. Paul's or Moorgate. Open M-Sa 9:30am-4:45pm. Free. Wheelchair accessible.)*

EXHIBITION SPACES

Barbican Art Gallery, Houses British and international art and photography. Exhibitions change every few months and generally include a variety of media. Two exhibits coexist in the gallery; admission covers both. Call ahead for the season's exhibit (some may not be suitable for young children). International pieces are showcased behind the concert hall on the first floor. *(☎084 5120 7500; www.barbican.org.uk/gallery, between London Wall, Beech St., Aldersgate, and Moorgate. ⊖Barbican or Moorgate. Open daily 10am-6pm except W open until 9pm. Last admission 15min. before closing. £8, concessions £6, disabled £4, under 12 free. Wheelchair accessible.)*

CLERKENWELL

CLERKENWELL QUICKFIND: Discover, p. 7; sights, p. 95; food, p. 169; pubs, p. 196; nightlife, p. 210; entertainment, p. 235; accommodations, p. 285.

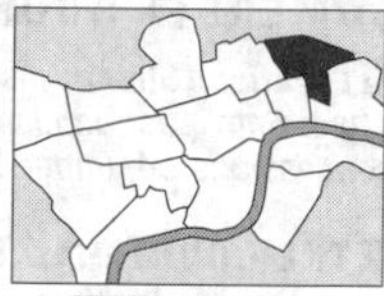

SEE MAP, p. 363

MUSEUM OF ST. BARTHOLOMEW'S HOSPITAL

West Smithfield. ☎7601 8152; www.bartsandthelondon.nhs.uk. ⊖Barbican, Farringdon, or St. Paul's. Open Tu-F 10am-4pm. Free. Tours including Smithfield area F 2pm; £5, concessions £4, children under 16 free. Wheelchair access by appointment.

Bart's, as the hospital is known, was established in 1123, when Henry I's courtier **Rahere** founded both the hospital and nearby **St. Bartholomew the Great** (see p. 96).The musty museum is largely skippable, although it is well-stocked with some gruesome old medical tools and free info packets devoted to such fascinating topics as "Nurses' Uniforms." Of note are the two huge paintings by Hogarth (who was born in nearby Bartholomew Close) which adorn the walls by the the Grand Staircase; if you need a close-up, take the tour. Also on hospital grounds is the church of **St. Bartholomew the Less,** mostly an 1820s restoration but still has a 15th-century tower.

MR.POLICEMAN, SIR. Talk to security guards, police, anyone like that (assuming they are allowed to talk to you—don't be annoying). They have great info plus they welcome questions that aren't "where's the loo?"

HOLBORN

HOLBORN QUICKFIND: Discover, p. 7; sights, p. 97; food, p. 170; pubs, p. 197; nightlife, p. 211; entertainment, p. 236; shopping, p. 257; accommodations, p. 286.

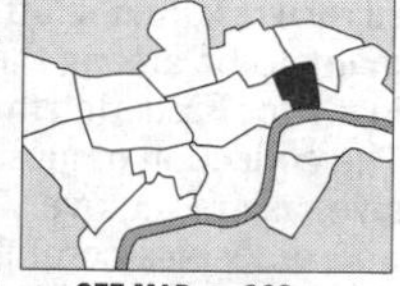

SEE MAP, p. 363

SIR JOHN SOANE'S MUSEUM

13 Lincoln's Inn Fields. ☎1405 2107. ⊖Holborn. Open Tu-Sa 10am-5pm, first Tu of month also 6-9pm. Tours Sa 2:30pm, tickets sold from 2pm; £3, students free. Free; £1 donation requested.

Eccentric architect John Sloane let his imagination run free when designing this intriguing museum for his own collection of art and antiquities. Three separate homes in Lincoln's Field Rd. had to be joined together to accommodate the collection. The result is

a bewildering, delightful maze. Framed by endlessly-mirrored walls, items range from the mummified corpse of his wife's dog to an extraordinary sarcophagus of Seti I, for which Soane personally outbid the British Museum. The Picture Room houses Hogarth's famous debauchery-fest, *The Rake's Progress*. In addition to the permanent collection, the museum holds two to five exhibitions a year in its gallery space.

HUNTERIAN MUSEUM

35-43 Lincoln's Inn Fields; the street numbers aren't marked—enter via the columned main entrance to the RCS building. ☎ 7869 6560; www.rcseng.ac.uk/services/museums. Holborn. Closed for redevelopment until December 2004, call for hours. Free. Wheelchair accessible.

Buried within the grandiose Royal College of Surgeons, this museum is not for the squeamish. John Hunter (1728-1793), considered the founder of modern surgery, had a keen interest in the anatomy of all living things. Only 3500 of his original 14,000 colorless pickled organs survived the Blitz, but that's enough to fill endless shelves. Among the viscera are some genuine marvels, generally of the freak-show variety—like the 7' 7" skeleton of the "Irish Giant" and the twisted bones of an anchylosed man. Since 2001, the menagerie has been undergoing a £3 million facelift, and its doors are scheduled to reopen in December 2004.

SOMERSET HOUSE

***Location:** Strand, just east of Waterloo Bridge; Charing Cross or Temple. **Open:** Daily 10am-6pm. Last admission to galleries 5-5:30pm. Ticket for one of the three collections £5, concessions £4, under 18 free. Two collections: £8/£7. Three collections: £12/£11. MC/V.*

THE COURTAULD INSTITUTE GALLERIES. The Courtauld's small but outstanding collection ranges from 14th-century Italian religious works to 20th-century abstractions. Not limited solely to paintings, the three floors of the Courtald house sculpture, decorative arts, prints, and drawings as well. Works are arranged by collector, not chronologically, so don't fret if you think you skipped a few hundred years. The **Renaissance** holdings feature some of the finest triptychs in Europe, and **15th- and 16th-century** highlights include Botticelli's *Christ on the Cross*, many of Rubens's works, and Peter Brueghel's cold and eerie *Christ and the Woman Taken in Adultery*. The undisputed gems of the collection, though, are from the **Impressionist and Post-Impressionist** periods: Manet's *A Bar at the Follies Bergères*, van Gogh's *Self-Portrait with Bandaged Ear*, and works by Cézanne, Monet, Degas, Renoir, and Gauguin. The newly expanded top floor also contains over 100 new 20th-century works, including some exquisite sculptures by Degas and an impressive collection of Kandinskys. *(☎ 7420 9400; www.courtauld.ac.uk. 1hr. tours held Sa 2:30pm; £6.50, concessions £6, including admission. Free M 10am-2pm. Last admission 5:15pm. Wheelchair accessible.)*

THE GILBERT COLLECTION. The Gilbert Collection of Decorative Arts opened in 2000 and houses some of the more exquisite nonpaintings you'll find on display in any museum. The emphasis here is on incomparable craftsmanship, and precious materials. The collection's 800 objects fall into three categories: mosaics, gold- and silverwork, and snuffboxes. Sir Arthur's collection of the latter is considered by many to be among the finest in the world, with over 200 examples—including six made for Frederick the Great, each encrusted with diamonds, rubies, and emeralds. The collection of mosaics, the most comprehensive ever formed, is equally impressive, as are the over 7 ft. tall "Russian Gates." Be sure to spend time viewing the micromosaics carefully. To fully appreciate the brilliant craftsmanship of these pieces, you'll need to pick up a complimentary magnifying glass at the front desk (you'll also get a free audioguide). You can also access the King's Barge House from here, a reminder that the Thames once came all the way up to the walls of Somerset House. *(☎ 7420 9400; www.gilbert-collection.org.uk. 1hr. tours held Sa 2:30pm; £6.50, concessions £6, including admission. Last admission 5:30pm. Wheelchair accessible.)*

THE HERMITAGE ROOMS. A unique chance to get a taste of the renowned Hermitage art museum without going to St. Petersburg, Russia. The five rooms in the south wing of the Somerset House have been recreated as smaller replicas of the Winter Palace in St. Petersburg, down to the door fittings and floor patterns, all of which were done by Russian craftsmen. All this recreated elegance almost overshadows the paintings on loan from the big brother in Russia, exchanged for new ones every six months to keep things fresh. In case you want to check your experience against the real thing, the main room has a live webcast from the museum in Russia. *(☎7485 4630; www.hermitagerooms.org.uk. Audioguide £1. Last admission 5pm.)*

KENSINGTON & EARL'S COURT

KENSINGTON & EARL'S COURT QUICKFIND: Discover, p. 8; sights, p. 100; food, p. 171; pubs, p. 198; entertainment, p. 236; shopping, p. 257; accommodations, p. 286. For the Victoria & Albert Museum, see, p. 138.

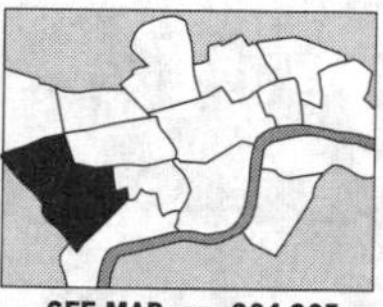

SEE MAP, pp. 364-365

South Kensington's Albertopolis is home to three of London's biggest and best museums: the **Victoria & Albert Museum,** the **Natural History Museum,** and the **Science Museum.** While it's tempting to try and "do" them in a day, visiting more than two is a feat of superhuman stamina (not to mention a waste of at least one perfectly good museum). A traveling note: while most people just take the sign-posted "Subway" feeder tunnels from the Tube to the museums, it's just as quick (and far more pleasant in good weather) to use the overland route.

SCIENCE MUSEUM

Location: *Exhibition Rd.* ***Contact:*** *☎0870 870 4868, IMAX ☎0870 870 4771; www.sciencemuseum.org.uk. ⊖South Kensington.* ***Open:*** *Daily 10am-6pm. Audioguides: "Soundbytes" cover* Power, Space, *and* Making the Modern World*; £3.50 each. IMAX: Shows usually every 75min., 10:45am-5pm daily; £7.50, concessions £6. Call to confirm showtimes and for bookings. Online booking available. Daily demonstrations and workshops in the basement galleries and theater.* ***Admission:*** *Free. Some special exhibits £6, concessions £4. Wheelchair accessible. MC/V.*

Dedicated to the Victorian ideal of Progress, the Science Museum focuses on the transformative power of technology in all its guises. There's something for everyone in this mix of state-of-the-art interactive displays and priceless historical artifacts. The gigantic **Making of the Modern World** entrance hall houses a collection of pioneering contraptions from "Puffing Billy" (1814), the oldest surviving steam locomotive, to the Apollo 10 command module. Unless you're a devoted space cadet, skip past this front area quickly on your way to the newer **Wellcome Wing** at the back, six stories of beeping, buzzing, futuristic diversions. It begins with the basement **Launch Pad,** a hands-on introduction to do-it-yourself science—communicate across the room using giant sound dishes, try building an arch, or solve the "hangover problem." Floor 1 offers **Who am I?** a series of (sometimes demoralizing) games and tests that let you figure out how smart, attractive, successful, and happy you are. The third-floor **Flight** gallery tells the story of air travel from Victorian attempts at steam-powered flight to jumbo jets, assisted by a supporting cast of dozens of airplanes and the hands-on **Flight Lab,** with a more mouth-on approach to aerodynamics. Children will love the basement **Garden** and **Things. The Science and Art of Medicine,** on the top floor, chronicles in impressive detail the history of medicine in its modern and cross-cultural incarnations. Or, forsake modern medicine and instead take a **SixEx** simulator ride through the plains of Africa (£3.75, concessions £2.75).

HIGHLIGHTS IN A HURRY: Breeze through the entrance hall on your way to the **Wellcome Center.** Enjoy **Who am I?,** decide who you are, then shoot up to the **Flight Lab** and finally the **Science of Art and Medicine.**

in recent news

Double-Decker Demise

Double-decker buses are a fixture in this city of high-profile public transportation. However, these distinctive buses are being quietly removed from the streets of London. This process began in late 2003, and now the London transportation authorities have announced that nearly all will be gone by early 2005. Replacement–single-decker "bendy buses" and bigger, boxier doubles–will lack the convenient open rear exit of their predecessors and will no longer employ the informative conductors, but they will be in compliance with European Union requirements of wheelchair accessibility and a lower floor that facilitates easy entrance/exit for people with disabilities.

Critics assert that the old buses offered a convenience and uniqueness that made the distinctly unsexy world of bus travel appealing to tourists and locals alike. In 2000, London mayor Ken Livingston was promising to *add* to the city's fleet, and as of 2002 the Transport Authority had "no intention" of withdrawing them. As it turns out, the sometimes-40 year old machines were just too dated to remain in circulation, and plans now call for a token few to remain in circulation on the heavily touristed "Heritage Routes." A grand era is London travel is coming to a close. Enjoy its last days.

NATURAL HISTORY MUSEUM

Location: *Cromwell Rd.* ***Contact:*** *☎7942 5011; www.nhm.ac.uk. ⊖South Kensington.* ***Open:*** *M-Sa 10am-5:50pm, Su 11am-5:50pm; last admission 5:30pm.* ***Tours:*** *45min. highlights tours hourly 11am-4pm; reserve places at the main info desk. Free.* ***Admission:*** *Free; special exhibits usually £5, concessions £3. Wheelchair accessible.*

Architecturally the most impressive of the South Kensington trio, this cathedral-like Romanesque building has been a favorite with Londoners since 1880. The entrance hall is dedicated to the **Wonders of the Natural History Museum,** a series of historically important skeletons including a diplodocus and a moa. The **Life Galleries** offer insight into the minds of the curators—the relative importance of the displays perfectly mirrors the natural inclinations of school-aged children. The **Dinosaur** galleries will not disappoint the Jurassic Park generation: the animatronic T-Rex (complete with bad breath) is so popular that he's secured an exhibit entirely for himself. And don't miss the semi-nauseating fun of **Creepy Crawlies,** with vomiting fly models right alongside a live webcast of the museum's ant colony.

The enormous **Human Biology** exhibition keeps adults and children intrigued with an endless succession of interactive and hi-tech displays, not to mention an extremely detailed reproduction gallery. Other galleries remind visitors of how much museum-going has evolved over the last century; the **bird, reptile,** and **mammal** exhibits favor Victorian style stuffed-and-mounted displays and are decidedly less pleasant than the newer areas. The uncontested centerpiece of the mammalian display is the massive blue whale suspended from the ceiling. The **Origin of Species** display on the first floor offers a detailed explanation of evolution, from Darwin's finches to genetic engineering.

Less comprehensive, but a bit more dynamic, the **Earth Galleries** are reached via a long escalator that pierces a giant model of the earth on its way to **The Power Within,** an exposition of the awesome volcanic and tectonic forces beneath our planet's surface. A walk-through model of a Japanese supermarket provides an amusement park-worthy recreation of the 1995 Kobe earthquake and, on the same floor, **Restless Surface** explores the gentler action of wind and water in reshaping the world. The history of the Earth itself, from the Big Bang to the way life has shaped the environment, is the subject of **From the Beginning,** on the first floor. The **Earth's Treasury** presents an enormous array of minerals, from sandstone to diamonds. Phase One of the cutting-edge **Darwin Centre** on the ground floor opened in September 2002 and now houses 100 scientists and 22 million specimens, many of which are on display.

HIGHLIGHTS IN A HURRY: Shudder from **Creepy Crawlies** through to the **Dinosaur** galleries, making sure to swing by the **blue whale** at some point. And perhaps the knowledge you gained at the **Darwin Centre** will help you through the **Kobe earthquake** upstairs.

EXHIBITION SPACES

Serpentine Gallery, off West Carriage Dr., Kensington Gardens (☎7402 6075; www.serpentinegallery.org). ⊖South Kensington or High St. Kensington. This 1934 tea pavilion, in the middle of the gardens is the unlikely venue for some of London's top contemporary art shows. It's tiny, so stop in and take a quick peek. Summer park nights also include architecture talks, live readings, and open-air film screenings; most £5, concessions £3. Open daily 10am-6pm, F late-view until 10pm. Free. Wheelchair accessible.

MARYLEBONE & REGENT'S PARK

MARYLEBONE & REGENT'S PARK QUICKFIND: Discover, p. 9; sights, p. 103; food, p. 173; pubs, p. 199; entertainment, p. 237; accommodations, p. 291.

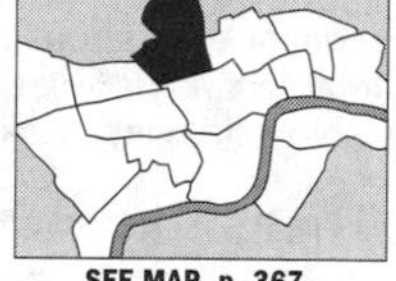

SEE MAP, p. 367

THE WALLACE COLLECTION

Location: *Hertford House, Manchester Sq.* ***Contact:*** *☎7563 9500; www.the-wallace-collection.org.uk ⊖Bond St. or Marble Arch.* ***Open:*** *M-Sa 10am-5pm, Su noon-5pm.* ***Tours:*** *daily at 1pm, plus W and Sa 11:30am and Su 3pm (1hr.); free. Talks: M-F 1pm and occasional Sa 11:30am; free. Audioguides: £3.* ***Admission:*** *Free (£3 suggested donation). Wheelchair accessible.*

Housed in palatial Hertford House, this stunning array of paintings, porcelain, and armor was bequeathed to the nation by the widow of Sir Richard Wallace in 1897. The impressive collection is rendered even more dazzling by its grand, gilded setting; the mansion has been restored to much of its 19th-century glory. Two minor drawbacks: poor labeling requires some sifting through long information sheets to learn more about a piece, and rotating gallery closings mean that you might miss out on what you came to see (call ahead). On the **ground floor** the most popular display is just through the gift shop: four **Armoury Galleries** threaten and enthrall visitors with scads of richly decorated weapons and burnished suits of armor. Don't miss the imposing 15th-century German Gothic horse model, with a complete, terrifying suit of armor for horse and rider. Through the hall, the Front State Room retains its original appearance, with sumptuous furnishings and society portraits, and china buffs will swoon at the collection of Sèvres porcelain in the Back State Room next door. Italian and Flemish works dominate the 16th-century Galleries and Smoking Room. The **first floor** is home to a world-renowned array of 18th-century French art, announced on the staircase by Boucher's works, including the *Rising and Setting of the Sun*, all billowing clouds and trembling pink flesh. More Bouchers accompany Fragonards and Watteaus in the West Room and West Gallery. The Small Drawing Room displays a series of Venice views by Canaletto and Guardi. The **Great Gallery,** once called "the greatest picture gallery in Europe" by Lord Clark, has a varied collection of 17th-century work, with scenes by van Dyck, Rembrandt, Rubens, and Velázquez as well as the collection's most celebrated piece, Frans Hals' *Laughing Cavalier*. In the modern basement, the tiny **Conservation Gallery** has a small display on the manufacture of furniture and armor, including some pieces you can try on. Hungry art appreciators can plop down in the swanky, gorgeous sculpture-garden restaurant **Café Bagatelle** *(mains £8-12; call for reservations ☎7563 9505).*

SHERLOCK HOLMES MUSEUM

"221b Baker St."; actually at 239. ☎7935 8866; www.sherlock-holmes.co.uk. ⊖Baker St. Open daily 9:30am-6pm. £6, age 7-16 £4.

Four floors of wildly cheesy decor culled meticulously from Sir Arthur Conan Doyle's literary descriptions. This museum claims to be the real 19th-century residence of Sherlock Holmes and Doctor Watson based the belief that these fictional characters existed at all. It doesn't take a master sleuth to see that there is more fiction than fact here, but die-hard fans may find it worth the six quid.

THE SOUTH BANK

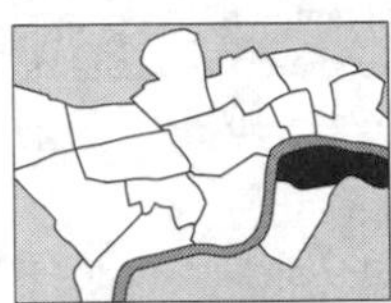

SEE MAP, pp. 368-369

SOUTH BANK QUICKFIND: Discover, p. 10; sights, p. 106; food, p. 176; pubs, p. 200; nightlife p. 212; entertainment, p. 247; accommodations, p. 292. For Tate Modern, see p. 137.

Anchored by the gigantic **Tate Modern** (see p. 137), the South Bank is home to some of London's top public contemporary art galleries, each in a totally unique space. Established masters hold court at the Hayward and promising newcomers at the Jerwood. In addition to the galleries listed below, there are also frequent exhibitions in the foyer and sculptural displays on the river terrace of the **Royal Festival Hall** (see p. 238). Design aficionados will drool at the **Design Museum** and fashionistas can check out the ever-evolving displays at the **Fashion and Textile Museum.**

IMPERIAL WAR MUSEUM

***Location:** Lambeth Rd., Lambeth. **Contact:** ☎7416 5320, recorded info ☎7416 5000; www.iwm.org.uk. ⊖Lambeth North or Elephant & Castle. **Open:** Daily 10am-6pm. Audioguide: £3, concessions £2.50. **Admission:** Free.*

Five floors of modern, exciting, always-respectful warfare education. Massive 15-inch naval guns guard the entrance to the building, formerly the infamous lunatic asylum known as Bedlam. Grab a free **floorplan** at the desk, then decide on your battle plan. The best and most publicized display is up on the third floor: the **Holocaust Exhibition** provides an honest and poignant look at all the events surrounding the tragedy. (Not recommended for children under 14.) The **Large Exhibits Hall** features an impressive array of military hardware, from "Little Boy" (an atomic bomb of the type dropped on Hiroshima) to Montgomery's tank to a German V-2 rocket, all clearly labeled and carefully explained. The **cinema** shows a rotating schedule of historical documentaries (free). In the basement, the **Trench Experience** and **Blitz Experience** recreate the conditions of WWI and life on the home front in WWII, respectively. On the first floor, the remarkably hi-tech **Secret War** is filled with the gadgets and gizmos of espionage, with a particularly gripping presentation of Operation NIMROD (the storming of a hostage-filled Iranian embassy in 1980 London). On the fourth floor, **Crimes Against Humanity** is a sobering interactive display with a 30min. film at the back. Temporary exhibitions **D-Day Remembered** and **Great Escapes** showcase detailed WWII presentations and famous POW escapes, respectively (through May 2005).

OTHER PERMANENT COLLECTIONS

DESIGN MUSEUM. Housed in an arrestingly white Art Deco riverfront building, this contemporary museum's installations fit right into the cool surroundings. The marvels in the Design Museum cater mostly to the young, hip, well-dressed crowd. You might find anything from avante garde furniture pieces to galleries on big-name graphic designers. Everyone will enjoy the **Interaction Space** on the airy top floor, which includes a colorful variety of household items (some hands-on) and a bay of **vintage video games** (which you can play) that inspired contemporary gaming. The

Museum Café on the first floor—not to be confused with the considerably pricier **Blue Print Café** next door—serves an array of sweet treats as aesthetically pleasing as anything you'll find in the galleries. *(28 Shad Thames, Butlers Wharf. ☎7403 6933; www.designmuseum.org. ⊖Tower Hill or London Bridge. Open daily 10am-5:45pm, last entry 5:15pm. £6, students £4, under 15 and over 60 £4, family of 4, £16. Wheelchair accessible.)*

FLORENCE NIGHTINGALE MUSEUM. On the grounds of St. Thomas' Hospital, where Florence Nightingale's first school of nursing opened in 1860. This one-floor tribute to the famous "Lady with the Lamp" is suitably reverent; well-labeled displays chart Nightingale's life from childhood to posthumous renown. With mostly personal effects and letters, with a few interactive displays and atmospheric enclaves pepper the way. Flo enthusiasts will be enthralled, but others might want to save the six quid. *(St. Thomas' Hospital, 2 Lambeth Palace Rd.; look for the ramp down to the museum near the corner of the hospital. ☎7620 0374; www.florence-nightingale.co.uk. ⊖Waterloo or Westminster. Tours M-F 2 and 3pm. Free. Open M-F 10am-5pm, Sa-Su 10am-4:30pm; last entry 1hr. before closing. £5.80, concessions £4.20, family of 4, £13. Wheelchair accessible. AmEx/MC/V.)*

THE CLINK PRISON MUSEUM. Satisfyingly onomatopoeic, the original jail on this site was so notorious that all English prisoners are said to be "in the clink." The private prison of the Bishop of Winchester from the 13th century; it's located a convenient 50 paces from his old castle. It was the first prison where women were confined for punishment—in a separate corner of course. The quirky and diverting museum in the basement of the old prison chills and disgusts visitors with tales of medieval punishments, complete with waxwork inmates and torture tools. Guides armed with ultra-grisly stories are often around, it's worth tagging along for a tour. Pride of the place goes to the original medieval torture chair and a well-used, retired, execution block. Just past the museum on Clink St. stand the remains of the Bishop's **Winchester Palace.** *(1 Clink St. ☎7378 1558; www.clink.co.uk. ⊖London Bridge. Open daily 10am-6pm. £5, concessions £3.50, family £12. Tours £1, usually available.)*

EXHIBITION SPACES

Saatchi Gallery, County Hall (☎7823 2363; www.saatchi-gallery.co.uk). ⊖Waterloo or Westminster. Charles Saatchi, famous for supporting young and provocative artists, remains true to his mission in this space. County Hall's wood-panelled rooms, showcases some of the most innovative contemporary Britart. The rotunda features edgy work by the most famous YBAs (young British artists) like Damien Hirst, Sarah Lucas and Tracey Emin. Focused on Saatchi's own collection, the Gallery is not for the faint-hearted; many of the pieces are pretty raw. That's what makes it incomparable. Open Su-Th 10am-8pm, F-Sa 10-10pm. £8.75, concessions £6.75, family £26.

Bankside Gallery, 48 Hopton St. (☎7928 7521; www.banksidegallery.com). ⊖Blackfriars. Entrance on Riverside Terr. This small riverside gallery is a watercolor haven. Run jointly by the Royal Watercolour Society and the Royal Society of Painter Printmakers, it mostly displays members' works, but any type of media is liable to be shown. The exception (and best exhibit) is the annual Open Exhibition (held in late spring and through July), when anyone can submit watercolors for inclusion. The wide range of works are all for sale and generally very good. There are also spring and autumn watercolor shows, and a yearly print show. Open Tu-F 10am-5pm, Sa-Su 11am-5pm. Wheelchair accessible.

Fashion and Textile Museum, 83 Bermondsey St. (☎7403 0222; www.ftmlondon.org). Housed in a can't-miss pink-and-orange building, this is a new space in an up-and-coming South Bank area. Smallish installations are top-quality displays of fashion and textiles from the 1950s to the present. Exhibits change about every 3-4 months and cover all aspects of the fashion world, including photography. The gallery will also feature an upcoming permanent collection, as well as a multimedia learning center; call or check website for dates. Open Tu-Su 11am-5:45pm, last admission 5:15pm. £5, concessions and children £3, family £13. Partially wheelchair accessible.

Hayward Gallery, South Bank Centre (☎7960 4242; www.hayward.org.uk). ⊖Waterloo, Embankment, or Temple. Hiding next to the Royal Festival Hall, this stark Modernist building is a distinctive maze of concrete blocks, topped with a twisting red roof sculpture. Contemporary art predominates, with occasional forays into the early or mid-20th century. Usually 2-3 shows run concurrently. Call ahead as the gallery closes between exhibitions. Open M 11am-7pm, Tu-W 11am-8pm, Th 11am-7pm, F 11am-9pm, Sa-Su 11am-8pm. Adults £9, seniors £7, concessions £4, 12-16 £3, under12 free.

Jerwood Space, 171 Union St. (☎7654 0171; www.jerwoodspace.co.uk). ⊖Southwark or Borough. Not to be confused with the **Jerwood Art Academy,** just down the street at 201 Union. The art academy often houses student exhibits, although they change all the time. Primarily a center for rehearsal of performing arts, the Jerwood Space gives promising young artists a leg up, most famously by hosting the prestigious Jerwood Painting Prize exhibition (early May to mid-June). Open M-F 9am-9pm, Su 10am-6pm. Free.

THE WEST END

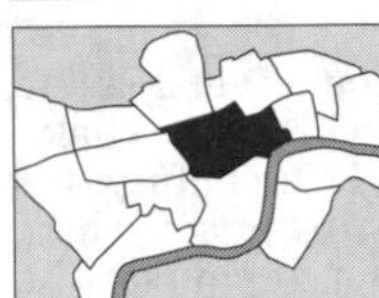

SEE MAP, p. 354

THE WEST END QUICKFIND: Discover, p. 10; sights, p. 111; food, p. 177; pubs, p. 201; nightlife p. 212; entertainment, p. 240; shopping, p. 261; accommodations, p. 292.

LONDON'S TRANSPORT MUSEUM

Location: *Southeast corner of Covent Garden Piazza.* ***Contact:*** *☎7565 7299; www.ltmuseum.co.uk.* ***Open:*** *M-Th and Sa-Su 10am-6pm, F 11am-6pm; last admission 5:15pm.* ***Admission:*** *£5.95, concessions £4.50, under 16 free with adult. Wheelchair accessible.*

From tram to tube, LTM glorifies the virtues of public transportation. While primarily geared toward kids, the LTM is surprisingly informative and grown-up friendly. Adults will be engrossed in the development of London's public transportation system over the last 200 years, including the earliest tube maps and displays on London's growth as a metropolis. Actual antique and modern carriages, trams, buses, trains, and tube cars invite curious little climbers. Wax models mine the coal that powered the first trams, and wax bus drivers collect passengers' "fare". Most of the interactive displays are conveniently located at kiddy-level. The "Fast Forward" display explores the future of transport, from sci-fi hovercars to teleportation. The museum shop sells must-have Tube-logo T-shirts (£13), as well as the world-famous London "Mind the Gap" Underground posters (£5-10) whose design was originally rejected by London Transport. Eventually, designer Harry Beck was paid for his 1933 creation—the handsome sum of £5.25.

THEATRE MUSEUM

Location: *Russell St.* ***Contact:*** *☎7943 4700; www.theatremuseum.org. ⊖Covent Garden.* ***Open:*** *Tu-Sa 10am-6pm, last admission 5:30pm. Free guided tours noon, 2, and 3:30pm. Wheelchair accessible.*

Heaven for travelers interested in the history and behind-the-scenes parts of theater; the top floor covers the emergence of British dramatic and musical theater and has vintage props and 18th-century ticket stubs. The maze-like downstairs is more interesting with costumes from famous shows like *Richard II*, and shoes and costumes from the Russian Ballet. Changing special exhibits are also excellent and may feature the life of a famous theater family or a tribute to a star recently departed. There are also daily make-up demos (11:30am, 1, 2:30, 3:30, 4:30pm and Sa noon) and costume workshops (12:30, 3 and 3:30pm).

EXHIBITION SPACES

Royal Academy of Art, Burlington House, Piccadilly (☎7300 8000; www.royalacademy.org.uk). ⊖Piccadilly Circus or Green Park. Founded in 1768 with King George III's patronage, the Academy was designed to cultivate sculpture, painting and architecture. Today the Academy shares courtyard space with the Royal Societies of Geology, Chemistry,

Antiquaries, and Astronomy. The academics who run the place are all accomplished artists or architects. Spacious and ornate main galleries hold the larger exhibitions and the minimalist top-floor Sackler Gallery holds the other. The **Summer Exhibition** (June-Aug.), held every year since 1769, is open-submission, providing an unparalleled range of contemporary art in every medium, much of which is available for purchase. Exhibitions for 2004-2005 include: *Ancient Art to Post-Impressionism* (Sept 18 2004-Dec. 10 2004); *William Nicholson: A Retrospective* (Oct. 2004-Jan. 2005); *The Turks 500-1500* (Jan. 22 2005–Apr. 15 2005). F nights the whole place stays open late; there's free jazz in Friends room after 6:30pm, and candlelit suppers in the cafe. Open Sa-Th 10am-6pm, F 10am-10pm. Wheelchair accessible.

Institute of Contemporary Arts (ICA), The Mall (☎7930 0493; www.ica.org.uk). ⊖Charing Cross or Piccadilly Circus. A grand neoclassical building just down the road from Buckingham Palace is the last place you'd expect to find Britain's national center for the subversion of the contemporary art. The ICA has a large ground level and small upstairs gallery for temporary exhibitions, an avant-garde cinema, a theater, a trendy cafe, and a relaxed bar that hosts frequent club nights and gigs. Open M noon-11pm, Tu-Sa noon-1am, Su noon-10:30pm; galleries close 7:30pm. "Day membership," giving access to galleries and cafe/bar M-F £1.50 (concessions £1), Sa-Su £2.50 (concessions £1.50). Cinema £6.50, M-F before 5pm £5.50; concessions £5.50/£4.50; no concessions on weekends.

The Photographers' Gallery, 5 and 8 Great Newport St. (☎7831 1772; www.photonet.org.uk). ⊖Leicester Sq. or Covent Garden. One of London's only public galleries devoted entirely to camerawork. Two exhibitions run concurrently at the larger location (No. 5). Displays usually feature a single artist's work, ranging from classic landscape to socially conscious photography. The gallery and small bookshop at (no. 8) houses an equally exemplary show and also has a good selection of photographic monologues. Frequent gallery talks, book readings and film screenings are free, occasional photographer's talks may charge admission. Open M-Sa 11am-6pm, Su noon-6pm. Free. Partially wheelchair accessible.

COMMERCIAL GALLERIES & AUCTION HOUSES

Mayfair is the center of London's art market—and despite the genteel aura it's not all Old Masters and Prince Charles's watercolors. Cork St., running parallel to Old Bond St. between Clifford St. and Burlington Gdns., is lined with dozens of small commercial galleries specializing in contemporary art of all types. The auction houses give insight into what is being bought and sold in the upper-crust art world today.

Christie's, 8 King St. (☎7839 9060; www.christies.com). ⊖Green Park. Like a museum but more crowded and all for sale, Christie's is the best of the auction houses. Open to the public on the days before an auction to display what's up for grabs; lots range from busts of Greek gods to Monets to sports memorabilia. Catalogues £14-27. Open M-F 9am-4:30pm; during sales also Tu to 8pm and Su 2-5pm. Free. Wheelchair accessible.

Gagosian Gallery, 8 Heddon St. (☎7292 8222). ⊖Piccadilly Circus. A branch of the famed New York Gagosian, this gallery holds solo shows of contemporary artists like Willem de Kooning and Cy Twombly. Sparse and spacious, the very modern Gagosian shows 1 exhibition on 2 floors. Works vary; however, social documentaries are common exhibits. Shows change monthly or every 2 months. Open Tu-Sa 10am-6pm, M by appointment only. Free.

Sotheby's, 34-35 New Bond St. (☎7293 5000; www.sothebys.com). ⊖Bond St. Before each auction, the items to be sold are displayed for viewing in the many galleries. Aristocratic Sotheby's is a busy place; auctions occur within days of each other. Each sale is accompanied by a glossy catalog (£6-30); old catalogs usually half-price. Open for viewing M-F 9am-4:30pm, Sa and some Su noon-4pm. Free. Wheelchair accessible.

Marlborough Fine Arts, 6 Albermarle St. (☎7629 5161; www.marlboroughgraphics.com). ⊖Green Park. Spacious gallery presents variety of contemporary artists, one at a time. Anything from sketches to mixed-media; anyone from Lucian Freud to Frank Auerbach. Open M-F 10am-5:30pm, Sa 10am-12:30pm. Free. Wheelchair accessible.

National Gallery

Tate Modern

British Museum

Robert Sandelson, 5a Cork St. (☎7439 1001; www.robertsandelson.com). ⊖Bond St. or Green Park. Small but quality exhibitions of big-time modern and contemporary artists like Tamara de Lempicka, Sam Francis, and Howard Hodgkin. One 2002 show was devoted entirely to Andy Warhol. Also holds lectures. Open M-F 10am-6pm, Sa 11am-4pm. Free.

WESTMINSTER

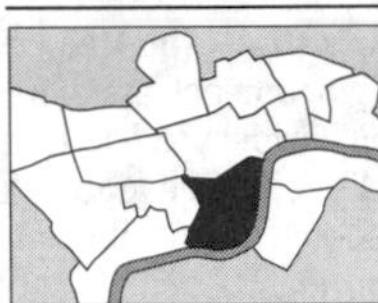
SEE MAP, p. 370

WESTMINSTER QUICKFIND: Discover, p. 11; sights, p. 116; food, p. 181; pubs, p. 202; entertainment, p. 244; accommodations, p. 293. For the National Gallery, see p. 135. For Tate Britain, see p. 136.

CABINET WAR ROOMS

***Location:** Clive Steps, far end of King Charles St. ⊖Westminster. **Contact:** ☎7766 0130; www.iwm.org.uk/cabinet. **Open:** Apr.-Sept. daily 9:30am-6pm; Oct.-Mar. 10am-6pm; last admission 5:15pm. **Admission:** £7.50, concessions and students £5.50, under 16 free.*

In 1939, what started as a government coal storage basement quickly became the bombproof nerve center of a nation at war. For six tense years, Churchill, his cabinet and generals, and dozens of support staff lived and worked in this dark labyrinth underground, while bombs wreaked havoc above. The day after the war ended in August 1945, the rooms were abandoned, shut up, and left undisturbed for decades until their reopening in 1984 by Margaret Thatcher. Thanks to journals, testimonies and photos, the space was able to be preserved and displayed EXACTLY as it was in those years. An indispensable free Churchillian-voiced audioguide talks you through the maze of rooms on show, supplemented with original recordings of Churchill's speeches and recreations that bring them to life. Highlights include "Churchill's personal loo"—a small room containing the top-secret transatlantic hotline and the defense and map rooms which were in operation for six years straight, night and day. Don't miss the case of Churchill's many decorations and metals too. The clocks on display read two minutes before five, the moment Churchill called the Cabinet's first official meeting, one day after a German blitz on London. Rarely are museums this real. A **Churchill Museum** will be opening here in January 2005, to commemorate the 40th anniversary of his death. It will be devoted exclusively to Churchill-ology, with all sorts of displays about the PM in his "finest hour."

NATIONAL PORTRAIT GALLERY

Location: *St. Martin's Pl., at the start of Charing Cross Rd., Trafalgar Sq. Leicester Sq. or Charing Cross.* ***Contact:*** *7312 2463; www.npg.org.uk.* ***Open:*** *M-W and Sa-Su 10am-6pm, Th-F 10am-9pm. Audioguides: Free; £3 suggested donation. Lectures: Sa,Su,Tu and Th 1:10pm and 3pm; free, but popular events require tickets, available from the info desk. Evening Events: Talks Th 7pm; free-£3. Live classical and jazz music every F 6:30pm; free.* ***Admission:*** *Free; exhibitions free-£6. Wheelchair accessible on Orange St.*

This artistic Who's Who in Britain began in 1856 and has grown to be the place to see Britain's freshest new artwork as well as centuries old portraiture. This portrait heaven was recently bolstered by the addition of the sleek Ondaatje Wing. New facilities include a **Micro Gallery,** with computers allowing you to search for pictures and print out a personalized tour, and a 3rd-floor **restaurant** offering some of the best views in London—although the inflated prices (meals around £15) will limit most visitors to coffee.

To see the paintings in historical order, take the escalator from the Ondaatje reception hall to the top-floor Tudor gallery, and work your way around the Stuarts and Hanoverians before moving down to the small sovereign gallery with Organ's great paintings of Prince Charles, Princess Diana and The Duke of Edinburgh. Contemporary works on the ground floor, starting with excellent rooms from WWI years and the 1920s. Don't miss the quiet portrait of Beatix Potter of Peter Rabbit fame. Rooms over will find you in the 1960s-1990s galleries with excellent Bill Brandt Photos and Sam Walsh's painting of Paul McCartney jokingly titled *Mike's Brother*. Sam was friends with Paul's bro Mike. The most fun section, however, is the 1990-present gallery which boasts work of **Lucian Freud,** and the young British artist Sam Taylor Wood. The size of the collection, however, makes a complete tour of the gallery an exhausting prospect, not helped by endless galleries upstairs of bewhiskered Victorians. In the summer there is a portrait contest for £25,000; most of the entries are on display, a final winner is chosen in June.

QUEEN'S GALLERY

Buckingham Palace Rd. St. James's Park or Victoria. 7766 7301. Open daily 10am-5:30pm, last admission 4:30pm. £7.50, concessions £6, family £19. Wheelchair accessible.

"God Save the Queen" is the rallying cry at this gallery dedicated to changing exhibitions of jaw-droppingly valuable items from the Royal Collection. A massive collection of portraits and belongings to King George III and his German wife Queen Charlotte will be displayed until January 2005. Five exquisite rooms are full of various artifacts dedicated to extolling the glory of the sovereign in numerous art forms. The friendly older guards can show you the finest pieces of the Royal Collection that the tourist can view, with the exception of the State Rooms. The rooms in this opulent museum are monochromatic and designed to look like the interior of the palace; a grand staircase and green marble pillars welcome visitors into the first room. Free audio guides are available, but be warned of the narrator's pompous voice.

NORTH LONDON

NORTH LONDON QUICKFIND: Discover, p. 12; sights, p. 120; food, p. 183; pubs, p. 203; nightlife, p. 218; entertainment, p. 244; shopping, p. 269; accommodations, p. 294.

THE IVEAGH BEQUEST

Kenwood House; for directions, see p. 123. 8348 1286. Audioguide £3.50, concessions £2.60, children £1.75; Open Apr.-Sept. Sa-Tu and Th 10am-6pm, W and F 10:30am-6pm; Oct. closes 5pm; Nov.-Mar. closes 4pm. Free. Wheelchair accessible.

The impressive Iveagh collection in Kenwood House was bequeathed to the nation by the Earl of Iveagh, who purchased the estate in 1922. The rooms themselves are works of art, especially the library. Highlights include one of 35 Vermeers in the world, Rembrandt's compelling self-portraits, and a beautiful Botticelli. The majority of these old masters is housed in the plush dining room. Georgian society portraits by Reynolds, Gainsborough, Hogarth and Romney fill the walls with faces of people who look as though they might have called Kenwood home.

ROYAL AIR FORCE MUSEUM

Grahame Park Way. ☎8205 2266; www.rafmuseum.org. Follow signs from the ⊖Colindale (Zone 4), it's a 10min. walk. Bus #303 goes from the station right to the museum's door. Open daily 10am-6pm; last admission 5:30pm. Free. Partially wheelchair accessible.

Although a hassle to get to, the RAF museum will delight plane fans and awe everyone else. This enormous museum contains three huge hangars of planes, from the first plane made in Europe to 1980s Harriers. Details of each plane's combat missions add to the realism, though it feels a bit like an oversized models exhibition. Galleries are divided into Jets, Fighter Planes, Helicopters, Bombers and Aquatic Machines. Torpedos, engines and missles are on display too. Beyond the planes, are portraits, timelines, medallions, and memorabilia. *Our Finest Hour*, a somewhat kitschy 15min. laser light show on the hour, is probably only worth it if there is no wait. Free tours at 1:45 and 2:45 and last 30min.

FREUD MUSEUM

20 Maresfield Gardens. ☎7435 2002; www.freud.org.uk. ⊖Swiss Cottage or Finchley Rd. Open W-Su noon-5pm. £5, concessions £2, under 12 free. Wheelchair accessible.

The comfortable home in which Sigmund Freud spent the last year of his life after fleeing the Nazis evokes a little more than most celebrity houses. In his later years, Freud delved into cultural analysis, evidenced by the anthropological collection of masks and random artifacts. He didn't drop his patients, however, and the infamous rug-covered couch in his dark study stands ready for the next session. Upstairs hangs Dalí's cranially exaggerated portrait of Freud alongside the room of Anna Freud, Sigmund's youngest daughter, who was an eminent psychoanalyst in her own right. A video of Freud in his Vienna garden plays on the hour.

ESTORICK COLLECTION

39a Canonbury Sq. ☎7704 9522; www.estorickcollection.com. ⊖Highbury and Islington. Open W-Sa 11am-6pm, Su noon-5pm. £3.50, concessions £2.50, students and under 16 free. Partially wheelchair accessible.

This collection, started by an American sociologist-cum-Italian art lover, focuses on the not widely shown Futurist art. The Futurists' revolutionary manifesto included destroying old buildings, abolishing museums, reinventing food (recipes included sausage cooked in black coffee and perfume), and making the universe affordable for everyone. Ninety years after their heyday, their paintings, drawings, etchings, and sculptures are tastefully displayed in an 18th-century Georgian mansion beside a secluded courtyard cafe that serves great food. There are also works from the Metaphysical school. Temporary exhibitions change about every three months.

THE JEWISH MUSEUM

129-131 Albert St. ☎7284 1997; www.jewishmuseum.org.uk. ⊖Camden Town. Open M-Th 10am-4pm, Su 10am-5pm; last admission 30min. prior to close; closed Su in Aug. and Jewish holidays. £3.50, seniors £2.50, students and children £1.50, family £8.

Actually two complementary museums; the **Jewish Museum, Camden,** focuses on the history of Jews in Britain, including a torah with the coat of arms of the first Jewish MP. The upstairs gallery houses regalia and artifacts relating to Jewish festivals and holidays; pride of place goes to a magnificent 16th-century Venetian synagogue ark that was discovered by accident while being used as a lord's wardrobe. The collection is small but high in quality. The smaller **Jewish Museum, Finchley,** focuses on Jewish social history and 19th- and early 20th-century life in London's East End. The small Holocaust Education gallery is particularly moving, detailing the life of London-born Auschwitz survivor Leon Greenman, who visits the museum most Sundays to answer questions. *(80 East End Rd. ☎8349 1143. ⊖Finchley Central (Zone 4). Take the "Regent's Park Rd." exit from the Tube, turn left into Station Rd., then right into Manor View, which runs into East End Rd. by the museum; 10min. Open M-Th 10:30am-5pm, Su 10:30am-4:30pm; closed Su in Aug. and Jewish holidays. £2, concessions £1, children free. Partially wheelchair accessible.)*

EXHIBITION SPACES

Crafts Council, 44a Pentonville Rd. (☎7278 7700; www.craftscouncil.org.uk). ⊖Angel or King's Cross. The centerpiece of craftwork in London, the Crafts Council Gallery showcases new and old designs by metalworkers, jewelers, glass artists, ceramicists and more. Shows might run along a theme (such as *Boys Who Sew*, focusing on male textile artists) or feature the work of a single craftsperson. The council also displays the work of the Jerwood shortlist artists in the fall. The Jerwood prize is given annually to an artist for outstanding work in a specific category. The reference area upstairs includes an excellent library and photo database where you can learn about featured artists and their work. Open Tu-Sa 11am-6pm, Su 2-6pm. Free. Wheelchair accessible.

SOUTH LONDON

SOUTH LONDON QUICKFIND: Discover, p. 14; sights, p. 125; food, p. 186; nightlife, p. 221; entertainment, p. 247; shopping, p. 271.

DULWICH PICTURE GALLERY

Location: *Gallery Rd., Dulwich.* ***Contact:*** *☎8299 8700; www.dulwichpicturegallery.org.uk. Rail: North Dulwich or West Dulwich, or ⊖Brixton and bus P4. From West Dulwich station, turn right onto Thurlow Park Rd., then left onto Gallery Rd. and follow the signs for a 15min. walk; from North Dulwich, turn left out of the station and a 10min. walk through Dulwich Village to the Gallery.* ***Open:*** *Tu-F 10am-5pm, Sa-Su 11am-5pm.* ***Tours:*** *Sa-Su 3pm; free.* ***Admission:*** *£4, seniors £3, students and under 16 free. Wheelchair accessible.*

Dubbed "the most beautiful small art gallery in the world" by the *Sunday Telegraph*, England's first public gallery is the unlikely legacy of Polish misfortune. In 1790, King Stanislaus Augustus of Poland decided to invest in a national art collection and commissioned two London dealers to buy the best pictures available. Unfortunately

the hidden deal

Just Swimmingly

Most of the water in London comes in the form of drizzle, but on those precious days of sun, there are actually quite a few places to get your watery kicks and tan, for not much cash. To swim head for a local lido. The ever-popular Serpentine Lido in **Hyde Park** has a great big pool, a little kids' area and plenty of grassy space to work on the tan. The Bathing Ponds in **Hampstead Heath** are also great hot weather options, and you can't beat the view from **Parliament Hill.** If swimming isn't your thing, you can opt to rent a boat, and work on your tan while afloat (though the life jacket might mess up the tan lines). The best boating options are usually in Hyde and Regent's Park.

While London is not the water-skiing capital of the world, it still has sailing facilities on various lakes around the city. You'll have to shell out a bit more for these activities, and you might want to wait for a tropical vacation to really get into hardcore watersports.

Call for times and prices: Hyde Park Boathouse; Regent's Park Boathouse ☎7724 4069; Serpentine Lido ☎7706 3422; Parliament Hill Lido ☎7485 3873; Royal Docks Water Ski Club ☎7511 2000; The Royal Yachting Association ☎0845 345 0400.

for the dealers (not to mention the Poles), the partition of Poland in 1795 left them with a full-blown, unpaid-for collection in hand. Rather than selling the works, they decided to put them on public display. The benefactors are buried in a domed mausoleum at the center of the gallery (designed by Sir John Soane), and the high-ceilinged halls house one of the finest collections of Old Masters in the world: mostly 17th- and 18th-century work from the Dutch, Spanish, Italian, French, and English schools of painting. Rubens, Veronese, and van Dyck feature prominently, while other Dutch masterpieces include Rembrandt's *A Girl at a Window*.

HORNIMAN MUSEUM & GARDENS

100 London Rd. ☎8699 1872; www.horniman.ac.uk. Rail: Forest Hill. Exit the station to Dartmouth Rd., cross it, and follow A205 until it becomes London Rd. (5min.) or ⊖Brixton and then bus P4 (request stop). Open daily 10:30am-5:30pm. Gardens open 7:15am-dusk. Free. Wheelchair accessible.

This eccentric museum is the legacy of 19th-century tea merchant Frederick Horniman; his eclectic collections are small, fascinating, and all over the map. The **African Worlds** gallery displays a tiny but rich selection of artifacts from past and present African cultures: Benin brass plaques are dwarfed by the world's largest *Ijele* (Nigerian masquerade costume) and a marvelous elephant's head mask. A marvel of taxidermy, the **Natural History** collection features stuffed animals and skeletons behind glass cases. A colorful assortment of fish in waterfall tanks constitutes the tiny **Living Worlds** aquarium, and the **Music Gallery,** which opened in 2002, displays instruments new and old alongside music boxes and other children's toys. The neighboring hillside **garden** holds a tiny domestic zoo and offers brilliant views of St. Paul's in the distance— pet the rabbits and goats, then go for a charming stroll through the 16 acres.

EAST LONDON

EAST LONDON QUICKFIND: Discover, p. 13; sights, p. 126; food, p. 187; pubs, p. 204; nightlife, p. 222; entertainment, p. 248; shopping, p. 271.

NATIONAL MARITIME MUSEUM

***Location:** Romney Rd. between the Royal Naval College and Greenwich Park. **Contact:** ☎8858 4422; www.nmm.ac.uk. **DLR:** Cutty Sark. **Open:** June to early Sept. daily 10am-6pm; early Sept. to May 10am-5pm; last entry 30min. before closing. **Admission:** Free.*

With around 2 million items in its possession, the NMM covers almost every aspect of seafaring history. Many of the galleries feel like a nautical theme park, the **Explorers** section recreates an Antarctic ice-cave and a ship's foredeck. Once children enter the **All Hands** interactive gallery, complete with morse code stations and cargo loading simulators, it's hard to get them—or the child within you—out. The **Trading and Empire** gallery displays goods from the slave trade and the far east. Under the glass canopy, naval instruments dating from as early as 1200 fill the cases. Prince Frederick's gold plated barge is also on display. The pride of the naval displays, naturally, is the top floor **Nelson Room,** which tells the stirring tale of Admiral Lord Nelson's life, from joining the Royal Navy as a 12-year-old midshipman. The cases chronicle his rise through the ranks, his brilliant major victories, and his scandalous love affair with the married Lady Emma Hamilton. In the starkly lit center of the room, music plays softly and a glass case displays the uniform Nelson died in, the bullet hole still evident and the stockings stained with blood.

OTHER PERMANENT COLLECTIONS

GEFFRYE MUSEUM. This "Museum of English Domestic Interiors," is completely non-Shoho-esque and pleasantly diverting. The setting—an elaborately restored terrace of a 17th-century almhouse—showcases a set of connecting rooms, each painstakingly recreating a specific period in interior design. Move through Elizabethan parlors, Victorian studies, and stark post-war sitting rooms.

The obsessive attention to detail can be amusing: the radio in the "1990-2000" loft plays 1990s pop, and the table is strewn with glossy women's magazines. The downstairs space houses temporary exhibits and a Design Centre for local artists' display. The manicured backyard garden is lovely; look out onto it from the popular glass-in lunch cafe **At Home** (food £3-6; open 10am-4:45pm). *(Kingsland Rd. ☎ 7739 9893; www.geffrye-museum.org.uk. ⊖Old St., then bus #243 or 10min. walk along Old St. and left into Kingsland Rd. or ⊖Liverpool St. and bus #149 or 242. Open Tu-Sa 10am-5pm, Su noon-5pm. Free. Wheelchair accessible.)*

MUSEUM OF CHILDHOOD. The place to be for the under-five set. Housed in the original V&A building, this museum is popular with families. The curators have managed to please both parents and children. Displays and galleries hold artifacts, puzzles, toys, dolls, and furniture from hundreds of years ago, accompanied by informative plaques. In order to make the museum more palatable to the thousands of children who visit it daily, the glass cases are interspersed with play areas where children can try out a rocking horse, dress up in fabulous costumes, put on their own puppet show, play games, and generally exhaust their parents. Areas are separated into child-friendly themes like *Babies* or *Who Will I Be?* *(Cambridge Heath Rd. ☎ 8980 2415; www.museumofchildhood.org.uk. ⊖Bethnal Green. Open M-Th and Sa-Su 10am-5:50pm. Free.)*

MAJOR EXHIBITION SPACES

Whitechapel Art Gallery, Whitechapel High St. (☎ 7522 7888; www.whitechapel.org). ⊖Aldgate East. Long the sole artistic beacon in a culturally and materially impoverished area, Whitechapel is now at the forefront of the buzzing art scene. Each summer the East End Academy exhibit features the best of local talent. Th late nights music, poetry, food and film. Open Tu-W and F-Su 11am-6pm, Th 11am-9pm. Partially wheelchair accessible.

Deluxe Gallery, 2-4 Hoxton Sq. (☎ 7729 8503; www.deluxe-arts.org.uk) ⊖Old St. Located on the 1st fl. of what looks like an office building, Hoxton's only public exhibition space provides a less ShoHocentric art experience. It shows a broad range of international contemporary art, often related to current new-media installations and various screenings. Open M-F 11am-6pm, Sa noon-5pm. Free. Wheelchair accessible.

COMMERCIAL GALLERIES

The small commercial galleries dotting the streets of Hoxton and Shoreditch, offer visitors their best chance to view the up-and-coming work of the "next big thing." To find even the most obscure and newest shows, arm yourself with the hugely helpful and artsy Shoreditch Map, available from most galleries in the area.

White Cube^2, 48 Hoxton Sq. (☎ 7930 5373; www.whitecube.com). ⊖Old St. One of the gems of Hoxton Sq., this stark white building has showcased some of the biggest names in international contemporary art. White Cube has an impressive list of alums; they've shown almost all major Brit artists from the last few years. Open Tu-Sa 10am-6pm. Free. Wheelchair accessible.

Victoria Miro, 16 Wharf Rd. (☎ 7336 8109; www.victoria-miro.com). ⊖Old St. or Angel. From Old St., take exit 8 and walk north up City Rd. toward Angel, then turn right after the McDonald's; ring the bell for entry. Don't be intimidated by the bell-ringing ex-warehouse feel; the exhibits here are spare and excellent. Gallery list include Jake and Dinos Chapman, Chris Ofili, and Peter Doig. Open Sept.-July Tu-Sa 10am-6pm. Call for Aug. hours.

COFFEE
OLD
COMPTON
CAFÉ

INSIDE

Food

Forget stale stereotypes about British food; in terms of quality and choice, London's restaurants offer a gastronomic experience as diverse, stylish, and satisfying as you'll find anywhere on the planet—until you see the bill. It's a sad truth that while the media scream about food being the new rock'n'roll, and chefs and restaurateurs have become household names, pound-for-pound, restaurants in London charge what would be deemed exorbitant prices across the Atlantic or the Channel. Any restaurant charging under £9 for a main course is relatively cheap by London's standards. With drinks and service, the bill for a simple meal nudges £15.

ICON	❶	❷	❸	❹	❺
PRICE	under £5	£5-9	£9-12	£13-16	£17+

FOOD BY TYPE

TIPS FOR EATING CHEAPLY

It is possible to eat cheaply the trick is knowing where and when to eat. If your hostel, B&B, or hotel includes a **"Full English Breakfast"** in its prices, you're half-way there—this cholesterol-laden feast of fried meat, eggs, and bread should fill you up long into the afternoon. If you want to spend a little more, lunchtime and early-evening special offers make it possible to dine in style affordably.

SANDWICHES. In many parts of central London sandwiches are the only affordable option. Chains such as Prêt-à-Manger and EAT (see p. 162) offer high-quality prepacked sandwiches, while hundreds of snack bars offer made-to-order "sarnies" for under £3. Note that, if you ask for a ham sandwich, in most cases, you'll get a slice of ham between two pieces of buttered bread: no lettuce, no mayo, and certainly not "overstuffed." Fixin's, most likely, will cost you another 50p.

PUB GRUB. For a proper sit down meal without the high bill, pubs offer hope. Far more than mere drinking, most pubs offer a range of hot and cold fare during the day and often in the evenings; for around £6 you can lunch on traditional English specials like bangers and mash or steak and kidney pie. "Pub grub" may be cheap but note that meals may be left under hot lamps for hours or microwaved from frozen. Find a pub where locals eat, and keep away from the tourist trail. More yuppified **gastropubs,** in contrast, place a higher priority on fresh, original dishes— although higher prices often reflect the change. For pub listings, see **Pubs,** p. 192.

EXOTIC TASTES. Many of the best budget meals can be found in the variety of **ethnic restaurants** the city has to offer. **Indian** food, at the top of the list, is recognized as Britain's unofficial national cuisine—when Prince Charles was asked to describe the archetypal British meal, he shared popular taste and chose the classic Anglo-Indian hybrid chicken tikka masala. **Turkish** restaurants are also experts at cooking up low-budget feasts (kebab stands are the Euroquivalent of American hot dog vendors), while some of the cheapest and tastiest sit-down dinners in town are **Chinese.** Recently, **Japanese** cuisine has shed its upmarket image with a proliferation of noodle bars—Wagamama most notable among them—offering giant bowls of ramen for £5-6. For the best and cheapest ethnic food, head to the source: Whitechapel for Bengali *balti*, Islington for Turkish *meze*, Marylebone for Lebanese *shwarma*, and Soho for Cantonese *dim sum.*

GROCERIES & SUPERMARKETS. Most hostels and student halls have kitchen facilities for residents, and cooking for yourself is almost always less expensive than eating out. The cheapest places to get the ingredients for your own meal in London are often the local markets; for listings of street markets see **Shopping**, p. 254. For all your food under one roof, London's largest supermarket chains are **Tesco, Safeway,** and **Sainsbury's. Asda, Kwik-Save,** and **Somerfield** are "budget" supermarkets, while **Waitrose** and **Marks & Spencer** are more upmarket and a good source of fancier ingredients. For night owls, the branches of **Hart's** stay open 24hrs. And if you're willing to splurge, the food halls of **Harrods, Harvey Nichols, Selfridges,** and **Fortnum & Mason's** are attractions in their own right.

TO GO PLEASE. Takeout is cheaper than staying in for many lunch places. Save yourself a few quid by using that option.

SNACKS. Favorite **chocolate bars** include Flake (a stick of flaky chocolate often stuck into an ice cream cone), Crunchie (honeycombed magic), and the classic Dairy Milk. If you're accustomed to the waxy brown stuff known as "chocolate" in America, high-quality Cadbury goods here will be a revelation. **Sweets** come in many forms—the fizzy Refreshers, the chewy Wine Gums, or frosted Fruit Pastilles. **Crisps** (potato chips to Americans) come in a range of flavors, including prawn cocktail, cheese & onion, chicken, bacon, and salt & vinegar. All this sugar and salt can be washed down with Lilt, a pineapple and grapefruit flavored **fizzy drink** (soda), or a drinkbox-ful of Ribena, a super-sweet blackcurrant manna from heaven. This latter beverage belongs to a family of drinks known as **squashes,** fruit-based syrups watered down to drink. The food that expatriate Britons miss most is **Marmite,** a yeast extract which is spread on bread or toast.

AFTERNOON TEA, SEE P. 163

ASIAN (SEE ALSO CHINESE)

Aki	HOL 2
busaba eathai	WEND 2
Galanga Thai Canteen	NL 2
Jenny Lo's Teahouse	K/B 2
Makan	NH 1
Mandalay	M/RP 1
New Culture Revolution	NL 1
Noodle, Noodle	WEMIN 2
Nusa Dua	WEND 2
Phât Phúc	CHEL 2
Soba Noodle Bar	WEND 2
tsu	WEND 2
Wagamama	BLOOM 2
Yelo	EL 1
Yo!Sushi	WEND 3

BREAKFAST

Black and Blue	NH 3
Buckingham Coffee Lounge	WEMIN 1
Cafe Pushkar	SL 1
Chelsea Bun Diner	CHEL 1
Chelsea Kitchen	CHEL 1
The Island Café	SB 1
Lazy Daisy Café	NH 1

CAFES

Al Café/Bar	CLERK 2
Bluebird	CHEL 2
Blue Room Café	WEND 1
Buckingham Coffee Lounge	WEMIN 1
Café 7	SB 2
Café 1001	EL 1
Café Emm	WEND 2
Candid Cafe	NL 1
Gloriette	K/B 2
The Island Café	SB 1
Lazy Daisy Café	NH 1
Lisboa Patisserie	NH 1
La Madeline	WEND 2
Maison Blanc	WL 1
Marketplace Restaurant	CHEL 3
Monmount Coffee Company	WEND 1
Notting Hill Gate Cafe	NH 2

CARIBBEAN

Mango Room	NL 2
Mr. Jerk	BAY 2

CHINESE & MONGOLIAN

Golden Dragon	WEND 2
Harbour City	WEND 2
Mr. Kong	WEND 2
Royal China	BAY, M/RP 3
Tiger Lil's	BAY, NL 3

EASTERN EUROPEAN

L'Autre	WEND 3
Patio	WL 2
Trojka	NL 3

FRENCH

Bleeding Heart Bistro & Restaurant	HOL 5
La Brasserie	KEN/EC 4
La Brasserie Townhouse	BLOOM 2
Le Cellier du Midi	NL 5
Gloriette	K/B 2
Gordon Ramsay	CHEL 5
La Madeline	WEND 2
Masion Blanc	NL 1
Le Mercury	NL 2
Patisserie Valerie	WEND 1
Poilâne	K/B 1
Raison d'Être	KEN/EC 1

GREEK

Aphrodite Taverna	BAY 3

INDIAN

Aladin	EL 2
Bar Bombay	CLERK 2
Café Spice Namaste	CITY 3
Diwana Bhel Poori House	BLOOM 2
Durbar Tandoori	BAY 2
Masala Zone	WEND 2
Tamarind	WEND 3
Zaika	KEN/EC 5

ITALIAN (SEE ALSO PIZZA)

Buonasera at the Jam	CHEL 3
Cantina del Ponte	SB 3
Carluccio's	WEND 2
ICCo	BLOOM 2
Spighetta	M/RP 3
Tomato	WEND 3

LATENIGHT

Bar Italia	WEND 1
Carmelli Bakery	NL 1
Grand Central	EL 1
Ranoush Juice	M/RP 1

MIDDLE EASTERN

Afghan Kitchen	NL 1
Al Casbah	NL 3
Alounak Kebab	BAY 2
Café Zagora	WL 2
Gallipoli	NL 2
Levantine	BAY 2
Manzara	NH 1
Patogh	M/RP 2
Ranoush Juice	M/RP 1
Shish	EL 2
Tas	SB 2

MODERN BRITISH

Babylon	HOL 4
Black and Blue	NH 3
Bleeding Heart Tavern	HOL 3
Bloom's	NL 2
Bluebird	CHEL 2
Books for Cooks	NH 1
Bug	SL 3

MODERN BRITISH (CONT.)

Goddard's Pie and Mash	EL ❶
Ivy	WEND ❺
People's Palace	SB ❹
St. John	CLERK ❺
SW9	SL ❷
Tiles	WEND ❸

PIZZA

Bar Italia	WEND ❶
Bar Room Bar	NL ❷
ECCo	WEMIN ❶
Gourmet Pizza Co.	SB ❷
Pizza Express	CHEL ❷
Pizzeria Oregano	NL ❷

SANDWICHES & SNACKS

Beigel Bake	EL ❶
La Bodega del Gelato	BAY ❶
Carmelli Bakery	NL ❶
La Crêperie de Hampstead	NL ❶
ECCo	WEMIN ❶
Futures	CITY ❶
The Grain Shop	NH ❶
Grand Central	EL ❶
Marine Ices	NL ❶
Neal's Yard	WEND ❶
The Place Below	CITY ❶
Poilâne	K/B ❶
Relish	WEMIN ❶
Spianata & Co.	CITY ❶
Tom's Delicatessen	NH ❷
Wolley's	HOL ❷

SEAFOOD

Delfina	SB ❸
George's Portabello Fish Bar	NH ❶
North Sea Fish Restaurant	BLOOM ❸
Pescatori	BLOOM ❹

SPANISH/LATIN AMERICAN

Anexo	CLERK ❷
L'Autre	WEND ❸
Café Pacifico	WEND ❸
Cuba Libre	NL ❷
Cubana	SB ❷
Goya	K/B, WEMIN ❸
Mô	WEND ❸
Navarro's Tapas Bar	BLOOM ❸

VEGETARIAN

Afghan Kitchen	NL ❶
Café Em	WEND ❷
Café Pushkar	SL ❶
Chelsea Bun	CHEL ❶
Diwana Bhel Poori House	BLOOM ❷
The Gate	WL ❸
The Greenery	CLERK ❶
The Place Below	CITY ❶
Relish	WEND ❶
Tas	SB ❷

WINE BARS

Gordon's Wine Bar	WEND ❷
Odette's Wine Bar	NL ❺
Vats	BLOOM ❸

WORLD

Giraffe	M/RP, NL ❷

NEIGHBORHOOD ABBREVIATIONS: BAY Bayswater **BLOOM** Bloomsbury **CHEL** Chelsea **CITY** The City of London **CLERK** Clerkenwell **HOL** Holborn **KEN/EC** Kensington & Earl's Court **K/B** Knightsbridge & Belgravia **M/RP** Marylebone & Regent's Park **NH** Notting Hill **SB** The South Bank **WEND** The West End **WEMIN** Westminster **NL** North London **SL** South London **EL** East London **WL** West London

NOTABLE CHAINS

ASK (www.askcentral.co.uk). A recent pretender to Pizza Express's throne with a similar emphasis on hip, design-conscious restaurants. Not quite as dependable, but with much more menu variety. Pastas, salads, and thin-crust pizzas £5-8. Open daily noon-11:30pm. AmEx/MC/V. ❷

Crussh Juice Bar, (☎7626 2175). This hole-in-the-wall makes smoothies and juices (£2-£4) and makes them well. Lunch is the best deal: sandwiches and wraps (£1-£4), salads and soups (£2-4) and some breakfast options (£1-2) are available. Open M-F 6:30am-4pm. ❶

EAT (www.eatrestaurant.co.uk). Despite the cheesy name (it stands for "Excellence And Taste"), this coffee bar/sandwich joint combo is a hit with Londoners. A small range of salads, soups, and sushi complements the sandwiches, all made fresh daily and preservative-free. Food £1.50-3.50; coffee from £1.10. AmEx/MC/V. ❶

Pizza Express (www.pizzaexpress.co.uk). Once a mini-chain famed for crisp, Italian-style pizza and modern design, Pizza Express has massively expanded across Europe; their pizzas have simultaneously shrunk in size (now around 8 in. diameter) and in quality. Nonetheless, Pizza Express continues to offer reasonably priced food in reasonably attractive surroundings. Pizzas and salads £5-8. AmEx/MC/V. ❷

Prêt-à-Manger (www.pret.com). These bustling, chrome-adorned sandwich bars are mobbed for their sandwiches, baguettes, and salads (£2-3), all made daily on the premises without "obscure" additives and preservatives. Eat-in prices 17.5% higher. AmEx/MC/V. ❶

Wagamama (www.wagamama.com). Pioneer of the noodle-bar revolution. It's not clear why, though—the transformation from one-hit wonder to international chain has brought with it a downward trend in food quality. That said, it's still good value (ramen from £6) and good fun. Wide vegetarian selection around £6. AmEx/MC/V. ❷

Yo!Sushi (www.yosushi.com). The original Yo!Sushi, at 52 Poland St. (⊖Oxford Circus), pioneered conveyor-belt sushi in London, and the chain has spread like wildfire. Diners sit at an island bar, picking from a never-ending stream of small plates, color-coded by price (£1.50-3.50). There's no doubt that it's fun, but portions are paltry (a filling meal will come to around £15 each), and there's no knowing how long that raw fish has been circling on the (unrefrigerated) conveyor belt. AmEx/MC/V. ❸

AFTERNOON TEA

The Ritz, Piccadilly (☎7493 8181). ⊖Green Park. See The Big Splurge: Tea at the Ritz (p. 182).

The Lanesborough, Hyde Park Corner (☎7259 5599). ⊖Hyde Park Corner. Full disabled access. This converted hospital astounds with both its opulent decor and its steep prices. See what it is to be proper, English, and appallingly well taken-care-of by your smartly-dressed waiter. Traditional afternoon tea served in the large, glass-ceilinged Conservatory, which was modelled on the Prince Regent's lurid oriental-fantasy Brighton Pavilion. Dent the pocketbook a tad less by ordering a la carte (scones with jam and clotted cream £7), min. charge £9.50 per person, or splurge for set tea (£25) or champagne tea (£32). Dress code is smart casual—no jeans or sneakers. Open 6:30am-midnight. MC/V/AmEx.

Fortnum & Mason, 181 Piccadilly (☎7734 8040; www.fortnumandmason.co.uk). This gourmet department store (and official royal grocery) has three restaurants; the fancy fourth-floor St. James Restaurant serves a lovely formal afternoon tea Tu-Sa 3-5:30pm. Classic set tea £19.50, Rare set tea £21.50. Wheelchair accessible. AmEx/MC/V.

St. Martin's Lane Hotel, 45 St. Martin's Ln. (☎7300 5588. ⊖Leicester Sq. Too cool for a sign (look for the yellow-lit revolving door), this white post-modern hotel ditches traditional for avant-garde. £14.50 gets you "Asian" (bento) or "Eurasian" tea. Bewilder your taste buds with the complex flavors. Dress code: casual. Tea served daily 3-5pm. Wheelchair accessible. AmEx/MC/V.

Brown's, Albemarle St. (☎7493 6020). ⊖Green Park. Opened by Byron's butler in 1837, London's first luxury hotel still oozes old-fashioned charm. Dress code: no jeans or sneakers. However, it is closed till March 2005 so call for time details. AmEx/MC/V.

The Orangery, Kensington Palace (☎7938 1406). ⊖High St. Kensington. Built for Queen Anne's dinner parties and full of white, high-ceilinged stateliness, this airy neoclassical building behind Kensington Palace is popular for light lunches (£8-11, set lunch £9) and afternoon teas (from £8) served to an admiring tourist-heavy clientele. Recently opened for light breakfasts as well (£2-5). Open daily 10am-noon for breakfast, noon-3pm for lunch, 3-6pm for tea. MC/V.

The Savoy, Strand (☎7420 2356; www.the-avoy-group.com). ⊖Charing Cross. One of London's most famous hotels, popular for afternoon tea. Noel Coward once performed in the elegant Thames Foyer, but now you'll have to make due with the Savoy pianist accompanying your tea. Su a band plays hits from the 20s to the 40s as the floor is opened up to dancers. Set tea of tasty sandwiches and pastries £24 M-F, £27 Sa-Su.; with champagne £31.50/

Menu Reader

ENGLISH	AMERICAN
peckish	hungry
aubergine	eggplant
bangers and mash	pork sausage and mashed potato
bap	soft bun
biscuit	cookie or cracker
chips	french fries
clotted cream	like butter but sweeter and better
Cornish pastries	pastry filled with meat, onions, and vegetables
courgette	zucchini
crisps	potato chips
crumpet	holier version of an English muffin
fry up	big English Breakfast of eggs, sausage or bacon, tomatoes, and more
gateau	cake
Haricots vert	green beans
ice lolly	popsicle
jacket potato	baked potato served with various toppings
kipper	smoked fish
Ploughman's lunch	pub grub of crusty bread with cheese or paté
prawn	shrimp
pudding	dessert
salt beef	corned beef
scotch egg	hard boiled egg fried with ground sausage and bread crumbs

£34.50. Dress code: no jeans, shorts, or sneakers; jacket and tie preferred. Tea daily 2:30-5:30pm. Reserve 1-2 days ahead M-F, 2 weeks Sa-Su. Wheelchair accessible. AmEx/MC/V.

RESTAURANTS BY NEIGHBORHOOD

BAYSWATER

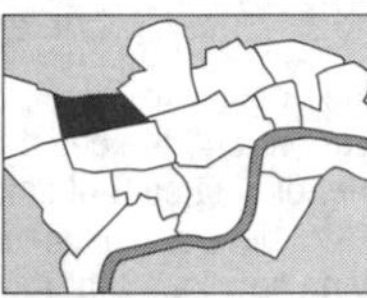

SEE MAP, p. 359

BAYSWATER QUICKFIND: Discover, p. 4; pubs, p. 193; entertainment, p. 233; shopping, p. 254; accommodations, p. 279.

Cheap and central, Bayswater was an immigrant magnet in the years after WWII, playing a pioneering role in developing Britain's tastebuds beyond meat pie and spotted dick. The **Standard Tandoori,** on Westbourne Grove, was one of London's first Indian restaurants. Hummus, kebabs, and other Middle Eastern delights were introduced to Londoners through Bayswater's large Arab population. **Westbourne Grove** and **Queensway** hold numerous cheap Chinese, Indian, and Persian restaurants; and a similar smattering of affordable flavor borders Paddington Station on **London Street.** For those who appreciate the appeal of good old-fashioned commercialism, **Whiteleys** mall (see p. 254) has a good selection of upscale chain restaurants. Bayswater draws the best balance between good ethnic food, ambience, and cost.

Mr. Jerk, 19 Westbourne Grove (☎7221 4678; www.mrjerk.co.uk). ⊖Bayswater or Royal Oak. **Branch** at 189 Wardour St. in the West End (☎7287 2878). No snickering, children: the name refers to their house specialty "jerk chicken" (£6.50), and this fantastic little Caribbean joint might even deserve a "Dr. Jerk" moniker instead. There's nothing fancy about the cafe-style setup, but mouthwatering smells and an inexpensive menu more than make up for tiny tables. Feast on Trinidadian *mutton roti* (£5) or the traditional combo of ackee (a savory Caribbean fruit) and saltfish (£6). All mains come with a hearty portion of rice and peas. Add fried plantains £1. Sip a Guinness Punch or go fully local with Soursap (both £2.50). Open M-Sa 10am-11pm, Su noon-8pm. AmEx/MC/V. ❷

Levantine, 26 London St. (☎7262 1111). ⊖Paddington. Enter to the faint aroma of incense and rose petals; a beautiful, elegant Lebanese restaurant that just wants to keep feeding you. Endless tiny courses make up the famous *mezze* set menu (lunches £8.50-15, dinners £19.50-28). *A la carte* the dishes start at £3.25. With loads of vegetarian options, featured nights of belly-dancing and *shisha* (water pipe), and even an ornate loo to boot; this is a splurge well worth making. £1 cover. Open daily noon-1am (last food orders midnight). MC/V. ❹

La Bottega del Gelato, 127 Bayswater Rd. (☎7243 2443). ⊖Queensway. Now in his 70s, Quinto Barbieri still gets up at 4:30am to make the best gelati this side of the Rubicon. Perfect to take on a stroll in the Kensington Gardens across the street; eat up as children stare at you with jealous eyes. 1-3 scoops £1.50-3.50. Open daily 10am-7pm, later in summer. ❶

Aphrodite Taverna, 15 Hereford Rd. (☎7229 2206). ⊖Bayswater. Pantelis and Rosanna have been running this Greek restaurant for 20 years, and it's got a homey warmth that's almost as striking as the madly over-zealous wall decorations. Fabulous menu is a grab-bag of multisyllabic treats. (mains £7.80-£19.50, set meals £13-27.) £1 cover isn't wasted; pre-meal bread and fixings are worth it. **Cafe Aphrodite,** next door, offers some of the specialties at cheaper prices and a full sandwich menu (£2.80-5). Restaurant open M-Sa noon-midnight. Cafe open daily 8:00am-5pm. AmEx/MC/V. Restaurant ❸ Cafe ❷

Royal China, 13 Queensway (☎7221 2535). ⊖Bayswater or Queensway. A micro-chain renowned for London's best dim sum (see p. 174). ❸

Durbar Tandoori, 84 Westbourne Grove. (☎7727 1947; www.durbartandoori.co.uk). ⊖Bayswater. Durbar's claim to fame is the extraordinary cooking of Shamin Syed, former International Indian Chef of the Year. Chow down in the simple dining room and revel in the low-priced goodness of it all. Veggie and meat mains £4-9, set lunch £8, bargain takeout lunch box £4. Chef's special dinner for two £22. Open Sa-Th noon-3pm and daily 6pm-midnight. AmEx/MC/V. ❷

Alounak Kebab, 44 Westbourne Grove (☎7229 0416). ⊖Bayswater or Royal Oak. A discreet gem among the scads of Persian restaurants in the area, with low prices to boot. Most dishes baked in the traditional clay oven by the door. Succulent, slow-grilled kebabs (from £5.60). Mouthwateringly fluffy saffron rice or fresh *taftaan* bread accompany with all meals. Open daily noon-midnight. MC/V. ❷

Tiger Lil's, 75 Bishop's Bridge Rd. (☎7221 2622). ⊖Bayswater. Same create-your-own-meal formula as the branch in Islington, North London (see p. 184). Open M-F noon-3pm and 6-11pm, Sa-Su noon-11pm. ❷

ENGLISH	AMERICAN
Shepherd's pie	baked meat and vegetables pie covered with gravy and mashed potatoes
Smarties	like M&Ms
spotted dick	sponge cake with fruit and raisins steamed with custard sauce
steak and kidney pie	pastry-topped pie of steak, kidneys and mushrooms in gravy
sticky toffee pudding	spotted dick without the fruit and served with warm butterscotch sauce
squash	a concentrated fruit drink, you have to add water to it to drink it
sultanas	raisin
sweets	candy
trifle	sponge cake soaked in sherry, layered with rasberry preserves, covered with custard sauce, and capped with whipped cream
Welsh rarebit	melted cheddar cheese and mustard or Worcestershire sauce served on toast
whitebait	small, whole, deep-fried fish
Yorkshire pudding	eggy pastry served with roast beef

BLOOMSBURY

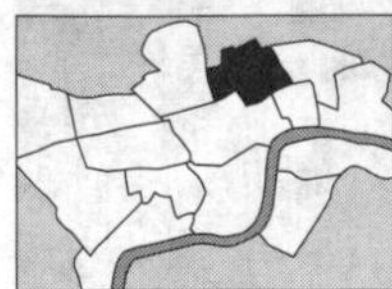
SEE MAP, p. 360

BLOOMSBURY QUICKFIND: Discover, p. 5; sights, p. 87; museums & galleries, p. 140; pubs, p. 193; entertainment, p. 234; shopping, p. 255; accommodations, p. 282.

At the heart of London's student community, Bloomsbury is overflowing with top-notch budget food. Running parallel to Tottenham Crt. Rd., **Charlotte Street** (⊖Goodge St.) has for decades been one of London's best-known foodie streets, with fashionable restaurants in all price ranges. A string of extremely cheap vegetarian Indian eateries and sweet shops lines **Drummond Street,** near Euston, while on the other side of Bloomsbury, bordering Holborn, **Sicilian Avenue** has some great sandwich and snack shops. Cheap ethnic food is everywhere, but **Euston Road** (near ⊖Warren St.), **Museum Street,** and **Cosmo Place** are particularly flavorful. Of course, on a sunny day, the ideal meal only requires a bit of takeout and a patch of grass on one of the numerous squares and gardens that dot the neighborhood.

ICCo (Italiano Coffee Company), 46 Goodge St. (☎7580 9688). ⊖Goodge St. Light-years ahead of its competition, ICCo serves delicious 11" pizzas, made to order, for an eye-popping £3. Pre-packaged sandwiches and baguettes, on in-store baked bread, start at £1.50 (rolls 50p), and pasta £2. Takeout available. A young student crowd generally fills the steel-tabled dining area. Buy any hot drink before noon and get a free fresh-baked croissant. Sandwiches half-off after 4pm. Pizzas available from noon. Open M-F 7am-11pm, Sa-Su 9am-11pm. MC/V. ❶

North Sea Fish Restaurant, 7-8 Leigh St. (☎7387 5892; www.northseafishrestaurant.co.uk). ⊖Russell Sq. or King's Cross St. Pancras. Real fish 'n' chips done right. The classy little restaurant offers a boatload of fresh, tasty seafood dishes in a warm, attractive setting, or the takeout shop sells heaping portions of the same for unbeatable prices (£3.50-5). Mains £8-17. Restaurant open M-Sa noon-2:30pm and 5:30-10:30pm; takeout M-Sa noon-2:30pm and 5-11pm. AmEx/MC/V. ❸

Vats, 51 Lambs Conduit St. (☎7242 8963). ⊖Russell Square. Move through the woody, front area to the classic main bar, flanked by an antique reading desk piled high with wine-related volumes. Friendly staff is happy to let you taste before you commit (for wines available by the glass). Food is quasi-pricey (starters £4-8, mains £10-16), but delicious and innovative. Vats has too many wines to fit them all on the list, so if you have something particular in mind, don't be afraid to ask. "Good ordinary claret" £3.50 per glass, £14.50 per bottle. Burgundy from £15 per bottle. Lunch served noon-2:30pm, dinner 6-9:30pm. Open M-F noon-11pm. AmEx/MC/V. ❸

Navarro's Tapas Bar, 67 Charlotte St. (☎7637 7713; www.navarros.co.uk). ⊖Goodge St. Enca and Paco's colorful, bustling tapas restaurant boasts the wrought-iron decor, tiled walls, and brightly painted furniture of a Seville original, and this gorgeous authenticity carries over to their excellent food—try the spicy and deliciously thick lentil stew. *Tapas* £3-6; 2-3 per person is plenty (£7.50 min.). Open M-F noon-3pm and 6-10pm, Sa 6-10pm. AmEx/MC/V. ❸

Diwana Bhel Poori House, 121-123 Drummond St. (☎7387 5556). ⊖Euston or Euston Sq. No frills or frippery here—just great, cheap south Indian vegetarian food and quiet, efficient service. Try the excellent all-you-can-eat lunch buffet (£6.50, served daily noon-2:30pm) or enjoy ample portions on the regular menu. Outside buffet hours, *thali* set meals are a good deal (£5.50-8). Open M-Sa noon-11:30pm, Su noon-10:30pm. AmEx/MC/V. ❷

La Brasserie Townhouse, 24 Coptic St. (☎7636 2731). ⊖Tottenham Crt. Rd. or Holborn. A bright pink and yellow facade welcome you into this tiny, mirrored eatery of simple delights. French-inspired offerings like Toulouse sausages or citron-grilled tuna and a cozy atmosphere. 2 course dinner £8 (lunch £5). Open M-F noon-3pm and 6-11pm, Sa 4-11pm, Su 1-10pm. MC/V. ❷

Pescatori, 57 Charlotte St. (☎7580 3289; www.pescatori.co.uk). ⊖Goodge St. Branch at 11 Dover St. in Mayfair (☎7493 2652). Don't let the tacky Tube ads fool you—Pescatori knows its fish. The seafood is consistently fresh, delicious, and pricey: pasta mains £12-17, others £12-30; if you don't mind the lunchtime crowd, try the 2 course special (£19). Open M-Tu noon-3pm and 6-11pm, W-Sa noon-3pm and 6-11:30pm. MC/V. ❹

TIP **CONDIMENT WARNING.** Before you order that comforting PB&J sandwich or slather your chips with ketchup, you might want to sample the prospective addition. British peanut butter, ketchup, yogurt and BBQ sauce may taste different from their overseas counterparts.

CHELSEA

CHELSEA QUICKFIND: Discover, p. 5; sights, p. 89; museums & galleries, p. 141; pubs, p. 195; entertainment, p. 234; shopping, p. 256, accommodations, p. 285.

TRANSPORTATION: *The only Tube station in Chelsea is Sloane Sq.; from here buses #11, 19, 22, 211, and 319 serve King's Rd.*

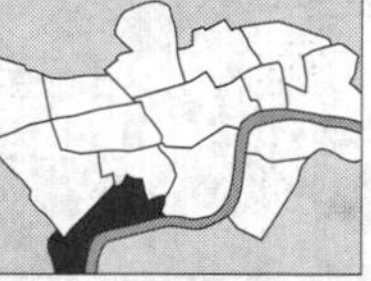

SEE MAP, p. 361

As with everything else in Chelsea, it's all happening on **King's Road.** The chic thoroughfare houses a surprising number of quality, affordable eateries catering to a wide range of budgets and tastes, with a particularly high concentration between Sydney St. and the World's End kink. Outdoor cafes are closer to Sloane Square.

Chelsea Bun, 9a Limerston St. (☎7352 3635). Spirited and funky casual diner that serves heaping portions of everything under the sun. Extensive vegetarian and vegan options include faux sausages with a full English breakfast. No need to set the alarm clock—early-bird specials available 7am-noon (£2-3). Sandwiches (£1.80-4) and breakfasts (from £4) are served until 6pm. Pasta, salads, burgers, and omelettes £6-8. Minimum £3.50 per person lunch, £5.50 dinner. Open M-Sa 7am-11:30pm, Su 9am-7pm. MC/V. ❶

Chelsea Kitchen, 98 King's Rd. (☎7589 1330). Hearty, unpretentious diner fare makes for one of the cheapest sit-down meals in London; mains, with fries and salad £3.30-5. Simple interior—charming cave-like booths downstairs. Soup, salads, and sandwiches £2-4, wine £1.40 per glass and £6.80 per bottle. Minimum charge £3 per person. Breakfast served until 11:30am. Open daily 7am-midnight. MC/V (£10 min.). ❶

Buonasera, at the Jam, 289a King's Rd. (☎7352 8827). The novelty of the bunk-style seating, patented by the owners, makes for a worthwhile experience in itself, as the waiters leap up the small ladders to your mid-air table. What's more, the mouth-watering Italian dishes on the menu should keep you flying high for hours after you've descended. Fish and steak dishes run £8-12, and sizable pasta plates (£6.80-12). Reservations recommended for weekends. Open Tu-F noon-3pm and 6pm-midnight, Sa-Su noon-midnight. MC/V. ❸

Gordon Ramsay, 68 Royal Hospital Rd. (☎7352 4441; www.gordanramsay.com). Gordon Ramsay—eccentric artist, former footballer, and celebrity chef. The man was only 18 when he gave up professional soccer for culinary school (he started in the league at 15), and it was a good move; Ramsay's light, innovative French concoctions have been awarded 3 Michelin stars (only 2 other UK restaurants can match that), and he's widely considered to be the best chef in England. The purple and glass-trimmed interior manages to avoid pretension, but the set lunch menu is £35, and multi-course dinners £65-80, so don't show up in anything but a jacket and tie. Reserve 2 weeks ahead for lunch and 1 month for dinner. Open M-F noon-2:50pm and 6:30-11pm. AmEx/MC/V. ❺

Bluebird, 350 King's Rd. (☎7559 1000; www.bluebird-store.co.uk). An auto-shop turned gastronomic pit stop, this food emporium includes a restaurant, an outdoor cafe, and a gourmet Sainsbury's—it's all been labeled the "Bluebird Gastrodome." The metallic-chic cafe serves salads, sandwiches, and steaks (£6.50-11), while the swanky skylit restaurant pushes eclectic gourmet (£12-21). Cafe open M-Sa 8am-10pm, Su 10am-6pm. Restaurant open M-F 12:30-3:30pm and 6-11:30pm, Sa noon-4pm and 6-11:30pm, Su noon-4pm and 6-10:30pm. Store open M-Sa 8am-10pm, Su 11am-5pm. AmEx/MC/V. Cafe ❷ Restaurant ❹

Phât Phúc, The Courtyard at 250 King's Rd., entrance on Sydney St. (☎7349 9696). Most giggly diners only eat here because of the homonymically hilarious name (sound it out, people), but the fresh courtyard seating and heaping portions of this Vietnamese noodle bar are more than just a gimmick. Dishes rotate daily (£4.95). Open daily noon-5pm. MC/V. ❷

ON THE MENU

Full English Breakfast

If you're after more food than you can imagine, there is little in life more fullfilling than a **full English breakfast** (a.k.a. the "fry-up") in the early morning. Variations abound, but an English breakfast typically consists of fried eggs and bacon in double servings, plus fried toast, baked beans, and a selection of other foods, which can include pork sausages, liver, kidneys, black or white pudding (not actually pudding, but sausages of the blood and non-blood variety), grilled or fried tomato, and mushrooms. All washed down with coffee or tea (or beer if you're the hardy type).

It may be traditional English breakfast fare, but very few British people actually eat a full English breakfast every morning–it's just too unhealthy to stomach daily. Quicker and healthier breakfast options have increasingly displaced this delicious English breakfast, exiling it mostly to hotels, B&Bs, and neighborhood haunts like diners where it's readily consumed by tourists and working men looking for an early-morning cholesterol fix.

Marketplace Restaurant, 125 Sydney St., in Chelsea Farms Mkt. (☎7352 5600). Set within a courtyard of spiffy restaurants and shops, this high-end cafe is best appreciated for its outdoor seating and appealing French-inspired menu. Large salads, burgers, and sandwiches £10-11.50, starters £5-7. Open M-F 9:30am-5pm, Sa-Su 9:30am-6pm. Wheelchair accessible. AmEx/MC/V (£10 min.). ❸

Pizza Express, 152 King's Rd. (☎7351 5031; www.pizzaexpress.co.uk). See Notable Chains, p. 163. Perhaps the most impressive of Pizza Express's locations; it's gigantic and ornate. The 3 atmospheric floors are located in the former home of dancer Princess Astafieva. A triumphal archway supported by caryatids and topped by a bronze chariot separates the large courtyard from the sidewalk. Open daily 11:30am-midnight. AmEx/MC/V. ❷

THE CITY OF LONDON

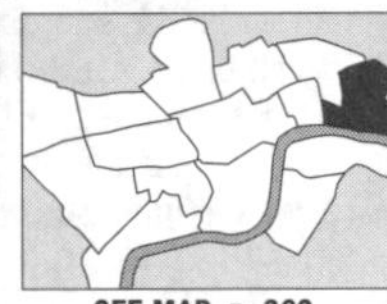
SEE MAP, p. 362

THE CITY OF LONDON QUICKFIND: Discover, p. 6; sights, p. 90; museums & galleries, p. 141; pubs, p. 195; entertainment, p. 235.

With almost none of the City's workforce sticking around for supper and with hardly any residents, it's not surprising that the vast majority of City eateries open only for weekday breakfast and lunch—it's nearly impossible to find a decent dinner here, although most pubs are open and serving food well into the evenings. Even at lunchtime, choices are limited: it comes down to a sandwich or a millionaire's banquet. If you're after the former, sandwich bars are on every corner and there are plenty of options from all cuisines and food groups. Side alleys have some of the best bargain food. Be warned, however, that long queues will form outside the better establishments between noon and 1:30pm on weekdays. If you can't decide what to eat, the alleyways of **Leadenhall Market,** just south of Leadenhall, pack in numerous mid-range chain restaurants, cafes, and pubs (see p. 163).

Futures, 8 Botolph Alley (☎7623 4529), between Botolph Ln. and Lovat Ln. ⊖Monument. Suits and their lackeys besiege this tiny takeaway during the lunch hour; come before noon to take advantage of the place. Weekly-changing variety of vegetarian soups (£2-3), salads (£1.50-£3), pre-packaged smoothies (£1.40), and hot dishes (£4) For breakfast you'll find a wide variety of pastries (80p), or porridges and cereals (£1). This is a rarity in the City: truly good food that is truly fresh. Open M-F 7:30-10am and 11:30am-3pm. Wheelchair accessible. ❶

Café Spice Namaste, 16 Prescot St. (☎7488 9242). ⊖Tower Hill or DLR: Tower Gateway. While hard to find, Café Spice is worth a bit of a trek. Bright, carnivalesque decoration brings an exotic feel to this old Victorian warehouse, and the classy service is a cut above. The extensive menu of Goan and Parsee specialities helpfully explains each dish. Meat dishes are on the pricey side (£11-13), but vegetarian meals (£7-9) are affordable, especially for an establishment of this quality. A varied wine list and excellent but expensive desserts (£3-£4) complete the experience. Open M-F noon-3pm, 6:15-10:30pm, Sa 6:30-10:30pm. AmEx/MC/V. ❸

The Place Below, Cheapside (☎7329 0789), in the basement of St. Mary-le-Bow. ⊖St. Paul's or Mansion House. Climb down the winding steps from the foyer of St. Mary-le-Bow, and you'll find yourself in a fantastic vegetarian restaurant, light-years away from the typical City sandwich joint. The food is the star here; be prepared to wait at lunchtime and count on taking your food with you. Fresh, elaborate sandwiches (£3-5), yummy porridge (£1.20), and a constantly changing menu of tasty mains (£4-6) There are also pastries (£1.30-£2.50) and plenty of hot drinks as well as the daily healthbowl, a concoction of various health-conscious foods (£4.50). Open M-F 7:30am-3:30pm. ❶

Spianata & Co., 73A Watling St. by Bow Lane (☎7236 3666). ⊖Mansion House. This eat-and-run sandwich shop also serves organic salads (£3), fruit and yogurt (£1-£3). The name, however, comes from the wide, flat sandwiches (£3-£4) served on Italian Spianata bread and made on the premisis. Daily offerings include a classic mozzarella and tomato or a slightly more elaborate shrimp and roasted pepper. All are good and all are a good deal. Open M-F 7:30am-3:30pm. Wheelchair accessible.❶

CLERKENWELL

CLERKENWELL QUICKFIND: Discover, p. 7; sights, p. 95; museums & galleries, p. 143; pubs, p. 196; nightlife, p. 210; entertainment, p. 235; accommodations, p. 285.

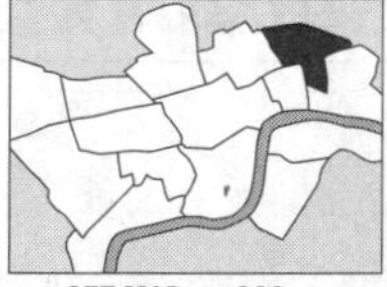

SEE MAP, p. 363

There's no shortage of fine dining in Clerkenwell—and even the best restaurants offer some affordable sustenance. Foregoing "fine" in favor of cheap, try one of the many sandwich bars south of Farringdon station, or along **Clerkenwell Green, St. John Street,** or **Charterhouse Street.** There are also inexpensive snack bars, pubs, and Chinese takeaways on West Smithfield just south of the market. For a proper sit-down meal, your best bet is **Exmouth Market,** a pedestrian street north of Clerkenwell Rd. flanked on both sides by all manner of eateries, from pie'n'mash joints to some of London's priciest restaurants.

Anexo, 61 Turnmill St. (☎7250 3401; www.anexo.co.uk). ⊖Farringdon. Funky and laid-back, this Spanish-flavored restaurant and bar serves up tasty Iberian concoctions all day long. The attractive, multi-tiered dining area (it expands outdoors in good weather) is all about wrought copper and edgy elegance, with an expansive menu to match. Gorge on authentic paella (£7.50-9), fajitas (£8.50-10), and tapas (£3.25-5). Mondays 2-for-1 tapas. Happy Hour, M-Sa from 5-7pm. 2- and 3-course lunch specials £7.50-9.50, 4-course "Tapas Menu" £15. Take away available. Open M-F 10am-10pm, Sa 6-11pm, Su 4:30-10pm. Bar open until 2am most nights. Wheelchair accessible. AmEx/MC/V.❷

St. John, 26 St. John St. (☎7251 0848; www.stjohnrestaurant.com). ⊖Farringdon. St. John has stormed the London restaurant scene, winning countless prizes for its eccentric English cuisine; they call it "nose to tail eating," and certainly few body parts are wasted. Hence, not a great place for vegetarians. Prices in the posh restaurant are high (mains £13-20), but you can enjoy similar bounty (in smaller quantities) in the airy bar outside, which was formerly a smokehouse used by the butchers at Smithfield Market. The menu changes daily, but some representative dishes include roast bone-marrow salad (£6.20), ox heart and green beans (£14.50), and rack of lamb (£19). A bakery at the back of the bar churns out delicious fresh loaves (£2.50). Bar menu £8-12. Open M-F noon-3pm and 6-11pm, Sa 6pm-11pm. Bar open M-F 11am-11pm, Sa 6-11pm. AmEx/MC/V. ❺

Al's Café/Bar, 11-13 Exmouth Market (☎7837 4821). ⊖Angel or Farringdon. This maroon-hued cafe/bar (with a basement club) is a favorite hangout for journalists from the nearby *Guardian*, *Face* and *Arena*. With comfortable leather loungers and windows all around, Al's is a prime spot to relax with a coffee (£1.20-2) and people-watch. Outdoor seating in good weather. Mains £10.50. All-day breakfast on weekends £1.50-6.50. DJs visit regularly. Open M-Tu 8am-midnight, W-Sa 8am-2am, Su 10am-10:30pm. Last food 10pm. Wheelchair accessible. AmEx/MC/V (£10 min.). ❷

The Greenery, 5 Cowcross St. (☎7490 4870). ⊖Farringdon. For the vegetarian and/or health fanatic in your party, this tiny restaurant and juice bar is a welcome bit of leafy heaven. And with salads only £2-4, savouries (like lasagna, pizzas, quiches) £2-4, and a combination platter £5, the prices are a bargain. Packed sandwiches start at £2 and vitamin-enriched smoothies run £2-4. Expect long 'queues' during lunch time. There are only a few tables in this busy shop; expect to take your organic goodies to-go. Open M-F 7am-5pm. ❶

Bar Bombay, 33-37 Charterhouse Sq. (☎7600 7277 or 7600 7278; www.barbombay.com). ⊖Farringdon. This pleasant eatery offers up traditional Indian fare in an attractive, airily bright setting looking out Charterhouse Sq. Prices go all the way up to the £32. Bombay Meal for 2 (a voluminous heaping of appetizers, main courses, and dessert), but you can also get a vegetable or meat meal for about £5-8. Soft crab with ginger, garlic and coconut (£10) is quite good. Takeout available. Open M-F noon-midnight, Sa 6pm-midnight. AmEx/MC/V. ❷

WATER EXPENSE. If you want water at a restaurant (and don't want to pay for it) specifically order 'tap water.' Otherwise you will probably end up with a gold-plated bottle of mineral water hand-squeezed from a rock by a beautiful nymph who charges per drop...you get the message.

HOLBORN

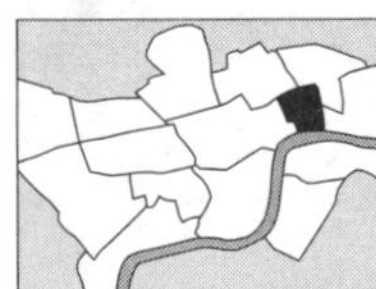

SEE MAP, p. 363

HOLBORN QUICKFIND: sights, p. 97; museums & galleries, p. 143; pubs, p. 197; nightlife, p. 211; entertainment, p. 236; shopping, p. 257; accommodations, p. 286.

In the 18th century, there was one tavern in Holborn for every five homes. They remain your best bet for atmospheric nourishment. Some pubs have fallen to the dark side under pressure from Holborn's masses of "young professionals," but others (including several of London's oldest) remain cozy enclaves of smoke-blackened wood, comfort food, and hand-pulled ales. If you're hungry and not up for pub grub, affordable eateries line the alleys around **Red Lion Street** and behind the **Holburn underground station,** cheap sandwich joints are plentiful along **Grey's Inn Road** (especially above Theobald's Road), and small cafes cater to the shoppers at **Leather Lane Market.** Whatever your cuisine, if it's in a box or a bag, take it over to **Lincoln's Inn Fields** or **Gray's Inn** for a fair-weather picnic.

Bleeding Heart Tavern, corner of Greville St. and Bleeding Heart Yard (☎7404 0333). ⊖Farringdon. When approaching customers are greeted by a menu-wielding maitre d', you can safely assume that this "tavern" is in fact a restaurant, and quite a good one. The name derives from the 1626 murder of Elizabeth Hatton by her jilted lover, the Spanish ambassador; the body was found in the yard, her heart "still pumping blood onto the cobblestones." This 2-level establishment is split between the slightly posh upstairs pub and the luxurious restaurant below, whose thick tablecloths, fresh roses, and candles make a romantic backdrop to hearty and delicious English fare. Highlights include the roast suckling pig with delicately spiced shards of apple (£11). Extraordinarily good service and fine ale round out your dining experience (mains £8-12). Open M-F 7-10:30am, noon-2:30pm and 6-10:30pm. Upstairs pub open M-F 11:30am-11pm. AmEx/MC/V. ❸

Woolley's, 33 Theobald's Rd. (☎7405 3028; www.woolleys.co.uk). Rear entrance on Lamb's Conduit Passage. ⊖Holborn. Narrow take-out joint in two parts: salads (£1.50-3.70), savories (£2-4), and jacket potatoes (£2.50-3.50) are dished out from the

Theobald's Rd. side, whilst Lamb's Conduit supplies fresh sandwiches (£2-3) made to order. You can walk through to the Lamb's Conduit side and eat in the charming passage, which makes for great rush-hour people-watching. Open M-F 7:30am-3:30pm. ❶

Aki, 182 Gray's Inn Rd. (☎7837 9281; www.akidemae.com). ⊖ Chancery Lane. The bambooified warmth of this smallish Japanese restaurant is only brightened by its value-packed menu. Noodle dishes (£4-6), chicken, fish, and meat meals (£4.20-10), and sushi meals (from £5) are a bargain, and set 3-course menus start at £6.50. Take out, or eat in and enjoy the bright eclectic decor. Open M-F noon-3pm and 6-11pm, Sa 6-10:30pm. Wheelchair accessible. AmEx/MC/V. ❷

Bleeding Heart Bistro and Restaurant, Bleeding Heart Yard (bistro ☎7242 8238, restaurant 7242 2056). ⊖ Farringdon. Around the corner from the Tavern (follow the signs). The Parisian cousins of the Tavern, this duo ranks among London's finest French cuisine; boasting "one of the finest wine lists in the world." The Bistro features a *prix-fixe* 3-course menu for around £20; *a la carte* mains £8-16. Mains at the Restaurant run £11-19. Weather permitting, eat outdoors and reap dividends of cobblestone-induced romanticism. Bistro and restaurant open M-F noon-2:30pm and 6-10:30pm. Wheelchair-accessible outdoor seating. AmEx/MC/V. Bistro ❹, Restaurant ❺

KENSINGTON & EARL'S COURT

KENSINGTON & EARL'S COURT QUICKFIND: Discover, p. 8; sights, p. 100; museums & galleries, p. 145; pubs, p. 198; entertainment, p. 236; shopping, p. 257; accommodations, p. 286.

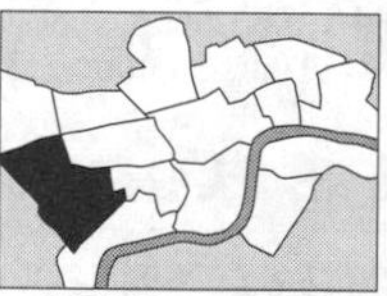

SEE MAP, pp. 364-365

Kensington is not known for food, budget or otherwise, but its uniform prettiness makes for a nice dining experience. The most attractive spot is **Kensington Court,** a short pedestrian street lined with budget and mid-range cafes, always popular on warm summer evenings. **Kensington High Street** is roughly split between overpriced yuppie hangouts and family-friendly pizzerias, both of which tend to be thoroughly mediocre, but **Kensington Square's** environs provide decent sit-down options. **South Kensington** is better; the area around the Tube overflows with sandwich bars and cheap restaurants. On **Bute Street,** just opposite the Institut Francais's lycée (high school), you're as likely to hear

the BIG $plurge

Up in Smoke

Tony Blair and other politicians are considering a ban on public cigarette smoking. As it stands today, patrons can (and do) light up in restaurants, bars, and cafes. Britons can even puff in the workplace.

Not surprisingly, the death toll due to smoking and secondhand smoking-related causes has skyrocketed in the last decade and now doctors and lobbying groups are pressuring lawmakers to do something about it.

A potential public smoking ban hits close to home for many Londoners, whether they're smokers or not. Angry nicotine-lovers have protested for their freedom while employees rights groups demand the right to health at work, especially for waitresses and the like.

With mayoral and general elections not far off, politicians are being forced to take a stand. Many candidates support a ban for the capital, and recently Tony Blair voted tentatively in favor of not banning smoking, but giving local councils the right to do so.

The relatively high number of smokers in England are upset while many non-smokers are delighted. The politicians, of course, are skirting around the issue to avoid stepping on any toes—or in this situation—any cigarette wielding fingers.

French as English in the sidewalk cafes, pâtisseries, and continental delis full of delicious cheap eats. In **Earl's Court,** both Earl's Court Rd. and Old Brompton Rd. have a good variety of affordable eateries, though they tend to be scruffier than their northern and eastern neighbors.

Zaika, 1 Kensington High St. (☎7795 6533; www.zaika-restaurant.co.uk). ⊖High St. Kensington. One of London's best Indian restaurants. About as far as can be imagined from the usual £5-lunch-buffet Indian dive: elegant coppertoned decor, attentive service, and food that is original, beautiful, and sophisticated. Try the coconut poached prawns (£12). Long, excellent wine list. Starters £3-12. Mains £12-20. Desserts £4-5 (2-course minimum for dinner). Set lunch menu £15 for 2 courses, £18 for 3. 5-course dinner menu £38, with wine £57. Dinner reservations recommended. Dress scruffy and you'll feel out of place, especially at dinner. Open M-F noon-2:45pm and 6:30-10:45pm, Sa 6:30-10:45pm, Su noon-2:45pm and 6:30-9:45pm. AmEx/MC/V. ❹

The Orangery, Kensington Palace (☎7938 1406). ⊖High St. Kensington or Queensway. See **Afternoon Tea,** p. 160.

Raison d'Être, 18 Bute St. (☎7584 5008). ⊖South Kensington. One of many small cafes on Bute St. catering to the local French community, this comfortable, quiet eatery might not live up to its name, but it does offer a bewildering range of filled *baguettes* and *foccacia* (£2.50-5). *Salades composées* (£3.20-5.20) and various other light dishes (like yogurt with fruit, £2.50) are all made to order. After your meal, enjoy a divine *cafe au lait* under the outside canopy. Open M-F 8am-6pm, Sa 9:30am-4pm. ❶

La Brasserie, 272 Brompton Rd. (☎7581 3089). ⊖South Kensington. This bustling, cheerful French brasserie, famous for its oyster bar and renowned for its steak tartare, serves large portions and usually buzzes with hungry locals. Mains, from vegetarian pasta and cheese *plats* to hearty steak and poultry offerings £8-22, and appetizers £4-9. The best value is the 2-course menu (£10, M-F noon-7pm). Also serves breakfast and afternoon tea. Open M-Sa noon-11:30pm, Su noon-10pm. AmEx/MC/V. ❹

Babylon, Kensington Roof Gdns. (☎7368 3993; www.roofgardens.com). 99 Kensington High St. entrance is on Derry St. There's nothing like a little verticality to render an otherwise-fine eatery quite special, and Babylon benefits enormously from its location 7 stories above the rest of Kensington among the beautiful Roof Gardens. Eat outside if you can, and gasp at the view. *A la carte* starters £7.50-14, mains £14.50-24. Their best deal is the £14 2-course lunch (3 courses £16, M-F noon-3pm). Reservations recommended. Open M-F noon-3pm and 7-11pm, Sa 7-11pm, Su noon-3:30pm. AmEx/MC/V. ❹

KNIGHTSBRIDGE & BELGRAVIA

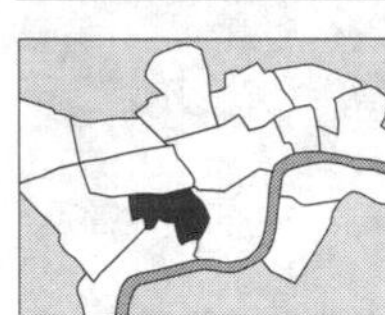

SEE MAP, p. 366

KNIGHTSBRIDGE & BELGRAVIA QUICKFIND: Discover, p. 8; sights, p. 102; pubs, p. 198; nightlife, p. 211; shopping, p. 258; accommodations, p. 172.

The jaw-dropping prices in Harrods's posh restaurants may deceive you into thinking that **Knightsbridge** is not promising territory for affordable eats. But cast your net a little wider, and you'll haul in the benefits. **Beauchamp** (BEE-cham) **Place,** off the Old Brompton Rd. and the surrounding streets are lined with cafes, noodle bars, and sandwich bars. **Belgravia** is a bit tougher—there's little chance of getting a sit-down meal at a restaurant for under £15. The mews behind **Grosvenor Place** cradle some popular pubs, and the gourmet delis and specialty food stores on **Elizabeth Street** will furnish a picnic basket fit for a prince. Some cheaper ethnic food also haunts the sidestreets around **Sloane Square.**

KNIGHTSBRIDGE

The Lanesborough, Hyde Park Corner (☎7259 5599). ⊖Hyde Park Corner. See **Afternoon Tea,** p. 160

Gloriette, 128 Brompton Rd. (☎7584 1182). ⊖Knightsbridge. This venerable pâtisserie offers hot meals and desserts in a bright cafe atmosphere. Eat outside, downstairs, or in the delicately ornate upper dining room. Leaf teas £2 per pot, delicious cakes and pastries £2.60-3.60, sandwiches £4.50-7.50. More substantial fare includes a rich goulash soup with bread (£4.95) and 2- and 3-course set meals (£8.90 and £10.95). Open M-F 7am-8pm, Sa 7am-7pm, Su 9am-5pm. AmEx/MC/V. ❷

BELGRAVIA

Jenny Lo's Teahouse, 14 Eccleston St. (☎7259 0399). ⊖Victoria. Right around the corner from Jenny's father's higher-end restaurant (Ken Lo is one of the most famous Cantonese chefs in the UK). The small modern interior here bustles on weekdays, but the delicious *cha shao* (pork noodle soup; £5.75) and the broad selection of Asian noodles from Vietnamese to Beijing style (£5.75-7.50) make it well worth the wait. Vegetarian options abound. Takeout and delivery available. Open M-F 11:30am-3pm and 6-10pm. ❷

Goya, 2 Eccleston Pl. (☎7730 4299; www.goya-restaurant.co.uk). ⊖Victoria. Pro: Goya is less than a minute from the Victoria tube station. Con: noisy, diesely Victoria Coach station is directly across the street. Solution: avoid the outdoor seating. Once indoors, enjoy London's most carefully prepared tapas menu (£3.50-6 per dish; order 2-3 per person). The other Spanish entrees (£10-15) include excellent vegetarian and seafood options, all served by friendly staff in a spacious tiered dining room. Sangria w/tapas of the day: £3.95. Open daily 11:30am-11:30pm. AmEx/MC/V. ❸

Poilâne, 46 Elizabeth St. (☎7808 4910; www.poilane.com). ⊖Victoria or Sloane Square. Paris's most famous boulangerie brings freshly baked delights to Belgravia. The shop is très petite, and only offers takeout service. Traditional round loaves can be as much as £6.50, but *pain au chocolat* is only 90p. Open M-F 7:30am-7:30pm, Sa 7:30am-6pm. MC/V. ❶

MARYLEBONE & REGENT'S PARK

MARLYEBONE & REGENT'S PARK QUICKFIND: Discover, p. 9; sights, p. 103; museums & galleries, p. 147; pubs, p. 199; entertainment, p. 237; accommodations, p. 291.

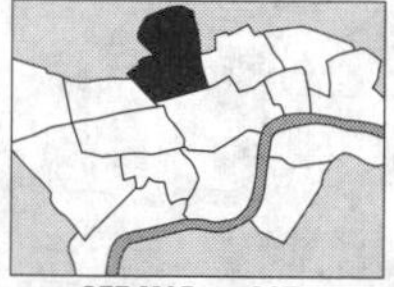

SEE MAP, p. 367

In an area long regarded as something of a food wilderness, numerous fashionable restaurants and modern sandwich bars have cropped up around **Marylebone High Street** to challenge that reputation. Apart from the Middle Eastern oasis of **Edgware Road,** this is not a place to go searching for great meals or great deals.

Mandalay, 444 Edgware Rd. (☎7258 3696). ⊖Edgware Rd. 5min. walk north from the Tube. Looks ordinary, tastes extraordinary—one of the best meal deals around. With huge portions of wildly inexpensive food, this down-to-earth Burmese restaurant is justly plastered with awards. Lunch specials are great value (curry and rice £3.90; 4 courses, including a banana fritter, £6). Be sure to ask for the full menu, which includes an explanation of Burmese cuisine. Mains £3-7.50. No smoking. Reservations recommended at peak hours. Open M-Sa noon-2:30pm and 6-10:30pm. AmEx/MC/V. ❶

Giraffe, 6-8 Blandford St. (☎7935 2333; www.giraffe.net). ⊖Bond St. or Baker St. One of a handful of Giraffe restaurants, a quirky and appealing gem like the rest. Decor is eclectic-modern (lots of bamboo and greenery), food is eclectic-tasty (from noodle dishes to Mexican burgers, £7-9). Earlybird specials 5-7pm: 2 course dinner £7, 2-for-1 drinks. Communal tables reduce privacy, but make the atmosphere even more cheerful. Open M-F 8am-4pm and 5-10:45pm, Sa-Su 9am-4pm and 5-10:45pm. Wheelchair accessible. AmEx/MC/V. ❷

Patogh, 8 Crawford Pl. (☎7262 4015). ⊖Edgware Rd. Persian for "meeting place," Patogh is too small and well-hidden to gather that many folks together. What it does offer is gastronomic perfection in an authentic (if tiny) space. Order the understated "bread" and get a delicious 14 in. flatbread with sesame seeds and subtle spices (£2). Mains like *kebab-e-koobideh* (minced-lamb kebab), with bread, rice, or salad, are £6-11 and worth every penny. Open daily noon-midnight. ❷

the hidden deal

Fresh Choice

The best food shopping in London lies far from the department stores and in the rich ethnic mini-neighborhoods, especially in the Northern and Eastern parts of the city. In most of these neighborhoods a main street serves as a thoroughfare of course, but more importantly as a vibrant, breathing food market. Make that twenty little markets, jostling for space and business on a crowded street, putting their sun-ripened fruits and vegetables on colorful display on the sidewalk. Due to the hectic competition the prices at the street side food stores are often much cheaper than the local Sainsbury's and the produce is fresh.

Head to one of the neighborhoods for everything from eggs to tomatoes to exotic delicacies. Beyond offering great deals on fruits and veggies, the stores that line the streets carry the ethnic foods typical of the neighborhood.

While you can see produce stands in more central areas, the goods offered there are often not particularly cheap. Heading to Zone 2 is the best option. Also, don't go for a lone little shop: part of the fun is walking around and seeing the options. Traditional British cuisine may not cherish the fresh fruit or veggie, but that doesn't mean they're not available.

Ranoush Juice, 43 Edgware Rd. (☎7723 5929; www.maroush.com). ⊖ Marble Arch. This affordable arm of the Maroush restaurant empire is commonly regarded as the best Lebanese joint on the Edgware Rd. Hugely popular (mostly for takeout), it offers cheap kebabs (£2.50-4) and full meals (£8-11). Open daily 9:30am-3am. ❶

Royal China, 24-26 Baker St. (☎7487 4688; www.royalchinagroup.co.uk). ⊖Baker St. An upscale, sleek, and attractive branch of the micro-chain renowned for London's best dim sum straddles the line between faux and real elegance. Unlike most, this dim sum is ordered from a menu rather than from a cart, gaining in freshness what it loses in charm. Keep your eyes open—this restaurant is crawling with MPs and minor celebs. If you're with a group and looking to splurge try the seafood 5-course prix-fixe (£36) or the standard and vegetarian versions (£28). Most mains £8-18; dim sum should set you back about the same. Open M-Sa noon-10:45pm, Su 11am-9:45pm; dim sum served until 4:45pm. AmEx/MC/V. ❸

Spighetta, 43 Blanford St. (☎7486 7340). ⊖Baker St. This charming, easy-to-miss subterranean Italian restaurant off Baker St. cooks up crunchy pizza (£7-9.50) in a wood-fired oven. Pasta (£7-9) and traditional Italian mainfare (£11-13). Open M-Th noon-2:30pm and 6:30-10:30pm, F noon-2:30pm and 6:30-11pm, Sa 12:30-3pm and 6:30-11pm, Su 6:30-10:30pm. AmEx/MC/V. ❸

NOTTING HILL

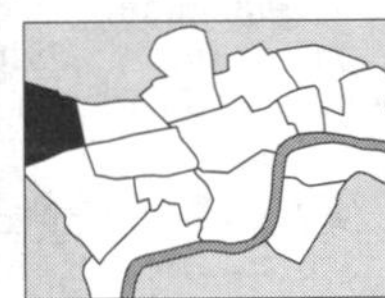

SEE MAP, p. 359

NOTTING HILL QUICKFIND: Discover, p. 9; sights, p. 105; pubs, p. 200; nightlife, p. 212; entertainment, p. 237; shopping, p. 259; accommodations, p. 292.

Food in Notting Hill basically comes down to a choice between numerous overpriced, and over-trendy eateries and the cheap but excellent bites serving the market crowds around Portobello Rd. Restaurant turnover here is incredibly high, especially for the pricier ones. So, every time you visit you're likely to find a whole new array of places. For the widest variety of food, hunt around at the southern end of the general market and under the Westway.

George's Portobello Fish Bar, 329 Portobello Rd. (☎8969 7895). ⊖Ladbroke Grove. George opened up here in 1961, and since then the little space has lived through various incarnations. It's (currently disguised as a 50s-style diner), and the fish 'n' chips are still as good as ever. Not much on ambience. Few types of freshly fried fillets on display, but you can ask your server to rustle up a new piece (£4-5). It comes with a huge scoop of chunky chips. Burgers, kebabs, and falafel are also available. Open M-F 11am-midnight, Sa 11am-9pm, Su noon-9:30pm. ❶

Books for Cooks, 4 Blenheim Crescent (☎7221 1992). ⊖Ladbroke Grove. At lunchtime, chef-owner Eric and his crew of culinary pros "test" recipes, filling the small store with warm smells. The cafe in back houses a few small tables, perfect for munching. There's no telling what will be on offer, but you can rely on the excellent cakes (£2). And the book selection isn't bad either. Food available Tu-Sa 10am-2:30pm or so. Bookstore open Tu-Sa 10am-6pm. Daily cookery workshops held in upstairs demo kitchen (£25; reservations essential). MC/V. ❶

Lazy Daisy Café, 59a Portobello Rd. (☎ 7221 8417). ⊖Notting Hill Gate. Tucked into an indoor alley, you'll be hard pressed to find a more pleasant place to eat. This cheery cafe serves a healthy selection of salads and pastries, and some fancier breakfast concoctions. All day breakfast, including a lazy fry-up (£6) and eggs florentine (£4.75). Service runs on the leisurely side, but the wide range of periodicals and bin of toys keep customers of all ages happily occupied. Open M-F 9:30am-5:30pm, Sa 9am-5pm, Su 12-2:30pm. Wheelchair accessible. ❶

Tom's Delicatessen, 226 Westbourne Grove (☎7221 8818). ⊖Ladbroke Grove or Notting Hill Gate. Look for the bright red storefront. An upstairs bakery and cafe, and a downstairs deli and mini market. Fills quickly during busy times, and the table-sharing policy makes for close encounters. A bite into the fresh sandwiches (£6-9) reveals why this deli attracts a constant flow of customers. No smoking. Open M-F 11am-7pm, Sa 10:30am-6:30pm, Su noon-5pm. MC/V (£5 min.). ❷

Lisboa Patisserie, 57 Golborne Rd. (☎0181 8968 5242). ⊖Ladbroke Grove. A sugar-happy Iberian cafe. At any hour, this little bakery is packed with Portuguese and Moroccan men chatting football over their coffee (80p). The decor is not much to look at and it gets extremely hot in late afternoon, but you can always get your goodies to go. The broad selection of cakes and pastries (from 5p) is impossible to resist—don't miss the Portuguese custard pie. Open M-Sa 8am-8pm, Su 8am-7pm. ❶

The Grain Shop, 269a Portobello Rd. (☎7229 5571). ⊖Ladbroke Grove. It's hard for anyone to ignore the aromatic smells of this mini-bakery, and during lunch the queue snaking out into Portobello Rd. People come for the breads. There's also a selection of homemade cakes and salads; mix as many dishes as you like in a takeout box for £2-5. Organic breads baked on-site (£1-2). Food available from noon onward. Open M-Sa 9am-6pm. MC/V. ❶

Nottinghill Gate Cafe, 19 Notting Hill Gate (☎7792 2521). The brightly painted walls and funky furniture make this a standout. On sunny days the front windows are flung open, turning it into a streetside dining room. Friendly staff serves salads and crepes (£3-5), and plenty of traditional grub (£7). MC/V. ❷

Manzara, 24 Pembridge Rd. (☎7727 3062). ⊖Notting Hill Gate. The streetside cafe vibe belies the menu of Turkish delicacies. Besides standard kebabs, Manzara specializes in *pide*, rolled pizza-like pastries filled with various delicacies (£4.25 takeout, £6 eat-in), as well as organic burgers and salads. Open daily 7am-11pm, last order 10:30pm. ❶

Makan, 270 Portobello Rd. (☎8960 5169; www.makan.com) ⊖Ladbroke Grove. This no- frills eatery serves heaping portions of greasy, delicious Malaysian food. Classic curries and chicken dishes are available, as well as appetizers like banana bread buttons and crab fingers. Choose from made to order dishes (£5-6) or the buffet of pre-made ones. Combos with noodles or rice £3.80 for 1, £4.50 for 2, £4.90 for 3. Open daily 11:30am-9:30pm. Wheelchair accessible. ❶

Black & Blue, 215-217 Kensington Church St. (☎7727 0004). ⊖Notting Hill Gate. All about the sleek and chic bistro feel, from the spotless glass tables right down to the stainless steel pepper mills. But, hey, it works: unpretentious food and an attractive setting. All-day English breakfast (£8), steaks (£12-20), vegetarian dishes (£8-12) and enormous burgers (£7-8). Appetizers and desserts £5-7. Open Su-Th noon-11pm, F-Sa noon-11:30pm. Wheelchair accessible. MC/V. ❸

THE SOUTH BANK

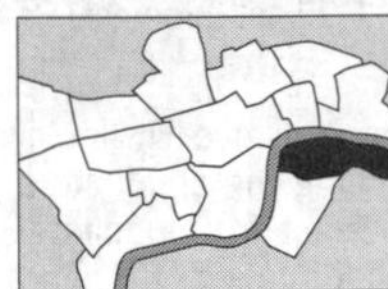

SEE MAP, pp. 368-369

THE SOUTH BANK QUICKFIND: Discover, p. 10; sights, p. 106; museums and galleries, p. 148; pubs, p. 200; nightlife, p. 212; entertainment, p. 238; accommodations, p. 292.

Until recently, Bankside wasn't on the restaurant radar. The choice was between overpriced restaurants in the big cultural complexes and the greasy spoons of Borough High St. But the rapid development of the area into a major cultural destination, not to mention increasing yuppification, have made this one of London's fine spots for eating out, and of course the views are unbeatable. Wharfside eateries are generally the priciest, buy food elsewhere and eat on one of the multitude of waterside benches. In addition to the places listed below, check out the **National Film Theatre** cafe under Waterloo Bridge (see p. 238) and the numerous pavement eateries of **Gabriel's Wharf,** between the National Theatre and the OXO Tower. If you venture farther from the river, follow the local crowds, they'll have the best ideas. Those who prefer to assemble their own meals can turn to the **Borough Market,** where stalls lay out fresh gourmet cheeses, breads, fruits and cured meats. (Off Borough High St. London Bridge. Open F 11am-6pm, Sa 9am-4pm, some stalls open daily; best on 3rd Sa of month.)

Cantina del Ponte, 36c Shad Thames, Butlers Wharf (☎7403 5403). Tower Hill or London Bridge. Amazing riverside location by Tower Bridge, without the superchain status of neighboring spots. The busy Mediterranean mural inside takes you away from the Thames, but given the quality of the classic Italian food it's okay if you can't get a riverside seat. The set lunch menu is a bargain at 2 courses for £11, 3 for £13.50 (available M-F noon-3pm). Pizzas £6-8. Mains £10-15. Open M-Sa noon-3pm and 6-10:45pm, Su noon-3pm and 6-9:45pm. Wheelchair accessible. AmEx/MC/V. ❸

Tas, 33 The Cut (☎7928 2111). Southwark. Also at 72 Borough High St. (☎7928 3300). **Tas Cafe,** 76 Borough High (☎7403 8559). **Tas Pide,** 20-22 New Globe Walk (☎7928 3300, www.tasrestaurant.com). London Bridge. A dynamic group of stylish and affordable Turkish restaurants. Generous soups and baked dishes–many vegetarian–outshine the respectable kebabs. Mains £6-9; set 2-course menu for £7.45 and *meze* menus (selection of starters) £7-10. *Pide,* an oval Anatolian pizza has myriad options (£6-7). Live music daily from 7:30pm. Evening reservations recommended at restaurants. Open M-Sa noon-11:30pm, Su noon-10:30pm. Wheelchair accessible. AmEx/MC/V. ❷

Gourmet Pizza Co., Gabriel's Wharf, 56 Upper Ground (☎7928 3188). Southwark or Waterloo. On the embankment, this adventurous pizzeria will have something for everyone. It offers "tradition with imagination" in the form of pizzas with unexpected toppings, like Thai chicken and eggplant (£6-9). Appetizers under £6. Also serves standard Italian pastas and salads. Friendly service, good sized portions. Reservations recommended. Open M-Sa noon-11pm, Su noon-10:30pm. Wheelchair accessible. AmEx/MC/V. ❷

People's Palace, Royal Festival Hall (☎7928 9999). Waterloo. Despite the communist name, this is the swankiest of the Festival Hall's many eateries. The minimalist decor is meant to highlight its chief virtue: the fantastic location on the 2nd fl. of the Festival Hall, with vast windows overlooking the river. The Mediterranean food is also top-notch. While dinner is pricey (mains from £15), luncheon mains (served noon-3pm) like cider-braised pork with apple, celery and summer truffle mash are all £9.50. Relative bargains on the pre-concert menu (5:30-7pm, starters from £6.25) or the children's menu (mains £6.50). Open daily noon-3pm and 5:30-11pm. Wheelchair accessible. MC/V. ❹

The Island Café, 1 Flat Iron Square (☎020 7407 2224). Southwark. At the junction of Union St. and Southwark Bridge Rd. One of the only places in the South Bank that serves lunch for under £4. Takeout breakfast (£1.80) and classic lunchbox-style sandwiches (£1.70), with tons of variations, like tuna with sweet corn and egg salad, or classic brie. There's also a substantial list of hot lunch specials, most around £3. Sit amid the chaos indoors or take your grub to the back patio. Open daily 6am-5pm. Wheelchair accessible. ❶

Cubana, 48 Lower Marsh (☎7928 8778; www.cubana.co.uk.). ⊖Waterloo. Look for the giant salsa dancer painted walls. Food takes second place to the spiky cocktails (£5, 2-pint jug £15): sample some classic drinks like the "Sputnik," originally mixed with cheap Cuban rum, now with Bacardi and Martell cognac. At lunch or happy hour get 2 tapas for £5.95, a 2-course meal for £6, and 3 courses for £8. Reservations recommended. Happy hour daily 5-6:30pm, 2-for-1 on select drinks. Salsa with live band W-Sa nights, F-Sa cover £5 with free plate of tapas. Open M-Tu noon-midnight, W-F noon-1am, Sa 6pm-1am. AmEx/MC/V. ❷

Delfina, 50 Bermondsey St (☎7357 0224; www.delfina.org.uk). Located on the ground floor of a chic brick building. The walls display the work of resident artists. The lunch mains (£10-14) are not cheap, but they certainly are good. Blue swimmer crab risotto and miso glazed mahi both made menu appearances; dessert puddings(£4.25) are also popular. Open daily 9am-5pm, lunch noon-3pm. Wheelchair accessible. AmEx/MC/V. ❸

Café 7, Tate Modern, Bankside (☎7401 5020). ⊖Southwark or Blackfriars. On the top (7th) fl. of Tate Modern (see **Museums & Galleries,** p. 137), windows on both sides provide mid-air views of the city and south London, while specially commissioned murals cover the end walls. Come here for a bird's eye view of the bank. The cafe does coffee and snacks, while the restaurant cooks modern British cuisine: smoke haddock and crab brioche £7.95; red snapper with braised fennel £13.50. Open Su-Th 10am-5:30pm (last order), F-Sa 10am-9:30pm, lunch from 11:30am, cafe earlier. Wheelchair accessible. AmEx/MC/V. ❷

THE WEST END

OXFORD STREET & REGENT STREET

OXFORD STREET & REGENT STREET QUICKFIND: Discover, p. 10; sights, p. 111; museums & galleries, p. 150; pubs, p. 201; nightlife, p. 212; entertainment, p. 240; shopping, p. 261; accommodations, p. 292.

SEE MAP, p. 354

Food on Oxford St. itself is predictable and tourist-oriented, with fast-food chains and dodgy kebab and pizza vendors. Fortunately, side streets offer plenty of better food and wider selections and are for the most part very affordable. Londoners have long kept quiet about **St. Christopher's Place**, reached by an innocuous-looking alleyway opposite Bond St. Tube. Less picturesque but just as wallet-friendly, **Kingly Street,** between Regent St. and Carnaby St., is popular with local diners as well.

Mô, 23 Heddon St. (☎7434 3999). ⊖Piccadilly Circus or Oxford Circus. A restaurant, tea room, and bazaar all in one, Mô is an aesthetic slice of Marrakesh. The two interior rooms are hung with traditional lanterns and decorated with Moroccan crafts; all is for sale. The carved chairs, floor cushions, and low tables used by diners add to the ambiance. Outdoor tables are the place to be seen in the summertime. Mix and match from their tapas-style dishes (£6-£7.50), and wash it down with some mint tea (£2.50). Sheesha (hookah) is also available (£9-20). Lunch is comparatively cheaper. No reservations, but very popular—arrive early or late. Open M-W 11am-11pm, Th-Sa noon-midnight. Wheelchair-accessible outside seating. AmEx/MC/V. ❸

Carluccio's, St. Christopher's Pl. (☎7935 5927; www.carluccios.com). ⊖Bond St. Refined Italian cooking in a pleasant and bustling environment. The short menu stocks many variations on pasta as well as a few choice meat dishes, plenty of appetizers, and scrumptious desserts. Choose from shared tables on the ground floor, the more formal indoor seating, or the piazza-style open patio that spills into St. Christopher's Courtyard. Antipasti £4-7, main dishes £5-10.50. Sandwiches and calzone for takeout (£3-4) and a deli with Italian hams, gourmet pastas, and olive oils. Carluccio's also has branches in Islington and The City, and delis all over London. Open M-F 8am-11pm, Sa 10am-11pm, Su 11am-10pm. Wheelchair-accessible patio. AmEx/MC/V. ❷

Soba Noodle Bar, 38 Poland St. (☎017 1734 6400; www.soba.co.uk). ⊖Oxford Circus. Also at 11/13 Soho St. (☎7827 7300; ⊖Tottenham Crt. Rd.). This narrow noodle bar with a long yellow communal table, bench seating, and walls covered with corrugated plastic. The

Soho St. Ideal for a meal on the run. Big bowls of noodles (£6-6.50), rice plates (£5.30-6.50), and lots of vegetarian options. Drop by during happy hour when all mains go for £4, M-W 5:30pm-7pm, Sa noon-5pm, Su all day. Open M-F noon-3:30pm and 5:30pm-11pm, Sa noon-10pm, Su noon-9pm. Wheelchair accessible. AmEx/MC/V. ❷

MAYFAIR & ST. JAMES'S

MAYFAIR & ST. JAMES'S QUICKFIND: Discover, p. 10; sights, p. 111; museums & galleries, p. 150; pubs, p. 201; entertainment, p. 240; shopping, p. 264; accommodations, p. 292.

One of the most pleasant places to eat and drink is in and around the winding cobblestone alleys of **Shepherd Market.** Within easy reach of the action and excitement around Oxford St. and Regent St. and Soho, Mayfair provides a pleasant alternative to the noise and bustle of the big city streets.

L'Autre, 5b Shepherd St. (☎7499 4680), in Shepherd's Market. ⊖Hyde Park Corner or Green Park. This charming restaurant has a confused identity. Although the name means "the other" in French, the menu is half-Polish and half-Mexican, and the décor is vintage Victorian. Hearty Polish fare (£9-12.50). In summer, sit on the pavement and munch the Mexican food (£8-12). L'Autre has a devoted neighborhood following, reservations sometimes necessary. Also specializes in fresh game in season. Open M-F 12:30pm-2pm and 5:30-10:30pm, Sa-Su 5:30-10:30pm. AmEx/MC/V. ❸

La Madeleine, 5 Vigo St. (☎7734 8353). ⊖Piccadilly Circus. A small French haven just off Regent St. This casual cafe invites you to spend the rest of the afternoon munching instead of shopping. Takeout or you can elect to be waited on in the cozy cafe. Lunchtime menu includes a daily, changing *plat du jour* (£7), omelettes (£7-8), sandwiches (£1.50-3.50), and a 2-course set meal with wine (£10.50). Scrumptious desserts (£2-3) fill the window and the display case. *C'est magnifique*. Open M-Sa 8am-8pm, Su 11am-7pm. Wheelchair accessible. AmEx/MC/V. ❷

Tamarind, 20 Queen St. (☎7629 3561). ⊖Green Park. One of only two Indian restaurants in the UK to receive a Michelin star, Tamarind is far from cheap. Sumptuous interior is classy but laid-back. Vegetarian dishes start at £6, meat kebabs from £13-28. For the best deal come for *prix-fixe* set lunch (2 courses for £15, 3 for £17). Open M-F noon-2:45pm and 6-11:30pm, Sa 6-11pm and Su 6-10:30pm. AmEx/MC/V. ❸

SOHO

SOHO QUICKFIND: Discover, p. 10; sights, p. 113; museums & galleries, p. 150; pubs, p. 201; nightlife, p. 214; entertainment, p. 240; shopping, p. 265; accommodations, p. 292.

All listings are near ⊖Piccadilly Circus, Leicester Sq., Tottenham Crt. Rd., and Oxford Circus.

One of the best places in London to eat and drink, Soho has restaurants, cafes, and bars to suit every taste and budget. Bustling **Chinatown's** main attractions are the dozens of Asian, especially Cantonese, restaurants. While **Gerrard Street** is considered Chinatown's heart, its eateries cater just as much to non-Chinese tourists; those on **Lisle Street,** one block south towards Leicester Sq., are often cheaper, less crowded, and more "authentic." Little Italy has pizza, pasta, and lots of garlic goodness on **Frith Street,** and various late-night and 24hr. options on **Wardour Street;** and the southern side of **Shaftesbury Avenue,** just north of Gerrard St., feed hungry post-clubbers. Midday, the outdoor cafes near Soho Sq. are perfect for lounging.

Masala Zone, 9 Marshall St. (☎7287 9966; www.realindianfood.com. Also in Islington at 80 Upper St.; 7359 3399). ⊖Oxford Circus. Masala Zone's softly lit interior and sexy sunken dining room feels very modern, as does the hindi-techno soundtrack. The food stems from a South-Indian tradition, with plenty of *masala* (spices), and is cooked in a kitchen visible from anywhere in the restaurant. The menu has typical favorites (£5-6) as well as "street food," which comes in small bowls (£3-5), or the large Thali (platter), which allows you to sample a variety of dishes (£8-11). Curries (£6-7) are particularly good. Open M-F noon-2:45pm and 5:30-11pm, Sa 12:30-3pm and 5-11pm, Su 12:30-3:30pm and 6-10:30pm. MC/V. ❷

hostelbookers.com
Great Hostels. Free Booking. No Worries.

Guaranteed lowest cost internet hostel booking

No booking fees

Genuine hostels featured

Fast and easy to use

Book Worldwide hostels online at

www.hostelbookers.com

GENERATOR HOSTELS

LONDON BERLIN

GENERATOR
generatorhostels.com

- Europe's largest hostels - over 800 beds. Great for meeting people!!
- Great locations for sightseeing and easy access to public transport
- Great value beds - from £10 (London) and 10 Euros(Berlin)
- Dorm rooms and private rooms available
- FREE "eat all you can" breakfast for all guests
- FREE bed linen and towels for all guests
- Famous Generator Bar open 6pm-2am
Happy Hour £1 a pint 6pm-9pm
- Events every night such as Karaoke,
DJ's, Drinking Games and Pool Comps
- Restaurant open 6pm-9pm, great value dinners
- 24 hour internet café and laundry
- Fantastic, friendly staff on hand to help 24hours
a day - no lock out or curfew
- Clean, safe and secure environment
- FREE luggage storage on arrival and departure, plus
lockers in all the rooms

BOOK ON-LINE AT

www.GENERATORhostels.com

or phone +44 207 388 7666 for London or +49 30 4172400 for Berlin

ON YOUR ARRIVAL SHOW THIS ADVERT AT RECEPTION TO RECEIVE 2 FREE DRINKS

GENERATOR - EUROPE'S FUNKIEST HOSTELS

busaba eathai, 106-110 Wardour St. (☎7255 8686). Brought to you by the founder of Wagamama; unlike its sibling, this wildly popular eatery has kept quality up and prices down. *Busaba* is a Thai flower, and *eathai...* well, you get the picture (for those who don't, not to worry: they explain this highly sophisticated bit of wordplay on the menu). Locals and students queue for marvelous Thai cuisine (£5-8) served at communal tables in a sea of polished wood. Open M-Th noon-11pm, F-Sa noon-11:30pm, Su noon-10pm. AmEx/MC/V. ❷

tsu, 103 Wardour St. (☎7479 4790; www.itsu.co.uk). Branches at 118 Draycott Ave. in Chelsea and Cabot Pl. East in Canary Wharf. A genuinely ground-breaking eating experience in a shiny retro-modern interior. A steel monorail shuttles color-coded fusion delights and traditional raw-fish plates (£2-4) right to your table. The perfection of *kaiten-sushi* (conveyor-belt sushi)—if only the monorail were chilled. Expect to spend about £12. Takeout available. Open M-Th noon-11pm, F noon-midnight, Sa 12:30pm-midnight, Su 1-10pm. AmEx/MC/V. ❸

Café Emm, 17 Frith St. (☎7437 0723; www.cafeemm.com). Just plain good. Cheap, generous portions in an unpretentious bistro setting with lots of vegetarian dishes (mostly salads and pastas). Main courses (£6-9) range from enormous salads (which come with extras) to rump steak (£9). Open M-Th noon-2:30pm and 5:30-10:30pm, F noon-2:30pm and 5-11:30pm, Sa 1-4pm and 5-11:30pm, Su 1-10:30pm. MC/V. ❷

Nusa Dua, 11 Dean St. (☎7437 3559). Named after a luxury Balinese resort, this is a prime destination for affordable Javanese and Singaporean cooking. Opt for the bright, airy ground floor, it is less crowded than downstairs. Fishtanks and Indonesian carvings complement the flavorful cuisine. Plentiful chicken and vegetarian dishes £5-7, duck and seafood £6-8. The 2-course £7 menu is a bargain. Open daily noon-midnight. AmEx/MC/V (£15 min). ❷

Patisserie Valerie, 44 Old Compton St. (☎7437 3466; www.patisserie-valerie.co.uk). Branches at 27 Kensington Church St., 215 Brompton Rd., Sloane Sq., 8 Russell St., and 105 Marylebone High St. Opened in 1926, this continental *patisserie* has become a London institution. The excellent pastries are *délicieuses*, and the smell of the place is an experience in itself. The recently opened upstairs restaurant offers more luxury, but without the sweet aromas of the bakery on the ground floor. Patrons swear the croissants (90p) are better than any French rival. Cakes and pastries £1.20-3.50. Mains £2.50-7. Open M-F 7:30am-8:30pm, Sa 8am-8:30pm, Su 9am-6:30pm. AmEx/MC/V. ❶

Bar Italia, 22 Frith St. (☎7437 4520). A fixture of the late-night Soho scene, this place is so popular the pop band Pulp immortalized it with a hit song called—you

ON THE MENU

Curry Cuisine

As the adopted national cuisine of England, Indian food has long been a favorite of London locals and tourists alike. Most, though, have little idea how these eateries prepare the dishes they love so well. Here is, a quick explanation of some key terms and concepts:

Paneer. A homemade cheese made by boiling whole milk, then curdling it with an acid (usually lemon juice). The whey is strained off and the curds pressed to get rid of moisture; that's why this mild cheese doesn't melt when heated.

Naan. This leavened bread is slapped onto the inner wall of the tandoor and cooks in just seconds.

Tandoor. A barrel-shaped clay oven traditionally fired with charcoal (gas is the modern alternative), the tandoor is where all your scrumptious **tandoori** dishes and fresh **naan** are cooked. With its enclosed space and thick walls, the heat inside can reach 250°C. In this heat, a full chicken quarter can cook within 10 minutes.

Tikka. Translating as "little pieces," tikka are small chunks of chicken or lamb marinated in yoghurt and spices and cooked in the tandoor. They can be served dry or in the familiar creamy *masala* sauce (as in the popular chicken tikka masala).

And some quick translations: aloo (potato), puri (deep fried unleavened bread), murgh (chicken), mutter (peas), palak (spinach), saag (spinach), samosa (savory stuffed pastry).

guessed it—"Bar Italia." Despite its name, you won't find anything stronger than an espresso (£1.80) here, but it's still the place for a post-club panini (£4-6) or pizza (£5.50-9). As long as the restaurant is open, the loud TV is never turned off—appropriate, since John Logie Baird gave the first-ever demonstration of television upstairs in 1922. Diplomatic Bar Italia accepts euros. Outdoor seating in good weather. Open 7am-5am daily. AmEx/MC/V (£10 min.). ❶

Tomato, 54 Frith St. (☎7437 0666; www.tomatogroup.com). Quintessential Italian fare with decent-sized pizzas and pasta dishes (£8-13) served in a simple, attractively modern interior. Lunch and pre-theater menu (2 courses £10.50). Ubiquitous tomatoes are the one decorative indulgence—seeing spots has never tasted so good. Try the *gnocchi gorganzola* (£8). Open daily noon-midnight. MC/V. ❸

Blue Room Café, 3-5 Bateman St. (☎7437 4827; www.blueroomcafe.com). Cosmopolitan regulars relax on the leather couches of this tiny hangout, absorbing the mellow music, sipping on smoothies (£3.25), and munching on sandwiches and salads (£3-5). Pasta £4-5 and jacket potatoes £3-5. Takeout prices 17% lower. Open M-F 8am-10:30pm, Sa 10am-10:30pm, Su noon-10pm. ❶

Yo!Sushi, 52 Poland St. See p. 163 and also **Nightlife,** p. 215. ❸

CHINATOWN

Leicester Sq.

Golden Dragon, 28-29 Gerrard St. (☎7734 2763). It's the ritziest and best-known dim sum joint in Chinatown. Golden Dragon's two large red-and-gold rooms are packed on the weekends with families and couples taking in the cheery atmosphere and shoveling in the dumplings—from veggie staples to minced prawn and sugarcane treats (each dish £2-3). Regular dinner items £5.50-9. Set dim sum meal £12.50-22.50. Open M-Th noon-11:30pm, F-Sa noon-midnight, Su 11am-11pm. AmEx/MC/V. ❷

Mr. Kong, 21 Lisle St. (☎7437 7341). If you're up for some duck's web with fish lips (£12) or spicy pig's knuckles with jellyfish (£8.80), this is the place to go. Less-adventurous eats (from £6), like fried Mongolian lamb, may not sound as impressive but are equally delicious. The menu is huge, and vegetarian options abound (try the mock crispy duck for £7 or mock pork for £5.90). £7 min. for dinner. Open daily noon-3am. AmEx/MC/V. ❷

Harbour City, 46 Gerrard St. (☎7439 7859). Gerrard St.'s biggest Cantonese restaurant, Harbour City offers up three floors of tasty dining. Popular for its menu-ordered dim sum, served daily noon-5pm (£2-3), and giant noodle dishes (£4-6). Other dishes £5.50-12. Open M-Th noon-11:30pm, F-Sa noon-midnight, Su 11am-10:30pm. AmEx/MC/V. ❷

COVENT GARDEN

CONVENT GARDEN QUICKFIND: Discover, p. 10; sights, p. 114; museums & galleries, p. 150; pubs, p. 201; nightlife, p. 216; entertainment, p. 240; shopping, p. 267; accommodations, p. 292.

Covent Garden unless stated otherwise.

Despite, or perhaps because of, its trendiness, Covent Garden is not known for its cuisine. The Piazza has unremarkable tourist-oriented cafes and overpriced restaurants catering to the theater- and opera-goers, while sandwich bars and theme pubs prevail on the side streets. An exception is **Neal's Yard,** a small open courtyard that has evolved into a wholesome haven of vegetarian, vegan, and organic delights.

St. Martin's Lane Hotel, 45 St. Martin's Ln. (☎7300 5588). Leicester Sq. See **Afternoon Tea,** p. 160.

Café Pacifico, 5 Langley St. (7379 7728; www.cafepacifico-laperla.com). The quest for good Mexican food in London is like trying to find a *taquito* in a haystack; *gracias* to the folks at Café Pacifico. The large, inviting, authentic (enough) eatery offers *muy grande* helpings of your favorite classics (burritos with rice, beans, and salad £10), and intricate surprises (lobster and papaya quesadillas with mango cream £10, char-chicken salad with fried cactus £7.50). Lunch special £6. M-F noon-4:30pm, £10 adds two beers or a giant margarita. Open M-Sa noon-11:45pm, Su noon-10:45pm. MC/V. ❸

Neal's Yard Bakery, Salad Bar & Tearoom, 1, 2, 8-10 Neal's Yard (☎7836 3233). It's a calculated bohemia, but in the midst of food-starved Covent Garden, it'll definitely do. A small, open-air counter sells fresh organic bread (loaves from £1.60) as well as vegan favorites like bean burgers (£3 eat-in, £2.50 takeout). The salad bar has more substantial vegan and vegetarian meal options, including *quiches* (£2) and *bruschetta* (£2). Wash it all down with a glass of fresh Brazilian juice (£3.50). Sit upstairs in the dim tea room or outside in wildly bright Neal's Yard, where you can duke it out with the pigeons. Eat-in minimum £1.50, M-F noon-3pm and Sa noon-4:30pm. Bakery open M-Sa 9:30am-5pm, salad bar and tea room M-Sa 10:30am-4:30pm. MC/V (£5 min.) ❶

The Ivy, 1-5 West St. (☎7836 4751). ⊖Leicester Sq. This celebrity-infested joint in central London can boast fans from Madonna to Noel Coward to Lawrence Olivier, and the waiting list for tables is even longer than the lines outside *Mamma Mia!* No one gets bored, though, because the superb modern British food remains mouthwatering no matter how old the novelty may be. The trademark: Shepherd's Pie (£12.50). The great deal: Su 3-course lunch (£18.50). The catch: reserve a table for next year if you're lucky. Open daily noon-3pm and 5:30pm-midnight. Wheelchair accessible. AmEx/MC/V. ❺

Monmouth Coffee Company, 27 Monmouth St. (☎7379 3516; www.monmouthcoffee.co.uk). It may be a chain, but at least it's not another Starbucks. Cozy Monmouth has huge sacks of beans, tiny wooden booths, and 17 different coffees to choose from. Coffee £1.50, double espresso £1. Get a bag of beans to go, or savor an aromatic cup in the "sample room" at the back. **Branch** at 2 Park St. open M-Sa 9am-6pm. MC/V (£5 min.). ❶

THE STRAND

Since The Strand is essentially one busy thoroughfare, it's not surprising that the bulk of dining is mediocre at best. A few key side streets are packed with restaurants and sandwich shops, though, so head to **Craven Passage** and **Villiers Street,** between the Strand and Victoria Embankment, if you're looking to grab a bite in the area.

Gordon's Wine Bar, 47 Villiers St. (☎7930 1408; www.gordonswinebar.com). ⊖Embankment or Charing Cross. A wine bar has been on the site since 1890, and the history is written on the walls—plastered with a century of newspaper articles about long-past coronations and marriages. Rudyard Kipling lived in this building during the 1890s, but the decor is less Jungle Book and more medieval-basement chic. Outdoor seating is limited, and the real attraction is the honeycomb of low, candle-lit vaults dripping with dark, smoky atmosphere. Choose a main dish, then pile on as much as you like from the self-serve salad bar for £6-10. Sherry and port from wood barrels around £3.50 per glass, wide selection of wine (£3.60 per glass, £14 per bottle). Open M-Sa 11am-11pm, Su noon-10pm. AmEx/MC/V (£10 min.). ❷

The Savoy, Strand (☎7836 4343). ⊖Charing Cross. See **Afternoon Tea,** p. 160.

WESTMINSTER

WESTMINSTER QUICKFIND: Discover, p. 11; sights, p. 116; museums & galleries, p. 152; pubs, p. 202; entertainment, p. 244; accommodations, p. 293.

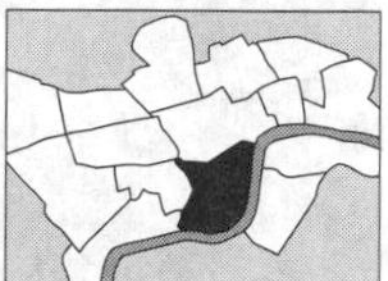

SEE MAP, p. 370

With one of London's highest concentrations of office workers, from tens of thousands of poorly paid clerks and civil servants to ministers, Lords, and business leaders; Westminster has no shortage of restaurants at every price range—at least for a weekday lunch. Come nighttime its a different story; sandwich bars close down and restaurants raise their prices, while many places shut down entirely over weekends. **Strutton Ground,** a short pedestrian road between Victoria and Great Peter St., has great sandwich/salad bars and cheap Chinese buffets. South of Victoria, **Tachbrook Street** has a number of cheap eats, as well as a tiny but excellent food market. (Open M-Sa 9am-5pm.) **Trafalgar Square's** eateries are hidden away inside its various historic buildings—**Crivelli's** restaurant, in the National Gallery (see p. 135), combines higher-end Ital-

the BIG $plurge

Tea at the Ritz

Those who want the ultimate afternoon tea experience should be sure to book a sitting at the Ritz (set tea £32). Long synonymous with luxury, an hour in the Palm Court allows you to play the part of nobility. The easy-listening piano tunes float in as the bespectacled maitre'd in tails leads you to your table, set of course with the finest, stainable linen.

What's most important is knowing your tools. The table is set with a tea cup and saucer, as well as a small scone-plate, a knife, stirring spoon, and dessert fork. That's for starters. After ordering your tea the rest of the cast emerges. A tray with housemade strawberry jam, sugar cubes, and clotted cream (like butter only sweeter and better) arrives. Tea service follows: a tea pot which you must let brew, a cream pitcher, another teapot with extra water should the tea get too strong, and the ever-important strainer. The strainer is crucial: it must be used otherwise the cup will become cluttered with tea leaves, and you might have to request another. This is an important point. At anytime should the tea be unsatisfactory in some way, any one of many attentive waiters will be happy to make a change.

ian favorites with a view of the Square. For cheaper fare, you may prefer the cafe in the crypt of St. Martin-in-the-Fields, which has a surprisingly varied menu. The plethora of pubs in the area provided good dining options too.

Goya, 34 Lupus St. (☎7976 5309). ⊖Pimlico. One of two corner Goya tapas bars, with earnest Spanish waiters serving food and drinks to the many locals who sit in or outside, or stake out the bar. Mirrors, large windows, and warm wood give the sunny interior an elegant aura. Plentiful vegetarian options. Generous, diverse tapas mostly £3-5; 3 per person is more than enough. Special sangria £3; alcohol is only served with food. Open daily noon-11:30pm. Wheelchair accessible. AmEx/MC/V. ❸

ECCo (Express Coffee Company), 40 Strutton Ground (☎7233 0557). ⊖Victoria or St. James's Park. The same great deals as the Bloomsbury original (see p. 166), including made-to-order 11 in. pizzas (start at £3), flavored French bread options (£1-2), cheap pastries (70p-£1.10) and sandwiches (£1.30-2.20) all served by a remarkably friendly staff. Buy any hot drink before 11am and get a free croissant. Open M-F 7am-7pm, Sa-Su 7am-4pm. Wheelchair accessible. ❶

Relish, 8 John Islip St. (☎071 828 0628). ⊖Pimlico. Lines often spill out of the door from outside this fresh lunchtime shop. The draw of the place is the cheap takeout sandwiches(£1.80-3.60): the ingredients are displayed in a big open case, point to what you want. Salads, deli options, and plenty of veggie fillings are available. Open M-Th 7:30am-3:30pm, F 7:30am-3pm. ❶

Noodle Noodle, 18 Buckingham Palace Rd. (☎7931 9911; www.noodle-noodle.co.uk) ⊖Victoria. A standout among the cheaper Chinese food in the area. Locals come for the massive portions and the noodle dishes. Takeout is possible, but most people stay and dig into their huge plates. Side dishes aren't a great deal at £3.95 but the noodle and rice plates could feed you 3 times over (£5-7). Open daily 11:30am-11pm. AmEx/MC/V. ❷

Tiles, 36 Buckingham Palace Rd. (☎7834 7761). ⊖Victoria. Despite its proximity to Buckingham Palace, the ambiance inside Tiles couldn't be more different. This tiny, cozy hole-in-the-wall is a great find. Upstairs, small round tables grace the blue-and-white tiled floor, and large mirrors add to the airy atmosphere. Downstairs, exposed brick, thick linen tablecloths, candles, and secluded couches raise the level of intimacy. Modern British cooking with a twist of French makes for an eclectic menu with mains £8-14. Free glass of wine with lunchtime main dish. Open M-F 11am-11pm, kitchen noon-2:30pm and 5:30-10:30pm. Wheelchair accessible. AmEx/MC/V. ❸

Buckingham Coffee Lounge, 19-21 Palace St. (☎7828 2665). ⊖Victoria or St. James' Park. Sitting on a corner among office buildings, this spacious coffee shop does most of its business with lunchtime sandwiches and homemade soups (£1.20-2.50). Made-to-order breakfasts are £1.50-3, but the modernist tables and futuristic chairs invite lazy coffee sipping all day. Open M-F 7am-5pm. Wheelchair accessible. ❶

NORTH LONDON

NORTH LONDON QUICKFIND: Discover, p. 12; sights, p. 120; museums & galleries, p. 153; pubs, p. 203; nightlife, p. 218; entertainment, p. 244; shopping, p. 269; accommodations, p. 294.

ISLINGTON

⊖Angel unless otherwise noted.

Upper Street has over 100 restaurants, and there are close to 200 nearby. Slightly more-down-market eateries line Islington Green on **Essex Road.** For a real taste of the ungentrified, pre-yuppie Islington, head to **Chapel Market,** just off Liverpool St. opposite Angel Tube. Here you can have an English meal with all the fixings for under £3 in any of the hole-in-the-wall restaurants that line the street. Don't expect linen tablecloths though. For the truly adventurous or seafood inclined, **M. Manze** eel house, at 70 Chapel Market, will give you a single serving of jellied eels with a side of mash to go for the small sum of £2.90. And you wonder why Indian food gained such rapid acceptance in England.

Gallipoli, 102 Upper St. (☎7359 0630), **Gallipoli Again,** 120 Upper St. (☎7359 1578) and the newest member of the family **Gallipoli Bazaar,** 107 Upper St. Deep-hued walls, patterned tiles and hanging lamps provide the authentic background to spectacular Turkish delights like *Iskender Kebap* (grilled lamb with yogurt and marinated pita bread in a top-secret sauce, £6). After the success of the first restaurant, they opened another on the same block; Again has the added bonus of an outdoor patio. Bazaar opened between the two and serves the same food in tearoom surroundings. Reservations recommended F-Sa. Open M-Th 10:30am-11pm, F-Sa 10:30am-midnight, Su 10:30am-11pm. Wheelchair accessible. MC/V. ❷

Le Mercury, 140a Upper St. (☎7354 4088). This sunny little corner restaurant offers delicious and delightfully presented French food at extremely affordable prices. The white-tablecloth service is excellent and the romantic ambience complete with dripping candles belies the price: dinner mains £6. The appetizers and desserts are not to be missed. Reservations recommended for evenings. Open daily noon-12:30am. Wheelchair accessible. MC/V. ❷

This brings us to the most important part of the event, the food, served on a three-tiered silver apparatus. The bottom tray holds finger sandwiches of varied types, and of course the eager waiters will continue re-stocking the plate until you force them to stop. The second tray holds the ever-popular scones. The top tray, the *piece de resistance,* holds a variety of tarts and specially selected tea pastries. Eat them all. They are excellent.

While drinking tea, your eyes will inevitably wander around. Be sure to take in the elegant dress of the other patrons, as well as the gilded fountains and red-vested waiters in tuxedos. This is what you're paying for. Don't forget to dress up yourself. Relax, breath easy, and realize that you may never feel this posh ever again. And while you are gawking, of course, don't spill. That would be embarrassing. At the end remember that you didn't have tea, you "took" tea.

The RItz, Piccadilly (☎7493 8181). ⊖Green Park. Arrive at noon for early tea. For later sittings reserve at least 6 weeks ahead for M-F, 3 months for Sa-Su, although there may be space closer to the date. Sittings at noon, 1:30, 3:30 and 5pm daily. Wheelchair accessible. AmEx/MC/V.

Candid Cafe, 3 Torrens St. (☎7837 2437). Signs point to the door beneath the horse sculpture; go up 2 floors to reach the cafe, part of the Candid Arts Trust. Quirky antique sofas and wax-covered victorian candlesticks decorate the room. The intellectual bohemian scene is ages away from the street-level bustle. Watercolors and sexually provocative paintings form the perfect background for serious discussions and romantic overtures. Large baguette sandwiches from £2.80; other hot dishes (£5.50-7). Open M-Sa noon-10pm, Su noon-5pm. ❶

Cuba Libre, 72 Upper St. (☎7354 9998) This colorful and spirited tapas bar/restaurant makes no secret of its political bent. Main course options are standard Latin dishes from various countries (the recipes here certainly aren't all Cuban); you can choose an appetizer and a main course for £10. Music plays loudly, Che posters hang, and exuberant waiters hover. The bar in the back has some dance space, or you can order tapas and eat them outside. 6 tapas for £7.95. Happy hour 5-8pm. Wheelchair accessible. MC/V ❷

Pizzeria Oregano, 18-19 St. Alban's Pl. (☎7288 1123). Two step away but almost hidden from Upper St. and its trendy eateries, Oregano relies on the loyal business of devoted regulars. Carefully prepared pasta and pizza £7-8, other mains around £10. The restaurant was recently redecorated, but thankfully they haven't changed the recipes. Open Tu-F 5:30-11pm, Sa 12:30-11pm, Su 1-11pm. MC/V. ❷

Afghan Kitchen, 35 Islington Green (☎7359 8019). This tiny restaurant sits on a busy street, but the cool mint walls and simple decor feel serene. "Traditional Afghan home cooking" equals manageable portions of spicy meat and vegetarian dishes; most are £5-6. Sides £2, yummy *bakhlava* is £1. Enjoy the food while sitting on stools and wooden planks either communally downstairs or more privately upstairs. Open Tu-Sa noon-3:30pm and 5:30-11pm. Partially wheelchair accessible. ❶

Giraffe, 29-31 Essex Rd. (☎7359 5999). The same successful formula as the Hampstead original (see p. 185), only bigger and more elegantly decorated. Open M-F 8am-11pm, Sa-Su 9am-11pm. AmEx/MC/V. ❷

Tiger Lil's, 270 Upper St. (☎7226 1118). ⊖Highbury and Islington. This Mongolian buffet chain lets you select raw ingredients (veggies, meats, fish, noodles and the accessories) before they stir-fry them with your choice of sauce. Appetizers (£1.50-5), desserts (£3). If you make the wrong choices you can go back as many times as you want during dinner (£12.50); lunch (£5) is only one serving, so there's less room for error. All ingredients are fresh. Open M-F noon-3pm and 6-11pm, Sa-Su noon-11pm. MC/V. ❸

CAMDEN TOWN

⊖Camden Town unless otherwise noted.

Camden Market and **Camden Canal Market** combine a fair selection of stands with some street or canalside seating, but the widest range of world food is in **Camden Lock** and in **Stables Market.** Turning off Camden High St. will lead you to some of the best restaurants. **Parkway,** running from the Tube toward Regent's Park, is home to several noodle bars and Inverness St. also has some good cafes. Though it's only a 15min. walk, the upper curve of **Regent's Park Road** towards posh Primrose Hill feels miles away. It has a burgeoning concentration of mid-priced restaurants catering to more refined tastes, as well as bakeries and pricey fruit stands.

Mango Room, 10-12 Kentish Town Rd. (☎7482 5065). A neighborhood favorite in an area where few restaurants last more than a year. Decor favors funky paintings and orange walls. The small Caribbean menu favors fish, complemented with plenty of mango, avocado, and coconut sauces (mains £9-12). Points for presentation. A wide array of potent tropical drinks are served from the tiny bar, but only at night. Reservations recommended for weekends. Open M 6pm-midnight, Tu-Sa noon-3pm and 6pm-midnight, Su noon-11pm. Wheelchair accessible. MC/V. ❷

New Culture Revolution, 43 Parkway (☎017 1267 2700). When this small restaurant first opened in 1994, it upgraded Londoners' perceptions of East Asian food. The revolution refers to the wealth of healthy menu options. Huge portions of noodles and steaming soups can be ordered from a menu that champions meats and veggies too. What's lost in authenticity is made up for with a clean, quiet environment and great value. Dumplings and noodle dishes all under £6. Open daily noon-11pm. AmEx/MC/V. ❶

Trojka, 101 Regent's Park Rd. (☎7483 3765; www.trojka.co.uk). Part restaurant, part Russian tea room, the 3-horse trap of its name could refer to the Russian, Ukrainian, and Polish influences tugging on the menu. If your budget doesn't stretch to the *sevruga* caviar *blinis* (£46), the lumpfish caviar makes an affordable substitute (£5.50); *Pelmeni* (pierogi £6.50) are perfect for a light supper, otherwise coffees, teas, and homemade desserts are also served. *A la carte lunch* offers 2 courses for £7.95. Open daily 9am-10:30pm. MC/V. ❷

Odette's Wine Bar, 130 Regent's Park Rd. (☎7586 5486). ⊖Chalk Farm. Odette's Restaurant, upstairs, is one of London's greats, with a modern British menu ranging from £14–25. The wine bar in the basement offers a cozy, more casual romantic setting and an exceptional range of wines, including many half bottles and some glasses. House wine starts at £12 per bottle. Open M-F 12:30-3:30pm and 5:30-10:30pm, Sa 5:30-10:30pm, Su 12:30-3:30pm. Partially wheelchair accessible. MC/V. ❺

Galanga Thai Canteen, 29-31 Parkway (☎7485 9933). Simple and sleek, this Thai restaurant pulls off a Modernist look with linoleum-like tiles and seablue table without looking like a canteen. The prices are reasonably canteen-like, if you stick to the basics. Pad thai starts at £5.20, while mains like deep-fried tilapia fish run from £5-7. Popular curries are £6-6.50. Open M-F noon-3pm and 6pm-11pm, Sa 1:30pm-11:30pm, Su 1pm-10pm. MC/V. ❷

Marine Ices, 8 Haverstock Hill (☎7482 9003). ⊖Chalk Farm. The Mansi family have been in charge here since 1930, and now supply their superb gelati to 1500 restaurants in and around London. Plenty of flavors abound £1.50 for a single scoop; more elaborate ice cream concoctions start at £2.50. The restaurant is the ultimate in family-friendly eating; Italian standards (£6-12). Gelateria open M-Sa 10:30am-11pm, Su 11am-10pm. Restaurant open M-F noon-3pm and 6-11pm, Sa noon-11pm, Su noon-10pm. AmEx/MC/V. ❶

HAMPSTEAD AND HIGHGATE

⊖*Hampstead unless otherwise noted.*

Hampstead High Street has no shortage of eating opportunities for the area's wealthy residents; most of the places are fairly high-end, but very good. The establishments know they have to maintain their quality to retain customers, and so Hampstead is perfect for a culinary splurge. For a small cluster of cheap restaurants, head to South End Rd. near the Hampstead Heath train station. **Highgate** is short on eating opportunities, you'll mostly just find pubs and convenience stores.

Le Crêperie de Hampstead, 77 Hampstead High St. (metal stand on the side of the King William IV; www.hampsteadcreperie.com). Don't let the slow-moving line deter you; these phenomenal crepes are worth any wait. French-speaking cooks take your order and leave to you wait and salivate while you watch them cook. Among many other varieties, mushrooms with ham and in tarragon cheese goes for £3.50, while the "Banana Butterscotch Cream Dream" is £2.60. 40p extra gets you gooey Belgian chocolate (plain, milk, or white) instead of syrup. Open M-Th 11:45am-11pm, F-Su 11:45am-11:30pm. Wheelchair accessible. ❶

Giraffe, 46 Rosslyn Hill (☎7435 0343; www.giraffe.net). With a menu as deliberately international as the world music they play, Giraffe orients itself as a place to please all world citizens. The menu represents at least 4 continents, ranging from Jamaican red vegetable curry (£7) to salmon fish fingers (£9) to a wide selection of burgers and an array of tropical smoothies. M-F 5-7pm 2 courses for £6.95 (7-11pm, £9.95) and 2-for-1 drinks. Open M-F 8am-11:30pm, Sa 9am-11:30pm, Su 9am-11pm. Wheelchair accessible. AmEx/MC/V. ❷

Al Casbah, 42 Hampstead High St. (☎7431 6356). Amid the rhythmic music and cushioned stools the Moroccan chef cooks up an array of *tajine* meat casseroles (£12.50-15) and couscous dishes (£12-14.50) large enough for two. Patrons lounge on the low-slung couches with ornate pillows, although eating at the not-so-low tables is a bit awkward. Gold lace tapestries and shisha pipes (£24 for two people) keep the mood. Sa belly dancing. Open daily 10am-11pm. MC/V. ❸

Wagamama

Chinatown

Old Spitafields Market

Bar Room Bar, 48 Rossyln Hill (☎7431 8802). A consciously hip but laid-back bar and art gallery, fills in the afternoon and stays pleasantly busy into the evening. Ponder the bizarrely cool teacup chandelier, or head out to the heated rear garden when it's sunny. Su live jazz from 8pm. Pizzas £5-7; 2-for-1 pizza special Tu, 2-for-1 drink special Th. Open M-Sa 11am-11pm, Su noon-10:30pm. Wheelchair accessible. MC/V. ❷

Le Cellier du Midi, 28 Church Row (☎017 1435 9998). Midi is a secret lair where French tradition is kept safe. Fancy white tablecloths and the rich wooden bistro interior complements the traditionally rich sauces, meats, and wines. Choose from the 3-course meal (£22) or 2-course meal (£19)–both of which allow you to mix and match any items on the menu. Single entree £16. Remarkably, prices here haven't been rising as they have at almost every other quality establishment in London. Open daily 6:30-11pm. AmEx/MC/V. ❺

GOLDERS GREEN

Golders Green (Zone 3). From the Tube exit, walk up to the big intersection and bear right.

Carmelli Bakery, 128 Golders Green Rd. (☎8455 2074). Carmelli's golden, egg-glazed challah (£1.25-2) is considered the best in London. With the bagels and sinfully good pastries (£1.50), it's hard to go wrong here. Packed F afternoons, as every Jewish mother in London scrambles to get bread for the Sabbath. Kosher. Hours vary, but generally open daily 6am-1am; Th and Sa 24 hours. Wheelchair accessible. ❶

Bloom's, 130 Golders Green Rd. (☎8455 1338). The waiter's signature black bow ties have been an essential part of the experience since 1920. The mains are varieties of roasted meat (£8.50-15)–simple, but delicious. Jewish favorites like gefilte fish (£3.50) and latkas (£2) served as side orders. Soups are excellent, and an extensive take-away menu saves time and cash. Kosher. Open Su-Th noon-10:30pm, F 11am-2 or 3pm. Wheelchair accessible. ❷

SOUTH LONDON

SOUTH LONDON QUICKFIND: Discover, p. 14; sights, p. 125; museums & galleries, p. 155; nightlife, p. 221; entertainment, p. 247; shopping, p. 271.

Brixton's mix of rich and poor means that there's very little between dodgy Caribbean dives and trendy, expensive new openings. Come during market hours (see p. 271) for traditional delights like curry goat or saltfish with ackee.

Bug (☎7738 3366; www.bugbar.co.uk), in the crypt of St. Matthew's Church, Brixton Hill. Brixton. Eerie lighting and decor give this small dining room and lounge a uniquely gothic atmosphere—then again, what else do you expect when dining in a crypt? The novel atmosphere and quasi-gourmet preparation doesn't come cheap. Mains like mango plantain curry, North African lamb, and Cajun chicken £7.50-13. Su special "Bug Roast" gets you 2 courses for £11.50. Evening reservations essential. Open Tu-Th 5-11pm, F-Sa 5-11:30pm, Su 1-9pm. MC/V. ❸

Café Pushkar, 424 Coldharbour Ln. (☎7738 6161). ⊖Brixton. A green cafe with a kick: this little vegetarian and vegan eatery serves scrumptious and affordable meatless wonders. An impressive list of cocktails to wash down all that goodhearted food. Attractive woody, plant-infused decor, and cheap mains (veggie burger with cheese and salad £4), and a fantastic "full vegetarian English breakfast" served until 5pm (£4.45). Open M-Tu 11am-5pm, W-Sa 11am-11pm. MC/V (£8 min.). ❶

SW9, 11 Dorrell Pl. (☎7738 3116). ⊖Brixton. SW9, the once-dreaded Brixton postal code, is now a stylish hangout for rich new residents. Attractive, friendly, and popular, serving heaping plates of food (£7-10) and great cocktails in the sleek dining area and on the isolated patio. Happy hour M 5pm-close, Tu-F 4:30-7pm, Su 7pm-close; £1.90 mixers, £2 pints. Live jazz F-Sa, jazz DJ Su. Open M-W 10am-11pm, Th 10am-11:30pm, F-Sa 10am-1am, Su 10am-11:30pm. AmEx/MC/V. ❷

EAST LONDON

EAST LONDON QUICKFIND: Discover, p. 13; sights, p. 126; museums & galleries, p. 156; pubs, p. 204; nightlife, p. 222; entertainment, p. 248; shopping, p. 271.

WHITECHAPEL AND THE EAST END

⊖Shoreditch (open rush hour and Su morning), or a 10min. walk from ⊖Aldgate East or Liverpool St.

For dirt-cheap, high quality Bangladeshi food **Brick Lane** can't be beat. Ignore the men aggressively inviting you in front of each establishment and go for the ones that seem most popular; amazingly, almost all of the 100 or so restaurants fill up on weekends. With so much competition the food is inexpensive and good. For a totally different and wonderfully delicious scene, **Spitalfields Market** is a must-eat (see **Sights,** p. 126). Here, the Edwardian market hall has a number of creatively decorated international food stalls offering daytime market browsers everything from goulash to guacamole; there's even a seating area. Most food stalls open only for lunch and close Saturdays, but otherwise the multitude of organic and original food stalls are open whenever the market is. With so many choices, it's best to leave some room for a second or third course.

Aladin, 132 Brick Ln. (☎7247 8210). Friendly service, nice decor and food that's a cut above the rest makes Aladin one of Brick Ln.'s more popular balti joints. Even the Prince of Wales has been here; a large commemorative photo rests in the window. You may not get photographed but you will get a reasonably priced and well-prepared meal. Mains £3-8.50, 3-course lunch £5.90. Open Su-Th noon-11:30pm, F-Sa noon-midnight. ❷

Café 1001, Dray Walk (☎7247 9679), off Brick Ln. Super popular Hipster hangout in the Truman Brewery complex, with an alley full of picnic tables in the summer. Inside 20-somethings gather on sofas and unwind to bumping garage beats. Everyone else comes for the yummy healthy food and finger-licking good cakes (slice £2.20). Parma ham and mozzarella sandwiches £3.20. Smoothies £2.50. The line moves fast. Food served until 8pm. Open M-F 8am-11pm, Sa-Su 10am-midnight. ❶

Beigel Bake, 159 Brick Ln. (☎7729 0616). Serving Jewish food in what was once the heartland of Jewish London. The quick-as-a-flash service keeps the line moving fast; if you make the wrong choice, get back in the queue for another go-it's worth it. The neighborhood has changed, but the prices haven't (bagels 15p). Also filled bagels, challah, brownies, and pastries, all under £1.50. No chairs or tables, but the best place to grab a 3am snack or two. Open daily 24hr. ❶

HOXTON & SHOREDITCH

Shoho's tone is shifting from can't-afford-to-eat artists to can't-be-bothered-to-cook artists, but the best meal remains the haute cuisine in the area's bars and drinking haunts.

Yelo, 8-9 Hoxton Sq. (☎7729 4626; www.yelothai.com). ⊖Old St. This popular Thai restaurant pulls off style, good service, and generous portions at an affordable price. Tried and true noodles, curries, rice dishes, and salads £4-5, small bowl of rice £1.50 extra. Eat outside overlooking the square in summer, or make new friends at the indoor communal benches amid hip minimalist decor. Open Tu-Sa noon-3pm and 6-11pm, Su-M closes at 10:30pm. Wheelchair accessible. ❶

Shish, 313-319 Old St. (☎7749 0990; www.shish.com). ⊖Old St. One of 2 popular Shish bar/restaurants, this establishment mixes Silk Rd. spice with slick modern decor. Usually abuzz with activity. The mezze-style small plate eating proves to be a hit with ShoHo-ians. Lunch deal offers 2 mezze dishes with a side and half-pint for £8, otherwise *mezze* dishes £3-4. Creative desserts such as muhallabia (rice pudding with coconut, pistachios, and cherry sauce, £3) round out the menu. Open M-Th 11:30am-midnight, Sa 10am-midnight, Su 10am-10:30pm. Wheelchair accessible. MC/V. ❷

Grand Central, 93 Great Eastern St. (☎7613 4228; www.grandcentral.org.uk). ⊖Old St. This trendy gastrobar is wildly popular with hungry pre- and post-clubbers, who dig the funky shapes of the walls and bright paintings. Feels very much like a bar. Tuck into standard sandwiches or burgers (£5-7) or the more creative haddock hash (£7). End of the week impromptu performances feature local bands and DJs. Su music brunch is helpfully designed to combat your hangover. Open M-F 8am-midnight, Sa 5pm-midnight, Su 11am-5pm. Wheelchair accessible. MC/V. ❶

GREENWICH

There's no shortage of places to eat in Greenwich, but many have a distinctly touristy feel (and price)—this is one of the few places in London where visitors outnumber locals. Ignore the dodgy snack and fish 'n' chips bars along Greenwich Church St. and duck into the market. Inside you can find all sorts of made-to-order goodies, from weekend booths or healthfood markets otherwise. Ice-cream stands and pubs along the small streets surrounding the park are also a good bet.

Goddard's Pie & Mash, 45 Greenwich Church St. (☎8293 9313). DLR: Cutty Sark. It doesn't get any more traditional than this. Saved from closure by a local campaign, Goddard's has been serving the good folk of Greenwich since 1890. All the original London working-class favorites are dished up cafeteria-style and eaten elbow-to-elbow on wooden benches. Five different eat-in lunch specials: pie with mash £2.00, fruit pie and ice cream £1.20. The adventurous can try various eels, jellied and otherwise (£2-4). Open M-F 10am-6:30pm, Sa-Su 10am-8pm. Wheelchair accessible. ❶

WEST LONDON

WEST LONDON QUICKFIND: Discover, p. 14; sights, p. 130; entertainment, p. 248; shopping, p. 273; accommodations, p. 295.

The most pleasant place to eat in the West is at one of the mid-range eateries on **Turnham Green Terrace,** extending to the left of the Tube station exit. If you're in **Shepherd's Bush,** the most variety is on Goldhawk Rd. (⊖Goldhawk Rd.), with a wealth of cheap ethnic eateries. **Hammersmith** is famous for the riverside pubs along the Upper and Lower Malls, west of the bridge. During the annual boat race between Oxford and Cambridge universities (late Mar. or early Apr.), thousands gather here to drink and watch the rowers speed by at the race's halfway point.

The Gate, 51 Queen Caroline St. (☎8748 6932). ⊖Hammersmith. It feels like a hidden find: go through the garden gate and up the external stairs on the right. One of London's top vegetarian restaurants with plenty of vegan options. Mains £8-13.50, starters £4-5. Deservedly popular at all times; reserve a table for dinner. Open M-F noon-3pm and 6-11pm, Sa 6-11pm. Wheelchair accessible. AmEx/MC/V. ❸

Café Zagora, 38 Devonshire Rd. (☎8742 7922). ⊖Turnham Green. From the Tube, walk south to Chiswick High Rd.; turn right, then left onto Devonshire Rd. From the attentive, discreet service to the warm North African interior (complete with mosaic tabletops and embroidered pillows), Café Zagora is a world away from London. The Lebanese-Moroccan cuisine is reasonably priced, with mains £9-13. Share several small dishes at £2.50-4 each. Desserts (£3.50) are worth every penny–the mint tea is heavenly and the scrumptiously sticky baklava melts in your mouth. Set dinner available 5-7:30pm; any 2 courses £12, 3 courses £15. Open daily 5-11pm. Wheelchair accessible. MC/V. ❷

Patio, 5 Goldhawk Rd. (☎8743 5194) Locally and critically acclaimed hidden deal. You wouldn't notice this place if you walked by it, but inside it's a cozy, quirky place. Samovars adorn the walls, mismatched porcelain sets the table and servers are happy to guide you along the menu. Polish delights from £4-7, great 3-course option for £12. With the huge portions you'll be stuffed, and you won't have spent more than £10-15. Open daily noon-3pm and 6-11:30pm, weekends for dinner only. Wheelchair accessible. AmEx/MC/V. ❷

Maison Blanc, 26-28 Turnham Green Terr. (☎8995 7220; www.maisonblanc.co.uk). This cute cafe does bread, pastries, lunch, and chocolate. The pink walls and tea tables turn it into a virtual cake box. Yummy sandwiches (£3.45-5) and pastries (£1-2.50). Good luck making out the waiter's impenetrable French accent. MC/V. ❶

INSIDE

Pubs

It's impossible to visit London and not see a pub—almost anywhere in the city is within a few blocks of one. Pubbing in London can be an incredible experience, allowing you to explore the different ways this 800-year-old institution has adapted to the present, while simultaneously downing some of the world's finest beer. It's all a bit daunting for the novice, what with the intimidation of lifelong Brits practically weaned *on the pint*, but the following pages should make pubbing a bit clearer.

PUBBING TIPS

WHAT TO AVOID

Avoid drinking in **chain pubs.** Most pubs are owned by big breweries, but the owners usually leave the publican to his own devices. Not so in chain pubs, whose proliferation in London is both worrying and inexplicable. Better food and better fun awaits at the real pub around the corner, although you might have to do without bright plastic menus or neon signs. The most common chain pubs are **All Bar One, Pitcher & Piano, Slug & Lettuce, O'Neil's,** and **It's A Scream;** avoid them all. Outposts of the **Firkin** chain all have "Firkin" in the title to warn you off.

ON THE MENU

Into the Pub, Off the Wagon

Sometimes, a glass of beer isn't just a glass of beer. In the exciting world of British pub life, ordering one might get you in trouble, at least if you're a lightweight.

The glass measurement doesn't follow here, as beers on tap are measured in pints and half-pints. A pint is a substantially large glass: order one and you'll be satisfied and perhaps a little more drunk than expected. As the pints add up sooner or later you'll realize just how large a quantity of beer you've consumed. Relative intoxication will follow.

A half-pint is more of an appetizer-sized beer, good for beginners and the like. Soft-core pubbers will find this size manageable and if the ale isn't having the desired effect, more is just as far away as the bar. Of course to avoid the delicate question of measuring beer intake in pint-terms, bottles can be ordered at most pubs (they are, however, a bit more expensive).

Similar size issues might come into play when ordering wine: here glasses come in two sizes and there are often options for half and full bottles too. Ask for a glass of wine and you may end up with a glass twice as large or half as big as you wanted. Specifying the desired size (175ml small or 275ml regular) should eliminate any confusion.

DRINK

BEERS. Every pub keeps a range of different beers on tap and has dozens more in bottles. There are three basic types of beer: lagers, stouts, and bitters. **Lagers** are light, gassy beers with little substance—most American beers are lagers. **Stouts** are dark and heavy; Guinness is the best-known stout, and one of the darkest. **Bitters** lie in the middle—they are rich and full-bodied with very little gas. Bitters are served at slightly below room temperature, and are normally hand-pulled from casks in the cellar. The bitter is the classic pub beer and what almost every Englishman drinks when he's at a pub. Most pubs have a half-dozen different bitters on tap; two of our favorites are **Old Speckled Hen** and **Adnams**.

OTHER DRINKS. All pubs have a fully stocked bar in addition to their beer taps. **Cider** is an alcoholic drink, about as strong as beer. A **Martini** in Britain is not a cocktail—it's just a glass of vermouth. **Lemonade** in Britain is a carbonated drink similar to ginger ale. Lemonade and beer can be mixed to form a **shandy,** which is very refreshing and perfect for a summer afternoon—but only an afternoon, thanks to...

THE UNWRITTEN RULES. It is considered effeminate for a **man** to drink anything except beer or straight hard liquor; ordering a cocktail will elicit strange looks and maybe some heckling. Shandies are especially girly. These rules relax during the afternoon, especially during the summer, when it's too hot to down a pint of bitter; in the evening, order that Bacardi Breezer at your own peril. (Note: all of these rules are thrown out the window on Old Compton St.— gay pubbing has its own, very different, unwritten code.) **Women** were once expected to shun beer in favor of wine, mixed drinks, and bottled cocktails. Now most ladies you encounter have a pint just like everyone else. While most pubs are perfectly friendly, **solo females** may feel unwelcome at some very traditional pubs. Almost all the pubs we list in *Let's Go* are friendly toward solo women.

HOW TO GET YOUR DRINK. Pubs have no waitstaff. You must order at the bar—try to catch the barman's eye, and wait your turn. If you're in a group, have one person order and pay for the entire group. Order at the bar, pay the bartender (never tip), and carry your drink anywhere in the pub. Most pubs reward exploration with deliciously cozy nooks and galleries or outdoor tables. Note that almost no pubs serve alcohol after 11pm; a bell will ring to announce last call.

FOOD

WHAT TO EXPECT. Standard pub grub consists of sandwiches in the afternoon, and British classics in the evening: sausages, meat pies, jacket potatoes, etc. Snack foods like chips, nuts, and crisps are usually available all day. The menu is usually written on a chalkboard above the bar, though there may also be printed menus. If there's a glossy color menu, beware: you're probably in a chain pub, and the food is probably lousy. In general, we'll note it specifically if a pub offers better-than-average food. Consider getting food at a pub if you're on a tight budget. Gastropubs like **The Eagle** (p. 197), in contrast, offer trendy, modern takes on traditional British cuisine, usually with excellent results and higher prices.

HOW TO GET YOUR FOOD. Pubs have no waitstaff. Choose your meal from the chalkboard menu, then order and pay at the bar. Bring your drink back to your table; the bartender will bring you your food when it's ready. Never tip.

PUBS BY NEIGHBORHOOD

BAYSWATER

BAYSWATER QUICKFIND: Discover, p. 4; food, p. 164; entertainment, p. 233; shopping, p. 254; accommodations, p. 279.

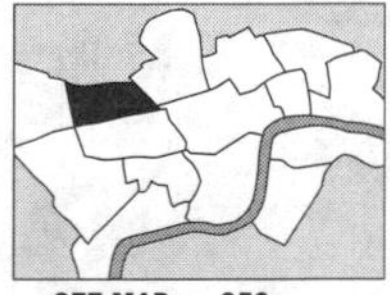

SEE MAP, p. 359

All listings are near ⊖Bayswater.

Mitre, 24 Craven Terr. (☎7262 5240). This comfortable, sprawling Victorian pub is perfect for a lazy afternoon. Perched on a quiet corner. this is a large mansion with booths and taps inside. Hearty pub grub £5-8. Open M-Sa 11am-11pm, Su noon-10:30pm. AmEx/MC/V. ❷

Bar Oz, 51 Moscow Rd. (☎7729 0647). "Oz" for Aussie; observe the distinctly un-British alien in its native habitat. With barbecue-style grub, "Lizard Warning" signs, and a windsurfing sail affixed to the ceiling, you'll get the picture even before you notice that the place is actually filled with authentic Ozfolk. A nice way to explore the true Bayswater expat experience. Live music Sa night. Food served daily noon-9:30pm. Open M-Sa 11am-11pm, Su noon-10:30pm. MC/V. ❷

The Shakespeare, 65 Westbourne Grove (☎7229 2233). The self-proclaimed "last traditional pub" in the area, Shakespeare displays little of the Bard's famous eloquence, but makes up for it in good cheer. Classic brass and wood set-up, with slightly extended pub grub offerings. Snacks and sandwiches £2.75-4.50, mains £4.75-7. Open M-Sa 11am-11pm, Su noon-10:30pm. MC/V. ❶

BLOOMSBURY

BLOOMSBURY QUICKFIND: Discover, p. 5; sights, p. 87; museums & galleries, p. 140; food, p. 166; entertainment, p. 234; shopping, p. 255; accommodations, p. 282.

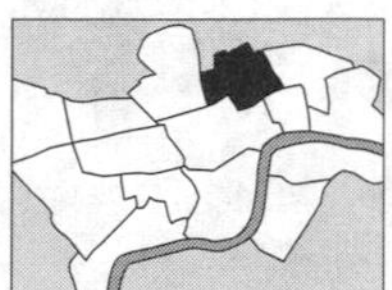

SEE MAP, p. 360

Newman Arms, 23 Rathbone St., entrance to pie room on Newman Passage (☎7636 1127). ⊖Tottenham Crt. Rd. or Goodge St. The real highlight in this tiny, ancient pub is the famous upstairs pie room and restaurant. In what was once (reportedly) a bordello, ten sought-after tables of connoisseurs dig into a selection of homemade meat pies (seasonal game fillings are most popular, although vegetarian and fish options available). Pie and a pint, with potatoes and veggies on the side £10. Book in advance or face a hungry 45min. wait. Pub open M-F 11am-11pm; pie room M-F noon-3pm and M-Th 6-9pm. MC/V. ❷

Aquarium

Enjoy a Cold Pint

At Docklands

Fitzroy Tavern, 16 Charlotte St. (☎7580 3714). ⊖Goodge St. Historically popular with artists and writers (Dylan Thomas was known to frequent the Tavern), this is the place to go to get a fix of intellectual stimulation along with your pint (both cost under £2). The center of Bloomsbury's "Fitzrovia" neighborhood (guess where the area's name came from). Umbrellaed outdoor seating in summer; comedy and other special events regularly. Open M-Sa 11am-11pm, Su noon-10:30pm. MC/V. ❶

The Queen's Larder, 1 Queen's Sq. (☎7837 5627). ⊖Russell Sq. A pub has stood on the premises since 1710; the present incarnation dates to the late 1700s, when Queen Charlotte rented out the cellar to store food for her ailing husband, King George III; the friendly proprietor is more than happy to tell the story. Traditional English fare, including a popular roast with Yorkshire pudding, is available in the tiny upstairs restaurant (mains £5.50-8). Open M-Sa 11:30am-11pm, Su noon-3pm and 7-10:30pm. AmEx/MC/V. ❷

Exmouth Arms, Starcross St. (☎7387 5440; www.exmouth-arms.co.uk). ⊖Euston. Sitting pretty on a quiet corner above Euston Station, it's a vision in magenta and purple. This welcoming neighborhood pub is notable for both its friendly quietude and the overflowing cascades of flowers that grace its outer walls in the warm months. Normal pub grub and snacks, plus good vegetarian options (£4-5). Open M-Sa 11am-11pm. MC/V (£10 min.). ❶

The Jeremy Bentham, 31 University St. (☎7387 3033). ⊖Goodge St. With 2 floors packed with students from nearby UCL, friendly staff, superior food, and a broad ale selection, this is an extremely popular pub. Sandwiches and burgers from £3.45. Food served until 9pm. Open M-F 11am-11pm, Sa noon-11pm, Su noon-10:30pm. AmEx/MC/V (£5 min.). ❶

The Lamb, 94 Lamb's Conduit St. (☎7405 0713). ⊖Russell Square. Popular with doctors from the many nearby hospitals and barristers from Holborn, this quiet, cozy pub is also a bit of a celebrity hangout—regulars include Peter O'Toole. The swiveling "snob screens"—pivoting panels of etched glass around the bar—once hid "respectable" men meeting with ladies of ill repute. Nowadays, those of any repute can enjoy the decent pub grub served noon-2:30pm and M-Sa 6-9pm. Open M-Sa 11am-11pm, Su noon-4pm and 7-10:30pm. AmEx/MC/V (£10 min.). ❶

The Museum Tavern, 49 Great Russell St. (☎7242 8987). ⊖Tottenham Crt. Rd., Russell Sq., or Holborn. Across the street from the British Museum, this pleasant, wood-paneled pub actually predates its namesake (it was known as the Dog & Duck until the museum's 1759 founding). The original carved fittings and cut glass lend it an authentic feel, although you'll undoubtedly be sharing the premises with scads of fellow tourists. Pub grub £5-7 but no great reason to visit. Open M-Sa 11am-11pm, Su noon-10:30pm. AmEx/MC/V. ❷

Rising Sun, 46 Tottenham Crt. Rd. (☎7636 6530). ⊖Goodge St. or Tottenham Crt. Rd. The place is over 150 years old, but a young crowd populates the Rising Sun's high-ceilinged old barroom. Enjoy the self-affirmed "jollity and conviviality" and munch on the homemade snacks (£4-7). Open M-F 11:30am-11pm, Sa noon-3pm and 7-11pm, Su noon-3pm and 7-10:30pm. MC/V (£10 min.). ❷

Of Dogs and Ducks

CHELSEA

CHELSEA QUICKFIND: Discover, p. 5; sights, p. 89; museums & galleries, p. 141; food, p. 167; entertainment, p. 234; shopping, p. 256; accommodations, p. 285.

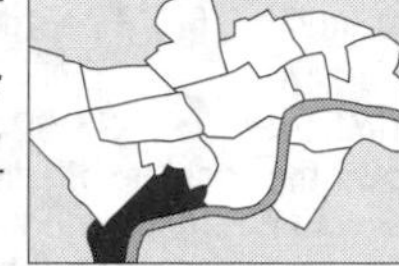
SEE MAP, p. 361

***TRANSPORTATION:** The only Tube station in Chelsea is Sloane Sq.; from here buses #11, 19, 22, 211, and 319 serve King's Rd.*

Grapes

The Chelsea Potter, 119 King's Rd. (☎7352 9479). This friendly, flowery old-style pub was once–surprise surprise–a potter's studio. Perfect for people-watching, with large open windows looking out onto King's Rd. Open daily 11am-11pm, with simple pub grub and snacks available all day. AmEx/MC/V. ❶

Pig's Ear Pub, 35 Old Church St. (☎7352 2908). Funky background music and a shiny new decor lend the Pig's Ear a bit of yuppified smartness to complement its generally young crowd. Wide variety of food goes along with the semi-upmarket theme (mains £6-11). Open M 5-11pm, Tu-Sa noon-11pm, Su noon-10:30pm; food closed Su night and M. MC/V. ❷

THE CITY OF LONDON

THE CITY OF LONDON QUICKFIND: Discover, p. 6; sights, p. 90; museums & galleries, p. 141; food, p. 167; entertainment, p. 235.

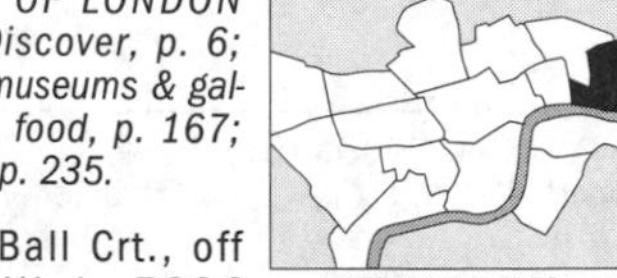
SEE MAP, p. 362

Simpson's, Ball Crt., off 38½ Cornhill (☎7626 9985). ⊖Bank. "Established 1757" says the sign on the alley leading to this pub; it remains so traditional that an employee stands in the door to greet you. The open space outside the entrance fills with people after 3pm; inside, different rooms divide the patrons: quaffers populate the basement wine bar (sandwiches £2-4), beer lov-

One Londoner's Experience

ers frequent the standing-only ground-floor bar, and diners relax in the ground-floor and upstairs restaurants (traditional main dishes £6-7). Simpson's has been a local favorite for years; it still sets the standard for city pubs. Wheelchair accessible. ❶

The Walrus and the Carpenter, 45 Monument St. at Lovat Ln. (☎7626 3362). ⊖Monument. Everything a pub should be and a little bit more: outside picnic tables and bright hanging plants ensure that patrons will spill over into the cobbled alleyway. Afternoons are the busiest; the post-lunch hour is the ideal time to visit the Walrus (as it is affectionately known). Solid selection of beers, wines, and cocktails draw a varied crowd; families often eat on the benches. Sandwiches (£4-£5), snacks (£1.25-£3) and mains (£4.50-£7) round out the menu. Open M-F 11am-11pm. AmEx/MC/V. Wheelchair accessible. ❷

The Black Friar, 174 Queen Victoria St. (☎7236 5650 5654). ⊖Blackfriars. The Black Friar's claim of being "London's most unique pub" rests upon its Art Deco imitation of the 12th-century Dominican friary that once occupied this spot. It was almost razed in the 1960s but thankfully survived. This is one of the City's coziest pubs: an open front room and a warm back dining area are inside. Outside cafe tables and umbrellas are very inviting, especially in sunny weather. Food served 11:30-9pm, mains £6-7. Open daily 11:30am-11pm. AmEx/MC/V. Wheelchair accessible. ❷

The Samuel Pepys, Stew Ln., off High Timber St. (☎7634 9841). ⊖Mansion House. This recently renovated gastro-pub juts out over the Thames, offering a phenomenal view south to the Tate Modern and west along the river to Westminster. Plush chairs by the window and larger tables in the restaurant section make it ideal for pubbers and grubbers alike. The modernist decor disguises a remarkably relaxed atmosphere. Respectable array of ales, a solid wine list, and excellent sandwiches on ciabatta (£5-6). Burgers, jacket potatoes and other mains are available too (£5-£9). Food served noon-9pm. Open M-F noon-11pm. AmEx/MC/V (£10 min.). Wheelchair accessible. ❶

The Hung Drawn and Quartered, 27 Great Tower St. at the corner of Byward and Great Tower. (☎7626 6123). ⊖Tower Hill. This pleasant establishment is that rarest of beasts: a City pub open on the weekend, and one of the most spacious pubs in the neighborhood. Its location, just a block or two from the Tower, means that Beefeaters have been known to stop in wearing full regalia. The rich red and gold decor is decadent and the vibe is comfortable. Serves jacket potatoes (£3-5), English standards (£4-6) as well as sandwiches and some veggie options (£5-6). Wine, cocktails and hot drinks are also available, although beer is the mainstay. Food served M-F noon-7pm, Sa-Su noon-3pm. Open M-F 11am-11pm, Sa-Su noon-6pm. AmEx/MC/V. Wheelchair accessible. ❶

The Golden Fleece, Queen's St. between Cheapside and Queen Victoria. (☎7236 1433). ⊖Mansion House. A genuine old-boy's pub, the very traditional Golden Fleece (or "The Fleece") has a distinct lounge-like feel. Like most pubs in the area, it's built for after-work socializing. Booths in the back offer privacy and raised chairs in the front are more open. A massive oak wood bar sits in the center of the room where bartenders circle to pour drinks; the Fleece has so many brews that it's hard to choose (£2-6). Sandwiches and full meals £2.50-£6.95. Monthly pool tournaments and occasional special events. Open M-F 11am-11pm. MC/V. ❶

CLERKENWELL

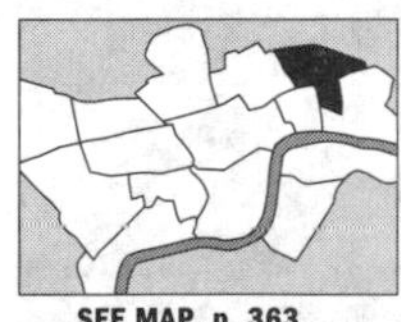

SEE MAP, p. 363

CLERKENWELL QUICKFIND: Discover, p. 7; sights, p. 95; museums & galleries, p. 143; food, p. 169; nightlife, p. 210; entertainment, p. 235; accommodations, p. 285.

The Jerusalem Tavern, 55 Britton St. (☎7490 4281; www.stpetersbrewery.co.uk). ⊖Farringdon. Tiny and wonderfully ancient, this Dickensian pub offers many niches in which to get your drink on, including a bizarre one-table balcony right across from the bar. The broad selection rewards the adventuresome with specialty ales (£2.40) like grapefruit, cinnamon and apple, elderberry, and the delicious Suffolk Gold. Taste cases of their speciality beer (£26). Solid pub grub runs £5-8. Popular with the locals, the small space fills up at night. Open M-F 11am-11pm, Sa 5-11pm, Su 11am-5pm. MC/V. ❷

The Eagle, 159 Farringdon Rd. (☎7837 1353). ⊖Farringdon. As the original gastropub, the always-packed Eagle kicked off the whole stripped-wood, mismatched-furniture craze, transforming pubs into hipster hangouts. Tasty Mediterranean dishes (£7.50-10) and down-to-earth atmosphere that appeals to both lunching businessmen and lingering locals. Open M-F 12:30-2:30pm and 6:30-10:30pm, Sa 12:30-3:30pm and 6:30-10:30pm, Su 12:30-3:30pm. Bar open M-Sa noon-11pm and Su noon-5pm. MC/V. ❷

The Three Kings, 7 Clerkenwell Close. (☎7253 0483). ⊖Farringdon. The bright tri-colored exterior captures the merry atmosphere of this local favorite. The pub is eccentrically decorated—check out the metal rhino head over the mantle and the authentic 1940s jukebox upstairs. Loud and crowded around the bar area at night; look for more privacy in the 2 upper-level rooms. Food £5.25-9. Open M-Th noon-11pm, F-Sa 7pm-11pm. Cash only. ❷

Fox & Anchor, 115 Charterhouse St. (☎7253 5075). ⊖Farringdon. One of the only places in London where you can get a beer with your breakfast (the £9.50 "Business Boy's Breakfast"), this pub is great for an early fix, it does a roaring trade before noon. Reservations are recommended, especially Th-F. Later in the day, expect a quiet and cozy affair. Open M-Th 7am-5pm, F 7am-11pm (may close earlier). AmEx/MC/V. ❷

HOLBORN

HOLBORN QUICKFIND: Discover, p. 7; sights, p. 97; museums & galleries, p. 143; food, p. 170; nightlife, p. 211; entertainment, p. 236; shopping, p. 257; accommodations, p. 286.

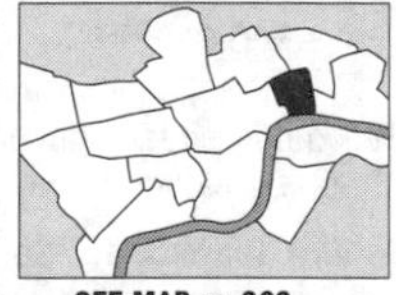

SEE MAP, p. 363

Ye Olde Mitre Tavern, 1 Ely Ct. (☎7405 4751). Off #8 Hatton Garden. ⊖Chancery Ln. To find the alley where this pub hides, look for the street lamp on Hatton Garden bearing a sign of a mitre. This classic pub fully merits its "ye olde"—it was built in 1546 by the Bishop of Ely. The corner still holds the cherry tree planted to divide the Bishop's land from that he rented to Christopher Hatton. With dark oak beams and spun glass, the 2 rooms are perfect for nestling up to a bitter, and you can forget the bustle of Holborn Circus entirely. Popular in the evenings, the pub and its tiny Ely Ct. generally fill with merriment and people during the summer months. Hot meals subject to availability (about £4), with bar snacks and superior sandwiches (£1.75) served until 9:30pm. Open M-F 11am-11pm. AmEx/MC/V (£10 min.). ❶

Ye Olde Cheshire Cheese, Wine Office Ct. (☎7353 6170; www.yeoldecheshirecheese.com). By 145 Fleet St., not to be confused with The Cheshire Cheese on the other side of Fleet St. ⊖Blackfriars or St. Paul's. A dark labyrinth of oak-paneled, low-ceilinged rooms on 3 floors, dating from 1667, the Cheese was once a haunt of Johnson, Dickens, Mark Twain, and Theodore Roosevelt. Not only does this pub have character; it has several: drink in the small front; munch on sandwiches (£4-5) in the Cheshire at the back; tuck into meaty traditional dishes in the Chop Room (mains £7-10); sup on daily hot specials (£4.95) on the long wooden benches of the downstairs Cellar; or savor fancier cuisine on the 2nd fl. Johnson Room (£7-13). Front open M-Sa 11am-11pm, Su noon-3pm. Cellar Bar open M-F noon-2:30pm, M-Th and Sa 5:30-11pm. Chop Room open M-F noon-9:30pm, Sa noon-2:30pm and 6-9:30pm, Su noon-2:30pm. Johnson Room open M-F noon-2:30pm and 7-9:30pm. AmEx/MC/V (1.5% surcharge). ❷

The Old Bank of England, 194 Fleet St. (☎7430 2255). ⊖Temple. Next to the Royal Courts of Justice and directly across from the entrance to The Temple. Opened on the premises of the 19th-century Bank of England, this pub takes full advantage of its predecessor's towering ceilings, massive oil paintings, and impressive chandeliers. Sweeney Todd, "the Demon Barber of Fleet St.," killed his victims in the tunnels beneath the modern pub; his mistress turned them into meat pies next door. The Old Bank of England is "extremely proud" of its own meat pies (£6.95-7.95). Mains £5-10, sandwiches £3-5. Reservations recommended for lunch. Open M-F 11am-11pm, kitchen closes at 9pm. AmEx/MC/V. ❶

The Punch Tavern, 99 Fleet St. (☎7353 6658). ⊖Blackfriars. This newish gastro-pub occupies the site of the 1840s tavern in which the famous political satire magazine *Punch* was conceived. The decor is suitably *Punch*-inspired, although you'll find no hint of irony in the salad. Buffet-style meals run about £5.50; take-out is cheaper. Open M-F 7am-11pm, food all day. Wheelchair accessible. AmEx/MC/V. ❷

Cittie of Yorke, 22-23 High Holborn St. (☎7242 7670). Next to the Gray's Inn gatehouse on High Holborn. ⊖Chancery Ln. Cittie of Yorke, with its towering raftered ceilings and chandelier from 1695, has served such patrons as Charles Dickens and Samuel Johnson—then again, hasn't everyone? Skip the front room in favor of either the airy, barn-like back bar (overlooking Gray's Inn) or the cozy subterranean Cellar Bar. The latter's lunch special (£5) features solid English fare with good vegetarian options. Open M-Sa 11am-11pm. AmEx/MC/V (£5 min.). ❷

KENSINGTON & EARL'S COURT

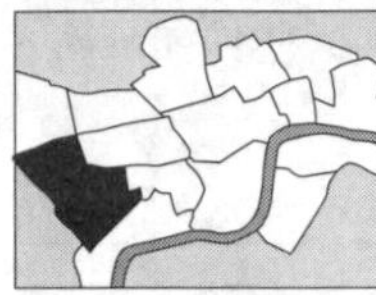

SEE MAP, pp. 364-365

KENSINGTON & EARL'S COURT QUICKFIND: Discover, p. 8; sights, p. 100; museums & galleries, p. 145; food, p. 171; entertainment, p. 236; shopping, p. 257; accommodations, p. 286.

The Troubadour, 265 Old Brompton Rd. (☎7370 1434; www.troubadour.co.uk). ⊖Earl's Court. A combination pub/cafe/deli, each wing is uniquely fantastic. Once upon a time the likes of Bob Dylan, Joni Mitchell, and Paul Simon played in the intimate basement club, and the whole place retains a bohemian appeal. The quirky, dusky decor is equally suited for morning espresso shots and evening vodka shots. Breakfast all day £3-5, meals £5.50-10. Open daily 9am-midnight. MC/V. ❷

The Scarsdale, 23a Edwardes Sq. (☎7937 1811). ⊖High St. Kensington. The pub is hidden down an alleyway off Earl's Court Rd.: turn onto Earl's Walk and follow it to the end, then turn right. Built by a French speculator to house Napoleon's officers following the inevitable conquest of Britain, it's now a picture-perfect pub. Always fantastically popular (dinner reservations are essential, even during the week) and for good reason, considering the elaborate food and great decor. Mains (£10-16) served noon-3pm and 6-10pm, bar food (salads and sandwiches, £5-10) served until 9pm. Open daily noon-11pm. MC/V. ❸

The Drayton Arms, 153 Old Brompton Rd. (☎7835 2301). ⊖Gloucester Rd. or South Kensington. A local favorite on a quiet stretch of shady Old Brompton Rd. This large and airy pub has a percussion motif—the low tables resemble large drums and other drums decorate the walls. Sandwiches (£4.50-7) and mains (£6.70-10) are a mouthful, and served all day. Live music Su nights. Open M-Sa noon-11pm, Su noon-10:30pm. MC/V. ❷

KNIGHTSBRIDGE & BELGRAVIA

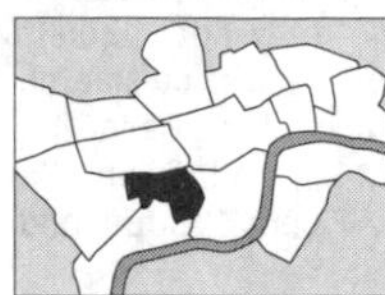

SEE MAP, p. 366

KNIGHTSBRIDGE & BELGRAVIA QUICKFIND: Discover, p. 8; sights, p. 102; food, p. 172; nightlife, p. 211; shopping, p. 258; accommodations, p. 290.

The Gloucester, 187 Sloane St. (☎7235 0298). ⊖Knightsbridge or Sloane Sq. Nestled snugly up against Cartier on devastatingly chic Sloane St., this bit of pleasant wood and brass offers welcome relief from the rarefied air that surrounds it. Advertising: "Homely foods" and cheap drinks, the Gloucester makes for a cheerful rest-stop on your tour of London's poshest. Get some "homeliness" for just £5-7, and a pint for £3-4. Outdoor seating in good weather. Open M-F 11am-11pm, Sa-Su noon-6pm; food daily noon-6pm. MC/V. ❶

The Talbot, Little Chester St. (☎7235 1639). ⊖Knightsbridge or Sloane Sq. Cheerful, bright, airy and peaceful the Talbot beckons both the errant traveler blundering into the quiet Grosvenor mews and the smartly clad professional Londoner taking a lunch break. Meals are simple, hot, and cheap: sandwiches with three fillings £3.25; and hot meals

£5.50. On a hot afternoon, sit outside with a pitcher of Pimm's and lemonade for £10. Takeout available. Open M-F 9am-11pm. MC/V. ❶

Wilton Arms, 71 Kinnerton St. (☎7235 4854). ⊖Knightsbridge or Hyde Park Corner. On a quiet residential street just a hop from Sloane St., this hearty traditional pub offers some cheap meals: Shepherd's Pie, curry dishes, vegetarian dishes, and steak and kidney pie run about £4.75, with lager or bitter starting at £2.60. Open M-Sa 11am-11pm, Su noon-10:30pm; food M-F noon-10pm, Sa noon-3pm. MC/V. ❷

Grouse & Claret, Little Chester St. (☎7235 3438). ⊖Hyde Park Corner or Victoria. A quiet pub on Belgravia mews, with lots of frosted-glass booths and polished wood. Menu changes daily; hot meat sandwiches start at £2.50 and meals from £5. Excellent gammon (roast pork steak) sandwiches (£3.15) and dinners (£6). Lager and bitter from £2.30. Open M-F 11am-11pm. MC/V. ❷

MARYLEBONE & REGENT'S PARK

MARLYEBONE & REGENT'S PARK QUICKFIND: Discover, p. 9; sights, p. 103; museums & galleries, p. 147; food, p. 173; entertainment, p. 237; accommodations, p. 291.

SEE MAP, p. 367

The Golden Eagle, 59 Marylebone Ln. (☎7935 3228). ⊖Bond St. The quintessence of "olde worlde" charm; one of the friendliest pubs around. Sidle up to the bar and enjoy honest-to-God pub singalongs Th-F nights around the much-used piano in the corner. Open M-Sa 11am-11pm, Su noon-7pm. MC/V. ❶

O'Conor Don, 88 Marylebone Ln. (☎7935 9311). ⊖Bond St. Well-known and well-loved authentic Irish pub, with a great big barroom and Guinness ads plastered over the walls. Come here instead of the shamrock-ed theme chains that dot the West End. Open daily noon-11pm. MC/V. ❶

The William Wallace, 33 Aybrook St. (☎7487 4937). ⊖Baker St. or Regent's Park. A true London rarity: a Scottish pub. And with *Braveheart* stills covering the walls and Scottish sporting paraphernalia behind the bar and, the reverence is *not* half-hearted. *Haggis* and black pudding feature prominently on the menu (mains £5-8). Charmingly quiet, except when Scottish sports are playing on the big-screen TV. Food served M-F noon-3pm and 6-11pm. Open M-Sa 11am-11pm, Su noon-10:30pm. MC/V. ❶

the local story

The Demon Barber

Attend the tale of Sweeney Todd.
His skin was pale and his eye was odd.
He shaved the faces of gentlemen
Who never thereafter were heard from again.

These opening lines, from the Stephen Sondheim-Hugh Wheeler musical *Sweeney Todd,* set the stage for a fanciful retelling of a legend. It's the story of a barber who slit the throats of his customers and had a trick chair that dumped their bodies down into storage so that his lover could grind them up and sell them in her meat pie shop. Sondheim's romantic plot and some other details may be a bit off, but there was indeed a Sweeney Todd, and he murdered over 160 people in his Fleet Street barbershop during the 1780s-90s (the site of his killings is the **Old Bank of England** pub). Todd and Lovett were jailed and the shocking details of their crime were revealed to a fascinated public. The suicide of an imprisoned Mrs. Lovett made for another dramatic delay in the trial, but eventually the prosecutors won their case. On January 25th, 1802, Todd was hanged in Newgate Prison. This bloody end was a fitting one for the murderous barber, but the story of his ghastly deeds never faded from the public eye. As Anna Pevord of the *London Observer* wrote in 1979, "Sweeney Todd will never die. We all need bogeymen, and he was bogier than most."

ON THE MENU

Fish 'n' Chips

In 1999, Brits ate nearly 300 million servings of the stuff, and there are currently over 8500 "chip shops" ("chippies" if you like) in the country–that's about 8 for every 1 McDonald's. A beginner's guide to fishy etiquette:

Don't point out the foreignness of it all. Sure, potatoes didn't make it to Europe until Sir Walter Raleigh brought them over from America a few centuries ago, and yes, it was the Belgians who first thought to "chip" their pommes de terre and then fry the shavings into bite-sized snacks, but Brits can get indignant when you question their gastronomic patriotism. Besides, they were the first ones to think to put the two meals together and sell them as a pair (first recorded around 1850).

Don't reach for the mayo. The traditional way to eat your crispy treats is with salt and vinegar. Unless you're Belgian and looking for a scowl, don't even think about adding the très-Continental mayonnaise.

What exactly am I eating? Cod is the classic fish of choice, but haddock is a common alternative.

Never cut off the supply! During WWI, fish 'n chips were two of the only food items *not* to be rationed. At the time, it was boasted that England's signature source of cheap protein and fat helped to fuel the nation to victory.

NOTTING HILL

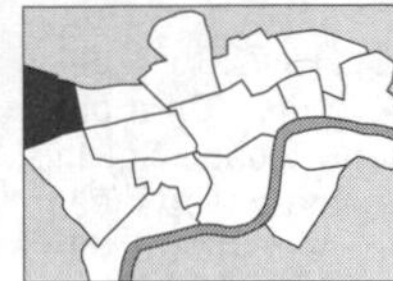

SEE MAP, p. 359

NOTTING HILL QUICKFIND: Discover, p. 9; sights, p. 105; food, p. 174; nightlife, p. 212; entertainment, p. 237; shopping, p. 259, accommodation, p. 292

Portobello Gold, 95-97 Portobello Rd. (☎7460 4900). ⊖Notting Hill Gate. Classic pub with a healthy selection of draughts and ales (£2.30-3). Also has Internet terminals (£1 per 30min.) so punters can surf and drink at the same time. The picturesque restaurant area in back serves lunch, tea, and dinner beneath a sunny glass ceiling. Open daily 10am-10:30pm. Wheelchair accessible. MC/V. ❷

Prince Albert Pub, 11 Pembridge Rd. (☎7727 5244). ⊖Notting Hill Gate. Euro-trendy meets blue-collar at bar-like Prince Albert's. It's comfortably crowded with stylin' 20-somethings. Stained-glass windows and plush sofas fill the lounges and front area. Open daily noon-11pm. ❶

THE SOUTH BANK

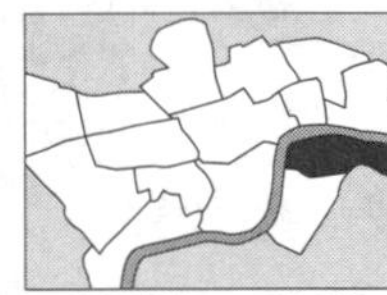

SEE MAP, pp. 368-369

SOUTH BANK QUICKFIND: Discover, p. 10; sights, p. 106; museums & galleries, p. 148; food, p. 176; nightlife, p. 212; entertainment, p. 238; accommodations, p. 292.

The George Inn, 77 Borough High St. (☎7407 2056). ⊖London Bridge. With a mention in Dickens's "Little Dorritt" and the honor of being the only remaining galleried inn in London, the George takes great pride in its historical tradition. A deceptively tiny interior leads out into a popular patio, full of migrants from the City across the river. The ale is excellent, the atmosphere is relaxed, and the proprietor is pleased to share his pub's storied past. Open M-Sa 11am-11pm, Su noon-10:30pm. Wheelchair-accessible patio. AmEx/MC/V. ❶

The Royal Oak, 44 Tabard St. (☎7357 7173). ⊖Borough. This is the real deal: voted the Best Pub of 2003 by the Campaign for Real Ale; the Royal Oak is one of the most pleasant establishments in London. It's not flashy, just family-run, with an intensely loyal group of local patrons in classic Victorian decor. Nostalgically traditional, yet welcoming to outsiders. Superior pub grub (£4-6) served from noon-2:15pm and 6-9:15pm. Open M-F 11:30am-11pm. MC/V. ❶

The Founders Arms, 52 Hopton St. (☎7928 1899). ⊖Southwark. A Young's pub, The Founders managed to snag the best pub real estate south of the Thames. From the open deck and tables on the water, you can order big portions of beer-battered fish 'n' chips (£7.50). The interior feels more like a hotel bar. Lunch served noon-8:30pm, Su noon-8pm; breakfast 9am-11am. Open M-Sa 9am-11pm, Su noon-10:30pm. Wheelchair accessible. MC/V. ❷

The Lord Nelson, Union St, just north of Blackfriar's. (☎ 7207 2701). This quiet pub is tucked into the industrial building surroundings, but it's carved out space enough for a circular outdoor seating area and plenty of games and tables inside. Sports play on the TVs. If it's sunny, you can't beat Lord Nelson for their their patio. Standard pub fare (around £5). Served noon-2:30pm. Senior citizens get beer discounts. Open M-F 11am-11pm, Sa 1-11pm, Su noon-3pm and 7-10:30pm. Wheelchair accessible. ❶

THE WEST END

WEST END QUICKFIND: Discover, p. 10 sights, p. 111; museums & galleries, p. 150; food, p. 177; nightlife, p. 212; entertainment, p. 240; shopping, p. 261; accommodations, p. 292.

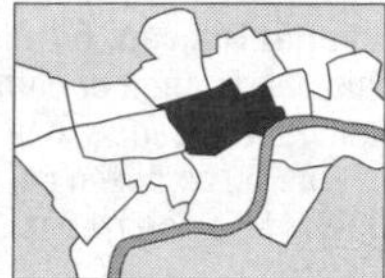

SEE MAP, p. 354

Dog and Duck, 18 Bateman St. (☎7494 0697). ⊖Tottenham Crt. Rd. This historic establishment sits on the past site of the Duke of Monmouth's Soho house, and is the smallest, oldest pub still standing in Soho. The name refers to Soho's previous role as Royal hunting grounds. The gorgeous Victorian tile interior surrounds a little hearth and four tables, more standing room is available near the bar. It's said that George Orwell drank here. Open M-Sa noon-11pm, Su noon-10:30pm. Wheelchair accessible. ❷

The Cross Keys, 31 Endell St. (☎7836 5185). ⊖Convent Garden. It's all about ambience at Cross Keys. The deep red lighting inside makes it the darkest pub around. Check out the strange collection of paintings and antiques and Beatles memorabilia. Outside, the flowers and vines surround picnic tables and umbrellas, ideal for beer in the sun. Food served noon-2:30pm daily. Open M-Sa 11am-11pm, Su noon-10:30pm. Wheelchair accessible. ❶

Lamb and Flag, 33 Rose St. (☎7497 9504). ⊖Leicester Sq. A neighborhood mainstay since the 1700s. Sitting at the end of a cul-de-sac the saloon-like interior serves pints to locals and visitors alike. Patrons spill outside and order beer from the open front window. Charles Dickens liked the Lamb. Regularly packed, but everyone's too happy to even notice. Food served daily noon-3pm. Live jazz upstairs Su from 7:30pm. Open M-Th 11am-11pm, F-Sa 11am-10:45pm, Su noon-10:30pm. Wheelchair-accessible outside seating. ❷

Comptons of Soho, 53 Old Compton St. (☎7479 7961). ⊖Leicester Sq. or Piccadilly Circus. The rainbow flag flies with pride outside Soho's oldest gay pub. Don't be surprised if strangers greet you at the door. Much larger than most pubs, Comptons fills early with a wonderfully friendly, predominantly male crowd of all ages. Horseshoe-shaped bar is open all the time, while the upstairs lounge (opens 6:30pm) has a more mellow scene and a break from the noise. Open M-Sa noon-11pm, Su noon-10:30pm. Wheelchair-accessible outside seating. MC/V. ❶

Maple Leaf, 41 Maiden Ln. (☎7240 2843). Need a break from the local pub scene? Maple Leaf pays homage to all things Canadian, even though the crowd is mostly British. The front-room showcases sports memorabilia (hockey anyone?) and the back "log cabin" room has pictures and uniforms of Canadian Mounties, and of course, a stuffed life size bear. Spacious tables invite you to down Alberta beef-burgers (£6.45), *quebecois poutine* (fries with cheese and gravy; £4) and any other of the Canadian classics on the menu. Oh, Canada! Open M-Sa 11am-11pm, Su noon-10:30pm. AmEx/MC/V. ❷

The Toucan, 19 Carlisle St. (☎7437 4123). ⊖Tottenham Crt. Rd. Small, snug, tight-knit pub right outside of Soho Sq., bursting with Irish pride and with blowzy, affable men swigging Guinness. You can order from the extensive menu of classic or rare Irish whiskeys (£2.50-50). Beer can be ordered to go and taken to Soho Park, 10 ft. away. Arrive before the early-evening crowds. Open M-F 11am-11pm, Sa noon-11pm. ❷

The Shepherds Tavern, 50 Hertford St. (☎7499 3017). ⊖Green Park. In 1735, Edward Shepherd of Shepherd Market fame also lent his name to this local watering hole. The Tavern takes a no-frills approach to pubbing with a well-stocked bar and plenty of space. Though unglamorous except for the random chandeliers hanging from the bright red ceiling, the pub is usually humming with activity both indoors and just outside. Extensive drink menu available. Kitchen (open until 30min. before closing) serves traditional favorites like spotted dick with custard (£3.25). Open M-Sa 11am-11pm, Su noon-3pm and 7-10:30pm. Wheelchair accessible. AmEx/MC/V. ❷

The Duke of York, 7 Dering St. (☎7629 0319). ⊖Bond St. This recently remodeled pub gives you lots of choices while you pack down the pints (£2.60-3). The 3 floors are connected by a spiral staircase right in the middle of the room—the ground floor has games, open space and a big bar. The first floor serves as a restaurant, and the basement as a "comfort zone" is perfect for some lazy lounging or a game of darts. Of course, pubbers are welcome to just lounge outside, as most do. Open M-Sa 11am-11pm; Su noon-10:30pm. MC/V. ❶

Admiral Duncan, 54 Old Compton St. (☎7437 5300). ⊖Leicester Sq. or Piccadilly Circus. This pub is another cornerstone of the Soho gay pub scene. Loyal local men hang out at the Admiral Duncan, a long funky narrow bar in the center of town. A relaxed crowd comes early, but the place doesn't fill until evening. Mostly standing room with space to dance in the back. Open M-Sa noon-11pm, Su noon-10:30pm. Wheelchair accessible. ❶

Bunker Bierhall, under Thomas Neal's at 41 Earlham St. (☎7240 0606; www.bunkerbar.com). One of London's few (and new) microbreweries. Patrons can get house beer or pretty much any other beer or liquor at Bunker. Long wooden tables and benches are perfect for large groups, and lend the pub its bunker-like feel. Small but classic menu draws a dining only crowd too. Lunch deal (£5) M-F noon-3pm offers a choice of mains with a half-pint or glass of wine included. This social, untraditional pub is in a mall, so evening visits are best. Open M-Sa noon-12am, Su 12-10:30pm. MC/V. ❶

WESTMINSTER

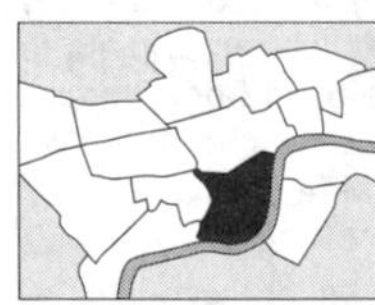

SEE MAP, p. 370

WESTMINSTER QUICKFIND: Discover, p. 11; sights, p. 116; museums & galleries, p. 152; food, p. 181; entertainment, p. 244; accommodations, p. 293.

The Old Shades, 37 Whitehall. (☎7321 2801). ⊖Charing Cross. The front and back rooms are more spacious than almost any other pub around. The rear lounge area has sofas and is a bit removed from the bustle of the open streetside front. Lunchtime crowds aside, The Old Shades offers up a great assortment of bitters and the perfect break from the throngs in Trafalgar Sq. The food is a cut above the usual pub standard, serving solid British fare (£5-7). Open M-Sa 11am-11pm, Su noon-3pm & 7-10:30pm. Wheelchair accessible. MC/V. ❶

Sherlock Holmes, 10-11 Northumberland St. (☎7930 2644); www.sherlockholmespub.homestead.com. ⊖Charing Cross. In the former Northumberland Hotel, as mentioned in the *Hound of the Baskervilles*. Numerous Holmesian "artifacts" are displayed in the pub, acquired with help from Sir Arthur Conan Doyle's family. There's no mystery in the excellent upstairs restaurant (mains £9-13), just à la carte Brit food, and patrons can even view a replica of Holmes's study. Cheaper pub food is served downstairs and is fairly standard. Sherlock Holmes Ale £2.30. Sandwiches £3.95-5.95. Hot meals £5.95. Food served daily noon-10pm. Open M-Sa 11am-11pm, Su noon-10:30pm. Restaurant open M-Th noon-3pm, and 5:30-10pm; F-Su noon-10pm. Groundfloor is wheelchair-accessible. MC/V. ❶

Red Lion, 48 Parliament St. (☎7930 5826). ⊖Westminster. TVs carrying the Parliament cable channel and portraits of politicians on the walls remind you that this is still the original politico's pub. MPs listen to the debates over a warm pint, while a "division bell" alerts them to drink up when a vote is about to be taken. Very chill place, despite the distinguished clientele, plus the food (sandwiches £3-4, hot dishes £6) is dependable, if not flashy. Downstairs cellar bar offers more space for crowded hours. Open M-Sa 11am-11pm, Su noon-7pm. Food served daily noon-2:30pm, snacks noon-3pm. Wheelchair accessible. MC/V. ❶

The Cask and Glass, 39-41 Palace St. ⊖St. James's Park or Victoria. As one of the smallest pubs around, it's certainly among the coziest. This pleasant, carpeted, quiet establishment is a second home to a loyal troop of patrons who throw back the pints while admiring the mix of political cartoons and model airplanes that decorate the place. Outdoor tables nestled among hanging plants are lovely in nice weather. Decent sandwiches £3.50. Ploughman's lunch £4.25. Open M-F 11am-11pm. Wheelchair accessible. ❶

The Phoenix, Corner of Palace and Stag Pl. ⊖St. James' Park or Victoria. (☎7834 3547) A huge, friendly pub just down the block from the palace and galleries. Serves a lunchtime work crowd and a steady stream of sports devotees and visitors. Large tables and chairs lining the walls add to the social atmosphere; screen projection TV plays whatever sporting event is going on. The food here is decent, two mains for £6 (otherwise £4.45 each) and great baguette sandwiches for £1.45-3. Any sandwich with crisps and a coke, £3.50. Open M-F 11am-11pm, Sa 10am-6pm. Wheelchair accessible. AmEx/MC/V (£3 min.). ❶

NORTH LONDON

NORTH LONDON QUICKFIND: Discover, p. 12; sights, p. 120; museums & galleries, p. 153; food, p. 183; nightlife, p. 218; entertainment, p. 244; shopping, p. 269; accommodations, p. 294.

Compton Arms, 4 Compton Ave. (☎7359 6883; www.comptonarms.net). ⊖Highbury or Islington. Removed enough from Upper St. to escape the hectic crowds. Low ceilings and multicolored bar stools enhance the amiable atmosphere. The big draw is the "beer garden" which is a picturesque outdoor patio where locals enjoy their sausages and mash. Diverse clientele. Su comedy video night. Food served daily noon-2:30pm and 6-8:30pm. Open M-Sa noon-11pm, Su noon-10:30pm. ❶

Duke of Cambridge, 30 St. Peter's St. (☎7359 3066). This pub is dedicated to the art of environmentally responsible dining, from the sophisticated gastropub menu to the must-try organic beer selection. Specializing in fresh dishes with surprise ingredients, the kitchen changes the menu twice a day. Mains £7-13. Dinner M-Sa 6:30-10:30pm, Su 6:30-10pm; lunch M-F 12:30-3pm, Sa-Su 12:30-3:30pm. Open M-Sa noon-11pm, Su noon-10:30pm. AmEx/MC/V. ❷

NO WORK ALL PLAY

Great British Beer Festival

The beer-lover's dream come true, the annual Great British Beer Festival houses over 450 ales under roof. If it's beer, and it's good, you'll find it here. The festival is organized by the Campaign for Real Ale (CAMRA) every year in early August. Obscure micro-breweries, big names, and international brands are all represented. Some breweries, including Courage, Fuller, and Adnams, even have their own bars. The budding connoisseur can learn from the experts with tutored beer tastings (tickets go quickly, book in advance).

The prestigious Champion Beer of Britain awards are also handed out for milds, bitters, best bitters, strong bitters, specialty beers, and real ales. The Champion award is considered the consumer's top choice award, and those at the festival get first taste of the winners.

Beer is obviously the main focus of the festival, but food, entertainment, and even non-alcoholic drinks get some space. Food stalls sell international fare, plus traditional pub foods like cornish pastries, sausages, and pork scratching. Entertainment includes live music, pub games, and street theatre, including the popular balloon twiddlers.

For tickets or more information, go to www.camra.org.uk or call ☎2786 7201.

The Wenlock Arms, 26 Wenlock Rd. (not Wenlock St.) (☎7608 3406; www.wenlock-arms.co.uk) ⊖Old St. or Angel. This award-winning traditional pub is the real deal, with a large array of ales, including many local brews. It also has the best hot salt beef sandwich in the city (£3). The atmosphere is warm and relaxed. Food served "until we run out of bread." Open Tu-F 11am-7pm, Sa 10am-4pm. Wheelchair accessible. MC/V. ❶

The Castle, 54 Pentonville Rd. (☎7713 1858) ⊖Angel. The Castle with the neighborhood pub mentality but the decor and style of a local bar optimizes the idea of the pub bar. Inside striped wallpaper, flower vases and funky decor give it a trendy edge; sofas make it lounge-like. Upstairs the roof terrace looks inviting from the street. Pub food (£2-7) and an extensive drink selection available, of course. Open M-Sa 11am-10pm, Su noon- 10pm. ❶

Camden Head, 2 Camden Walk (☎7359 0851). ⊖Angel. This pub gets its Victorian identity from the chintzy rose wallpaper and plenty of etched glass. Bridging the gap between the antique market and the rest of the area, it's removed from most Islington yuppie hangouts. Jug of Pimms with vodka and Red Bull £10. Food served daily noon-9:30pm, 2 meals for £6. Also offers comedy nights upstairs starting daily around 9pm, W and Su around 8. Open M-Sa 11am-11pm, Su noon-10:30pm. Wheelchair accessible. ❶

King William IV (KW4), 77 Hampstead High St. (☎7435 5647). The buttercup yellow exterior and the rainbow flag fluttering outside the well-kept, 18th-century facade says it all—a rocking gay bar in the body of a Victorian pub. The most popular event here is the traditional British Su lunch (£6.50). During the summer KW4 hosts barbecues in the sizable beer garden (Sa-Su). Pub food served daily noon-4pm. Open M-Sa noon-11pm, Su noon-10:30pm. Wheelchair accessible.❶

The World's End, 174 Camden High St. (☎7482 1932). ⊖Camden Town. Although Camden doesn't have the most vibrant pub scene, this one is smack in the middle of all the Camden Town action. The World's End is permanently buzzing, but with two massive rooms, a restaurant, club, and a balcony, this huge space can feel a little empty, and it claims to be "probably the largest pub in the world." Located below the pub, The Underworld venue hosts live bands. Open M-Th 11am-11pm, F-Sa 11am-midnight, Su noon-10:30pm. Partially wheelchair accessible. ❶

The Flask, 77 Highgate West Hill (☎8348 7346). Bus #214 from Kentish Town or #210 from Archway. Walking will take twice as long as you think. Built in 1663, the low-ceilinged, intricate interior of this pub is perfect for winter evenings or a little bit of quiet. In summer, drinkers mingle on the extensive patio or in the park across the street. The changing menu mixes Olde English (sausage and mash £8) with modern British (sandwiches around £5). Open M-Sa 11am-11pm, Su noon-10:30pm. MC/V. ❷

Freemason's Arms, 32 Downshire Hill (☎7433 6811). ⊖Hampstead. All that you'd expect from a pub, but much larger, with a fuller menu and a sizable beer garden. The inside was designed by Erno Goldfinger, of nearby 2 Willow Rd. fame, in what was obviously one of his boring, traditional moments. Open M-Sa noon-11pm, Su noon-10:30pm. AmEx/MC/V. ❷

EAST LONDON

EAST LONDON QUICKFIND: Discover, p. 13; sights, p. 126; museums & galleries, p. 156; food, p. 187; nightlife, p. 222; entertainment, p. 271; shopping, p. 271.

Prospect of Whitby, 57 Wapping Wall (☎7481 1095). ⊖Wapping. From tube exit turn right, follow the street around the bend, right turn onto Wapping Wall and walk about 3 blocks down. A little out of the way, but worth it. This fantastic 1520 pub should be visited just for the spectacular river view, but it has the added advantage of 2 inside dining spaces and a brilliant outdoor patio. The ship-like interior is friendly, and the food jumps between the ultra-traditional and more modern. Mains £6-7, sandwiches £3-5. Food M-Sa noon-9pm, Su noon-3pm and 6-9pm. Open M-F 11:30am-11pm, Su noon-10:30pm. AmEx/MC/V. ❶

The Macbeth, 70 Hoxton Street (☎7739 5095). ⊖Old St. The exterior is underwhelming, but inside the friendly bartenders and patrons chatter away at the bar, pool table, and worn-in couches. There's a stage and small dance space for F-Su DJs and music. W karaoke nights are another weekly staple as is the Su traditional roast lunch. Food served M-Sa 11am-7pm. Open M-Sa 11am-11pm, Su noon-10:30pm. Wheelchair accessible. MC/V. ❶

Cat and Canary, 1-24 Fisherman's Walk (☎7512 9187). DLR: Canary Wharf. Follow signs to the North Promenade; it's at the far left end of the walk. A fairly standard Fuller's pub, the Cat and Canary has an expansive river view, plenty of outdoor tables, and a classy interior. The patrons are mostly business people relaxing after leaving the Docklands office towers. The food is a step beyond fish 'n' cips, with specials like goat cheese salad. Specials and mains £5.25-7.50. Food served M-F 11am-11pm, Sa 11am-4pm. Open M-Sa 11am-11pm, Su noon-10:30pm. Wheelchair accessible. AmEx/MC/V. ❷

NESCAFE
.co.uk
McDonalds
GAP
GAP

INSIDE

Nightlife

NIGHTLIFE BY TYPE

BARS (DRINKING)

Brits *love* to drink, and these days, drinking is the new dancing, and bars are the new nightclubs. The range of styles and ambiances that you can find is incredible. An explosion of club-bars has invaded the previously forgotten zone between pubs and clubs, offering stylish surroundings and top-flight DJs, with plentiful lounging space and a wide selection of bottled lagers (the current "in" drink). In fact, these places are the most fun to frequent. Often incorporating both restaurants and dance floors, the new bars are designed as one-stop nightspots, combining all you need for an evening's entertainment under one roof. They tend to close earlier than clubs, usually between midnight and 2am, so you'll need to move on to a "real" nightclub for late night early morning action.

DRINK FREELY, DRINK EARLY. It is enormously easier to find a bar without a cover charge around 10pm than it is just an hour later.

NIGHTCLUBS (DANCING)

Most major DJs in the world either live in London or make frequent visits to the city. While the US may have introduced house music to the world, the UK has taken the lead in developing and experimenting with new types of dance music, and club culture in London is all pervasive—18 to 30 year old Londoners are the audience for DJs. Such is the variety and fast-changing nature of London nightlife that even weekly publications have trouble keeping up—even *Time Out*, the Londoner's clubbing bible, only lists about half the club happenings in London on any given night. The shelf-life of clubs is understandably not too long, don't be surprised if something's opened and closed within the calendar year. Instead, walk down the street and you're sure to find another venue that will probably be just as fun.

DRESS. London clubs often fall into one of two categories: those for dancing, and those for lounging. In the former, dress codes are generally relaxed; it's not uncommon to find clubbers dressed in nothing fancier than jeans, a stylish T-shirt, and trainers (sneakers), although women are usually expected to make more of an effort and pulling on a pair of "proper" shoes is a good idea (many clubs allow jeans but not sneakers). At loungers/posers' clubs, however, dress is crucial, and what's expected depends very much on the scene. If you're not sure what to wear, call up the club beforehand (although answers like "New York super-funk glam" aren't always that helpful); otherwise, black and slinky is generally safe. The exception to the categorization are theme nights, especially retro clubs—you're unlikely to get in unless you look like an extra from *Saturday Night Fever*. If a bouncer says it's "members and regulars only," he thinks you're not up to scratch; however, that's rare (especially if you're female or in the company of many females) and persistence can pay off, especially when accompanied by a sob story—like how it's your best friend's birthday and she's already inside. Theme nights are not the standard though, and most any night you'll be fine without a getup.

PLANNING. Planning is important for the discriminating clubber. Look before you leap, and especially before you drink. Avoid the bright glitzy clubs of Leicester Sq. (e.g. Equinox and Hippodrome), in which no Londoner would be seen dead—they're crowded with out-of-town English youth looking to get lucky. Plus, drinks are pricey and the music predictable. Instead, comb through listings in *Time Out* which also prints the weekly "TOP" club pass. The latter gives you discounts on entry to many of the week's shenanigans. Call or check online for guest list entry, sometimes it's as easy as a double click. For popular clubs, it's worth learning the names of the DJs (not to mention the type of music) just to prove to the bouncer that you're part of the scene. Go a little early to the popular night spots. Just because there's no queue outside doesn't mean there won't be one later. Working out **how to get home** afterwards is crucial; remember that the Tube and regular buses stop shortly after midnight, and after 1am black cabs are like gold dust. If there's no convenient night bus home, ask the club in advance if they can order a minicab (unlicensed taxicab) for you later on the night; otherwise, order your own (see **Service Directory,** p. 338 for phone numbers). Although it's technically illegal for minicabs to ply for hire, whispered calls of "taxi, taxi" or honking horns signal their presence outside clubs and in nightlife-heavy neighborhoods—however, you've no guarantee that the driver is reputable or even insured. If you have no other option, agree on a price before you get in, and never ride alone. The best option is to take a minute or two to look at the **night bus map** before you leave home so you know how to get back.

FLIER EDUCATION. Don't go straight for the dustbin when you get a bit of pushy advertising thrust on you at a street corner. Various nightspots have a reduced admission price for those entering with their specific flier.

SELECTED CLUB NIGHTS

London clubbing revolves around promoters and the nights they organize rather than the bricks-and-mortar clubs themselves. For this reason you're liable to see posters advertising four events with different names at the same venue. This gives London clubbing both its incredible range and its infuriating/charming (take your pick) ephemeral nature, as promoters arrange one-off events, move regular nights between clubs, or just get married and find a "proper" job. Below is a selection of some club nights; however, it's inevitable that some will move to different clubs or different nights, shift from weekly to monthly, or simply fold altogether. Always call ahead to check the details still hold, and don't forget that these listings barely scrape the surface of what's offered.

GAY NIGHTS

G-A-Y, see Soho, p. 216.

Fusion, every other F at the Fridge. The best gay night this side of Fabric's *DTPM*, it's a shiny happy antidote to the dirtier feel of much of London's gay scene. The boys are hot and hunky, yes, but there's a friendly good-time vibe that's reflected a thousand times over in the Fridge's ubiquitous disco balls. Open 10pm-5am. Cover £12 with flyer, £10 in advance, £5 before 10:30pm.

Popstarz, F at Scala (www.popstarz.org). A long-running gay/mixed extravaganza. Covers the whole musical spectrum, for better or worse: the Rubbish Room is devoted to the most embarrassing hits of the 80s, the Love Lounge hosts 70s funk and disco, indie lives in the Common Room, while house stays home in the Big Beat Bar. A few current hits are sprinkled around in each room. Open 10pm-5am. Cover £8.

DANCE

Shake, Sa at the Electric Ballroom (see p. 220). With space for over 1000 people, there's plenty of room (sometimes too much) on the 3 floors. Happy dancers groove to a range of 70s, 80s, and 90s disco music. Open 10:30pm-4am. Cover £10.

FUNK AND JAZZ

Deep Funk, F at Madame Jojo's (see p. 215). Resident Keb Darge's legendary funk jam night: funkier than an evening with James Brown, plumbing the depths of 60s and 70s music. The vibe is an unpretentious and jolly anecdote to the mega-disco-tech-club headache of some of the more self-serious nightspots. Most of the laid-back student crowd is content to sit back and watch the amazing feats of the dedicated movers and shakers on the sunken dance floor. Things get churning around 11:30pm. Open 10pm-3am. Cover £8; £6 before 11pm.

the hidden deal

Cheap Groovin'

Like many things in London, clubbing is an expensive pastime. Cover charges run £10-15, and you'll probably spend as much again on drinks—even a beer will set you back £3-5. Add in a taxi home, and an evening's out can easily set you back £50.

There are ways of limiting the damage. First, **arrive early**—cover charges rise after 10 or 11pm. Since most clubs don't get busy until midnight, though, it's easy to lose the savings in extra drinks until the dance floor fills up.

Bring a **club flyer** along. Usually available in dance-music shops, presenting a flyer often saves you pounds at the door.

Avoid weekends and instead opt for **midweek clubbing** when cover charges are lower. London has enough students, slackers, and devoted party people to pack a few clubs even Sunday-Wednesday.

Alternatively, skip nightclubs altogether and head to a **bar.** Increasingly popular, these have smaller dance floors (and more couches), but still attract top DJs for covers that tend to be lower, varying from free to £5.

THIS! (That's How It Is), M at Bar Rumba (see p. 215). On a Monday you won't do better than THIS! Eclectic sounds all night, from Miles Davis to dance, jazz-funk with other genres thrown in. You could chill and listen for hours, and most people do, though there's no shortage of freestylers bopping and swerving on the floor, which opens up as the night progresses. Open 9pm-3:30am. Cover £5.

INDIE & ALTERNATIVE

Sincity, F at the Electric Ballroom (see p. 220). London's oldest and best-known alternative night; goths flock to this festival of leather, ripped lace, and pierced flesh. Mostly alternative, industrial techno, and punk beats. Open 10:30pm-4am. Cover £7, student £5.

NIGHTLIFE BY NEIGHBORHOOD

CLERKENWELL

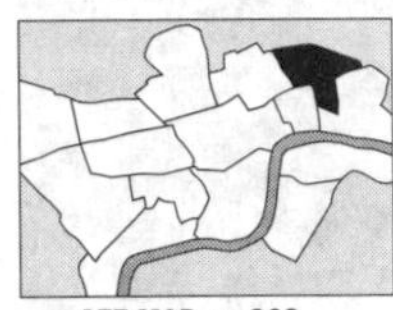

SEE MAP, p. 363

CLERKENWELL QUICKFIND: Discover, p. 7; sights, p. 95; museums & galleries, p. 143; food, p. 169; pubs, p. 196; entertainment, p. 235; accommodations, p. 285.

If London's fashionable epicenter has shifted east to Hoxton, so much the better for Clerkenwell—less posing, more partying! Most nightspots are found around Charterhouse St. and St. John's St., with a lower concentration on Clerkenwell Rd. Be aware that this isn't the most pleasant area to walk at night; while it doesn't have a particularly dangerous reputation, the streets tend to be narrow, winding, and dark, so you may feel uncomfortable by yourself, especially females. A few ambitious drug dealers like to hang out by Farringdon station to offer their wares to the club crowd; they'll generally leave you alone if you ignore them.

DRINKING

Cafe Kick, 43 Exmouth Market (☎7837 8077; www.cafekick.co.uk). ⊖Farringdon or Angel. Dedicated to the twin goals of drinking and football (soccer), Kick has covered its every available surface with footy paraphernalia. There's a jovial, Latin American feel to this cafe-bar, dominated by multiple foosball tables (50p per game) which play host to monthly table football contests. Happy Hour daily 4-7pm (beer of the day £1.50, cocktails £4.50). Otherwise, beers and cocktails £2.50-5.50. Open M-F noon-11pm, Sa 1-11pm, Su 1-10:30pm. MC/V.

Match EC1, 45-47 Clerkenwell Rd. (☎7250 4002; www.matchbar.com). ⊖Farringdon or Barbican. With an original drink list full of exclusive concoctions created by Match bartenders and NYC's Dale DeGroff ("The King of Cocktails" of Rainbow Room fame), Match has made its reputation with quality cocktails (£6-10) and a yuppie-tastic following. The family-style "big bowl" dishes (£7-20) are ideal for group meals, while the sunken bar and plush setting make it an ideal spot for lounging. Open M-Sa 11am-midnight. AmEx/MC/V.

DANCING

Fabric, 77a Charterhouse St. (☎7336 8898; www.fabriclondon.com). ⊖Farringdon. One of London's premier clubbing venues; expect lines. Fabric is large, loud, and boasts a vibrating "bodysonic" dance floor that is actually one giant speaker (a unique experience that will hammer some rhythm into even your most uptight friends). Chill-out beds, multiple bars, and three dance floors crammed with up to 1900 hopping Londoners complete the scene; the rather young crowd is generally dressed down. F Fabric Live (hip-hop, breakbeat, "soundclash;" 9:30pm-5am; cover £12), Sa (house, techno, electro; 10pm-7am; £15), Su DTPM polysexual night (house; 10pm-5am; £15; www.dtpm.net). Wheelchair accessible. MC/V (only at bar; £15 min.).

Fluid, 40-42 Charterhouse St. (☎7253 3444). ⊖Farringdon or Barbican. Sushi bar by day, intimate nightclub by night, Fluid is the perfect antidote to megaclub madness (and the restaurant, with dishes ranging £3-15, isn't bad either). The basement dance floor, adorned with a Tokyo cityscape at one end and a glowing bar at the other, is too small for serious dancing. Chill upstairs on the fabu leather couches under soft projections. Th Orient Express beats and breaks; F Fluid Session friendly funk; Sa Eye Candy funky house. Generally free before 10pm (Sa 11pm), cover £3. Restaurant open Tu-W noon-midnight, Th-F noon-3pm and 5-10pm; club Th-Sa 8pm-2am. Wheelchair accessible. MC/V.

Turnmills, 63b Clerkenwell Rd. (☎7250 3409; www.turnmills.co.uk). ⊖Farringdon. Clubbing Tomb-Raider style: enter through a Spanish restaurant into a subterranean maze of themed zones, from post-industrial jungle to French bistro. The glammed-up, affluent crowd is more intent on eyeing up than getting down. Dress code: no sportswear, white sneakers, or light jeans. Tu Salsa (classes from 6:30pm-midnight); F The Gallery mainstream house with art show (10:30pm-7:30am; £12 before 11:30pm, £15 after); Sa Headstart heavier, deeper sounds with an artier crowd (10pm-5am; £15-20). Open M-Th varying hours (free-£8). 18 and over. MC/V at bar.

HOLBORN

HOLBORN QUICKFIND: Discover, p. 7; sights, p. 97; museums & galleries, p. 143; food, p. 170; pubs, p. 197; entertainment, p. 236; shopping, p. 257; accommodations, p. 286.

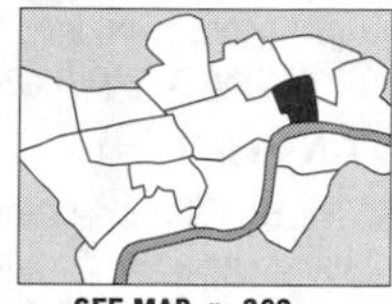

SEE MAP, p. 363

DRINKING

Na Zdrowie, 11 Little Turnstile (☎7831 9679). ⊖Holborn. Hidden in the pub-filled alleyways behind the Holborn Tube station—when you see Pu's Brasserie, look to the left. The name (pronounced nah-ZDROVE-yeh) is a Polish toast, and everything about this classy, well-hidden gem cries out for the mother country. That means the food menu is packing some impressive kielbasa and pirogues (hearty dishes and substantial helpings £5-7; sandwiches with salad start at £2.50), and chrome Polish eagles scowl down at you from the mosaic-mirrored walls. But best of all is the bar's bold alcoholic salute to its homeland's favorite beverage: over 65 types of vodka are available at about £2.10 a shot (add a mixer for 60p). Popular at night--but come anytime and you'll enjoy this different type of Eastern experience. (But don't worry, no polka, we promise.) Open M-F 12:30-11pm, Sa 6-11pm. Wheelchair accessible. MC/V.

The Three Tuns, Houghton St. (☎7476 1672). ⊖Holborn. From Holborn walk south on Kingsway and turn left onto Aldwych, then turn left onto Houghton St.; it's in the LSE's Clare Market Bldg. on the right. Miss dorm life? Wish you could experience the dingy exhilaration of the college social scene? Head over to this student bar (part of the London School of Economics) and bask in the booze and bookishness. Open during schoolyear M-Th 11am-11pm, F 11am-2am, Sa 7:30pm-2am. Holidays 11am-7:30pm. Wheelchair accessible.

KNIGHTSBRIDGE & BELGRAVIA

KNIGHTSBRIDGE & BELGRAVIA QUICKFIND: Discover, p. 8; sights, p. 102; food, p. 172; pubs; shopping, p. 258.

SEE MAP, p. 366

DRINKING

Blue Bar, Berkeley Hotel, Wilton Pl. (☎7201 1680). ⊖Knightsbridge. Swankified Knightsbridge is not the place to go for a low-key night of inexpensive drinking, so you might as well do it up high-style and take your liquor with the celebrity and jet-setting crowds do. Blue Bar is suitably marine-hued for its moniker, with a sumptuous decor that can best be described as eclectic expensive. A cocktail list including over 50 types of finely aged whiskey. This is rich London at its best (dress code: no jeans, sneakers, or T-shirts). No food served. Open M-Sa 4pm-1am. Wheelchair accessible. MC/V.

NOTTING HILL

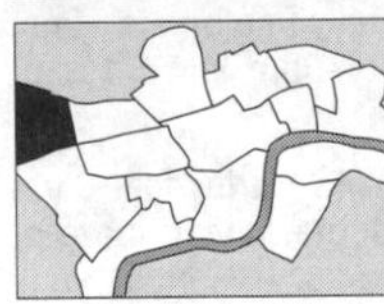
SEE MAP, p. 359

NOTTING HILL QUICKFIND: Discover, p. 9; sights, p. 105; food, p. 174; pubs, p. 212; entertainment, p. 237; shopping, p. 259, accommodations, p. 292.

DRINKING

The Market, 240A Portobello Rd. (☎7229 6472). ⊖Ladbroke Grove. Look for the strange iron-like sculpture above the door. It's consistently the loudest spot on Portobello, and that's saying alot. The Market has a rowdy, unpretentious atmosphere in tune with the local Caribbean vibe. Huge mirrors, dripping candles and plenty of space make it a fine place to appreciate the West Indian/Notting Hill atmosphere. Make some friends while downing a cool Cuban punch (£3). Thai food weekdays noon-3pm. Open M-Sa 11am-11pm, Su noon-12:30am. Wheelchair accessible.

Visible, 299 Portobello Rd. (☎8969 0333) ⊖Ladbroke Grove. None of the reggae madness of the other area bars, but equally appealing. Visible has a sexy red-and-blue interior and some of the softest, slouchiest couches around. You won't be able to get up for drinks, and at £6.50 a pop, you won't want to. Delectable drinks like the Pixie (raspberry and cinnamon vodka, orange and mango juice) fill the menu. MC/V.

DANCING

Notting Hill Arts Club, 21 Notting Hill Gate (☎7460 4459). ⊖Notting Hill Gate. Excellent place for relaxed grooving: turntables on folding tables, a dance floor, and minimal decoration, this no-frills basement still manages to rock. Not at all touristy, and very chill. A friendly, casual venue for rock stars and Rastafarians to sip cocktails (£2.50-5) and move to a range of eclectic music. Acts vary daily; DJs are also great. As the night goes on the doormen operate a 1 in 1 out policy. Get there early to claim some space and avoid a wait. M cover £4, before 9pm free; Tu-Th £5, before 8pm free; F £6, before 8pm free; Sa-Su £5, before 6pm free. Open M-W 6pm-1am, Th-F 6pm-2am, Sa 4pm-2am, Su 4pm-12:30am.

THE SOUTH BANK

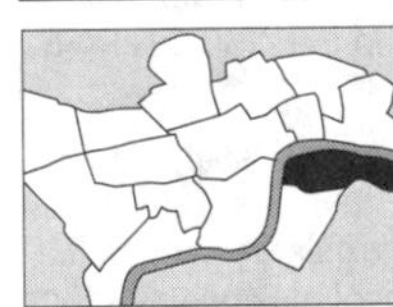
SEE MAP, pp. 368-369

SOUTH BANK QUICKFIND: Discover, p. 10; sights, p. 106; museums & galleries, p. 148; food, p. 176; pubs, p. 200; entertainment, p. 238; accommodations, p. 292.

Ministry of Sound, 103 Gaunt St. (☎7378 6528; www.ministryofsound.co.uk). ⊖Elephant and Castle. Take the exit for South Bank University. Mecca for serious clubbers worldwide—arrive before it opens or queue all night. It's the crowd and the atmosphere they come for. Emphasis on dancing rather than decor, with a massive main room, smaller 2nd dance fl., and always-packed overhead balcony bar. Dress code generally casual, but famously unsmiling door staff make it sensible to err on the side of smartness (no jeans or sneakers, especially Sa). F Smoove garage and R&B (10:30pm-5am; cover £13); Sa Rulin US and vocal house (11pm-8am; cover £17).

THE WEST END

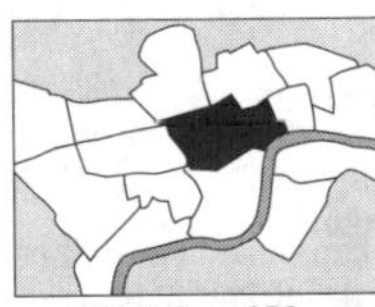
SEE MAP, p. 354

OXFORD ST. & REGENT ST.

OXFORD ST. & REGENT ST. QUICKFIND: Discover, p. 10; sights, p. 111; museums & galleries, p. 150; food, p. 177; pubs, p. 201; entertainment, p. 240; shopping, p. 261; accommodations, p. 292.

DRINKING

Trap, 201 Wardour St. (☎7434 3820, www.traplondon.com). ⊖Oxford Circus or Tottenham Crt. Rd. The coolest new bar/club in town, Trap took the place of the now-defunct Propaganda. Upstairs bar area invites lounging, and of course, drinking amid the mood lighting and beautiful people. The downstairs bar and dance floor

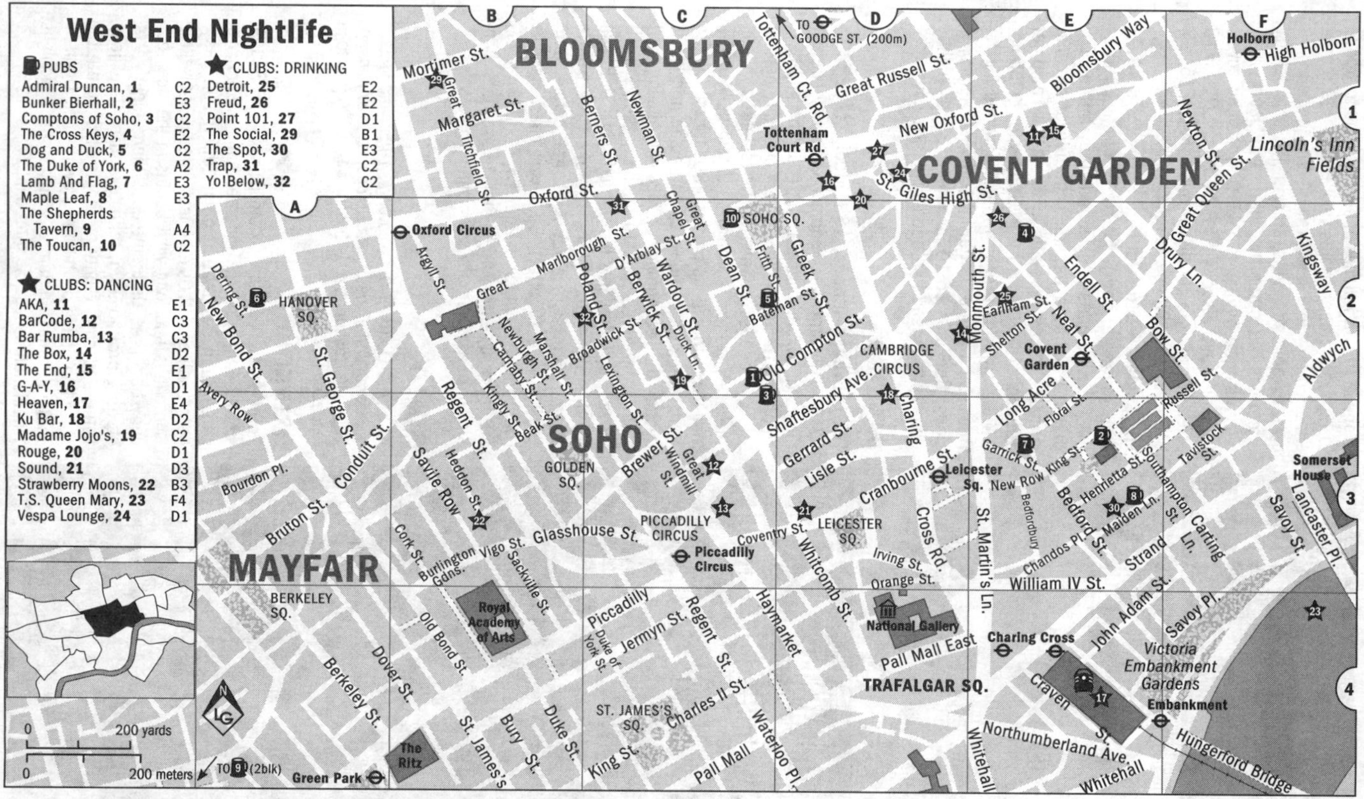

West End Nightlife

PUBS

Admiral Duncan, **1**	C2
Bunker Bierhall, **2**	E3
Comptons of Soho, **3**	C2
The Cross Keys, **4**	E2
Dog and Duck, **5**	C2
The Duke of York, **6**	A2
Lamb And Flag, **7**	E3
Maple Leaf, **8**	E3
The Shepherds Tavern, **9**	A4
The Toucan, **10**	C2

CLUBS: DANCING

AKA, **11**	E1
BarCode, **12**	C3
Bar Rumba, **13**	C3
The Box, **14**	D2
The End, **15**	E1
G-A-Y, **16**	D1
Heaven, **17**	E4
Ku Bar, **18**	D2
Madame Jojo's, **19**	C2
Rouge, **20**	D1
Sound, **21**	D3
Strawberry Moons, **22**	B3
T.S. Queen Mary, **23**	F4
Vespa Lounge, **24**	D1

CLUBS: DRINKING

Detroit, **25**	E2
Freud, **26**	E2
Point 101, **27**	D1
The Social, **29**	B1
The Spot, **30**	E3
Trap, **31**	C2
Yo!Below, **32**	C2

BLOOMSBURY
COVENT GARDEN
SOHO
MAYFAIR
TO GOODGE ST. (200m)
Holborn
High Holborn
Tottenham Court Rd.
Oxford Circus
Piccadilly Circus
Leicester Sq.
Covent Garden
Charing Cross
Embankment
Green Park
TO 9 (2blk)
HANOVER SQ.
SOHO SQ.
GOLDEN SQ.
BERKELEY SQ.
LEICESTER SQ.
ST. JAMES'S SQ.
TRAFALGAR SQ.
CAMBRIDGE CIRCUS
PICCADILLY CIRCUS
Lincoln's Inn Fields
Somerset House
Royal Academy of Arts
National Gallery
The Ritz
Victoria Embankment Gardens
Oxford St.
Regent St.
Piccadilly
Shaftesbury Ave.
Charing Cross Rd.
Strand
Whitehall
Haymarket
0 200 yards
0 200 meters

is one of the only places in the West End to groove to hip-hop. Super exclusive VIP and Red rooms are open only to a select few. The huge spaces fill up on weekend nights. Rockin' list of celebrity attendees has made this the new "it" spot. Tu-W bar and food available, R&B DJ spins; no cover. Th soul, funk, disco. F R&B club night (Th-F £10 after 10pm). Sa *Sintillate* mix (cover £15; £7 before 10pm). Wheelchair accessible.

The Social, 5 Little Portland St. (☎7636 4992; www.thesocial.com). ⊖Oxford Circus. One of three UK Socials, this small, labyrinthine DJ-driven bar has a packed schedule of musical guests and DJs. Upstairs fosters a low-key diner atmosphere complete with booths for grubbing; it's the only room open on less crowded nights. Downstairs has a harder edge and is more spacious. Cocktails £5.10, shooters £3. DJs nightly from 7pm. Open M-Sa noon-11pm. No cover.

DANCING

Strawberry Moons, 15 Heddon St. (☎7437 7300; www.strawberrymoons.co.uk). ⊖Piccadilly Circus or Oxford Circus. Loud, eccentric, hip bar/club with theatrical lighting effects,. Clubbers of all ages come to dance to the feel-good music. The staff performs impromptu routines on the mini-stage to various pop and 80s tunes. The fun starts early, with a non-stop hit parade from every decade that encourages enthusiastic singing (and yelling) along as well. Tu hip-hop, garage, R&B (cover £5, ladies free before midnight); Th Reach for the Stars mixed hits, karaoke (free before 10pm, £5 after); F Body Heat (free before 9pm, £5 9-10pm, £7 after); Sa Fever! chart classics (free before 8pm, 8pm-9pm £5, 9pm-10pm £7, £9 after). Open M and W 5pm-11pm, Tu and Th-Sa 5pm-3am. Partially wheelchair accessible.

SOHO

SOHO QUICKFIND: Discover, p. 14; sights, p. 113; museums & galleries, p. 150; food, p. 178; pubs, p. 201; entertainment, p. 240; shopping, p. 265; accommodations, p. 292.

DRINKING

Point 101, 101 New Oxford St. (☎7379 3112). ⊖Tottenham Crt. Rd. Underneath the unattractive, gargantuan Centrepoint office tower, 101 has a cosmopolitan 1970s retro feel, with low, faux-futuristic chairs and long vinyl booths in the sleek balcony bar. The 70s theme ends there—nightly DJs, starting around 9pm, tend toward chill-out jazz, Latin, and soul. Plenty of people pack in, but the sprawling space dilutes the crowd factor. Open M-Th 8am-2am, F-Sa 8am-2:30am, Su 8am-midnight. Wheelchair accessible. AmEx/MC/V.

the insider's
CITY

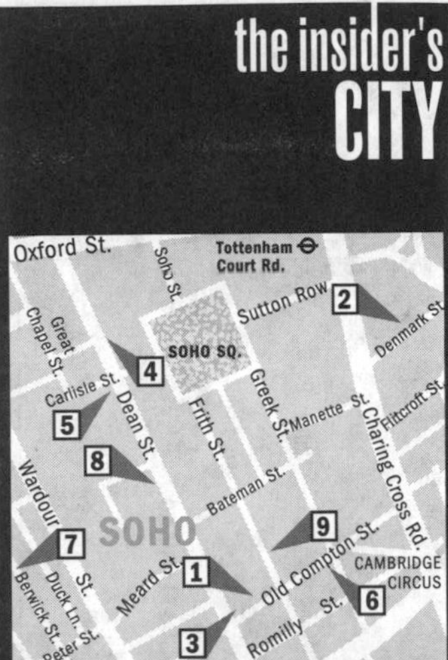

The Soho People-Watching Tour

Soho is often hailed as the center of the West End experience, and for good reason. It's the beating heart of London nightlife, and the daylife isn't so bad either. No other neighborhood in the city has quite the same flavor of excitement, acceptance, and devil-may-care attitude. There's also great food, gay fun, and phenomenal people-watching. And here is how we recommend you to do it:

1) You've woken up midmorning like a true Soho-er. Head to one of the many cafes on **Old Compton** for a latte and snack. Most have window-bar seating, so you can watch people scurrying off to work as you lazily drink your tea.

2) **Denmark Street** has a huge concentration of the best guitar stores. Wander around checking out the luxe electric guitars and the men and women who play them.

3)Emulate the browsers: Soho has plenty of cutting edge shops and book stores. Start at **Soho Books.**

Yo!Below, 52 Poland St. (☎7439 3660; www.yobelow.com), below Yo!Sushi. ⊖Piccadilly Circus. Another concept-driven Yo! venture (see p. 163). Professionals en masse chill in funky blue booths and floor-sunk tables, complete with self-service beer taps (£1.30 for a small glass). This unpretentious bar can feel kitsch-y, but it works. Staff members belt out karaoke, give tarot readings, and do their best to hype up the crowd. Since the public got jealous, Tu night Karayo!ke has been added to the weekly quirky repertoire. Impressive selection of sake sticks (£5-5.50) and other drinks (£3-5.50) from the long sunken bar. Open daily 5pm-1am, food served until 11pm (£1.50-6.50). £3 cover after 11pm. AmEx/MC/V.

DANCING

Madame Jojo's, 8-10 Brewer St. (☎7734 3040; www.madamejojos.com). ⊖Piccadilly Circus or Leicester Sq. This place does it all: comedy, disco, jazz and the famous deep funk. The crowd here is loyal and happy and the atmosphere can't be duplicated. Sa, Soho's premiere drag cabaret, "Kitsch Cabaret" (doors open 7pm) draws a crowd. The drag queen performers work the audience and dazzle in sparkly costumes and belt out songs anyone can sing to. Reservations recommended, although standing room is usually available. Th Electrodisco with DJs Mark Moor and Frankie D; cover £5 at door, £4 with flyer. F Deep Funk (£6 before 11, £8 after) says it all (see p. 209), Sa Groove Sanctuary deep soulful house, nu-jazz, samba soul, and Latin (10pm-3am; £8, £6 before 11).

Bar Rumba, 36 Shaftesbury Ave. (☎7287 6933; www.barrumba.co.uk). ⊖Piccadilly Circus. Rumba has weathered 11 years of London existence, impressive for any club. It now draws a young crowd that makes good use of the industrial-strength interior for dancing. Rumba prides itself on the quality of its DJs, for good reason: many of the best spin here. The excellent sound system goes for high fidelity over volume. Arrive early or you'll have to queue. M This! (see p. 210) starts off the week with a bang. Tu Rumba Pa'Ti with salsa-rap and techno-merengue (open 8:30pm-3am, dance class 6:30-8:30; cover £4, club and class £7); W 70s-80s classics 10pm-3am (£5 all students all night, £3 with flyer before 11pm, £4 with flyer after 11pm); Th perpetual sexy drum&bass (open 8:30pm-3am; £6, £3 before 10pm); F the hip-hop Get-Down (open 10pm-4am; £8, £6 before 11pm); Sa Funk Asylum (open 10pm-6am; £12, £7 before 11pm); Su street soul and R&B (8pm-1am; £5, men £3 and women free before 10pm).

Sound, 10 Wardour St. (☎7287 1010; www.soundlondon.com). ⊖Leicester Sq. or Piccadilly Circus. In keeping with its commercial Leicester Sq. location, this maze of a club is both glitzy and glittery—in

4) Head to Dean St. **Tesco** for picnic fixings. Then plant yourself in **Soho Square.** As the afternoon goes on the lawn will fill with people, from street performers to corporate suits post-workday.

5) A pint at **Nellie Dean** will put you in the thick of things. Grab your pint and stand among everyone on the corner.

6) **Boheme Kitchen and Bar** is the best place to park for people watching with its cozy one-side tables facing the street.

7) By now you 'll want to take a walk on the seedier side. A stroll along the streets and alleys west of **Wardour,** and up into **Berwick Street,** will put you in contact with all the sex shops and "entertainment" you'll want.

8) Time for the bar hop. Do it like the locals and find one of the many hidden bars. **Downstairs Akbar** (77 Dean St.) does it just right.

9) After you've drunk and danced your way to oblivion, finish off the night (or early morning) with a stop at perpetually open **Bar Italia** (22 Firth St.). You can watch the trickle (then flood) of midnight patrons while you drink your coffee and pat yourself on the back for a job well done.

keeping with its name, the music is always loud. "Sound" actually covers 2 venues: the Sound Bar and Restaurant and Club Sound. The Club is a giant maze of main dance floors, balcony bars, and a ground floor bar. Theme nights abound (check website for all the listings): F School Disco at Club Sound (over 21; open 10pm-3am; £15, £12.50 advance); Sa Club Fantastic joins the two venues for 80s and 90s hits (over 17; open 5pm-4am; £12, £8 advance). Wheelchair accessible.

Rouge, 144 Charing Cross Rd. (☎7240 1900; www.rougeclublondon.com), down the alleyway. ⊖Tottenham Crt. Rd. After merging with the live-music Studio Club, Rouge is now a revamped warehouse-style venue with 5 bars, and 6 dance floors. If you like the underground feel of it all, you'll have a blast. Cocktails £4.50-6.80. F Funky house, R&B classics, eclectic beats (£15, £10 before 11pm), Sa Guest DJs choose the beat (£15). Dress is smart-casual (no sneakers, no light jeans–they keep a strict door watch). Open W-Su 9pm-4am.

GAY AND LESBIAN

Ku Bar, 75 Charing Cross Rd. (☎7437 4303; www.ku-bar.co.uk). ⊖Leicester Sq. Don't be fooled by the naked-lady mosaic; this fashionable hangout is definitely gay. Offers a moderately dim interior, plus a loungy outdoor area. Happy hour noon-9pm offers discounted cocktail jugs (£7) and beer refills (£1). Get your tickets to G-A-Y. (see below) and Heaven to skip the queue. Bottled beer from £2.90. Open M-Sa 1-11pm, Su 1-10:30pm. MC/V.

BarCode, 3-4 Archer St. (☎7734 3342). ⊖Piccadilly Circus. On a dark alley in the seedier side of Soho is this bustling, men's-only bar. The overflow crowd on the street is a testament to BarCode's popularity and to the undying love affair between gay men and sleeveless t-shirts. Come to pose and preen, stay to preen and pose. F-Sa the action shifts to the downstairs dance floor, open 10pm. Comedy club Tu evenings. Open daily 1pm-1am. Wheelchair accessible. MC/V.

Vespa Lounge, 15 St. Giles Ct. (☎7836 8956). ⊖Tottenham Crt. Rd. Above the Conservatory, a gay bar/restaurant, at the foot of Centrepoint tower. Small, relaxed lesbian lounge bar with blue walls, comfy seats, and a giant big-screen TV. Gay men welcome. A laidback feel, and pool tables in the back. Spirits and mixers from £2.40. Th live music, F-Sa DJ from 8pm. Open Su-Th noon-midnight, F-Sa noon-1am. MC/V (£5 min.).

G-A-Y, 157 Charing Cross Rd. (☎7434 9592; www.g-a-y.co.uk). ⊖Tottenham Crt. Rd. London's biggest gay/lesbian night, 4 nights a week. Frequently besieged by teenage girls on weekends–the Spice Girls and Boyzone both played here, G-A-Y (you spell it out when you say it) is a bouncing bit of fluff that enjoys mainstream popularity. M Pink Pounder 90s classics with 70s-80s faves in the bar (open 10:30pm-4am; cover £1 with flyer or ad, available at most gay bars, students 50p w/ID); Th Music Factory house, dance, and a little pop (open 11pm-4am; £1 with flyer or ad, students 50p w/ID); F Camp Attack attitude-free 70s and 80s cheese with a second room devoted to 90s music (open 11pm-4am; £2 with flyer, £3 after midnight); Sa G-A-Y big night out, rocking the capacity crowd with commercial-dance DJs and live pop performances (open 10:30pm-5am; £10, £8 with flyer). Wheelchair accessible.

COVENT GARDEN

COVENT GARDEN QUICKFIND: Discover, p. 10; sights, p. 114; museums & galleries, p. 150; food, p. 180; pubs, p. 201; entertainment, p. 240; shopping, p. 267; accommodations, p. 292.

Covent Garden's popularity with tourists means easy money for bars and clubs, which translates into a widespread epidemic of high prices and low quality. Serious partiers and wise locals head to Soho or over to Clerkenwell for a night out, but there are enough quality establishments to fill time with some liquor, some laughs, and maybe a dance move or two.

DRINKING

Freud, 198 Shaftesbury Ave. (☎7240 9933). Not to be confused with the metalworks store on the ground floor, this basement hipster hangout is accessed via a dodgy set of stairs. The sand-blasted walls occasionally echo to live jazz (M 5pm) and the crowd is uncommonly laid-back. Drink a toast to Freud's namesake and invigorate your psyche with cheap cocktails (from £3.40). In terms of hourly costs, this is one cheap shrink. All bottled beers less than £3. Light meals noon-4:30pm (£3.50-6). Open M-Sa 11am-11pm, Su 1-10:30pm. MC/V.

The Spot, 29 Maiden Ln. (☎7379 5900). Frequent live acts include singers and stand-up at this 3-floor club-bar. Dance in the velvet-trimmed basement, drink in the sparkling bar or lounge in the wood-paneled Oval Room. Weekday after-work business crowd gives way to young, dance-happy revelers. DJs spin dance music (soul, R&B, some garage) W-Su. Cover £5 F-Su after 9pm. Happy hour daily noon-7pm (beers from £2.25). Open M-Sa noon-1am, Su 6pm-1am. AmEx/MC/V (£5 min.).

Detroit, 35 Earlham St. (☎7240 2662; www.detroit-bar.com). A set of imposing double doors swing open to reveal a subterranean den full of cave-like enclaves. Low ceilings, powerful speakers, and futuristic lighting add to the cavernous appeal when DJs start spinning deep and funky house around 8pm weekend nights. Top-notch cocktails £4-7. Open M-Sa 5pm-midnight, restaurant open 5:30pm-10:30pm (2 courses £11, snacks £3-7). AmEx/MC/V (£10 min.).

DANCING

AKA, 18 West Central St. (☎7836 0110; www.akalondon.com), next to e (see below). ⊖Tottenham Crt. Rd. or Holborn. From Holborn, walk west along High Holborn and turn right onto Museum St.; look for the lavender building. A sleek DJ-bar full of attractive, 20-somethings. The loungy decor makes for a decidedly chill dance floor. Cocktails £5-10. Casual dress. Tu 'The Players' twisted house; W R&B and some funk; Th Spirit house (cover £5); F DJs from the 4 corners of London (£7, £5 before 10pm, free before 9pm); Sa joins with The End for As One (£15 for both clubs, £10 after 9pm for AKA only). Check website for details. Open Su-F 6pm-3am, Sa 7pm-7am; club nights start at 10pm. Wheelchair accessible. MC/V (£10 min.).

The End, 16A West Central St. (☎7419 9199; www.endclub.com), next to AKA. ⊖Tottenham Crt. Rd. or Holborn. With speaker walls capable of earth-shaking bass, a huge dance floor, and a second lounge bar, The End is a cutting-edge clubber's paradise full of hard house and pumping dancing. Thankfully hidden from most tourists. M Trash glam rock to disco (open 10pm-3am; cover £4). W Swerve, funky drum and bass (open 10pm-3am, cover £6 after 11pm). Th mixed/gay clubbing Discotec (open 10pm-4am; cover £7, £5 before midnight); happy hour 10-11:30pm. Sa As One joins up with AKA (see above). Wheelchair accessible. MC/V (£10 min.).

GAY

The Box, 32-34 Monmouth St. (☎7240 5828). Bright, friendly, and—despite the name—quite spacious, this gay/mixed bar and brasserie has an airy charm that keeps its hip clientele loyal. Wink at a cute bartender for us. Food specials change daily (mains £8-9). Also sells club tickets. Outdoor seating in good weather. Food served M-Sa until 5pm, Su until 6pm. Open M-Sa 11am-11pm, Su noon-10:30pm. MC/V.

THE STRAND

DANCING

Heaven, The Arches, Craven Terr. (☎7930 2020; www.heaven-london.com). ⊖Charing Cross or Embankment. Though it runs regular mixed nights, "the most famous gay nightclub in the world" dispels any doubts about its orientation with the ubiquitous boyz magazine and ambitiously attired clientele. Things get pumping at about midnight, and stay pumping well on to 3am. Intricate interior rewards explorers—try every unguarded door to discover the fantastically lit main floor, 3 additional bars/dance floors, a coffeebar with Internet access, and an elusive chill-out room (depending on when you find it, it may have become a make-out room). M mixed Popcorn with chart-toppers, 70s-80s disco hits, commercial house, and £2 drinks (cover £4, £2 before 11:30pm); W gay Fruit

the local story

Eric Miller, DJ

Mr. Miller has been DJing in the UK for over 20 years. He founded "nu funky people," a group that encourages experimental musicians.

Q: What are your favorite venues in London?

A: Among others, I enjoy the Tongue&Groove, because it's a very intimate venue, and it feels like you're dancing with the crowd in there, which is very unusual. It reminds you that you're there having fun and it's great–though not when people spill drinks on you, of course.

Q: Why do you think the clubbing scene is so big in London?

A: In London, everything is extremely fast-paced and cosmopolitan, and I think it's reflected in the music. You go to a techno night, and you could have a Brazilian techno DJ who puts latin sounds in his music. The eclectism here really makes a difference.

Q: What do you think of pop music?

A: I tend to go for good songwriting and musicanship. I've got nothing against pop music; I just don't like the churned-out, conveyor-belt, boy/girl band crap. My favorite genre is jazz, as well as drum&bass, anything funky. That's one of the beauties of

Machine house, glam soul, and swing (£2 before 11:30pm); F School Disco (£15); Sa gay/lesbian Heaven dance, trance, house, and disco (£12, £10 with flyer). Open M, W, F 10:30pm-3am, Sa 10pm-5:30am.

T.S. Queen Mary, Waterloo Pier, Victoria embankment. (☎7240 9404; www.queenmary.co.uk). ⊖Embankment or Temple. This 1930s Turbine Steamer, now moored permanently on the north bank of the Thames, provides a breezy drinking experience. While the occasionally swaying deck and loud creaking noises can be disconcerting, after a few pints, you'll barely notice. On weekends T.S. becomes a floating disco called, appropriately enough, "Hornblower's." Open M-W noon-11pm, Th-Sa noon-2am, Su noon-10pm (6pm in winter). Cover varies disco nights, check the website. Wheelchair accessible. MC/V.

NORTH LONDON

NORTH LONDON QUICKFIND: Discover, p. 12; sights, p. 120; museums & galleries, p. 153; food, p. 183; pubs, p. 203; entertainment, p. 244; shopping, p. 269; accommodations, p. 294.

Nightlife in Islington is good for loungers and drinkers: it mostly means bar-hopping around Upper St. If you're in need of some booty-shaking Clerkenwell's superclubs are just a short jaunt away. In recent years, however, the seedy area on the Islington side of King's Cross has developed some popular superclubs of its own. Famous as a proving ground for new bands, and with swarms of young people in the area, it comes as a surprise that **Camden Town's** late-night scene is limited to a handful of clubs and club-bars. Music is the main reason to be in Camden at night. The local council loathes to hand out late licenses; the burgeoning bar scene is abruptly cut short at 11pm, so you're likely to be partying with local professionals while the area's pierced youth go elsewhere.

DRINKING

Filthy MacNasty's Whiskey Café, 68 Amwell St. (☎7837 6067). ⊖Angel or King's Cross. Shane MacGowan, U2, and the Libertines have all played in this laid-back Irish pub. The last two still drop by periodically; Shane just lives here. Filthy's has become the new trendy neighborhood spot. Outside red picnic benches catch the rowdy overflow. It's actually 2 spaces with separate entrances, linked by the passage marked "toilets." Live music and occasional literary readings add to the bad-boy cum-intellectual atmosphere. More whiskey than cafe, 14 varieties all go for around £2. Bar food mostly £5-6. Open M-Sa noon-11pm, Su noon-10:30pm.

Bar Vinyl, 6 Inverness St. (☎7681 7898). ⊖Camden Town. One of the only bars in London with its own decks. DJs spin a loud mix music in a narrow space dominated by a blue bar counter running down one wall. Tiny dance space always has a few takers, the rest of the crowd hangs out towards the quieter front of the room. During the day, a relaxed spot for a coffee or lunch, with an open kitchen at the rear (most food £3-6). Most drinks under £5. DJs W-F night and Sa-Su from 3pm. Food served until 9pm. Open M-Th noon-11pm, F-Sa noon-midnight, Su noon-10:30pm.

Lush, 31 Jamestown Rd. (☎7424 9054). ⊖Camden Town. Classy pub/bar with a more romantic and subdued atmosphere than the Camden standard. Sexy red candles, warm walls, and mirrors look down at couples seated at the jumble of tables. Great exotic and creative cocktails £6. Happy hour 2-for-1 5-7pm. Food served until 10:30pm. Open M-Sa 11am-11pm, Su noon-10:30pm. Wheelchair accessible.

The Purple Turtle, 61-65 Crowndale Rd. (☎7383 4976). ⊖Mornington Crescent. A young, eclectic crowd frequents this purple drinking haven, which turns into a packed dance space on weekend nights (8pm-2am). Downstairs area is where clubbers shake it to the music. Even if you don't feel like jumping around with the masses, there's always the upstairs chill-space, not to mention close to 50 shooters to choose from at the bar. For the relaxed, truly turtle experience forgo the sweaty crowds and come during the week or earlier on weekends for drinks. Club cover £3, free before 10. Open M-Th and Su noon-midnight; F-Sa noon-2am.

The Garden, 179 Upper St. (☎7226 6276). ⊖Angel. Until 11pm the sizable outdoor patio and deck fill with happy international yuppies at home in Islington. Inside, the large side booths provide cushions from which you can watch the drinkers get down. Dark maroon and wood interior has lots of corners and tables for two. Th-Sa DJs spin from the lacquered library cove starting around 9pm. On Th student nights, many drinks go for £1.50. The eclectic pub menu (most items £6) offers more than your standard pies and mash. Open M-W noon-11pm, Th-Sa noon-1am, Su noon-midnight.

DANCING: KING'S CROSS

Canvas and The Cross, King's Cross Freight Depot, off Goods Way. (Canvas ☎7833 8301; The Cross ☎7837 0820)). ⊖King's Cross. Walk up York Way (to the right of King's Cross station), turn left on Goods Way, then right about 100m later through the iron gates, and follow the road left and down (10min.). Prostitutes and drug dealers often frequent this area after dark; travel in groups or take a taxi. This space used to be known as Bagley's, it's now been renamed (twice over) but is still one of London's biggest and most popular club venues,

dance music today: people are a lot more open-minded about these different genres.

Q: What do you think of the Ministry of Sound?

A: I would like to do it just for the sound system. They were one of the pioneers of bringing the dance floor to the masses. They were quite businesslike about their approach, so what they did was introduce the whole club culture to the masses, which I think is a good thing. In a way, it's like a popular culture that's an alternative to pop music.

Q: Do you get a lot of chicks as a DJ?

A: Well, yes. You are approached by lots of girls—you're on stage, you're like a mini-god for a while, and it's very exciting. But they don't do that when I'm not working.

Q: Why London?

A: There's also this sense here that anything goes; that you're free to do what you want to do. There's no set way of living here. I've lived in Hoxton, Islington, Notting Hill—and then I fell in love with South London when I first came. There's a real sense of community here, even if everyone's from different parts of the world; that's why I came to London in the first place.

accommodating over 2000 people on up to 5 cavernous, hot dance floors. The scene is heaven for dayglo and rave gear, but hip-hop and reggae slip in among the house and trance beats. Clubbers dance in an outdoor terrace is set up in the summer. Dress is funky and mostly casual. Different promotions means there's no set schedule. The only regular is Friday Fiction, funky house music in all rooms (11pm-all night; cover £15, £9 before 11:30pm, £11 before midnight with flyer). Wheelchair accessible.

Scala, 275 Pentonville Rd. (☎7833 2022, tickets 0870 060 0100; www.scala-london.co.uk). ⊖King's Cross. Booze and beats filled nights in a seedy area guaranteed to scare out-of-towners—what more could a Londoner ask for? The huge main floor embraces its movie-theater past: DJs spin from the projectionist's box, tiered balconies make great people-watching, and giant screens pulse with mood-enhancing visuals as enormous speakers detonate the bass. A 3rd level has a bar that overlooks the dancefloor. So much space means that sometimes it's empty, but there's always room to dance. The club can get pretty sticky and dirty later in the night; come around midnight and you'll get the best of Scala. F Popstarz is a night of musical eclectica (see p. 209); on Sa constantly changing DJs and promotions brings a blend of hip-hop and R&B (no caps, sneakers, or sportswear; £10 in advance, around £15 at the door); every Su another club night called Text Me (10pm-3am; £10). Every M The Jump Off, doors at 9pm, show 10pm-midnight, party midnight-2am (cover £6 before 10, £8 after). Occasional live events during the week. No sneakers or sportswear.

DANCING: CAMDEN TOWN

Electric Ballroom, 184 Camden High St. (☎7485 9006; www.electric-ballroom.co.uk). ⊖Camden Town. The Ballroom hasn't been fashionable for a while, but no one here cares—they're just out for a good time. You won't find the latest sound systems or particularly stylish decor, but free Sega Dreamcast machines, not to mention foosball and pinball, help make up for it. There are 2 floors of dancing and 1 floor for relaxing with an expensive drink. F Sincity (see p. 220) attracts a regular crowd of alternatively styled patrons while Sa Shake (see p. 220) provides a generic 70s and 80s night and tends to double as a raucous singalong.

The Koko Club, 1a Camden High St. (☎0870 432 5527). ⊖Mornington Crescent. The newly reincarnated face of the old landmark Camden Palace, the Koko Club opened Sept 2004. In a converted Victorian theater, now with space for 1500, it's a dance club with a stage, side-view balconies and 6 bars and lounges. A favorite with students, foreign, and British alike. This new space will be carving out a niche in the Camden area nightlife.

Jazz Café, see Entertainment, p. 245.

Mint Bar, 18 Kentish Town Rd. (☎7284 3660; www.mint-bar.co.uk). ⊖Camden Town. Another place new on the Camden scene, Mint Bar doubles as a music venue on the weekends. Two self-consciously cool floors host funky flavored live music and DJs every night. The rooms are done up in—what else?—minty green, with mostly dance space downstairs and tables upstairs. Food served noon-2pm. Happy hour 5-7pm; M student night, cheap house drinks. DJs favor hiphop and R&B. F Regal, a hiphop, reggae, funk and soul party, with DJs from nearby MTV studios. Cover £5, £3 online, ladies free before 11, dress up. Su all-day BBQ then a nighttime party; families welcome before 8pm. Cover £3 before 6pm, £5 after.

GAY

The Black Cap, 171 Camden High St. (☎7428 2721; www.theblackcap.com). ⊖Camden Town. North London's most popular gay bar and cabaret is always buzzing and tends to draws an eclectic male and female crowd. The upstairs rooftop patio is the highlight of the place with plenty of tables for outside pint-downing. Live shows and club scene downstairs F-Su nights, some weekdays, times vary call for details. Cover for downstairs £3, before 11pm £2; F-Sa £4, before 11pm £3. Food served daily noon-6pm. Open M-Th noon-2am, F-Sa noon-3am, Su noon-12:30am. Partially wheelchair accessible.

Bar Fusion, 45 Essex Rd. (☎7688 2882). ⊖Angel. Laid-back gay and lesbian bar with comfy black sofas and mellow purple walls; a great place for anyone to chill. It gets raucous on the weekends though—jump on the sinuous bar and dance along with the bartenders. Open daily 1pm-midnight. MC/V.

SOUTH LONDON

SOUTH LONDON QUICKFIND: Discover, p. 14; sights, p. 125; museums & galleries, p. 155; food, p. 186; entertainment, p. 247; shopping, p. 271.

Nightlife features most prominently in Brixton's renaissance, with an ever-increasing number of bars and clubs luring London's choosiest and largest concentration of under 40s. Lounging generally takes priority over dancing, though the recent proliferation of DJ-bars signals a shift back to good old-fashioned booty-shaking. While many nightspots are little different from their Hoxton or Clerkenwell brethren, there are still plenty of places that have escaped yuppification. Of course, walking to and from whatever joint you end up in will *not* look like north London at all. Though there are just too many people for it to be thought of as dangerous, **be prepared** to wave off the drug dealers who approach you on the street.

DRINKING

Fridge Bar, 1 Town Hall Parade, Brixton Hill (☎7326 5100; www.fridge.co.uk). ⊖Brixton. Next to the Fridge nightclub (see below). Stylish Brixtonians from both sides of the fence mingle in this bright, narrow bar, occasionally nipping downstairs to the DJ-driven dance floor; the place is fantastic for upstairs lounging, but the dance basement has limited appeal until you've downed a few. Happy hour M-F 6-9pm (½ price drinks). DJs spin from 9pm nightly: M roots and reggae; Tu salsa (with free classes downstairs) W 80s Brixton; Th soulful house and R&B; F-Sa hip-hop, rap, and R&B (21+); and Su 70s-80s faves (22+). Occasional after-parties early morning for Fridge Club (check website for dates). Dress code F-Sa: no sneakers or tracksuits. M-Th no cover; F-Sa free before 10:30pm, £5 before 11pm, £7 before midnight, £10 after; Su free before 10:30pm, £5 after; cheaper with flyer; after-parties £6. Open M-Th 6pm-2am, F-Sa 6pm-4:30am, Su 6pm-3am. MC/V (£10 min.).

Satay Bar, 447-455 Coldharbour Ln. (☎7326 5001; www.sataybar.com). ⊖Brixton. Sharing space with an Indonesian restaurant specializing in—you guessed it—*satay* (mains £5-6). One of Brixton's more relaxed bars; quiet enough for chatting but sometimes verging on dull. All strata of local society mix beneath Balinese masks and modern art. Happy hour daily 5-8pm; cocktails £4.25, jugs £12. Restaurant open M-Th noon-3pm and 6-11pm, F noon-3pm and 6pm-1:30am, Sa 1pm-1:30am, Su 1-11pm; bar open M-Th noon-11pm, F noon-2am, Sa 1pm-2am, Su 1-11pm. MC/V (£10 min.).

Living, 443 Coldharbour Ln. (☎7326 4040; www.livingbar.co.uk). ⊖Brixton. Loud, dark, and thumping. This popular newcomer to the Brixton party scene is regularly packed even on weekday nights. The upstairs dance floor has club pretensions, but it's ultimately a DJ-driven drinking den for 20-somethings homesick for the sofa-bars of North London. Bootytastic video projections remind you that you're not in Shoreditch anymore. F-Sa cover £5 after 10pm, (£7 after 11pm for F); no cover Su-Th. Open M-Th 5pm-2am, F 5pm-4am, Sa noon-4am, Su noon-2am. Music starts pumping around 9pm nightly. MC/V (£10 min.).

DANCING

Tongue&Groove, 50 Atlantic Rd. (☎7274 8600; www.tongueandgroove.org). ⊖Brixton. Unself-consciously trendy club-bar so popular and narrow that people dance on the speakers. Arrive early if you ever want to claim a seat. Soak up the brothel chic—huge black leather sofas lining one wall, red lighting, and chandeliers—and anticipate early-morning partying. Do not underestimate the cocktails (£5 doubles)! W US house; Th special guests and Euro house; F house-based mix of African, Cuban, and Brazilian vibes; Sa soulful house, jazz breaks, some disco; Su funk and electronica. Cover £2 Th after 11pm; £3 F, Sa after 10:30. Open Su-W 7pm-3am, Th-Sa 7pm-5am. MC/V (£10 min.).

Bug Bar, Crypt, St. Matthew's Church (☎7738 3184; www.bugbar.co.uk). ⊖Brixton. The antithesis of most self-labeled "cool" nightspots, the intimate space in this whitewashed former church crypt holds an extremely laid-back, friendly, student-heavy crowd. The crypt setting is fantastically atmospheric, though not for the claustrophobic: the single dance floor is nowhere near big enough to contain all the movers and shakers. W live acts, from poetry slams to breakbeats (cover £4-5, free before 8pm); Th funk, jazz, and R&B (free before 8pm, £2.50 before 10pm, £5 after 10pm); F rare beats and breaks and old skool house (£6, before 11pm £4, before 9pm free); Sa one-offs (£6, before 11pm £4, before 9pm free); Su "Simply Boogie" classics (£3, before 10pm free). Open M-W 7pm-1am, Th 7pm-2am, F-Sa 7pm-3am, Su 7pm-1am. Wheelchair accessible.

The Fridge, 1 Town Hall Parade, Brixton Hill (☎7326 5100; www.fridge.co.uk). ⊖Brixton. A revered institution that just got a much-needed face-lift. This converted cinema was the first venue played by hallowed rockers the Eurythmics and the Pet Shop Boys. Now, the fully-restored original rococo features are complemented by luxurious lounge areas and a mirror-balled dance floor. Popular theme nights rotate (check website); cover £5-15. Dress code relaxed, but err on the side of spangly to fit in. Occasional after-party Sa-Su mornings from 5:30am at the Fridge Bar, £6 (see above). Wheelchair accessible.

The Dogstar, 389 Coldharbour Ln. (☎7733 7515; www.thedogstar.com). ⊖Brixton. One of the first nightspots to cash in on Brixton's new-found popularity as a bohemian hangout for aspiring media-types. Every night around 9pm the big open bar transforms into a full-out club with projectors and a good-sized dance floor—it always looks as if clubbers have taken over a trendy pub and refused to give it up. M Afterglow funk, 80s, and indie fare; Tu Souled Out funk and soul; W Offshore brokebeats and world; Th Brixton High old skool 80s jams; F Shoot from the Hip house classics; Sa Latin Quarter Latin house and party; Su Funk to Punk. Cover F-Sa £3 after 10pm, after 11pm £5. Open Su-Th noon-2am, F-Sa noon-4am. Wheelchair accessible. MC/V (£10 min.).

Mass, St. Matthew's Church, Brixton Hill (☎7738 7875; www.massclub.com), entrance to the left of Bug Bar. ⊖Brixton. Renovated in early 2003 and now billed as the "New Mass," these 2 funkily decorated rooms fill quickly with a happy crowd intent on gyrating the night away. W reggae; Th live underground; F Friday Nite Mass R&B and slow jams; Sa hard dance and house. Cover W £5 before 11pm, £7 after; Th £6; F £10 before midnight, £12 after, ladies free before midnight; Sa £13. Open W 10pm-2am, Th 8:30pm-1am, F-Sa 10pm-6am.

EAST LONDON

EAST LONDON QUICKFIND: Discover, p. 13; sights, p. 126; museums & galleries, p. 156; food, p. 186; pubs, p. 204; entertainment, p. 248; shopping, p. 271.

As the self-proclaimed capital of the London scene—and there aren't too many dissenters—**Shoreditch** and **Hoxton,** or "Shoho" as their trendier elements prefer to call it, is now London's main nighttime destination outside Soho. While the West End does theatre and North London does super-clubs, ShoHo does trendy (and the crowds aren't super friendly). Fashion was always about exclusivity, so if locals scowl at you for joining the party, get an expertly messy haircut, dress in your best grunge/sexy art-student outfit, and pout right back.

DRINKING

Vibe Bar, 91-95 Brick Ln. (☎7426 0491; www.vibe-bar.co.uk). ⊖Aldgate East or Liverpool St. One of the Truman Brewery's 2 happening nightspots, this funky clubby bar has all of the style and none of the pretension. The interior is straight out of a hipster magazine. DJs spin M-Sa from 7:30pm and Su from 6:30pm; in summer, fun extends outside with a 2nd DJ working the shady courtyard where white tents and picnic benches create a totally different ambience. The youngish crowd grooves to hip-hop, soul, acoustic, funk, and jazz. Plop on a comfy sofa, or get there early for an outside table. Open Su-Th 11am-11pm, F-Sa 11am-1am. Free Su-Th, £3 F-Sa after 8pm.

Cantaloupe, 35 Charlotte Rd. (☎7729 5566; www.cantaloupe.co.uk). ⊖Old St. Archetypal, self-aware, hip Shoho hangout, with dim lighting and funky wooden chairs. This place is surprisingly homey, with sofas in the back and 2 separate bar areas. Red walls and the raw industrial ceiling set the mood. Tapas from all over the world £3-4, great creative cocktails £6. Open M-F 11am-midnight, Sa noon-midnight, Su noon-11:30pm. Wheelchair accessible. AmEx/MC/V.

Cargo, Kingsland Viaduct, 83 Rivington St. (☎7739 3440; www.cargo-london.com). ⊖Old St. With great acoustics, an intimate candlelit lounge, a front restaurant (mains around £5), and 2 enormous arched rooms, pre- and post-club hangout is frequented by ShoHoians. A mix of DJs and live music, manages to drag almost every lounger onto the dance floor at some point. The cool cave interior means that the only thing missing is the light. Open M-Th noon-1am, F noon-3am, Sa 6pm-3am, Su noon-midnight. Live music M-Sa from 8pm, Su from 6pm. Cover free-£10. Wheelchair accessible.

93 Feet East, 150 Brick Ln. (☎7247 3293; www.93feeteast.com). ⊖Aldgate East or Liverpool St. Part of the Truman Brewery complex, 93 rocks the post-tandoori Brick Ln. night scene. The main bar area houses the DJ; the bar and curved wooden benches serve as both tables and chairs. Don't be afraid to climb over someone on your way back to the bar. The main dance fl. is sparsely decorated but has cool blue lights; the Terrace Bar is a chill, sofa-laden room. Outside there's plenty of space to dance or set up camp at the patio tables. Music style changes virtually every night; call or check website for details. Free before 11, varying cover after. Open daily until 1am.

Hoxton Square Bar & Kitchen, 2-4 Hoxton Sq. (☎7613 0709). ⊖Old St. This spacious bar manages to be a lounge, restaurant, and drinking destination in one. Incredibly popular at night, you can come early or late and sink into retro swivel chairs and low-slung leather couches. The pleasant outdoor patio is packed with funkified, art-chic drinkers every evening. Mediterranean food served in the open-plan kitchen (£2-10), drinks poured at the long sleek bar. Open M-Sa noon-midnight, Su noon-10:30pm. Wheelchair accessible. MC/V.

DANCING (AKA MORE PLACES TO DRINK AND LOUNGE)

Herbal, 12-14 Kingsland Rd. (☎7613 4462; www.herbaluk.com). ⊖Old St. Herbal is less flagrantly trendy than most of its neighbor, and therefore usually more fun. The action is divided onto 2 floors—the smaller, loft-like upstairs room fills first (around midnight). Downstairs has an equally well-stocked bar with more space to dance. The DJ and events calendar hits everything you could want; most weekdays have guest DJs or particular themes. Set of rotating monthly events that change every season. Cover rarely over £7; check website or call.

333, 333 Old St. (☎7739 1800; www.333mother.com). ⊖Old St. Although no longer the cornerstone of Shoho nightlife, 333 still pulls in the late-night crowds with a vengeance. 3 floors, each with its own DJ and style. The plain basement goes a little more retro and the size makes it feel like a personal party. In the self-assuredly cool upstairs lounge, called Mother-Bar, you'll find super hipsters and their artist friends seated in distressed lounge chairs and sofas. The top fl. has a lovely but strange wrap-around mural of the Statue of Liberty and central Manhattan. Cover £10, £5 before 11pm. Open daily 10pm-5am.

RSC in
LONDON'S
LONGEST RUNNING
COMEDY HIT
CRITERION
CRITERION
'A delight'
AMERICA
LONDON'S BEST COMEDY

INSIDE

Entertainment

When a man is tired of London, he is tired of life; for there is in London all that life can afford.
—Samuel Johnson, 1777

Johnson said it. On any given day or night in London, you can choose from the widest range of entertainment a city can offer. The West End is the undisputed theater capital, supplemented by an adventurous "fringe" and a justly famous National Theatre, while new bands spring eternal from the fountain of London's many music venues. There are tons of comedy clubs, movie theaters, and pretty much anything else you could think of.

ENTERTAINMENT BY TYPE

ANNUAL FESTIVALS	
City of London Festival	CITY
Greenwich & Docklands Int'l Festival	EL
Holland Park Shakespeare Festival	KEN/EC
Music on a Summer Evening	NL
▧ The Proms	KEN/EC
CINEMA	
Barbican Cinema	CITY
BFI London IMAX	SB
Curzon Soho	WEND
CINEMA CONTINUED	
▧ Electric Cinema	NH
Everyman Cinema	NL
Gate Cinema	NH
ICA Cinema	WE
▧ National Film Theatre	SB
Prince Charles Cinema	WEND
Renoirs	BLOOM
▧ Riverside Studios	WL
▧ Tricycle Cinema	NL

COMEDY

Canal Cafe Theatre	NL
Chuckle Club	HOL
Comedy Cafe	EL
Downstairs at the King's Head	NL

DANCE

(*see also* Opera & Ballet)

Barbican Theatre	CITY
Peacock Theatre	HOL
The Place	BLOOM
Sadler's Well	CLERK

MUSIC: CLASSICAL

Barbican Hall	CITY
Purcell Room	SB
The Proms	KEN/EC
Queen Elizabeth Hall	SB
Royal Albert Hall	KEN/EC
Royal Festival Hall	SB
St. John's, Smith Square	WEMIN
St. Martin-in-the-Fields	WEMIN
Wigmore Hall	M/RP

MUSIC: JAZZ

100 Club	WEND
606 Club	CHEL
Jazz Café	NL
Pizza Express Jazz Club	WEND
Ronnie Scott's	WEND
Spitz	EL

MUSIC: ROCK, POP, & FOLK

Borderline	WEND
Brixton Academy	SL
Carling Apollo Hammersmith	WL
Dublin Castle	NL
Forum	NL
Garage	NL
Hammersmith Irish Centre	WL
London Arena	EL
London Astoria (LA1)	WEND
Shepard's Bush Empire	WL
Spitz	EL
The Swan	SL
The Water Rats	BLOOM

OTHER

BBC Television Centre	WL
Cycle Rickshaws	WEND
Earl's Court Exhibition Centre	KEN/EC
London Skate Centre	BAY
Queen's Ice Bowl	BAY
Puppet Theatre Barge	NL

OPERA & BALLET

English National Opere.	WEND
Holland Park Theatre.	KEN/EC
Royal Opera House. WE	

THEATER: "WEST END"

The Aldelphi	WEND
Aldwych Theatre	WEND
Apollo Victoria Theatre	WEMIN
Barbican Theatre	CITY
Criterion Theatre	WEND
Dominion Theatre	WEND
Fortune Theatre	WEND
Her Majesty's Theatre	WEND
London Apollo	WL
London Palladium	WEND
Lyceum Theatre	WEND
National Theatre	SB
New London Theatre	HOL
Old Vic	SB
Open-Air Theatre	M/RP
Palace Theatre	WEND
Pheonix Theatre	WEND
Picadilly Theatre	WEND
Prince Edward Theatre	WEND
Prince of Whales	WEND
Queen's Theatre	WEND
Royal Court Theatre	CHEL
St. Martin's Theatre	WEND
Shakespeare's Globe	SB
Theatre Royal, Drury Lane	WE
Victoria Palace Theatre	WEMIN

THEATER: "OFF-WEST END"

The Almeida	NL
Battersea Arts Centre	SL
Donmar Warehouse	WEND
Hackney Empire	EL
Hampstead Theatre	NL
Lyric Hammersmith	WL
RADA	BLOOM
Riverside Studios	WL
Soho Theatre	WEND
Tricycle	NL
Young Vic	SB

THEATER: FRINGE

The Bush Theatre	WL
Etcetera Theatre	NL
The Gate	NH
The King's Head	NL
New End Theatre	NL
The Old Red Lion	NL
The Plt	CITY

NEIGHBORHOOD ABBREVIATIONS: BAY Bayswater **BLOOM** Bloomsbury **CHEL** Chelsea **CITY** The City of London **CLERK** Clerkenwell **HOL** Holborn **KEN/EC** Kensington & Earl's Court **K/B** Knightsbridge & Belgravia **M/RP** Marylebone & Regent's Park **NH** Notting Hill **SB** The South Bank **WEND** The West End **WEMIN** Westminster **NL** North London **SL** South London **EL** East London **WL** West London

THEATER

The stage for a national dramatic tradition over 500 years old, London theaters maintain unrivaled breadth of choice. Knowing what's on is easy enough: pick up the week's *Time Out*, look through the newspapers' weekend sections, or check out www.officiallondontheatre.co.uk. Knowing what to pick, however, is tougher. For many people, a visit to London isn't complete without going to see a big musical, for others it requires a trip to the National Theatre or Royal Shakespeare Company; play to your tastes, and you're unlikely to be disappointed. The variety is immense, so the key to spending your money lies in knowing what's what. At a **West End** theater (a term referring to nearly all the major stages, whether or not they're actually in the West End), you can expect a professional, (usually) mainstream production, top-quality performers, and ticket prices in the £20-40 range (cheaper for standby and student seats). Be warned, though, of two recent trends on the West End scene: money-hungry stinkers headlined by B-list Hollywood talent (think Molly Ringwald and Luke Perry) have carved out a niche that's best to be avoided; and pre-packaged megamusicals made up of well-known pop songs (from Queen to Elvis to Rod Stewart) now nearly own the musical market— some are great fun *(Mamma Mia!)*, but most are distressingly awful. **Off-West End** theaters generally present more challenging work, while remaining every bit as professional as their West End brethren. The Almeida and the Donmar Warehouse regularly attract big-name Hollywood stars the West End can only dream of. The **Fringe** refers to the scores of smaller, less commercial theaters around the city, often just a room in a pub basement with a few benches and a team of dedicated amateurs. With so many fringe productions going on all the time, few even get reviewed by newspapers and magazines; it's hit-or-miss whether you'll stumble across the next Tom Stoppard, but even if it turns out to be a flop, you're rarely more than £5 the worse for it.

YOU'RE LATE. At the theater or at a restaurant, lateness is not appreciated. Most shows refuse to seat latecomers until intermission, and restaurants give away reservations within minutes of a no-show.

LONG-RUNNING SHOWS

London's West End is dominated by musicals and plays that run for years, if not decades. Below we list both shows that have proved their staying power, plus recent arrivals that look set to settle down for the long haul. Despite what the ever-increasing number of ticket peddlers would have you believe, you'll **almost always get the best deal by going to the theater directly,** especially on the day of the show and with a student ID—phone bookings (and virtually all transactions through an agent) will attract a supplementary fee of £1-3 per ticket. The one quasi-exception is the **tkts** booth in Leicester Square (see p. 242), which is run by the theaters themselves and releases half-price tickets on the day of the show (they still charge a fee, though). **Ticket touts** who hawk tickets outside theaters charge sky-high prices for tickets of dubious authenticity or of obstructed views; moreover, selling (and by extension buying) tickets from an unauthorized source is a crime. All theaters, and the tkts booth, accept AmEx/MC/V, except on some same-day student discounts. Also all theatres are wheelchair accessible unless noted otherwise.

MUSICALS

Billy Elliot: The Musical, Victoria Palace Theatre, Victoria St. (☎0870 895 5577). ⊖Victoria. Local boy makes good—in tights. Opening in Mar. 2005, it may be another movie-to-musical adaptation, but this little show boasts some distinguished talent: new songs by Elton John, and directed by the Oscar-nominated director of the film, Stephen Daldry. Shows M-Sa 7:30pm, Th and Sa 2:30pm. £17.50-50.

Covent Garden

Empire Cinema, Leicester Square

Royal Opera House

Blood Brothers, Phoenix Theatre, Charing Cross Rd. (☎0870 060 6629; www.theambassadors.com/phoenix). ⊖Tottenham Crt. Rd. Nearing 20 years old, it's the British mega-hit that most foreigners have never heard of. Twins separated at birth, passionate melodrama, and a dash of 1980s social commentary—Willy Russell's songs are fantastic. Shows M-Sa 7:45pm plus Th 3pm, Sa 4pm. £15-42.50 student and senior standby £15 1hr. before curtain.

Chicago, The Adelphi, Strand (☎087 0403 0303; www.chicagothemusical.com). ⊖Charing Cross. The musical that inspired the movie that inspired the Oscars. Merry murderesses want their name in lights: slinky costumes, fantastic Fosse, continuous showstoppers. Some dodgy American accents, though. M-Th and Sa 8pm, F 5 and 8:30pm, plus Sa 3pm. £15-35.

Chitty Chitty Bang Bang, London Palladium, Argyll St. (☎0870 890 1108; www.chittythemusical.com). ⊖Oxford Circus. Another movie-turned-musical, this one a bit silly; a flying car and some mad scientists make for a crowd-pleasing spectacle, though. Geared towards children. Shows Tu 7pm, W-Sa 7:30pm; mats W and Sa-Su 2:30pm. £15-40.

Fame—The Musical, Aldwych Theatre, Aldwych St. (☎0870 400 0805; www.aldwychtheatre.com). ⊖Charing Cross. Based on the classically cheeseball film about New York theater students, you'll recognize the tunes but wonder when all the caffeine and saccharine were added. Energetic dancing, though. Shows M-Th 7:30pm, F 5:30pm and 8:30pm, Sa 3 and 7:30pm. £15-38.50. Day-of student discounts.

Jailhouse Rock: The Musical, Piccadilly Theatre, Denman St. (☎7369 1734). ⊖Piccadilly Circus. Based on the film and full of 1950s rock classics, this is the well-known tale of an ex con who becomes a star. Elvis, we feel, would not be pleased, but big fans of the King might be. Shows M-Sa 7:30pm, W and Sa 3pm. £19.50-45.

Joseph and the Amazing Technicolor Dreamcoat, New London Theatre, Drury Ln. (☎0870 4000 650). ⊖Holborn. Andrew Lloyd Webber's 2nd most famous biblical extravaganza. Songs in every style imaginable, plus the titular eye-catching overcoat. Majorly campy Egyptian saga. Shows Tu-Th 7:30pm, also W 2:30pm; F 5pm and 8pm; Sa 2, 5, 8pm. £20-40.

The Lion King, Lyceum Theatre, Wellington St. (☎0870 243 9000; www.disney.co.uk/MusicalTheatre/The Lion King). ⊖Covent Garden. Same old script, gorgeous new puppets. Disney has adapted its movie into a sometimes innovative and aesthetically pleasing show, while still retaining the Disney pop appeal. Shows Tu-Sa 7:30pm plus W and Sa 2pm, Su 3pm. £17.50-47.50. Day-of standing-room tickets released at noon.

Mamma Mia!, Prince of Wales Theatre, Coventry St. (☎7839 5987; www.delfont-mackintosh.com. ⊖Leicester Sq. A revue of ABBA's music strung together with a simple plotline, it's by far the best of the "pop's greatest hits"-style megashows. Charming, irresistible, and always nearly sold out. Shows M-Th 7:30pm, F 5 and 8:30pm, Sa 3 and 7:30pm. £25-49.

Mary Poppins, Prince Edward Theatre, Old Compton St. (☎7447 5458). ⊖Leicester Sq. The nanny, the parasol, the irritating British schoolchildren: it all comes to the London stage in Dec. 2004. We're fairly confident there will be more than just a 'spoonful of sugar.' Shows M-Sa 7:30pm, Th and Sa 2:30pm. £15-49.

Les Misérables, Queen's Theatre, Shaftesbury Ave. (☎0870 534 4444, US 800-334-8457; www.lesmis.com). ⊖Piccadilly Circus. A rather polarized look at good and evil in 19th-century France, or "The Most Successful Musical on the Planet." A tradition and still well-loved. If you don't recognize "I Dreamed a Dream" and "On My Own," you've missed a few decades. Shows M-Sa 7:30pm, plus Sa 2:30pm. £15-45. Day-of student discounts.

Phantom of the Opera, Her Majesty's Theatre, Haymarket (☎7494 5400). ⊖Piccadilly Circus. Andrew Lloyd Webber's famously romantic take on love and deformity at the Paris Opera. The chandelier still falls and the crowds still flock. Shows M-Sa 7:30pm, plus Th and Sa 3pm. £10-42.50.

The Producers, Theatre Royal, Drury Ln. (☎0870 890 1109). ⊖Covent Garden. Mel Brooks's über-smash Broadway comedy, newly planted in London. Two money-hungry producers set out to stage a flop but end up with the unlikeliest of Hitler-based hit musicals. An irreverent gutbuster. Shows M-Sa 7:30pm, W and Sa 2:30pm. £20-49.

Saturday Night Fever, Apollo Victoria, Wilton Rd. (☎0870 4000 650). ⊖Victoria. The Bee-Gee's tunes, the polyester suits, and that disco-hungry hunk Tony Manero are all back on stage again, after a brief hiatus. In the grand tradition of *Footloose: The Musical*, SNF takes iconic movie images and renders them painfully dull, to the delight of thousands. Shows M-Th 7:30pm, F 5:30pm and 8:30pm, Sa 3pm and 7pm. £10-45.

We Will Rock You, Dominion Theatre, Tottenham Crt. Rd. (☎0870 607 7400). ⊖Tottenham Crt. Rd. Adapted from Ben Elton's book and incorporating the popular chart-toppers of Queen, this futuristic tale pits a rock rebel against a globalized, conformist world. The sci-fi gaudiness of it all would make Freddie Mercury proud. Shows M-Sa 7:30pm, plus W and Sa 2:30pm. £22.50-50.

The Woman in White, Palace Theatre, Shaftesbury Ave. (☎0870 895 5579). ⊖Leicester Sq. The hotly-anticipated latest from Andrew Lloyd Webber is based on a Wilkie Collins Victorian thriller; a mysterious woman, a dashing young hero, and a villainous count encounter romance and intrigue. Later, of course, they sing about intrigue and romance. Shows M-Sa 7:30pm, plus W and Sa 2:30pm. £17.50-50.

DISCOUNT TICKET BOOTHS. The only real deal you'll be getting on West End theater come from the tkts booth in the center of Leicester Sq. The "official half-price ticket booths" that cluster everywhere usually get you much worse deals than just going to the box office of the show you want to see.

NON-MUSICALS

The Complete Works of William Shakespeare (Abridged) and **The Complete History of America (Abridged),** Criterion Theatre, Piccadilly Circus (☎7369 1747). ⊖Piccadilly Circus. Monumental topics in a lightning-quick 2hr.; high-octane and high-energy irreverence by a trio of funnymen. Shakespeare W 8pm, Th 3pm, F 5:45pm and 8pm, Sa 5 and 8pm, Su 4pm; America Tu 8pm. £10-33. Day-of student discounts.

The Mousetrap, St. Martin's Theatre, West St. (☎7836 1443). ⊖Leicester Sq. By Agatha Christie. After half a century on the stage, is there anyone left in London who doesn't know whodunnit in this, the world's longest-running play? Shows M-Sa 8pm plus Tu 2:45pm and Sa 5pm. £11.50-32. Day-of student tickets.

Take Your Seats

Americans can easily be confused by the terminology used in English theaters and concerts. First, seating terminology: **Stalls** are what Americans call orchestra seats, and are nearest the stage. The **dress circle** (mezzanine) is the first tier of balcony above the stalls. This section often has better views of the stage; stalls and dress circle are usually the most expensive seats. Above the dress circle comes the **upper circle,** while the cheapest seats at the top of the theater are **slips** or in the **balcony** (also known as gallery). Patrons usually refer to them as **the gods,** a reference to their closeness to heaven.

The **interval** (intermission) is the time for gin or the loo; within seconds the entire theater empties into the appropriately named **crush bar.** Instead of joining the undignified scramble, you can order interval drinks before the show and find them waiting for you—usually on an unguarded side table marked with your name. Fortunately, London theatergoers do not seem to be of the drink-snatching variety.

Also remember **programmes** here usually cost £1-3 and that **return line** is set up on the day of a performance to sell those seats that have been returned before use. **House seats** are saved for important people. If no one shows up, they often go for sale just before curtain and are the best seats in the house.

The Woman in Black, Fortune Theatre, Russell St. (☎7836 2238). ⊖Covent Garden. Proving that good writing is scarier than any amount of cinematic gore, an aging detective recalls the ghost of a dead woman. Shows M-Sa 8pm plus Tu 3pm and Sa 4pm. £10-30. Day-of student and senior discounts, £10 1hr. before curtain.

FILM

London's film scene offers everything. The heart of the celluloid monster is **Leicester Square** (p. 240), and its surrounding streets, which are lined with cinemas. It's best to avoid cinemas on the square itself, given that prices are generally £2-3 higher than anywhere else. The dominant chain is **Odeon** (☎0870 5050 007; www.odeon.co.uk); Odeon does much more than just mainstream fare and each branch has its own character. Tickets to West End cinemas cost £5-10; weekday screenings before 5pm (and all day Monday) are usually cheaper and many cinemas offer regular student discounts (except on the weekends). The annual **London Film Festival** (www.lff.org.uk), UK's biggest and held in November, takes place at the National Film Theatre (see p. 238). Hollywood fans will see many pictures released concurrently on both sides of the Pond, and just as many arriving in the UK months later. In any case, film buffs will be pleased at the large number of repertory cinemas screening classics and obscure art house works. The two most prolific theaters for independent flicks are the **NFT** (p. 238) and **ICA** (p. 151). Both tend to have different movies every single night. *Time Out* publishes reviews and schedules for all cinemas, as do many other newspapers. Online, www.viewlondon.com also posts schedules.

COMEDY

Capital of a nation famed for its (often baffling) sense of humor, London takes its comedy seriously. On any given night of the week, you'll find at least 10 comedy clubs in operation; **stand-up** is the mainstay, but **improvisation** is also hot. Most clubs only run once a week or once a month in an otherwise unfunny venue, so check listings in *Time Out* or a newspaper to keep up to speed. However, as comedy goes more mainstream, a few purpose-built, full-time comedy venues have cropped up, of which the **Comedy Store** (p. 241) is the most famous.

Summertime comedy seekers should note that London empties of comedians in **August,** when most head to Edinburgh to take part in the annual festival (trying to win an award); but **June** and **July** are full of feverish comic activity as performers test out new material prior to heading north.

MUSIC

CLASSICAL

Home to 4 world-class orchestras, 3 major concert halls, 2 opera houses, two ballet companies, and more chamber ensembles than Simon Rattle could shake his baton at, London is rightfully renowned for serious music—and there's no need to break the bank. Most venues have scads of cheap seats, and when music is the attraction, bad views of the stage are less important. The London Symphony Orchestra remains the marquee orchestra but has competition from the Philharmonia, London Philharmonic, and the Royal Philharmonic, all of which play at the **Barbican Centre** (see p. 235) and **South Bank Centre** (see p. 238). Smaller chamber groups like the Academy of St. Martins in the Fields and the Gabrieli Consort provide different classical pleasures. The serious opera buffs who populate "the Gods" (so called because the seats are so far from the stage, you may as well be in heaven) in the **Royal Opera House** (see p. 241) and the **Coliseum** (see p. 241) wouldn't dream of descending to rub shoulders with the wealthy poseurs below. Every evening for most of July and August queues snake all the way around Royal Albert Hall for the **Proms** (see p. 236), the world's largest festival of classical music; others brave the elements to enjoy some outdoor **Music on a Summer Evening** (see p. 245) on Hampstead Heath. Beyond the major concert halls, smaller venues offer music of all periods and standards—almost every church in central London has a regular concert program, often for free. To hear some of the world's top choirs, head to Westminster Abbey (see p. 78) or St. Paul's Cathedral (see p. 80) for Evensong. As a double bonus, you'll also get into the cathedral for free.

MOVIE TIME. Most cinemas sell tickets with assigned seat numbers on a first-come-first serve basis, so it is a good idea to show up early to purchase your tickets and grab those Jujifruits while you're at it.

JAZZ, FOLK AND WORLD

London's jazz scene is small but serious; this ain't Chicago, but hallowed clubs like **Ronnie Scott's** (see p. 241) pull in big-name performers from across the world, while the **606 Club** (see p. 234) focuses on hot local players. For the most part, the scene is low-key and home-grown, with performances taking place in various bars and pubs around town, often in the suburbs. The **Pizza Express** chain of restaurants (see p. 163) often features jazz in its larger and swankier branches, in addition to operating a full-time jazz club (see p. 241) which attracts top talent. **Folk** (which in London usually means **Irish**) and **world** music keep an even lower profile, though big-name acts make occasional appearances at major concert venues. The **South Bank Centre** (see p. 238) runs a strong and varied program in its three halls. In general, folk and world outings are restricted to pubs and community centers. The **Swan** in Stockwell (see p. 248) and the **Hammersmith Irish Centre** (see p. 249) are two of the best-known venues for Celtic music.

ROCK & POP

Birthplace of the Rolling Stones, the Sex Pistols, Madness, and the Chemical Brothers, home to Madonna (or should we call her Esther?) and Paul McCartney, London is a town steeped in rock'n'roll history. Every major band and singer in the world has played at least one of its major venues; dates for the biggest acts are usually booked months in advance and often sell out within days of tickets being released, so you need to start planning well before arriving in London to have a chance at bagging a seat.

Stadium-filling acts are only the tip of the giant iceberg that is London's music scene. For the best of the bands that can't sell out whole arenas yet, check out the **London Astoria** (see p. 241) or the **Forum** (see p. 246). Other well-known traveling acts frequently stop at the **Borderline** (seep. 241). Every night in dozens of pubs and smaller venues, hopeful bands play to a devoted crowd of followers and friends, hoping the record-company scout is somewhere in the audience. The **Water Rats** (see p. 234) and the **Dublin Castle** (see p. 245) are both pubs with good records of talented new acts.

SPECTATOR SPORTS

Britain may not produce the best sportsmen in the world (or even in Europe)—it's been over 60 years since a local won Wimbledon, 35 since the English team lifted the football World Cup, and almost 20 since they last won the Ashes in cricket—but Brits are some of the best, most enthusiastic fans around. While this has occasionally been less than positive (deportation due to football hooliganism comes to mind), for the most part watching sports is fun, loud and social, whether its on television or live.

FOOTBALL

Many evils arise which God forbid.
—Edward II, banning football in London in 1314

Whether or not football (soccer) was invented here, there's no doubt that the sport in its current form is heavily influenced by the English football tradition. Almost a million people attend professional matches, most dressed with fierce loyalty in team colors. The vast majority of games takes place on Saturdays, with some on Sundays and the odd mid-week matches. However, the most popular way to watch is on TV in a local bar or pub, where you get the benefit of multiple cameras and commentators. Though violence at stadiums has been a problem for years, the atmosphere has become tamer now that stadiums sell seats rather than standing spaces. Also the increasing (though still proportionally tiny) number of women attending matches has calmed things down. Most of these fans attend the matches of one of five London teams in England's **F.A. Premier League.**

The big three London teams are **Arsenal,** Highbury Stadium, Avenell Rd. (☎7413 3366; ⊖Arsenal, Zone 2); **Chelsea,** Stamford Bridge, Fulham Rd. (☎7386 7799; ⊖Fulham Broadway, Zone 2); and **Tottenham Hotspur,** White Hart Ln. (☎8365 5000; ⊖Seven Sisters, Zone 3 or Rail: White Hart Ln.). Generally tickets are £10-40, but they are difficult to get on short notice. Buying from scalpers is not a good idea. The odds of your getting a ticket may be better for one of London's other slightly less popular Premiership teams, though travel times to the stadiums are usually greater: **Charlton**, The Valley (☎8333 4010; Rail: Charlton or DLR: North Greenwich, Zone 3 plus bus: #422, 472 or 486), and **Fulham,** Loftus Rd. (☎7442 1234; ⊖White City). For the best of the next rung of teams try **West Ham,** Upton Park (☎8548 2700; ⊖Upton Park, Zone 3), or **Crystal Palace** and **Wimbledon,** who both play at Selhurst Park, Whitehorse Ln. (☎8771 8841; Rail: Selhurst).

FOOTBALL NIGHTS. England takes its football seriously, and you should too. Find out when the big matches are, because you'll be encountering drunken hordes of fans after each one—and that's just when they win.

RUGBY

An excellent rowdy sport. Rugby was allegedly created when an inspired (or confused) Rugby School student picked up a regular football and ran it into the goal. Never as popular in London as it is in the north, locals still turn out loyally to support the four big London teams who play from August to May on weekend afternoons: **London Wasps**

(☎8993 8298); **NEC Harlequins** (☎8410 6000); **Saracens** (☎0192 347 5222); and **London Broncos** (☎09 0683 3303). January to March brings the **Six Nations Championship** (featuring England, Scotland, Wales, Ireland, France, and Italy). Tickets for the championship matches at **Twickenham** (☎8892 2000; Rail: Twickenham) are nearly impossible to get.

CRICKET

For non-Commonwealth visitors who have no understanding of the game, cricket can seem baffling. Either get someone with a lot of time to explain it to you or just give up. But who cares? The sun is (hopefully) shining, the beer is warm, and there's little enough action that you can read the newspaper and still not miss a thing. In a bid to attract younger viewers, one-day matches have been introduced, with risk-taking players dressed in gaudy colors, but purists denounce the new versions. Cricket does, however, get lots of press attention. During the summer there are matches nearly every day at the famous **Lord's Cricket Grounds** (see **Sights,** p. 124) and the **Oval,** in south London (☎7582 7764; ⊖Oval, Zone 2). Many matches (except the **International Test Matches**) are free or affordable.

TENNIS

Every year, for the last week of June and the first week of July, tennis buffs all over the world focus their attention on **Wimbledon** (or, as it's known in England, "The Championships"). Demand for tickets so exceeds supply that pre-sold tickets are lotteried in December; only 500 Centre, no. 1 and no. 2 Court tickets are saved for each day (except the final 4, when none are). To be assured of one of these seats (£30-53 for Centre Court depending on the day, £23-48 for no. 1 and no. 2 Courts), overnight queueing is recommended. To secure a grounds ticket (£13-15) for the outer courts, fantastically exciting during the first few days, when hundreds of matches are going on, less so as the field dwindles—show up by 7am. Gates open at 10:30am. You can then enter the queue atop "Henman Hill" where returned Centre Court and no. 1 court tickets are resold for a cool £9 at 5pm for early evening action. (All England Lawn Tennis and Croquet Club. ☎8971 2473; www.wimbledon.org. ⊖Southfields, Zone 3, then a 15min. walk along Wibledon Park Rd. or an 80p shuttle ride; or Rail: Wimbledon.)

ENTERTAINMENT BY NEIGHBORHOOD

BAYSWATER

BAYSWATER QUICKFIND: Discover, p. 4; food, p. 164; pubs, p. 193; shopping, p. 254; accommodations, p. 279.

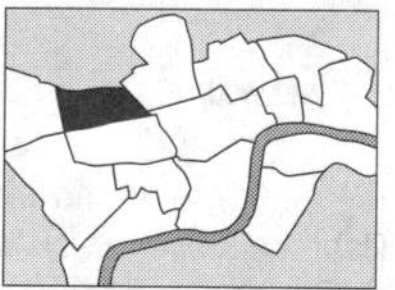

SEE MAP, p. 359

Hyde Park and Kensington Gardens next door are perfect for lazy summer days; when it rains, try the UCI cinema in Whiteleys (see p. 255).

Queen's Ice Bowl, 17 Queensway (☎7229 0172). ⊖Queensway or Bayswater. Channels the American suburban experience into urban British cheesiness; there's something for everyone in this all-in-one entertainment center: central London's only ice rink. 12 lanes of 10-pin bowling, a video-game arcade, pool tables, and a bar. Ice rink sessions daily 10am-2pm, 2-5pm, and 5-7pm, M-Th 8-11pm, F-Sa 7:30-11pm, Su 8-10pm. £5.50 per session, £6.50 F-Sa nights; £1 skate rental (free F-Sa). Live DJ skating sessions Th-Su. Bowling open daily 10am-11:30pm, £5.50 per game, children free before 6pm. MC/V.

London's Skate Centre, 35 Queensway (☎7727 4669; www.lonskate.com). For those tired of walking or eager for some wheels, this boards-and-blades store rents in-line skates by the day (£7 per 2hr., £10 per day, £15 overnight; only day rentals on weekends). Deposit required: passport, photo ID with credit card, or £30 cash. Return skates by 6pm. Open M-F noon-6:30pm, Sa-Su 11am-6:30pm. MC/V (£12 min.).

BLOOMSBURY

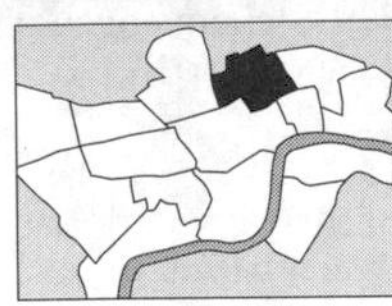
SEE MAP, p. 360

BLOOMSBURY QUICKFIND: Discover, p. 5; sights, p. 87; museums & galleries, p. 140; food, p. 166; pubs, p. 193; shopping, p. 255; accommodations, p. 282.

The Water Rats, 328 Grays Inn Rd. (☎7837 7269; www.plumpromotions.co.uk). ⊖King's Cross St. Pancras. A hip pub/cafe by day, a stomping venue for top new talent by night—this is where young indie-rock bands come in search of a record deal. Oasis was signed here after their first London gig, although the place has been spiffed up since. Open for coffee M-F 8:30am-midnight. Excellent, generous gastro-pub lunches (£5-6) M-F noon-3pm. Music M-Sa 8pm to late (headliner 9:45pm). Cover £5-6, £4-5 with flyer. MC/V (£7 min.).

RADA (Royal Academy of the Dramatic Arts), 62-64 Gower St., entrance on Malet St. (☎7908 4800; www.rada.org). A cheaper alternative to the West End, Britain's most famous drama school has 3 on-site theaters, and productions throughout the year—catch the next Kenneth Branagh or Ralph Fiennes before they hit the big time. Box office open M-F 10am-6pm, until 7:30pm performance nights. Call ahead for event details. £3-10, concessions £2-7.50. Regular Foyer events during the academic year including plays, music, and readings M-Th at 7 or 7:30pm (free-£4). Wheelchair accessible. MC/V.

Renoir, Brunswick Sq. (☎7837 8402; www.renoir.co.uk). ⊖Russell Sq. This independent movie house emphasizes current European (especially French) cinema. Only two screens, but the regular turnover makes this a standout. Doors and bar/cafe open 30min. before each screening. £8.50; 1st performance of the day M-F £6, concessions £4. MC/V.

The Place, 17 Duke's Rd. (☎7387 0031; www.theplace.org.uk). ⊖Euston or King's Cross St. Pancras. A top venue for contemporary dance, attracting companies from both the UK and abroad. Seasons Jan.-July and Sept.-Nov. Box office/phone bookings open M-F 10:30am-6pm, Sa 12:30-6pm; until 8pm on performance nights. 24 hr. online booking. Performances £5-15, depending on seats and advance booking; students and concessions £7. Day-of standbys available from 6pm (£7). Wheelchair accessible. MC/V.

CHELSEA

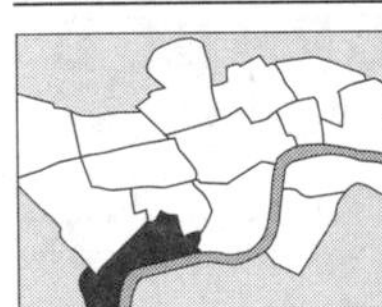
SEE MAP, p. 361

CHELSEA QUICKFIND: Discover, p. 5; sights, p. 87; museums & galleries, p. 141; food, p. 167; pubs, p. 195; shopping, p. 256; accommodations, p. 285.

TRANSPORTATION: *The only Tube station in Chelsea is Sloane Sq.; from here buses #11, 19, 22, 211, and 319 run down the King's Rd.*

Royal Court Theatre, Sloane Sq. (☎7565 5000; www.royalcourttheatre.com). Called "the most important theater in Europe" by *The New York Times*, this venerable stage is dedicated to challenging new writing and innovative interpretations of classics. Their 1956 production of John Osborne's *Look Back in Anger* is universally acknowledged as the starting point of modern British drama. In the past few seasons, the Royal Court has premiered award-winning new works from such luminaries as Caryl Churchill, Connor McPherson, and Martin McDonagh. As part of their project they also sponsor young writers' contests and workshops; they've helped launch the careers of many influential playwrights. Main auditorium £7.50-31.50 26; concessions £9; standing room 10p 1hr. before curtain. 2nd venue Upstairs £12.50-16, concessions £9. M all seats £7.50, though you can only book M upstairs tickets on the day of the performance. Box office open M-Sa 10am-7:45pm, closes 6pm non-performance weeks. Wheelchair accessible. MC/V.

606 Club, 90 Lots Rd. (☎7352 5953; www.606club.co.uk). Hard to find; look for the brick arch labeled 606 opposite the "Fire Access" garage across the street; ring the doorbell to be let downstairs. The intrepid will be rewarded with brilliant British and European jazz in a smoky, candle-lit basement venue. Entrance F-Su is with a meal only; M-Th you can choose to just order drinks. Mains run £8-15, and the music charge (added to the bill) is £7 M-Th, £9 F, £8 Sa-Su. Reservations highly recommended. Closing times are for the kitchen—the music continues until the musicians don't want to play anymore. M-W doors open 7:30pm, 1st band 8-10:30pm, 2nd 10:45pm-1:00am; Th-Sa doors open 8pm, music 9:30pm-1:30am; Su (vocalists) doors open 8pm, music 9pm-midnight. MC/V.

THE CITY OF LONDON

THE CITY OF LONDON QUICKFIND: Discover, p. 6; sights, p. 90; museums & galleries, p. 141; food, p. 168; pubs, p. 195.

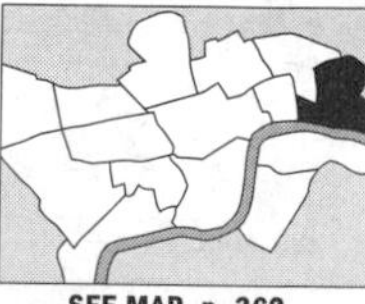

SEE MAP, p. 362

With 39 churches, the City is not short of venues for lunchtime concerts or choral evensong; see separate church listings under **Sights,** p. 90, for details. Most churches have at least one musically inclined event a week. Less well-known as venues are the 24 livery halls—occasional concerts provide the only opportunity for most people to see inside these bastions of tradition. Contact the **City of London Information Centre** (☎7332 1456) for information. In June and July, the **City of London Festival** (see below) provides another occasion to get into places like the Mansion House (typically only for mayoral events) and Middle Temple Hall. The City's primary entertainment venue, though, is the massive **Barbican** arts complex.

Barbican Centre, Barbican; main entrance on Silk St. (box office ☎0845 120 7500; cinema 7382 7000; www.barbican.org.uk). ⊖Barbican or Moorgate. See also **Sights,** p. 92, and **Museums & Galleries,** p. 141. Equally famous for the quality of its very diverse offerings and its mildly confusing layout, the Barbican is a one-stop cultural powerhouse. Call in advance for tickets, especially for very popular events. Otherwise, the online and phone box office sometimes have good last minute options. The Barbican is also the place to go for information on **festivals and season specific events**. Many occur in the summer so it's worth checking out what's going on around April or so as many summer events sell out.

Barbican Theatre: A futuristic auditorium that hosts touring companies and short-run shows, as well as frequent short-run multicultural and contemporary dance performances. Prices vary considerably by seat, day, and production; £7-30, cheapest M-F evening and Sa matinee. Student and senior standbys from 9am day of performance.

The Pit: A small, intimate theater used primarily for new and experimental (read: can be pleasantly or unpleasantly eccentric) productions. (£10-15.)

Barbican Hall: Recently refurbished, the Barbican Hall is one of Europe's leading concert halls, with excellent acoustics and a nightly performance program. The resident **London Symphony Orchestra,** plays here frequently; the hall also hosts concerts by international orchestras, jazz artists, and world musicians. (£5-35.)

Barbican Cinema: 2 smallish screens, offering a rotation of the latest blockbusters with-arthouse, international, and classic movies. (£8, seniors and students £6, under 15 £4.)

CLERKENWELL

CLERKENWELL QUICKFIND: Discover, p. 7; sights, p. 105; museums & galleries, p. 143; food, p. 169; pubs, p. 196; nightlife, p. 210; accommodations, p. 285.

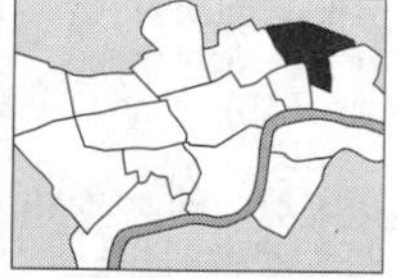

SEE MAP, p. 363

Sadler's Wells, Rosebery Ave. (☎7863 8000; www.sadlerswells.com). ⊖Angel. Exit left from the tube, cross the road, and take the 2nd right on Roseberry Ave. Recently rebuilt as a brick-and-glass megalith, historic Sadler's Wells remains London's premier dance theater, with everything from classical ballet to contemporary tap and the occasional operas. Two smaller stages within the complex also offer nightly performances. 10/10 for transportation: Sadlers Wells Express (SWX) bus to Waterloo via Farringdon and Victoria leaves 8min. after the end of each mainstage evening show (£1.50, £1 with period Travelcard); those arriving by regular bus can have their fare refunded (and get cash for the journey home) at the box office. Box office open M-Sa 9am-8:30pm. £6-45; student, senior, and under-16 standbys £15 1hr. before curtain (cash only). Online booking available. Wheelchair accessible. AmEx/MC/V.

HOLBORN

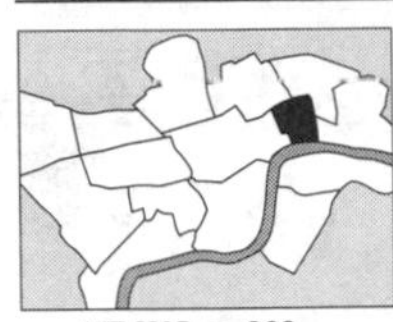

SEE MAP, p. 363

HOLBORN QUICKFIND: Discover, p. 7; sights, p. 97; museums & galleries, p. 143; food, p. 236; pubs, p. 197; nightlife, p. 211; shopping, p. 257; accommodations, p. 286.

Chuckle Club, at the Three Tuns Bar, Houghton St. (☎7476 1672; www.chuckleclub.com). ⊖Holborn. From Holborn walk south on Kingsway and turn left onto Aldwych, then turn left onto Houghton St.; it's in LSE's Clare Market Bldg. on the right. Located in the Three Tuns bar, this is not one of those "comedy is hip" clubs. A changing lineup of at least 3 headline acts and many tryouts guarantees more belly laughs than chuckles. Expect quality heckling from student-heavy audience. Show Sa 8:30pm; doors 7:45pm, line up 15min. earlier. Ticket admits you to the club/disco that follows the show (until 3am). £10, students £8.

Peacock Theatre, Portugal St. (☎0870 737 7737; www.sadlerswells.com). ⊖Holborn. Program leans toward contemporary dance, ballet, and popular dance-troupe shows. Some wheelchair accessible seats (£9) can be booked 24hr. in advance. Box office open M-Sa 10am-6:30pm, 10am-8:30pm on performance days. £10-35; cheaper rates M-Th and Sa matinee. Standbys (1 hr. before show) £15 and other discounts for students, seniors, under 16. Cheapest tickets at Box Office; fees for telephone and online booking. AmEx/MC/V.

KENSINGTON & EARL'S COURT

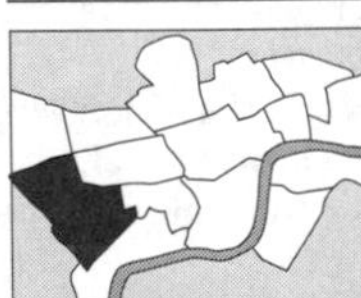

SEE MAP, pp. 364-365

KENSINGTON & EARL'S COURT QUICKFIND: Discover, p. 8; sights, p. 100; museums & galleries, p. 145; food, p. 171; pubs, p. 198; shopping, p. 257; accommodations, p. 286.

MUSIC: CLASSICAL AND OPERA

The Proms (☎7589 8212; accessibility info ☎7589 3853; www.bbc.co.uk/proms), at the Royal Albert Hall (see below). The summer season of classical music has been held every year since 1895, with concerts every night from mid-July to mid-Sept. "Promenade" refers to the tradition of selling dirt-cheap standing tickets, and it's the presence of up to 1400 dedicated prommers that gives the concerts their unique, informal atmosphere—that and the lack of A/C. Seats for popular concerts sell out months in advance, while lines for standing places often start mid-afternoon. If you plan on standing, the **arena,** immediately in front of the orchestra, tends to be most popular; the nosebleed-inducing **gallery** has more space, but you need binoculars to see the musicians. The famous **Last Night** is an unabashedly jingoistic celebration complete with Union Jack-painted faces, flag-waving, and mass sing-a-longs of "Rule Britannia." Regarded with horror by "serious" music lovers, it's so popular that you have to have attended at least 6 other summer concerts before they'll let you take part in a lottery for Last Night tickets. Tickets for seats go on sale in mid-May (£5-75; occasional discounts for under 16); standing places sold the morning of the performance, with 500 saved for 90min. before the concert (£4; cash only). Season ticket £160 arena, £135 gallery; half-season £90/£75. All concerts are transmitted live on BBC Radio 3 (91.3FM), and the Last Night is broadcasted on a big screen in Hyde Park.

Holland Park Theatre, Holland Park (☎7361 3057, box office ☎0845 230 9769; www.rbkc.gov.uk/hollandpark). ⊖High St. Kensington or Holland Park. Open-air performance space in the atmospheric ruins of Holland House, grounds of a Jacobean mansion. Outdoor setting aside, the program is generally a bit less adventurous, and the prices are steep. No need to fear the rain—everything is held under a huge white canopy. Performances from June to early Aug. Tu-Sa 7:30pm, occasional matinees Sa 2:30pm. For 2 weeks in Aug., the **Holland Park Shakespeare Festival** (www.openairshakespeare.co.uk) takes over. Box office located in the Old Stable Block just to the west of the opera; open from late Mar. M-Sa 10am-6pm or 30min. after curtain. Tickets £26-42; concessions £33 (selected dates only). Special allocation of tickets for wheelchair users. AmEx/MC/V.

GENERAL VENUES

Earl's Court Exhibition Centre, Warwick Rd. and **Olympia Exhibition Centre,** Hammersmith Rd. (for both: ☎7385 1200; www.eco.co.uk). ⊖Earl's Court for Earl's Court, Kensington/Olympia for Olympia. London's main venues for trade fairs and mega-expos, from the London Car Show to the Great British Beer Festival (see **All Play No Work,** p. 203). Earl's Court is also popular with pop acts (Madonna and Justin Timberlake played here in 2004), while Olympia generally sticks to Flower Expos and the odd Erotica Exposition. Wheelchair accessible.

Royal Albert Hall, Kensington Gore (see p. 101 for details). 5300-seat Victorian mega-venue holding anything from trade fairs to pop concerts. From mid-July to mid-Sept., the hall rocks to the sound of the **Proms** (see above).

MARYLEBONE & REGENT'S PARK

MARYLEBONE & REGENT'S PARK QUICKFIND: Discover, p. 9; sights, p. 103; museums & galleries, p. 147; food, p. 173; pubs, p. 199; accommodations, p. 291.

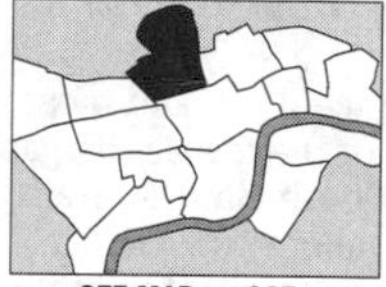

SEE MAP, p. 367

Open-Air Theatre, Inner Circle, Regents Park (☎0870 060 1811; www.openairtheatre.org). ⊖Baker St. Charming, occasionally magical venue in the middle of Regent's Park. Bring blankets and raingear to this open-air stage—performances get cancelled only in the most extreme weather conditions. Well-reviewed program runs early June to early Sept. and always includes 2 Shakespeare plays, a musical, and a children's performance. BBQ before evening shows. Performances: M-Sa 8pm; matinees most Th and every Sa 2:30pm. £8-28; discounts for groups and under 16; student and senior standby £9 from 1hr. before curtain. Box office open Apr.-May M-Sa 10am-6pm; Jun.-Sept. M-Sa 10am-8pm, Su (only performance days) 10am-8pm. Wheelchair accessible. AmEx/MC/V.

Wigmore Hall, 36 Wigmore St. (☎7935 2141; www.wigmore-hall.org.uk). ⊖Oxford Circus. London's premier chamber-music venue, in a beautiful setting with excellent acoustics; occasional jazz recitals. Newly refurbished in summer 2004. Box office open M-F 10am-5pm; during performance weeks M-Sa 10am-8:30pm and Su 10:30am-5pm. Phone bookings (£1.50 extra) open mid-Mar. to Oct. M-Sa 10am-7pm, Su 10:30am-6:30pm; Nov. to mid-Mar. M-Sa 10am-7pm, Su 10:30am-6pm. Season Oct.-Jul.; concerts most nights 7:30pm. Prices vary greatly with event (£2-35). Wheelchair accessible. AmEx/MC/V.

NOTTING HILL

NOTTING HILL QUICKFIND: Discover, p. 9; sights, p. 105; food, p. 174; pubs, p. 200; nightlife, p. 212; shopping, p. 259; accommodations, p. 292.

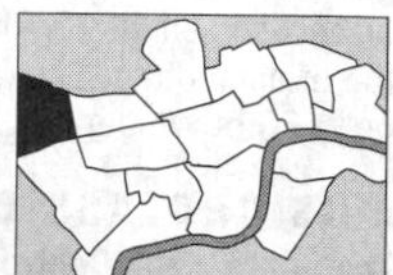

SEE MAP, p. 359

Electric Cinema, 191 Portobello Rd. (☎7908 9696; www.the-electric.co.uk). ⊖Notting Hill Gate or Ladbroke Grove. The improved version of London's oldest cinema (built 1910), recently reopened after a 15-year hiatus. The Baroque splendor of a stage theater paired with a sleek big screen. Leather armchairs and loveseats make for a luxurious cinematic experience. Independent and international films, including docudramas, classics, and recent raves. Double bills Su 2pm (£7.50). Kids Club films Sa 1pm (£4.50). M £7.50, Tu-Su £12.50; 2-seat sofa M £20, Tu-Su £30; front 3 rows M £5, Tu-Su £10. Wheelchair accessible.

The Gate, 11 Pembridge Rd. (☎7229 0706; www.gatetheatre.co.uk). ⊖Notting Hill Gate. In a tiny room above the Prince Albert pub. Famous for supporting fledgling international writers, the Gate's aim is to "discover the hidden riches of international drama"—they often premiere new foreign works (in English translation) before they've been performed in their home countries. Performances M-Sa 7:30pm. Happy M: first 30 customers "pay what you can" at the door. Box office open for phone bookings M-Sa 10am-6:30pm, in person from 6:30pm. £14, concessions £7. MC/V.

Gate Cinema, 87 Notting Hill Gate (☎7727 4043; www.picturehouses.co.uk). ⊖Notting Hill Gate. Opened in 1911, Gate's drab exterior is a result of post-war reconstruction. Fortunately, the lovely Victorian interior remains intact. Small lobby leads to an intimate theatre. Admire the ceiling details while waiting for the film to start. This theater hosted the world premiere of *Notting Hill*. Art-house, international and discerning Hollywood flicks on daily rotation. £7, 1st show M-F £5, concessions £3.50 only M-F before 6pm and F-Sa latest shows. Wheelchair accessible. MC/V (80p surcharge).

THE SOUTH BANK

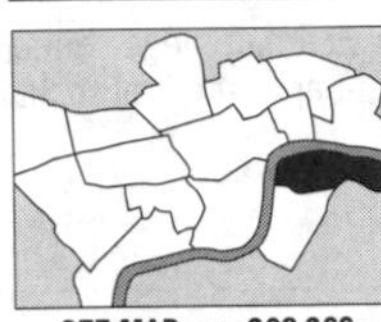

SEE MAP, pp. 368-369

SOUTH BANK QUICKFIND: Discover, p. 10; sights, p. 106; museums & galleries, p. 148; food, p. 176; pubs, p. 200; nightlife, p. 212; accommodations, p. 292.

The South Bank is hard to beat in classical entertainment; it offers the most concentrated array of theater, music, and serious film in Britain. If you're in the mood for something more lighthearted, try out the massive BFI IMAX cinema, or relax to the free jazz that often fills the South Bank Centre foyers. On nice days, and most weekends street musicians become wharf musicians and play for the masses. Organized by the community developers responsible for much of the South Bank's vitality, the **Coin Street Festival** (☎7401 2255; www.coinstreetfestival.org) runs in late summer. A sporadic succession of independent events, the festival celebrates ethnic diversity, modern design, and world music in and around Gabriel's Wharf and OXO Tower Wharf (see p. 109), finishing in mid-September with the **Mayor's Thames Festival** along the South Bank embankment.

CINEMA

National Film Theatre (NFT; ☎7928 3232; www.bfi.org.uk/nft). ⊖Waterloo, Embankment, or Temple. Underneath Waterloo Bridge. This is a one-stop shop for alternatives to the summer blockbusters: European art-house retrospectives, old American flicks and special director's series fill the program. 6 different shows hit 3 screens every evening (9 shows on weekends), starting around 6pm (2pm on weekends). The sprawling super popular cafe and bar on the ground floor serve up goodies to the masses. Annual membership (£22, concessions £14) gives £1 off movies, priority booking, and a free ticket when you join. All films £7.50, concessions £5.70. Wheelchair accessible.

BFI London IMAX Cinema, 1 Charlie Chaplin Walk (box office ☎0870 787 2525; www.bfi.org.uk/imax). ⊖Waterloo. At the south end of Waterloo bridge, accessed via underground walkways from the South Bank and the Tube station. This theatre sticks out like a glass enclosed sore thumb: it rises in the center of a traffic roundabout. It houses the UK's biggest screen: at 20m high and 26m wide, it's taller than 5 double-decker buses stacked on top of each other. Shows start every 1-1¼hr.; last show 8pm daily. £7.90, concessions (M-F only) £6.50, under 16 £5.

MUSIC: CLASSICAL, WORLD & JAZZ

The South Bank Centre (☎7960 4242, or 0870 380 9988; www.rfh.org.uk). ⊖Waterloo or Embankment. This megaplex of concert halls features all kinds of music. Tickets for all events can be purchased from the Royal Festival Hall box office (open daily 11am-8pm, until 9pm on performance days, even though the venue is closed until 2007); Queen Elizabeth Hall and Purcell Room box offices open 45min. before performance, but tickets can be purchased from that phone number. Some discounts for concessions and under 18; some £5-10 standbys from 2hr. before performance.

Royal Festival Hall: Closing from July 2005 until January 2007 for major improvements on acoustics, education department, and the waterside facade. It's a 2700-seat concert hall with the best acoustics in London, soon to be even better. Some of the cheapest seats are the choir benches, which put you right behind the orchestra. The 2 resident orchestras, the **Philharmonia** and the **London Philharmonic,** predominate, but big-name jazz, latin, and world-music groups also visit. While under construction, all the events will take place in the halls below. Classical concerts £6-50; others £10-30.

Queen Elizabeth Hall: Mid-sized venue used for smaller musical ensembles; more varied and multicultural program than the Festival Hall. World-class jazz soloists and Indian DJs share the space with choirs and classics. Occasional literary evenings. With the renovations, tickets may be hard to come by. Call as early as possible. £10-25.

Purcell Room: Intimate hall for chamber music, soloists, and small groups, with the usual varied South Bank repertoire. Same availability warning as above applies. Most shows around £15.

THEATER

Shakespeare's Globe Theatre, 21 New Globe Walk (☎7401 9919; www.shakespeares-globe.org). ⊖Southwark or London Bridge. Innovative, top-notch performances at this faithful reproduction of Shakespeare's original 16th-century playhouse. Aside from the classic dramas, some shows modernize the script or have an all-female cast. Choose among 3covered tiers of hard, backless wooden benches (cushions £1 extra) or stand through a performance as a "groundling." The latter costs less, allows a historical communion with the Elizabethan peasantry, and puts you much closer to the stage. It can be a tad uncomfortable; come 30min. before the show to get as close as you can. Should it rain, however, the show must go on, and umbrellas are prohibited. For **tours** of the Globe, see p. 107. Performances mid-May to late Sept. Tu-Sa 7:30pm, Su 6:30pm; June-Sept. also Tu-Sa 2pm, Su 1pm. Box office open M-Sa 10am-6pm, 8pm on performance days. Seats £12-27, concessions £10-24, yard (i.e. standing) £5. Raingear £2.50. Weekend performances can sell out early, especially the seats. Wheelchair accessible.

National Theatre, (info ☎7452 3400, box office ☎7452 3000; www.nationaltheatre.org.uk). ⊖Waterloo or Embankment. Founded by Laurence Olivier, the National Theatre opened in 1976 and has been at the forefront of British theater ever since. Popular musicals and hit plays, often transfer to the West End, although the dramatic productions are what it's famous for. Bigger shows are mostly staged on the **Olivier,** which seats 1160 in a fan-shaped open-stage layout; the 890-seat **Lyttleton** is a proscenium theater, while the **Cottesloe** offers flexible staging for new works. Box office open M-Sa 10am-8pm. Complicated pricing scheme, which is liable to change from show to show: Olivier/Lyttelton £10-34, Cottesloe £10-27, standby (90min. before curtain) £10 all theaters, standing places (only available if all seats sold) £6. Numerous concessions include: matinees seniors £16, under-18 £10; M-Th evenings under 25 £15; disabled £8-16; student standby £8 from 45min. before curtain. Wheelchair accessible.

Old Vic, Waterloo Rd. (☎7369 1722; www.oldvictheatre.com). ⊖Waterloo. Still in its original 1818 hall (the oldest theater in London), the Old Vic is one of London's most historic and most beautiful theaters. The elegant front facade leads to an equally fancy Victorian lobby. These days, it hosts touring companies like the Royal Shakespeare Company, which set their own prices and show schedules. There are also often guest directors and actors, for 2004-05 Kevin Spacey is the artistic director, and will be acting as well. Check website for listings. Box office generally M-Th 10am-7pm, F-Sa until 7:30pm.

Young Vic, 66 The Cut (☎7928 6363; www.youngvic.org). ⊖Waterloo. Close to the Old Vic but completely independent, the Young Vic is conducive to experimental theater. It closed in July 2004 for extensive renovations and is set to open in 2006. Historically one of London's top off-West End companies. The new venue will have more seats and better acoustics. Check online for updates.

STUDENT DISCOUNTS. Often on the day of a West End show, students can get best available seats for £15-20. Show up at the box office well before the show and ask about it.

THE WEST END

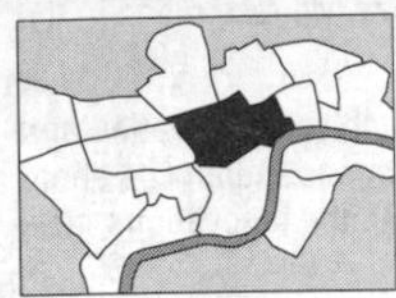

SEE MAP, p. 354

WEST END QUICKFIND: Discover, p. 10; sights, p. 111; museums & galleries, p. 150; food, p. 177; pubs, p. 201; nightlife, p. 212; shopping, p. 261; accommodations, p. 292.

So prominent is the West End in London's entertainment industry that the term "West End Theatre" now refers to any major mainstream London theater, whether or not it's actually in the West End. **Shaftesbury Avenue** in Soho, **Drury Lane** and the **Aldwych** in Covent Garden, and the **Strand** have been synonymous with the London stage for centuries, ever since the crown ended Theatre Royal's legal monopoly on the area in the 19th century. **Leicester Square** is home to the essential **tkts** (see p. 242), which peddles coveted discount tickets to budget theatergoers (although it is nearly always cheaper to **go to the theatre itself**), as well as London's largest first-run cinemas. If you worry that the entertainment in the West End is too mainstream, off-West End and fringe theaters lie just yards from *Mamma Mia!* and *Les Misérables*, while art-house and repertory indie films play just a stone's throw from Leicester Sq. and Piccadilly Circus.

CINEMA

Cinemas abound in the West End, most of them concentrated in gaudy Leicester Sq. Unless you've booked early for a premiere, it's best to avoid the megaplex cinemas on the square itself—they all charge a few pounds more than those on the surrounding streets. Also, it pays to buy tickets in advance (or at least show up early to purchase); seating in most cinemas is assigned according to first-come, first-choice.

Curzon Soho, 93-107 Shaftesbury Ave. (☎7734 2255; www.curzoncinemas.com). ⊖Leicester Sq. This huge cinema has a cafe on the ground floor and a fully-loaded bar for ticket holders on the lower level. It retains the same good taste in good films– watch the latest hot independent and international films from your plush, highbacked seat (plus Su classic and repertory double bills). Frequent talks and Q&A sessions from big-name indie directors. 3 screens. Tu-Su £8.50; M all day and Tu-F before 5pm £5.50; Su matinees and double bills £6; M-Th concessions £5.50; under 14 £4.50. Wheelchair accessible. AmEx/MC/V.

Prince Charles Cinema, 7 Leicester Pl. (☎7957 4009 or 7420 0000; www.princecharlescinema.com). ⊖Leicester Sq. Just off blockbuster-ridden Leicester Sq., the Prince Charles couldn't offer more of a contrast. Most notably, they host the offbeat sing-along screenings of *The Sound of Music* (F 7:30pm; £13.50) with a costumed host and dress competitions (www.singalonga.com). Other times feature second-run Hollywood films and recent independents for unbelievably low prices. Tickets £3-4.

ICA Cinema, Institute of Contemporary Arts. See p. 151.

COMEDY

Comedy Store, 1a Oxendon St. (Tickets: TicketMaster booking number ☎0870 060 2340; www.thecomedystore.co.uk). ⊖Piccadilly Circus. The UK's top comedy club (founded in a former strip club) sowed the seeds that gave rise to *Absolutely Fabulous, Whose Line is it Anyway?*, and *Blackadder*, while Robin Williams did frequent improv acts here in the 80s. A large venue (400 seats), with an intimate feel. Tu Cutting Edge (contemporary news-based satire), W and Su *Comedy Store Players* improv, Th-Sa standup. With former *Whose Line...* costar Josie Lawrence among the top draws, the players are widely acknowledged to produce the best improv in London. Grab food at the bar before shows and during interval (burger £6), and bring it back to your seat. Loosen up before the show with happy hour 6:30-7:30pm. Shows Tu-Su 8pm, plus F-Sa midnight. Book ahead. Over-18s only. Tu and W £12, concessions £8; Th, F early show, and Sa £15, no concessions; F late show and Su £13, concessions £8. Box office open Tu-Su 6:30-9:30pm, F-Sa 6:30pm-1:30am. 100 seats always available at the door. MC/V.

MUSIC: CLASSICAL, OPERA, AND BALLET

English National Opera, the Coliseum, St. Martin's Ln. (☎7632 8300; www.eno.org). ⊖Charing Cross or Leicester Sq. The newly re-opened London Coliseum is staggering—huge, ornate, and complete with 500 £10 seats for sale at every performance—and the ENO has proven it can fill the venue with its innovative productions of the classics and some more contemporary, avant-garde work. All performances in English. Box office open M-Sa 10am-8pm. £5-9; under-18 half-price with adult, students £12.50. Cheap standbys bookable on performance days, by phone from 12:30pm, 10am in person; 1 per person. Wheelchair accessible. AmEx/MC/V.

Royal Opera House, Bow St. (☎7304 4000; www.royaloperahouse.org). ⊖Covent Garden. Known as "Covent Garden" to the aficionado, the Royal Opera House is also home to the Royal Ballet. Productions tend to be conservative but lavish, just like the patrons. Late 2004-2005 will see *Cinderella* at the ballet, and *Faust* and *Cosi Fan Tutte* at the Opera. Prices for the best seats (orchestra stalls) regularly top £100, but standing room and restricted-view seating in the upper balconies can be under £5. Tickets unsold 4hr. before curtain available at half-price to everyone; student, senior, and under-18 standby £12.50 ballet, £15 opera. 67 seats available from 10am on day of performance, limit 1 per person. Discounts available online. Box office open M-Sa 10am-6pm. AmEx/MC/V.

MUSIC: JAZZ

Ronnie Scott's, 47 Frith St. (☎7439 0747; www.ronniescotts.co.uk). ⊖Tottenham Crt. Rd. or Leicester Sq. The reputation justifies the prices. This intimate venue is London's oldest and most famous jazz club, having hosted everyone from Dizzy Gillespie to Jimi Hendrix. 2 bands alternate 4 sets every M-Sa night, the support starting at 9:30pm, the headline act around 11pm; Su brings lesser-known bands from 7:30pm. Table reservations essential for big-name acts, though there's limited unreserved standing room at the smoky bar—if it's sold out, try coming back at the end of the main act's first set, around midnight. Ask for a non-smoking table to be (probably) right by the stage. Food £6-25, cocktails £7-9. Box office open M-Sa noon-5:30pm. Club open M-Sa 8:30pm-3am, Su 7:30-11pm. M-Th £15, F-Sa £25, Su £8-12; M-W students £10. AmEx/MC/V.

100 Club, 100 Oxford St. (☎7636 0933; www.the100club.co.uk). ⊖Tottenham Crt. Rd. Stage, audience, and bar are all bathed in sallow orange light in this jazz venue that makes frequent excursions into indie rock. Weekdays see the serious indie and jazz, while weekends tend to become more "date-friendly" and mellow. Punk burst onto the scene at a legendary gig here in 1976, when the Sex Pistols, the Clash, and Siouxsie and the Banshees all shared the stage in 1 evening. Regular nights include M night Stompin', Sa night swing. Open F 8:30pm-2am, Sa-Su 7:30pm-midnight, other nights vary. Cover £7-15, concessions £5-10. AmEx/MC/V.

Pizza Express Jazz Club, 10 Dean St. (☎7439 8722; www.pizzaexpress.co.uk/jazz.htm). ⊖Tottenham Crt. Rd. Underneath a branch of the popular chain (see p. 163), sophisticated diners dig into pizzas while feasting their ears on music. Surprisingly one of the better places to hear innovative contemporary jazz, with the classy trappings of an old-time club. Big names have included Van Morrisson and Diana Krall, along with more on-topic headliners. Table reservations recommended, especially F-Sa. Doors normally open 7:45pm, music 9-11:30pm; some F-Sa have 2 shows, with doors opening at 6 and 10pm. Cover (£15-20) added to the food bill. AmEx/M/V.

MUSIC: ROCK AND POP

London Astoria (LA1), 157 Charing Cross Rd. (☎7344 0044; www.londonastoria.com). ⊖Tottenham Crt. Rd. Former pickle factory, strip club, and music hall before turning to full-time rock venue in the late 1980s. Now basking in an air of somewhat faded glory, the 2000-capacity venue only occasionally hosts big names (such as the Red Hot Chilli Peppers and Blink182). At this point, it's more famous for the popular G-A-Y M, Th-Sa clubnight (see p. 209.)

Borderline, Orange Yard, off Manette St. (☎7534 6970; www.borderline.co.uk) ⊖Tottenham Crt. Rd. Warm, funky, smoky basement space—175 seats set around a small stage—used for well-known groups with strong folk-rock flavor. Past luminaries include Oasis,

the hidden deal

No Pence? No Problem?

Do you have a fine ear for Figaro, a good grasp of Giselle? Or maybe you're not quite up on your dead composers and iconic ballets. No worries, beginners and experts alike can enjoy the vast talents of London's prestigious **Royal Opera** and delight in the wizardry of the **Royal Ballet** without the debilitating commitment of a gigantic bill to keep you away.

The Royal Opera House's 'Performance in the Park' series is a welcome relief for the penny-pinching connoisseur of high culture. Every summer, dates are announced for a number of live giant-screen broadcasts that bring the ROH's acclaimed main-stage performances to delighted audiences in Trafalgar Square, Covent Garden Piazza, and Victoria Park.

The ROH brings at least one performance of each of its main-stage productions to the masses, and 2005's schedule will be announced on their official website (www.royaloperahouse.org) by late 2004. Check the schedule, plan your picnic, and prepare to soak in all that high culture without putting a dent in your pocketbook.

More information at the Royal Opera House, Bow St. in Covent Garden (☎ 7304 4000; www.royaloperahouse.org). Box Office open M-Sa 10am-8pm.

Pearl Jam, and Spinal Tap. Music M-Sa usually 7pm-3am. Box office open M-Sa 10am-6pm. £10-25 in advance. AmEx/MC/V.

THEATER

tkts, on the south side of Leicester Sq. (www.tkts.co.uk). ⊖Leicester Sq. First off, we'll say it again: **you'll most likely get the best deal, especially with less popular shows, by going directly to the theater.** Now for tkts: run jointly by London theaters, tkts (formerly the Half-Price Ticket Booth) is the only place where you can be sure your half-price tickets are genuine. The catch is that theaters only release the most expensive tickets to the booth, which means that it's a good deal for the best seats in the house, but rarely under £15 (most musicals around £23, plays £20-22). In addition, you can only buy day-of tickets in person, with little seating choice. There's no way of knowing in advance what shows will have tickets available that day, but there is almost always a wide range (they'll usually offer some full-price tickets and smaller discounts in order to increase options). Notice-boards display what's going on; up to £2.50 booking fee per ticket. No limit on the number of tickets you can buy. Open M-Sa 10am-7pm, Su noon-3pm. Wheelchair accessible. MC/V.

Donmar Warehouse, 41 Earlham St. (☎ 7369 1777; www.donmarwarehouse.com). ⊖Covent Garden. In the mid-90s, artistic director Sam Mendes (later of *American Beauty* fame) transformed this gritty space into one of the best theatres in the country. Serious contemporary stuff with an edge. Past productions have starred the likes of Nicole Kidman and Colin Firth, so it's not surprising that this nondescript warehouse rarely has difficulty filling its 251 seats. Nov. 2004 will see the musical Grand Hotel make an entrance here. £13 -29; concessions and under-18 standby 30min £12. before curtain; £5 standing-room tickets available once performance is sold out. Box office open M-Sa 10am-7:30pm. Wheelchair accessible. AmEx/MC/V.

Soho Theatre, 21 Dean St. (☎ 0870 429 6883; www.sohotheatre.com). ⊖Tottenham Crt. Rd. With a focus on new writers and plenty of low-priced tickets, this populist, modern "off-west end" theater intends to introduce people of all ages to theater. These aren't generally well-known plays, but that's what the excitement of a new writers' theatre is all about. The associated writers' center will read any script you send them and provide comments. M nights and matinees £5; Tu-Th £14, concessions £10; F-Sa £15/£12.50. Online prices Tu-Th £12. Late night stand-up comedy £6-15. Box office open M-Sa 10am-last performance. MC/V.

Long-running shows, see p. 227.

Theatreland

THEATRES

Theatre	Grid	Theatre	Grid
The Adelphi **1**	F3	Phoenix, **14**	D1
Aldwych, **2**	G2	Piccadilly, **15**	C3
Comedy Store, **3**	D4	Prince Edward, **16**	D2
Criterion, **4**	C4	Prince of Wales, **17**	D3
Dominion, **5**	D1	Queen's, **18**	C3
Donmar Warehouse, **6**	E2	Royal Opera House, **19**	F2
English National Opera, **7**	E3	Savoy, **20**	G3
Fortune, **8**	G2	Soho Theatre, **21**	C1
Her Majesty's, **9**	D4	Strand, **22**	G2
London Palladium, **10**	A1	St. Martin's, **23**	E2
Lyceum, **11**	G3	Theatre Royal, Drury Lane, **24**	G2
New London, **12**	F1	tkts, **25**	D3
Palace, **13**	D2		

Map: See **Theatreland** Map.

The Adelphi, Strand. *Chicago.*

Aldwych Theatre, Aldwych St. *Fame: The Musical.*

Apollo Victoria Theatre, Wilton Rd. *Saturday Night Fever*

Criterion Theatre, Piccadilly Circus. *The Complete Works of William Shakespeare (Abridged) and The Complete History of America (Abridged).*

Dominion Theatre, Tottenham Crt. Rd. *We Will Rock You.*

Donmar Warehouse, Earlham St. Grand Hotel (opens Feb. 2005).

Fortune Theatre, Russell St. *The Woman in Black.*

Her Majesty's Theatre, Haymarket. *Phantom of the Opera.*

London Palladium, Argyll St. *Chitty Chitty Bang Bang.*

Lyceum Theatre, Wellington St. *Disney's The Lion King.*

New London Theatre, Drury Ln. *Joseph and the Amazing...*

Palace Theatre, Shaftesbury Ave. *The Woman in White.*

Phoenix Theatre, Charing Cross Rd. *Blood Brothers.*

Piccadilly Theatre, Denman St. *Jailhouse Rock.*

Prince Edward Theatre, Old Compton St. *Mary Poppins.*

Prince of Wales, Coventry St. *Mamma Mia!*

Queen's Theatre, Shaftesbury Ave. *Les Misérables.*

St. Martin's Theatre, West St. *The Mousetrap.*

Theatre Royal, Drury Lane, Catharine St. *The Producers.*

OTHER

Cycle Rickshaws (☎0870 240 5719; www.londonpedicabs.com) bring a touch of Bangkok to an area now largely denuded of strip joints and sex shops. If you'd rather not explore Soho on foot, flag down a pedicab driver to cart you around. Marvel as your driver nimbly evades cars screeching past. Rickshaws congregate at various points around the West End, but the most popular pick-up spot is the corner of Firth St. and Old Compton St. (⊖Piccadilly Circus or Leicester Sq.), Su-Th 6pm-1am, F-Sa 6pm-4am. Short spins around Soho £2.50-3 per person; longer trips £5 per person per mi. 2 full-sized people per rickshaw. Agree to a price before you go.

WESTMINSTER

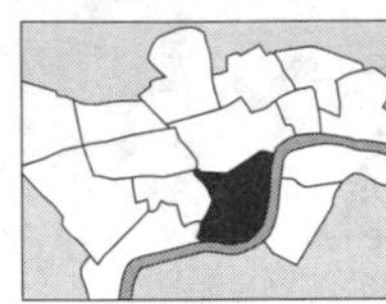

SEE MAP, p. 370

WESTMINSTER QUICKFIND: Discover, p. 11; sights, p. 116; museums & galleries, p. 152; food, p. 181; pubs, p. 202; accommodations, p. 293.

St. John's, Smith Square, Smith Sq. (☎7222 1061; www.sjss.org.uk). ⊖Westminster or St. James's Park. A former church (see p. 119), now a full-time concert venue with a program weighted toward chamber and classical music; rarely sold-out but highly regarded by critics. Excellent acoustics. Restaurant in the undercroft serves concert suppers, a great value at £13.50 for 2 courses, £16.50 for 3. Concerts Sept. to mid-July daily, mid-July to Aug. 1-2 per week. Performances generally start 7:30pm. £8-15; concessions sometimes available. Box office open M-F 10am-5pm.

St. Martin-in-the-Fields, Trafalgar Sq. (see p. 117; box office ☎7839 8362). Frequent concerts and recitals are given in this ornate 18th-century church, home to the acclaimed Academy of St. Martin-in-the-Fields, which occasionally plays here. Music includes Baroque, chamber, solo or group recitals. Free lunchtime concerts most weekdays 1:05pm. Tourist-oriented candlelit evening concerts Tu–Sa 7:30pm, £6-18.

NORTH LONDON

NORTH LONDON QUICKFIND: Discover, p. 12; sights, p. 120; museums & galleries, p. 153; food, p. 183; pubs, p. 203; nightlife, p. 218; shopping, p. 269; accommodations, p. 294.

CINEMA

Tricycle Cinema, (box office ☎7328 1000, film info ☎7328 1900); entrance on Buckley Rd. Specializes in independent and foreign films, with the occasional Hollywood blockbuster. Films stay for a week or two, buy tickets in advance for popular flicks. A few movies play on a rotating schedule. Recline on the plush pink seats and enjoy the show. Tricycle print rugs and decor complete the picture. Singles night 1st Th of the month including pre-movie champagne and post-movie bar (£12, concessions £9). Family films Sa 1pm (£4, concessions £3). Supercheap matinees Th and F 2:30pm (£3.50, concessions £3). Regular features £7, £4.50 bargain M and Tu-F before 5pm; concessions £1 less M-F before 8pm and Sa-Su before 5pm. Wheelchair accessible. MC/V.

Everyman Cinema, 5 Holly Bush Vale (☎08700 664 777; www.everymancinema.com). ⊖Hampstead. One of London's oldest movie theaters, this 1930s picture house was recently revamped and is now hipper and more comfortable than ever. Lean back on the pillowed leather sofas on the "luxury" balcony, or snuggle into one of the velvet stall seats. Bars and lounges offer pre-, or post-show drinks. Mostly new independent films. Box office open daily noon-11pm. Cafe/bar open daily 2pm-11pm. Gallery with drink £15, Standard/loveseats £9, concessions £7.50 M-F and Sa-Su matinees only. Wheelchair accessible. MC/V.

COMEDY

Canal Cafe Theatre, (☎7289 6054) above the Bridge House pub, Delamere Terr. ⊖Warwick Ave. One of the few comedy venues to specialize in sketch, as opposed to stand-up. Cozy red velvet chairs and a rear raised balcony means that everyone gets a good view of the small stage. Grab dinner below and enjoy your drinks around the small tables. Box office opens 30min. before performance. Weekly changing shows W-Sa 7:30 and 9:30pm (£5, concessions £4). *Newsrevue,* Th-Sa 9:30pm and Su 9pm, is London's longest-running comedy sketch show, a hilarious satire of weekly current events since 1979 (£9, concessions £7). Both shows together cost £12. £1 membership included in ticket price.

Downstairs at the King's Head, 2 Crouch End Hill (☎8340 1028; www.downstairsattheking-shead,cin). Bus #W7 from Finsbury Park tube, take the Wells Terrace exit and get on the bus, get off after the bus turn right. One of London's oldest comedy clubs, in a cozy space under a pub. Shows start 8 or 8:30pm, doors 30min. earlier. Try-outs every Th give up to 16 new acts (£4, concessions £3); Sa-Su "comedy cabarets" mix up to 5 acts, from stand-up to songs to ventriloquism (Sa cover £8, concessions £6; Su £7/, £5). Sunday afternoons lunchtime jazz 1-5pm, M nights Salsa class and dancing (£7/£5).

MUSIC: CLASSICAL, FOLK AND JAZZ

Jazz Café, 5 Parkway (☎7344 0044; www.jazzcafe.co.uk). ⊖Camden Town. Famous and popular. Crowded front bar and balcony restaurant overlook the dance floor and stage, both of which are just the right size. Shows can be pricey at this night spot but the top roster of jazz, hip-hop, funk, and Latin performers (£10-30) explains it. Jazzy DJs spin on club nights following the show F-Sa (cover £8-9, £5 with flyer), until 2am. Awesome jam session open to all young musicians Su noon-4pm (cover £3 or £1 with musical instrument). Open M-Th 7pm-1am, F-Sa 7pm-2am, Su 7pm-midnight. Partially wheelchair accessible. MC/V.

Music on a Summer Evening, in Kenwood Highgate (see p. 123; ☎7413 1443; www.picnic-concerts.com). Classical, jazz, R&B and classic tunes concerts along with lakeside fireworks held here July-Aug. 7:30pm, call/go online for schedule. The tender-eared might shrink from the amplified sound system. If you don't need to see, stay outside the enclosure and listen for free—music is audible for miles around. Deckchairs £21-25, concessions £19-22.50. You can't bring your own chairs; promenade (bring a groundsheet or risk a wet bum) £17/£15. Order ahead for most events, they sell out close to the date.

MUSIC: ROCK AND POP

Dublin Castle, 94 Parkway. (☎7485 1773) There's music in the back of this pub every night, which saves the pub from an otherwise dull existence. They find good up-and-coming acts and record execs and talent scouts often descend looking for the next big thing. After the bands finish the pub turns dance club until 1am. On weekends it gets crowded; get there

the hidden deal

The Student Scene

All that classy high-culture comes with a price tag heavy enough to smother the budget traveler beneath its weight. So when you don't feel like paying £10 to comtemplate Vin Diesel's lack of facial expression or £35 to sing along with *Mamma Mia!'s* dancing queens (although the latter we might recommend), try turning to London's most talented pre-famous artists and see what some world-renowned arts colleges are offering.

The **Royal College of Art.** Touted by Vogue as "a great place to discover big names of the future," Admission is usually free. (*www.rca.ac.uk. Open 10am-6pm daily, mid-Mar. to July. Kensington Gore. ☎7590 4444.*)

The **Royal College of Music.** Likely home to scads of future **Prom** performers. Popular "lunchtime concerts" at midday. Tickets free-£15. (*Prince Consort Rd. www.rcm.ac.uk. ☎7591 4314. MC/V.)*

The **Royal Academy of Dramatic Arts (RADA).** Catch the next Ralph Fiennes before he hits the big time. Regular Foyer events, with plays, music, and readings M-Th at 7pm or 7:30pm throughout the academic year (free-£4). *(62 64 Gower St., entrance on Malet St. ☎7908 4800. www.rada.org. Box office open M-F 10am-6pm, 7:30pm on performance nights. MC/V.)*

early to avoid a queue. 3 bands nightly 8:45-11pm; doors open 8:30pm. Cover Su-Th £5, students £4.50, F-Sa £6/£4.50. Wheelchair accessible.

Forum, 9-17 Highgate Rd. (☎7284 1001, box office 7344 0044; www.meanfiddler.com). ⊖Kentish Town. Turn right out of Tube station, go over the crest of the hill and bear left–you'll see the marquee. The outside looks grungy but inside it's a lavish Art Deco theater. The winning sound system and clear stage view has attracted some big names in the past: Van Morrison, Björk, Oasis, Jamiroquai, among others have played here. Many shows are random smaller groups, but famous bands still play relatively often. Tickets around £12-35.

The Garage, 20-22 Highbury Corner. Enter on Holloway Rd. (box office ☎7607 1818, upstairs 0870 150 0044; www.meanfiddler.com). ⊖Highbury and Islington. Hard core and indie rock groups play F-Sa and often weeknights too. There's also an occasional smattering of American punk and emo bands. Lesser acts play the upstairs room (gigs around £5). Music 8-11pm, F-Sa followed by an indie clubnight until 3am (included in gig ticket; clubnight alone F £6, £4 with flyer, Sa £7, £5 with flyer). F night Statik, punk, indie and eclectic contemporary music; Sa night International Hi-Fi. Gigs £5-20.

THEATRE

The Almeida, Almeida St. (☎7359 4404; www.almeida.co.uk). ⊖Angel or Highbury and Islington. The top fringe theater in London, if not the world; always comes up with novel scripts and quality shows, both dramatic and opera. Hollywood stars, including Kevin Spacey and Nicole Kidman, have both established acting credentials here. The metallic sparkling bar and foyer areas were part of the expensive 2003 renovations. Theatre seats 325-350. Shows M-Sa at 7:30pm, Sa matinees 3pm. Tickets £6-27.50, concessions £10 M-F and Sa matinees. Wheelchair accessible.

Etcetera Theatre, upstairs at the Oxford Arms, 265 Camden High St. (☎7482 4857; www.etceteratheatre.com). ⊖Camden Town. Aptly nicknamed the smallest theatre in the capital, it's got only 42 seats leading straight to a good-sized stage. Two plays per night of anything from drama to comedy. Mostly experimental stuff from new writers and unsolicited scripts, though there have been some famous directors and pieces featured here. Box office opens 30min. before the show. Shows M-Sa 7 or 7:30 and 9 or 9:30pm, Su 6:30 and 8:30pm. £8-10, concessions £5-8; includes 1yr. membership giving £1.50 off future tickets.

Hampstead Theatre, Eton Ave. (☎7722 9301; www.hampsteadtheater.com). ⊖Swiss Cottage. Take the Eton Ave. Tube exit. This theater features works selected from hundreds of unsolicited scripts by budding unknowns from around UK. Acting alumni include John Malkovich. Shows M-Sa 7:45pm and Sa 3pm. M £13, Tu-F and Sa 3pm £17.50, Sa 8pm £21. Limited concession, day of and student tickets (£10 off).

The King's Head, 115 Upper St. (☎7226 1916). ⊖Angel or Highbury and Islington. Above a hip pub, the theater focuses on new writing and rediscovered gems. The King's head has enjoyed good reviews in the press and successful productions often transfer to the West End. Alums include Hugh Grant, Gary Oldman, and Anthony Minghella. 3-course meal (£14) is available to ticket holders 1hr. before the show. Shows Tu-Sa 8pm, Sa 3:30pm; £10-20, concessions M-Th and matinees £5 cheaper. Occasional lunchtime shows and M night short run shows might be playing, call for exact schedule.

New End Theatre, 27 New End (☎7794 0022; www.newendtheatre.co.uk). ⊖Hampstead. New work skillfully produced by local and touring companies tends to have a historically or socially conscious bent. Tu-Sa night (Sa-Su matinee). Box office open M 10am-6pm, Tu-F 10am-7pm, Sa 11am-7pm, Su noon-3pm. £12-16, concessions available in advance £10-14.

The Old Red Lion, 418 St. John St. (☎7837 7816; www.oldredliontheatre.co.uk). ⊖Angel. Experimental plays and quirky adaptations in this closet of a theatre. Occasional film screenings and readings from new scripts. Shows change monthly or bimonthly. Performances Tu-Su 7:45 or 8pm (£12, Su and Tu-Th concessions £10), occasional M events. Call or drop by in advance.

Puppet Theatre Barge, colorful barge moored in Little Venice next to Blomfield Rd. (☎7249 6876; www.puppetbarge.com). ⊖Warwick Ave. Puppet and shadow-puppet shows beneath the bright red-and-yellow awnings of this Little Venice institution have thrilled children for years, while adult-oriented shows recall the ribald history of puppetry as a serious performance art. The boat makes it that much cooler. Children's shows most weekends and daily during holidays at 3pm; call for program. Reservations recommended for weekends. £7, children and concessions £6.50.

Tricycle, 269 Kilburn High Rd. (☎7328 1000; www.tricycle.co.uk). ⊖Kilburn or Rail: Brondesbury Park. A marvelous 3-in-1, with cinema (see above), art gallery, and a theater known for cutting edge work and new minority playwrights. One of the most fun places to see a show. Box office open M-Sa 10am-9pm, Su 2-9pm. Performances M-F 8pm, Sa 4 and 8pm. Tickets £10-17; concessions Tu-F £2 less, Tu evenings and Sa matinees pay-what-you-can (first 30 seats). Wheelchair accessible.

SOUTH LONDON

SOUTH LONDON QUICKFIND: Discover, p. 14; sights, p. 125; museums & galleries, p. 155; food, p. 186; nightlife, p. 221; shopping, p. 271.

Battersea Arts Centre (BAC), Old Town Hall, 176 Lavender Hill (☎7223 2223, www.bac.org.uk). ⊖Clapham Common or Stockwell, then 15min. bus ride on the #345 (get off at Lavender Hill right outside BAC); bus: #345, 77, 77a, 156, and G1 stop at the door; or Rail: Clapham Junction. From Clapham Junction, take the shopping center exit, turn left and walk straight up Lavender Hill for 10min. BAC is right after the junction with Latchmere Rd. One of London's top off-West End venues, best known for experimental theater and new works. Also hosts comedy, opera, and "mainstream works" (generally radical reinterpretations of canonical texts). Plenty of family-friendly selections. On occasional 'Scratch Nights,' guinea pigs can see works in progress for free (advance booking essential). Box office open M-Sa 10:30am-6pm, Su 4-8pm. Tickets usually £13, concessions £7. MC/V.

Brixton Academy, 211 Stockwell Rd. (bookings on Ticketweb, ☎7771 3000; www.brixton-academy.co.uk). ⊖Brixton. 4300-seats, 1929 Art Deco ex-cinema with a sloping floor ensures even those at the back have a chance to see the band. In 2004, named *Time Out's* "Live Venue of the Year." Recent names include Maroon5, PJ Harvey, Dido, and the Pogues. Box office open only on performance evenings; order online or by telephone, or go to the Shepherd's Bush Empire box office, Shepherd's Bush Green, M-Sa noon-5pm. £15-20, sometimes up to £33. Ocassionally hosts F-Sa club nights, call or check website for details.

The Swan, 215 Clapham Rd. (☎7978 9778; www.theswanstockwell.co.uk). ⊖Stockwell. Opposite the Tube. Large, dark pub venue with shabby but comfortable furnishings and a devoted crowd of regulars. Th "Thank God It's Thursday" essential rock, pop, and indie dance anthems; F live bands; Sa-Su rock and indie bands. Recently leaning heavily towards tribute bands. Music starts 10pm. Open Th 6pm-2am, F 6pm-3am, Sa 7pm-3am, Su 7pm-2am. Cover: F £3.50, before 8pm free; Sa £6, before 9pm £3; Su £3, free before 10pm. No admittance after 2am. MC/V (£10 min.).

EAST LONDON

EAST LONDON QUICKFIND: Discover, p. 13; sights, p. 126; museums & galleries, p. 156; food, p. 187; pubs, p. 204; nightlife, p. 222; shopping, p. 271.

Comedy Cafe, 66 Rivington St. (☎7739 5706; www.comedycafe.co.uk). One of London's best venues for stand-up; come see both established stars and hot young talent. The outside is painted in comedically bright colors; the inside holds a bar and music space as well as the comedy stage. Skip the food and stick to beers (£2.70). If you run up the bar bill, at least you'll be laughing all the way to the ATM. Reserve F-Sa. W no cover try-out night, Th £5, F £10, Sa £14. Group packages W-Sa £16-30. Happy hour 6-7 F-Sa nights, F-Sa nights include disco and dancing. Doors open 7pm W-Th, 6pm F-Sa, show 9pm, dancing to 1am. MC/V.

Hackney Empire, 291 Mare St. (☎8985 2424; www.hackneyempire.co.uk). Rail: Hackney Central or ⊖Bethnal Green, then bus #D6, 106, or 253. An unfortunately out of the way site for such an ornate and beautiful theater, but it's pulled in the stars for years. Charlie Chaplin performed here early in his career. It features a wide range of performing arts: comedy, musicals, opera, and drama. The Empire is currently in the final stages of a multi-million-pound overhaul, the main theatre is open as usual, but the project continues. Call or check website for shows and prices.

Greenwich and Docklands International Festival (☎8305 1818, bookings 8858 7755; www.festival.org). For the first 2 weeks in July the GDIF brings international musicians, dancers, and theatrical troupes to outdoor stages and alternative venues all over East London. The performances span genres and cultures, finishing with a spectacular fireworks display. Individual events free-£20.

London Arena, Limeharbour (☎7538 1212, 24hr. recording 087 0512 1212; www.londonarena.co.uk). DLR: Crossharbour and London Arena. The Arena has established itself as London's leading megavenue for commercial pop and large-scale performances. A multi-million pound refurbishment 7 years ago increased seating space and sound quality. When not hosting chart-toppers the arena serves as the base of the London Knights hockey team. Box office open M-F 9am-6pm, Sa 9am-2pm, Su event days only. £10-25.

Spitz, 109 Commercial St. (☎7392 9032; www.spitz.co.uk). ⊖Liverpool St. The eclectic Spitz is a restaurant in Old Spitalfield's with an upstairs venue and bar with food downstairs. Fresh range of live music, from klezmer, jazz, and world music to indie pop and rap. All profits help refugees worldwide and other worthy causes through the Dandelion Trust. Music most nights at 8pm. Check the website for details. Cover £3-15. MC/V.

WEST LONDON

WEST LONDON QUICKFIND: Discover, p. 14; sights, p. 130; food, p. 188; shopping, p. 273; accommodations, p. 295.

Riverside Studios, Crisp Rd. (☎8237 1111; www.riversidestudios.co.uk). ⊖Hammersmith. From the Tube, take Queen Caroline St. under the motorway and follow it right past the Apollo (15min.) towards the Thames. Crisp Rd. is on the left. One of the best, if least-known, entertainment venues in London, it's very popular with locals and understandably so. The 4 **theaters** offer international work, as well as home-grown fringe productions and comedy. The BBC often films live shows here. The superb, plush **cinema** plays international art-house, with an excellent program featuring new stuff and many classics (some with live piano) entirely in double bills. Box office open daily noon-9pm. Plays £12-18, concessions £5-12; films £5.50/£4.50. Wheelchair accessible.

BBC Television Centre, Wood Ln. (☎8576 1227; www.bbc.co.uk). ⊖White City. (See **Sights,** p. 130). The BBC records over 600 shows with live studio audiences every year. Book 6 weeks ahead, though less popular shows often have tickets available nearer showtime. With the exception of children's shows, participants must be over 18. Apply by phone or write to: Audience Services, P.O. Box 3000, BBC Television Centre, London W12 7RJ. Send your name, address, daytime phone, number of tickets requested, and the age range of those attending; you will be added to a waiting list. If approved, your tickets will arrive 2 weeks before the date of the show. You can also apply online–www.bbc.co.uk/tickets. Free. Wheelchair accessible.

The Bush Theatre, Shepherd's Bush Green (☎7602 3703; www.bushtheatre.co.uk). ⊖Shepherd's Bush. This theatre's off-beat, brand spankin' new and controversial programs derive from their policy of actively encouraging unsolicited submissions from new writers. Kate Beckinsale acted here in 1996. Telephone booking M-Sa 10am-7pm. Box office open M-Sa 5-8pm, on performance days 1:30-8pm. £3.50-10.

Hammersmith Irish Centre, Black's Rd. (info ☎0181 563 8232, tickets ☎8741 3211; www.lbhf.gov.uk/irishcentre). ⊖Hammersmith. Due to the brick facade, it's a bit hard to find. It's across from the Coke building as you walk towards the spire of the church. Run by the local council, this claims to be London's foremost Irish cultural center. Houses a small Irish lending library, an art gallery, and frequently screens Irish films. The large hall hosts Irish bands, dance sessions, and *ceilidhs*, as well as comedians and literary readings. Library open Th-F 11am-4pm. Most performances F-Sa 8:15pm. Free-£10. Wheelchair accessible.

Lyric Hammersmith, King St. (☎08700 500 511; www.lyric.co.uk). ⊖Hammersmith. Behind a concrete facade, this recently renovated, ornate 1895 theater is known for classy, controversial productions. Above the main theater, the small **Lyric Studio** stages experimental drama. Box office open M-Sa 10am-6pm, theater £10-20, students and concessions £7-9. Studio usually £7, concessions £5. M all £7. Wheelchair accessible.

Shepherd's Bush Empire, Shepherd's Bush Green (☎0905 020 3999; Ticketweb bookings, ☎0870 771 2000; www.shepherds-bush-empire.co.uk). ⊖Shepherd's Bush. Turn-of-the-century theater right on the green. Once famous for hosting BBC gameshows, it is now a major music venue (capacity 2000). Everyone has played here–from Maroon 5 to Blondie. Box office open M-Sa noon-5pm. £13.50-28, most £15-20.

Carling Apollo Hammersmith, Queen Caroline St. (24hr. Ticketmaster ☎0870 606 3400; www.cclive.co.uk). ⊖Hammersmith. In the shadow of the Hammersmith Flyover, this utilitarian venue hosts a huge array of musical and theatrical diversions, from the Beach Boys to the Wu-Tang Clan. Box office only open on performance days, from 4pm-start of show. Usually £18.50 and up.

INSIDE

Shopping

From its earliest days, London has been a trading city, its wealth and power built upon commerce. Today even more so than at the Empire's height, London's economy is truly international—and thanks to the outward-looking and eclectic nature of Londoners' diverse tastes, the range of goods on offer is unmatched anywhere in the world. From Harrods's proud boast to supply "all things to all people," to African crafts on sale in Brixton market, you could shop for a lifetime.

The major mainstream shopping areas in Central London are Covent Garden, Oxford St., Carnaby St., Bond St. (The West End); King's Rd. (Chelsea); Old Brompton Rd. and Sloane St. (Knightsbridge & Belgravia); Kensington High St. (Kensington & Earl's Court); and Tottenham Court Road (Bloomsbury). For the market-oriented shopper Central London offers Portobello Market (Notting Hill) while Greater London has Camden Market (North London), Brick Ln. and Petticoat Ln. Markets (East London).

The shopping areas vary greatly in character. At the beginning of each Neighborhood entry is an overall outline of what to expect. Find what you want and fulfill those spending impulses, or just window-shop and browse to your heart's content.

SHOPPING BY TYPE

NEIGHBORHOOD ABBREVIATIONS: BAY Bayswater **BLOOM** Bloomsbury **CHEL** Chelsea **CITY** The City of London **CLERK** Clerkenwell **HOL** Holborn **KEN/EC** Kensington & Earl's Court **K/B** Knightsbridge & Belgravia **M/RP** Marylebone & Regent's Park **NH** Notting Hill **SB** The South Bank **WEND** The West End **WEMIN** Westminster **NL** North London **SL** South London **EL** East London **WL** West London

ACCESSORIES

Annie's	NL
The British Hatter	KEN/EC
Hoxton Boutique	EL
Jauko	KEN/EC
Willma	NH

ALCOHOL

The Beer Shop	EL
Gerry's	WEND

BOOKS

Blackwell's	WEND
Fosters Bookshop	WL
Foyles	WEND
Gay's the Word	BLOOM
Hatchard's	WEND
Mega City Comics	NL
Shipley	WEND
Sotheran's of Sackville Street	NL
Stanfords	WEND
The Travel Bookshop	NH
Unsworth	BLOOM
Waterstone's	BLOOM,WEND

CLOTHES: NEW

Ad Hoc	CHEL
Apple Tree	WEND
Browns Labels for Less	WEND
Cyberdog	NL
Daisy and Tom	CHEL
Energie	WEND
Hoxton Boutique	EL
Jauko	KEN/EC
The Laden Showroom	EL
Mango	WEND
Miss Sixty	WEND
Oscar Milo	WEND
Paul Smith Sale Shop	WEND
Proibito Sale Shop	WEND
Savage London	WEND
Teaze	NH
Ted Baker	WEND
Therapy	WEND
Willma	NH
World's End	CHEL
Zara	WEND

CLOTHES: VINTAGE

Annie's	NL
Cinch	WEND
Delta of Venus	BLOOM
Dolly Diamond	NH
One of a Kind	NH
Pandora	K/B
Steinberg and Tolkein	CHEL

DEPARTMENT STORES

Fortnum and Mason	WEND
Hamley's	WEND
Harrods	K/B
Harvey Nichols	K/B

DEPARTMENT STORES (CONT.)

John Lewis	WEND
Liberty	WEND
Marks and Spencer	WEND
Selfridges	WEND

GIFTS & MISCELLANY

Butler and Wilson	WEND
Fortnum and Mason	WEND
James Smith and Sons	BLOOM
L. Cornelissen and Son	BLOOM
Neal's Yard Dairy	WEND
Neal's Yard Remedies	WEND
Penhaligon's	WEND
Tea and Coffee Plant	NH
Twining's	HOL

MARKETS

Bayswater	BAY
Berwick Street	WEND
Brick Lane	EL
Brixton	SL
Camden Canal	NL
Camden Lock	NL
Camden Passage	NL
Chapel	NL
Covent Garden	WEND
Greenwich Markets	EL
Goldborne Road	NH
Inverness Street	NL
Leather Lane	HOL
Portabello	NH
Spitalfields	EL
Stables	NL

MUSIC

Black Market	WEND
Blacker Dread Muzik/CD Link	SL
Delta of Venus	BLOOM
HMV	WEND
Honest Jon's	NH
Music Zone	WEND
Out on the Floor	NL
Reckless Records	WEND
Rough Trade	NH
Sister Ray	WEND
Tower Records	WEND
Turnkey	WEND
Uptown Records	WEND
Vinyl Addiction	NL
Virgin Megastore	WEND

SHOES

Egoshego	WEND
Office	WEND
One of a Kind	NH
Sukie's	CHEL
Tabio	CHEL

SPORTING GOODS

Lillywhite's	WEND

NOTABLE CHAINS

As in almost any major city, London retailing is dominated by chains. Fortunately, local shoppers are picky enough that buying from a chain doesn't mean abandoning the flair and quirky stylishness for which Londoners are famed. Plus, in such an expensive city chain stores are often a great place for deals. Stores have an eagle eye for trends and change lines often enough to keep punters coming back. Most chains have a flagship on or near Oxford St., usually with a second branch in Covent Garden. The branches will have slightly different hours, but almost all the stores listed below are open daily 10am-7pm, starting later (noon) on Su and staying open an hour later one night of the week (usually Th).

Lush (☎01202 668 545; www.lush.co.uk). Seven London locations including 123 King's Rd. ⊖Sloane Sq.); Covent Garden Piazza Unit 11 (⊖ Covent Garden); 40 Carnaby St. (⊖Oxford Circus); 96 Kensington High St. (⊖High St. Kensington); Quadrant Arcade, 80-82 Regent St. (⊖Piccadilly Circus); and the concourses of Victoria Station (⊖Victoria) and Heathrow. All-natural cosmetics look good enough to eat: soap is hand-cut from blocks masquerading as cakes and cheeses (£2-5), and facial masks are scooped from guacamole-like tubs. Giant, fizzing bath-beads too. Vegan cosmetics are marked with a green dot. New products come out every season.

FCUK, flagship 396 Oxford St. (☎7529 7766; www.frenchconnection.com). ⊖Bond St. 16 branches in London. The home of the 90s advertising coup has an extensive collection sporting their vaguely offensive, subversive moniker. Very popular with everyone around, and somehow they manage to keep coming up with new ways to exploit those four letters. Many designs have UK specific references. AmEx/MC/V.

Oasis, flagship 292 Regent St. (☎7323 5978; www.oasis-stores.com). ⊖Oxford Circus. 19 branches. Colorful, sexy clothes for work and play, plus shoes and accessories. A favorite with students and 20-somethings. AmEx/MC/V.

Topshop/Topman/Miss Selfridge, 400 Oxford St. (☎7499 2917). ⊖Bond St., also 36-38 Great Castle St. (☎7606 7700) ⊖Oxford Circus. Dozens of locations in central London. Cheap fashions for young people—over-25s will feel middle-aged. The flagship store brings them all under 1 roof, though very popular Topshop dominates with a huge range of casual clothes, strappy shoes and skimpy clubwear spread over 3 floors. Miss Selfridge, on the ground fl., has an even younger feel; Top Man is all club clothes and cargo pants, at low prices. Occasional 10% student discount. AmEx/MC/V.

Karen Millen, (☎0870 1601 830; www.karenmillen.co.uk). Eight central locations including: 262-264 Regents St. (⊖Oxford Circus); 22-23 James St. (⊖Covent Garden); 33 Kings Rd. (⊖Sloane Sq.); 57 South Molton St. (⊖Bond St.); Jubilee Place, Canary Wharf and Barker's Arcade (⊖High St. Kensington). Best known for richly embroidered brocade suits and evening gowns, but recently edging towards a more casual line. Seems like they're looking to extend their classic look toward a younger market.

Jigsaw, flagship 126-127 New Bond St. (☎7491 4484; www.jigsaw-online.com). ⊖Bond St. 22 branches in London. The essence of Britishness, distilled into quality mid-priced womenswear. Restrained, classic cuts that prize elegance over fad-based fashions, though there has been a move toward more edgy designs. AmEx/MC/V.

Muji (www.muji.co.uk). 8 locations including 187 Oxford St. (☎7437 7503; ⊖Oxford Circus), 41 Carnaby St. (☎7287 7323; ⊖Oxford Circus); 135 Long Acre (☎7379 0820; ⊖Covent Garden); 157 Kensington High St. (☎7376 2484; ⊖High St. Kensington); 118 King's Rd. (☎7823 8688; ⊖Sloane Sq.); and 6-17 Tottenham Crt. Rd., Unit 5 (☎7436 1779; ⊖Tottenham Crt. Rd.). Escape the High Street frenzy. Minimalist lifestyle stores, with a sleek Zen take on everything from chilled oolong tea to futons. AmEx/MC/V.

Marks and Spencer, (☎0845 302 1234; www.marksandspencer.com) Oxford St. Pantheon, 173 Oxford St. (☎7437 7722; ⊖Oxford Circus), and 107-115 Long Acre (☎7240 9549; ⊖Covent Garden). Once the definition of shopping in London, Marks and Spencer is established and famous. Its popularity has waned in recent years, but it's undergoing a major overhaul. Hundreds of locations around London. New food stores *Simply Food* are also popular. AmEx/MC/V.

Window Shopping

Harrods

Fly Shoes

Shellys, 266-270 Regent St. (☎7287 0939; www.shellys.co.uk). ⊖Oxford Circus. Smaller stores at: 159 Oxford St. (⊖Oxford Circus); 40 Kensington High St. (⊖High St. Kensington); 14-18 Neal St. (⊖Covent Garden); and 124b King's Rd. (⊖Sloane Sq.). The Topshop of shoes, boasts a good selection of reasonably priced, funky footwear. Women's selection better than men's, although they're working on it. Up there with Office as one of the top shoe shops. AmEx/MC/V.

UNIQLO, 84-86 Regent St. (☎7434 9688; www.uniqlo.co.uk). ⊖Piccadilly Circus. Also at 163-169 Brompton Rd. (☎7584 8608, ⊖Knightsbridge). "The clothes store from Japan" has simple, casual clothing for men, women, and children. Nothing flashy: similar to the GAP clothing but cheaper. A safe bet. AmEx/MC/V.

Sainsbury's, www.sainsburys.co.uk. Two central locations at 3-11 Southampton St. (⊖Covent Garden), and 113-117 Oxford St (⊖Oxford Circus). Traditionally a supermarket, some of the larger stores also have furniture, clothes, toys, and even car insurance. Still one of the best supermarkets, especially because they seem to be everywhere. Some open 24hr. MC/V.

SHOPPING BY NEIGHBORHOOD

BAYSWATER

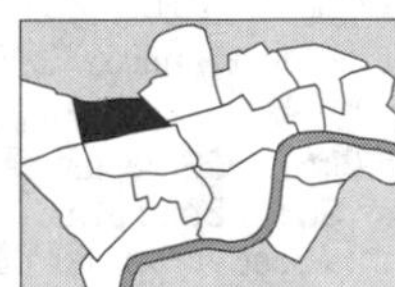

SEE MAP, p. 359

BAYSWATER QUICKFIND: Discover, p. 4; food, p. 164; pubs, p. 193; entertainment, p. 233; accommodations, p. 279.

For all its gastronomic and earthy charms, Bayswater really doesn't hold much attraction for the die-hard shopper: if you're up for a bit of charge card aerobics, you'd do well to check out posher districts to the south and west. Two exceptions: the weekly outdoor artists' market and central London's biggest shopping mall.

Bayswater Market, (www.bayswater-road-artists.com), along Bayswater Rd. from Clarendon Pl. to Queensway. Every Su for the past 50 years, this open-air art show—the largest weekly expo of its kind in the world—has been parked along the gates of Kensington Gardens. The location and atmosphere are beautiful, even if the artwork isn't; over 250 painters, photographers, and various others ply their trade with a depressingly firm eye on the tourist market. Surprises and delights lurk everywhere. Open Su 10am-6pm, all weather.

Whiteleys Shopping Centre, Queensway (☎7229 8844; www.whiteleys.com). ⊖Bayswater. High street variety, with absolutely none of the charm. Upscale shopping mall with over 70 restaurants and stores including Oasis, Karen Millen, H&M, Jigsaw, and Muji, along with a Marks & Spencer **grocery store** and a **UCI** multiplex cinema. Concerts and art exhibitions on occasion. Open M-Sa 10am-10pm (some stores close at 8pm), Su noon-6pm.

PAPER OR PLASTIC? At most supermarkets, you're expected to bag your own groceries at the checkout. Don't stand there gawking—grab a bag!

BLOOMSBURY

BLOOMSBURY QUICKFIND: Discover, p. 5; sights, p. 87; museums & galleries, p. 140; food, p. 166; pubs, p. 193; entertainment, p. 234; accommodations, p. 282.

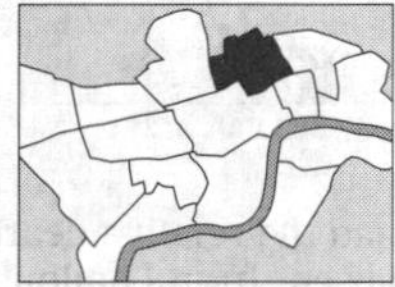

SEE MAP, p. 360

As home to the British Library and most of London's academic institutions, Bloomsbury's main commodity (other than A-level acumen) is **books;** the streets around the British Museum are crammed with specialist and cut-price bookshops, while the Waterstone's on Gower St. (see below) is one of London's largest. Also, if you're after **electronic** equipment, head to **Tottenham Court Road** and haggle away—it's expected.

BOOKS

Gay's the Word, 66 Marchmont St. (☎7278 7654; www.gaystheword.co.uk). ⊖Russell Sq. As the UK's largest gay and lesbian bookstore (no behemoth, mind you, just a few well-stocked rooms), GTW boasts a well-informed staff, and a large enough inventory to devote entire sections to queer detective fiction. Erotic postcards, secondhand fiction, serious movies, and free magazines. Weekly events and discussion groups. Noticeboard with accommodations listings. Open M-Sa 10am-6:30pm, Su 2-6pm. AmEx/MC/V.

Waterstone's, 82 Gower St. (☎7636 1577). ⊖Goodge St. Cafe, infinite rows of magazines, and frequent high-profile signings are additional attractions of this comprehensive 5-floor monstrosity– size *does* matter. Make sure to check the large used and remainder section on the 2nd floor, and the excellent travel section on the ground fl. Open M and W-F 9:30am-8pm, Tu 10am-8pm, Sa 9:30am-7pm, Su noon-6pm. Wheelchair accessible. AmEx/MC/V.

Unsworths, 12 Bloomsbury St. (☎7436 9836; www.unsworths.com). ⊖Tottenham Crt. Rd. Branch at 101 Euston Rd. Up to 90% off publishers' prices on a wide range of fictional and academic books. An excellent used selection upstairs, rare and antiquarian books in the basement. Open M-Sa 10:30am-8pm, Su 11am-7pm. AmEx/MC/V.

CLOTHES

Delta of Venus, 151 Drummond St. (☎7387 3037; www.deltaofvenus.co.uk). ⊖Euston or Euston Sq. A small but unbeatable array of vintage clothes for both sexes from the 60s to the early 90s. Dresses £25-50, shirts £22-30, men's jackets from £35. Worth every penny if you happen to find your new favorite jeans. Just as exciting as the clothes is the small, but mouth-watering selection of vinyl, with everything from the Doors to the Sex Pistols to Velvet Underground at great prices (most LPs £15). Also some books, jewelry, and accessories. Be sure to chat with the friendly and knowledgeable proprietor. Open M-Sa 11am-7pm. MC/V.

GIFTS AND MISCELLANY

James Smith & Sons, 53 New Oxford St. (☎7836 4731; www.james-smith.co.uk). ⊖Tottenham Crt. Rd. Groucho Marx once quipped that he hated London when it wasn't raining. The Smith family, in the umbrella business since 1830, must agree. There's a lovely time-warp feel about the ornate shop: signature handmade brollies (from £35) and walking sticks (from £25) share shelf-space with the newest rain-repelling models. Open M-F 9:30am-5:25pm, Sa 10am-5:25pm. AmEx/MC/V.

L. Cornelissen & Son, 105 Great Russell St. (☎7636 1045). ⊖Tottenham Crt. Rd. With its original 1855 interior, Cornelissen's looks more like an apothecary's than an art store. Jars of raw pigment, crystals, and lumps of evil-smelling "dragon's blood" reach to the ceilings, while mahogany drawers hide a fantastic array of brushes, nibs, paints, and crayons. An artist's dream. Open M-F 9:30am-5:30pm, Sa 9:30am-5pm. MC/V.

CHELSEA

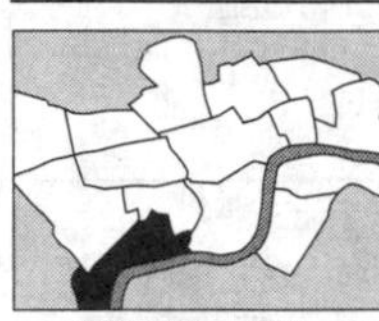

SEE MAP, p. 361

CHELSEA QUICKFIND: Discover, p. 5, sights, p. 89; museums & galleries, p. 141; food, p. 256; pubs, p. 195; entertainment, p. 234, accommodations, p. 285.

***TRANSPORTATION:** The only Tube station in Chelsea is Sloane Sq.; from here buses #11, 19, 22, 211, and 319 run down the King's Rd.*

No serious shopper can come to London and ignore Chelsea, even if it's lost much of its punk rock edge in recent years. The abundance of quirky one-off boutiques and the relative dearth of large chain stores give the area a vitality and diversity absent from London's other shopping meccas. On the east side, **Sloane Square** is extremely "Sloaney" (the English equivalent of American Preppy), while to the west **King's Road** gave us both the miniskirt and the Sex Pistols in previous decades. Today, alternative styles have given way mostly to more mainstream trendy cuts, but the notorious Vivienne Westwood hasn't fled yet (see **World's End**), so hope remains for wannabe rebels. Things generally become more downmarket the farther west you move from Sloane Sq., and popular antique shops are ubiquitous towards the center of the neighborhood.

CLOTHES

Steinberg & Tolkien, 193 King's Rd. (☎7376 3660). London's largest collection of vintage American and European clothing. The place has the feel of a fantastic museum where touching, trying on, and buying the displays is encouraged. With everything from a £2500 golden gown from the film *Erke* to one of Jackie Kennedy's Givenchy classics, from authentic Victorian accessories to early-1990s jean shorts (£15). Check out the half-off sale rooms downstairs. Open Tu-Sa 11am-6:30pm, Su noon-6pm. AmEx/MC/V.

Ad Hoc, 153 King's Rd. (☎7376 8829; www.adhoclondon.com). With glitter and confetti spilling out into the sidewalk, Ad Hoc displays baggy cargoes and ultra-short minis. A rainbow collection of wigs dominate the cluttered neon space. Check out the plastic retro jewelry (£5-10) and the basket of irreverent pins (50p) by the register. Clothing mostly £15-60. Open M-Tu 10am-6:30pm, W 10am-7pm, Th-Sa 10am-6:30pm, Su noon-6pm. AmEx/MC/V.

World's End, 430 King's Rd. (☎7352 6551). This small store's past legendary incarnations include SEX and Let it Rock, but other than the huge clock spinning wildly backwards, not much remains of the punk store that launched the careers of the Sex Pistols. Owned by the notorious Vivienne Westwood (who recently got an entire special exhibit devoted to her at the Victoria and Albert Museum), the shop is now a pricey, slightly funky showplace for her latest designs (most items £100-300). Open M-Sa 10am-6pm. AmEx/MC/V.

Daisy & Tom, 181 King's Rd. (☎7352 5000; www.daisyandtom.com). This multi-level kiddie paradise stocks toys, books, nursery goods, clothing, and even a hairdressing salon. The in-store carousel and marionette shows (every 30min. in the clothing department) are bound to please, although upmarket prices are included as well. Open M-W:30am-6pm, Th 10am-7pm, F 9:30am-6pm, Sa 10am-7pm, Su 11am-5pm. MC/V.

SHOES

Sukie's, 285 and 289 King's Rd. (female dept. ☎7352 3431, men's dept. 7376 7129). Too much style for just one store, Sukie's 2 locations carry a brilliant selection of funky-to-formal footwear, in both classic and contemporary styles with unusual colors, materials, and textures. Many designed specifically for the store. Shoes starting from £30. Open M-Sa 10am-6pm, Su noon-6pm. Wheelchair accessible. MC/V.

Tabio, 94 King's Rd. (☎7591 1960; www.tabio.co.uk). Two levels of perfectly arranged socks (£2-10), plus an extensive collection of tights in every imaginable color. The yin-yang rock garden at the foot of the stairs hints at the store's Japanese roots. Open M-Sa 10am-7pm, Su noon-6pm. AmEx/MC/V.

BOOKS

World's End Bookshop, 357 King's Rd. (☎7352 9376). All the charm a closet-sized, used bookstore can offer (a lot), with especially good holdings in architecture, art, biography, cinema, and cooking. Bargain bins are perfect for finding that 10p diversion for the teary plane ride home. Open daily 10am-6pm. MC/V.

HOLBORN

HOLBORN QUICKFIND: Discover, p. 7; sights, p. 97; museums & galleries, p. 143; food, p. 170; pubs, p. 197; nightlife, p. 211; entertainment, p. 236; accommodations, p. 286.

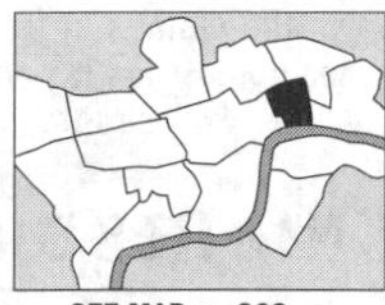
SEE MAP, p. 363

With Covent Garden so close—and barristers not renowned for their dress sense— Holborn is not a top shopping destination. **High Holborn** is a busy road with a few common high-street chains, while **Fleet Street** has a number of indistinguishable clothing shops serving lawyers who just spilled port down their shirtfronts. **Leather Lane Market** is a local favorite, though.

Leather Lane Market. Confusingly enough, the name of the street actually has nothing to do with leather (it's a corruption of the 13th-century "Le Vrunelane"); but you can still buy yourself some shoes or a handbag at this 300-year-old market. Not well known to tourists, this free-for-all serves the local and business communities, who come out to browse the clothes, food, electrical goods, and cheap CDs/DVDs on display. Open M-F 10:30am-2:30pm.

Twining's, 216 Strand (☎7353 3511). ⊖Temple. Proportionately London's narrowest shop, Twining's is the oldest family-run business in Britain to stay on the same premises (since 1706), and takes its legacy seriously. In addition to a small tea museum in the back, Twining's has its own epic lay, including the stirring: "Note, by the way, it was not *Twining's* tea the Boston rebels tossed into the sea." The real draw is, of course, the tea: rows of Earl Grey (£1.20-1.70 per 125g), Prince of Wales (£1.40-1.90 per 100g), and other noble blends recall the Queen's official patronage. Open M-F 9:30am-4:45pm. AmEx/MC/V.

SALE CRAZY. Twice a year, in January and July, London goes sale crazy. Prices are slashed in almost every shop and crowds take advantage of the extended hours. This might be your chance to buy those haute jeans.

KENSINGTON & EARL'S COURT

KENSINGTON & EARL'S COURT QUICKFIND: Discover, p. 8; sights, p. 100; museums & galleries, p. 145; food, p. 171; pubs, p. 198; entertainment, p. 236; accommodations, p. 286.

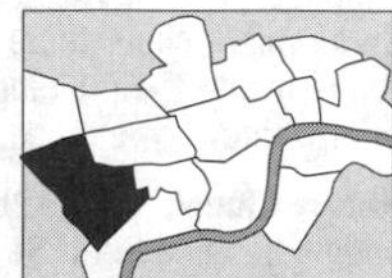
SEE MAP, pp. 364-365

Some people prefer **Kensington High Street** to Oxford St. It offers a similar, albeit more limited, range of mid-priced UK and international chains compared to its West End rival in a smaller and less crowded area—although Saturdays here can certainly approach sardine-tin crowding as well. Karen Millen, Monsoon, Next, Diesel, Benetton, Urban Outfitters, and Zara are all here. On the other hand, High St. Ken generally lacks the trendy one-off boutiques, and **Barkers,** the only department store, is positively tiny compared to the West End behemoths—if you're looking for anything other than mainstream clothes, go elsewhere. **Kensington Church Street** provides a mildly alternative, if pricey, experience: it's mostly clothing stores in the south, crafts and specialty shops in the middle, and antiques and oriental art as it winds north towards Notting Hill Gate.

CLOTHES

The British Hatter, 36b Kensington Church St. (☎7361 0000). ⊖High St. Kensington. Attending a smart wedding or the Royal Ascot? Pamela Bromley's superb hats will make sure that your headgear complements you perfectly—you'll emerge from this exquisite, tiny store looking altogether British. Hats of all shapes and sizes and colors here, festooned with feathers, ribbons, and bows; also stocks accessory essentials: pins and combs to anchor your hat discreetly in place. Dapper gentlemen take note: there is a small selection of men's hats. Headgear from £90-190. Open M-Sa 10:30am-6pm, Th 11am-6:30pm. AmEx/MC/V.

Jauko, 34c Kensington Church St. (☎7376 1408). ⊖High St. Kensington. Like its name says, the clothes in this tiny boutique are a clever melding of Japanese, UK, and Korean styles from Hello Kitty and Astro Boy-logo tees to bright flower-print dresses. All with soft, flowing lines. Prices run from £25-270. Open M-Sa 10am-6pm. MC/V.

KNIGHTSBRIDGE & BELGRAVIA

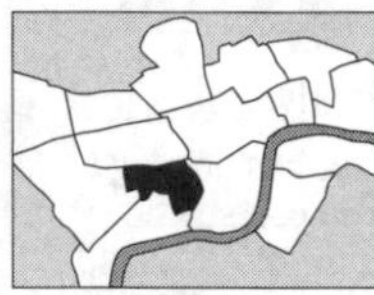

SEE MAP, p. 366

KNIGHTSBRIDGE & BELGRAVIA QUICKFIND: Discover, p. 8; sights, p. 102; food, p. 172; pubs, p. 198; nightlife, p. 211; accommodations, p. 290.

Brompton Road dominates Knightsbridge's shopping arteries, with representatives of most upmarket chains between Harvey Nichols and Harrods. Explore the side streets for spectacular deals on designer clothing, or blow a cool thousand on ultra-exclusive **Sloane Street,** which rivals Bond St. for designer boutiques. Window shop Armani, Chanel, Dior, Gucci, Hermès, Kenzo, Versace, and Yves St. Laurent.

CLOTHES

Pandora, 16-22 Cheval Pl. (☎7589 5289). See p. 259. ⊖Knightsbridge.

DEPARTMENT STORES

Harrods, 87-135 Old Brompton Rd. (☎7730 1234; www.harrods.com). ⊖Knightsbridge. Big things start small: in 1849, Mr. Harrod opened a small grocery store, and by 1901 had done well enough to construct the terra-cotta behemoth that now bears his name. In the Victorian era, this was the place for the wealthy to shop; over a century later, it's less a provider of goods and more a tourist extravaganza. Given the sky-high prices, it's no wonder that only tourists and oil sheiks actually shop here. (Prices near normal during sales in Jan. and July.) Do go, though; it's an iconic bit of London that even the cynical tourist shouldn't miss. If nothing else, ride the Egyptian escalator in the middle, which leads down to the eerie "Diana and Dodi" memorial, with Diana's engagement ring and a wine glass she drank out of her last night alive. Some might claim there's an unwritten dress code in this poshest of establishments, but if you're inside the building, chances are everyone already knows you're a tourist; may as well wear whatever you'd like. Open M-Sa 10am-7pm. Wheelchair accessible. AmEx/MC/V.

Harvey Nichols, 109-125 Knightsbridge (☎7235 5000; www.harveynichols.com). ⊖Knightsbridge. Imagine Bond St., Rue St. Honoré, and Fifth Ave. all rolled up into one store. Five of its seven floors are devoted to the sleekest, sharpest fashion, from the biggest names to the hippest unknowns. Needless to say, the prices discourage much more than starry-eyed browsing, but even the poorest of wanderers can have an amusing time determining which department boasts the most hollow-cheeked, devastatingly attractive attendants. 5th-floor food hall has a swanky restaurant, a Yo!Sushi (see p. 163), and the chic 5th Floor Café; there's a juice bar on the main floor and a Wagamama in the basement (see p. 163). Open M-F 10am-8pm, Sa 10am-7pm, Su noon-6pm. Wheelchair accessible. AmEx/MC/V.

NOTTING HILL

NOTTING HILL QUICKFIND: Discover, p. 9; sights, p. 105; food, p. 174; pubs, p. 200; nightlife, p. 212; entertainment, p. 237; accommodations, p. 292.

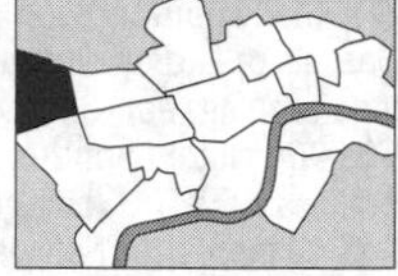

SEE MAP, p. 359

The best reason to visit Notting Hill is the world-renowned **Portobello Market,** which brings bursts of weekend color to an otherwise gentrified residential area. Portobello Rd. is home to a number of distinct markets, occupying different parts of the street and operating on different days. To make sure you see it all, come on a Friday or Saturday when everything is sure to be open, otherwise there's no real telling what might be around. Don't expect it all to start by the Gate, in fact the shops don't begin in earnest until quite a bit farther up. The **antiques market** is what most people associate with Portobello Rd.; it stretches north from Chepstow Villas to Elgin Crescent. Most of what's on display otherwise is cheap bric-a-brac. *(⊖Notting Hill Gate, Open Sa 7am-5pm.)* Farther north, from Elgin Crescent to Lancaster Rd., is the **general market,** with food, flowers, and household essentials. Gourmet stalls selling continental breads and organic produce show up to compete with local eateries. *(⊖Westbourne Park or Ladbroke Grove (both Zone 2). Open M-W 8am-6pm, Th 9am-1pm, F-Sa 7am-7pm.)* North of Lancaster Rd., with arms stretching along the Westway, is the **clothes market,** with a wide selection of second-hand clothes, ethnic gear, and kitsch fashions, oddly interspersed with dodgy used electronics. *(⊖Ladbroke Grove. Open F-Sa 8am-3pm.)* Finally, north of the Westway, the **Golborne Road market** has a dowdier, local air, while Golborne Rd. itself shows Moroccan influence with stalls selling gourmet olives, steaming couscous, and Berber handicrafts. *(⊖Ladbroke Grove. F-Sa 9am-5pm, busiest Sa.)* Helpful signs let you know what's available where.

BOOKS

The Travel Bookshop, 13-15 Blenheim Crescent (☎7229 5260; www.thetravelbookshop.co.uk). This is heaven for travelers both professional and amateur. More than just a Grantophile destination, the specialist bookshop featured in *Notting Hill* is packed with all the books you need to plan your next trip. Everything from Amsterdam to Zambia. They also carry a small selection of fiction. Open M-Sa 10am-6pm. MC/V.

the hidden deal

Pandora's Hocks

Are you a fabulously wealthy fashion-plate looking to open up a bit of room in your wardrobe? Does your appetite for haute couture exceed your closet space?

If you answered no, well, good for you; it's time to benefit from our most fashionable hidden deal. You see, the ladies at **Pandora** and other dress agencies resell clothes and accessories on behalf of those unnamed wealthy women and celebrities whose designer garments have become too voluminous to house.

That leaves their Chanel suits, their Gucci handbags, and their Gaultier sunglasses available to the woefully underprivileged folks who generally get their high-fashion fix courtesy of Joan Rivers and her catty friends on E! The good stuff is all "seasonally correct," under two years old, and often barely worn. And the best part: prices are about a quarter of what they would be a few blocks over on Sloane St. So if you're tired of your GAPtastic duds, or you just need a little something special to perk up your under-accessorized self, make your way to Pandora stat. You can practice your red-carpet posing later.

16-22 Cheval Pl. ☎7589 5289. ⊖Knightsbridge. Open M-Sa 10am-7pm. AmEx/MC/V.

the BIG $plurge

Life Centre

Tired of walking? To escape the insanity of Portobello Market, try **The Life Centre,** a bonafide relaxation haven. The Life Centre offers a wide range of soothing therapies perfect for the weary, backpack-laden, jet-lagged traveler.

The complex philosophy behind many of the therapies may not make much sense, but the word "massage" transcends all belief systems. An hour of deep tissue massage, aromatherapy, therapeutic massage, or reflexology will set you back at least £55. For a truly deep and relaxing experience, try the chavutti thirumal massage, originated in India, in which the therapist uses his feet to massage the body (£75 for 1½ hours). Those who can't afford a full body treatment can go for an Indian head massage (£25-30 for 30 minutes), which covers the scalp, face, and shoulder areas. Walk-ins are welcome as long as there are therapists available. Massage therapies are all cash-only.

For something more active, the center offers 6 yoga classes daily (£9 an hour) at varying skill levels.

For more information, go to www.thelifecentre.org or call ☎7221 4602. 15 Edge St. Open M-F 6:30am-10pm, Sa-Su 9am-8pm.

CLOTHES AND ACCESSORIES

Dolly Diamond, 51 Pembridge Rd. (☎7792 2479; www.dollydiamond.com). ⊖Notting Hill Gate. Jackie Onassis or Audrey Hepburn? This shop specializes in vintage eveningwear. Choose your look from Dolly's classic 50s-70s clothing and elegant 20s-40s evening gowns. Dresses £50-120, ball gowns from £75. Smaller selection of men's formalwear upstairs, as well as shoes, bags, and even some swimwear. Open M-F 10:30am-6:30pm, Sa 9:30am-6:30pm, Su noon-6pm. MC/V.

One of a Kind, 259 Portobello Rd. (☎7792 5853). ⊖Ladbroke Grove. Heaven for discriminating vintage shoppers. Vintage clothing, shoes, and accessories line every available inch of wall space, with more hanging from the ceiling. You can find anything you want from any decade, but it will cost you. Shoes start at £25, clothes around £35, and prices rise rapidly into the stratosphere—some pieces on display are literally priceless. Most hover in the £100-150 range. Open daily 11am-6pm. MC/V.

Willma, 339 Portobello Rd. (☎8960 7296; www.willma.co.uk). You can't miss the blindingly pink storefront. Fluorescent cases present an exclusive range of intricate accessories and clothes. All are sourced from up-and-coming designers around the world, mostly one-offs. Come here for an inkling of the next big thing. Prices run high, with some affordable pieces mixed in: tops from £20, novelty knickers from £10. Open Tu-Sa 11am-6pm. Wheelchair accessible. AmEx/MC/V.

Teaze, 47 Pembridge Rd. (☎7727 8358). ⊖Notting Hill Gate. Wide range of anti-slogan T-shirts with sexual overtones; novelty lingerie, with themes from Che Guevara to Playboy; and last but not least, tubs of liquid latex (£13) for the true skin-tight look. Open M-Sa 10:30am-6:30pm, Su noon-5pm. AmEx/MC/V.

GIFTS AND MISCELLANY

The Tea and Coffee Plant, 180 Portobello Rd. (☎7221 8137). ⊖Ladbroke Grove. The rich smell of freshly ground coffee permeates this small but uncluttered shop, which offers a wide selection of coffees and teas (£1-3). All are fairly traded and organic—the staff in this politically conscious shop wouldn't have it any other way. Chew on some beans before committing to a kilo (£8-11), smell the tea varieties, or sip on a fresh espresso (75p). Mail order available. Open M-Sa 8:15am-6:30pm, Su 10am-4pm.

MUSIC

Rough Trade, 130 Talbot Rd. (☎7229 8541). ⊖Ladbroke Grove. Choosing from the wide selection of music is made easier by the small reviews tacked to most CDs and records (£5-13). Try the in-store turntables or test out CDs at the listening station. Open M-Sa 10am-6:30pm, Su 1-5pm. AmEx/MC/V.

Honest Jon's, 276-278 Portobello Rd., W10 (☎8969 9822). ⊖Ladbroke Grove. Still loud and funky after all these years. Subterranean 276 holds an impressive jazz, latin, and "outer-national" collection, while 278 carries a wide selection of reggae, hip-hop, house, and garage on vinyl and CD. Some soul and funk. You'll be drawn in by the cool selections always playing. Most CDs and LPs £8-13 range. Open M-Sa 10am-6pm, Su 11am-5pm. AmEx/MC/V.

BUSES. While some buses still have conductors who will take cash, most forgo on-board ticket sales. Make sure you either have a pass or you've purchased your bus ticket from the roadside ticket machine before you hop on. Also buses don't automatically stop at every bus-stop. Check whether you will need to pull a cord, press a button, or simply holler.

THE WEST END

OXFORD STREET & REGENT STREET

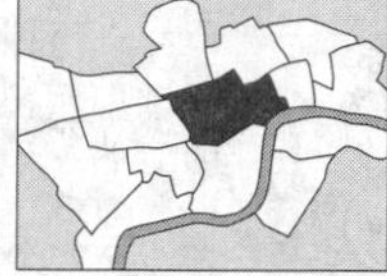

SEE MAP, p. 354

OXFORD STREET & REGENT'S STREET QUICKFIND: Discover, p. 10; sights, p. 111; museums & galleries, p. 150; food, p. 261; pubs, p. 201; nightlife, p. 212; entertainment, p. 240; accommodations, p. 292.

Shopping in London, as in many cities, is concentrated around a number of busy high streets, and these might be the highest of them all. A bona-fide shopping nirvana, **Oxford Street** has an amazing atmosphere and buzz. "Crowded" would be an understatement. Tourists and Londoners alike flock to the flagships of all the mainstream British chains—from Marks & Spencer to FCUK—on what is essentially a massive British High Street. The street's popularity is undoubtedly a part of the priceless Oxford St. experience; if you prefer a less frantic atmosphere, try **Kensington High Street.** Many Londoners head to Oxford St. for the massive **department stores** that line its northern edge (between Oxford Circus and Marble Arch) and the fashionable boutiques of **South Molton Street,** stretching south into Mayfair from Bond St. Tube. East of Oxford Circus, especially near Tottenham Court Road, things are more downmarket, with budget chains and dodgy "sale shops" alongside the Virgin and HMV music megastores.

Regent Street is altogether a more refined affair, despite the presence of a Disney Store. There are plenty of shops aimed at rich tourists, but it's balanced with venerable names such as Aquascutum and Liberty, not to mention the toy shop of the gods, Hamley's. **Oxford Circus,** where Regent St. and Oxford St. cross, is home to mega-flagships of international brands such as Nike and Benetton (if you fear crowds in the least, don't come within 500 yards). Behind Regent St., swinging **Carnaby Street** has a decent selection of youth fashions from famous-but-still-credible brands such as Diesel, though you'll find more interesting and obscure designer pickings in nearby **Foubert's Place** and **Newburgh Street.**

CLOTHES

Cinch, 5 Newburgh St. (☎7287 4941; www.levi.com). ⊖Oxford Circus. Specializes in classic Levi's cuts from the 40s to the 70s, with a mixture of both vintage and modern gear. Pick up an unworn pair of 1960s 505s for £850, but there are also affordable pairs from £50. The showcase of strategically hung clothing also includes limited edition Kubrick t-shirts (£50) and some shameless bins of "collectible" junk. Open M-Sa 10:30am-6:30pm. MC/V.

Mango, 106-112 Regent St. (☎7434 1384; www.mango.com). ⊖Piccadilly Circus. Also at 225-235 Oxford St. (⊖Oxford Circus) and 8-12 Neal St. (⊖Covent Garden). A UK foothold for a Spanish fashion empire which is quickly becoming a popular London mainstay, Mango's bright and keenly priced female line is cut with classy, sensible designs appropriate for all occasions. Most casual tops and bottoms go for under £40, some as low as £10. Open M-W 10am-8pm, Th 10am-9pm, F-Sa 10am-8pm, Su noon-6pm. AmEx/MC/V.

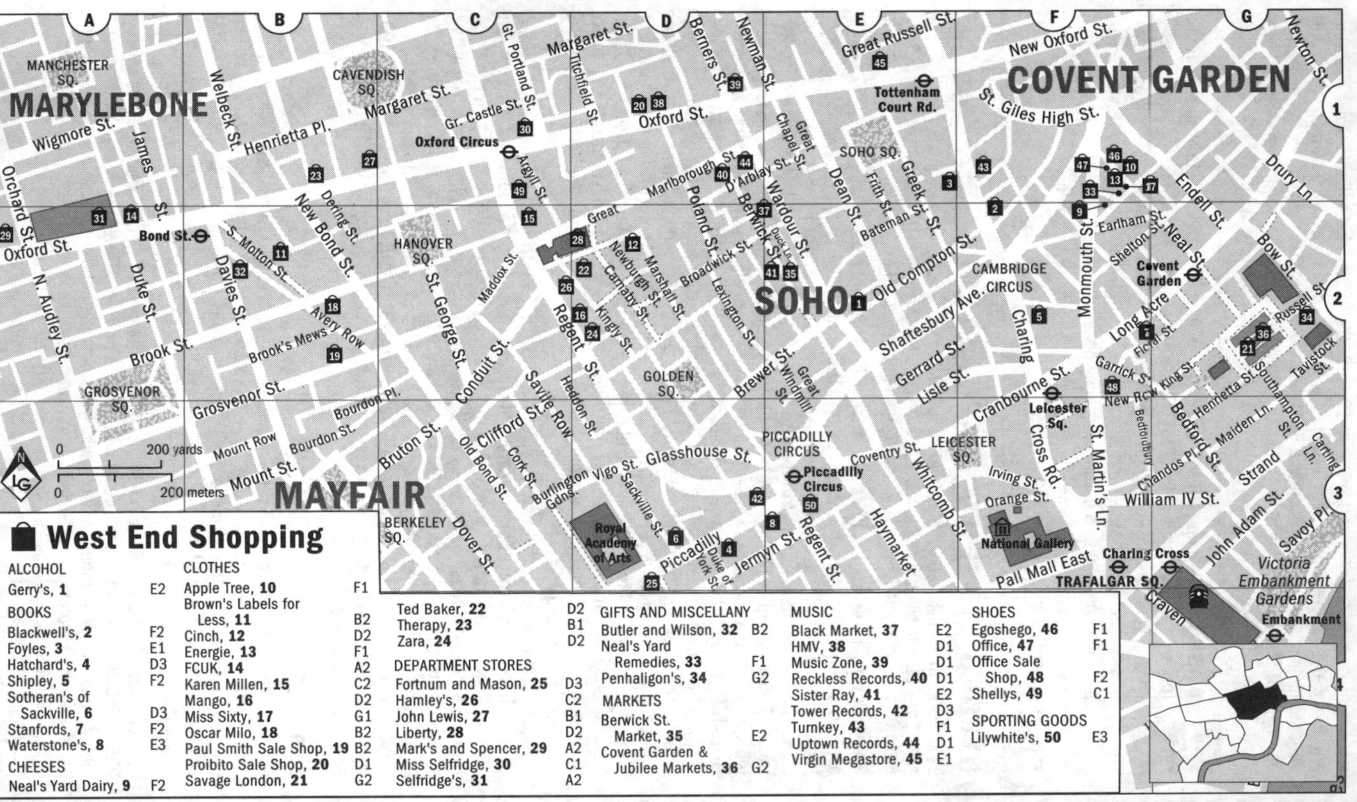
MARYLEBONE
COVENT GARDEN
SOHO
MAYFAIR
MANCHESTER SQ.
CAVENDISH SQ.
HANOVER SQ.
SOHO SQ.
GOLDEN SQ.
GROSVENOR SQ.
BERKELEY SQ.
CAMBRIDGE CIRCUS
PICCADILLY CIRCUS
LEICESTER SQ.
TRAFALGAR SQ.
Oxford Circus
Bond St.
Tottenham Court Rd.
Covent Garden
Leicester Sq.
Piccadilly Circus
Charing Cross
Embankment
Royal Academy of Arts
National Gallery
Victoria Embankment Gardens
0 200 yards
0 200 meters
West End Shopping
ALCOHOL
Gerry's, 1 E2
BOOKS
Blackwell's, 2 F2
Foyles, 3 E1
Hatchard's, 4 D3
Shipley, 5 F2
Sotheran's of Sackville, 6 D3
Stanfords, 7 F2
Waterstone's, 8 E3
CHEESES
Neal's Yard Dairy, 9 F2
CLOTHES
Apple Tree, 10 F1
Brown's Labels for Less, 11 B2
Cinch, 12 D2
Energie, 13 F1
FCUK, 14 A2
Karen Millen, 15 C2
Mango, 16 D2
Miss Sixty, 17 G1
Oscar Milo, 18 B2
Paul Smith Sale Shop, 19 B2
Proibito Sale Shop, 20 D1
Savage London, 21 G2
Ted Baker, 22 D2
Therapy, 23 B1
Zara, 24 D2
DEPARTMENT STORES
Fortnum and Mason, 25 D3
Hamley's, 26 C2
John Lewis, 27 B1
Liberty, 28 D2
Mark's and Spencer, 29 A2
Miss Selfridge, 30 C1
Selfridge's, 31 A2
GIFTS AND MISCELLANY
Butler and Wilson, 32 B2
Neal's Yard Remedies, 33 F1
Penhaligon's, 34 G2
MARKETS
Berwick St. Market, 35 E2
Covent Garden & Jubilee Markets, 36 G2
MUSIC
Black Market, 37 E2
HMV, 38 D1
Music Zone, 39 D1
Reckless Records, 40 D1
Sister Ray, 41 E2
Tower Records, 42 D3
Turnkey, 43 F1
Uptown Records, 44 D1
Virgin Megastore, 45 E1
SHOES
Egoshego, 46 F1
Office, 47 F1
Office Sale Shop, 48 F2
Shellys, 49 C1
SPORTING GOODS
Lilywhite's, 50 E3

Ted Baker, 5-7 Foubert's Pl. (☎7437 5619; www.tedbaker.co.uk). ⊖Oxford Circus. Also at 1-4 Langley Ct., Covent Garden (☎7497 8862; ⊖Covent Garden). Mid-priced modern classics for both sexes, from one of Britain's best-known and most influential names. Shirts £35-70, jeans £70-90. Open M-W 10:30am-7pm, Th 10:30am-7:30pm, F-Sa 10:30am-7pm, Su 11am-5pm. AmEx/MC/V.

Therapy, 318 Oxford St. (☎0870 160 7258; www.houseoffraser.co.uk), lower ground floor of the House of Fraser. All the high street women's fashion brands in one place, with flashing lights and in-store DJ. Clothes from Diesel and DKNY to budget high-street names like Morgan and Warehouse, with prices dipping occasionally below the £10. Open M-W 10am-8pm, Th 10am-9pm, F-Sa 10am-8pm, Su noon-6pm. MC/V.

Zara, 118 Regent St. (☎7534 9500; www.zara.com). ⊖Piccadilly Circus. Also at 242-248 and 333 Oxford St. (☎7318 2700; ⊖Oxford Circus); and 48-52 Kensington High St. (☎7368 4680; ⊖High St. Kensington). Yet another stylish Spanish brand that has taken Europe by storm with its sleek, relatively inexpensive clothing. Prices similar to its neighbor Mango (shirts from £13, sweaters from £17, jackets from £25), but with brighter and younger designs. Menswear is especially popular. Open M-W 10am-7pm, Th 10am-8pm, F-Sa 10am-7pm, Su noon-6pm. Wheelchair accessible. AmEx/MC/V.

CLOTHES: SALE SHOPS

Browns Labels for Less, 50 South Molton St. (☎7514 0052; www.browsfashion.com). ⊖Bond St. Remainders from the Browns mini-empire that's taking over South Molton St. The range is small, especially for menswear, but high fashion is reduced to low prices: D&G jeans dropped to £50, and trouser suits for £55. Open M-W 10am-6:30pm, Th 10am-7pm, F-Sa 10am-6:30pm. AmEx/MC/V.

Proibito Sale Shop, 42 South Molton St. (☎7941 3244) ⊖Bond St. Casual, club, and jeanswear from top designer names for up to 70% off–get a pair of Moschino jeans for only £39. Also stocks D&G, Calvin Klein, Guess, Valentino, and Versace for both men and women. Open daily 10am-6:30pm. AmEx/MC/V.

DEPARTMENT STORES

Hamley's, 188-189 Regent St. (☎7734 3161; www.hamleys.co.uk). ⊖Oxford Circus. Quite simply one of the best toy shops in the world. Opened in 1760, Hamley's has 7 floors filled with every conceivable toy and game, plus dozens of strategically placed product demonstrations to tempt the young (and not-so-young) with flying airplanes and rubber bugs that stick to the walls. The Bear Factory lets you personalize a stuffed toy by choosing the animal and voice; it's then stuffed and sewn on the site (from £10). 4th fl. has enough model cars, planes, and trains for the most die-hard enthusiast; the basement has Lego stations and video game consoles, and, of course, there's an in-house candy shop in the middle. Open M-F 10am-8pm, Sa 9:30am-8pm, Su noon-6pm. Wheelchair accessible. AmEx/MC/V.

Selfridges, 400 Oxford St. (☎0870 837 7377; www.selfridges.com). ⊖Bond St. The total department store–tourists may flock to Harrods, but Londoners head to Selfridges. Fashion departments are not cheap (there's an admission line just to get into Gucci), but run the gamut from traditional tweeds to space-age clubwear. Departments specialize in every product imaginable, from antiques to scented candles (not to mention key cutting and theater tickets), and it's all stylish. With 18 cafes and restaurants, a hair salon, a bureau de change, and even a hotel, shopaholics need never leave. Massive Jan. and July sales. Open M-F 10am-8pm, Sa 9:30am-8pm, Su noon-6pm. Wheelchair accessible. AmEx/MC/V.

Liberty, 210-220 Regent St. (☎7734 1234; www.liberty.co.uk), main entrance on Gt. Marlborough St. ⊖Oxford Circus. Liberty's timbered, Tudor chalet (built in 1922) sets the tone for this unique department store. The focus on top-quality design and handicrafts makes it more like a giant boutique than a full-blown department store. Liberty is famous for custom fabric prints–now 10,000 Liberty prints in the archive–sewn into everything from shirts to pillows, but they also have a wide array of other high-end contemporary designer lines, home accessories, and assorted gadgets. Open M-W 10am-7pm, Th 10am-8pm, F-Sa 10am-7pm, Su noon-6pm. Wheelchair accessible. AmEx/MC/V.

John Lewis, 300 Oxford St. (☎7629 7711; www.johnlewis.com). ⊖Oxford Circus. The employees collectively own John Lewis, with predictable results. They have a somewhat questionable fashion sense but are famed for service and guarantees, with a "Never Knowingly Undersold" policy that will refund you the difference if you find the same item cheaper elsewhere. Great for houseware and electronics, and the best haberdashery department in London. Open M-W, F-Sa 9:30am-7pm, Th 9:30am-8pm, Su noon-6pm. Wheelchair accessible. MC/V.

GIFTS AND MISCELLANY

Butler and Wilson (B&W), 20 South Molton St. (☎7409 2955; www.butlerandwilson.com). ⊖Bond St. A magpie's paradise and a masterpiece of Oriental kitsch. Brilliant range of costume jewelry (most pieces £35-90), including ornate chokers, tiaras, pendants, and body chains. Also Indian-style beaded handbags, colorful print tops, and "vintage Chinese jackets" (£193). This is about as cool as costume jewelry can get, especially with the flapper mannequins gazing coquettishly from every angle. Open M-W 10am-6pm, Th 10am-7pm, F-Sa 10am-6pm, Su noon-6pm. AmEx/MC/V.

MUSIC

HMV, 150 Oxford St. (☎7631 3423; www.hmv.co.uk). ⊖Oxford Circus. 3 massive floors with a huge range of new vinyl especially dance music. Games department has free consoles from every game maker. Music madness done right. Open M and W 9am-8pm, Tu 9:30am-8pm, Th 9am-9pm, F-Sa 9am-8pm, Su noon-6pm. Wheelchair accessible. AmEx/MC/V.

Virgin Megastore, 14-16 Oxford St. (☎7631 1234). ⊖Tottenham Crt. Rd. With 4 floors it fully deserves the name (the 2nd half, at least). Covers the entire musical spectrum, including the related books, magazines, and posters, plus lots of DVDs, videos, and computer games on the 1st fl. Internet cafe on ground fl. (£1 per 50min. before noon, £1 for 20min. after). Open M-Sa 9am-9pm, Su noon-6pm. Wheelchair accessible. AmEx/MC/V.

MAYFAIR & ST. JAMES'S

MAYFAIR & ST. JAMES'S QUICKFIND: Discover, p. 10; sights, p. 111; museums & galleries, p. 150; food, p. 178; pubs, p. 201; entertainment, p. 240; accommodations, p. 292.

Stiff pricetags and starched collars abound; nowhere is Mayfair's aristocratic pedigree more evident than in its scores of high-priced boutiques; many bearing Royal Warrants to indicate their status as official palace suppliers. **New Bond Street** is the location of choice for the biggest designer names. Its southern end **(Old Bond Street)** is equally renowned for its jewelers, art dealers, and silversmiths. Less mainstream designers—like Vivienne Westwood, Alexander MacQueen, and Yohji Yamamoto—set up shop on **Conduit Street,** where Old Bond St. meets New Bond St. **Savile Row,** which runs south off Conduit St., and **Jermyn Street,** one block south of Piccadilly, are the home of old-fashioned elegance, with tailor-made suits whose understated style belies their four-figure price-tags. Near Piccadilly, a number of Regency and Victorian **arcades** are lined with boutiques whose less-interesting wares have changed little in the last hundred years.

BOOKS

Waterstone's, 203-206 Piccadilly (☎7851 2400; www.waterstones.co.uk). ⊖Piccadilly Circus. If you're going to do megastore, do it like this. The 8 floors house Europe's largest bookshop, with specialty sections in just about everything. In addition to a cafe, there's a swanky basement restaurant. The top floor is dedicated to the store's frequent special events, including book signings by big-name authors (£2-4). Open M-Sa 10am-10pm, Su noon-6pm. Wheelchair accessible. AmEx/MC/V.

Sotheran's of Sackville Street, 2-5 Sackville St. (☎7439 6151; www.sotherans.co.uk). ⊖Piccadilly Circus. Founded in 1761 in York, Sotheran's moved to London in 1815, when Dickens began to frequent these stacks; the selection of collectible and rare books hasn't changed much since. And while the atmosphere of hushed voices and locked shelves might give the impression of an exclusive library, there are some affordable newer books (£5-30). Antique prints available downstairs. Open M-F 9:30am-6pm, Sa 10am-4pm. AmEx/MC/V.

Hatchard's, 187 Piccadilly (☎7439 9921; www.hatchards.co.uk). ⊖Green Park or Piccadilly Circus. Although London's oldest bookshop (est. 1797) has been bought by Waterstone's, the establishment is still most respected in London. Renowned for its selection of signed bestsellers, many by authors who frequent the store. As you'd expect from Prince Charles's official bookseller, the fiction and royalty sections are particularly strong. Open M-Sa 9:30am-6:30pm, Su noon-6pm. AmEx/MC/V.

CLOTHES

Oscar Milo, 19 Avery Row (☎7495 5846). ⊖Bond St. Particularly good menswear boutique with clothes that may not be cheap but are a bargain for what you get: well-cut jeans and shirts and seriously smooth footwear (separates and shoes £50-110). Open M-W and F-Sa 10:30am-6:30pm, Th 10:30am -7pm, Su 1-5pm. AmEx/MC/V.

Paul Smith Sale Shop, 23 Avery Row (☎7493 1287; www.paulsmith.co.uk). ⊖Bond St. Small range of last-season and clearance items from the acknowledged master of modern British menswear. More formalwear than not, at least 30% off original prices: grab a shirt or a pair of jeans for £45. Open M-W 10am-6pm, Th 10am-7pm, F-Sa 10am-6pm, Su 1-5pm. AmEx/MC/V.

DEPARTMENT STORES

Fortnum & Mason, 181 Piccadilly (☎7973 4133; www.fortnumandmason.com). ⊖Green Park or Piccadilly Circus. Founded in 1707, Fortnum is famed for its sumptuous food hall, with liveried clerks, chandeliers, and fountains. This is the official grocer to the royal family, but don't come here to do the weekly shopping—prices aside, the focus is very much on gifts and luxury items, especially chocolates, preserves, and teas. Open M-Sa 10am-6:30pm, Su noon-6pm (food hall and patio restaurant only). **Fountain Restaurant** open M-Sa 8:30am-8pm. AmEx/MC/V.

MUSIC

Music Zone, 104/106 Oxford St. (☎7631 5393; www.musiczone.co.uk). ⊖Tottenham Crt. Rd. The only London branch of Russ Grainger's independent music-chain-with-a-message. Music Zone's mascot is "Underdog" and its strategy-cum-philosophy is to undercut the megastores by selling all albums for £11 or less (with suprisingly good music available at £6). No 5-story mega-madness here, but you get 2 floors of mega-bargains. Open M-W, F-Sa 10am-7:30pm, Th 10am-9pm, Su noon-6pm. 1st floor is wheelchair-accessible. MC/V.

Tower Records, 1 Piccadilly Circus (☎7439 2500; www.tower.co.uk). ⊖Piccadilly Circus. London's first music megastore has lower prices and better discount sections than most. Tower also has a particularly good alternative selection, and every other type of media imaginable. Open M and Sa 8:30am-midnight, T-F 9am-midnight, Su noon-6pm. Wheelchair accessible. AmEx/MC/V.

SPORTING GOODS

Lillywhite's, 24-36 Lower Regent St. (☎0870 0333 9600; www.lillywhites.co.uk). ⊖Piccadilly Circus. A 7-floor sporting goods mecca, selling everything from polo mallets to Polo™ shirts. With slow lifts and no escalators, only the sportiest will ever make it to the top floor. Open M-F 10am-9pm, Sa 9am-9pm, Su noon-6:30pm. AmEx/MC/V.

SOHO

SOHO QUICKFIND: Discover, p. 10; sights, p. 113; museums & galleries, p. 150; food, p. 178; pubs, p. 201; nightlife, p. 214; entertainment, p. 240; accommodations, p. 292.

Despite Soho's eternal trendiness, its shopping options are decidedly mediocre—between all the bars and cafes, there's precious little space left for boutiques (rubbertastic sex shops not included). The main exceptions to this rule in central Soho are the record stores of **D'Arblay** and **Berwick Street,** not surprising given the area's

Street Chic

The Travel Bookshop, Notting Hill

Camden Market

integral position in the British entertainment industry. **Denmark Street,** on the eastern fringe of Soho, has been dubbed London's "Tin Pan Alley" due to its many musical instrument and equipment shops. **Charing Cross Road,** meanwhile, remains London's bookshop central.

ALCOHOL

Gerry's, 74 Old Compton St. (☎7734 2053). ⊖Piccadilly Circus or Leicester Sq. Gerry's stocks a staggering selection of beer and hard liquor, in all sizes from miniatures to magnums. With 50 different tequilas, 150 vodkas, a revolving bottle display, and an incendiary Bulgarian absinthe that's 89.9% alcohol by volume (half-liter £40), you can get drunk just looking. Open M-F 9am-6:30pm, Sa 9am-5:30pm.

MARKETS

Berwick St. Market, ⊖Leicester Sq. or Piccadilly Circus. Begun in the 1840s, this southernmost strip of Berwick is Central London's best-known fruit and vegetable market. The produce men advertise their stock loudly, and they have a right to be proud: they've got the best fruit and vegetable prices for miles. Especially lively at lunchtime. Open M-Sa 9am-5pm.

BOOKS

Shipley, 70, 72, and 80 Charing Cross Rd. (☎7836 4872; www.artbook.co.uk). ⊖Leicester Sq. Formerly Zwemmer, this art-specialist tri-fecta of stores spreads its media over 2 city blocks. 80 Charing Cross Rd. contains the photography, film, and fashion; 72 busies itself with graphic design and typography; and 70 finishes up with paintings. All open M-Sa 10am-6:30pm. AmEx/MC/V.

Blackwell's, 100 Charing Cross Rd. (☎7292 5100; www.blackwell.co.uk). ⊖Tottenham Crt. Rd. or Leicester Sq. Get blissfully lost in the London flagship store of Oxford's top academic bookshop, with everything on 1 enormous floor. Go for the postmodern theory, stay for the huge selection of fiction. Open M-Sa 9:30am-8pm, Su noon-6pm. Wheelchair accessible. AmEx/MC/V.

Foyles, 113-119 Charing Cross Rd. (☎7437 5660; www.foyles.co.uk). ⊖Tottenham Crt. Rd. or Leicester Sq. With over 30 mi. of shelving, this self-proclaimed "world's greatest bookshop" could host a marathon within its walls—if running wasn't discouraged on the premises. The 5 floors can make finding the book you want quite a challenge, but you can be sure it's there somewhere. There's also a strong sheet music department and a small art gallery. Relax with a new book in Ray's Jazz Cafe, on the first floor. Open M-Sa 9:30am-8pm, Su noon-6pm. AmEx/MC/V.

MUSIC

Black Market, 25 D'Arblay St. (☎7437 0478; www.blackmarket.co.uk). ⊖Oxford Circus. Metal-clad walls and massive speakers characterize this all-vinyl dance emporium. House and garage upstairs, phenomenal drum & bass section below with more underground garage. Give the turntables on the counters a spin. Also sells club tickets and own-label merchandise (£12-40). Open M-W and Sa 11am-7pm, Th-F 11am-8pm. AmEx/MC/V.

Reckless Records, 26 and 30 Berwick St. (☎7434 3362 and 7734 3144; www.reckless.co.uk). ⊖Tottenham Crt. Rd. or Oxford Circus. It may not be under the same roof, but this second-hand buyer/seller covers it all. 30 is the DJs' favorite exchange shop, with bucketfuls of used soul, dance, hip-hop, and reggae (vinyl and CDs). 26 is big in the rock/indie department, including rarities. Used DVDs are cheap and eclectic. Other locations at 92 Camden High St. and 79 Upper St. Open M-Sa 10am-8pm, Su 10am-7pm. AmEx/MC/V.

Sister Ray, 94 Berwick St. (☎7287 8385; www.sisterray.com). ⊖Oxford Circus, Piccadilly Circus, or Tottenham Crt. Rd. Put on your too-cool-for-school scowl and saunter into this crowded outlet of rare indie and alternative music on both vinyl and CD; lots of goth, metal, and punk. Decent dance selection with ambient, trance, and techno beats. Open M-Sa 10:30am-7pm, Su 11am-5pm. MC/V.

Uptown Records, 3 D'Arblay St. (☎7434 3639; www.uptownrecords.co.uk). ⊖Oxford Circus. Ever wondered what top DJs do in the daytime? Descend a rickety spiral staircase in this small all-vinyl store and you'll find scads of them huddled in the basement, advising shoppers on the latest house, garage, and hip-hop happenings. Bags and DJ equipment £50-100. Open M-Sa 10:30am-7pm. AmEx/MC/V.

Turnkey, 114-116 Charing Cross Rd. (☎7419 9999; www.turnkey.co.uk). ⊖Tottenham Crt. Rd. A creative dance DJ's paradise, with a basement crammed with synthesizers, turntables, PA machines, amps, and a mix station. Upstairs, play to your heart's content on dozens of dedicated analyzers, processors, and PCs. Massive range of guitars and keyboards on the first floor. Open M-W 10am-6pm, Th 10am-7pm, F-Sa 10am-6pm. AmEx/MC/V.

COVENT GARDEN

COVENT GARDEN QUICKFIND: Discover, p. 10; sights, p. 114; museums & galleries, p. 150; food, p. 267; pubs, p. 201; nightlife, p. 216; entertainment, p. 240; accommodations, p. 292.

All listings are near ⊖Covent Garden unless otherwise noted.

Once the hottest proving ground for new designers, Covent Garden is gradually being overtaken by large clothing chains: almost every store with an eye on the youth market has a second shop in the area, in addition to its main branch around Oxford St. and Regent St. Mid-priced chains and horrid souvenir shops fill the piazza, though there are still enough quirky specialty shops left to make it worth a quick wander. Still a top destination for funky footwear and mid-priced clubwear, **Neal Street** led the regeneration of Covent Garden back in the 90s, but is now indistinguishable from Carnaby St. (see p. 261). The fashion focus has shifted to nearby streets such as **Short's Gardens** to the east for chic menswear and **Earlham** and **Monmouth Street** to the west for a similarly stylish selection of women clothing.

BOOKS

Stanfords, 12-14 Long Acre (☎7836 1321; www.stanfords.co.uk). Second location at 1 Regent St. The self-proclaimed best map store in the world, Stanfords covers every corner, nook, and cranny of the universe. With a staggering range of hiking maps, city maps, road maps, flight maps, star maps, wall maps, and globes, you'll never be lost again. Also a massive selection of travel books (including the Let's Go series). Open M, W-F 9am-7:30pm, T 9:30am-7:30pm; Sa 10am-7pm: Su noon-6pm. MC/V.

CLOTHES

Apple Tree, 51 and 62 Neal St. (☎7836 6088; www.appletree.uk.com). Locations across the street from each other. Cute, wildly colorful clothing that verges on the punk, with an emphasis on cartoon-character designs from Hello Kitty to Pucca. So gaudy and garish that it's 150% hip. Pick up a pair of Powerpuff Girls pajamas (£20), underwear (£8), a matching wallet and purse (£20), and "save the world before bedtime." Open M-Sa 10am-7:30pm, Su 11am-6:30pm. AmEx/MC/V.

Miss Sixty, 39 Neal St. (☎7836 3789; www.misssixty.com). The newest in Italian streetwise clothing is nothing if not form-fitting. Purchase one eye-catching item and you may have to sacrifice your savings to the fashion gods. Long and skinny jeans around £75, shirts around £40. Open M-W 10am-6:30pm, Th-Sa 10am-7pm, Su noon-6pm. AmEx/MC/V.

Energie, 47-49 Neal St. (☎7836 7719; www.energie.it). This male companion to **Miss Sixty** (see above) offers the casual man chain boutique fashions at chic-boutique prices; pick up a £50 polo shirt or £85 jeans if you have money to burn. Open M-W and F-Sa 10am-6:30pm, Th 10am-7:30pm, Su 12:30-4:30pm. AmEx/MC/V.

Savage London, Unit 14, Covent Garden Market Pl. (☎7240 4582; www.savagelondon.com). Small corner store that focuses on funny, printed t-shirts (all £20). Logos range from neighborhood pride ("Brixton") to the irreverent ("Jesus loves hip-hop"). Also carries a small selection of purses, urbanwear, baggy sweatshirts, and jackets. Obviously targeted at tourists, but do you really care so long as "Jesus loves your mum"? Open M-Sa 10:15am-7pm, Su 11am-5pm. Branch at 14a Newburgh St. Wheelchair accessible. AmEx/MC/V.

GIFTS AND MISCELLANY

Neal's Yard Dairy, 17 Short's Gardens. (☎7240 5700; www.nealsyarddairy.co.uk). You'll smell it from a mile off—and that's a good thing. The enormous array of mostly British and Irish cheeses are all produced in small farms by traditional methods; massive wheels of stilton and cheddar line the shelves and countertops. Also sells preserves, organic milk, and yogurts. Drop in to escape the summer heat—the chilly shop is essentially a walk-in refrigerator to keep the cheese fresh. Open M-Th 11am-6:30pm, F-Sa 10am-6:30pm. MC/V.

Neal's Yard Remedies, 15 Neal's Yard (☎7379 7222; www.nealsyardremedies.com). A fragrant alternative medicine mecca: if it exists in nature it has probably been captured by Neal's in some soap, lotion or fragrance. What started with this little yard shop has now grown to a national chain, complete with books and pamphlets on natural healthcare. Most of the herbs are fairly recognizable (think lavender lotion and the like) but of course there is bladder wrack and pilewort, just in case you need some. Most of the employees are licensed natural healthcare practitioners. There's also a do-it-yourself ingredients section where beeswax pellets and henna powder are available to make your own remedy. Also, each Neal's has rooms available for private therapeutic sessions. Gift boxes from £8. Open M-W 10am-7pm, Th 10am-8pm, F-Sa 10am-7pm, Su 11am-6pm. AmEx/MC/V.

Penhaligon's, 41 Wellington St. (☎7836 2150; www.penhaligons.com). Branches on Bond St. and Piccadilly Circus. Founded by former palace barber William Henry Penhaligon in 1870, this aristocratic shop still provides the elite with scents and grooming products. Churchill never left home without a dab of the English classic Blenheim Bouquet—get a jar of shaving cream (with a silver plated lid of course) for £24. Super snobby but deliciously so: call in to make a personal scent-layering appointment. Framed pictures of style icons are on display—who wouldn't want to smell like Audrey Hepburn? Penhaligon's also sells female fragrances, scented candles, and exquisite, incredibly expensive toilette accessories. Open M-W and F-Sa 10am-6pm, Th 10am-7pm, Su noon-6pm. Wheelchair accessible. AmEx/MC/V.

MARKETS

Covent Garden Market and Jubilee Market Hall, inside the center of Covent Garden Piazza. Large covered markets, where anything and everything is sold. Covent Garden Market has mostly artwork and jewelry, while Jubilee has more clothing and accessories retailers. There are antiques on M and arts and crafts on the weekends; the rest of the week is general market. This is no flea market; it's a gentrified mix of clothes, souvenirs, and other goods from aspiring designers. Open daily 10am-6pm. Wheelchair accessible.

SHOES

Office, 57 Neal St. (☎7379 1896). One of London's foremost fashion footwear retailers, this Office store has a larger selection than most of the shoe stores on the street. They carry their own brand as well as other brands like Camper and LaCoste. Office's own broad range of high heels, low heels, and no heels is colorful, stylish, and mostly wearable. Women's shoes £20-145 with £50-80 being the average, men's £60-130. The **sale shop** at 61 St. Martin's Ln. (☎7497 0390; ⊖Leicester Sq. or Covent Garden) has good deals on all types of styles and includes mid-season reductions and older shoes. Techno soundtracks make it extra-funky. Neal St. store open M-W and F-Sa 10am-7:30pm, Th 10am-8pm, Su noon-6pm. Sale shop open M-Sa 10am-7pm, Su noon-6pm. Wheelchair accessible. AmEx/MC/V.

Egoshego, 76 Neal St.(☎7836 9260) www.egoshego.co.uk. One of the many Neal St. shoe havens, Egoshego carries both women's and men's shoes from lots of different brands. Not cheap (similar to Office) but a wide selection. Shoes range from the spiky/sparkly/pointy to the ultra-comfy walking shoe variety. And of course everything is sufficiently up-to-the moment trendy. The salespeople are also the kind every shoe store needs: helpful but not pushy. Open M-W 10:30am-7pm, Th 10:30am-8pm, F-Sa 10:30am-7pm, Su 12pm-6pm. AmEx/MC/V.

NORTH LONDON

NORTH LONDON QUICKFIND: Discover, p. 12; sights, p. 120; museums & galleries, p. 153; food, p. 183; pubs, p. 203; nightlife, p. 218; entertainment, p. 244; accommodations, p. 294.

North London has some of the best cheap, non-chain shopping. **Camden Town**—renowned for its markets that radiate out from Camden High St., with stores spilling out onto the street. Most of the stores are alternative, concentrating on cheap clothes and accessories for a young crowd. Even if it's not your style, you're bound to find something you want. Serious music shoppers will also revel here, particularly those interested in vinyl. There are a number of specialized DJ shops on **Inverness Street** Islington. Markets spread out from the lower part of Upper St., around the Angel Tube station. Moving north on Upper St. brings you to scads of boutiques.

in recent news

And Your Total Comes to...An Arm and a Leg

After a trip to London, visitors are left asking: where did all the money go? This isn't a reference to the scary number of pickpockets in the city, rather, it's rooted in the fact that London is one of the most expensive places to live and work in the world.

A series of articles published by BBC coined London as the second most expensive city in the world, the first being Tokyo, Japan. London used to sit tight at number seven before exploding to second place in 2004.

The huge price tags are attached to everything, from groceries to clothes to public transportation, and most importantly to rent and housing. The average two-bedroom apartment in London costs almost £2000 per month; try buying one and it will set you back hundreds of thousands of pounds in the 'burbs and likely close to a million in the center of things. While the housing problem is significant, visitors will feel the pinch while simply eating and shopping.

However, Londoners merrily consume and purchase and life goes on. Prices rise, but stores are still full. While economists may wonder how long it can last, visitors are left to tally their losses on the ride home.

CAMDEN TOWN

Camden Markets. Make a sharp right out of the Tube station to reach Camden High St. where most of the markets start. All stores are accessible from ⊖Camden Town.

Cyberdog, arch 14, Stables Market (☎7482 2842). Ever wonder what the world would be like if it happened in the mind of a clubber? These people made that world. The pounding music draws you from stalls away, enter the cave/shop and find endless caverns with flashing lights, and glowing clubbing clothes in museum-like displays. They also have an enormous dance floor in the silver-plated entrance lobby, where guest DJs spin on Sa. Open M-F 10:30am-6pm, Sa-Su 10am-7:30pm. Wheelchair accessible. AmEx/MC/V.

Stables Market, farthest from the tube station and the best of the bunch. No matter which entrance you pick you'll find yourself lost among the myriad stalls, shops, and food peddlers offering anything under the sun. Stables manages to avoid the tackiness trap so many markets fall into. Toward the back, at the horse hospital, you'll find some remaining independent artists as well as a two-story antique market. The railway arches sell outrageous club- and fetish-wear, plus a good selection of vintage clothes. Open F-Su, with a few shops open daily. Wheelchair accessible.

Camden Lock Market, extends from the railway bridge to the canal. The main draw of the Lock is the food; stalls and restaurants perfume the air with everything from Carribean plantains to chocolate strawberry waffles to Japanese dumplings. This is the original market and still the place to catch a bite (or a few bites from different vendors) along Regent's Canal. While there isn't much seating, the canal bank is pleasant and there are stand-up tables for passing munchers. The non-tourist stores focus on carpets, books, and household goods. Open daily 10am-6pm.

Camden Canal Market, opposite Camden Lock. Follow it down past the first shops which sell little more than cheap club gear and tourist trinkets. At the bottom, the more independent stores and restaurant stalls are open, but most of the stuff here can be found on High St. or at another market. Open F-Su. Wheelchair accessible.

The Camden Market, the nearest to Camden Town Tube stop, and correspondingly the most crowded and least innovative. This is the first market you see, the brightly painted sign welcomes you to the maze of stands separated by curtains and competing boomboxes. The clothes hang on racks 6 ft. high; it's like swimming in a sea of Tommy Hilfiger imitations. Predictably oriented toward teenagers, with jeans, sweaters, and designer fakes at average prices. You can also find jewelry and some pretty unique stuff if you head to the back. Vendors loudly hawk their wares, and most will be ready to cut you a deal, the major downside is the crowds. Open daily 9:30am-5:30pm, though not everything opens during the week. Wheelchair accessible.

Inverness Street Market, off Camden High St. opposite the Tube. What once was just a daily fruit 'n' veg market has become a mini extension of Camden Market, although it's thankfully less crowded and still has the cheap and fresh produce. Unconnected to the madness surrounding it, you'll still find plenty of trinket shops and some stalls selling random goods like shampoo. Open M-Sa 8am-5pm. Wheelchair accessible.

Mega City Comics, 18 Inverness St. (☎7485 9320; www.megacitycomics.co.uk). ⊖Camden Town. New series and comics in mint condition, from collector's items to the latest imports, starting at 50p. Covers the entire spectrum from Tintin to erotic Manga; most books are American. They also have animated videos, DVDs, posters and t-shirts with comic book characters. Open M-W and Sa 10am-6pm, Th-F 10am-7pm. MC/V (£10 min.).

Out on the Floor, 10 Inverness St. (☎7267 5989). ⊖Camden Town. Two tiny but full floors of used records and CDs, specializing in 60-70s rock, soul, reggae, and funk on vinyl, as well as some tapes and CDs. Vintage posters from the same eras are both on the walls and for sale. Open daily 10am-6pm. MC/V.

Vinyl Addiction, 6 Inverness St. (☎7482 1230). ⊖Camden Town. Underneath Bar Vinyl (see p. 219); a shop for professional DJs and those who wish to be. The shoppers all seriously know their beats. Many records have a staff description on the jacket, and there are numerous tables with mixers to take a test spin; join the pros with your big headphones, too. Open daily 11am-7:30pm.

ISLINGTON

Camden Passage Market, Islington High St. ⊖Angel. Turn right from the Tube; it's the alleyway that starts behind "The Mall" antiques gallery on Upper St. Not to be confused with Camden Market. The place for antiques; London's premier antique shops line these quaint alleyways. Smaller items may dip into the realm of the affordable, especially old prints and drawings and small knick-knacks. Stalls are only open W and Sa 8:30am-6pm; some stores are open daily, but W is the best day to go by far. Try **Annie's,** 12 Camden Passage (☎7359 0796). *Vogue* and *Elle* regularly use these vintage frocks in their photo shoots; movie costume designers often drop by, too. 1920s dresses are pricey (£350-600), but the less flashy 1930s pieces are more affordable (£60-150). Bags, shoes and hats start at £30. Open M and Th 11am-6pm, Tu and F 10am-6pm, W and Sa 8am-6pm. AmEx/MC/V.

Chapel Market, Chapel Market. ⊖Angel. A major contrast to the boutiques and mini-mall of Islington; this down-to-earth street market is all about inexpensive practical needs. Stalls hawk fruit 'n' veg, household goods, books, clothes and shoes. No-frills budget eateries line the road behind the market stalls. Come early as the grounds get tired and dirty in the afternoon. Open M-Sa 9am to mid-afternoon. Wheelchair accessible.

SHOPPING. Think of the neighborhoods like this: Mayfair for all the designer goods, Convent Garden for high end chains and boutiques, Oxford St. for affordable chains, and Camden for flea-market style.

SOUTH LONDON

SOUTH LONDON QUICKFIND: Discover, p. 14; sights, p. 125; museums & galleries, p. 155; food, p. 186; nightlife, p. 221; entertainment, p. 247.

If you're looking for the fruits of West Indian cultures or cheap club-wear, **Brixton** is the place to be. Actually, if you're looking for fruit in general, Brixton Market is still the place to be. Shops along Brixton Rd. and Coldharbour Ln. blast hip-hop and reggae and peddle skanky tops, tight pants, and gaudy accessories perfect for a night out on the town.

MARKETS

Brixton Market, along Electric Ave., Pope's Rd., and Brixton Station Rd., and inside markets in Granville Arcade and Market Row. ⊖Brixton. To experience Brixton fully in the daytime, stroll through the crowded streets of the market, where stalls hawk everything from cheap household items to bootlegged films. London's best selection of Afro-Caribbean fruits, vegetables, spices, and fish. Negotiate with the vendors for some unbelievable deals on meat and produce. Open daily 8am-6pm; closes W at 3pm.

MUSIC

Blacker Dread Muzik Store/CD Link, 404/406 Coldharbour Ln. (☎7274 5095; www.blackerdreadmuzikstore.co.uk). ⊖Brixton. Plastered wall-to-wall with record and CD covers, these 2 tiny shops literally vibrate with Caribbean beats and boast a remarkable selection of R&B, hip-hop, UK garage, gospel, and soul. Specializes in pre-releases: singles around £4, albums £15. Mail-order service available. Open M-W 9:30am-9pm, Th-Sa 9:30am-10pm, Su noon-6pm. AmEx/MC/V.

EAST LONDON

EAST LONDON QUICKFIND: Discover, p. 13; sights, p. 126; museums & galleries, p. 156; food, p. 187; pubs, p. 204; nightlife, p. 222; entertainment, p. 248.

In East London, the **street-market** tradition is alive and well, helped along by large immigrant communities, like the South Asian-dominated Brick and Petticoat Lanes. The scene here is very different than Camden, as it is less touristy. You can find cheap clothes and goods in Petticoat, but Spitalfields is the most pleasant and well organized of the bunch and has great street-food. For **leather** you can't beat the deals on the block of Brick Ln. just below Bethnal Green. Jackets are pre-made or tailor- made, and all are a fraction of what they'd cost elsewhere. In **Hoxton, Shoreditch,** and especially the stretch of Brick Ln. just north of the Truman Brewery, independent young designers have opened up boutiques frequented by local artists and arty pretenders. These places are great for clubbing gear or ideas on how to modify your wardrobe. Corporate **Docklands** has gone in the opposite direction, with the huge **Cabot Place and Canada Place** shopping malls offering the full range of British and international clothing chains and mainstream designer stores.

ALCOHOL

The Beer Shop, 14 Pitfield St. (☎7739 3701). ⊖Old St. Over 600 beers from around the world line the walls of this store, the one-stop shop for beer lovers. The distinctive hoppy smell comes from the successful Pitfield Brewery next-door, which brews all organic ales (and beer) from centuries old recipes. The friendly staff is happy to make recommendations and guide you through the overwhelming selection. Bottles, glasses, and organic wines, ciders and do-it-yourself beer making equipment is available to start your own personal brewery. Open Tu-F 11am-7pm, Sa 10am-4pm. MC/V.

CLOTHES AND ACCESSORIES

The Laden Showroom, 103 Brick Ln. (☎7247 2431; www.laden.co.uk). ⊖Aldgate East or Liverpool St. Fashion meets lifestyle at Laden, where local designers have their own racks, and there are plenty of them. This hip shop is a fitting favorite of celebs like Posh Spice, who calls it one of London's hidden finds. Up-to-the-minute casual and clubwear for both men and women shares space with choice accessories. Staff is dedicated and highly trend-conscious. New and recently used items, mostly under £50; and all original. Open M-Sa noon-6pm, Su 10:30am-6pm. AmEx/MC/V.

Hoxton Boutique, 2 Hoxton St. (☎7684 2083; www.hoxtonboutique.co.uk). ⊖Old St. If your current gear isn't fit for even 1 night on the town in Shoho, let this pricey but ultra-hip boutique funkify you. Alternatively, you could rip up, decorate, or throw paint on your own outfit and you'd look fine and save money. Most items £50-150. There's also a small but excellent selection of jewelry, starting at around £10. Open Tu-F 10am-6pm, Sa 11am-5pm, Su noon-5pm.

MARKETS

Spitalfields Market. ⊖Shoreditch or Liverpool St. Formerly 1 of London's main wholesale vegetable markets, Spitalfields has matured to be the best of the East End markets. It's now a crafts market with a wide range of made-to-order and pre-made food stalls, plus an organic food market twice a week. On Su, the foodstuffs share room with burgeoning independent clothing designer stalls. Crafts market M-F 11am-3:30pm, Su 10am-5pm. Organic market F and Su 10am-5pm.

Brick Lane Market. ⊖Shoreditch or Aldgate East. At the heart of Whitechapel's sizeable Bangladeshi community, Brick Ln. hosts a large Su market. In its glory days it worked the South Asian motif (food, rugs, spices, bolts of fabric, strains of sitar). Now most of the stands sell bargain household goods and trinkets, although rare gems can be found among them. Food remains the best reason to stop by. Open Su 8am-2pm.

Greenwich Markets. Numerous weekend markets converge on Greenwich, and on Su it is blanketed with stalls and shoppers looking for deals among the multitudes of goods.

> **Greenwich Market,** in the block surrounded by King William Walk, Greenwich Church St., College Approach, and Romney Rd. DLR: Cutty Sark. Th antiques and collectibles, F-Su arts & crafts. Open Th-Su 10am-6pm.
>
> **Antiques Market,** Greenwich High Rd. Rail: Greenwich or DLR: Cutty Sark. Mostly 20th-century stuff, lots of which dips into the range of affordable; busiest in the summer. Open Sa-Su 9am-5pm.

Village Market, Stockwell St. DLR: Cutty Sark. International food court is the best part here, but there are also used clothes and bric-a-brac, in this hodge-podge indoor market. Everything from gramophones to used books. Indoor stalls F-Sa 10am-5pm, Su 10am-6pm; outdoor market Sa 7am-6pm, Su 7am-5pm.

Petticoat Lane Market. ⊖Liverpool St., Aldgate, or Aldgate East. Streets of stalls, mostly cheap clothing and household appliances, with lots of leather jackets between Bishopsgate and Whitechapel High St. Hectic shopping scene begins around 9:30am and is mobbed by 11am. Open Su 9am-2pm.

WEST LONDON

WEST LONDON QUICKFIND: Discover, p. 14; sights, p. 130; food, p. 188; entertainment, p. 248; accommodations, p. 295.

Fosters Bookshop, 183 Chiswick High Rd. (☎8995 2768). ⊖Turnham Green. One of the most amusing used book shops in London, full of great finds. This small family-run business is a treasure trove for serious (and not so serious) readers of all ages. From vintage children's literature to antique angler's manuals. Open Th-Sa 10:30am-5pm. MC/V.

INSIDE

Accommodations

Sorry folks, but this isn't going to be pretty. Just as real estate prices make Londoners clutch their heads and scream, London's hotels and hostels are incredibly expensive. However, with a little bit of searching and a lot of planning, it is possible to find comfortable and affordable rooms. Between the inexpensive and institutional residence halls, and the exorbitant and cozy B&Bs, there are tons of non-budget-killing options that will leave you with enough money to spend on your tourist-y adventures. The price ranges are represented by the five different **Price Diversity Icons** and the icons are based on the cost of a single per night.

ICON	❶	❷	❸	❹	❺
PRICE	under £20	£21-34	£35-49	£50-74	£75+

ACCOMMODATIONS BY PRICE

NEIGHBORHOOD ABBREVIATIONS: BAY Bayswater **BLOOM** Bloomsbury **CHEL** Chelsea **CITY** The City of London **CLERK** Clerkenwell **HOL** Holborn **KEN/EC** Kensington & Earl's Court **K/B** Knightsbridge & Belgravia **M/RP** Marylebone & Regent's Park **NH** Notting Hill **SB** The South Bank **WEND** The West End **WEMIN** Westminster **NL** North London **SL** South London **EL** East London **WL** West London

UNDER £20 (PRICE ICON ❶)

Ashlee House	BLOOM
The Generator	BLOOM
Hyde Park Hostel	BAY
International Student House	M/RP
Leinster Inn	BAY
Palace Hotel	BAY
Pickwick Hall Int'l Backpackers	BLOOM
Quest Hostel	BAY
St. Christopher's Inn	NL
University of Westminster Halls	M/RP
YHA Earl's Court	KEN/EC
YHA Holland House	KEN/EC
YHA Oxford Street	WEND

£20-34 (PRICE ICON ❷)

Carr-Saunders Hall	BLOOM
City University Finsbury Residences	CLERK
Commonwealth Hall	BLOOM
High Holborn Residence	WEND
Indian YMCA	BLOOM
Jury's Inn	NL
LSE Bankside House	SB
Roseberry Hall	CLERK
Windsor Guesthouse	WL
YHA Hampstead Heath	NL
YHA St. Pancras International	BLOOM
YHA South Kensington	KEN/EC

£35-49 (PRICE ICON ❸)

Abbey House Hotel	K/B
Admiral Hotel	BAY
Alexander Hotel	WEMIN
Balmoral House Hotel	BAY
Camden Lock Hotel	NL
Dalmacia Hotel	WL
Edward Lear Hotel	M/RP
Garden Court Hotel	BAY
The Gate Hotel	NH
George Hotel	BLOOM
Georgian House Hotel	WEMIN
Greenville House Hotel	HOL
Guilford House Hotel	HOL
Hotel Orlando	HOL
Hyde Park Court Hotel	BAY
IES Student Residence	CHEL
Kandora Guesthouse	NL
Kensington Gardens Hotel	BLOOM
The Langland Hotel	BLOOM
Luna Simoe Hotel	WEMIN
Melbourne House	WEMIN
Morgan House	K/B
Mowbray Court Hotel	KEN/EC
Oxford Hotel	KEN/EC
Philbeach Hotel	KEN/EC
Star Hotel	WL
Vicarage Hotel	KEN/EC
Westminster House Hotel	K/B

£50-74 (PRICE ICON ❹)

Cardiff Hotel	BAY
Hamden Village Guest House	NL
James and Cartref House	K/B
Jenkins Hotel	BLOOM
Lincoln House Hotel	M/RP
Royal National Hotel	BLOOM
Seven Dials Hotel	WEND
Swiss House Hotel	KEN/EC
Thanet Hotel	BLOOM
Travel Inn County Hall	SB
Vancouver Studios	BAY

£75+ (PRICE ICON ❺)

Amsterdam Hotel	KEN/EC
Five Summer Place Hotel	KEN/EC

ACCOMMODATIONS TIPS

PLAN AHEAD. No matter where you plan to stay, it is essential to plan ahead, especially in summer. Tourist offices can help you find a room (see **Service Directory,** p. 339), while private hostels might grant you a patch of floorspace if all else fails. Generally, though, showing up in town without reservations means spending far more than you'd like on a room. When reserving in advance, it's worth the price of a phone call or fax to confirm a booking. Be sure to check the cancellation policy before handing over the deposit.

DISCOUNTS. Most B&Bs offer discounted rates for **long-term** stays (over a week), though not all advertise the fact—be sure to ask, and insist, if necessary. Most private hostels offer super-cheap weekly rates for guests staying over a month, or sometimes less. Another good source of discounts is traveling in the **low season,** October through March, excepting Christmas. If you're brave enough to arrive in London without prearranged accommodation and lucky enough to find a hotel with a vacancy in the afternoon or early evening, you're in a strong bargaining position—if you don't take the room, it will likely go empty. (Hint: don't be that brave. Reread "Plan ahead," above.)

PAYMENT. It's perfectly normal for accommodations in London to demand full payment on arrival—that way, you can't just leave if you don't like the room or find somewhere nicer. For this reason, always insist on being shown the room before handing over any money; that way, you'll only lose your one-night deposit should the room turn out to be unacceptable.

The vast majority of accommodations accept payment by either cash, credit card, or sterling traveler's checks. A number of lower-end accommodations don't take credit cards, so be sure to find out before checking in; those that do sometimes levy a 3-5%. Conversely, you may be able to negotiate a small reduction for cash payments (but don't count on it).

TYPES OF ACCOMMODATION

HOSTELS

Hostels offer a bed in a shared dormitory and are a great way of meeting fellow travelers; if you're traveling alone. A hostel is certainly your cheapest option. Shared dorms can hold anything from 3 to 20 beds, typically on a sliding price scale with smaller rooms being more expensive. Many also offer singles, though they are generally about as expensive as a cheap bed and breakfast room would be. If you plan on reserving a place in a large dorm (10-20 beds), ask the hostel if they can put you down for a corner bed. Sleeping (and waking) are easier when you're not in the middle of action. Hostels in London are either run by the **Youth Hostel Association** (YHA), an affiliate of Hostelling International (HI), or are independent **private hostels;** the difference is explained below.

YHA/HI HOSTELS

YHA hostels (www.yha.org.uk) are invariably more expensive than private ones, but are generally better kept, with more facilities, and knowledgeable staff; under 18 discounts make them popular with families. On the other hand, they tend to be feel more institutional, and draw a less bohemian crowd. While bedding is included in the price at all London hostels. All hostel rooms are equipped with large lockers that require your own padlock (available for purchase at hostels, £3). Most YHA hostels operate cheap cafeterias for dinner, and can supply a picnic lunch.

MEMBERSHIP. To take full advantage of YHA hostels, you need to be a member of the YHA or another HI-affiliated hostelling association, such as the American Youth Hostels (AYH). Non-members can stay in YHA hostels, but must purchase a "Welcome Stamp" (£2.20 per night stayed until payment equals £15), after which you become a full member for one year; you can also purchase membership straight away. In addition to being able to stay at YHA hostels, HI members are eligible for a range of discounts on sights and activities in London.

RESERVATIONS. YHA hostels in London are invariably oversubscribed; in the summer, beds fill up months in advance, and sometimes hostels have not been able to accommodate every written request for reservations, let alone walk-ins. However, hostels occasionally hold a few beds free until a few days before, and in a large hostel there's a good chance that someone will fail to show up or check-out early. If you want to risk it without reservations, turn up as early as possible and expect to queue. Reserving, however, is especially easy: online booking at www.yha.org.uk.

PRIVATE HOSTELS

Private hostels vary widely in price and quality, but as a rule are cheaper and have a more "fun" feel than their YHA equivalents. With a few exceptions, they also have fewer facilities and a less family-friendly atmosphere (many have a minimum age of 16 or 18). On the other hand, a lack of formal rules and the general laissez-faire attitude means that those who value privacy, quiet, and tidiness should think again about staying at a private hostel—though a few are as well-run as any YHA equivalent. As with YHA hostels, prices generally include sheets but not towels, and most have kitchens in various states of repair.

RESIDENCE HALLS

Over summer vacation, many of London's universities and colleges turn their student residences into vast budget hotels, at hostel prices. Most residence halls have student-priced bars, TV lounges, and games rooms with pool, ping-pong, and foosball tables. The only downside is that rooms tend to be fairly ascetic—standard student digs—and shared baths feel rather institutional. Additionally, the bulk of accommodation is single rooms, with the occasional twin and triple, so they're not ideal for couples or large groups. All halls have shared "pantries" (small kitchens), but they're mostly designed for students to eat tins of baked beans in.

Given their low prices, great locations, and good facilities, it's not surprising that residence halls fill extremely rapidly; it's often necessary to book months in advance. Moreover, many halls don't take walk-ins, so some form of advance booking is required, even if just the night before. A good number of residence halls require a **minimum stay**—find out if you should even bother calling. Bookings and accommodations information can be found on many colleges' **websites**.

University College London Residential Services, www.ucl.ac.uk/residences/. Site contains description and contact information for 8 halls, mostly around Bloomsbury. Rooms available Apr. and mid-June to mid-Sept.

London School of Economics, (☎7955 7575; www.lse.ac.uk/collections/vacations). Central information site for 6 halls, spread out over central London. Rooms available Apr. and mid-June to mid-Sept.

King's College Conference and Vacation Bureau, (☎7848 1700; www.kcl.ac.uk/services/conbro/Accommodation/Accommodation.html). Accommodations at the halls of King's College London, mostly located on the South Bank.

B&BS & HOTELS

Bed and Breakfasts—or B&Bs—are smallish hotels, usually a converted townhouses, run by a family or a proprietor. The term "B&B" encompasses accommodations of wildly varying quality and personality, often with little relation to price. Some are nothing more than budget hotels that serve breakfast, with small, dreary rooms. Others (often on the same street as their nightmarish doubles) are unexpected oasis of comfort, beautifully decorated and with excellent facilities. A **basic room** means that you share the use of a shower and toilet in the hall. An **ensuite** room contains a private shower or bath and a toilet, and tends to cost £10-20 more. Be aware, however, that in-room showers are sometimes awkward prefab units jammed into a corner. **Family room** in B&B lingo generally means a single-room quad or quint with at least one double bed and some single beds. Most B&Bs serve **English breakfasts**—eggs, bacon, toast, fried bread, baked beans, tomato (baked or stewed), and tea or coffee. **Continental breakfast** means some form of bread, cereal, and a hot drink.

Apart from B&Bs, a few **hotels** descend into the realms of the affordable—or at least, overlap in price with London's ridiculously expensive B&Bs. In general, these fall into two categories. The first is once-grand hotels that never modernized. On the one hand, you've got lifts, bars, restaurants, and sometimes even bellhops; on the other, it can be like a trip back in time to the 1970s, with aging decor, dodgy plumbing, and a radio pre-set to stations that haven't broadcast for 20

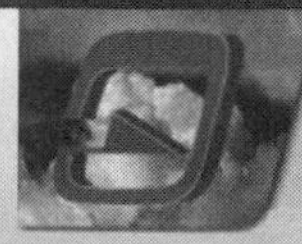

the new way to go on holiday

welcome to the new gateway for world travelling

Book Hostels all over the World!

Hostelsclub provides budget travellers and backpackers with an online booking engine for destinations all over the world:

Europe, North America, South America, Asia, Oceania, and Africa

You can make secure, guaranteed bookings for hostels, hotels and camping grounds for thousands of locations in just minutes.

www.hostelsclub.com

years. The second category are the increasingly numerous and ultra-modern **chain hotels,** which offer large well-equipped rooms. The downside to these, aside from a lack of character and a general leaning towards £100 per night or more, is that they're only economic for travelers in groups of two or more, since they usually charge a flat rate per room. Additionally, breakfast is rarely included in the prices. Advance booking is strongly recommended.

ACCOMMODATIONS BY NEIGHBORHOOD

BAYSWATER

BAYSWATER QUICKFIND: Discover, p. 4; food, p. 164; pubs, p. 193; entertainment, p. 233; shopping, p. 254.

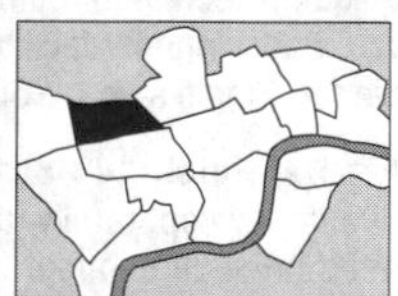
SEE MAP, p. 359

The budget traveler's dream neighborhood; friendly, safe, and full of cheap beds. Bayswater is a charming area in itself, and it's flanked by the twin attractions of expansive Hyde Park and posh Notting Hill, but the decidedly downmarket property prices mean that almost every side street is lined with converted Victorian houses offering rooms. (Enjoy the place while it lasts; gentrification is just beginning to take hold.) The greatest variety of rooms, and all the cheaper hostels, can be found around **Queensway;** try **Inverness Terrace, Kensington Square Gardens,** and **Leinster Square.** On the other side of Bayswater, the area around **Paddington** is convenient for travelers arriving on the Heathrow Express: **Sussex Gardens** is lined with affordable B&Bs, while marginally cheaper hotels surround the Tube station itself.

A word of warning: almost all the establishments are in converted 5- or 6-story townhouses with **very steep staircases.** Those who may have physical difficulty making the climb should ask for a room on a lower floor.

HOSTELS

Quest Hostel, 45 Queensborough Terr. (☎7229 7782; www.astorhostels.com). ⊖Bayswater or Queensway. A good chunk of long-term visitors, with comfortable, snazzy bunkbeds, and more space than the Hyde Park Hostel (see below). Dorms are mostly mixed-sex (2 female-only rooms available), and nearly all are ensuite. Otherwise, facilities on every other floor. Laundry, luggage storage, Internet (50p per 15min.) and kitchen available. Continental breakfast, linen, and lockers included. 4- to 8-bed dorms £14-17; twins £42. MC/V. ❶

Hyde Park Hostel, 2-6 Inverness Terr. (☎7229 5101; www.astorhostels.com). ⊖Queensway or Bayswater. There's nothing fancy about the tightly bunked dorms, but with 260 beds and a veritable theme park of diversions, this colorful and backpacker-friendly hostel is tons of fun. The recently renovated, jungle-themed basement bar and dance space hosts DJs and parties (open W-Sa 8pm-3am). Continental breakfast and linen included. Kitchen, laundry, TV lounge, secure luggage room. Ages 16-35 only. Reserve 2 weeks ahead for summer; 24hr. cancellation policy. Internet access 50p/7min. Online booking with 10% non-refundable deposit. 24hr. reception. 10- to 12-bed dorms £11-14; 8-beds £14.50-16; 6-beds £15.50-17; 4-beds £16.50-18; twins £43-50. 10% ISIC discount, weekly rates around 30% discount. MC/V. ❶

Leinster Inn, 7-12 Leinster Sq. (☎7729 9641; www.astorhostels.com). ⊖Bayswater. Mid-sized rooms are decent, and some are ensuite. Small bar that stays open W-Sa until 3am. TV/pool room. Internet access (£1-1.60 per hr.). Linen and Continental breakfast included. Safe-deposit boxes, kitchen, luggage room and laundry. £10 key deposit. 24hr. reception. 10-bed with shower £12; 4- to 8-bed dorms £13-16, with shower £16.50-18.50; singles £27.50-35/£33-40; twins £44-50/£55-58; triples £54/£57-63. 10% ISIC discount. Weekly discounts. MC/V. ❶

Palace Hotel, 48-49 Princes Sq. (☎7229 1729; www.hostelworld.com). ⊖Bayswater. One of the numerous dingier hostels around Princes and Leinster Squares. Decent-sized rooms equipped with wardrobe, sink, fridge, and table. No private baths. Linen included. Laundry, large kitchen, TV room, terrace. Book at least 1 week ahead in summer for a private room. 24hr. reception. 8-bed dorms £9; 4-to 6-bed dorms £9-10; 3-bed dorms £11; doubles £25; single (only one) £15. ❶

HOTELS AND BED & BREAKFASTS

Vancouver Studios, 30 Prince's Sq. (☎7243 1270; www.vancouverstudios.co.uk). ⊖Bayswater. Boasting the "convenience of a hotel, with the privacy of an apartment," Vancouver offers fully-serviced studios. It's a fantastic idea for anyone who craves a bit of self-sufficient convenience and the prices are comparable to hotels which offer a great deal less. Light, uniquely decorated rooms vary in size but all come with kitchenette, TV, hair dryer, phone, private bath, laundry facilities, and daily maid service. The "Balcony Studio" for two (£95) is to die for. Single studio £65; doubles £85-95; triples £120. AmEx/MC/V. ❹

Admiral Hotel, 143 Sussex Gdns. (☎7723 7309; www.admiral-hotel.com). ⊖Paddington. Beautifully kept family-run B&B; all rooms with shower, toilet, hairdryer, TV, and kettle, decorated in warm summer colors. If you're picky ask for a tiled bathroom rather than linoleum. Non-smoking. English breakfast included. Call 10-14 days ahead in summer; 4-day cancellation policy. Singles £40-50; doubles £58-75; triples £75-90; quads £88-110; quints £100-130. Be sure to ask about their winter and long-stay discounts. MC/V. ❸

Balmoral House Hotel, 156-157 Sussex Gdns. (☎7723 7445; www.balmoralhousehotel.co.uk). ⊖Paddington. Spacious, well-kept rooms. Rooms have smallish bathroom, satellite TV, kettle, and hair dryer. English breakfast included. Singles £40; doubles £65; triples £80; family suites for 4 £100, for 5 £120. MC/V (5% surcharge). ❸

Garden Court Hotel, 30-31 Kensington Gdns. Sq. (☎7229 2553; www.gardencourthotel.co.uk). ⊖Bayswater. Newly refurbished rooms with crisp, attractive decor vary widely in size (the quad is an especially tight fit); all have sink, TV, hair dryer, and phone. Rare conve-

Welcome to

Abbey House

Hospitality, Quality & Genuine Value in the Heart of London.

If you are planning a trip to England and looking for a B&B in London Abbey House is the place to stay. Situated in a quiet garden square adjacent to Kensington Palace, this elegant Victorian house retains many of its original features including the marble entrance hall and wrought iron staircase. Once the home of a Bishop and a member of Parliament it now provides well maintained quality accommodation for the budget traveller who will be well looked after by its owners the Nayachs.

Write or call for a free colour brochure.

Recommended by more travel guides than any other B&B.

ABBEY HOUSE HOTEL

11 Vicarage Gate, Kensington, London W8 4AG

Reservations: 020-7727 2594

Fax: 020-7727 1873

www.AbbeyHouseKensington.com

nience alert: elevator, and ensuite rooms have full bathtubs. Access to the patio garden. English breakfast included. Strict 14-day cancellation policy. Singles £40 with bath £62; doubles £64/£92; triples £84/£114; family quad (2 double beds) £94/£135. MC/V. ❸

Kensington Gardens Hotel, 9 Kensington Gdns. Sq. (☎7221 7790; www.kensingtongardenshotel.co.uk). ⊖Bayswater. Handsomely decorated, well-equipped rooms with kettle, TV, phone, mini bar, fan and hair dryer on demand, and even a bowl of snacks. Rooms are similarly sized, so singles feel more spacious. All rooms have shower; the 4 shower-only singles share 3 hall toilets. Continental breakfast included; English breakfast £5.50. 48hr. cancellation policy. 24hr. reception. Singles £50; doubles £75; triples £95. Shower only singles £45. £5 discount after 7 days. AmEx/MC/V. ❸

Cardiff Hotel, 5-9 Norfolk Sq. (☎7723 9068; www.cardiff-hotel.com). ⊖Paddington. Clean, simple rooms come with shower, TV, kettle, and phone (cheery staff included in the price). Singles can run on the small side, though, and tiny bathrooms border on space-age oddness. English breakfast included. 48hr. cancellation policy. 24hr. reception. Singles £55, with hall toilet £49; doubles £85; triples £95; quads £110. MC/V. ❹

Hyde Park Court Hotel, 48 Norfolk Sq. (☎7723 3050; www.hydeparkcourthotel.com). ⊖Paddington. Tired decor shows signs of wear, but rooms are reasonably sized with shower, toilet, TV, and phone. The ingenious, duplex-style family rooms are especially spacious, but the standard bathroom setup is boat-cabin tiny— the entire plasticized cubicle becomes your shower space. Continental breakfast included. Singles £38, on the weekend £42; doubles £55/£65; triples £65/£75; quads £71/£85. AmEx/MC/V. ❸

BLOOMSBURY

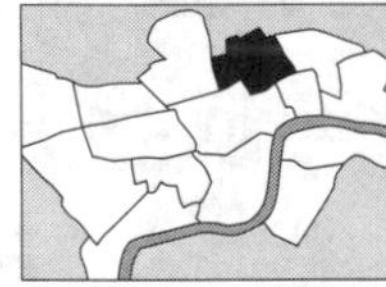

SEE MAP, p. 360

BLOOMSBURY QUICKFIND: Discover, p. 5; sights, p. 87; museums & galleries, p. 140; food, p. 166; pubs, p. 193; entertainment, p. 234; shopping, p. 255.

Bloomsbury's quiet squares and Georgian terraces are home to an endless and varied assortment of accommodations, from dodgy sinkholes near King's Cross charging by the hour to London's self-appointed "coolest" hotel (the pricey Myhotel, on Bedford Sq.). A plethora of quasi-affordable B&Bs line leafy **Cartwright Gardens** and quiet **Bedford Place,** while depopulated university halls dot the area around UCL. If you opt for a hostel or B&B in the King's Cross area, be warned that the local nightlife consists partly of drug-dealing and prostitution—though locals report that it's not as dangerous as it is disquieting. The southern part of Bloomsbury, by contrast, abuts the more socially acceptable nightlife of the West End.

HOSTELS

The Generator, Compton Pl., off 37 Tavistock Pl. (☎7388 7655; www.generatorhostels.com). ⊖Russell Sq. or King's Cross St. Pancras. The ultimate party hostel, you might be greeted by the "Welcome Host" with a complimentary beer and a grin. Under-18 not allowed unless part of a family group. Mixed-sex dorms (all-female available), a hopping bar (6pm-2am), cheap pints (£1, 6-9pm), dinner specials, and well-equipped common rooms. Rooms have small mirrors and washbasins; private doubles have tables and chairs. Continental breakfast included. Fax and photocopy machines, luggage storage, lockers (bring your own lock), free towels and linens, laundry, kitchen, cash machine, and an in-house travel shop that sells Tube and train tickets. Internet £1 per 8min. Reserve 1 week ahead for weekends. 24hr. reception. Dorms £12.50-17. Mar.-Oct. singles £42; doubles £53; triples £67.50; quads £90; quints £112.50; six-person £135. Smaller rooms are cheaper in the off-season. Discounts for long stays, online booking, student IDs, or VIP Backpacker card-holders. Credit card required with reservation, MC/V. ❶

Ashlee House, 261-265 Gray's Inn Rd. (☎7833 9400; www.ashleehouse.co.uk). ⊖King's Cross St. Pancras. All about quiet, laid-back mellowness. Mixed-sex (all-female available) dorms are airy and bright, while private rooms include table, sink, kettle, luggage room, safe, laundry, kitchen. Brand new bathrooms, plus an elevator, and TV room. Continental breakfast included. Linen included, towels £1. No lockers, but all rooms lock. 2-week maximum stay. Internet £1 per hr. 24hr. reception. May-Sept. 16-bed dorms £15; 8- to10-bed £17; 4- to 6-bed £19. Singles £36; doubles £48. Oct.-Apr. subtract £2. MC/V. ❶

Indian YMCA, 41 Fitzroy Sq. (☎7387 0411; www.indianymca.org). ⊖Warren St. or Great Portland St. Standard student-dorm affair, an institutional (and somewhat musty) feel, but price includes both continental breakfast and an Indian (or Western) dinner. Laundry, lounge, and games room are all new and attractive. Deluxe rooms are substantially larger and feature TV, fridge, desk, and kettle. Reserve ahead during summer. £1 temporary membership fee payable on arrival. 1-night deposit required with reservations. £10 cancellations fee. Dorms £20; singles £34, ensuite £52; doubles £49, ensuite £55, with bath £72. AmEx/MC/V. ❷

Pickwick Hall International Backpackers, 7 Bedford Pl. (☎7323 4958; www.pickwickhall.co.uk). ⊖Russell Sq. or Holborn. Aside from a single 6-bed room, most accommodation is in 3- to 4-bed single-sex "dorms." Small, simple rooms are clean and include minifridge and microwave. Rules include no smoking and no guests. Continental breakfast and linen included. Laundry room, kitchen, TV lounge, Internet access. Reception approx. 8am-10pm. Call 2-3 days ahead, 3 weeks ahead for July-Aug. Singles £25, ensuite £45; doubles £44/£50; triples £60/£66; quads £80/£88. Discounts for longer stays. AmEx/MC/V. ❶

YHA St. Pancras International, 79-81 Euston Rd. (☎7388 9998; stpancras@yha.org.uk). ⊖King's Cross St. Pancras. Away from the seediest part of King's Cross, opposite the British Library. Triple glazing and comfortable wooden bunks. Most of the (single-sex) dorms have bath and A/C; all have lockers (bring your own lock). Lounge with video games. Dinner 6-9pm £5.50. English breakfast and linen included. Laundry, kitchen, and elevators. Internet £1 per

REGENCY
HOUSE HOTEL
JVM HOTELS
A GEORGIAN TOWN HOUSE IN
THE HEART OF LONDON'S HISTORIC BLOOMSBURY
A SHORT STROLL AWAY FROM
THE BRITISH MUSEUM, WEST END THEATRES
AND OXFORD STREET SHOPS.

All rooms have colour T.V, direct dial telephones,
tea and coffee making facilities.
Room rates are inclusive of all taxes and English breakfast.

71 GOWER STREET LONDON WC1 E6HJ
TEL: 020 7637 1804 FAX: 020 7323 5077
www.regencyhouse-hotel.com

15min. 10-day maximum stay. Reserve 1 week ahead for weekends or summer, 2 for doubles. Dorms £24.60, under 18 £20.50. Doubles £56, ensuite £61.50. £3 discount with ISIC or NUS card. Non-HI members add £2 per night. AmEx/MC/V. ❷

RESIDENCE HALLS

Commonwealth Hall, 1-11 Cartwright Gdns. (☎7685 3500; www.lon.ac.uk/services/students/halls1/halls2/vacrates.asp). ⊖Russell Sq. Post-war block housing: 425 nicely sized, recently refurbished student singles with telephones; a good value, especially with the included English breakfast and garden tennis/squash courts. Pantry on each floor, elevators, bar and cafeteria. Open mid-Mar. to late Apr. and mid-June to mid-Sept. (check website for dates). Generally reserve at least 3 months ahead for July-Aug. No walk-ins. Singles £24, half-board £28; UK students half-board £20. MC/V. ❷

Passfield Hall, 1-7 Endsleigh Pl. (☎7107 5916/5915; www.lse.ac.uk/vacations). ⊖Euston or Euston Sq. Three converted Georgian blocks arranged around a garden courtyard. Singles fairly small, but clean and with sink and phone; doubles and triples are much bigger. Unisex baths and kitchen on each floor. TV lounge, game room, laundry. English breakfast included. Open Easter (Mar. 19-Apr. 24) and early Jul. to late Sept. Book at least 1 month ahead, though walk-ins generally get a room. Singles £27; doubles £48; triples £62. MC/V. ❷

Carr-Saunders Hall, 18-24 Fitzroy St. (☎7107 5888; www.lse.ac.uk/vacations). ⊖Warren St. Old and somewhat creaky hall, but rooms are larger than most and include sink and phone. TV lounge, games room, and lift to all floors, including the panoramic roof terrace, used for breakfast. English breakfast included. Reserve 6-8 weeks ahead for July-Aug., but check for openings any time. Internet access. Open Easter (Mar. 25-Apr. 23) and late-June to late-Sept. 30% deposit required. Discount for stays over 5 weeks. Singles £27 in summer, £25 Easter; doubles £45/£40, ensuite £50/£45. MC/V. ❷

HOTELS AND BED & BREAKFASTS

Jenkins Hotel, 45 Cartridge Gdns., entry on Barton Pl. (☎7387 2067; www.jenkinshotel.demon.co.uk). ⊖Euston or King's Cross St. Pancras. Each room is unique—size and decor may vary, but all are airy, pleasant, and attractive. The cheery staff will be happy to show you a few. Guests can use the tennis courts in Cartwright Gardens at a reduced rate (£5). Rooms have TV, kettle, phone, fridge, hair dryer, and safe. English breakfast included. Non-smoking. Reserve 1-2 months ahead for summer. 24hr. cancellation policy. Singles £52, ensuite £72; doubles ensuite (some with tub) £85; triples ensuite £105. MC/V. ❹

The Langland Hotel, 29-31 Gower St. (☎7636 5801; www.langlandhotel.com). ⊖Goodge St. A comfortable B&B that distinguishes itself with lower rates. The friendly staff keep their large rooms spotless, and guests have access to a lounge with satellite TV. Recently refurbished rooms have TV, kettle, and fan. English breakfast included. 48hr. cancellation policy. Singles £45, ensuite £65; doubles £55/£80; triples £75/£95; quads £85/£105. Discounts available for longer stays, students, advance booking, and in winter. AmEx/MC/V. ❸

George Hotel, 58-60 Cartwright Gdns. (☎7387 8777; www.georgehotel.com). ⊖Russell Sq. Meticulous blue and yellow rooms with satellite TV, radio, kettle, phone, and sink, plus hair dryers and iron on request. The forward-facing 1st-floor rooms are the best, with high ceilings and tall windows. Free Internet. English breakfast included. Reserve 3 weeks ahead for summer; 48hr. cancellation policy. Singles £47.50, with shower only £60, fully ensuite £70; doubles £66.50/£74/£89; triples £79/£89/£99; basic quad £89. 15% discount for stays over 5 days. MC/V. ❸

Thanet Hotel, 8 Bedford Pl., Russell Sq. (☎7636 2869; www.thanethotel.co.uk). ⊖Russell Sq. or Holborn. The same quality rooms and services as other listed B&Bs, but without the cheaper rooms. On the flip side: rooms are all bright, especially toward the back with views of the garden. All ensuite, with TV, hair dryer, kettle, and phone. Breakfast included. Reserve 1 month in advance. Singles £72; doubles £96; triples £105; quads £116. AmEx/MC/V. ❹

Royal National Hotel, Bedford Way (☎7637 2488, reservations 7278 7871; www.imperialhotels.co.uk). ⊖Russell Sq. London's largest hotel, with 1335 rooms, the Royal National occupies almost an entire block, with 2 lobbies and corridors that vanish into the horizon.

CENTRAL LONDON
Atlantic Paddington
Youth Hotel
Near Hyde Park and within walking distance of major attractions.
Excellent transport links to the rest of the city.
Single, double, triple and multishare rooms.
All cleaned daily with TV and phone.
Continental Breakfast included.
Internet Access and Bar.
From £12.50 per person
Call free +44 (0) 800 085 1932
www.atlantic-paddington.com

Recently redecorated, the hotel has large rooms that B&Bs do not, but with a distinct loss of personality. All rooms ensuite with satellite TV. Continental breakfast included. Singles £66; doubles £85; triples £102.50. Wheelchair accessible. MC/V. ❹

CHELSEA

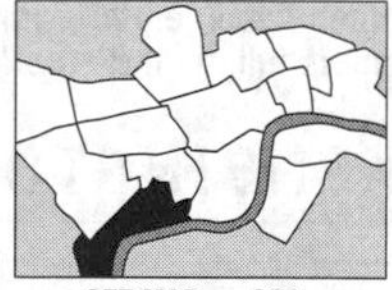
SEE MAP, p. 361

CHELSEA QUICKFIND: Discover, p. 5; sights, p. 89; museums & galleries, p. 141; food, p. 167; pubs, p. 195; entertainment, p. 234; shopping, p. 256.

The only Tube station in Chelsea is Sloane Sq.; from here buses #11, 19, 22, 211, and 319 serve King's Rd.

IES Student Residence, corner of Manresa Rd. and King's Rd. (☎7808 9200; www.iesreshall.com). Brand new university residence hall (built 2002-2003) offers clean and spacious dorm rooms year round. In the heart of uber-posh Chelsea, these prices are unheard of. All rooms are ensuite, with data ports (free, unlimited Internet if you've got a computer), phone, kitchen and laundry access, and a number of TV/DVD-loaded student lounges. 72hr. cancellation policy. Reservations recommended. 2-night minimum stay. Singles £45; doubles £60. Over 4-weeks stay £40/£50. 20 wheelchair-accessible rooms. AmEx/MC/V. ❸

CLERKENWELL

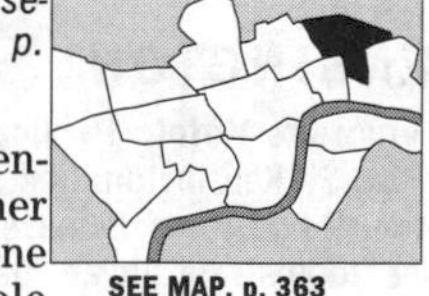
SEE MAP, p. 363

CLERKENWELL QUICKFIND: Discover, p. 7; sights, p. 95; museums & galleries, p. 143; food, p. 169; pubs, p. 196; nightlife, p. 210; entertainment, p. 235.

Clerkenwell boasts two smashing bargains in its inexpensive university dormitories (only open during the summer and Easter holidays), but otherwise this boho-trendy zone generally lacks budget accommodations. For affordable hotels and B&Bs, look to nearby Bloomsbury and into the King's Cross area.

City University Finsbury Residences, 15 Bastwick St. (☎7040 8811; www.city.ac.uk/ems/accomm/fins.html). ⊖Barbican. Don't judge a building by its facade—this might be a grim 1970s tower block, but the inside is freshly renovated, and it's within walking distance of City sights, Islington restaurants, and Clerkenwell nightlife. Singles in the main building have shared shower, toilet, kitchen access, and a laundry room. English breakfast included. Evening meals available (£4.70). Earlier reservation recommended. £21, students £19. 3night min. stay. Wheelchair accessible. MC/V. ❷

Rosebery Hall, 90 Rosebery Ave. (☎7955 7575; www.lse.ac.uk/collections/vacations). ⊖Angel. Exit left from the Tube, cross the road, and take the 2nd right onto Rosebery Ave. Buzz for entry. Modern student residence in 2 buildings arranged around a sunken garden. "Economy twins" are singles with an extra bed. Rooms in the newer block are more spacious, with handicap-accessible baths. TV lounge, laundry, and bar. Common rooms pool tables. English breakfast included. Open Dec. 11, 2004-Jan. 8, 2005; Mar. 25-Apr. 24 and early July-late Sept. 2005. Reserve 6 weeks ahead for July with 1 night or 25% deposit; £10 cancellation fee. Online request form available. Singles from £30; doubles £48, economy £37, with bath £58; triples £60. Wheelchair accessible. ❷

HOLBORN

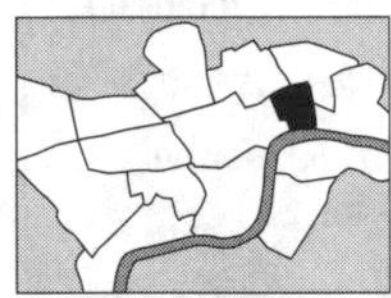

SEE MAP, p. 363

HOLBORN QUICKFIND: Discover, p. 7; sights, p. 97; museums & galleries, p. 143; food, p. 170; pubs, p. 197; nightlife, p. 211; shopping, p. 257.

Guilford House Hotel, 6 Guilford St. (☎7430 2504; www.guilford-hotel.co.uk). ⊖Russell Sq. or Holborn. Situated nicely in between Holborn's low-profile charms, the Guilford House is a friendly mid-range hotel that distinguishes itself with immaculate quarters and a number of welcome conveniences. Rooms all come with a tiny, spotless shower, kettle, TV, hair dryer, and telephone. Continental breakfast is included. 24hr. reception. Single £45, double £58, triple £68, quad £78-89, and "family room" up to 6 people £88-99. Reserve about 2 weeks ahead June-Aug. Check-in after noon, check-out at 11am. Pay on arrival. AmEx/MC/V. ❸

Grenville House Hotel, 4 Guilford St. (☎7430 2504; www.grenvillehotel.co.uk).⊖Russell Sq. or Holburn. Affiliated with the Guilford House, this next-door neighbor offers the same amenities in equally immaculate, well-priced rooms. Same prices and indications apply. If one is full, try the other! ❸

KENSINGTON & EARL'S COURT

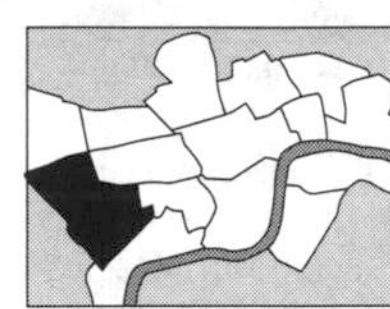

SEE MAP, pp. 364-365

KENSINGTON & EARL'S COURT QUICKFIND: Discover, p. 8; sights, p. 100; museums & galleries, p. 145; food, p. 171; pubs, p. 198; entertainment, p. 236; shopping, p. 257.

For such a posh neighborhood, Kensington is not entirely devoid of affordable accommodations—a few streets removed from the mansions are dotted with mid-priced B&Bs. Then again, it's a big place and a "Kensington" address doesn't necessarily put you within walking distance of the main sights and shops. Decidedly less exclusive **Earl's Court** remains popular with backpackers and budget travelers, with a quick connection (Piccadilly Line) to the center of London.

KENSINGTON

Vicarage Hotel, 10 Vicarage Gate, (☎7229 4030; www.londonvicaragehotel.com). ⊖High St. Kensington. Beautifully kept Victorian house with ornate hallways, TV lounge, and charming bedrooms: all have solid wood furnishings and luxuriant drapes, with kettle and hair dryer (rooms with private bath also have TV). English breakfast included. Reserve several

Best apartments.
Affordable prices.
reservation@1st-london-flats.com
UK calls - Tel. 0871 990 3045
International Calls - Tel. +34 93 310 6686
www.1st-london-flats.com

months ahead with 1 night's deposit; US$ personal checks accepted for deposit with at least 2 months notice. Singles £46, with private facilities £75; doubles £78/£102; triples £95/£130; quads £102/£140. ❸

YHA Holland House, Holland Walk, (☎7937 0748; www.hihostels.com). ⊖High St. Kensington or Holland Park. A picturesque location makes this one of the better hostels in the city. In the middle of Holland Park, with half the rooms in a gorgeous 17th-century mansion and overlooking a large flowery courtyard. Standard 12- to 20-bed single-sex dorms are less alluring (some bunks are 3-tiered), but a cleaner facility would be hard to find. Caters mostly to groups. Facilities include Internet (7p per min.), TV room, luggage storage, lockers, laundry, and kitchen. Breakfast included; dinners £5-6. Book 2-3 weeks ahead in summer, although there are frequent last minute vacancies. 24hr reception. Dorms £21.60, under 18 £19.30. Some private rooms available, book 14 days in advance: Singles £30; doubles £50; triples £70; quads £90; 6-beds £135. £3 discount w/student ID. MC/V. ❶

Five Sumner Place Hotel, 5 Sumner Pl. (☎7584 7586; www.sumnerplace.com). ⊖South Kensington. Boasts the amenities of a luxury hotel without losing the charm of the converted Victorians in the area. All accessible by lift, the spacious rooms have elegant ceiling moldings and large windows; all have private bath, TV, fridge, phone, and hair dryer. English breakfast served in the beautiful conservatory dining room. The location is fantastic as well, but there's no doubt that you'll be paying for all these charms. 14-day cancellation policy; book 1 month ahead in summer. Singles £85; doubles £130, add a bed for £22. AmEx/MC/V. ❺

Abbey House Hotel, 11 Vicarage Gate (☎7727 2594; www.abbeyhousekensington.com). ⊖High St. Kensington. Spacious, pastel-themed rooms with TV, desk, and sink. 5 baths between 16 rooms. 24hr. free tea, coffee, and ice room. English breakfast included. Hospita-

If you are on a budget, but still have high standards, come to the

Euro Hotel

And here's why...

The hotel dates from 1807

- Clean comfortable rooms with TV, tea & coffee and telephone
- Superb all-you-can-eat full English breakfast
- A quiet and safe neighborhood
- A short walk from Central London's attractions, nightlife, and shopping
- Special rates for children
- Discount for long stays
- Prices from £49 to £115 per room

Everyone gets a friendly welcome at the Euro Hotel. Visitors from every country of the world return time and again because of its friendly staff, its fantastic location, and its reasonable prices. If you are travelling outside the peak season, be sure to ask for a special price!

The breakfast parlor overlooks the garden

EURO HOTEL
53 Cartwright Gardens
London WC1H 9EL
Tel: 011 44 207 387 4321
Fax: 011 44 207 383 5044
email: reception@eurohotel.co.uk

Visit our web site at www.eurohotel.co.uk

ble staff will gladly provide you with bus routes and sightseeing directions. Singles £45; doubles £74; triples £90; quads £100. Winter discounts available. No credit cards; personal checks in US$ or euros accepted for deposit with at least 1 month notice. ❸

Swiss House Hotel, 171 Old Brompton Rd. (☎7373 2769; www.swiss-hh.demon.co.uk). ⊖Gloucester Rd. or South Kensington. On a quiet, shady part of Old Brompton Rd. 10-15min. walk from the nearest Tube station. All of the large, wood-floored rooms have TV, phone, fan, toilet, and shower. Book 1 month ahead for summer. Continental breakfast included; English breakfast £6.50. Singles £56, with bath £78-114; doubles with bath £97; triples with bath £132; quads with bath £147. 5% discount for stays over 7 nights and cash payments. AmEx/MC/V. ❹

YHA South Kensington, 65-67 Queensgate (☎7584 7031; www.yha.org). ⊖Gloucester Rd. In the heart of museumland, this decent hostel (housed in a post-war fixer-upper) offers tidy and tight single-sex dorms. They're more expensive than some, but the great location is a plus. Facilities include laundry, cafe, luggage storage, and a rooftop terrace. Full English breakfast included. Open Feb.-Dec. Reception 7am-10pm. 6- to 20-bed dorms £30.50, under 18 £20. Wheelchair accessible. MC/V. ❷

EARL'S COURT

⊖All Earl's Court.

Oxford Hotel, 24 Penywern Rd. (☎7370 1161; www.the-oxford-hotel.com). Midsized, bright rooms, all with at least a shower. Furnishing is minimal but generally of high-quality, with comfortable beds, TV, kettle, safe, chair, and clothes rail, although some share a toilet in the hall. Continental breakfast included. Rooms in the annex down the road are a little less splendid, but still good. 24hr reception. Reserve 2-3 weeks ahead for June. Singles with shower only £37.50, with bath £53; doubles £59/£69; triples £72/£81; quads £90/£96; quints £110/£120. Discount on stays over 1 week. AmEx/MC/V. ❸

Amsterdam Hotel, 7 Trebovir Rd. (☎7370 5084, within UK 0800 279 9132; www.amsterdam-hotel.com). Accommodations are split into rooms and suites, and further between "standard" and "executive." Suites have a kitchenette and sitting area. Rooms have bath, TV, kettle, and phone, and are served by an elevator. Continental breakfast included. Singles standard £62, executive £84; doubles £87/£97; triples £114/£124. Suites: studios standard £102, executive £108; doubles £108/£120; triples £146/£156; 2-bedroom £173/£186. 10% discount on stays 7 nights or more. Wheelchair accessible. AmEx/MC/V. ❺

YHA Earl's Court, 38 Bolton Gdns. (☎7373 7083; www.yha.org; earlscourt@yha.org.uk). Rambling Victorian townhouse that's considerably better-equipped than most YHAs. The bright, tidy, single-sex dorms (4-8 people) have wooden bunks, lockers (bring your own lock), and sink. Features a small garden, kitchen, 2 spacious TV lounges and luggage storage. Linen and laundry included. Internet access available (at an ungodly 7p per min.). Breakfast included only for private rooms; otherwise £3.50. 2-week max stay. 24hr. cancellation policy; £5 cancellation charge. Dorms £19.50; under 18 £17.20. Private rooms (only bookable online; book at least 48hr. in advance): doubles £52; quads £76. MC/V. ❶

Mowbray Court Hotel, 28-32 Penywern Rd. (☎7373 8285; www.mowbraycourthotel.co.uk). Large B&B with 80 rooms, elevator, TV lounge, and bar. Rooms vary from smallish to enormous, but facilities include TV, trouser press, hair dryer, safe, and phone. Baths are big. Continental breakfast included. Reserve a week ahead; 24hr. cancellation policy. 24hr reception. Singles £45, with bath £52; doubles £56/£67; triples £69/£80; quads £84/£95; quints £100/£110; sextuples £115/£125. Discounts for 7 nights or more. AmEx/MC/V. ❸

Philbeach Hotel, 30-31 Philbeach Gdns. (☎7373 1244; www.philbeachhotel.freeserve.co.uk). The rooms in London's largest gay and lesbian B&B vary greatly: "budget singles" are very basic (phone and sink), while 1 double with private bath features a cast-iron bedframe, desk, and full bay window. Wireless Internet throughout and a garden out back. Standard rooms have TV, phone, kettle, and sink. Continental breakfast included, served in

Welcome to London
Hyde Park Rooms Hotel

Nice Central Location
Full English Breakfast
Clean, Comfortable and Friendly
From:
Single: £30.00 • Double: £45.00 • Family: £60.00
137 Sussex Gardens, Hyde Park W2 2RX
Tel 0207 723 0225 • 0207 723 0965
reception@hydeparkrooms.com www.hydeparkrooms.com

the Thai restaurant downstairs. Reserve 1-2 weeks ahead; 48hr. cancellation policy. Budget singles £35. Singles £55, with bath £65; doubles £70/£90; triples £85/£117.50. 10% discount for online booking. AmEx/MC/V. ❸

KNIGHTSBRIDGE & BELGRAVIA

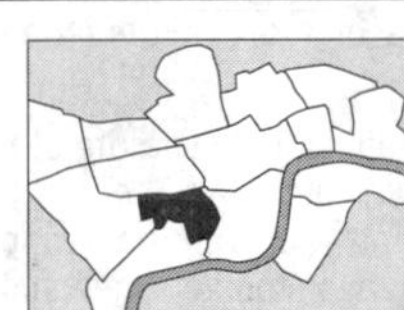

SEE MAP, p. 366

KNIGHTSBRIDGE & BELGRAVIA QUICKFIND: Discover, p. 4; sights, p. 102; food, p. 290; pubs, p. 198; nightlife, p. 290; shopping, p. 258.

Belgravia's B&Bs are concentrated on **Ebury St.,** a fairly busy road of Georgian terraces as close to Victoria and Sloane Sq. as it is to Belgravia proper. That's not a disadvantage—on the contrary, with Westminster's sights and Chelsea's shops within walking distance, you'd be hard pressed to do better. We've listed three of Ebury's best, but if none of these is available, chances are you'll find a vacancy in a comparable establishment somewhere on the road.

Westminster House Hotel, 96 Ebury St. (☎7730 7850 or 7730 4302; www.westminsterhousehotel.co.uk). ⊖Victoria. Extreme cleanliness, prime location, and a charming family staff make this a standout. The 10 mid-sized rooms have TV, tea trays, coffee and hot chocolate; almost all have private bath. English breakfast included. 48hr. cancellation policy. Reserve well ahead; some scattered availability last minute. Single £45, with bath £50; doubles £75/£85; triples with bath £95; quad with bath £110. AmEx/MC/V. ❸

Morgan House, 120 Ebury St. (☎7730 2384; www.morganhouse.co.uk). ⊖Victoria. Rooms are quite clean with TV, sink, kettle, and phone for incoming calls (pay phone downstairs). English breakfast included. Reserve 2-3 months ahead. 48hr. cancellation policy. Singles £46; doubles £66/£86; triples £86/£110; quad with bath £122. MC/V. ❸

James and Cartref House, 108 and 129 Ebury St. (☎7730 7338; www.jamesandcartref.co.uk). ⊖Victoria. Really two separate B&Bs on opposite sides of Ebury St. under the same family's ownership. Both have sparkling, mid-sized rooms and well-kept hallways. The James has a bright breakfast room overlooking the garden; the Cartref feels older but has more rooms with private bath and an ornate dining room with fireplace. All rooms come with TV, tea/coffee kettle, hair dryer, and fan and are non-smoking. English breakfast included. Reserve with 1-night deposit; 10% non-refundable, the rest refundable with 2 wk. notice. Singles £52, with bath £62; doubles £70/£85; triples £95/£110; family room (1 double and 2 bunks for under-12s) with bath £135. AmEx/MC/V. ❹

MARYLEBONE & REGENT'S PARK

MARYLEBONE & REGENT'S PARK: Discover, p. 9; sights, p. 103; museums & galleries, p. 141; food, p. 173; pubs, p. 199; entertainment, p. 237.

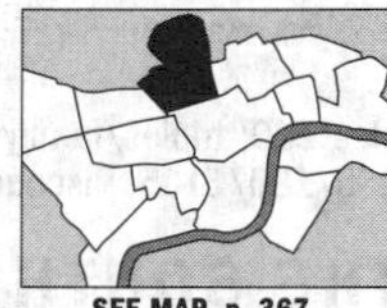

SEE MAP, p. 367

Marylebone's West End-fringe location means that it has plenty of accommodations. However, they're usually beyond the price range of the less-than-posh. There are a number of attractive B&Bs, but don't expect the bang-for-the-buck ratio you'd find in Bloomsbury or Bayswater. Here, you're paying to be in walking distance of Oxford St. The area's student accommodations are a good deal. Little happens after dark but you're never more than a short night-bus ride away from Soho.

HOSTELS

International Student House, 229 Great Portland St. (☎7631 8310; www.ish.org.uk). ⊖Great Portland St. More institutional than most institutions; it functions like a little city, with regulations and staff everywhere. Great location near Regent's Park and fantastic rates make it all worth it. Most rooms are of similar size—singles seem huge, bunk-bedded quads less so—and have desk, sink, phone, and fridge. Shared facilities. Dorms have sink but no lockers. Facilities include: 3 bars (M-W noon-2pm and 5-11pm, Th noon-2pm and 5pm-1am, F noon-2pm and 5pm-3am); nightclub/venue; cheap cafeteria; fitness center (£5 per day, £3 concessions); cinema (Su only); laundry; Internet access £2 per hr. 3 wk. maximum stay. Continental breakfast included except for dorms (£2); English breakfast £3. £10 key deposit. Reserve 3 months ahead during the summer; singles and doubles are mostly booked throughout the school year. Dorms £12. Singles £33.50; doubles £51; triples £61.50; quads £74. ISIC discounts for singles and doubles. Wheelchair accessible. MC/V. ❶

RESIDENCE HALLS

University of Westminster Halls, 35 Marylebone Rd. (☎7834 1172/1169; www.wmin.ac.uk/comserv/marylebone.htm). ⊖Baker St. Typical student singles: not much character but mid-sized and incredibly convenient. Laundry, kitchen, lounges and shared bathrooms. Linen included. Students only. Available early June to mid-Sept. Book 1wk. in advance, but occasional last-minute availability. Singles £24.50, under 26 £19.25. MC/V.

HOTELS AND BED & BREAKFASTS

Edward Lear Hotel, 28-30 Seymour St. (☎7402 5401; www.edlear.com). ⊖Marble Arch. This was once the home of Ed Lear. A flowery front, friendly service, and a free email lounge. although rooms can vary. Clean mid-sized rooms but showers are tiny boxes. Singles £47.50, with shower only £60; doubles £66.50/£74, with shower and WC £89; triples £79/£89/£99; family quad with shower £99, with full bath £105. 15% discount on stays of 5 nights; ask about shorter-term discounts as well. AmEx/MC/V. ❸

Lincoln House Hotel, 33 Gloucester Pl. Marble Arch (☎7486 7630; www.lincoln-house-hotel.co.uk) ⊖Marble Arch. Located 5 min. walk up from Oxford St. and Marble Arch, Lincoln House is within easy reach of the tube, buses, and Hyde Park. Naval-themed decor hangs on the walls; the rooms are clean and no-frills. All have phone, TV, kettle, fridge and private toilet and shower. Full English breakfast included. Singles £59-79; doubles £69-95; twins £95-105; triples £105-115; family (4) £115-125. Discounts on stays of over 7 nights. Some wheelchair-accessible rooms. AmEx/MC/V. ❹

NOTTING HILL

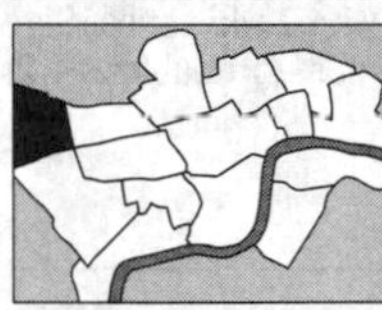

SEE MAP, p. 359

NOTTING HILL QUICKFIND: Discover, p. 9; sights, p. 105; food, p. 174; pubs, p. 200; nightlife, p. 212; entertainment, p. 237; shopping, p. 259.

The Gate Hotel, 6 Portobello Rd. (☎7221 0707; www.gatehotel.com) On the corner of Portobello Rd. Clean, relatively spacious, and a very good deal for the area. Rooms are ensuite with TV/DVD, desk, and phone. The sunny location and friendly staff make staying here a pleasure. A great base for Notting Hill and West End exploits. Continental breakfast included. 1 week cancellation required. Doubles £80; triples/family £95. Sa-Su £75/£90/£110. Nov-Apr. M-F £55/£75/£90, Sa-Su £65/£80/£105. Discounts on stays 2 nights or longer. AmEx/MC/V (3% surcharge). ❸

THE SOUTH BANK

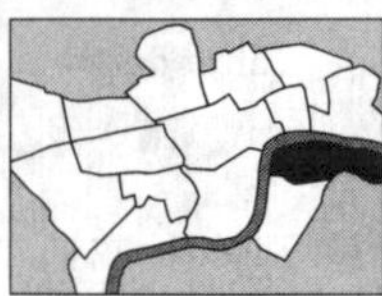

SEE MAP, pp. 368-369

THE SOUTH BANK QUICKFIND: Discover, p. 10; sights, p. 106; museums & galleries, p. 148; food, p. 176; pubs, p. 200; nightlife, p. 212; entertainment, p. 238.

Though the South Bank has some of the best views in the city, its cheaper hotels don't—cost is directly proportional to the river's proximity. Still, where else in London could you roll out of bed and be breakfasting by the Thames in five minutes? What it lacks in bar-hopping nightlife it makes up for in accessibility; all the lively central neighborhoods are a stone's throw away: the City, West End, and Westminster all just across the bridge,.

Travel Inn County Hall, Belvedere Rd. (☎0870 238 3300; www.travelinn.co.uk). ⊖Westminster or Waterloo. Expect no grand views (the river front is hogged by a Marriott). Seconds from the South Bank and Westminster though, and this hotel has all the class without the cost. All rooms are clean, fairly spacious, and modern with full bath and color TV. Facilities include elevator, restaurant, and bar. Prices by the room make it a great family deal. Reserve 1 month ahead; cancel by 4pm on day of arrival. English Breakfast £7, Singles/doubles and family rooms, M-Th £85, F-Su £80. AmEx/MC/V. ❹

LSE Bankside House, 24 Sumner St. (☎7107 5750; www.lse.ac.uk/vacations). ⊖Southwark or London Bridge. The largest of London School of Economics' student halls, this one is facing the back of the Tate Modern. The 3 wings sleep over 800 and offer more privacy than the average dorm. Facilities include elevator, laundry, TV lounge, games room, restaurant, and bar. Open from the first week of July to the last week in Sept. English breakfast can be included in the rate for a daily charge of £3. Singles (shared bath between 2 rooms) £30, with bath £42; doubles with bath £60; triples with bath £78; quads with bath £93. MC/V. ❷

THE WEST END

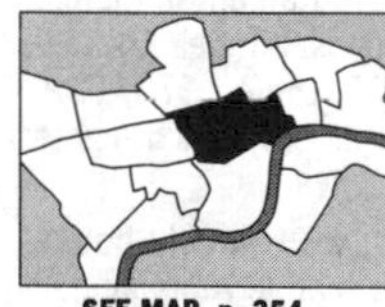

SEE MAP, p. 354

THE WEST END QUICKFIND: Discover, p. 10; sights, p. 111; museums & galleries, p. 150; food, p. 177; pubs, p. 201; nightlife, p. 212; entertainment, p. 240; shopping, p. 261.

Unless you have tons of money, accommodations in the West End are scarce and unless you book months in advance, you won't find a bed here. You may get lucky on short term notice, but don't count on it. If you want to be close to the Soho action, don't forget that many Bloomsbury accommodations are a walk away and probably cheaper.

YHA Oxford Street, 14 Noel St. (☎0870 770 5984; www.yhalondon.org.uk). ⊖Oxford Circus. Small, clean, sunny rooms with limited facilities but an unbeatable location for Soho nightlife. The double rooms have bunkbeds, sink, mirror, and wardrobe. Triple-decker bunk beds may feel cramped. Spacious and comfy TV lounge; toilets and showers are off the hallways. Internet terminal, and well-equipped kitchen available. Linen included. Towels £3.50. Prepacked continental breakfast £3.60. Reserve at least 1 month ahead. 3- to 4-bed dorms £22.60 per person, under-18s £18.20; 2-bed dorms £24.60 per person. ❶

Seven Dials Hotel, 7 Monmouth St. (☎7240 0823, reservations 7681 0791, fax 7681 0792). ⊖Covent Garden. The fantastic location of this tiny B&B compensates for the smaller-than-average rooms; it's in the heart of Covent Gardens and close to Soho, Piccadilly and Theatreland. Each room is different: the front rooms are brighter, with triple glazing to keep out the noise, and have better views. Size varies considerably and some doubles are rented as singles too. Asking to see available rooms is a good idea. All have TV, phone, kettle, and sink; most have ceiling fan. Full English breakfast included. Reserve a few months ahead; 72hr. cancellation policy. Singles £65, with shower £75, with bath £85; doubles £75/£85/£95; twin with bath £100; triple with bath £115. AmEx/MC/V. ❹

High Holborn Residence, 178 High Holborn (☎7379 5589; www.lse.ac.uk/collections/vacations). ⊖Holborn or Tottenham Crt. Rd. Social and well-situated university dorm-that converts into a hostel during the end of summer. Perfect location for Covent Garden and other West End exploits. Rooms are organized into clusters of 4-5 singles (some twins), each with phone and shared kitchen and bath. Rooms with private bath are much larger. Bar, elevator, laundry, TV room, and game room. Continental breakfast included. Open Aug.-Sept. 2005, depending on when summer school ends. Singles £30; twins £48, with bath £58; triples with bath £68. Some wheelchair-accessible rooms. MC/V. ❷

WESTMINSTER

WESTMINSTER QUICKFIND: Discover, p. 11; sights, p. 116; museums & galleries, p. 152; food, p. 181; pubs, p. 202; entertainment, p. 244.

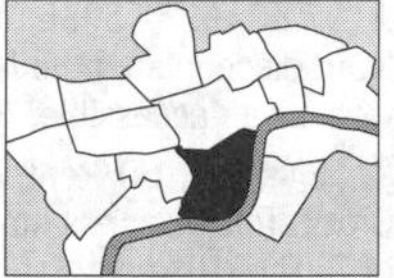

SEE MAP, p. 370

Pimlico, south of Victoria station, is a grid-like district of late Georgian and early Victorian terraces that are home to dozens of B&Bs—among them some of London's best. The cream colored buildings line block after block, many are generic hotels but tucked between them are some charming and affordable B&Bs. Very few have elevators, so if stairs are a problem, be sure to request a ground-floor room. While ultra-residential Pimlico itself has little to offer the visitor, Westminster Abbey, Parliament, the Tate Britain, and Buckingham Palace are close by, and Victoria's fantastic transportation links puts the rest of London within easy reach.

Melbourne House, 79 Belgrave Rd. (☎7828 3516; www.melbournehousehotel.co.uk). ⊖Pimlico. The pick of the area: recently refurbished establishment with a superbly friendly staff. The rooms vary in terms of size and shape. Super clean, non-smoking rooms all with TV, phone, coffee-maker, hair dryer, and kettle; the pride and joy is the luxurious basement double, with triangular bathtub large enough for two. 24 hour reception. Continental breakfast included. Reserve 2 weeks ahead; 48hr. cancellation policy. Singles £38, with bath £60; doubles with bath £85; triples with bath £100; quad with bath £120. Substantial discounts for week-long stays or for large groups. MC/V (payment on arrival; cash preferred). ❸

Alexander Hotel, 13 Belgrave Rd. (☎7834 9738; www.alexanderhotel.co.uk). ⊖Victoria. Good sized rooms, eclectically furnished with quality fittings, solid oak dressers, comfy beds, and satellite TV. Some singles are very small. A friendly plastic suit of armor keeps order in the sunny and pleasant breakfast room, where breakfast is served 7:30-9am (included). Prices vary according to demand. Singles £48; doubles £65; triples from £75; quads and quints £110. MC/V. ❸

Luna Simone Hotel, 47/49 Belgrave Rd. (☎7834 5897; www.lunasimonehotel.com). ⊖Victoria or Pimlico. Stuccoed Victorian facade conceals pleasant yellow rooms with desk, big closets, TV, phone, kettle, safety deposit box, and hair dryer. Meticulously clean bathrooms. On the downside, some singles are cramped. Twins and doubles, however, are bigger than average. English breakfast included. Reserve 2 weeks ahead; 48hr. cancellation policy. Singles £40, with bath £55; doubles £75; triples £100. 10% discount for stays over 7 nights in low season. AmEx/MC/V. ❸

Georgian House Hotel, 35 St. George's Dr. (☎7834 1438; www.georgianhousehotel.co.uk). ⊖Victoria. Well-equipped rooms, with TV, phone, hair dryer, kettle, and matching furniture. Top-floor "student" rooms, available to all, are smaller with fewer amenities. Very popular, rooms fill in the summer and in surrounding months. Lounge-room portraits commemorate the family in charge since 1851. Professional staff and elegant decor make this B&B seem like a fancy hotel. English breakfast included. Internet access. Reserve 1 month ahead for Sa-Su and student rooms. Singles £50; doubles £72; triples £90; quads £100. MC/V. ❸

NORTH LONDON

NORTH LONDON QUICKFIND: Discover, p. 12; sights, p. 120; museums & galleries, p. 153; food, p. 183; pubs, p. 203; nightlife, p. 218; entertainment, p. 244; shopping, p. 269.

YHA Hampstead Heath, 4 Wellgarth Rd. (☎0870 770 5846; hampstead@yha.org.uk). ⊖Golders Green (Zone 3). This gorgeous manorial hostel is surrounded by lovely shaded gardens. Rooms are fresh and relatively spacious. It feels a bit far from the center, but transport links are easy. Great for those traveling in large groups or with children. Common rooms (both smoking and non-smoking), lockers, laundry, currency exchange, kitchen, and snack bar. Linen and breakfast included. 24hr. reception. Internet access. 4- to 8-bed dorms £21, under 18 £18.50; doubles £48.50, ensuite £52.50; triples £69/£73; quads £87/£91; quints £107.50/£111.50; 6-beds £129; 7-beds £150.50. Families with 1 child under 18 get significant discounts on the larger rooms, single parent families also get discounted stays. Partially wheelchair accessible. AmEx/MC/V. ❷

Jurys Inn, 60 Pentonville Rd. (☎7282 5500; www.jurysdoyle.com). ⊖Angel or Kings Cross. This business hotel offers true 3-star luxury for B&B prices—at least if you're in a group of 3. The decked-out lobby gives way to an Inn pub and elegant restaurant. Private bath, TV, kettle, A/C, and hair dryer are standard. Non-smoking except for 5th fl. Room rates can be augmented to include breakfast. 3 adults or 2 adults and 2 children, £99 per night; when you book online rooms are much cheaper. AmEx/MC/V. ❷

Kandara Guesthouse, 68 Ockendon Rd. (☎7226 5721; www.kandara.co.uk). From ⊖Angel take bus #38, 56, 73, 341; be alert, it's a small stop. Far from the Tube—but with so many buses to the West End, and even more options if you take the bus down to Angel, it's a blessing in disguise. Classically decorated family-run B&B. Sparkling clean rooms and a friendly, bustling atmosphere with plenty of privacy. 5 baths between 11 rooms. Breakfast included. Hairdryer and iron on request. Reserve well ahead; call for family quad. One week cancellation notice. Singles £41-49; doubles/twins £51-62; triples £64-72. MC/V. ❸

St. Christopher's Inn, 48-50 Camden High St. (☎7407 1856; www.st-christophers.co.uk). ⊖Mornington Crescent. The reception in Belushi's Bar downstairs serves as a fitting entrance to this party-friendly, backpacker hostel. Nicknamed the "hostel with attitude" they get you started right with 10% off all food and drinks at the bar. While the street it's on is a little dreary, its location is perfect for hitting the Camden Town bars and Clerkenwell clubs. Even with the commotion, the rooms are surprisingly fresh, cheerful, and spacious. Most have private bath; if not, showers are close by. Luggage room, safe deposit boxes, lockers, laundry, and common rooms. Linen and continental breakfast included. 24hr. reception. Internet access. 10-bed dorms £15; 8-bed £16; 6-bed £17, doubles £23. Discount with online booking. ❶

Hampstead Village Guest House, 2 Kemplay Rd. (☎7435 8679; www.hampsteadguesthouse.com). ⊖Hampstead. Hidden on a little sidestreet off the main road, the house has 8 good-sized rooms in a well-maintained Victorian house with a touch of old-fashioned elegance. All rooms have TV, fridge, phone, iron, and kettle. The studio apartment, in a converted garage, sleeps 5 and has a small kitchen. It can be a little dark but the garden is bright. English breakfast £7. Reservations essential. Singles £48-54, with bath £66; doubles £72/£84; studio £90 for 1 person, £120 for 2, £138 for 3, £150 for 4, £162 for 5. ❹

Camden Lock Hotel, 89 Chalk Farm Rd. (☎7267 3912; www.camdenlockhotel.co.uk) ⊖Chalk Farm. The decor is dowdy and faded, but the prices are good and all rooms have very clean ensuite bathrooms; twins and doubles are the most spacious. Phone, tea and coffee in room, safe deposit box, and TV in lobby. 24hr. reception. Not luxury by any standards but good value and privacy in a brilliant location 2min. from the Tube and a few steps from the Chalk Farm and Camden action, as well as Regent's Park. Breakfast included. Singles from £47, doubles and twins from £64, triples £74. Quads upon request. Reserve a few weeks in advance. AmEx/MC/V. ❸

WEST LONDON

WEST LONDON QUICKFIND: Discover, p. 14; sights, p. 130; food, p. 188; entertainment, p. 248; shopping, p. 273.

Reasonably central and relatively cheap, with good transport links, **Shepherd's Bush** is popular with budget travelers (especially Australians), but they have to compete with builders and other workers who also favor the B&Bs on **Shepherd's Bush Road.**

Star Hotel, 97-99 Shepherd's Bush Rd. (☎7603 2755; www.star-hotel.net). ⊖Hammersmith. Rooms are relatively spacious; all have TV, kettle, hair dryer, and large bath, as well as wood furniture and new carpeting. A family-run B&B. English breakfast included, served in a sky-lit dining area. Book 1-2 months ahead July-Aug. and Easter. 48hr. cancellation policy. Singles £42; doubles £62; triples £75; quads £95. Stays over 2 nights receive a substantial discount. MC/V (3% surcharge). ❸

Family-run since 1970

Convenient to Buckingham Palace, Westminister Abbey, The London Eye, theaters, parks & night clubs

Rooms as low as £35 / night

Cosy & Family-like atmosphere

47/49 Belgrave Road
London SW1V 2BB

+44 20 7834 5897 *(call between 7:00-23:00 hrs)*
FAX: +44 20 7828 2474

www.lunasimonehotel.com

Hotel Orlando, 83 Shepherd's Bush Rd. (☎/fax 7603 4890; www.hotelorlando.co.uk). ⊖Goldhawk Rd. Clean, pleasant rooms are decently-sized, with modern baths. Small beds. Helpful and considerate staff. Rooms have TV, phone, and bath. Most have a mini-fridge. English breakfast included. 5-day cancellation policy. Singles £40; doubles £52; triples £70; family (1 double and 2 single beds) £88. AmEx/MC/V. ❸

Dalmacia Hotel, 71 Shepherd's Bush Rd. (☎7603 2887; www.dalmacia.co.uk). ⊖Goldhawk Rd. The aspiring-rock-star accommodation of choice (Nirvana stayed here before they became famous), the Dalmacia provides each room with kettle, TV, phone, and hair dryer. English breakfast included. Singles £49; doubles £69; triples £81. 30% discount if staying 2 or more nights. MC/V. ❸

Windsor Guest House, 43 Shepherd's Bush Rd. (☎/fax 7603 2116; neven@windsorghs.freeserve.co.uk). ⊖Goldhawk Rd. Small, unpretentious family-run B&B catering to a mixture of tourists and workmen. Basic rooms are small, but are well-kept and have TVa; baths are reasonably clean, and modern. Small beds. English breakfast included. Reserve 1-2 months ahead in summer. Singles £30; doubles £50; triples £67.50. ❷

FINDING SOMEWHERE TO LIVE

There's a good reason that every year a long-ignored, distant suburb is "outed" as the Next Big Thing in London living. Inexorably rising property prices are pushing the urban hip further and further from the center of town. It's the same old story: struggling artists move to a long-depressed borough, then a few years later it's "discovered" by the style magazines and the next thing you know it's all bankers, Starbucks, and BMWs. The people who made it hip, meanwhile, have long since been forced to move to a more distant zone. This year's hapless neighborhood is Camden; next on the list looks to be Hoxton. Luckily, London is large enough that there are still enough terminally uncool neighborhoods where you might actually be able to afford to live; if you're lucky, you might pick just at the start of the upswing.

COST

Take a deep breath. If you want to live alone, you'll probably end up in a **bedsit,** a single room in a converted townhouse, typically miniscule, and usually with a shared kitchen and bath. For this privilege, you won't get away paying less than £60 per week in the most distant, depressed suburb; count on at least £100 for anywhere within striking distance of the center. **Flat shares** are not very different from bedsits, and cost £60-80 per week in the suburbs and £110-200 in a fashionable area. **Short-term** housing is pricier and harder to find; it's almost impossible to rent for under a month. When deciding how much you can afford, don't forget to figure in **transport costs.** If you work in the center, living in the suburbs could add £30-50 to your monthly Travelcard cost; if you work outside Zone 1, you'll save if you don't have to go through Zone 1 to get there.

COUNCIL TAX

Local taxes are another factor that shouldn't be ignored when choosing a place to live. In England, council tax is levied on each "dwelling," with the amount owed being set by the local council and dependent on the market price of the dwelling. A dwelling is defined as any self-contained living unit—so a house converted into independent flat counts as numerous dwellings, but a house converted into bedsits that share kitchen and bathroom facilities counts as only one dwelling. Who is liable to pay the tax is a complicated matter; in rented flats it's generally the tenant, though if the landlord lives on the premises, he or she is normally liable. In any case, who is responsible for paying the tax should be clearly worked out before moving into any flat. If everyone in the dwelling is a full-time student, or earns less than a certain amount, it may be exempt from council tax; however this is not an automatic exemption and must be applied for. If your dwelling is liable for council tax, expect to pay around £600 per year for a small flat.

TENANTS' RIGHTS

All tenants have certain rights. For example, the landlord is responsible for keeping the accommodation in habitable condition and paying for necessary repairs; it's also illegal for landlords to threaten or harass tenants. Asserting your rights is another matter. Few tenants can afford a court dispute with a landlord, and some may even face eviction. It's best to get advice from your local CAB before demanding action. Note that terms set out in the **tenancy agreement** (lease) cannot override rights laid out by law. Oral agreements have the force of law, but are hard to enforce; it's best to get a signed document. For free advice on housing rights, or if you have a dispute with your landlord, go to your local **Citizens' Advice Bureau (CAB),** or check www.citizensadvice.org.uk.

RESOURCES

Do-it-yourselfers willing to put in some time and footwork should rush to the newsagent the morning that London's **small-ads papers** are published, and immediately begin calling. **Loot** is published daily, as is the **Evening Standard** (which, despite its name, can be bought in the morning). Both have the best listings for short rentals (1-2 month). Other sources of vacancies are **Time Out** (published Tu) and **NME** (Th). Bulletin boards in **newsagents** frequently list available rooms, as do the classified sections of major and local newspapers. Beware of ads placed by **letting agencies;** they may try to sell you something more expensive when you call. Though they save a lot of legwork, agencies generally charge one to two weeks' rent as a fee, and it's in their interest to find high-priced accommodations. There are few laws regulating letting agencies, and tales of unscrupulous practices are common. Be sure to deal only with agencies that are members of the **National Approved Letting Scheme (NALS),** which must adhere to a strict set of standards. Always thoroughly read the contract before signing anything—you might find yourself responsible for repairs that are normally the landlord's responsibility. Note that agencies may legally charge you only once you rent a room through them. Don't pay just to register, or to get a list of rooms available. Many London boroughs run **information offices,** which often have listings of reliable local agencies. Helpful websites to begin your search are: www.intolondon.com, www.fish4uk.co.uk, www.easyroommate.com, www.interlet.com. For a listing of accommodations agencies in London, see the **Service Directory,** p. 335.

INSIDE

Daytripping

For all the capital's many and varied charms, even the most die-hard London-lover needs to get out of the city occasionally. With Britain's comprehensive transportation network capable of spiriting you anywhere in the country in under a day, there's no excuse for staying cooped up in London when the historic and bucolic charms of England await. But first, a word of explanation about the organization of this chapter. **Short Daytrips Near London** covers sights and towns that are close (and small) enough to be easily covered in a day; you can leave after breakfast and return in time for dinner without breaking a sweat. If you're pressed for time, **Overnight Trips** could be done as long full-day trips, but their distance and/or size make it worth staying over.

SHORT DAYTRIPS FROM LONDON

HAMPTON COURT

Travel time from central London: *30min. from Waterloo by train, 24 min. from Clapham Junction; 4hr. by boat (Apr.-Sept., Westminster Passenger Cruises ☎7930 2062).* ***Contact:*** *☎087 0752 7777; www.hrp.org.uk.* ***Open:*** *late Mar. to late Oct. M 10:15am-6pm, Tu-Su 9:30am-6pm; late Oct.-late Mar. closes 4:30pm; last admission 45min. before closing. Gardens open until dusk or 9pm.* ***Admission:*** *Palace and gar-*

dens £11.80, concessions £8.70, children £7.70, family of 5 £35; Maze or South Gardens only £3.50, children £2.50; gardens (excl. South Gardens) free. Free admission for worshippers at Chapel Royal services, held Su 11am and 3:30pm. Audio tours and guided tours are included in the ticket.

HAMPTON COURT PALACE

Although a monarch hasn't lived here for 250 years, Hampton Court still feels royal. The sprawling palace and carefully manicured gardens appeal to everyone from nature lovers to history buffs from art fans to horticulturalists. The palace is unique because it showcases the tastes and styles of many of its royal inhabitants at once. Cardinal Thomas Wolsey built the first structure here in 1514, showing young Henry VIII how to act the part of a splendid and powerful ruler—a lesson Henry learned quite well; confiscating the palace in 1528 and embarking on a massive building program. His rooms remain the most grandiose in the palace. In 1689, William III and Mary II employed Christopher Wren to bring Hampton Court up to date, utilizing a more subdued Baroque style. They originally planned on tearing down Henry's castle, but decided instead to embellish it.

The palace itself stands around three central courtyards. Visitors walk up the long green driveway and enter through the **Base Court,** which survives from Wolsey's original Tudor-style building; Henry VIII's own lavish apartments are off this courtyard. Many of Henry's private rooms were damaged by fire or demolished in later renovations, but the glorious Great Hall survives. Below the royal apartments are the countless rooms of the **Tudor Kitchens.** Greens, fish, spices, and wild boar carcasses lie strewn about, adding to the impression that the kitchens were in the midst of preparing a Midsummer's Day feast.

A walk through the Boleyn gate leads to the **Clock Court**—so named because of the colorful astronomical clock that adorns the tower. It was built in 1540 for Henry. Half of the Tudor yard has been overtaken by Wren's colonnades; it's here that you can see the overlap of architectural styles. The courtyard leads to the apartments of King William III and the Wolsey Rooms. The latter have been renovated to look as they did in Wolsey's time. They also hold the impressive Renaissance picture gallery, which includes a self-portrait by Raphael, among other treasures.

The last courtyard, the **Fountain Court,** is the only Baroque courtyard completed by William and Mary. Unlike the other two, it features grass and a simple fountain. Just off this courtyard are the dark and sumptuous **Queen's Apartments** and the **Georgian Rooms,** which were used by George II and Queen Caroline the last time they stayed at the Palace in 1737. These rooms also house the palace's most extensive collection of paintings and silver. Guides in full historical costume can be seen wandering around the halls of the courtyard.

HAMPTON COURT GARDENS

In the sunshine (or the light-drizzle time) the palace has to compete with the equally lavish gardens. Palace tickets are required for entry to the flower-rich **South Gardens,** the first of which is the ornate Privy Garden, built for the private enjoyment of William III and now available for public enjoyment. The stunning **Pond Gardens** are off- limits to visitors, but you can stand at the rail and stare longingly at the posies. Nearby, the giant Great Vine is housed in its own terrace; it is the world's oldest vine, planted by Lancelot "Capability" Brown sometime between 1768 and 1774. It still produces 500-700 pounds of grapes every year, which are sold in the shop in late summer and early fall. Secreted away in the neighboring Lower Orangery is Andrea Mantegna's series *The Triumphs of Caesar* (1484-1505). Among the most important works of the Italian Renaissance, the nine paintings are displayed in almost total darkness to protect the fragile colors. The rest of the gardens are open to all. The Home Park stretches beyond the impeccably manicured trees, paths, and fountains of the **East Front Gardens.** North of the palace, the **Wilderness,** a pseudo-natural area earmarked for picnickers, holds the ever-popular Maze, planted in 1690. It's been known to boggle even the most astute of wanderers. Another popular area here is the **Tiltyard Tearoom,**

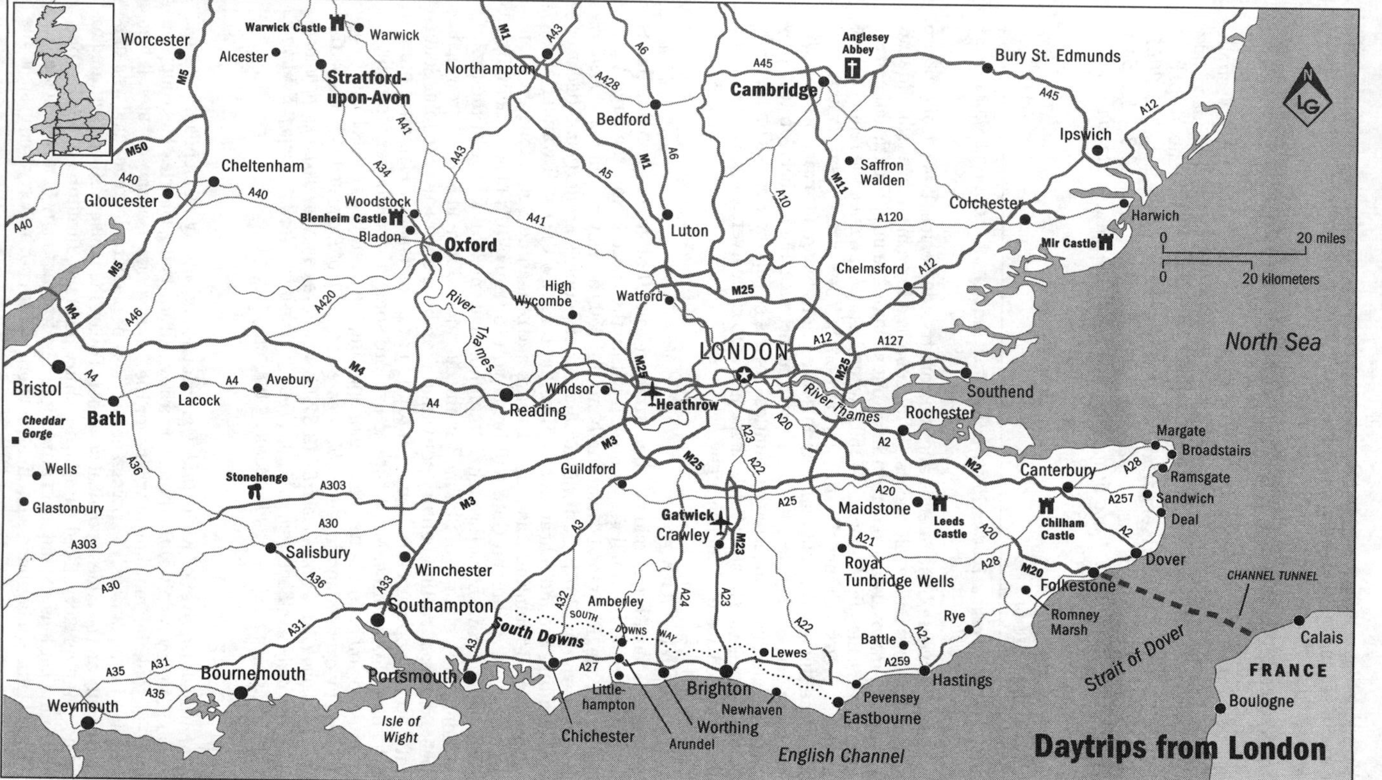
Daytrips from London
North Sea
English Channel
Strait of Dover
CHANNEL TUNNEL
FRANCE
Calais
Boulogne
LONDON
Heathrow
Gatwick
Crawley
Worcester
Warwick Castle
Warwick
Alcester
Stratford-upon-Avon
Northampton
Bedford
Cambridge
Anglesey Abbey
Bury St. Edmunds
Ipswich
Harwich
Mir Castle
Colchester
Saffron Walden
Chelmsford
Luton
Watford
Cheltenham
Gloucester
Woodstock
Blenheim Castle
Bladon
Oxford
High Wycombe
River Thames
Windsor
Reading
Bristol
Bath
Lacock
Avebury
Cheddar Gorge
Wells
Glastonbury
Stonehenge
Salisbury
Winchester
Southampton
Guildford
South Downs
SOUTH DOWNS WAY
Amberley
Portsmouth
Isle of Wight
Bournemouth
Weymouth
Chichester
Little-hampton
Arundel
Worthing
Brighton
Newhaven
Lewes
Eastbourne
Pevensey
Battle
Hastings
Rye
Romney Marsh
Royal Tunbridge Wells
Maidstone
Leeds Castle
Chilham Castle
Rochester
Southend
Canterbury
Margate
Broadstairs
Ramsgate
Sandwich
Deal
Dover
Folkestone
0 20 miles
0 20 kilometers
M1
M2
M3
M4
M5
M11
M20
M23
M25
M50
A2
A3
A4
A5
A6
A10
A12
A20
A21
A22
A23
A24
A25
A27
A28
A30
A31
A32
A33
A34
A35
A36
A40
A41
A43
A45
A46
A120
A127
A257
A259
A303
A420
A428

where jousting matches used to take place—it's really a sandwich cafeteria with beautiful seating by the gardens; it serves tea in the afternoon of course. The palace also hosts the annual Hampton Court Palace Flower Show every August.

TRANSPORTATION. The fastest way is to take the **train** to Hampton Court from Waterloo; the palace is a 5min. walk. *(30min., every 30min. Day return £4.90; big reductions with Travelcard.)* More relaxing, scenic, and slower, **boats** from Westminster run April through October. It's a 4hr. trip; to leave time to see the Palace, take it one-way and return by train, or board at Kew (p. 128) or Richmond (p. 302) instead. *(Westminster Passenger Association, Westminster Pier. ☎7930 2062; www.wpsa.co.uk. ⊖Westminster. Departures mid-Apr. to Sept. daily 10:30, 11:15am, noon, and 2pm returning 3, 4, and 5pm. Tides may affect schedules; call to confirm. £12, return £18; ages 5-15 £6/£9; 33% discount with Travelcard.)*

RICHMOND

Travel time from central London: *25min. by tube from Earl's Court; 2hr. by boat. Most sites are wheelchair accessible.*

Richmond is where London ends and the countryside begins. It is a leafy suburb along the Thames that, while accessible by Tube, is a town in its own right. Edward III built the first royal palace here in 1358, but a major fire in 1497 burned the place down. It was called the Sheen, until 1501, when Henry VII named the rebuilt palace (later destroyed by Cromwell) after his earldom in Yorkshire. Only the gateway of that palace still remains, but many durable attractions linger: **Richmond Bridge** is the oldest spanning the Thames, and the view from **Richmond Hill** has been protected by an act of Parliament since 1902. Countless artists set up their easels on the 17th-century terrace. Neighboring **Twickenham,** just across the river, is the well-loved and oft-pummelled home of English rugby.

RICHMOND PARK

Perhaps the most breathtakingly beautiful area in all of greater London, this is the closest to nature you'll get while still within the capital. Now the largest city park in Europe, Richmond's lush and beautiful 2500 acres were first enclosed by Charles I, who in 1637 built a wall around other people's property and declared it his hunting ground. Large herds of red and fallow **deer** still wander about (unthreatened—hunting was banned years ago). Heading right along the main footpath from Richmond Gate will bring you to **Henry VIII's Mound,** actually a bronze-age barrow. Look through a small hole cut into the foliage at the top of the mound for a glimpse of St. Paul's in the distance. Bertrand Russell grew up in **Pembroke Lodge,** an 18th-century conversion job by the versatile Sir John Soane that's now a popular cafe. Deeper into the park, the **Isabella Plantation** bursts with color in the spring. Make sure to explore some of the smaller footpaths—not only do you have a better chance of spotting the deer, you're less likely to be run over by cyclists and joggers. *(Main gate at the top of Richmond Hill. Bus # 371 from Richmond (75p. Park office ☎8948 3209; www.royalparks.gov.uk/parks/richmond-park. Open daily Mar.-Sept. 7am-dusk; Oct.-Feb. 7:30am-dusk.* ***Health warning:*** *Tick-borne Lyme disease is a risk in the park; wear long trousers.)*

HAM HOUSE

Some way down river of Richmond, Ham House sits among resplendent gardens. William Murray received the house as a reward for being Charles I's "whipping boy"—he took the punishment whenever the future king misbehaved. Later, it was occupied by the famously extravagant Duchess of Lauderdale, renowned as a dazzling beauty and a ruthless political schemer. Today, the house has been returned to the height of its glory, filled with 17th-century portraits, furniture, and tapestries, though the gardens are the main attraction. The formal **Cherry Garden** is actually a diamond lattice of lavender, santolina, and hedges with not a cherry tree in sight. **The**

Wilderness is even less aptly named, an orderly array of trimmed hedges surrounding nooks of roses and wildflowers, with newly-restored 17th-century statuary standing guard. And for those who love the practical gone extravagant, the **Kitchen Garden** offers endless rows of fresh fruit and vegetables. *(At the bottom of Sandy Ln., Ham. Bus #65 (then a 15min. walk) or #371 (then a 10min. walk) from Richmond station, or a beautiful 30min. walk along the Thames. A ferry crosses the river from Marble Hill, Twickenham, Sa-Su 10am-6:30pm or dusk; Feb.-Oct. also M-F 10am-6pm; 70p, children 35p. ☎8940 1950; www.nationaltrust.org.uk/hamhouse. House open Apr.-Oct. M-W and Sa-Su 1-5pm, gardens year-round M-W and Sa-Su 11am-6pm or dusk. House and gardens £7, children £3.50, family £17.50; gardens only £3/£1.50/£7.50. MC/V.)*

Ashmolean Museum

RICHMOND THEATRE

A popular and well-lauded regional theater, Richmond Theatre is a pre-West End tryout ground for a number of popular shows. From straight drama to musical theater, see West End quality for about half the price. *(On Richmond Green, just above George St. ☎8939 9277; www.richmondtheatre.net. Performances M-Sa 7:45pm; W and Sa 2:30pm. £8-26, concessions £2 off M-Th perfs and mats. From 1hr. before curtain, students get best available seats for £8. Box office open M-Sa 10am-8pm.)*

Sheldonian Theatre

OTHER SIGHTS

Quite the hidden treasure, the **Museum of Richmond** has a small but fascinating array of exhibits on the history of Richmond, from the days of Queen Elizabeth to its Blitz legacy. *(Whittaker Ave. ☎8332 1141; www.museumofrichmond.com. Open Tu-Sa 11am-5pm; May-Sept. also Su 1-4pm. Free.)* Across the river from Ham House, **Marble Hill** was built in 1724 by Henrietta Howard, using an allowance from her former lover, George II. *(Marble Hill Park, Richmond Rd. Bus #33, H22, R68, R70, or 490 from Richmond; alternatively, a ferry crosses from Ham House, Richmond (see above), or 15min. walk from the town center– turn right onto Richmond Br. from Hill St., then left onto Richmond Rd. ☎8892 5115; www.english-heritage.org. House open Apr.-Oct. W-F 10am-6pm, Sa 10am-5pm, Su 10am-2pm. Grounds open daily 7am-dusk. £3.70, concessions £2.80, kids £1.90.)* The **Museum of Rugby and Twickenham Stadium Tours** offers a twofer: see the 75,000-seat epicenter of English rugby and then learn about the history of the game. Until Nov. 2005, the **Rugby World Cup** will be on display here. *(Rugby Rd. Follow Richmond Rd. unitl it becomes York St., then take bus #281 up London Rd. ☎8892 8877; www.rfu.com/microsites/*

Pembroke College

museum. Open Tu-Sa 10am-5pm, Su 11am-5pm (last tour 4:30pm). £8, concessions £5, family £25. MC/V.) Only James Gibbs's richly decorated Octagon Room survives of 18th-century **Orleans House.** Louis Philippe, Duc d'Orleans, rode out the French Revolution here before becoming king in 1830. *(Riverside, Twickenham. Transportation as for Marble Hill. ☎8831 6000; www.richmond.gov.uk/orleanshouse. House open Apr.-Sept. Tu-Sa 1-5:30pm, Su 2-5:30pm; Oct.-Mar. closes 4:30pm. Grounds open daily 9am-dusk. Free.)*

TRANSPORTATION. Richmond is at the end of the District line; the quickest route there is by **Tube** or **Silverlink train** *(Zone 4)*. For a more leisurely, scenic journey, **boats** make the 2hr. cruise upriver from Westminster. Travelcard holders receive a 33% discount on most riverboat fares—be sure to ask. *(Westminster Passenger Association, Westminster Pier. ☎020 7930 2062; www.wpsa.co.uk. ⊖Westminster. Departures mid-Apr.-Sept. daily 10 and 10:30am; returning 4, and 6pm. Tides may affect schedules;* ***call to confirm.*** *£10.50, return £16.50; concessions £7/£11; ages 4-15 £5.25/£8.25. MC/V.)*

ORIENTATION AND PRACTICAL INFORMATION. From **Richmond** station, turn left onto The Quadrant, which becomes George St. and then Hill St. Turning right from Hill St. onto Bridge Rd. takes you across Richmond Bridge into **Twickenham,** while bearing left onto Hill Rise leads to Richmond Hill and Richmond Park. Running from Hill St. to the river, Whittaker Ave. is home to the **Tourist Information Centre,** where you can pick up your best friend—a **free map** of the town and the surrounding sites. Brochures abound, and **free Internet** as well. *(Old Town Hall, Whittaker Ave. ☎020 8940 9125; www.visitrichmond.co.uk. Open May-Sept. M-Sa 10am-5pm, Su 10:30am-1:30pm; Oct.-Apr. M-Sa 10am-5pm. Audiotours of the area £4, concessions £2.50.)*

FOOD. The **Quadrant** and **George St.** are mini London high streets, complete with all the chain restaurants and fast-food joints you could ever want. For more atmospheric dining, try any one of the tiny side streets surrounding **Richmond Green.** The charming, leafy corner of **Golden Court** (off George St.) and the Green offers a number of quiet pubs and cafes. **The Prince's Head** is the best of them, with a classic neighborhood pub feel and outdoor seating on the Green. Sandwiches £4, snacks from £4, mains £6.25-9. *(28 The Green. ☎8940 1572. Open M-Sa 11am-11pm, Su noon-10:30pm; food M-Sa noon-9pm. MC/V. ❷)* For a picnic, there' s no question: head to Richmond Park.

WINDSOR AND ETON

Travel time from central London: *40min. from Victoria and Paddington by train.*

The town of Windsor and its attached village of Eton are overshadowed by two bastions of the British class system, Windsor Castle and Eton College. Windsor is filled with specialty shops, tea houses, and pubs, which despite all their charm, pale beside the fortress by the Thames.

WINDSOR CASTLE

Built by William the Conqueror in the 1070 and 80s as a fortress rather than a residence, Windsor is the largest inhabited castle in the world. The castle's main attractions are found in the **Upper Ward.** Stand in the left queue as you enter to detour past **Queen Mary's Doll House,** an exact replica of a grand home down to tiny books in its library handwritten by their original authors. The **state apartments** are filled with works by Holbein, Rubens, Rembrandt, Van Dyck, and Queen Victoria herself. A stroll to the **Lower Ward** brings you to the 15th-century **St. George's Chapel,** with delicate vaulting and exquisite stained glass. The site of Edward and Sophie's wedding, 10 sovereigns lie here, including George V, Edward IV, Charles I, and Henrys VI and VIII. *(24hr. info ☎017 5383 1118. As a "working castle," large areas may be closed at short notice. Open daily Mar.-Oct. 9:45am-5:30pm; Nov.-Feb. 9:45am-4pm; last admission 1¾hr. before close. £12, children £6. Audioguide £3.50.)*

ETON COLLEGE

Founded by Henry VI in 1440 as a school for paupers, Eton is now England's pre-eminent public (i.e. private) school. Pupils still wear tailcoats to every class and raise one finger in greeting to any teacher they pass. For all its air of privilege, Eton has shaped some notable dissidents, including Aldous Huxley and George Orwell. *(Across Windsor Bridge, and along Eton High St. ☎017 05367 1177. Open daily late Mar. to mid-Apr. and July-Aug. 10:30am-4:30pm; mid.-Apr. to June and Sept. to late Mar. 2-4:30pm. Schedule varies due to academic calendar. £3, under 16 £2.25. Daily tours 2:15 and 3:15pm; £4, under 16 £3.10.)*

TRANSPORTATION. Windsor has two train stations, both in walking distance of the castle. Trains (☎084 5748 4950) to **Windsor** and **Eton Central** arrive from both **Victoria** and **Paddington** stations via Slough (40min., 2 per hr., return £7.30), while those to **Windsor** and **Eton Riverside** come direct from **Waterloo** (50min., 2 per hr., return £6.90).

ORIENTATION AND PRACTICAL INFORMATION. Windsor village slopes downhill in an elegant crescent from the foot of its castle. **High Street,** which becomes **Thames Street** at the statue of Queen Victoria and continues downhill to the Thames, spans the top of the hill; the main shopping area, **Peascod Street,** meets High St. at the statue. The **Tourist Information Centre,** near Queen Victoria, has numerous free brochures and sells local maps, guides, and tickets to Legoland. *(24 High St. ☎017 5374 3900; www.windsor.gov.uk. Open daily May-Aug. 10am-5:30pm; Sept.-Apr. 10am-4pm.)*

OVERNIGHT TRIPS

BATH

Travel time from central London: *1½hr. from Paddington by train; 2¼hr. from Waterloo by train; 3½hr. from Victoria Coach Station by bus.*

Early in their occupation of Britain, the Romans built an elaborate complex of baths to house the curative waters at the town they called Aquae Sulis. In 1701, Queen Anne's trip to the hot springs reestablished the city as a prominent meeting place for artists, politicians, and intellectuals. Though damaged in WWII, the city has been painstakingly restored and today's thoroughfares remain utterly elegant, with modern shops and salons laced seamlessly into the fabric of its Georgian architecture.

ROMAN BATHS

Bath flourished for nearly 400 years as a Roman spa city, but it was not until 1880 that sewer diggers inadvertently uncovered the first glimpse of advanced Roman engineering. Underneath the baths, the **museum** features exhibits on Roman building design, including central heating and internal plumbing. Penny-pinching travelers can view one of the baths in the complex for free by entering through the **Pump Room.** *(Stall St. ☎012 2547 7785; www.romanbaths.co.uk. Open daily July-Aug. 9am-10pm; Sept.-Oct. and Mar-June 9am-6pm; Jan.-Feb. and Nov.-Dec. 9:30am-5:30pm. Last admission 1hr. before close. Hourly guided tour included. £9, seniors £8, children £5, family £29.)*

BATH ABBEY

An anomaly among the city's Roman and 18th-century Georgian sights, the 15th-century abbey still towers over its neighbors. The abbey saw the crowning of Edgar, "first king of all England," in AD 973. *(Next to the Baths. ☎012 2542 2462; www.bathabbey.org. Open Apr.-Oct. M-Sa 9am-6pm, Su 1-2:30pm and 4:30-5:30pm; Nov.-Mar. M-Sa 9am-4pm, Su between services. Free; requested donation £2.50.)* Below the abbey, the **Heritage Vaults** detail the abbey's history and its importance to Bath. *(Open M-Sa 10am-4pm; last admission 3:30pm. £2.50, concessions £1.50.)*

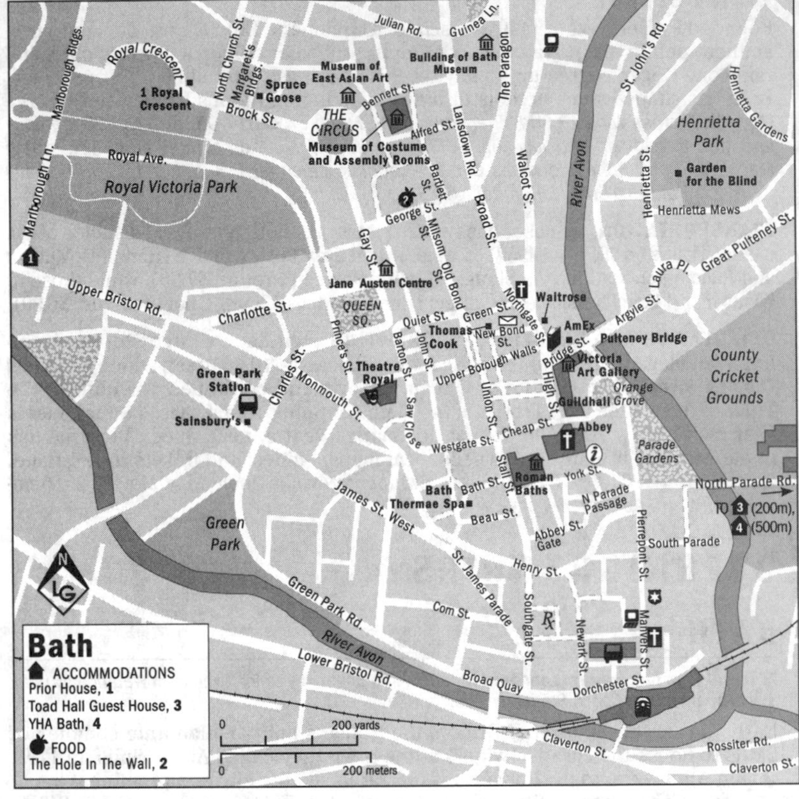

OTHER SIGHTS

The Museum of Costume hosts a dazzling, albeit motionless, 400-year parade of catwalk fashions, with everything from silver tissue garments to the revealing Dolce&Gabana dresses worn by J.Lo and Geri Haliwell. *(Bennett St. ☎012 2547 7789; www.museumofcostume.co.uk. Open daily Mar.-Oct. 10am-5pm; Nov.-Feb. 11am-4pm. £6, concessions £5, children £4, family £16.50.)* The museum is in the basement of the **Assembly Rooms,** which staged fashionable events in the 18th century. *(☎012 2547 7789. Open daily 10am-5pm. Free.)* The **Jane Austen Centre** invites dilettantes to experience the city as it was in 1806. Tours of the sights in her novels run daily 1:30pm from Abbey Churchyard. *(40 Gay St. ☎012 2544 3000; www.janeausten.co.uk. Open M-Sa 10am-5:30pm, Su 10:30am-5:30pm. £4.65, concessions £4.15, children £2.50, family £12.50. Tours £4.50/£3.50/£2.50/£8.)* Walk up Gay St. to **The Circus,** which has attracted illustrious residents for two centuries. Blue plaques mark the houses of Gainsborough, Pitt the Elder, and Dr. Livingstone. Proceed from there up Brock St. to **Royal Crescent,** a half-moon of Georgian townhouses. The interior of **1 Royal Crescent** has been painstakingly restored to a replica of a 1770 townhouse. *(☎012 2542 8126. Open mid-Feb. to Oct. Tu-Su 10:30am-5pm; Nov. Tu-Su 10:30am-4pm. £4, concessions £3.50, family £10.)*

TRANSPORTATION. Trains from **Paddington** are the fastest way to get to Bath, but those from **Waterloo** are much cheaper. *(Railway Pl., at the south end of Manvers St. Paddington: 1½hr., 2 per hr., £45. Waterloo: 2-2¼hr., 3 per day, £25.)* Even slower and cheaper are **National Express buses** from **Victoria Coach Station.** *(☎0870 580 8080. 3hr., every hr., £14.)*

LONDON TO PARIS OR BRUSSELS DIRECT

*From **$90*** round trip no taxes*

When you visit Europe, you want to go beyond the tourist traps. *So why travel like a tourist?*

Take Eurostar™ from the heart of London to the centre of Paris or Brussels and you'll glide there effortlessly, station to station. No coach transfers or long airport check-ins. Just a scenic journey – from London to Paris in 2 hours 35 or Brussels in 2 hours 15.

Visit **eurostar.com** or your travel agent

London

Paris

Brussels-Midi/Zuid

Disneyland® Resort Paris

*Price subject to change.
Fastest timetabled journeys quoted
[2271/04]

Visit us at http://www.letsgo.com

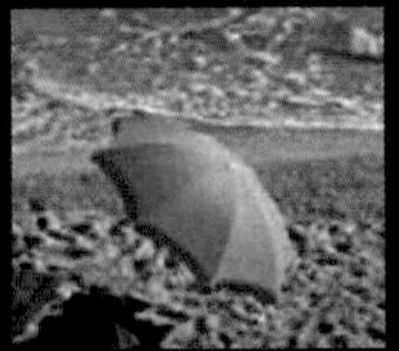

LET'S GO
Travel Guides

Be sure to check out our new website, beyondtourism.com, for a searchable database of international volunteer, work and study opportunities, a blog from fellow travelers and feature articles highlighting a variety of destination-specific opportunities.

Purchase one of our 48 guides online or at your local bookstore

Alaska - Amsterdam - Australia - Austria & Switzerland - Barcelona - Britain & Ireland - Brazil - California - Central America - China - Chile - Costa Rica - Ecuador - Eastern Europe - Egypt - Europe - France - Germany - Greece - Hawaii - India & Nepal - Ireland - Israel & the Palestinian Territories - Italy - Japan - London - Mexico - Middle East - New York City - New Zealand & Fiji - Paris - Peru - Pacific Northwest - Puerto Rico - Roadtrip USA - Rome - San Francisco - South Africa - Southeast Asia - Southwest USA - Spain, Portugal & Morocco - Thailand - Turkey - Vietnam - USA - Washington D.C. - Western Europe

http://www.letsgo.com

ORIENTATION AND PRACTICAL INFORMATION. Beautiful **Pulteney Bridge** and **North Parade Bridge** span the River Avon, which bends around the city. The **Roman Baths,** the **Pump Room,** and **Bath Abbey** cluster in the city center, while the **Royal Crescent** and **The Circus** lie to the northwest. The **Tourist Information Centre** offers the usual services. *(Abbey Chambers. ☎087 0444 6442; www.visitbath.co.uk. Open May-Sept. M-Sa 9:30am-6pm, Su 10am-4pm; Oct.-Apr. M-Sa 9:30am-5pm, Su 10am-4pm.)*

ACCOMMODATIONS AND FOOD. B&Bs cluster on **Pulteney Road** and **Pulteney Gardens.** From the stations, walk up Manvers St., which becomes Pierrepont St., right onto North Parade Rd., and past the cricket ground to Pulteney Rd. For a more relaxed (and more expensive) setting, continue past Pulteney Gdns. (or take the footpath from behind the train station) to **Widcombe Hill.** **Prior House ❸** has friendly proprietors and inviting rooms, complete with board games and hairdryers. *(3 Marlborough Ln. Take bus #14 from the station to Hinton Garage or walk 15min. ☎012 2531 3587; www.greatplaces.co.uk/priorhouse. Breakfast included. Doubles £50-55. AmEx/MC/V.)* **YHA Bath ❶** is in a secluded Italianate mansion overlooking the city. In summer, reserve a week ahead. *(Bathwick Hill. From North Parade Rd., turn left onto Pulteney Rd., right onto Bathwick Hill, and then 40min. up a steep footpath, or take bus #18 or 418 (6 per hr., return £1.20) from the bus station or the Orange Grove roundabout. ☎012 2546 5674. Dorms £11.80, under 18 £8.50; doubles £32, with bath £36.)* **Toad Hall Guest House ❸** is a friendly B&B with spacious doubles and hearty breakfasts. *(6 Lime Grove. Make a left off Pulteney Rd. after passing through the overpass. ☎012 2542 3254. Doubles £45.)*

Although restaurants in Bath tend to be expensive, reasonably priced cafes and eateries dot the city, many with outdoor seating. For fruits and vegetables, visit the **market** at Guildhall. *(☎012 2547 7945. Open M-Sa 9am-5:30pm.)* Stop by the **The Hole in the Wall ❹** for some succulent Anglo-Euro fusion. Lunches and dinner before 6:30pm have reasonable two- and three-course meals (£10-15). *(16-17 George St. ☎01225 425 242; www.theholeinthewall.co.uk. Open M-Sa noon-2:30pm and 5-10pm, Su 11am-4pm.)*

BRIGHTON

Travel time from central London: *1hr. by train from Victoria; 2hr. by bus from Victoria Coach.*

The undisputed home of the sketchy weekend, Brighton sparkles with a risqué, tawdry luster. Back in 1784, the future George IV sidled into town for some hanky-panky. Having staged a fake wedding with a certain "Mrs. Jones" (Maria Fitzherbert), he headed off to the farmhouse known today as the Royal Pavilion, and the royal rumpus began. Kemp Town (jokingly called Camp Town), among other areas of Brighton, has a thriving gay population, while the immense student crowd, augmented by flocks of foreign youth purportedly learning English, feeds Brighton's decadent clubbing scene. Lovingly known as "London-by-the-Sea," Brighton's open demeanor and youthful spirit make it a memorable visit for adventurous travelers.

SIGHTS

In 1750, Dr. Richard Russell wrote a treatise on the merits of drinking seawater and bathing in brine. Thus began the transformation of sleepy Brighthelmstone into a fashionable town with a hedonistic ben. **The Royal Pavilion** is the epitome of Brighton gaudiness; the prince enlisted John Nash to turn an ordinary farmhouse into the Oriental/Indian/Gothic/Georgian palace visible today. *(☎012 7329 2880. Open daily Apr.-Sept. 9:30am-5:45pm; Oct.-Mar. 10am-5:15pm. Last admission 4:30pm. £5.95, concessions £4.20, children £3.50, family £15.40. Tours daily 11:30am and 2:30pm, £1.50.)* The Pavilion's gaudiness reaches the beachfront, where the **Palace Pier** has slot machines and video games, with a roller coaster thrown in for good measure. Farther along, the now decrepit **West Pier** lies abandoned out in the sea. Even though Brighton was the original seaside resort, don't expect too much from the **beach**—the weather can be nippy even in summer, but yet on sunny days visitors have to fight for a patch of rock. Inland, fishermen's cottages once thrived in **the Lanes,** a jumble of 17th-century streets south of North St. constituting the heart of Old Brighton. Those looking for shopping opportunities should head towards **North Laines,** off Trafalgar St., where alternative merchandise and colorful cafes still dominate.

TRANSPORTATION. Trains leave from London's Victoria Station. *(☎084 5748 4950; 1hr., 2 per hr., £14.40.)* The Brighton Train Station is uphill at the northern end of Queen's Rd. **National Express buses** leave from London's Victoria Coach and stop at Pool Valley, at the southern angle of Old Steine; buy tickets from **One Stop Travel.** *(16 Old Steine. ☎012 7370 0406; National Express ☎087 0580 8080. 2hr., 15 per day, return £18.)*

ORIENTATION AND PRACTICAL INFORMATION. Queen's Road connects the train station to the English Channel, becoming **West Street** at the intersection with **Western Street.** Funky stores and restaurants cluster around **Trafalgar Street.** The narrow streets of **the Lanes,** left off Prince Albert St., provide an anarchic setting for Brighton's nightlife. **Old Steine,** a road and a square, runs in front of the Royal Pavilion, while **King's Road** runs along the waterfront. The **Tourist Information Centre** can help you find accommodation. *(10 Bartholomew Sq. ☎0906 711 2255; www.visitbrighton.com. Open June-Sept. M-F 9am-5:30pm, Sa 10am-5pm, Su 10am-4pm; Oct.-May M-F 9am-5pm, Sa 10am-5pm, Su 10am-4pm.)*

ACCOMMODATIONS AND FOOD. Frequent conventions make rooms scarce—book early or consult the TIC upon arrival. Many mid-range B&Bs line **Madeira Place;** shabbier B&Bs and hotels collect west of **West Pier** and in Kemp Town east of **Palace Pier.** **Baggies Backpackers ❶** has live jazz, spontaneous parties, murals, and spacious dorms, plus some doubles. *(33 Oriental Pl. ☎012 7373 3740. Key deposit £5. Dorms £12; doubles £30. MC/V.)* At **Hotel Pelirocco ❹,** rock-star longings are filled with over-the-top, hip-to-be-camp style in their 19 swanky individually-themed rooms. *(10 Regency Sq. ☎012 7332 7055. Singles £50-58; doubles £90-130. AmEx/MC/V.)* **Cavalaire Guest House ❸** has comfortable rooms ideal for a lazy weekend in town. *(34 Upper Rock Gdns. ☎012 7369 6899. Singles from £29; doubles from £70. AmEx/MC/V.)* Lively and social **Brighton Backpackers Hostel ❷** has a great location with many rooms overlooking the ocean. *(75-76 Middle St. ☎012 7377 7717. Dorms £15, weekly £80; doubles £25-£30. MC/V.)*

The Lanes area is full of suspiciously trendy places waiting to gobble tourist cash. The chippers along the beachfront avenues or north of the Lanes usually have better deals. **Food for Friends ❷** serves large vegetarian portions, based on Indian and East Asian cuisine. Mains £8-13. *(17a-18a Prince Albert St. ☎012 7320 2310. Open daily 11:30am-10pm. MC/V.)* **Nia Restaurant and Cafe ❸** is recognized for its generous portions and unique menu: everything from French pastries to Mediterranean dishes (mains £10-14). *(87 Trafalgar St. ☎012 7367 1371. Open daily 9am-11pm. MC/V.)*

NIGHTLIFE. Even Londoners come to club in Brighton. For the latest happenings, check *The Punter*, a local monthly, and *What's On*, a poster-sized flysheet. Gay and lesbian venues are found in the *Gay Times* (£2.75) and *Capital Gay* (free). Most clubs are open M-Sa 10pm-2am. **The Beach** adds big beats to the music on the shore. *(171-181 King's Rd. Arches ☎021 7372 2272. Cover £5-10.)* **Casablanca** lures students with live bands, playing everything from jigs to jazz. *(3 Middle St. ☎012 1733 2187. Th-Sa cover £7.)* **Event II** is among the most technically armed, crammed with the London crowd looking for wild thrills. *(West St. ☎01273 732627. Cover £5 and up.)*

CAMBRIDGE

Travel time from central London: *45min. from King's Cross by train; 1¼hr. from Liverpool St. by train; 2hr. from Victoria Coach Station by bus.*

Cambridge was a typical market town until the 13th century, when an academic schism sent Oxford's refugees to the banks of the Cam. In contrast to metropolitan Oxford, Cambridge is determined to retain its pastoral academic robes; as a town it's smaller, quieter, and more beautiful. Visitors can enter most colleges from 9am to 5:30pm, though virtually all close during the exam period from May to mid-June.

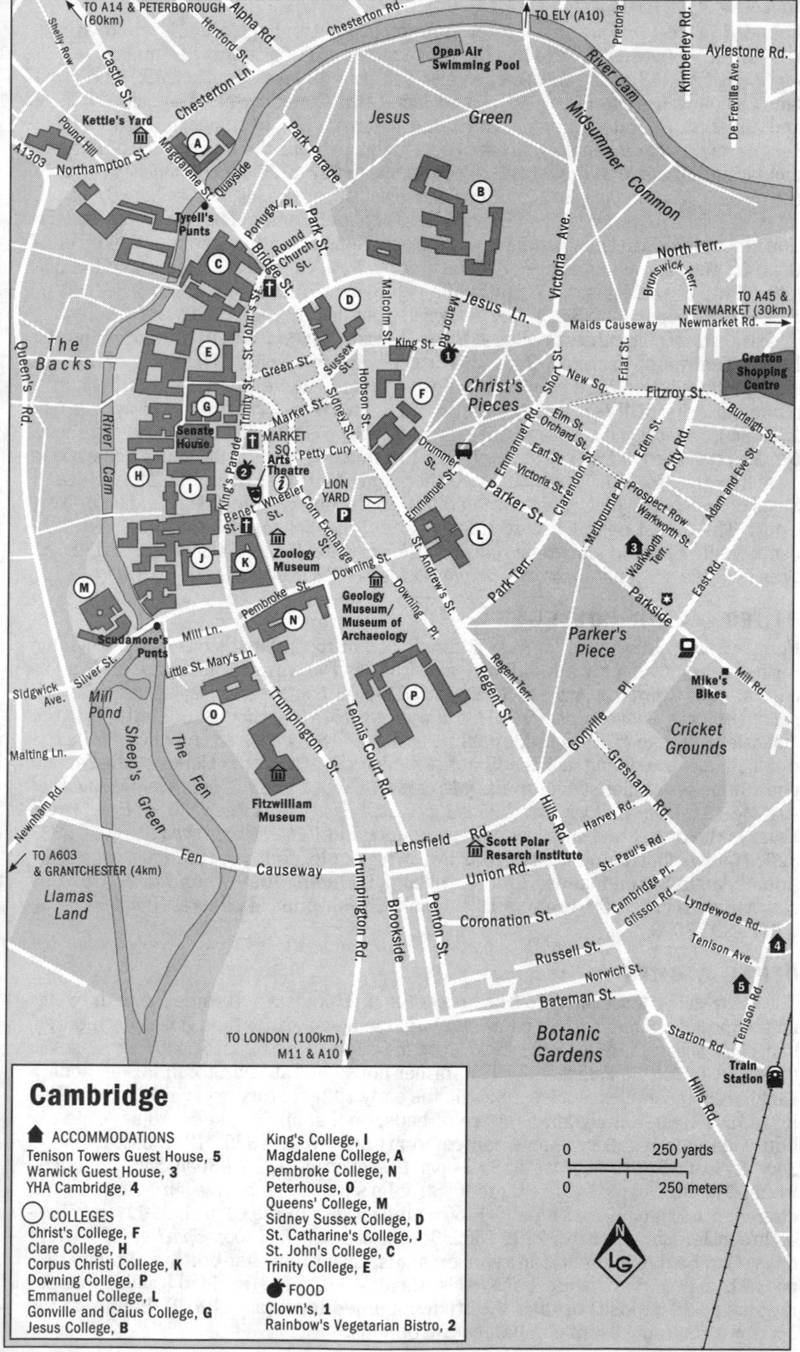

Cambridge
ACCOMMODATIONS
Tenison Towers Guest House, 5
Warwick Guest House, 3
YHA Cambridge, 4
COLLEGES
Christ's College, F
Clare College, H
Corpus Christi College, K
Downing College, P
Emmanuel College, L
Gonville and Caius College, G
Jesus College, B
King's College, I
Magdalene College, A
Pembroke College, N
Peterhouse, O
Queens' College, M
Sidney Sussex College, D
St. Catharine's College, J
St. John's College, C
Trinity College, E
FOOD
Clown's, 1
Rainbow's Vegetarian Bistro, 2
TO A14 & PETERBOROUGH (60km)
TO ELY (A10)
TO A45 & NEWMARKET (30km)
TO A603 & GRANTCHESTER (4km)
TO LONDON (100km), M11 & A10
Open Air Swimming Pool
Jesus Green
Midsummer Common
River Cam
Kettle's Yard
Tyrell's Punts
Scudamore's Punts
The Backs
Christ's Pieces
Senate House
MARKET SQ.
Arts Theatre
LION YARD
Zoology Museum
Geology Museum/ Museum of Archaeology
Fitzwilliam Museum
Scott Polar Resarch Institute
Parker's Piece
Mike's Bikes
Cricket Grounds
Grafton Shopping Centre
Mill Pond
Sheep's Green
The Fen
Llamas Land
Botanic Gardens
Train Station
Chesterton Rd.
Alpha Rd.
Hertford St.
Shelly Row
Castle St.
Chesterton Ln.
Pound Hill
A1303
Northampton St.
Magdalene St.
Quayside
Park Parade
Portugal Pl.
Round Church St.
Bridge St.
Park St.
St. John's St.
Trinity St.
Green St.
Sussex St.
Sidney St.
Malcolm St.
Hobson St.
King St.
Manor Rd.
Jesus Ln.
Victoria Ave.
Maids Causeway
Newmarket Rd.
North Terr.
Brunswick Terr.
Aylestone Rd.
Kimberley Rd.
Pretoria
De Freville Ave.
Friar St.
Short St.
New Sq.
Fitzroy St.
Burleigh St.
Queen's Rd.
Market St.
Petty Cury
King's Parade
Benet St.
Wheeler St.
Corn Exchange St.
Drummer St.
Emmanuel Rd.
Elm St.
Orchard St.
Earl St.
Victoria St.
Clarendon St.
Emmanuel St.
Parker St.
Eden St.
City Rd.
Melbourne Pl.
Prospect Row
Warkworth St.
Warkworth Terr.
Adam and Eve St.
East Rd.
Parkside
Park Terr.
Downing St.
Pembroke St.
St. Andrew's St.
Downing Pl.
Mill Ln.
Little St. Mary's Ln.
Silver St.
Sidgwick Ave.
Trumpington St.
Tennis Court Rd.
Regent Terr.
Regent St.
Gonville Pl.
Mill Rd.
Gresham Rd.
Hills Rd.
Malting Ln.
Newnham Rd.
Fen Causeway
Lensfield Rd.
Harvey Rd.
St. Paul's Rd.
Union Rd.
Cambridge Pl.
Glisson Rd.
Lyndewode Rd.
Trumpington Rd.
Brookside
Panton St.
Coronation St.
Russell St.
Tenison Ave.
Tenison Rd.
Norwich St.
Bateman St.
Station Rd.
0
250 yards
250 meters
N
LG

KING'S PARADE TO ST. JOHN'S ST.

Founded twice—by Queen Margaret of Anjou in 1448 and again by Elizabeth Woodville in 1465—**Queens' College** has the only unaltered Tudor court in Cambridge. *(Silver St. ☎012 2333 5511. College open Mar.-Oct. daily 10am-4:30pm. £1.30.)* The most famous colleges are found along the east side of the Cam between Magdalene Bridge and Silver St. Founded, along with Eton, by Henry VI, **King's College** features most heavily on postcards thanks to its soaring chapel, perhaps the finest piece of Perpendicular architecture in the world. *(King's Parade. ☎012 2333 1100. Chapel and grounds open M-Sa 9:30am-4:30pm, Su 10am-5pm. Evensong 5:30pm most nights. Contact TIC for tours. £4, concessions £3, under 12 free.)* Behind King's chapel, **Senate House** is where graduation ceremonies are held. *(Closed to visitors.)* Just opposite, you can climb the tower of **Great St. Mary's,** the university's official church, for a view of the greens and the colleges. Pray the 12 bells don't ring while you're ascending. *(Tower open M-Sa 9:30am-5pm, Su 12:30-5pm. £2, children 75p, family £5.)* Founded by Henry VIII, **Trinity College** is the largest and wealthiest college. Isaac Newton heads a list of alumni including Byron, Tennyson, Nabokov, Russell, Wittgenstein, and Nehru. The pride of the college is Christopher Wren's Library, whose treasures include A.A. Milne's handwritten manuscript of *Winnie the Pooh* and Newton's own *Principia*. *(Trinity St. ☎012 2333 8400. Chapel and courtyards open daily 10am-5pm. Library open M-F noon-2pm. Easter-Oct. £2, concessions £1; otherwise free.)* Next to Trinity, arch-rival **St. John's College** was established in 1511 by Henry VIII's mother, Lady Margaret Beaufort. The Bridge of Sighs connects the older part of the college to the neo-Gothic extravagance of New Court. The oldest complete building in Cambridge, **School of Pythagoras,** is a 12th-century pile of wood and stone hiding in the gardens. *(St. John's St. ☎012 2333 8600. Open daily 10am-5:30pm. Evensong 6:30pm most nights. £2, concessions £1.20, family £4.)*

OTHER MAJOR COLLEGES

Founded as "God's-house" in 1448 and renamed in 1505, **Christ's** has since won fame for its association with John Milton, and Charles Darwin's rooms were on G staircase in First Court. *(St. Andrews St. ☎012 2333 4900. Gardens open daily summer 9:30am-noon; term-time 9am-4:30pm. Free.)* Occupying a 15th-century Benedictine hostel, **Magdalene College** (MAUD-lin), one time home of C.S. Lewis, is renowned for its traditionalism—the dining hall is still entirely candlelit. The **Pepys Library** in the second court houses the diarist's journals. *(Magdalene St. ☎012 2333 2100. Library open Easter-Aug. M-Sa 11:30am-12:30pm and 2:30-3:30pm; Sept.-Easter M-Sa 2:30-3:30pm. Free.)* **Peterhouse** is the oldest and smallest college, founded in 1294. *(Trumpington St. ☎012 2333 8200.)* **Corpus Christi,** founded in 1352 by townspeople, contains the snazziest collection of Anglo-Saxon manuscripts in England, including the *Anglo-Saxon Chronicle*. Alums include Sir Francis Drake and Christopher Marlowe. *(Trumpington St. ☎012 2333 8000.)*

OTHER SIGHTS

The **Fitzwilliam Museum** has a fine array of Impressionists and some Blake drawings and woodcuts, along with ancient statuary, medieval armor, and far-eastern porcelain. *(Trumpington St. ☎012 2333 2900. Open Tu-Sa 10am-5pm, Su 2:15-5pm. Free, suggested donation £3. Tours Sa 2:45pm; £3.)* The former house of Tate curator Jim Ede, **Kettle's Yard** hardly resembles a museum at all; the early 20th-century art is displayed as Ede left it, among a homely atmosphere of beds, books, and trinkets. Adjacent to the house, a modern gallery shows contemporary art. *(☎012 2335 2124. House open Apr.-Sept. Tu-Su 1:30-5pm; Oct.-Mar. Tu-Su 2-4pm. Gallery open Tu-Su 11:30am-5pm. Free.)* The **Round Church,** where Bridge St. meets St. John's St., is one of five surviving circular churches in England, first built in 1130 on the pattern of the Church of the Holy Sepulchre in Jerusalem. *(☎012 2331 1602. Open Su-M 1-5pm, Tu-F 10am-5pm.Free.)* On warm days, Cambridge takes to the river on **punts,** traditional flat-bottomed boats propelled by a pole. You can rent at **Tyrell's,** Magdalene Bridge (☎01480 394 941; £12 per hr. plus a £60 deposit) or take the student-punted **tours** (about £10). Inquire at the TIC for a complete list of companies and options.

TRANSPORTATION. Every 30min. **trains** leave from **King's Cross** (45min.) and from **Liverpool St.** (1¼hr.) and arrive at the station on Station Rd.—beware it is a 30min. walk from the center of town and city buses (£1) are rare after 6pm and on Sundays. *(☎084 5748 4950. Day return £16.40.)* **Buses** are much slower, but drop you right in the center; **National Express** arrives from **Victoria Coach Station.** *(Drummer St. ☎087 0580 8080. 2hr., 2 per hr., from £9.)* **Taxi** services in Cambridge include Cabco *(☎012 2331 2444)* and Camtax *(☎012 2331 3131)*, both available 24hr.

ORIENTATION AND PRACTICAL INFORMATION. Cambridge has two main avenues, both suffering from multiple personality disorder. The main shopping street starts at **Magdalene Bridge** and becomes **Bridge Street, Sidney Street, St. Andrew's Street, Regent Street,** and finally **Hills Road** as it nears the train station. The other street—**St. John's Street,** then **Trinity Street, King's Parade,** and **Trumpington Street**—is the academic thoroughfare, parallel to the river but separated from it by colleges. The **Tourist Information Centre**, a block south of Market Sq., sells mini-guides (50p) and maps (£0.50-4.30). The TIC also books accommodations. *(Wheeler St. ☎090 6586 2526; www.tourismcambridge.com. Open M-Sa 10am-5pm, Su 11am-4pm.)*

ACCOMMODATIONS AND FOOD. Hostel and B&B reservations are essential in summer. Located two blocks from the train station, **Tenison Towers Guest House** ❷ is a welcoming house; breakfast includes homemade bread and marmalade. *(148 Tenison Rd. ☎012 2356 6511. Singles £25-28; doubles £50-56.)* **Warwick Guest House** ❸ offers sunny, ensuite rooms near the bus station. *(Warkworth Terr. ☎012 2336 3682. Singles £39-45; doubles £56-62. MC/V.)* At **YHA Cambridge** ❶, the staff fosters a relaxed atmosphere, although more showers wouldn't hurt. *(97 Tenison Rd. ☎012 2335 4601. Reserve ahead. Dorms £17.50, under 18 £13.50. MC/V.)*

There are plenty of cheap Indian and Greek restaurants dotting the town. Also, **Market Square** has bright pyramids of cheap fruit and vegetables. (Open M-Sa 9:30am-4:30pm.) **Clown's** ❶ serves a variety of pasta (£3-7) and northerly European cuisine. *(54 King St. ☎012 2335 5711. Open daily 7:30am-midnight.)* **Rainbow's Vegetarian Bistro** ❷ is a tiny burrow featuring delicious vegan and vegetarian fare and all dishes are £7.25. *(9a King's Parade. ☎012 2332 1551; www.rainbowcafe.co.uk. Open Tu-Sa 10am-10pm; last order 9:30pm.)*

CANTERBURY

Travel time from central London: *1½hr. from Victoria, Waterloo, and Charing Cross by train; 2hr. from Victoria Coach Station by bus.*

Flung somewhere between the cathedral and the open road, the soul of Canterbury is as flighty as the city's itinerant visitors. Saint Thomas à Becket met his demise in Canterbury Cathedral after an irate Henry II asked, "Will no one rid me of this troublesome priest?" and a few of his henchmen took the hint. In the near millennium since, the site has become a pilgrimage dedicated to the "the hooly blisful martir."

CANTERBURY CATHEDRAL

The focal point of English Christianity since St. Augustine consecrated it in the 6th century, Canterbury Cathedral became the nation's primary pilgrimage destination following the 1170 murder of Archbishop (now Saint) Thomas à Becket. The murder site is closed off by a rail—a kind of permanent police line—around the Altar of the Sword's Point. In the adjacent **Trinity Chapel,** a solitary candle marks where Becket's body lay until 1538, when Henry VIII burned his remains and destroyed the shrine to show how he dealt with bishops who crossed the king. In a structure plagued by fire and rebuilt time and again, the 12th-century **crypt** remains intact. The **Corona Tower,** 105 steps above the easternmost apse, is recently renovated. *(☎012 2776 2862; www.canterbury-cathedral.org. Cathedral open Easter-Oct. M-Sa 9am-6:30pm; Oct.-Easter M-Sa 9am-5pm; also Su 12:30-2:30pm and 4:30-5:30pm year-round. 3 1¼hr. tours per day; check nave or welcome center for times. Evensong M-F 5:30pm, Sa-Su 3:15pm. £4.50, concessions £3.50. Tours £3.50/£2.50. 40min. audiotour £3/£2.)*

OTHER SIGHTS

Inevitably, someone had to come up with an attraction called **The Canterbury Tales.** Let the gap-toothed Wife of Bath and her waxen companions entertain you with abbreviated versions of the tales. *(St. Margaret's St. ☎012 2747 9227; www.caterburytales.org.uk. Open daily Mar.-June 10am-5pm; July-Aug. 9:30am-5pm; Sept.-Oct. 10am-5pm; Nov.-Feb. 10am-4:30pm. £7, concessions £6, family £22.40.)* Soaring arches, crumbling walls, and silent altars are all that remain of **St. Augustine's Abbey,** founded in AD 598. Don't miss St. Augustine's humble tomb under a pile of rocks. *(Outside the city wall near the cathedral. ☎012 2776 7345. Open daily Apr.-Sept. 10am-6pm; Oct.-Mar. 10am-4pm. £3.50, concessions £2.60, children £1.80.)* Just around the corner from St. Augustine's on North Holmes St. stands the **Church of St. Martin.** King Ethelbert married the Christian Princess Bertha here in AD 562, paving the way for England's conversion to Christianity. Joseph Conrad lies in an underground heart of darkness. *(North Holmes St. ☎012 2745 9482. Open daily 9am-5pm. Free.)* The **Museum of Canterbury** spans town history from its earliest days to the beloved children's-book character Rupert Bear. *(Stour St. ☎012 2745 2747. Open June-Sept. M-Sa 10:30am-5pm, Su 1:30-5pm; Nov.-May M-Sa 10:30am-5pm. £3.10, concessions £2.10.)* England's first Franciscan friary, **Greyfriars** was built over the River Stour in 1267 by Franciscan monks who arrived in the country in 1224, two years before Saint Francis of Assisi died. A museum and chapel are found inside the building. *(Stour St., follow signs from the Westgate gardens. ☎012 2746 2395. Open summer M-F 2-4pm. Free.)* Near the city walls to the southwest lie the remnants of **Canterbury Castle,** built for the Conqueror himself.

TRANSPORTATION. Canterbury has two **train** stations. **Connex South** runs to **Canterbury East** from **Victoria.** *(Station Rd. East, off Castle St. Station open M-Sa 6:10am-8:20pm, Su 6:10am-9:20pm. National Rail Enquiries ☎084 5748 4950. 1¾hr., 2 per hr., £17.30.)* Connex also serves **Canterbury West** from **Charing Cross** and **Waterloo.** *(Station Rd. West, off St. Dunstan's St. Station open M-F 6:15am-8pm, Sa 6:30am-8pm, Su 7:15am-9:30pm. 1½hr., 1 per hr., £17.30.)* **National Express buses** arrive at St. George's Ln. from **Victoria Coach Station.** *(☎087 0580 8080. 2hr., 2 per hr., £10.50.)*

ORIENTATION AND PRACTICAL INFORMATION. Canterbury is roughly circular, as defined by the eroding city wall. An unbroken street crosses the city from northwest to southeast, changing names from **St. Peter's Street** to **High Street** to **The Parade** to **St. George's Street.** The **tourist information centre** gives out a free mini-guide. *(The Buttermarket, 12/13 Sun St. ☎012 2737 8100. Bed booking £2.50 plus 10% deposit. Open M-Sa 9:30am-5:30pm, Su 10am-4pm.)*

ACCOMMODATIONS AND FOOD. Reserve ahead, or arrive mid-morning to grab recently vacated rooms. B&Bs are concentrated around the lanes stemming from High St., with a few scattered near West Station. **Kipps Independent Hostel ❶** is a 10min. walk from the city center. *(40 Nunnery Fields. ☎012 2778 6121. Key deposit £10. Dorms £13; singles £18.50; doubles £32.)* **Let's Stay ❷** has hostel-style lodgings and a delightful Irish hostess. Ask about the origin of the name! *(26 New Dover Rd. ☎012 2746 3628. £14 per person.)* The **Castle Court Guest House ❷,** a few minutes from Eastgate in the old town, serves vegetarian breakfasts. *(8 Castle St. ☎ 012 2746 3441. Singles £25, doubles £42-50. 5% discount for* Let's Go *users.)* For some English food with a Mexican twist, stop by **Marlowe's ❷.** *(55 St. Peter's St. ☎012 2746 2194. Burgers £6.50, veggie dishes £6-9. Open M-Sa 9am-10:30pm, Su 10am-10:30pm.)* **Jaques ❸** has live music and candelit tables. *(71 Castle St. ☎012 2778 1000. Mains £11-16. Open M-F 11am-2:30pm and 6-9:30pm, Su 10am-10:30pm. MC/V.)*

NEAR CANTERBURY: LEEDS CASTLE

23 mi. west of Canterbury on the A20. Trains run from Canterbury West to Bearsted (every hr., £9.70); a shuttle goes from station to castle (£4). Shuttles leave the train station M-Sa 10:35am-2:35pm on the "35," Su 10:55am-2:55pm on the 55's; and return shuttles leave the castle M-Sa 2-6pm on the hr., Su 2:15-6:15pm on the quarter hr. ☎016 2276 5400 or 087

0600 8880. Castle open daily Mar.-Oct. 11am-7:30pm; Nov.-Feb. 10:15am-5:30pm. Grounds open daily Mar.-Oct. 10am-7pm; Nov.-Feb. 10am-5pm; last admission 2hr. before close. Castle and grounds £12.50, concessions £11, children £9, family £39.

Billed as "the Loveliest Castle in the World," Leeds Castle was built immediately after the Norman Conquest. Henry VIII made it a lavish dwelling whose woodlands and gardens still host unusual waterfowl, including black swans. Outside, lose yourself in a maze of 2400 yew trees; the sculpted grounds, vivid gardens, and forests, meanwhile, are almost a labyrinth in themselves.

OXFORD

Travel time from central London: *1hr. from Paddington by train; 1¾hr. from Victoria Coach Station, Marble Arch, and near Baker St. by bus.*

Oxford had been a center of learning for a century before Henry II founded the university in 1167. Though tourists now outnumber scholars, Oxford has irrepressible grandeur and pockets of tranquility, most famously the perfectly maintained quadrangles ("quads") of the university's 39 colleges. Most colleges are free to enter, though some charge admission in high season. However, opening hours for visitors are restricted, especially April to early June as students prepare for exams.

ASHMOLEAN MUSEUM

Opened in 1683, the Ashmolean was Britain's first public gallery, and now plays host to familiar favorites including Leonardo, Monet, Manet, Van Gogh, Michelangelo, Rodin, and Matisse. Renovated galleries also house ancient Islamic, Greek, and Far Eastern art. *(Beaumont St. From Carfax, head up Cornmarket St., which becomes Magdalene St.; Beaumont St. is on the left. ☎018 6527 8000. Open Tu-Sa 10am-5pm, Su noon-5pm; in summer Th until 7:30pm. Free, tours £2.)*

MAJOR COLLEGES

Christ Church, grand enough for Charles I to make it his capital during the Civil War, is centered around **Tom Quad,** named for the bell which has rung at 9:05pm (the original student curfew) every evening since 1682. The college's art gallery includes works by Tintoretto and Vermeer, with Leonardo and Michelangelo occasionally coming out of hiding. *(Just down St. Aldates St. from Carfax; for gallery only, enter at Canterbury Gate off Oriel St. College ☎018 6528 6573, gallery 018 6527 6172; www.chchox.ac.uk. College open M-Sa 9am-12:45pm and 2-5pm, Su noon-5:30pm. No entry after 4pm. Gallery open Apr.-Sept. M-Sa 10:30am-1pm and 2-5:30pm, Su 2-5pm; Oct.-Mar. 4:30pm close. College £4, concessions £3; gallery £2/£1.)* Merton College has Oxford's oldest quad, the 14th-century Mob Quad, and an equally ancient library holding the first printed Welsh Bible. *(Merton St. ☎018 6527 6310. Open M-F 2-4pm, Sa-Su 10am-4pm. Closed around Easter and Christmas. Free.)* University College dates from 1249 and vies with Merton for the title of oldest college; misbehaving alums include Shelley, expelled for his pamphlet *The Necessity of Atheism*, and a non-inhaling Bill Clinton. *(High St. ☎018 6527 6602.)* Around since 1341, Queen's College was later rebuilt by Wren and Hawksmoor in orange, white, and gold. A trumpet call summons students to dinner. *(High St. ☎018 6527 9120; www.queens.ox.ac.uk. Open only to tours.)* Only Oxford's best are admitted to **All Souls College.** The prestigious graduate students who survive the admission exams are invited to dinner, where it is ensured that they are "well-born, well-bred, and only moderately learned." **The Great Quad,** with its fastidious lawn and two spare spires, may be Oxford's most serene. *(Corner of High St. and Catte St. ☎018 6527 9379; www.all-souls.ox.ac.uk. Open M-F Nov.-Feb. 2-4pm; Apr.-Oct. 2-4:30pm. Free.)* **Magdalen College** (MAUD-lin), with flower-laced quads and a private deer park, is considered Oxford's handsomest, and thus a natural choice for budding aesthete Oscar Wilde. *(On High St. near the River Cherwell. ☎018 6527 6000; www.magd.ox.ac.uk. Open daily Oct.-Mar. 1pm to dusk; Apr.-June 1-6pm; July-Sept. noon-6pm. £3, concessions £2.)* Founded in 1379, **New College** is actually one of Oxford's oldest colleges. The bell tower has equally grotesque

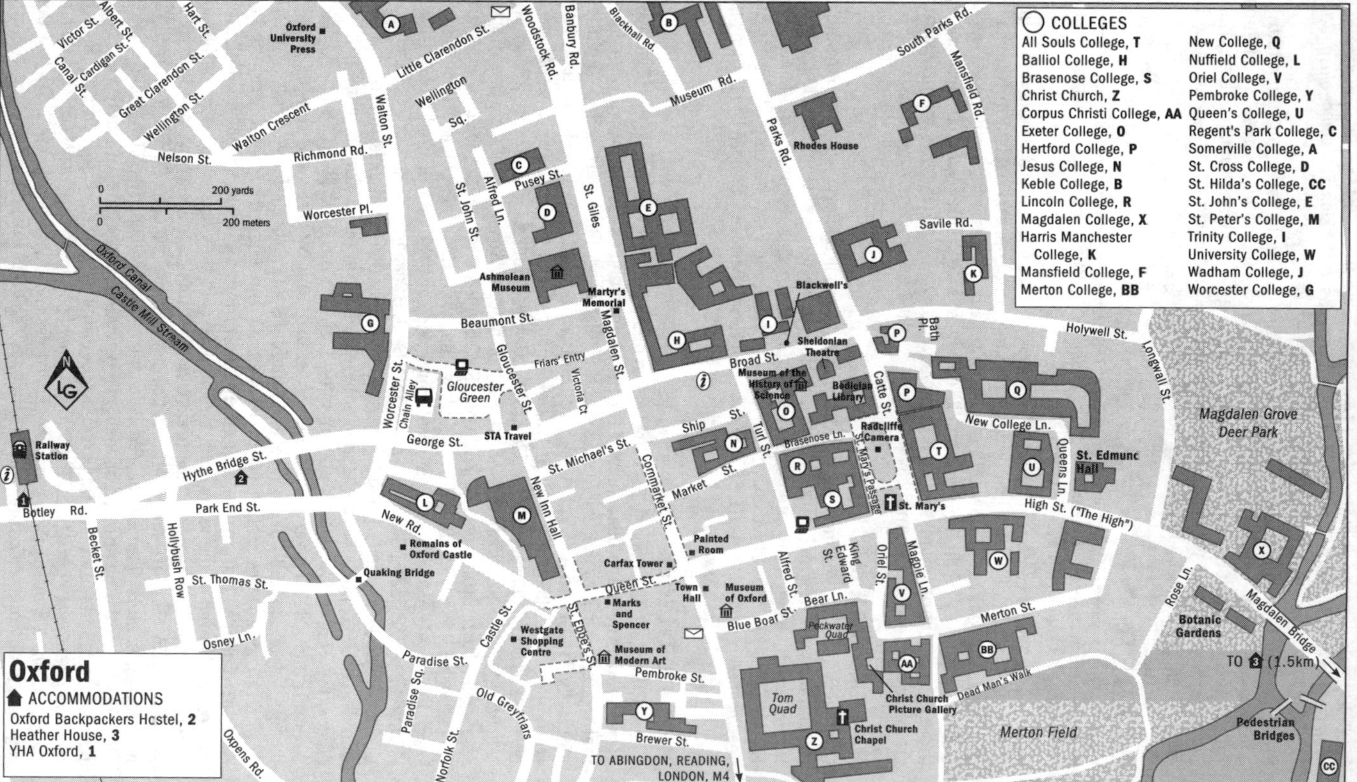
Oxford
ACCOMMODATIONS
Oxford Backpackers Hostel, 2
Heather House, 3
YHA Oxford, 1
COLLEGES
All Souls College, T
Balliol College, H
Brasenose College, S
Christ Church, Z
Corpus Christi College, AA
Exeter College, O
Hertford College, P
Jesus College, N
Keble College, B
Lincoln College, R
Magdalen College, X
Harris Manchester College, K
Mansfield College, F
Merton College, BB
New College, Q
Nuffield College, L
Oriel College, V
Pembroke College, Y
Queen's College, U
Regent's Park College, C
Somerville College, A
St. Cross College, D
St. Hilda's College, CC
St. John's College, E
St. Peter's College, M
Trinity College, I
University College, W
Wadham College, J
Worcester College, G
0 200 yards
0 200 meters
Oxford University Press
Victor St.
Albert St.
Hart St.
Canal St.
Cardigan St.
Great Clarendon St.
Wellington St.
Walton Crescent
Nelson St.
Richmond Rd.
Walton St.
Little Clarendon St.
Wellington Sq.
Woodstock Rd.
Banbury Rd.
Blackhall Rd.
Museum Rd.
South Parks Rd.
Mansfield Rd.
Parks Rd.
Rhodes House
Savile Rd.
Worcester Pl.
St. John St.
Alfred Ln.
Pusey St.
St. Giles
Oxford Canal
Castle Mill Stream
Ashmolean Museum
Martyr's Memorial
Blackwell's
Beaumont St.
Magdalen St.
Sheldonian Theatre
Bath Pl.
Holywell St.
Longwall St.
Broad St.
Museum of the History of Science
Bodleian Library
Catte St.
New College Ln.
Queens Ln.
St. Edmund Hall
Magdalen Grove Deer Park
Worcester St.
Chain Alley
Gloucester Green
Gloucester St.
Friars' Entry
Victoria Ct
STA Travel
George St.
Railway Station
Hythe Bridge St.
Botley Rd.
Park End St.
St. Michael's St.
Ship St.
Turl St.
Brasenose Ln.
Radcliffe Camera
St. Mary's Passage
St. Mary's
High St. ("The High")
Cornmarket St.
Market St.
New Inn Hall
New Rd.
Remains of Oxford Castle
Painted Room
Carfax Tower
Becket St.
Hollybush Row
St. Thomas St.
Quaking Bridge
Queen St.
Town Hall
Museum of Oxford
Alfred St.
King Edward St.
Oriel St.
Magpie Ln.
Rose Ln.
Magdalen Bridge
Marks and Spencer
Bear Ln.
Blue Boar St.
Merton St.
Botanic Gardens
Osney Ln.
Castle St.
Westgate Shopping Centre
St. Ebbe's St.
Museum of Modern Art
Peckwater Quad
TO 3 (1.5km)
Paradise St.
Paradise Sq.
Pembroke St.
Old Greyfriars
Tom Quad
Christ Church Picture Gallery
Dead Man's Walk
Merton Field
Pedestrian Bridges
Christ Church Chapel
Brewer St.
Oxpens Rd.
Norfolk St.
TO ABINGDON, READING, LONDON, M4

gargoyles of the Seven Deadly Sins on one side and the Seven Virtues on the other. *(New College Ln., use the Holywell St. Gate. ☎01865 279 555. Open daily Easter to mid-Oct. 11am-5pm; Nov.-Easter 2-4pm £2, children £1.)*

OTHER SIGHTS

The **Bodleian** was endowed in 1602 and is Oxford's principal library. No one has ever been allowed to take out even one of its five million volumes. Only scholars may enter the reading rooms; student ID may suffice, but an academic letter of introduction is recommended. *(Broad St. ☎018 6527 7000. Library open M-F 9am-10pm, Sa 9am-1pm; summer M-F 9am-7pm, Sa 9am-1pm. Tours leave from the Divinity School, in the main quadrangle; in summer M-Sa 4 per day, in winter 2 per day, in the afternoon. Tours £4, audio guide £2.)* A teenage Christopher Wren designed the Roman-style **Sheldonian Theatre,** now the site of graduation ceremonies; its cupola affords an inspiring view. The stone heads on the fence behind the theater are a 20th-century study of beards. *(Broad St. ☎018 6527 7299. Open roughly M-Sa 10am-12:30pm and 2-4:30pm; in winter, until 3:30pm. £1.50, under 15 £1. Purchase tickets from Oxford Playhouse ☎018 6530 5305. Box office open M-Tu and Th-Sa 9:30am-6:30pm or 30min. before last showing, W 10am-6:30pm. Shows £15.)*

TRANSPORTATION. The railway station, a 10min. walk from the historic center, is served by **Thames Trains** from **Paddington.** *(Botley Rd., down Park End. Trains ☎08457 484 950. 1hr., 2-4 per hr., return £14.90.)* Oxford CityLink **buses** from London arrive and leave Oxford from the station on Gloucester Green. *(☎01865 785 400; www.oxfordbus.co.uk. 1¾hr., 3 per hr. £9, students £7.)* Another option are the Oxford Tube buses from **Victoria Coach Station.** *(☎018 6577 2250. 2hr., 3-5 per hr., £9).*

ORIENTATION AND PRACTICAL INFORMATION. While Oxford is a fair-sized town, the historic center is easily walkable. The easiest way to orient yourself is to locate the colossal **Carfax Tower,** from which most colleges lie to the east. The **Tourist Information Centre,** beside the bus station, sells a £1.25 street map and guide with a valuable index. *(15-16 Broad St., Gloucester Green. ☎018 6572 6871; www.visitoxford.org. Open M-Sa 9:30am-5pm, Easter-Oct. also Su 10am-3:30pm.)*

ACCOMMODATIONS AND FOOD. From June to September book at least a week ahead. The superbly located **Oxford Backpackers Hostel** ❶ fosters the best of backpacker social life with an inexpensive bar, pool table, and music. *(9a Hythe Bridge St., between the bus and train stations. ☎018 6572 1761. Dorms £13-14. MC/V.)* **YHA Oxford** ❶ is an immediate right from the station onto Botley Rd. *(2a Botley Rd. ☎018 6572 7275. Breakfast included. Dorms £19, under 18 £14.)* **Heather House** ❷ has sparkling rooms and exceptionally helpful staff. *(192 Iffley Rd. Walk 20min. or take the "Rose Hill" bus from the bus or train station or Carfax Tower (70p). ☎/fax 018 6524 9757. Singles £33; doubles £66, discounts on longer stays.)* The owners of Oxford's bulging eateries know they have a captive market; students fed up with bland college food are easily seduced by a bevy of budget options. The **Covered Market,** between Market St. and Carfax, has fresh produce and deli goods (open M-Sa 8am-5pm). Across Magdalen Bridge, cheap restaurants line the first four blocks of **Cowley Road,** serving Chinese, Lebanese, and Polish food, as well as generic fish 'n' chips. Keep an eye out for after-hours **kebab vans,** usually at Broad St., High St., Queen St., and St. Aldates.

NEAR OXFORD: BLENHEIM PALACE

The palace is in Woodstock, 8 mi. north of Oxford; take the Stagecoach from Gloucester Green bus station. (☎018 6577 2250. 30-40min., every 30min. 8:15am-5pm, return £3.70.) Palace ☎019 9381 1091. House open mid-Feb. to mid-Dec. daily 10:30am-5:30pm. Last admission 4:45pm. Grounds open daily 9am-9pm. £12.50, children £7, family £33, concessions £10. Free tours every 5-10min.

The largest private home in England, Blenheim (BLEN-em) was built in appreciation of the Duke of Marlborough's victory over Louis XIV at the Battle of Blenheim in 1704. Another family scion, **Winston Churchill** grew up here; his baby curls

St. Mary's Church

Great Kitchen, Hampton Court

Musician in Fountain Court

are on display, while he rests in the nearby village churchyard of Bladon. **"Capability" Brown** designed the 2100 acres of gardens.

SALISBURY & STONEHENGE

Travel time from central London: *1½hr. from Waterloo by train; 3hr. from Victoria Coach Station by bus.*

Salisbury's fame comes from two remarkable monuments: its cathedral, with the highest spire in Europe, and the mysterious monoliths of nearby Stonehenge.

SALISBURY CATHEDRAL

Salisbury Cathedral rises from its grassy close to a neck- and record-breaking height of 404 ft. Built in just 38 years, starting in 1320, the cathedral has a singular and weighty design. The bases of the marble pillars bend inward under the strain of 6400 tons of limestone. Nearly 700 years have left the cathedral in need of structural and surface repair, and scaffolding shrouds parts of the outer walls where the stone is disintegrating. The chapel houses the oldest functioning mechanical clock, a strange collection of wheels and ropes that has ticked 500 million times over the last 600 years. Much to King John's chagrin, the best-preserved of four surviving copies of the *Magna Carta* rests in the Chapter House. *(33 The Close. ☎ 017 2255 5120. Cathedral open June-Aug. M-Sa 7:15am-8:15pm, Su 7:15am-6:15pm; Sept.-May daily 7:15am-6:15pm. Chapter House open June-Aug. M-Sa 9:30am-5:30pm, Su noon-5:30pm; Sept.-May daily 9:30am-5:30pm. Free tours May-Oct. M-Sa 9:30am-4:45pm, Su 4-6:15pm; Nov.-Feb. M-Sa 10am-4pm. 1½hr. roof tours May-Sept. M-Sa 11am, 2, 3pm, and Su 4:30pm; June-Aug. M-Sa also 6:30pm; winter hours vary, so call ahead. Suggested donation £3.80. Roof tour £3, concessions £2.)*

STONEHENGE

A ring of submerged colossi amid swaying grass and indifferent sheep, Stonehenge stands unperturbed by whipping winds. The present stones—22 ft. high—comprise the fifth temple constructed on the site. The first probably consisted of an arch and circular earthwork furrowed in 3050 BC, and was in use for about 500 years. Its relics are the **Aubrey Holes** (white patches in the earth) and the **Heel Stone** (the rough block standing outside the circle). The current monument is still more impressive considering that its stones, weighing up to 45 tons, were hauled all the way from Wales and erected by a tedious process of rope-and-log leverage—legend holds that the stones were magically transported here by Merlin. In 300 BC, Celts arrived from the Continent and claimed Stonehenge as their shrine; today, Druids are permitted to enter Stonehenge in midsummer to perform ceremonial exercises. *(☎019 8062 4715. Open June-Aug. daily 9am-7pm; mid-Mar to May and Sept. to mid-Oct. 9:30am-6pm; mid-Oct. to mid-Mar. 9:30am-4pm. £5.20, concessions £3.90, children £2.60, family £13.)* Getting to Stonehenge from Salisbury doesn't require much effort—as long as you don't have a 45-ton rock in tow. Wilts and Dorset **bus #3** runs from Salisbury station (☎017 2233 6855; 40min., return £5.25). An **Explorer** ticket (£6) allows you to travel all day on any bus, including those stopping by **Avebury,** Stonehenge's less-crowded cousin. The most scenic walking or cycling route from Salisbury is the **Woodford Valley Route.** Go north on Castle Rd., bear left just before Victoria Park onto Stratford Rd., and follow the road over the bridge through Lower, Middle, and Upper Woodford. After about 9 mi., turn left onto the A303 for the last mile. If Stonehenge isn't enough rock for you, look right to see Sting's Jacobean mansion.

TRANSPORTATION. Trains leave every 30min. from **Waterloo**. *(South Western Rd., across the Avon. ☎08457 484 950. 1½hr., £24-32.)* **National Express buses** make the trip from **Victoria Coach Station.** *(8 Endless St. Bus station ☎01722 336 855; National Express ☎08705 808 080. 2¾hr., 4 per day. Return £14.)*

ORIENTATION AND PRACTICAL INFORMATION. That all roads in Salisbury seem to lead to its cathedral gates is no accident—the streetplan was charted by Bishop Poore in the 13th century. The **Tourist Information Centre** is in the Guildhall, Market Sq., and runs 1½hr. city tours. *(Fish Row. ☎01722 334 956; www.visitsalisbury.com. Tours Apr.-Oct. 11am and 8pm; June-Aug. also 6pm; £2.50, children £1. Open June-Sept. M-Sa 9:30am-6pm, Su 10:30am-4:30pm; Oct.-May. M-Sa 9:30am-5pm.)*

ACCOMMODATIONS AND FOOD. Salisbury's proximity to Stonehenge breeds B&Bs, most of them comfortable and reasonably priced, though they fill quickly in summer. **YHA Salisbury ❶** is tucked into a cedar grove; reserve ahead in the summer. *(Milford Hill House, Milford Hill. ☎017 2232 7572. Lockout 10am-1pm. Dorms £15, under 18 £11.60.)* **Matt and Tiggy's ❶** is a welcoming 450-year-old house with warped floors and ceiling beams and an overflow house nearby. Both buildings have mellow, hostel-style, 2- to 4-person rooms. *(51 Salt Ln., just up from the bus station. ☎017 2232 7443. Breakfast £3. Dorms £12.)* **Farthings B&B ❷** is a peaceful haven with a lovely garden. *(9 Swaynes Close, a 10min. walk from city center. ☎017 2233 0749. Singles £25-27; doubles £46-55.)* Even jaded pub dwellers can find a pleasing venue among Salisbury's 60-odd watering holes. Most serve food (£4-6) and many offer free live music. **Market Square** in the town center fills on Tuesdays and Saturdays, with vendors hawking everything from peaches to posters (open 7am-4pm). **Harper's "Upstairs Restaurant" ❷** serves inventive English and international dishes (£6-10) and has a two-course "Early Bird" dinner: £8.50 before 8pm. *(6-7 Ox Rd., Market Sq. ☎017 2233 3118; www.harpersrestaurant.co.uk. Open M-F noon-2pm and 6-9:30pm, Sa noon-2pm; June-Sept. also Su 6-9pm.)*

STRATFORD-UPON-AVON

Travel time from central London: *2¼hr. from Paddington by train; 3hr. by bus.*

Shakespeare lived here. Admittedly, he got out as soon as he could, but even so millions make the pilgrimage here every year, showing their dedication by purchasing "Will Power" T-shirts, dining on faux-Tudor fast food, and dutifully traipsing through all the many sights vaguely connected to the Bard and his family. Yet for all that Stratford has milked its one cow, it still deserves a visit for the grace of the weeping Avon and the excellence of the Royal Shakespeare Company's productions.

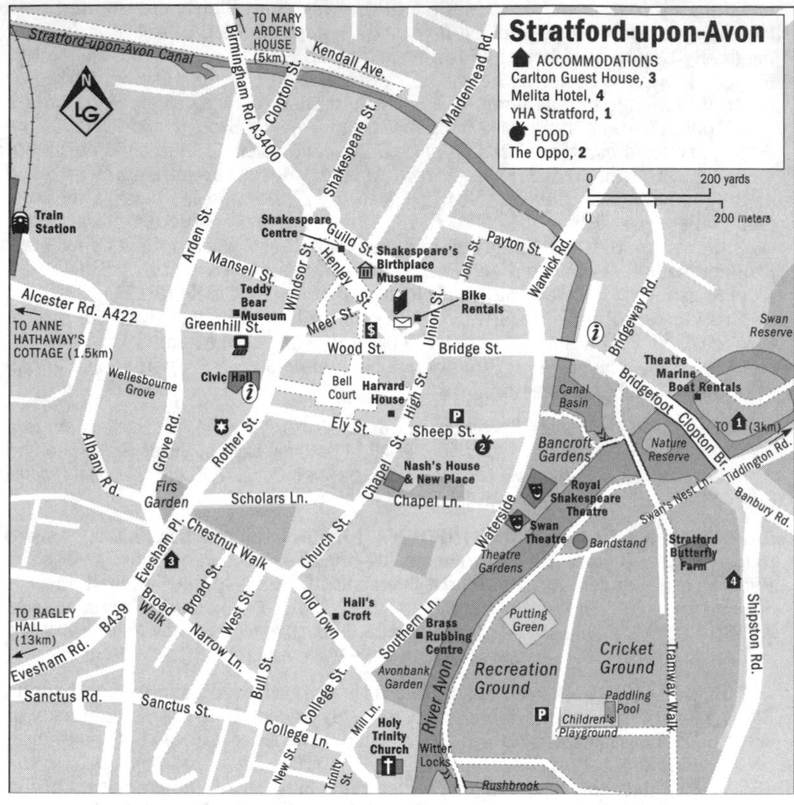

SHAKESPEAREAN SIGHTS

Two combination tickets are available for Will-seekers. The **Three In-Town Houses** ticket covers the "official" Shakespeare sights in town—the Birthplace, Hall's Croft, and Nash's House and New Place. *(£10, concessions £8, children £5, family £20.)* For fanatics, the **All Five Houses Ticket** throws in the more distant Anne Hathaway's Cottage and Mary Arden's House. *(£13, concessions £12, children £6.50, family £29.)* The least crowded way to pay homage is to visit the Bard's tiny grave in **Holy Trinity Church,** though groups still pack the arched door at peak hours. *(Trinity St. ☎017 8920 1823. £1, students and children 50p.)* **Shakespeare's Birthplace** is half period recreation and half life-and-work exhibition. *(Henley St. ☎017 8920 4016. Open Nov.-Mar. M-Sa 10am-4pm, Su 10:30am-4pm; Apr.-May and Sept.-Oct. M-Sa 10am-5pm, Su 10:30am-5pm; June-Aug. M-Sa 9am-5pm, Su 9:30am-5pm. £7.60, concessions £5.50, children £2.50, family £15.)* **Hall's Croft** follows the work of Dr. John Hall, who aside from being Shakespeare's son-in-law was one of the first doctors to keep detailed records of his patients—frogs were a frequent prescription. *(Old Town. ☎017 8929 2107. Open Nov.-Mar. daily 11am-4pm; Apr.-May and Sept.-Oct. daily 11am 5pm; June-Aug. M-Sa 9:30am 5pm, Su 10am-5pm. £3.50, concessions £3, children £1.70, family £8.50.)* The first husband of Shakespeare's granddaughter Elizabeth, Thomas Nash has only a tenuous connection to the bard, but a ticket to **Nash's House** also gets you a peek at what little remains of **New Place,** Stratford's hippest home when Shakespeare bought it in 1597. *(Chapel St. Opening hours same as Hall's Croft. £3.50, concessions £3, children £1.70, family £9.)* Will's wife's birthplace, **Anne Hathaway's Cottage** is one mile north of Stratford along ill-marked footpaths. This is the thatched cottage on all the posters; it boasts old Hathaway furniture and a new hedge maze. *(☎017 8929 2100. Opening hours same as Hall's Croft. £5, concessions £4, children £2, family £12.)*

THE PLAY'S THE THING

One of the world's finest repertory companies, the acclaimed **Royal Shakespeare Company (RSC)** is what makes Stratford more than an exploitative tourist trap. They even perform plays by other dramaturges, but only the Bard's work graces the stage at the towering **Royal Shakespeare Theatre,** Waterside. Renaissance and restoration plays are given at the neighboring **Swan Theatre,** built to resemble a 16th-century playhouse. If you don't manage to get tickets in advance, join the queue for the main box office about 20min. before opening for same-day sales. A happy few get returns and standing-room tickets for evening shows; queue 1-2hr. before curtain. The RSC also conducts **backstage tours** that cram camera-happy groups into the wooden "O"s of the RST and the Swan. *(The box office in the foyer of the Royal Shakespeare Theatre handles the ticketing for both theaters. Ticket hotline ☎087 0609 1110; www.rsc.org.uk. Open M-Sa 9:30am-8pm. Tickets £5-40. Both theaters have £5 standing room tickets; student and under 25 half-price same-day tickets in advance for M-W performances and on the day of the show otherwise. Standby tickets are also available; low season £12, high season £15. Tours: ☎01789 403 405. Daily 5:30pm, 11am on matinee performance days and also M-Sa 1:30pm and Su noon, 1, 2, 3pm. £4, concessions £3.)*

TRANSPORTATION. **Thames Trains** serve Stratford's rail station from **Paddington.** *(Station Rd., off Alcester Rd. ☎084 5748 4950. 2¼hr., 5 per day, return £34.)* **National Express buses** stop at Riverside Car Park, off Bridgeway Rd. near the Leisure Centre; buy tickets at the tourist centre. *(☎087 0580 8080. 3hr., 3 per day, £13.50.)*

ORIENTATION AND PRACTICAL INFORMATION. To get to the **Tourist Information Centre** from the train station, turn left onto Alcester Rd., which becomes Greenhill St., Wood St., Bridge St., and finally Bridgefoot. *(☎017 8929 3127. Maps, guidebooks, tickets, and accommodations list. Books rooms for £3 plus 10% deposit. Open Apr.-Oct. M-Sa 9am-5:30pm, Su 10:30am-4:30pm; Nov.-Mar. M-Sa 9am-5pm.)* There is another **branch** in the Civic Hall. *(14 Rother St. ☎017 8929 9866. Same hours as above.)*

ACCOMMODATIONS AND FOOD. Be sure to make reservations well ahead in summer. **B&Bs** in the £15-26 range line Grove Rd., Evesham Pl., and Evesham Rd.; if that fails, try Shipston Rd. and Banbury Rd. across the river. **YHA Stratford** ❶ is 2 mi. from town, but makes up with attractive grounds, a 200-year-old building, and friendly staff. *(Hemmingford House, Wellesbourne Rd., Alveston. Follow the B4086 road for 35min., or take the hourly bus #X18 from Bridge St., return £1.80. ☎017 8929 7093. Midnight lockout. Breakfast included. Dorms £17, under 18 £12.30.)* For more privacy, **Carlton Guest House** ❷ offers spacious rooms and spectacular service at a great price. *(22 Evesham Pl. ☎017 8929 3548. Singles £20-26; doubles £40-52.)* **Melita Hotel** ❸ is an upscale B&B with a gorgeous garden. *(37 Shipston Rd. ☎017 8929 2432. Singles £39; doubles £72.)*

Baguette stores and bakeries are scattered throughout the town center, while a **Somerfield** supermarket is located in Town Square. *(☎2017 8992 604. Open M-W 8am-7pm, Th-Sa 8am-8pm, Su 10am-4pm.)* The first and third Saturdays of every month, the river Avon's banks welcome a **farmer's market**. For a more substantial meal, try **The Oppo** ❸. Receiving raves from locals, this classy restaurant serves platters of lasagne (£9) and lamb cutlets (£13.50). *(Open M-Sa noon-2pm and 5-10pm, Su noon-2pm and 6-9pm. MC/V.)*

MONTY

INSIDE

Alternatives to Tourism

Let's Go believes that the connection between travelers and their destinations is an important one. We've watched the growth of the 'ignorant tourist' stereotype with dismay, knowing that many travelers care passionately about the communities and environments they explore—but also knowing that even conscientious tourists can inadvertently damage natural wonders and harm cultural environments. With this "Alternatives to Tourism" chapter, *Let's Go* hopes to promote a better understanding of London and enhance your experience there.

There several different options for those who seek to participate in Alternatives to Tourism. Opportunities for **volunteering** abound, both with local and international organizations. **Studying** can also be instructive, either in the form of direct enrollment in a local university or an independent research project. **Working** is a way to both immerse yourself in the local culture and finance your travels.

Eight percent of London's GDP is produced by tourist dollars, along with eight percent of employment. One-fourth of the people using the Tube in central London are tourists, a whopping 20% of these tourists coming from the US. Since the economic downturn of 2001, London has seen some strain on its citizen's pockets and patience. During the past 3 years, London has undergone strikes by British Airways workers, London Underground and Rail Drivers, and even British firefighters. At the same time, the city endeavors for reforms in order to improve the standard of living. Tony Blair's Labour government along with local councils are currently in the process of improving the state of London's schools, particularly in the poorer boroughs of Islington, Hackney, Southwark, and Lambeth. The debate, however, continues as to whether improvement could best be achieved through local fundraising or nationalization. Central London's infamously congested roads are headed for a change with London's £5 congestion charges of for driving at certain hours through the city.

As the political center of the country, London is the place for movers and shakers to make an impact on representatives in Westminster. For those interested in **political activism** we provide the contact information for several influential parties in Parliament; from the well-known Labour and Conservative parties, to the nationalist parties of Ireland, Scotland, and Wales, to the non-affiliated Trade Justice movement. Contact the party offices to inquire how you can become involved in London campaigns. For those interested in **environmental issues,** we list organizations at the forefront of current concerns, including the GM food debate, the protection of endangered species, conservation legislation ratified through the European Union, urban pollution, and waste management. Finally, we list organizations dedicated to **community assistance** and working for the London poor. As poverty is concentrated most in those areas with high populations of West African refugees, South Asians, and Eastern Europeans, it is a concern closely intertwined with continuing high rates of immigration. However, altruists can choose organizations which focus on a variety of different community segments, including recent immigrants and homeless youth. Later in this section, we recommend ways to find organizations that best suit your interests, whether you're looking to pitch in for a day or a year.

Studying at a college or in a language program is another way to integrate yourself into the London scene. Many travelers also structure their trips by the **work** they can do along the way—either odd jobs as they go, or full-time stints in cities where they plan to stay for some time. **Internships, teaching,** and **au pair** opportunities await the persistent. With the help of temp agencies, a job in the service or clerical sector is yours for the taking, provided you have the right visa documentation. For more on volunteering, studying, and working in London and beyond, consult Let's Go's alternatives to tourism website, **www.beyondtourism.com.**

Before handing your money over to any volunteer or study abroad program, make sure you know exactly what you're getting into. It's a good idea to get the names of **previous participants** and ask them about their experience, as some programs sound much better on paper than in reality. The **questions** below are a good place to start:

- -Will you be the only person in the program? If not, what are the other participants like? How old are they? How much will you be expected to interact with them?
- -Is room and board included? If so, what is the arrangement? Will you be expected to share a room? A bathroom? What are the meals like? Do they fit any dietary restrictions?
- -Is transportation included? Are there any additional expenses?
- -How much free time will you have? Will you be able to travel around the island?
- -What kind of safety network is set up? Will you still be covered by your home insurance? Does the program have an emergency plan?

VOLUNTEERING

Volunteering can be one of the most fulfilling experiences in life, especially when combined with the thrill of travel. London offers a rich array of options, from political campaigning to working on urban issues. Volunteer jobs are fairly easy to secure. However, if you receive room and board in exchange for your labor, you are "employed" and must get a **work visa.**

Most people who volunteer in London do so on a short-term basis, at organizations that make use of drop-in or once-a-week volunteers. There are two main types of organizations—religious and non-sectarian—although there are rarely restrictions on participation for either. A good place to begin your search for openings in London is on **www.volunteerabroad.com,** which allows you to search specifically within the city. Another useful engine for broadening your search is **www.idealist.org.**

ENVIRONMENTALISM

Wary of GM (Genetically Modified) food? Advocates for GM praise their potential for lowering costs, improving the quality and size of produce, and aiding farmers by reducing the need for pesticides. Environmental groups, on the other hand, raise concerns over the long-term consequences of GM foods, calling for more extensive research. The organizations listed below participate in a variety of environmental issues including and beyond the GM debate.

British Trust for Conservation Volunteers (BTCV), c/o 80 York Way, King Cross, London, N1 9AG (☎8808 8865; www.btcv.org). The largest volunteer organization in Britain, BTCV also sponsors community and school programs, training for employment, as well as regular sessions of conservation activities through Green Gym.

Friends of the Earth, 26-28 Underwood St., London, N1 7JQ (☎7490 1555; www.foe.co.uk). Circulates news events, networks with local groups. Also works on the water problem and on creative ideas for sustainable development.

Greenpeace UK, Canonbury Villas, London, N1 2PN (☎7865 8100; www.greenpeace.uk). Active in a wide range of regional campaigns; contact the London central office for calendar and volunteer openings.

Sustain, 94 White Lion St., London, N1 9PF (☎7837 1228; www.sustainweb.org). Launched in 1999 as a merger of the National Food Alliance, and the Sustainable Agriculture Food and Environment (SAFE) Alliance, Sustain relies on volunteers to maintain a network of over 100 organizations committed to safe food production.

POLITICAL ACTIVISM

For the politically-minded, London is the ideal place to participate in a party campaign. Your best bet is to contact the party directly to inquire what kind of tasks are needed. Often volunteers are recruited for clerical support, fundraising, and publicity. Usually no fee is required to participate, though you may be solicited to contribute to "the cause." *Let's Go* does not endorse the views of any of these parties, though we do have a soft spot for the Monster Raving Loony Party.

The Labour Party, 16 Old Queen St., London, SW1H 9HP (☎7490 4904; www.londonlabor.org.uk). Currently Her Majesty's government, Labour is led by Prime Minister Tony Blair. Originally founded by the Labour Movement, the now center-left party continues to advocate for increased social services, though recently it has been criticized by Leftist groups for its moderate stance.

The Conservative Party, 32 Smith Sq., London, SW1P 3HH (☎7984 8162; www.conservative-party.org.uk). The oldest political party in the world, the Tories hold sway over the moderate right, having locked horns with Labour over social and fiscal spending for a decade.

Liberal Democrats, 4 Cowley St., London, SW1P 3NB (☎7227 1335; www.libdems.org.uk). Britain's third-largest political party, the center-left Liberal Democrats advocate changing the voting system for a "fairer distribution of power" and has aggressively lobbied for improved public transportation in London.

Communist Party of Britain, 94 Camden Rd., London, NW1 9EA (☎7428 9300; www.communist-party.org.uk). Advocating unabashed socialism for the past 83 years, the Communist Party remains vehemently opposed to the so-called right-wing tactics of the Labour Party.

The Green Party of England and Wales, 1a Waterlow Rd., London, N19 5NJ (☎7272 4474; www.greenparty.org.uk). Aiming for a "just and sustainable society," this ecologically-minded, leftist party advises volunteers to mail an application to the Green Party Volunteer Manager.

UK Independence Party, Bridgeman House, 54 Broadwick St., London W1F 7AH (☎/fax 7434 4559; mail@ukip.org). If the EU doesn't do it for you, join the party that seeks UK's withdrawal from the European Union.

Scottish National Party Headquarters, 107 McDonald Rd., Edinburgh EH7 4NW, Scotland (☎131 525 8900; www.snp.org.uk). Like most nationalist parties, the SNPH endorses decentralized government and increased power in local assemblies.

Plaid Cymru, (Westminster Office) 4/5 Norman Shaw Bank, Victoria Embankment, London, SW1A 2JF (☎029 2064 6000; post@plaidcymru.org). Plaid Cymru promotes the revival of the Welsh language, along with a platform of "decentralist socialism." Head office is located in (surprise!) Wales at Ty Gwynfor, 18 Park Grove, Cardiff, CF10 3BN, Wales.

Trade Justice Movement, (secretariat ☎7404 0530; www.tradejusticemovement.org.uk). An umbrella organization for numerous British, Scottish, and Welsh charity organizations dedicated to fighting world poverty and promoting fair trade. Political campaigns often address the UK's position in the WTO. In June 2003, Radiohead demonstrated their support by encouraging UK MPs to join the TJM lobby marathon. TJM provides links to member organizations, including Save the Children, Action Aid, and the World Development Movement. Volunteer positions, when available, are usually at the Fairtrade Foundation offices in central London.

Monster Raving Loony Party, The Dog & Partridge, 105 Reading Road, Yateley, Hampshire, GU46 7LR, (☎012 5287 8382; www.omrlp.com). Questions why there is only one female Smurf, pressures the Olympics to include the Egg and Spoon Race and promotes the Annual Witch-ducking Championships.

URBAN ISSUES

Large economic discrepancies exist within London. Listed below are some organizations that work on urban issues like youth homelessness in London. A good website to search for volunteering opportunities in London is **www.do-it.org.uk.**

Alone in London, 188 Kings Cross Rd., London WC1X 9DE (☎7278 4224 or 7841 3719 for volunteering; www.als.org.uk). Committed to the young homeless and specializing in family support, ALS volunteer posts are 3-6 months and require an application.

Church on Poverty, Central Buildings, Oldham St., Manchester M1 1JT (☎016 1236 9321; www.church-poverty.org.uk). A national Christian social justice charity based in Manchester, CAP operates throughout the UK with churches and directly with those in poverty. Also maintains a Parliamentary Office in Westminster.

Community Service Volunteers (CSV), Head Office, 237 Pentonville Rd., London N1 9NJ (☎7278 6601; www.csv.org.uk). Offers both full and part-time volunteer positions, including teaching citizenship courses, broadcasting, and support for troubled youth and homeless. Several local offices in London; check the website. CSV cannot guarantee placement but can help in obtaining visas (only after placement). Provides £27.00 allowance plus free room and board. No fee.

Concordia International Volunteer Projects, Heversham House, 20-22 Boundary Rd., Hove, BN3 4ET, England (☎012 7342 2218; www.concordia-iye.org.uk). A small, not-for-profit charity, Concordia sponsors volunteer projects chiefly for residents of the UK, worldwide and locally. Volunteers pay subscription fee £6-10, project fee £75-80.

Oxfam, UK Poverty Programme, Central office, 274 Banbury Rd., Oxford OX2 7DZ (☎0870 333 2700; www.oxfam.co.uk). The UK's largest secular organization supporting the poor; contact Oxfam for your nearest regional office. Download an application online. No fee.

The Salvation Army UK Headquarters, 101 Newington Causeway, London SE1 6BN (☎0845 634 0101 or 7367 4500; www.salvationarmy.org.uk). A Christian organization dedicated to providing emergency and social services, including youth programs and family tracing. Open M-F 8:15am-4:30pm.

STUDYING

Study abroad programs in London range from basic language and culture courses to college-level classes. In order to choose a program that best fits your needs, research all you can before making your decision—ascertain costs and duration, inquire what kinds of students participate in the program and if accommodation is provided. A good resource for finding programs that cater to your particular interests is **www.studyabroad.com,** which has links to various semester abroad programs based on a variety of critera, including desired location and focus of study. Other useful links include **www.studyabroaddirectory.com** and **www.internationalstudent.com.**

STUDENT VISAS

Non-EU nationals intending to study in the UK generally must be enrolled by a qualifying British educational institution before applying for student status. **Non-visa nationals** (foreigners who do not require visas to enter the UK as visitors) are permitted to enter the country as tourists and then apply for student status once they have been admitted to a course of study. If they have already been accepted on a course, they may apply for student status when entering the UK. To do this, at the port of entry you will need to show a letter of admittance from the school, university, or college and proof of adequate financial support to cover tuition and maintenance. **Visa nationals** are required to obtain a student visa from their local British Consulate before entering the country; to do so, they must provide proof of admittance to a course of study and financial support.

WORKING ON A STUDENT VISA. Non-EU students may work up to 20hr. per week during term-time, and full-time in vacation. However, longer hours may be authorized if deemed a necessary part of the course of study (e.g., as part of medical school training). EU citizens enjoy the same working rights as British citizens.

UNIVERSITIES

With dozens of institutions, from the sprawling colleges of the University of London to the vast collections of the British Library, you can study almost any subject at any level in London. It's not surprising that every year hundreds of international students choose to make London their academic home-away-from-home. Even if you didn't come to London to study, taking evening courses—whether in medieval architecture or jazz dance—can be a great way to broaden your horizons and meet similarly minded people. For a comprehensive list of part-time and evening classes, the annual **Floodlight** directory lists over 40,000 courses in Greater London (www.floodlight.co.uk, also available from news agents). The following list of organizations can help place students in university programs abroad, or have their own branch in London.

AMERICAN PROGRAMS

American Institute for Foreign Study, College Division, River Plaza, 9 West Broad St., Stamford, CT 06902, USA (☎800-727-2437, ext. 5163; www.aifsabroad.com). Organizes programs for high school and college study in British and Irish universities.

Arcadia University for Education Abroad, 450 S. Easton Rd., Glenside, PA 19038, USA (☎866-927-2234; www.arcadia.edu/cea). Operates programs both within London and throughout Britain and Ireland. Costs range from $2200 (summer) to $29,000 (full-year).

Association of Commonwealth Universities (ACU), John Foster House, 36 Gordon Sq., London WC1H OPF (☎7380 6700; www.acu.ac.uk). Publishes information about Commonwealth universities, including the UK and Canada.

Center for Cultural Interchange, 17 North Second Avenue, St. Charles, IL 60174, USA (☎888-227-6231; www.cci-exchange.com). High school study abroad program, independent homestay, internship program.

Central College Abroad, Office of International Education, 812 University, Pella, IA, 50219, USA (☎800-831-3629 or 641-628-5284; www.central.edu/abroad). Offers internships, as well as summer, semester, and year-long programs in London and throughout Britain. US$25 application fee.

Council on International Educational Exchange (CIEE), 7 Custom House St., 3rd Floor, Portland, ME 01401, USA (☎800-407-8839; www.ciee.org/study). Sponsors work, volunteer, academic, and internship programs in Britain and Ireland.

International Association for the Exchange of Students for Technical Experience (IAESTE), 10400 Little Patuxent Pkwy. Suite 250, Columbia, MD 21044-3519, USA (☎410-997-2200; www.aipt.org). 8- to 12-week programs in London and throughout Britain and Ireland for college students who have 2 yrs. of technical study. US$25 application fee.

Institute for the International Education of Students (IES), 33 N. LaSalle St., 15th fl., Chicago, IL 60602, USA (☎800-995-2300; www.IESabroad.org). Year-long, semester, and summer programs in London for college students. Internships offered. Scholarships available. US$50 application fee.

School for International Training, College Semester Abroad, Admissions, Kipling Rd., P.O. Box 676, Brattleboro, VT 05302, USA (☎800-257-7751 or 802-257-7751; www.sit.edu). Semester- and year-long programs in London run US$10,600-13,700. Also runs the **Experiment in International Living** (☎800-345-2929; www.usexperiment.org), 3- to 5-week summer programs that offer high-school students cross-cultural homestays, community service opportunities, ecological adventure, and language training in London. US$1900-5000.

BUNAC
has the answer

Longing to travel?
Don't let a limited budget stop you.

BUNAC's work/travel programs enable US students and non-students to experience other cultures while giving you the freedom to choose your own way.

BRITAIN ✈ IRELAND ✈ CANADA
AUSTRALIA ✈ NEW ZEALAND ✈ SOUTH AFRICA

For further information or to request a brochure and application, contact:
BUNAC USA, PO Box 430, Southbury CT 06488

BUNAC™
WORKING ADVENTURES WORLDWIDE

Tel: 1-800-GO-BUNAC www.bunac.org

PROGRAMS IN LONDON

Combined, the University of London and the London Institute encompass the vast majority of London's universities and colleges, though there are also numerous independent specialist institutions. Many offer **special programs** for international students on exchange visits, semesters abroad, and **summer schools.**

Enrolling for a **degree course** can present problems to those raised in a different system. UK universities will want to see evidence that you have attained the same educational standard as British 18-year-olds, either by passing the British A-level exams or a recognized equivalent, such as the International Baccalaureate; EU credentials are generally admissible. Americans may have problems, since SAT scores and high-school diplomas are not normally accepted; frequently, students must have completed a year of college in the US before being considered equivalent to European high-school graduates. The **British Council** (see p. 327) can often arrange for people to take British exams in their home countries.

Fees for degree programs for non-EU students depend on the subject and school, from around £8500 per year for humanities to £18,000 for medicine; EU residents pay the same as UK students, currently £1150 per year for all subjects. In addition you need £5000-7000 per year for accommodation and living expenses.

EducationUK, (www.educationuk.org), a slick website run by the British Council (see below) explaining the British education system.

London School of Economics, The Admissions Officer, London School of Economics, P.O. Box 13401, Houghton St., London WC2A 2AS (☎020 7955 7124; www.lse.ac.uk). Year- long courses for international students (about £10,000).

The London Institute, 65 Davies St., London W1K 5DA (☎7514 6000; www.linst.ac.uk). 5 of London's best-known art and design schools, including Central St. Martins College, Chelsea College of Art, and the London College of Fashion.

Universities and Colleges Admissions Services (UCAS), P.O. Box 28, Cheltenham, Gloucestershire, GL52 3ZA (☎01242 227 788; www.ucas.ac.uk). The centralized admissions service for all undergraduate degree courses in the UK. Also provides impartial information to international students on the application process.

University College London, Gower St., London WC1E 6BT (☎7679 7765; www.ucl.ac.uk) The biggest of U of L's schools (and one of the UK's top universities), with a complete academic curriculum. Special programs are offered for international affiliate students on semester or 1yr. leaves from their home universities; affiliates must normally have completed 2yr. of university at time of admission to UCL.

The University of London, (www.lon.ac.uk) is an umbrella organization uniting the vast majority of London's academic institutions, with 17 constituent universities and colleges.

University of Westminster, International Education Office, 16 Little Tichfield St., London W1W 7UW (☎0207 911 5769; www.wmin.ac.uk/international). Offers a range of semester (£3300) and full-year (£6600) programs of study in schools of biosciences, integrated health, computer science, digital technology,- and design.

THE BRITISH COUNCIL

The British Council is the arm of the government charged with promoting education opportunities in Britain, among other responsibilities. Its offices are an invaluable source of information for those intending to study in Britain at a secondary school or university level, or for those enrolling in language classes in Britain. They also offer the opportunity to take British exams for university admission. For branches in countries not listed here, call the London office or check www.britishcouncil.org.

London: 10 Spring Gdns., London SW1A 2BN (☎7389 4383, inquiries 0161 957 7755; general.enquiries@britcoun.org).

Australia: P.O. Box 88, Edgecliff NSW 2027 (☎016 301 204; www.bc.org.au).

Canada: 80 Elgin St., Ottawa, Ontario K1P 5K7 (☎613-237-1530; www.ca.britishcouncil.org).

Ireland: Newmount House, 22/24 Lower Mount St., Dublin 2 (☎01 676 4088 or 01 676 6943; www.britishcouncil.org/ireland).

New Zealand: 44 Hill St., P.O. Box 1812, Wellington 6001 and 151 Queen St., Private Bag 92014, Auckland 1001 (both ☎04 472 6049; www.britishcouncil.org.nz).

United States: British Embassy, 3100 Massachusetts Ave. N.W., Washington, D.C. 20008 (☎800-488-2235 or 202-588-6500; www.britishcouncil-usa.org).

LANGUAGE SCHOOLS

Unlike American universities, language schools are frequently independently run organizations or divisions of foreign universities that rarely offer college credit. Language schools are a good alternative to university study if you desire a deeper focus on a new language or a slightly less-rigorous courseload. **Eurocentres** offer language programs for beginning to advanced students with homestays in London, Brighton, Cambridge, and Oxford (☎8318 5633).

SHORT VOCATIONAL PROGRAMS

Many of London's elite **art, music,** and **drama** academies supplement their income by offering part-time and summer courses to motivated amateurs. Typically there are no admissions requirements (though some courses fill up quickly); the flipside is that you will rarely receive any recognition other than a certificate of attendance for the work you put in. Always check whether you'll be taught by the same master artists who teach the colleges' regular offerings. Numerous private **vocational schools** also run short courses that are wildly popular with an international crowd.

Central St. Martins College of Art and Design, Southampton Row, London WC1B 4AP (☎7514 7015; www.csm.linst.ac.uk). Dozens of evening courses throughout the year as well as a comprehensive summer program covering all aspects of fine art, graphic design, fashion, and film. £150-300 per week.

Courtauld Institute, Somerset House, Strand, London WC2R ORN (☎7848 2413; www.courtauld.ac.uk). 12 week-long summer courses in art history. Courses include gallery visits, focusing on the Courtauld's own impressive collections. Also offers a year-long Master's program in Art History and Art Restoration.

London School of Journalism, 22 Upbrook Mews, London W2 3HG (☎7706 3790; www.lsj.org). 3-month full-time and 6-month part-time post-graduate diploma courses (from £2750) and a 4-week summer school (£1295). All courses are recognized by the National Union of Journalists, entitling students to NUJ membership.

Royal Academy of the Dramatic Arts (RADA), 62-64 Gower St., London WC1E 6ED (☎7636 7076; www.rada.org). The alma mater of Ralph Fiennes, Kenneth Branagh, and Anthony Hopkins offers 4- and 8-week summer courses in acting, set design, and scriptwriting. Applicants must be at least 18; no experience required. Around £2250 per 4 weeks.

Slade School of Fine Art, part of University College London, Gower St., London WC1 E6BT (☎7679 7772; www.ucl.ac.uk/slade). A range of general and specialized art courses over the summer, 1-10 weeks. The 2-month Alternative Foundation course offers a complete introduction to drawing, painting, sculpting, and printing (£2500).

Vidal Sassoon Academy, 56-59 Davies Mews, London W1Y 1AS (☎7318 5202). 8-month diploma course for beginners £10,750; shorter advanced courses around £1000.

COURSES IN ARCHAEOLOGY

Every quest for the Holy Grail should begin with a trustworthy guide; that guide should be *Current Archaeology* (www.archaeology.co.uk), a reliable publication on current and upcoming excursions and innovations in the UK.

Last year's winner, Eleanor Glass, spent a summer volunteering with children on an island off the Yucatan Peninsula. Read the rest of her story and find your own once-in-a-lifetime experience at **www.beyondtourism.com!**

"... I was discovering elements of life in Mexico that I had never even dreamt of. I regularly had meals at my students' houses, as their fisherman fathers would instruct them to invite the nice gringa to lunch after a lucky day's catch. Downtown, tourists wandered the streets and spent too much on cheap necklaces, while I played with a friend's baby niece, or took my new kitten to the local vet for her shots, or picked up tortillas at the tortilleria, or vegetables in the mercado. ... I was lucky that I found a great place to volunteer and a community to adopt me. ... Just being there, listening to stories, hearing the young men talk of cousins who had crossed the border, I know I went beyond tourism." - Eleanor Glass, 2004

LG
LET'S GO

Birkbeck College, Faculty of Continuing Education, 26 Russell Sq., London, WC1B 5DQ (☎7631 6627; www.bbk.ac.uk/fce). Offers courses in field archaeology and Egyptology; day and weekend schools and surveying courses. Be sure to check out their annual urban training excavation during June or July (£155 per week).

Bromley & West Kent Archaeological Group, 5 Harvest Bank Rd., West Wickham, Kent, BR4 9DL (☎/fax 8462 4737). Opportunities for volunteers to participate in weekend excavations and as guides at the Crofton Roman Villa in Orpington. Open to the public Apr.-Oct.

Bloomsbury Summer School or **Bloomsbury Academy,** University College London, Gower St., London WC1E 6BT (☎7679 3622; www.egyptology-uk.com/bloomsbury). Offers intensive summer courses on Eygptology.

WORKING

Casual work, such as bartending, baby-sitting, and waiting tables is the easiest to find, though it remains poorly paid. Working without a work visa or permit is unlawful, though unscrupulous employers may take on illegal workers. Those who gain illegal employment find that their right of redress against any abuses or malpractice by their employer is severely limited. If you work legally, you will enjoy the protection of UK labor laws. You'll pay 23% tax and 10% National Insurance on all but the lowest-paid jobs.

YOUR RIGHTS. The **minimum wage** varies with age and length of employment. Ages 18 to 21 and those receiving accredited training within six months of starting a new job may not be paid less than £3.60 per hr.; otherwise the rate is £4.20. **Full-time workers** may not be forced to work over 48hr. per week, 13hr. per day, or six days per week. They are also entitled to four weeks paid vacation per year. **Part-time workers** are now entitled to many of the benefits an employer accords full-time employees, including paid vacation on a pro-rated basis. For more information, including details of **maternity leave** and **anti-discrimination laws,** the **Tailored Interactive Guide on Employment Rights** (TIGER; www.tiger.gov.uk) offers information on employment law in the UK.

COMMONWEALTH CITIZENS. Commonwealth citizens ages 17-27 are eligible for a **working holidaymaker visa,** allowing them to stay and work in the UK for up to two years provided that employment is "incidental to a holiday." Essentially, this means that no more than half your stay can be spent in full-time work. (See FCO form INF 5 for details.) Those aged 17 and up who have at least one **UK-born grandparent** (including Ireland if born before March 31, 1922) are eligible for a **UK Ancestry Visa,** which gives the right to reside and work in the UK for an initial period of four years. (see FCO form INF 7 for details.) Canadian citizens should also refer to the **Student Work Abroad Programme** (SWAP; www.swap.ca), which has 40 offices in Canada administered by the Canadian Universities Travel Service. This program is similar to the BUNAC program available to US citizens (see below).

US STUDENTS. In general, US citizens are required to have a work permit (see below) to work in the UK. However, American citizens who are full-time students and are over 18 can apply for a special permit from the **British Universities North America Club (BUNAC),** which allows them to work for **up to six months.** Contact BUNAC at: P.O. Box 430, Southbury, CT 06488 (US ☎203-264-0901, UK 020 7251 3472; www.bunac.org.uk). BUNAC also offers limited assistance in finding housing and employment and organizes regular social events. You will need to enter the UK within one semester of graduation and have at least US$1000 on entry. BUNAC also has a very helpful bulletin board in their London office, 16 Bowling Green Ln. (☎7251 3472), with housing and job postings.

WORK PERMITS & WORK VISAS. If you do not fall into one of the above categories, you will need a **work permit** in order to work in the UK. If you require a visa to travel to the UK, you will also need a **work visa.** You must already have a job set up in the UK before obtaining a work permit, which can only be applied for through your employer. For further information, consult www.workpermits.gov.uk.

VISA INFORMATION

The **Foreign and Commonwealth Office's (FCO)** Joint Entry Clearance Unit (JECU; www.ukvisas.gov.uk) has info on visa and work permit requirements and downloadable application forms. Information for visitors already in the UK is also available from the **Home Office Immigration and Nationality Directorate** (www.ind.homeoffice.gov.uk). The **Immigration Advisory Service,** County House, 190 Great Dover St., London SE1 4YB (☎7357 6917; www.iasuk.org), is an independent charity providing free advice and assistance to UK visa applicants.

LONG-TERM WORK

If you're planning on spending a substantial amount of time (more than three months) working in London, search for a job well in advance. Currently teachers and specialists in the medical field, such as nurses, doctors and paramedics are in particularly high demand. For those outside the UK, a good place to begin your search online is on **www.tntmagazine.com/uk/jobs.**

INTERNSHIPS

Finding an internship in London is not difficult—finding a paid one is. If you are interested in interning, use college career offices and the Internet to investigate options. London's status as a financial hub means that there are hundreds of overpaid summer positions in banks and consultancies, but competition is fierce: applications must normally be completed by February for work starting in June. There is a smaller number of (normally unpaid) internship positions in media and publishing companies, though duties will typically be limited to menial tasks. Be wary of advertisements or companies abroad that claim the ability to get you a job for a fee.

Council Exchanges, 52 Poland St., London W1F 7AB, UK (☎7478 2000, US 888-268-6245; www.councilexchanges.org), charges a US$300-475 fee for arranging short-term working authorizations (generally valid for 3-6 months) and provides extensive information on different job opportunities in London.

IAESTE–US, 10400 Little Patuxent Pkwy., Ste. 250L, Columbia, MD 21044, USA (☎410-997-3068; www.aipt.org/iaeste.html). Arranges internships, especially in technical fields.

interExchange, 161 Sixth Ave., New York, NY 10013, USA (☎212-924-0446; www.interexchange.org). US students only. Fees for unpaid internships US$1150; for placements in hotel training US$700 extra. Fees include BUNAC Blue Card work permit (see p. 330).

International Exchange Programs (IEP), 196 Albert Rd., South Melbourne, Victoria 3205, Australia (☎03 9690 5890), and P.O. Box 1786, Shortland St., Auckland, New Zealand (☎09 366 6255; www.iepnz.co.nz). Helps Aussies and Kiwis on working holidaymaker visas (see p. 330) find employment, lodging, and friends. AU$300/NZ$340 fee.

Intern Exchange International (IEI), 2606 Bridgewood Circle, Boca Raton Florida 33434, USA (☎561 477 2434; www.internexchange.com). This co-educational program accepts high school students (aged 16-18 years) from US and Canada for various career internships in business, the professions, and the arts; in London for a summer. Combined with an exploration of the sights and culture of England. Application required, cost US$ 5795 plus airfare (see **London a la mode**, p. 333)

Tate, 7 Hanover Sq., London W1S 1HQ (☎7408 0424; www.tate.co.uk), arranges secretarial placements for foreigners in London.

Internships International, 1612 Oberlin Rd. # 5, Raleigh, NC 27608, USA (January- May) (☎919 832 1575; www.internshipsinternational.org). Unpaid internships in various fields and locations, including London. Fee US$1100.

TEACHING

Teaching jobs abroad are rarely well-paid. Volunteering as a teacher in lieu of getting paid is also a popular option; teachers often get some sort of a daily stipend to help with living expenses. In almost all cases, you must have at least a bachelor's degree to be a full-fledged teacher, although college undergraduates can often get summer positions teaching or tutoring. The British school system is comprised of state (public, government-funded), "public" (independent, privately funded), and international (often for children of expatriates in the UK) schools, as well as universities. Applications to teach at state schools must be made through the local government; independent and international schools must be applied to individually. University positions are typically only available through fellowship or exchange programs. Placement agencies are often a good way to find teaching jobs in Britain, although vacancies are also listed in major newspapers. An alternative is to make contacts directly with schools or just to try your luck once you get there. If you are going to try the latter, the best time of the year is several weeks before the start of the school year. The following organizations may help in your search.

Independent Schools Information Service, 56 Buckingham Gate, London SW1E 6AG (☎7630 8793; www.iscis.uk.net). A list of British independent schools and further information on teaching opportunities.

International Schools Services (ISS), 15 Roszel Rd., Box 5910, Princeton, NJ 08543-5910, USA (☎609-452-0990; www.iss.edu). Candidates should have experience teaching or with international affairs. 2yr. commitment expected.

European Council of International Schools, 21B Lavant St., Petersfield, Hampshire GU32 3EL (☎0730 268 244; www.ecis.org). Contact details for British international schools, as well as placement opportunities.

AU PAIR WORK

Au pairs are typically women, ages 18-27, who work as live-in nannies, caring for children and doing light housework in exchange for room, board, and a small spending allowance or stipend (around £40-70 per week). Typically they work 25-40hr. per week with one or two nights off. Citizens of certain countries may not be eligible for au-pair work in the UK, but may find placement instead as a **Mother's Helper.** Mother's helpers work 40-50 hours per week caring for children under the supervision of a parent. They are also responsible for light housework and a few nights of babysitting. People with childcare qualifications can find much more lucrative work as **live-in nannies,** making up to £250 per week in addition to food and lodging. Most former au pairs speak favorably of their experience, and of how it allowed them to get to know the country without the high expenses of traveling. Drawbacks include long hours on-duty and the somewhat mediocre pay. Much of the au pair experience really does depend on the family you're placed with. The agencies below are a good starting point for looking for employment as an au pair.

Au Pair Homestay, World Learning, Inc., 1015 15th St. NW, Suite 750, Washington, DC 20005, USA (☎800-287-2477). Covers Britain and Ireland.

Au Pair in Europe, P.O. Box 68056, Blakely Postal Outlet, Hamilton, Ontario, Canada L8M 3M7 (☎905-545-6305; www.princeent.com). Covers Britain and Ireland.

Childcare International, Ltd., Trafalgar House, Grenville Pl., London NW7 3SA (☎8906 3116; www.childint.co.uk). Arranges childcare placements for Commonwealth and European applicants.

InterExchange, 161 Sixth Ave., New York, NY 10013, USA (☎212-924-0446; www.interexchange.org).

SHORT-TERM WORK

A good place for foreigners to get their start is by checking newspapers such as **The Guardian, The Times,** and **The Evening Standard.** Other good (and free!) employment-specific publications include **TNT Magazine UK,** which appears every Monday, and **Metro,** found in blue bins at Tube stations. The jobs published may vary by day: Secretarial on Mondays, Financing on Tuesdays, etc. Most often, these short-term jobs are found by word of mouth, or simply by talking to the owner of a hostel or restaurant. Many places, due to the high turnover in the tourism industry, are eager for help, even if temporary.

HOTEL/CATERING. There's no shortage of jobs in London waiting tables, tending bars, or filling less glamorous behind-the-scenes roles in kitchen and cleaning positions. What these all have in common is that they are poorly paid (typically minimum wage, as little as £3.60 per hr., or even less for illegal employees) with anti-social hours. And don't expect to boost that much with tips: bartenders are not tipped in the UK, and many restaurants have "service included" in their prices—money which may or may not find its way into your pay. Another popular option is to work several hours a day at a **hostel** in exchange for free or discounted room and/or board. You can also begin your search with the **Blue Speed Employment Agency,** which specializes in the hotel and leisure industries. (☎/fax 084 564 433 04; www.bluespeed.co.uk).

SECRETARIAL WORK. If you can type like a demon, then **temping** can be a good way to pay the bills. Temps are temporary secretaries on short-term placements (from as little as one day to a few weeks); you'll need to register with a temping agency who'll match available positions to your skills.

LONDON A LA MODE

Cheers. It's a single word meaning hello, thank you, and have a nice day. I had imagined the word's versatility to be indicative of London's charm—just as this one word encompasses many greetings, I saw London as encapsulating many ages and cultures. I remember when the word first slipped out of my mouth without effort—I felt like a true Londoner.

When I was 17, I interned for a summer in the marketing department of Mulberry, Ltd., a fashion company headquartered in London. I was employed through a program that offers interning opportunities in different professional industries for America high school students. Working under a sales director at Mulberry, I lived for a month as a member of London's fashion world. I quickly adapted to my new work environment, noticing that on the third day a friendly "cheers" spilled out of my mouth as I left the office.

That night over dinner with American friends I shared my inadvertent slip into the London vernacular. However, on our walk home, I overheard a man on the street mumbling, "Russell Square—backpacker central." The area that we considered to be typical of the rest of the city turned out to be a mere glimpse of what London had to offer. There was more to the city's culture than I first thought; to experience the real London I would have to explore beyond the sightseeing packs of tourists. Through my work at Mulberry I caught a clear view of London—a city with much more to offer than unique expressions and tony neighborhoods.

Becoming a member of London's working citizenry during the day and touring its landmarks with American friends at night revealed to me two very different pictures of the city. While I expected to see most of London's culture on weekend trips and evening walks through famed Piccadilly Circus and Leicester Square, I could never have expected to learn so much about London through daily interactions at work. It was in the office on New Bond St. that I immersed myself in the fast-paced work culture of one of the most powerful cities in the world.

Shadowing my boss allowed me to experience the average day of a Londoner with authenticity. Assisting with fashion shows, schmoozing with buyers, and preparing sales pitches was all part of my work. While most of my friends were out after work meandering from one tourist spot to another, I was experiencing and even contributing to the evolving London fashion image. I wasn't among the throngs of tourists searching for a souvenir at Harrods; I was presenting Mulberry's newest line of accessories to the buyers charged with maintaining Harrods's posh image.

My boss's biggest project of the year was selling the season's new line to European buyers. My second and third weeks of work coincided with this biannual event. Even as a newcomer I shared in the anticipation of the arrival of the people who would determine the success of Mulberry's latest designs. Sales days began early, with buyers arriving from all around the continent, eager to see the latest fashions and choose which bags, skirts, jeans, colors, and styles would sell best in their respective countries. Amongst this international crowd saw the appreciation Londoners have for cultural diversity. Prices were easily converted from pounds to euros; cultural subtleties were understood and wittily noted.

With all the diversity present in the Mulberry offices those weeks, there emerged a feeling of European camaraderie. In the office I could mingle with French, German, Spanish, and Italian buyers. I found a deeper understanding of London culture —beyond "cheers," the Tube, and Buckingham Palace. As an intern, I viewed London as the meeting place of many societies and styles, a city where something distinctly British like the Mulberry brand could be modified to suit all of Europe. Despite Britain's traditional desire to separate herself from Europe, her capital city is soaked with European flavor.

I enjoyed the weekend trips to tourist hotspots and even flattered myself by easily picking up on the London style and way of speech. However, it was not a visit to the Tower of London or the Millennium Wheel but my work that brought me closer to London's history and future. I spent my last day in London as a tourist—taking a trip down to Kensington, then doing some last minute shopping on Oxford Street. When my walk brought me right outside my Mulberry office, however, I appreciated the time I spent at work and cherish the insights and opportunities my alternative London experience afforded me.

Russell Graney spent June of 2002 in London interning in the Marketing and Sales Department at Mulberry, Co Ltd. He is now a student at Harvard College.

UNDERGROUND
UNDERGROUND
SUBWAY
SUBWAY
HOTELS
TELEPHONE
TELEPHONE
TELEPHONE
PULL
PULL
PULL

Service Directory

ACCOMMODATION AGENCIES

Accommodation Outlet, 32 Old Compton St. (☎7287 4244; www.outlet4holidays.com). ⊖Piccadilly Circus or Leicester Sq. Organizes short and long term vacation accommodations (both shared and private) in Soho and Covent Garden for gays, lesbians, and gay-friendly travelers. Double bedrooms from £50, £65 with private bath. Studio apartments from £75 per night, 1-bedroom from £100, 2-bedroom from £120, 3-bedroom from £150. 3 nights min. Office open M-F 10am-6pm, Sa noon-5pm. Up to 30% discount for long stays. (www.outlet4homes.com).MC/V.

University of London Accommodations Office, Senate House, Room B, Malet St. (☎7862 8880; www.lon.ac.uk/accom). ⊖Russell Square. Keeps a list of summer room and apartment vacancies. Information on residence halls on website; services available only during vacations to students with valid ID. Open M, W 9:30am-5:30pm; Th 10:30am-5:30pm.

BANKS

See **Essentials,** p. 27.

BICYCLE RENTAL

London Bicycle Tour Company, 1a Gabriel's Wharf, off 56 Upper Ground (☎7928 6838; www.londonbicycle.com). ⊖Blackfriars or Waterloo. Bikes and blades £2.50 per hr. £14 for first 24hr., £7 per day thereafter. Credit-card deposit. Open Apr.-Oct. daily 10am-6pm; call ahead Nov.-Mar. AmEx/MC/V.

Scootabout, 1-3 Leeke St. (☎7833 4607). ⊖King's Cross. Moped and scooter rentals. Riders must be experienced. 21+ only; rates include insurance coverage and vary with age. 50-125cc bikes £23 per day; 2-day minimum. Credit-card deposit. Helmets occasionally available (£2); inquire when booking. MC/V.

BUDGET TRAVEL AGENCIES

Make sure any travel agencies you use are members of the Air Travel Organizer's License so that tickets will still be good if the agency goes bankrupt.

CTS Travel, 30 Rathbone Pl. (☎7290 0630; www.ctstravel.co.uk). ⊖Goodge St. Open M-F 9:30am-6pm.

Flightbookers, 177 Tottenham Crt. Rd. (☎0870 814 0000; www.ebookers.com). ⊖Warren St. Open M-F 8am-7pm, Sa 8:30am-5:30pm, Su 10:30am-4:30pm.

STA Travel (☎0870 1600 599; www.statravel.co.uk). 14 London branches; largest at 85 Shaftesbury Ave. (☎7432 7474). ⊖Piccadilly Circus. Open M-W and F 11am-7pm, Th 11am-8pm, Sa 11am-6pm. Other **branches** at 11 Goodge St.; 86 Old Brompton Rd.; 117 Euston Rd.; London School of Economics, East Building.

Travel CUTS, 295A Regent St. (☎7255 1944). ⊖Oxford Circus. Open M-W and F 9am-6pm, Th 9am-7pm, Sa 11am-4pm. Other **branch** at International Student House 209 Portland St. (☎7436 0459).

BUSES

See **Transport Information,** p. 339.

CALLING CARDS

See **Telephone Services,** p. 339.

CAR RENTAL

Foreigners over 17 may drive in the UK for up to one year if in possession of a valid driving licence (some exceptions apply).

Budget (☎087 0153 9170; www.budget.co.uk). Locations include Heathrow Airport (☎208 8991 000; fax 208 750 2525), Gatwick Airport (☎870 010 4068; fax 1293 562 613), and numerous London branches. Minimum age 25.

easyRentACar.com (www.easyrentacar.com). Internet-only rentals. 3 central London locations. Minimum age 21. From £7 per day, plus £5 preparation fee.

Europcar (☎087 0607 5000; fax 011 3242 9495; www.europcar.com). 5 London locations, including 245 Warwick Rd. ⊖Earl's Court. Minimum age 23.

CHEMISTS

Most chemists keep standard store hours (approx. M-Sa 9:30am-5:30pm); one "duty" chemist in each neighborhood will also open on Sunday, though hours may be limited. Late-night and 24hr. chemists are extremely rare; two are as follows.

Bliss, 5-6 Marble Arch (☎7723 6116). ⊖Marble Arch. Open daily 9am-midnight.

Zafash Pharmacy, 233 Old Brompton Rd. (☎7373 2798). ⊖Earl's Court. Open 24hr.

CINEMA

West End Cinemas: see **Entertainment,** p. 240.

The Empire, Leicester Sq. (☎0870 010 2030).

Odeon Leicester Sq., Leicester Sq. (☎0871 22 44 007).

CLINICS

Jefferiss Centre for Sexual Health, St. Mary's Hospital, Praed St. (☎7725 6619; www.st-marys.nhs.uk). ⊖Paddington. Open for walk-ins M-Tu 8:45am-6:15pm, W 11:45am-6:15pm, Th 8:45am-6:15pm. F 8am-1pm.

West London Center for Sexual Health, Charing Cross Hospital, Fulham Palace Rd. (☎8846 *1567).* ⊖Baron's Court or Hammersmith. NHS-run sexual and women's health clinic. By appointment only.

CONSULATES

See **Essentials,** p. 23.

CURRENCY EXCHANGE

See also **Essentials**, p. 27.

American Express (www.americanexpress.com). ☎0800 52 13 13. 30 London locations including:

- **84 Kensington High St.** (☎7795 6703). ⊖High St. Kensington. Open M-Sa 9am-5:30pm.
- **30-31 Haymarket** (☎7484 9610). ⊖Piccadilly Circus. Open M-F 9am-7pm, Sa 9am-6pm, Su 10am-5pm.
- **Terminal 3 & 4 Heathrow** (☎8897 0134). ⊖Heathrow Terminal 4 (Zone 6). Open daily 5:15am-10pm.

7 Wilton Rd (☎7630 6365). ⊖Victoria. Open M-Sa 9am-5:30pm.

56a Southampton Row (☎7837 4416). ⊖Holborn. Open M-Sa 9am-5:30pm

Thomas Cook (☎0870 750 5711; www.thomascook.com). For **traveler's check refunds,** call ☎0800 622 101.

DENTAL CARE

Dental Accident & Emergency, Guy's Hospital, 23 fl., Guy's Tower, St. Thomas St. (☎7188 7188). ⊖London Bridge. Adults treated up until patient quota (usually M-F 9-11am), children M-F 9am-noon and 2-4pm. Sa-Su and holidays use paying services at Emergency Dental Clinic (ground floor). Open Sa-Su and holidays 9am-6pm.

Dental Emergency Care Service (☎7955 2186). Refers callers to the nearest open dental surgery. Open M-F 8:45am-3:30pm.

DISABILITY RESOURCES

See **Essentials,** p. 51.

EMBASSIES

See **Essentials** p. 23.

EMERGENCY SERVICES

In an emergency, dial ☎**999** from any fixed phone or ☎**112** from a mobile to reach ambulance, police, and fire services.

GAY & LESBIAN RESOURCES

Accommodation Outlet. Finds accommodations for gays and lesbians. See p. 335.

GAY to Z (www.gaytoz.co.uk). Online and printed directory of gay-friendly resources and businesses throughout Britain.

Gay's the Word. The largest gay and lesbian bookshop in the UK, see **Shopping,** p. 255.

gingerbeer.co.uk. Lesbian web portal for London, with listings of clubs, bars, restaurants, and community resources.

London Lesbian & Gay Switchboard (☎7837 7324; www.queery.org.uk). 24hr. helpline and information resource.

HEALTH & FITNESS

London has hundreds of fitness clubs, from council-run gyms to lavish private clubs. Use Yellow Pages (under "Leisure Centres" or search online).

Barbican YMCA, 2 Fann St. (☎7628 0697). ⊖Barbican. Weights, Nautilus machines, treadmills, and bikes. Non-members £5 per session. Membership £55 per yr.; £27 for 3 mo.; plus £3.50 per use. Open M-F 7am-9:30pm, Sa-Su 10am-6pm.

Chelsea Sports Centre, Chelsea Manor St. (☎7352 6985). ⊖Sloane Square or South Kensington. Pool, solarium, gym, tennis, ping-pong, volleyball, basketball, football, and badminton. Numerous classes. Open M-F 7am-10pm, Sa 8am-6:30pm, Su and holidays 8am-10pm. Call for prices.

Kensington Leisure Centre, Walmer Rd. (☎7727 9747). ⊖Ladbroke Grove. In Notting Hill, despite the name. Pool, sauna, weights, badminton, and squash, plus aerobics, self-defense, and scuba-diving classes. Open M-F 7am-10pm, Sa 8am-6:30pm, Su and holidays 8am-10pm.

Queen Mother Sports Centre, 223 Vauxhall Bridge Rd. (☎7630 5522). ⊖Victoria. 1hr. intro course (non-members £28) required for use of weights. Pool open M 6:30am-8pm, Tu 6:30am-9:30pm, W-F 6:30am-7:30pm, Sa-Su 8am-5:30pm. Membership £40 per mo.; non-members £2.45 per use. Open M-F 6:30am-10pm, Sa 8am-8pm.

HELPLINES

Rape Crisis Centre: ☎7837 1600.

Samaritans: ☎08457 90 90 90. Emotional support for depression and suicide. 24hr.

Victim Support: (☎0845 303 0900; www.victimsupportline.org.uk). Emotional help and legal advice for crime victims. Open M-F 9am-9pm, Sa-Su 9am-7pm.

HOSPITALS

For urgent care, go to one of the 24hr. **Accident & Emergency** departments listed below. For non-urgent care, or to see a specialist, you will need a referral from your primary care doctor.

Charing Cross, Fulham Palace Rd., entrance on St. Dunstan's Rd. (☎8846 1234). ⊖Hammersmith, or Bus 220 or 295.

Chelsea and Westminster, 369 Fulham Rd. (☎8746 8000). ⊖Fulham Broadway, or South Kensington then bus #14 or 211. Or Bus C3, 11, 19, 22, 31, 49.

Royal Free, Pond St. (☎7794 0500). ⊖Belsize Park or Rail: Hampstead Heath.

St. Mary's, Praed St. (☎ 7886 6666). ⊖Paddington or Edgware.

St. Thomas's, Lambeth Palace Rd. (☎7188 7982 or 7188 8899). ⊖Waterloo.

University College Hospital, Grafton Way (☎7387 9300). ⊖Warren St.

Whittington, Highgate Hill (☎7272 3070). ⊖Archway.

INTERNET ACCESS

Independent cyber cafes are on almost every business street in London. If you're paying more than £2 per hour you're paying too much. The big chains are listed below.

easyEverything, easyInternet cafes (☎7241 9000; www.easyeverything.com). 5 locations, each with hundreds of terminals: 9-16 Tottenham Crt. Rd. (⊖Tottenham Crt. Rd.); 456/459 Strand (⊖Charing Cross); 358 Oxford St. (⊖Bond St.); 9-13 Wilton Rd. (⊖Victoria); 160-166 Kensington High St. (⊖High St. Kensington); Unit G1, King's Walk, King's Rd. (⊖Sloane Square). Prices vary with demand, from £1 per 15min. during busy times; usually around £1.60/hr. Minimum charge £1. Generally open until 11pm.

Virgin Megastore, Oxford St. See p. 264.

BT Multi.phones, installed in Tube and rail stations throughout London. Internet-enabled payphones with touch-screen control. These are ridiculously expensive, generally around £1 for 5-10 min.

Internet Exchange, (☎8742 4000) Around 20 locations in libraries all over London. Call for the nearest one.

LEGAL RESOURCES

Embassies may provide legal advice and services to citizens under arrest.

Citizen's Advice Bureaux (www.nacab.org.uk). Independent nationwide network of offices giving free advice on legal and consumer issues. London bureaux include 140 Ladbroke Grove (☎8960 3322; ⊖Ladbroke Grove); 32 Ludgate Hill (☎7236 1156; ⊖Blackfriars). Opening hours limited, appointments often necessary; call ahead.

Community Legal Service (☎084 5345 4345; www.clsdirect.org.uk). Government-run online advice and directory of legal advisors.

Release, 388 Old St. (☎7729 9904; www.release.org.uk). Advice and info on the law and drugs. Open daily 10am-5:30pm.

Victim Support. See **Helplines,** p. 337.

LOST PROPERTY

See also **Police,** p. 338.

Public Carriage Office, 15 Penton St. (☎7833 0996; www.transportforlondon.gov.uk/pco). ⊖Angel. For articles left in licensed taxicabs (black cabs). Open M-F 9am-4pm.

Transport for London Lost Property Office, 200 Baker St., NW1 5RT (☎7941 4500; fax 7918 1028). Items left on public transport are first held 48hr. at the bus garage or the Tube station where they were found, then forwarded to the above address. Reclamation fee. Open M-F 9:30am-2pm.

MINICABS

See also **Taxis,** p. 339.

Lady Cabs (☎7254 3501). Providing female drivers but not limited to women passengers. Pick-up North London only. Open M-F 8am-10pm, Sa 9am-10pm, Su 10am-10pm.

Liberty Cars, 330 Old St. (☎7734 1313). Shoreditch-based cab service catering to gays and lesbians. 24hr. pick-up anywhere in London. Central London to Airports: Heathrow £32, Gatwick £44, Stansted/ Luton £48; £10 more from airport to central London.

London Radio Cars (☎8905 0000, or ☎8204 4444). Large, well run service with pick up anywhere in London. Prices similar to above.

MINORITY RESOURCES

See also **Gay & Lesbian Services,** p. 337, and **Religious Resources,** p. 339.

Africa Centre, 38 King St. (☎7836 1973; www.africacentre.org.uk). ⊖Covent Garden. Pan-African cultural center, with a full program of events.

Black Cultural Archives, 378 Coldharbour Ln. (☎7738 4591). ⊖Brixton.

BLINK (www.blink.org.uk). Web resource for the UK's Black and Asian communities, from art and culture to human rights.

POLICE

In an **emergency,** dial ☎**999** from any land phone, or ☎**112** from a mobile phone. London is covered by two police forces: the **City of London Police** (☎7601 2222; www.cityoflondon.police.uk) for the City, and the **Metropolitan Police**

(☎7230 1212; www.met.police.uk). For **general inquiries,** write to: New Scotland Yard, Broadway, London SW1H 0BG. In the event of police misconduct, contact the **Police Complaints Authority**. There is at least 1 police station in each of the 32 boroughs open 24hr. (☎7230 1212 to find the nearest station).

POSTAL SERVICES

For information on **Royal Mail** services, see **Essentials,** p. 46.

FedEx (☎0800 123 800). Cheapest express service is International Priority. 500g envelope £25-35 depending on destination.

RELIGIOUS RESOURCES

Anglican/Episcopal: The vast majority of churches in London; there's almost always one within walking distance. **London Diocese,** London Diocesan House, 36 Causton St. (☎7932 1100; www.london.anglican.org), for London north of the Thames. **Southwark Diocese,** 4 Chapel Ct., Borough High St. (☎7939 9400; www.dswark.org), for South London.

Buddhist: Buddhapadipa Temple, Calonne Rd., Wimbledon Parkside (☎8946 1357). ⊖Wimbledon Park (Zone 3).

Hindu: Shree Swaminarayan Mandir, 105-119 Brentfield Rd. (☎8965 2651). ⊖Neasden (Zone 3). Also has a cultural center.

Jewish: Orthodox: Central Synagogue, Great Portland St. (☎7580 1355; www.brijnet.org/centralsyn). ⊖Great Portland St. or Oxford Circus. Can also advise on kosher restaurants and hotels. **Reform:** West London Synagogue, 33 Seymour Pl. (☎7723 4404; www.wls.org.uk). ⊖Marble Arch.

Muslim: London Central Mosque, 146 Park Rd. (☎7724 3363; www.islamicculturalcentre.co.uk). ⊖Baker St. Also houses the **Islamic Cultural Centre.**

Roman Catholic, Vaughn House, 46 Francis St. (☎7798 9009; www.rcdow.org.uk).

TAXIS

The listings below refer to licensed taxicabs ("black cabs"). All operate throughout London and charge the same rates (see **Essentials,** p. 44). For **Minicabs,** see p. 338.

Computer Cabs: ☎7286 0286.

Dial-a-Cab: ☎7253 5000.

Radio Taxis: ☎7272 0272.

TELEPHONE SERVICES

For info on making calls in Britain and useful numbers, see **Essentials,** p. 47.

Calling card access numbers: If calling from a British Telecom phone, use ☎0800; if using Cable & Wireless, use ☎0500.

AT&T: see calling card for details.

Canada Direct: ☎0800/0500 890 016.

MCI Worldcom: ☎0800/0500 890 222.

Telecom NZ Direct: ☎0800/0500 890 064.

Sprint: ☎0800/0500 890 877.

TICKETS

Ticketmaster (☎7344 4444; www.ticketmaster.co.uk) is the UK's largest telephone ticketing agency. Tickets to almost every event, show, mainstream movie theater, and major nightclub in the country.

tkts, Leicester Sq. Half-price theater tickets to almost every play on the day, see p. 227. Most venues also offer day-of student rates: usually for less than £20 .

TOURIST INFORMATION

Britain Visitor Centre, 1 Regent St. (www.visitbritain.com). ⊖Oxford Circus. Run by the British Tourist Association. Open M 9:30am-6:30pm, Tu-F 9am-6:30pm, Sa-Su 10am-4pm.

London Information Centre, 1 Leicester Pl. (☎7930 6769; www.wondoninformation.org). ⊖Leicester Sq. Right next to the Leicester Sq.'s half-price ticket booth. Right in the middle of the action, and full of all the helpful advice and info a wandering visitor might need. Open daily 8am-midnight.

TRANSPORT INFORMATION

See also **Essentials,** p. 40. For listings, see **Bicycle Rental,** p. 335; **Car Rental,** p. 336; **Minicabs,** p. 338; and **Taxis,** p. 339.

Transport for London (info ☎7222 1234; www.londontransport.co.uk) operates information centers in 8 central London Tube stations and also at Heathrow Airport and Greenwich.

WOMEN'S RESOURCES

Lady Cabs. Taxi service for women. See **Minicabs,** p. 338.

West London Center for Sexual Health, health clinic. See **Clinics,** p. 336.

Index

D

E

I

J

K

L

M

N

O

P

Q

R

S

Y

Z

Map Appendix

INSIDE:

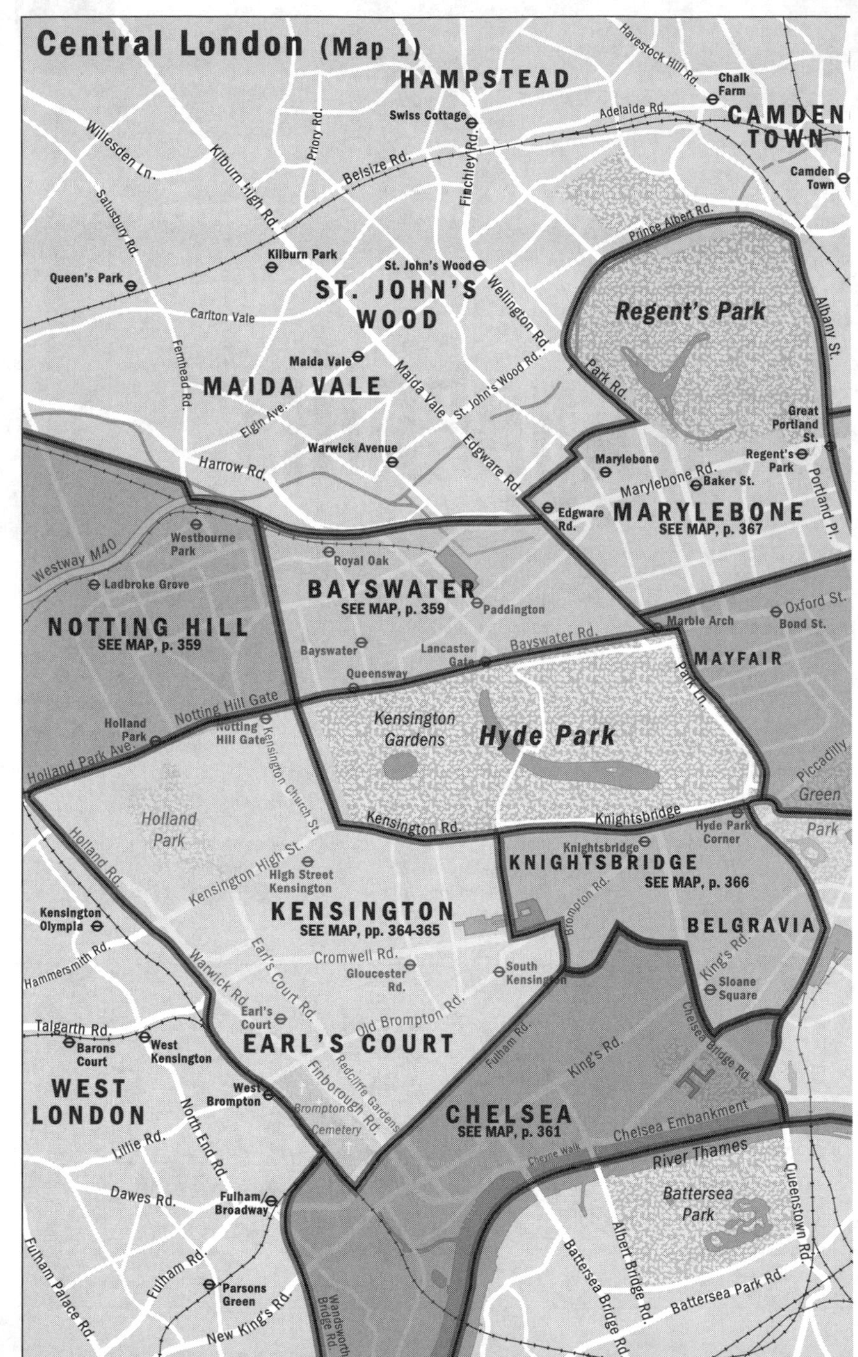
Central London (Map 1)
HAMPSTEAD
CAMDEN TOWN
ST. JOHN'S WOOD
MAIDA VALE
Regent's Park
MARYLEBONE
SEE MAP, p. 367
BAYSWATER
SEE MAP, p. 359
NOTTING HILL
SEE MAP, p. 359
MAYFAIR
Kensington Gardens
Hyde Park
Holland Park
KNIGHTSBRIDGE
SEE MAP, p. 366
BELGRAVIA
KENSINGTON
SEE MAP, pp. 364-365
EARL'S COURT
WEST LONDON
CHELSEA
SEE MAP, p. 361
Battersea Park
Brompton Cemetery
River Thames
Swiss Cottage
Chalk Farm
Camden Town
Kilburn Park
St. John's Wood
Queen's Park
Maida Vale
Warwick Avenue
Marylebone
Baker St.
Regent's Park
Great Portland St.
Edgware Rd.
Westbourne Park
Royal Oak
Ladbroke Grove
Paddington
Marble Arch
Oxford St.
Bond St.
Bayswater
Lancaster Gate
Queensway
Holland Park
Notting Hill Gate
Hyde Park Corner
Knightsbridge
High Street Kensington
Kensington Olympia
Gloucester Rd.
South Kensington
Sloane Square
Earl's Court
Barons Court
West Kensington
West Brompton
Fulham/Broadway
Parsons Green
Havestock Hill Rd.
Adelaide Rd.
Willesden Ln.
Kilburn High Rd.
Priory Rd.
Belsize Rd.
Finchley Rd.
Salusbury Rd.
Prince Albert Rd.
Wellington Rd.
Albany St.
Carlton Vale
Fernhead Rd.
Park Rd.
St. John's Wood Rd.
Elgin Ave.
Maida Vale
Edgware Rd.
Harrow Rd.
Marylebone Rd.
Portland Pl.
Westway M40
Bayswater Rd.
Park Ln.
Notting Hill Gate
Holland Park Ave.
Kensington Church St.
Piccadilly
Green
Park
Kensington Rd.
Knightsbridge
Holland Rd.
Kensington High St.
Brompton Rd.
King's Rd.
Hammersmith Rd.
Warwick Rd.
Earl's Court Rd.
Cromwell Rd.
Old Brompton Rd.
Talgarth Rd.
Fulham Rd.
King's Rd.
Chelsea Bridge Rd.
Redcliffe Gardens
Finborough Rd.
Chelsea Embankment
Cheyne Walk
North End Rd.
Lillie Rd.
Dawes Rd.
Queenstown Rd.
Albert Bridge Rd.
Battersea Bridge Rd.
Battersea Park Rd.
Fulham Rd.
Fulham Palace Rd.
New King's Rd.
Wandsworth Bridge Rd.

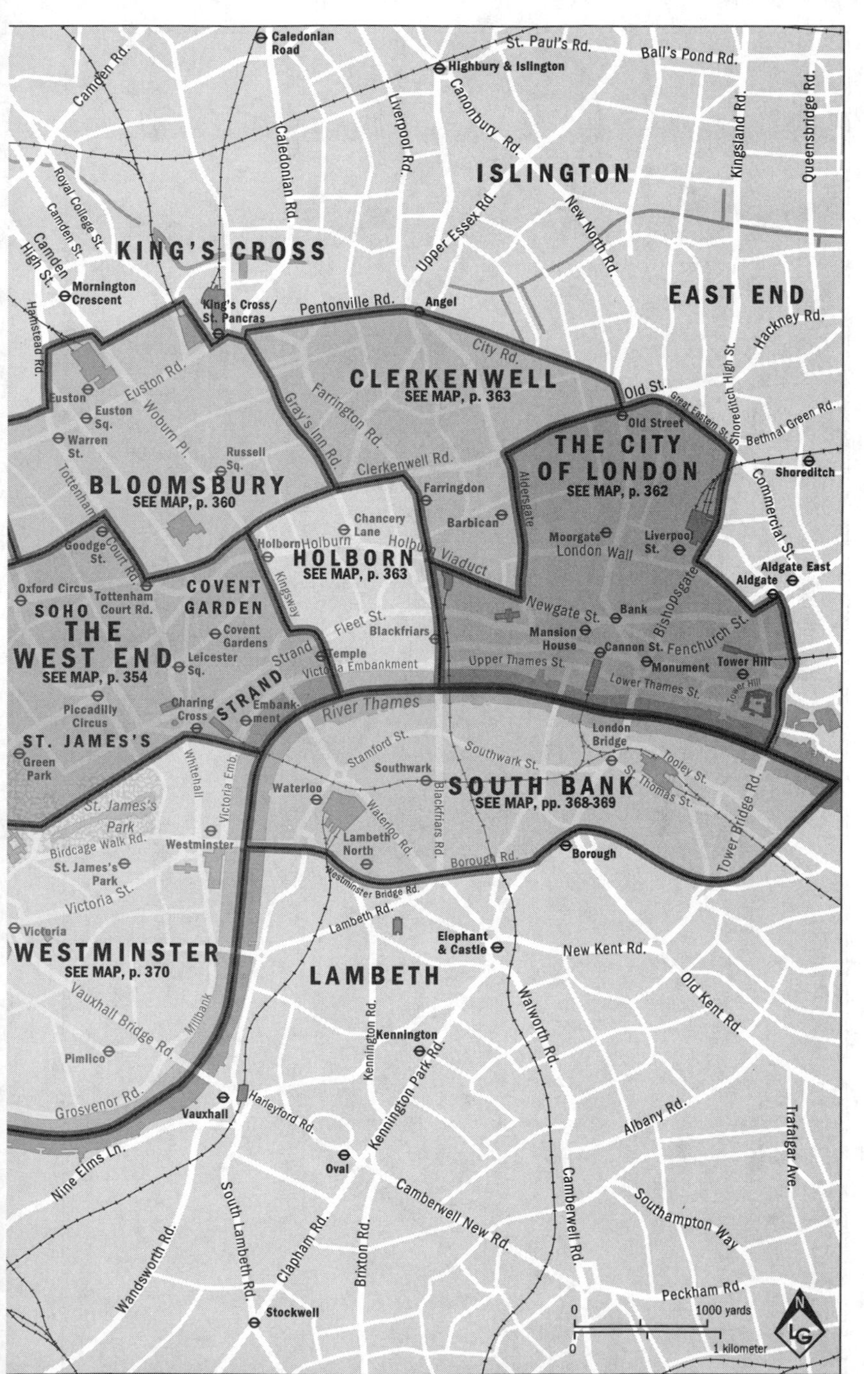

ISLINGTON
KING'S CROSS
EAST END
CLERKENWELL
SEE MAP, p. 363
THE CITY OF LONDON
SEE MAP, p. 362
BLOOMSBURY
SEE MAP, p. 360
HOLBORN
SEE MAP, p. 363
COVENT GARDEN
SOHO
THE WEST END
SEE MAP, p. 354
STRAND
ST. JAMES'S
SOUTH BANK
SEE MAP, pp. 368-369
WESTMINSTER
SEE MAP, p. 370
LAMBETH
Caledonian Road
Highbury & Islington
St. Paul's Rd.
Ball's Pond Rd.
Camden Rd.
Caledonian Rd.
Liverpool Rd.
Canonbury Rd.
Kingsland Rd.
Queensbridge Rd.
Royal College St.
Camden St.
Camden High St.
Upper Essex Rd.
New North Rd.
Mornington Crescent
Hamstead Rd.
King's Cross/ St. Pancras
Pentonville Rd.
Angel
Hackney Rd.
City Rd.
Euston Rd.
Euston
Euston Sq.
Warren St.
Woburn Pl.
Gray's Inn Rd.
Farringdon Rd.
Old St.
Great Eastern St.
Shoreditch High St.
Bethnal Green Rd.
Old Street
Shoreditch
Russell Sq.
Clerkenwell Rd.
Tottenham Court Rd.
Farringdon
Aldersgate
Commercial St.
Chancery Lane
Barbican
Goodge St.
Holborn
Holborn Viaduct
Moorgate
London Wall
Liverpool St.
Aldgate East
Aldgate
Kingsway
Oxford Circus
Tottenham Court Rd.
Bishopsgate
Newgate St.
Bank
Covent Gardens
Fleet St.
Blackfriars
Mansion House
Fenchurch St.
Leicester Sq.
Strand
Temple
Cannon St.
Monument
Tower Hill
Victoria Embankment
Upper Thames St.
Lower Thames St.
Piccadilly Circus
Charing Cross
Embankment
River Thames
Green Park
Whitehall
Victoria Emb.
Stamford St.
Southwark St.
London Bridge
Tooley St.
St. Thomas St.
Southwark
Waterloo
Blackfriars Rd.
Tower Bridge Rd.
St. James's Park
Waterloo Rd.
Birdcage Walk Rd.
Westminster
Lambeth North
Borough Rd.
Borough
St. James's Park
Westminster Bridge Rd.
Victoria St.
Lambeth Rd.
Victoria
Elephant & Castle
New Kent Rd.
Old Kent Rd.
Vauxhall Bridge Rd.
Millbank
Kennington Rd.
Kennington
Walworth Rd.
Kennington Park Rd.
Pimlico
Grosvenor Rd.
Vauxhall
Harleyford Rd.
Albany Rd.
Trafalgar Ave.
Nine Elms Ln.
Oval
Camberwell New Rd.
Camberwell Rd.
Southampton Way
South Lambeth Rd.
Clapham Rd.
Brixton Rd.
Wandsworth Rd.
Peckham Rd.
Stockwell
0
1000 yards
0
1 kilometer
N
LG

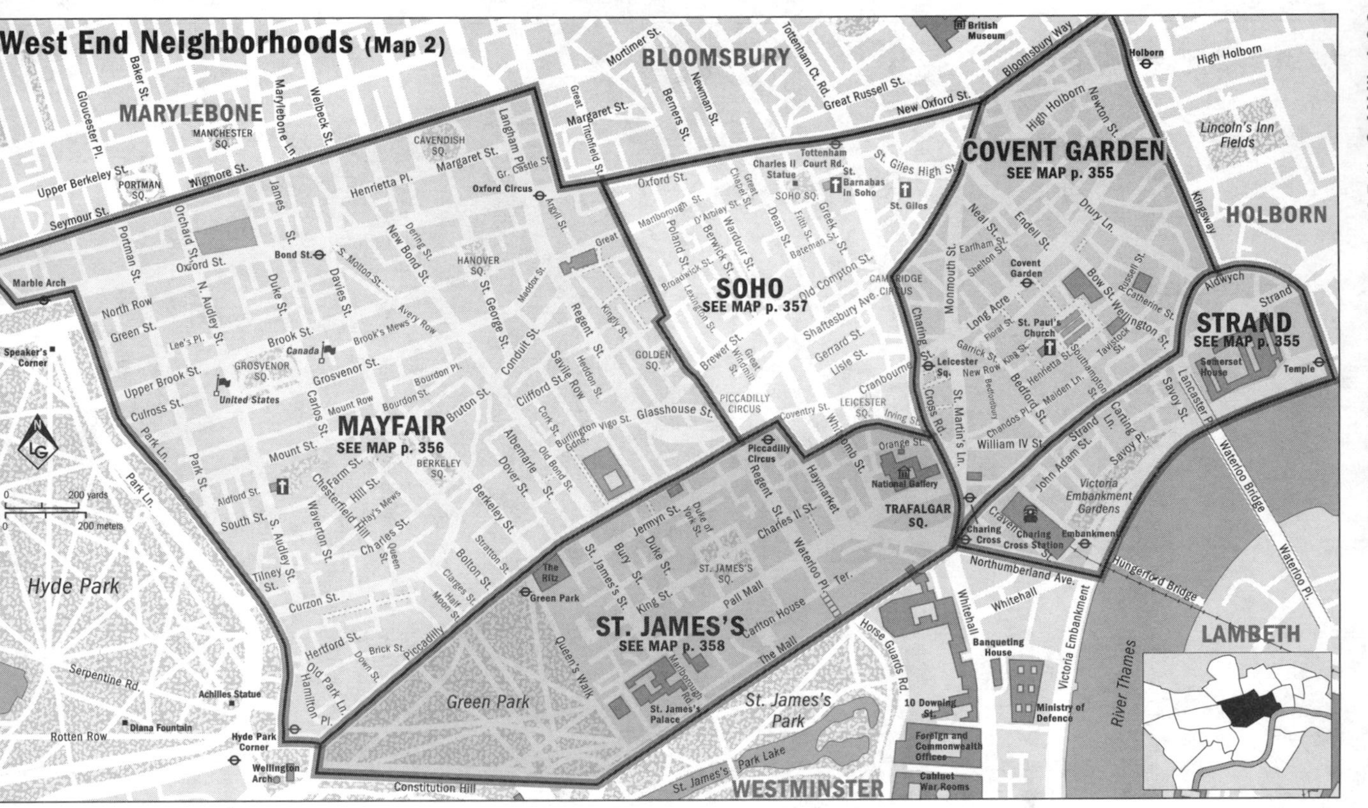
West End Neighborhoods (Map 2)
MARYLEBONE
BLOOMSBURY
HOLBORN
COVENT GARDEN
SEE MAP p. 355
STRAND
SEE MAP p. 355
SOHO
SEE MAP p. 357
MAYFAIR
SEE MAP p. 356
ST. JAMES'S
SEE MAP p. 358
TRAFALGAR SQ.
PICCADILLY CIRCUS
LAMBETH
WESTMINSTER
Hyde Park
Green Park
St. James's Park
River Thames
Lincoln's Inn Fields
Victoria Embankment Gardens
British Museum
National Gallery
Oxford St.
Regent St.
Piccadilly
Park Ln.
Charing Cross Rd.
Strand
Whitehall
The Mall
Constitution Hill
Waterloo Bridge
Hungerford Bridge
Victoria Embankment
0 200 yards
0 200 meters

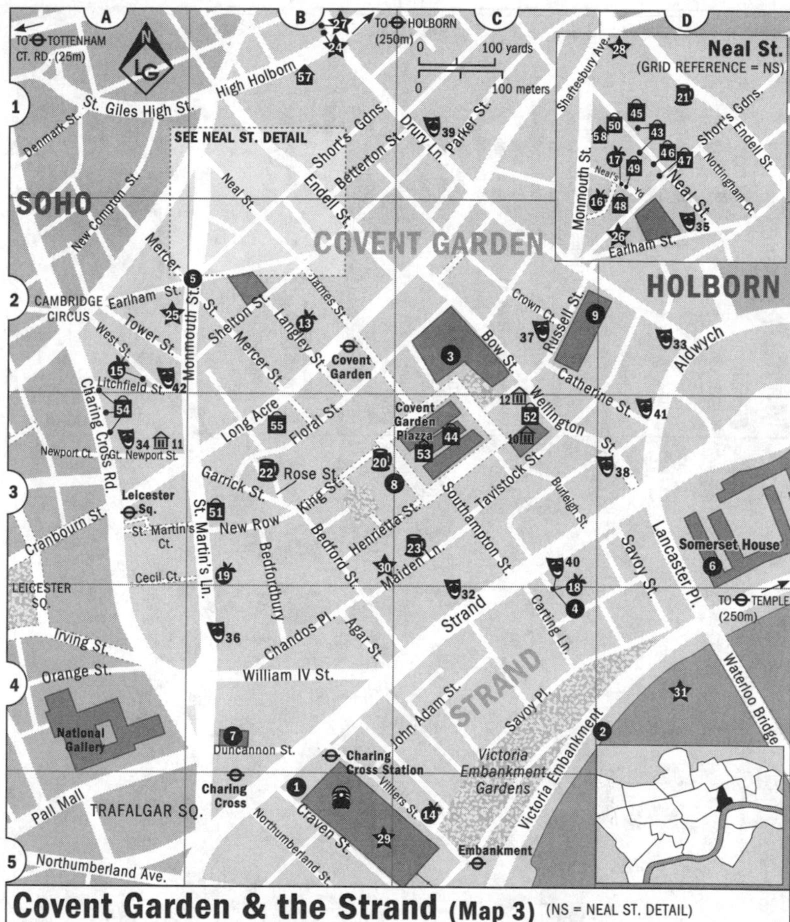

Covent Garden & the Strand (Map 3) (NS = NEAL ST. DETAIL)

SIGHTS

Charing Cross, **1**	B5
Cleopatra's Needle, **2**	D4
Royal Opera House, **3**	C2
The Savoy, **4**	C4
Seven Dials, **5**	B2
Somerset House, **6**	D3
St. Martin-in-the-Fields, **7**	B4
St. Paul's, **8**	B3
Theatre Royal, Drury Lane, **9**	C2

MUSEUMS AND GALLERIES

London's Transport Museum, **10**	C3
The Photographers' Gallery, **11**	A3
Theatre Museum, **12**	C3

FOOD

Café Pacifico, **13**	B2
Gordon's Wine Bar, **14**	C5
The Ivy, **15**	A2
Monmouth Coffee Company, **16**	NS
Neal's Yard Bakery, Salad Bar & Tearoom, **17**	NS
The Savoy, **18**	C4
St. Martin's Lane Hotel, **19**	B3

PUBS

Bunker Bierhall, **20**	B3
The Cross Keys, **21**	NS
Lamb and Flag, **22**	B3
Maple Leaf, **23**	C3

NIGHTLIFE

AKA, **24**	B1
The Box, **25**	A2
Detroit, **26**	NS
The End, **27**	B1
Freud, **28**	NS
Heaven, **29**	B5
The Spot, **30**	B3
T.S. Queen Mary, **31**	D4

ENTERTAINMENT

The Adelphi, **32**	C4
Aldwych Theatre, **33**	D2
Arts Theater, **34**	A3
Donmar Warehouse, **35**	NS
English National Opera, **36**	B4
Fortune Theatre, **37**	C2
Lyceum, **38**	D3
New London Theatre, **39**	C1
Savoy Theater, **40**	C3
Strand Theatre, **41**	D3
St. Martin's Theatre, **42**	A2

SHOPPING

Apple Tree, **43**	NS
Covent Garden & Jubilee Markets, **44**	C3
Egoshego, **45**	NS
Energie, **46**	NS
Miss Sixty, **47**	NS
Neal's Yard Dairy, **48**	NS
Neal's Yard Remedies, **49**	NS
Office, **50**	NS
Office Sale Shop, **51**	B3
Penhaligon's, **52**	C3
Savage London, **53**	C3
Shipley, **54**	A3
Stanfords, **55**	B3

ACCOMMODATIONS

High Holborn Residence, **57**	B1
Seven Dials Hotel, **58**	NS

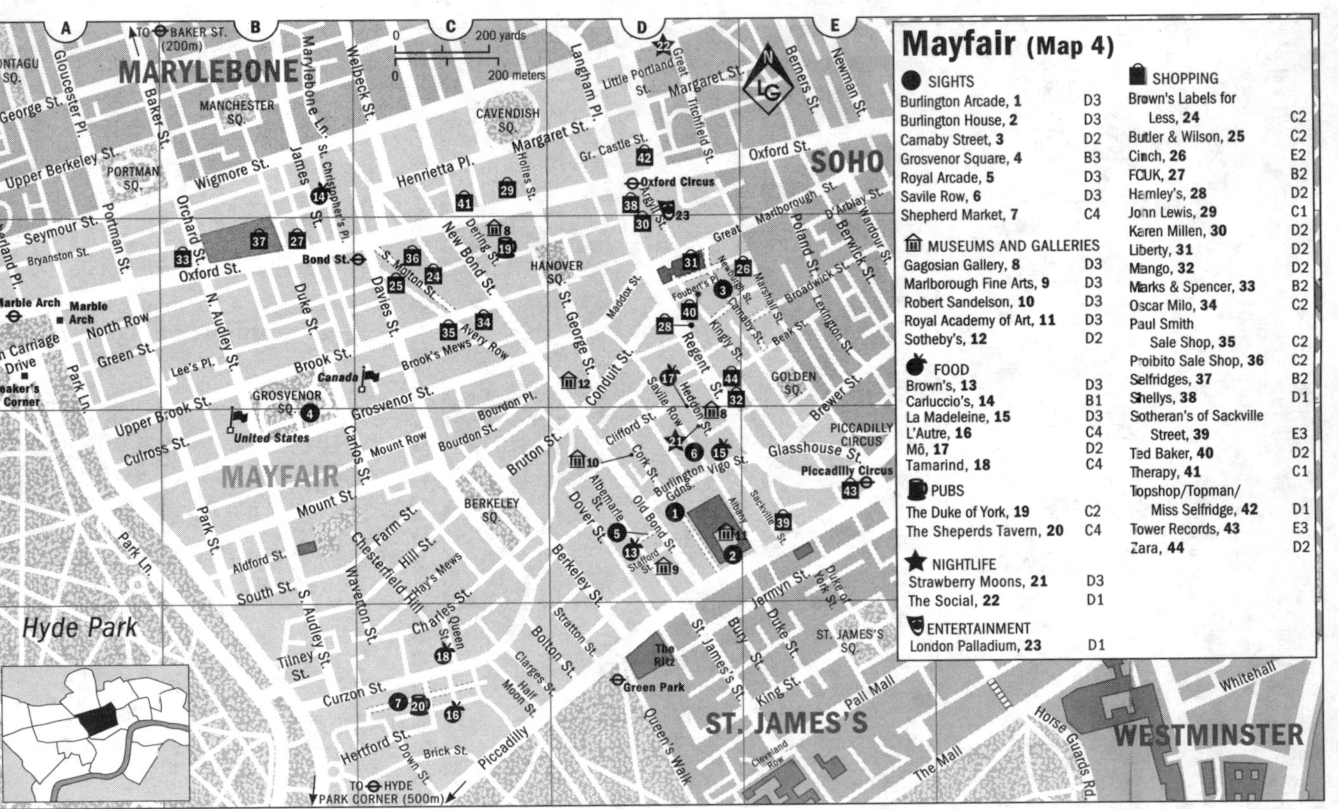
Mayfair (Map 4)
SIGHTS
Burlington Arcade, 1 D3
Burlington House, 2 D3
Carnaby Street, 3 D2
Grosvenor Square, 4 B3
Royal Arcade, 5 D3
Savile Row, 6 D3
Shepherd Market, 7 C4
MUSEUMS AND GALLERIES
Gagosian Gallery, 8 D3
Marlborough Fine Arts, 9 D3
Robert Sandelson, 10 D3
Royal Academy of Art, 11 D3
Sotheby's, 12 D2
FOOD
Brown's, 13 D3
Carluccio's, 14 B1
La Madeleine, 15 D3
L'Autre, 16 C4
Mô, 17 D2
Tamarind, 18 C4
PUBS
The Duke of York, 19 C2
The Sheperds Tavern, 20 C4
NIGHTLIFE
Strawberry Moons, 21 D3
The Social, 22 D1
ENTERTAINMENT
London Palladium, 23 D1
SHOPPING
Brown's Labels for Less, 24 C2
Butler & Wilson, 25 C2
Cinch, 26 E2
FCUK, 27 B2
Hamley's, 28 D2
John Lewis, 29 C1
Karen Millen, 30 D2
Liberty, 31 D2
Mango, 32 D2
Marks & Spencer, 33 B2
Oscar Milo, 34 C2
Paul Smith Sale Shop, 35 C2
Proibito Sale Shop, 36 C2
Selfridges, 37 B2
Shellys, 38 D1
Sotheran's of Sackville Street, 39 E3
Ted Baker, 40 D2
Therapy, 41 C1
Topshop/Topman/Miss Selfridge, 42 D1
Tower Records, 43 E3
Zara, 44 D2
MARYLEBONE
SOHO
MAYFAIR
ST. JAMES'S
WESTMINSTER
Hyde Park
TO BAKER ST. (200m)
TO HYDE PARK CORNER (500m)
0 200 yards
0 200 meters
Oxford Circus
Bond St.
Marble Arch
Piccadilly Circus
Green Park
Speaker's Corner
United States
Canada
The Ritz

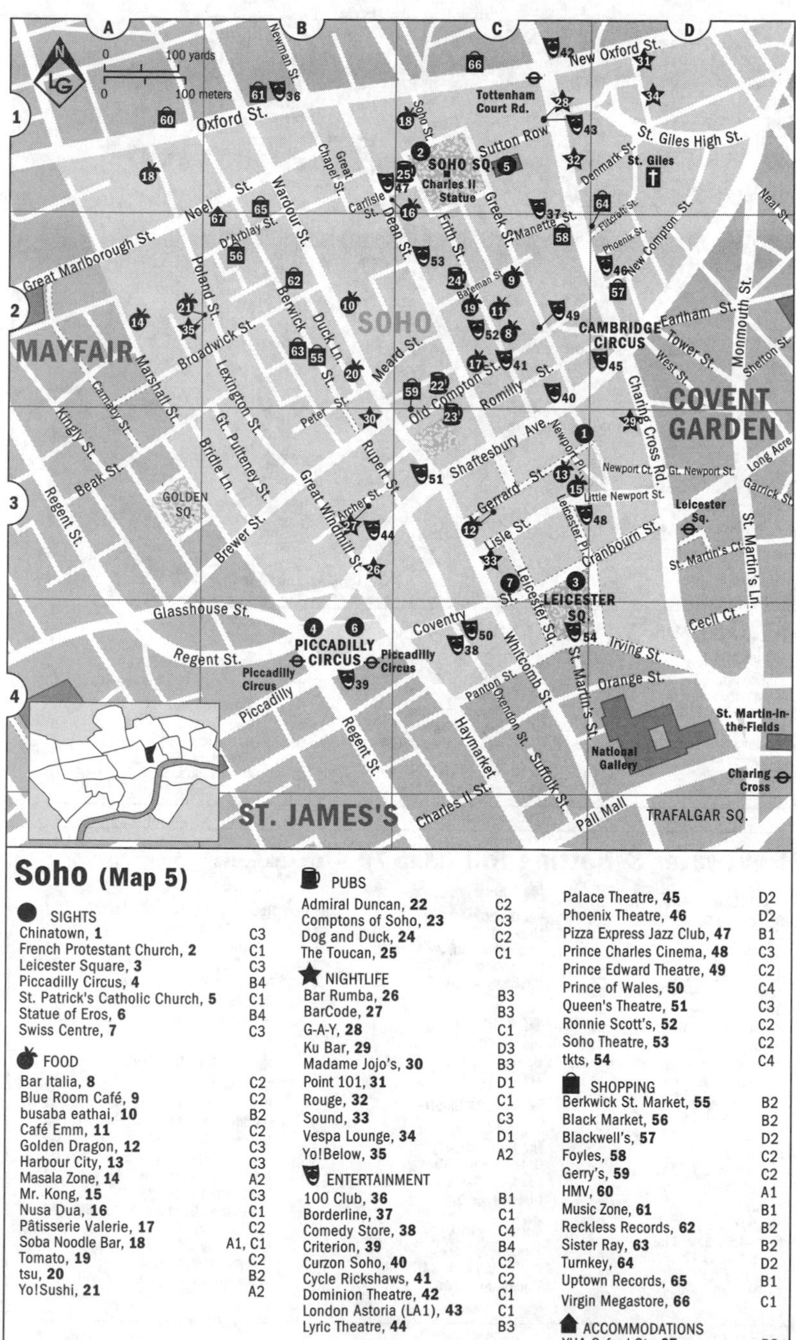

Soho (Map 5)

SIGHTS

Chinatown, **1**	C3
French Protestant Church, **2**	C1
Leicester Square, **3**	C3
Piccadilly Circus, **4**	B4
St. Patrick's Catholic Church, **5**	C1
Statue of Eros, **6**	B4
Swiss Centre, **7**	C3

FOOD

Bar Italia, **8**	C2
Blue Room Café, **9**	C2
busaba eathai, **10**	B2
Café Emm, **11**	C2
Golden Dragon, **12**	C3
Harbour City, **13**	C3
Masala Zone, **14**	A2
Mr. Kong, **15**	C3
Nusa Dua, **16**	C1
Pâtisserie Valerie, **17**	C2
Soba Noodle Bar, **18**	A1, C1
Tomato, **19**	C2
tsu, **20**	B2
Yo!Sushi, **21**	A2

PUBS

Admiral Duncan, **22**	C2
Comptons of Soho, **23**	C3
Dog and Duck, **24**	C2
The Toucan, **25**	C1

NIGHTLIFE

Bar Rumba, **26**	B3
BarCode, **27**	B3
G-A-Y, **28**	C1
Ku Bar, **29**	D3
Madame Jojo's, **30**	B3
Point 101, **31**	D1
Rouge, **32**	C1
Sound, **33**	C3
Vespa Lounge, **34**	D1
Yo!Below, **35**	A2

ENTERTAINMENT

100 Club, **36**	B1
Borderline, **37**	C1
Comedy Store, **38**	C4
Criterion, **39**	B4
Curzon Soho, **40**	C2
Cycle Rickshaws, **41**	C2
Dominion Theatre, **42**	C1
London Astoria (LA1), **43**	C1
Lyric Theatre, **44**	B3
Palace Theatre, **45**	D2
Phoenix Theatre, **46**	D2
Pizza Express Jazz Club, **47**	B1
Prince Charles Cinema, **48**	C3
Prince Edward Theatre, **49**	C2
Prince of Wales, **50**	C4
Queen's Theatre, **51**	C3
Ronnie Scott's, **52**	C2
Soho Theatre, **53**	C2
tkts, **54**	C4

SHOPPING

Berkwick St. Market, **55**	B2
Black Market, **56**	B2
Blackwell's, **57**	D2
Foyles, **58**	C2
Gerry's, **59**	C2
HMV, **60**	A1
Music Zone, **61**	B1
Reckless Records, **62**	B2
Sister Ray, **63**	B2
Turnkey, **64**	D2
Uptown Records, **65**	B1
Virgin Megastore, **66**	C1

ACCOMMODATIONS

YHA Oxford St., **67**	B2

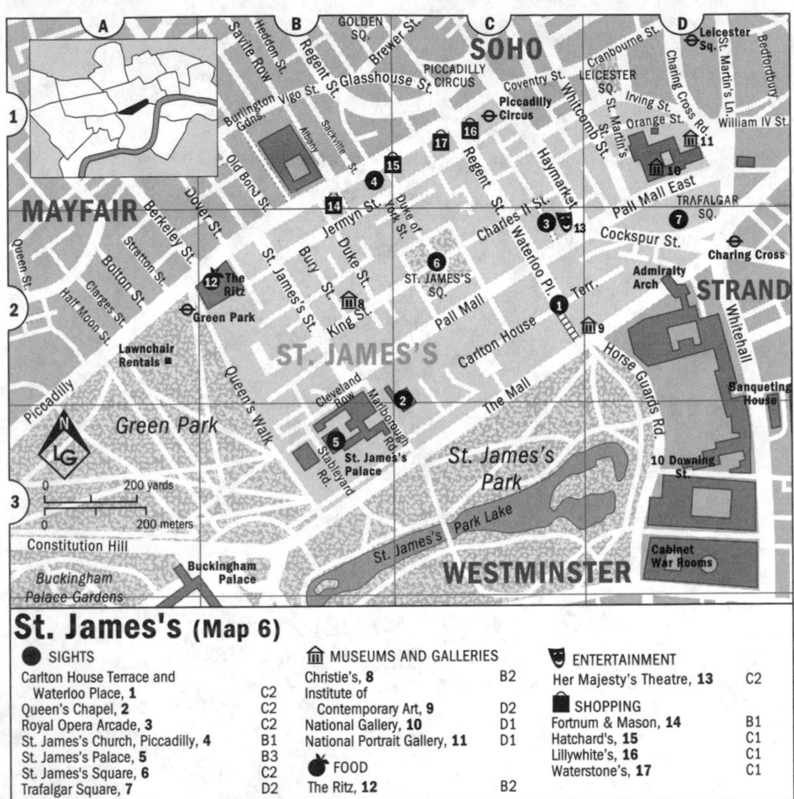

St. James's (Map 6)

SIGHTS

- Carlton House Terrace and Waterloo Place, **1** — C2
- Queen's Chapel, **2** — C2
- Royal Opera Arcade, **3** — C2
- St. James's Church, Piccadilly, **4** — B1
- St. James's Palace, **5** — B3
- St. James's Square, **6** — C2
- Trafalgar Square, **7** — D2

MUSEUMS AND GALLERIES

- Christie's, **8** — B2
- Institute of Contemporary Art, **9** — D2
- National Gallery, **10** — D1
- National Portrait Gallery, **11** — D1

FOOD

- The Ritz, **12** — B2

ENTERTAINMENT

- Her Majesty's Theatre, **13** — C2

SHOPPING

- Fortnum & Mason, **14** — B1
- Hatchard's, **15** — C1
- Lillywhite's, **16** — C1
- Waterstone's, **17** — C1

Bayswater & Notting Hill (Map 7)

SEE MAP, p. 359

MUSEUMS AND GALLERIES

- Serpentine Gallery, **1** — G4

FOOD

- Alounak Kebab, **2** — D2
- Aphrodite Taverna, **3** — D2
- Black and Blue, **4** — C4
- Books for Cooks, **5** — B2
- Durbar Tandoori, **6** — D2
- George's Portobello Fish Bar, **7** — A1
- The Grain Shop, **8** — B2
- La Bottega del Gelato, **9** — D3
- Lazy Daisy Café, **10** — C3
- Levantine, **11** — G2
- Lisboa Patisserie, **12** — A1
- Makan, **13** — B1
- Manzara, **14** — C3
- Mr. Jerk, **15** — D2
- Nottinghill Gate Cafe, **16** — D4
- Royal China, **17** — E3
- Tiger Lil's, **18** — E2
- Tom's Delicatessan, **19** — B2

PUBS

- Bar Oz, **20** — D3
- Mitre, **21** — F3
- Portobello Gold, **22** — B3
- Prince Albert Pub, **23** — C3
- The Shakespeare, **24** — D2

NIGHTLIFE

- The Market, **25** — B2
- Notting Hill Arts Club, **26** — C4
- Visible, **27** — A1

ENTERTAINMENT

- Electric Cinema, **28** — B2
- The Gate, **29** — C4
- Gate Cinema, **30** — C4
- London's Skate Centre, **31** — E3
- Queen's Ice Bowl, **32** — E3

SHOPPING

- Bayswater Market, **33** — F3
- Dolly Diamond, **34** — C3
- Honest Jon's, **35** — A1
- One of a Kind, **36** — B2
- Rough Trade, **37** — B2
- The Tea and Coffee Plant, **38** — B2
- Teaze, **39** — C3
- The Travel Bookshop, **40** — B2
- Whiteleys Shopping Centre, **41** — D2
- Willma, **42** — A1

ACCOMMODATIONS

- Admiral Hotel, **43** — G2
- Balmoral House Hotel, **44** — G2
- Cardiff Hotel, **45** — G2
- Garden Court Hotel, **46** — D2
- The Gate Hotel, **47** — C3
- Hyde Park Court Hotel, **48** — G2
- Hyde Park Hostel, **49** — E3
- Kensington Gardens Hotel, **50** — D3
- Leinster Inn, **51** — D2
- Palace Hotel, **52** — D3
- Quest Hostel, **53** — E3
- Vancover Studios, **54** — D3

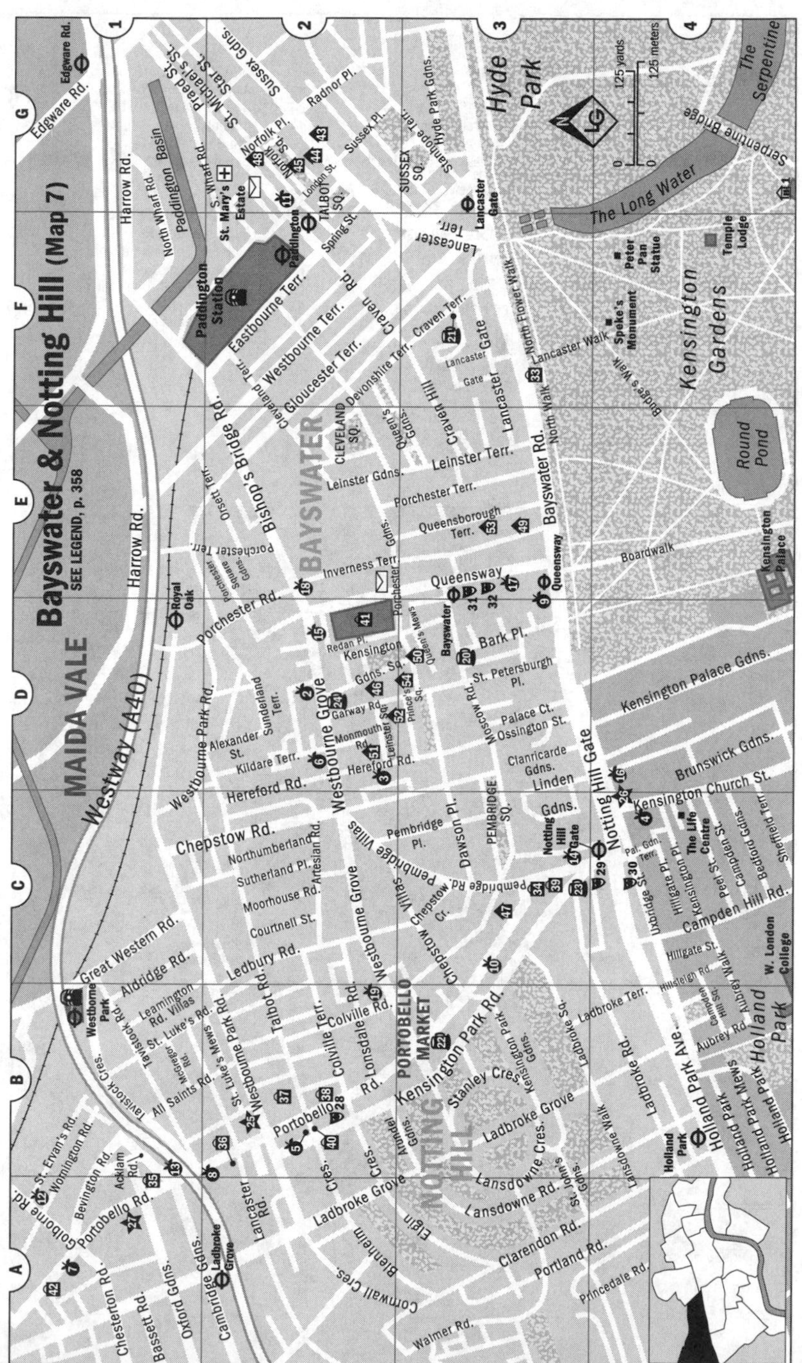
Bayswater & Notting Hill (Map 7)
SEE LEGEND, p. 358
MAIDA VALE
BAYSWATER
NOTTING HILL
PORTOBELLO MARKET
Hyde Park
Kensington Gardens
Holland Park
The Long Water
The Serpentine
Serpentine Bridge
Round Pond
Kensington Palace
Peter Pan Statue
Speke's Monument
Temple Lodge
Paddington Station
Paddington Basin
St. Mary's Estate
The Life Centre
W. London College
Westway (A40)
Harrow Rd.
Edgware Rd.
Bayswater Rd.
Notting Hill Gate
Kensington Church St.
Kensington Park Rd.
Kensington Palace Gdns.
Westbourne Grove
Westbourne Park Rd.
Westbourne Terr.
Bishop's Bridge Rd.
Porchester Rd.
Queensway
Ladbroke Grove
Portobello Rd.
Holland Park Ave.
Pembridge Rd.
Chepstow Rd.
Ledbury Rd.
Talbot Rd.
Great Western Rd.
Lancaster Gate
Lancaster Terr.
Craven Rd.
Gloucester Terr.
Eastbourne Terr.
Leinster Terr.
Leinster Gdns.
Inverness Terr.
Moscow Rd.
Campden Hill Rd.
Lansdowne Rd.
Clarendon Rd.
Portland Rd.
Elgin Cres.
Blenheim Cres.
Walmer Rd.
Princedale Rd.
Chesterton Rd.
Oxford Gdns.
Golborne Rd.
Royal Oak
Westbourne Park
Ladbroke Grove
Holland Park
Queensway
Bayswater
Notting Hill Gate
Paddington
Lancaster Gate
Edgware Rd.
125 yards
125 meters
A B C D E F G
1 2 3 4

Bloomsbury (Map 8)

SIGHTS

British Library, **1** C1
Coram's Fields, **2** D3
Senate House, **3** C3
St. George's Bloomsbury, **4** C4
St. Pancras Station, **5** C1
University College London, **6** B2

MUSEUMS AND GALLERIES

British Library Galleries, **7** C1
British Museum, **8** C4
Brunei Gallery, **9** C3
Percival David Foundation of Chinese Art, **10** C2
Pollock's Toy Museum, **11** B3

FOOD

Diwana Bhel Poori House, **12** B2
ICCo, **13** B4
La Brasserie Townhouse, **14** C4
Navarro's Tapas Bar, **15** B4
North Sea Fish Restaurant, **16** C2
Pescatori, **17** B4
Vats, **18** D3
Wagamama, **19** C4

PUBS

Exmouth Arms, **20** B2
Fitzroy Tavern, **21** B4
The Jeremy Bentham, **22** B3
The Lamb, **23** D3
The Museum Tavern, **24** C4
Newman Arms, **25** B4
The Queen's Larder, **26** C3
Rising Son, **27** B4

ENTERTAINMENT

The Place, **28** C2
RADA, **29** B3
Renoir, **30** C3
The Water Rats, **31** D1

SHOPPING

Delta of Venus, **32** B2
Gay's the Word, **33** C2
James Smith & Sons, **34** C4
L. Cornelissen & Son, **35** C4
Unsworths, **36** C4
Waterstone's, **37** B3

ACCOMMODATIONS

Ashlee House, **38** D1
Carr-Saunders Hall, **39** A3
Commonwealth Hall, **40** C2
The Generator, **41** C2
George Hotel, **42** C2
Indian YMCA, **43** A3
Jenkins Hotel, **44** C2
The Langland Hotel, **45** B3
Passfield Hall, **46** B2
Pickwick Hall International Backpackers, **47** C3
Royal National Hotel, **48** C3
Thanet Hotel, **49** C3
YHA St. Pancras International, **50** C1

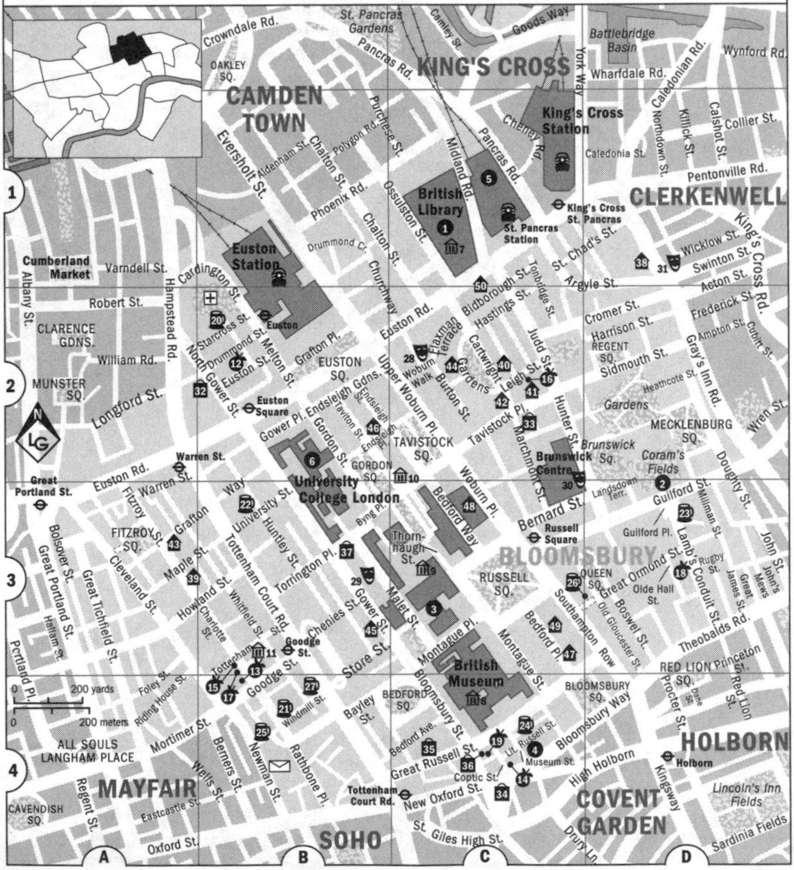

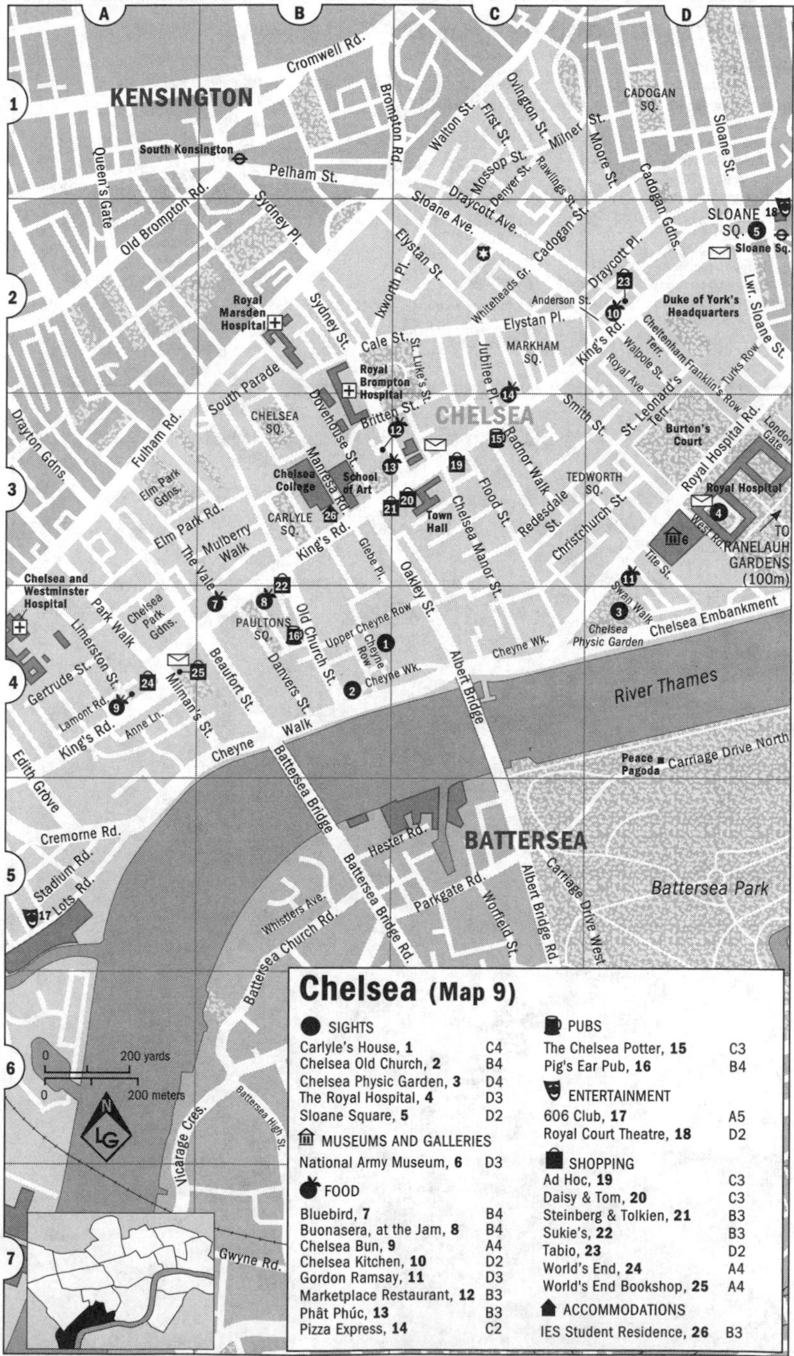
A
B
C
D
1
2
3
4
5
6
7
KENSINGTON
CHELSEA
BATTERSEA
Cromwell Rd.
South Kensington
Pelham St.
Queen's Gate
Old Brompton Rd.
Sydney Pl.
Brompton Rd.
Walton St.
First St.
Ovington St.
Milner St.
Moore St.
CADOGAN SQ.
Sloane St.
Mossop St.
Denyer St.
Rawlings St.
Draycott Ave.
Sloane Ave.
Cadogan St.
Cadogan Gdns.
SLOANE SQ.
Sloane Sq.
Elystan St.
Ixworth Pl.
Whiteheads Gr.
Anderson St.
Draycott Pl.
Duke of York's Headquarters
Lwr. Sloane St.
Royal Marsden Hospital
Sydney St.
Cale St.
St. Luke's St.
Elystan Pl.
Jubilee Pl.
MARKHAM SQ.
King's Rd.
Cheltenham Terr.
Franklin's Row
Turks Row
Walpole St.
Royal Ave
St. Leonard's Terr.
Royal Brompton Hospital
South Parade
Dovehouse St.
Britten St.
CHELSEA SQ.
Smith St.
Burton's Court
Royal Hospital Rd.
London Gate
Drayton Gdns.
Fulham Rd.
Radnor Walk
Chelsea College
Manresa Rd.
School of Art
TEDWORTH SQ.
Royal Hospital
Elm Park Gdns.
Elm Park Rd.
CARLYLE SQ.
Town Hall
Chelsea Manor St.
Flood St.
Redesdale St.
Christchurch St.
West Rd.
TO RANELAUH GARDENS (100m)
Mulberry Walk
The Vale
King's Rd.
Glebe Pl.
Oakley St.
Tite St.
Chelsea and Westminster Hospital
Park Walk
Chelsea Park Gdns.
PAULTONS SQ.
Old Church St.
Upper Cheyne Row
Cheyne Row
Swan Walk
Chelsea Physic Garden
Chelsea Embankment
Cheyne Wk.
Limerston St.
Gertrude St.
Lamont Rd.
Milman's St.
Beaufort St.
Danvers St.
Albert Bridge
River Thames
King's Rd.
Anne Ln.
Cheyne Walk
Battersea Bridge
Peace Pagoda
Carriage Drive North
Edith Grove
Cremorne Rd.
Hester Rd.
Battersea Bridge Rd.
Stadium Rd.
Lots Rd.
Parkgate Rd.
Worfield St.
Albert Bridge Rd.
Carriage Drive West
Battersea Park
Whistlers Ave.
Battersea Church Rd.
200 yards
200 meters
Vicarage Cres.
Battersea High St.
Gwyne Rd.
Chelsea (Map 9)
SIGHTS
Carlyle's House, 1 C4
Chelsea Old Church, 2 B4
Chelsea Physic Garden, 3 D4
The Royal Hospital, 4 D3
Sloane Square, 5 D2
MUSEUMS AND GALLERIES
National Army Museum, 6 D3
FOOD
Bluebird, 7 B4
Buonasera, at the Jam, 8 B4
Chelsea Bun, 9 A4
Chelsea Kitchen, 10 D2
Gordon Ramsay, 11 D3
Marketplace Restaurant, 12 B3
Phât Phúc, 13 B3
Pizza Express, 14 C2
PUBS
The Chelsea Potter, 15 C3
Pig's Ear Pub, 16 B4
ENTERTAINMENT
606 Club, 17 A5
Royal Court Theatre, 18 D2
SHOPPING
Ad Hoc, 19 C3
Daisy & Tom, 20 C3
Steinberg & Tolkien, 21 B3
Sukie's, 22 B3
Tabio, 23 D2
World's End, 24 A4
World's End Bookshop, 25 A4
ACCOMMODATIONS
IES Student Residence, 26 B3

The City of London (Map 10)

SIGHTS

- All Hallows-By-The-Tower, **1** D5
- Bank of England, **2** C4
- Barbican Centre, **3** B2
- Guildhall, **4** B3
- Lloyd's of London, **5** D4
- Lower Thames St., **6** C5
- Monument, **7** C4
- Royal Exchange, **8** C4
- St. Dunstan-in-the-East, **9** D5
- St. Giles Cripplegate, **10** B3
- St. Magnus-the-Martyr, **11** C5
- St. Margaret Lothbury, **12** C3
- St. Mary-le-Bow, **13** B4
- St. Mary Woolnoth, **14** C4
- St. Paul's Cathedral, **15** A4
- St. Stephen Walbrook, **16** C4
- Stock Exchange, **17** C4
- Temple of Mithras, **18** B4
- Tower of London, **19** D5

MUSEUMS AND GALLERIES

- The Clockmakers' Museum & Guildhall Library, **20** B3
- Bank of England Museum, **21** C4
- Guildhall Art Gallery, **22** B3
- Museum of London, **23** B3

FOOD

- Café Spice Namaste, **24** D4
- Crussh Juice Bar, **25** C4
- Futures, **26** C5
- Leadenhall Market, **27** C4
- The Place Below, **28** B4
- Spianata and Co., **29** B4

PUBS

- The Black Friar, **30** A4
- The Golden Fleece, **31** B4
- The Hung Drawn and Quartered, **32** D5
- The Samuel Pepys, **33** B5
- Simpson's, **34** C4
- The Walrus and the Carpenter Pub, **35** C5

ENTERTAINMENT

- Barbican Centre, **36** B2

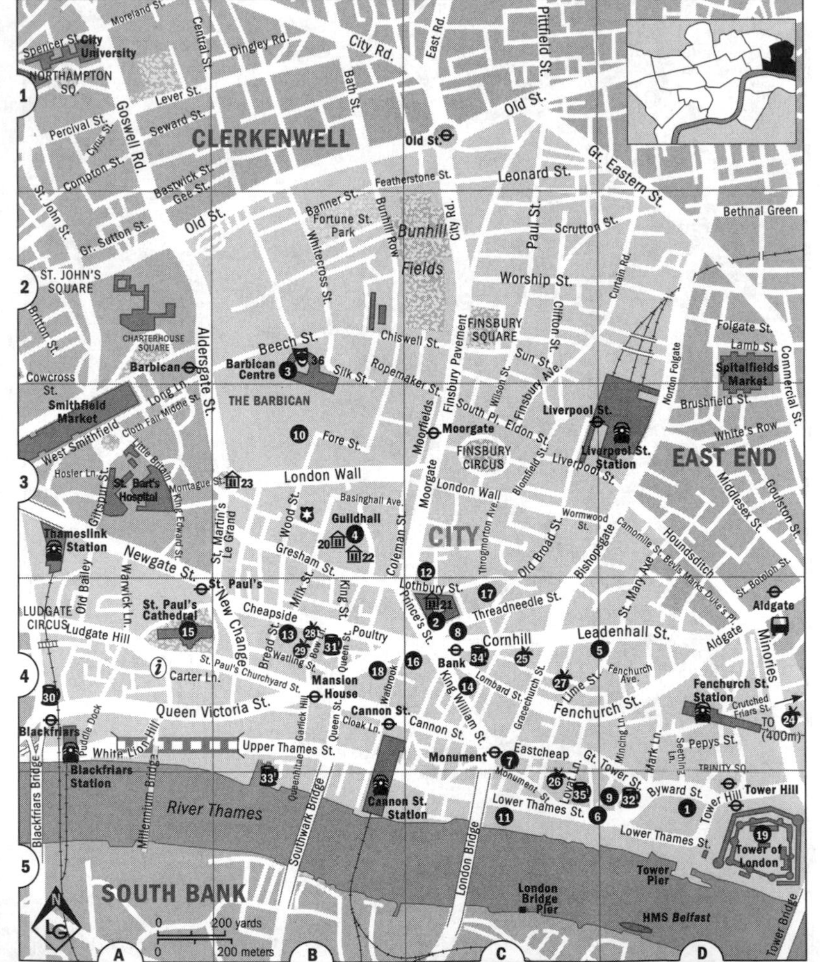

Holborn & Clerkenwell (Map 11)

SIGHTS

The Charterhouse, **1**	D3
Clerkenwell Green, **2**	C2
Clerkenwell Visitor Centre, **3**	C2
Elm Court, **4**	B5
Ely Place, **5**	C3
Fleet Street, **6**	B4
Gray's Inn, **7**	B3
Gray's Inn Chapel, **8**	B3
Leather Lane Market, **9**	B3
Lincoln's Inn, **10**	A4
Marx Memorial Library, **11**	C2
Middle Temple Garden, **12**	B5
Middle Temple Hall, **13**	B5
Priory of St. John, **14**	C2
Royal Courts of Justice, **15**	B4
St. Bartholomew The Great, **16**	D3
St. Bride's, **17**	C5
St. Clement Danes, **18**	B5
St. Dunstan-in-the-West, **19**	B4
St. Etheldreda's, **20**	C3
St. John's Gate, **21**	C2
St. John's Square, **22**	C3
The Temple, **23**	B5
Temple Church, **24**	B5

MUSEUMS AND GALLERIES

Courtauld Institute Galleries, **25**	A5
Gilbert Collection, **26**	A5
Hermitage Rooms, **27**	A5
The Hunterian Museum, **28**	A4
Museum of St. Bartholomew's Hospital, **29**	D4
Sir John Soane's Museum, **30**	A4
Somerset House, **31**	A5

FOOD

Al's Café/Bar, **32**	B2
Aki, **33**	B2
Anexo, **34**	C2
Bar Bombay, **35**	D3
Bleeding Heart Bistro and Restaurant, **36**	C3
Bleeding Heart Tavern, **37**	C3
The Greenery, **38**	C3
St. John, **39**	C3
Woolley's, **40**	A3

PUBS

Cittie of York, **41**	B3
The Eagle, **42**	B2
Fox & Anchor, **43**	D3
The Jerusalem Tavern, **44**	C2
The Old Bank of England, **45**	B4
The Punch Tavern, **46**	C4
The Three Kings, **47**	C2
Ye Olde Cheshire Cheese, **48**	C4
Ye Olde Mitre Tavern, **49**	C3

NIGHTLIFE

Café Kick, **50**	B1
Fabric, **51**	C3
Fluid, **52**	C3
Match EC1, **53**	C2
Na Zdrowie, **54**	A4
The Three Tuns, **55**	A4
Turnmills, **56**	C2

ENTERTAINMENT

Chuckle Club, **57**	A4
Peacock Theatre, **58**	A4
Sadler's Wells, **59**	B1

SHOPPING

Twining's, **60**	B5

ACCOMMODATIONS

City University Finsbury Residences, **61**	D2
Grenville House Hotel, **62**	A2
Guilford House Hotel, **63**	A2
Rosebery Hall, **64**	C1

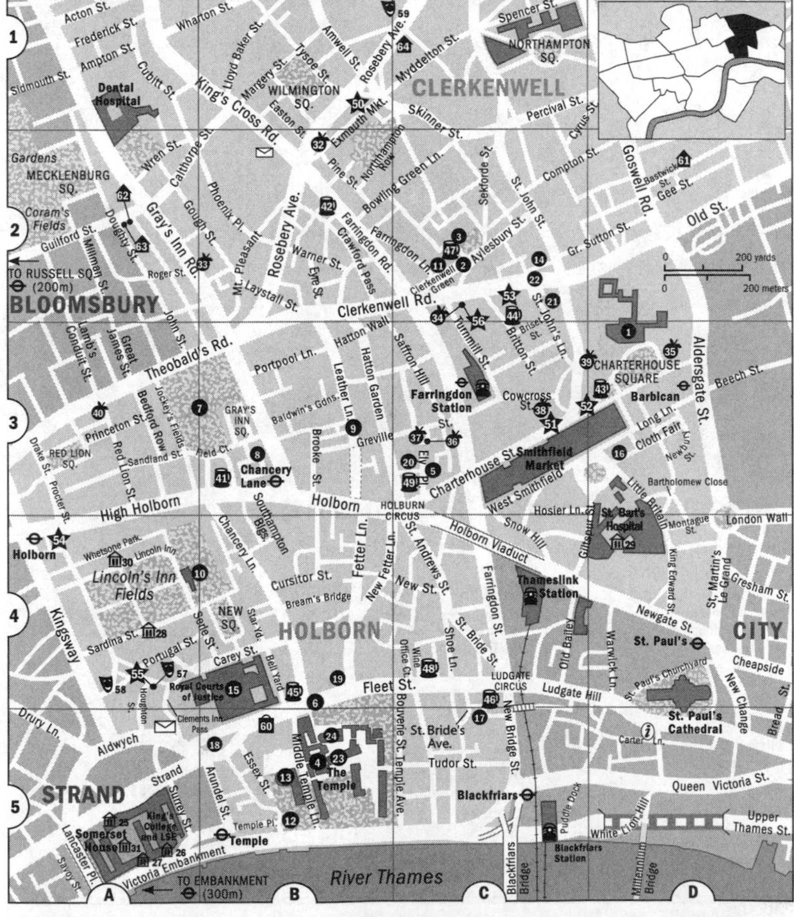

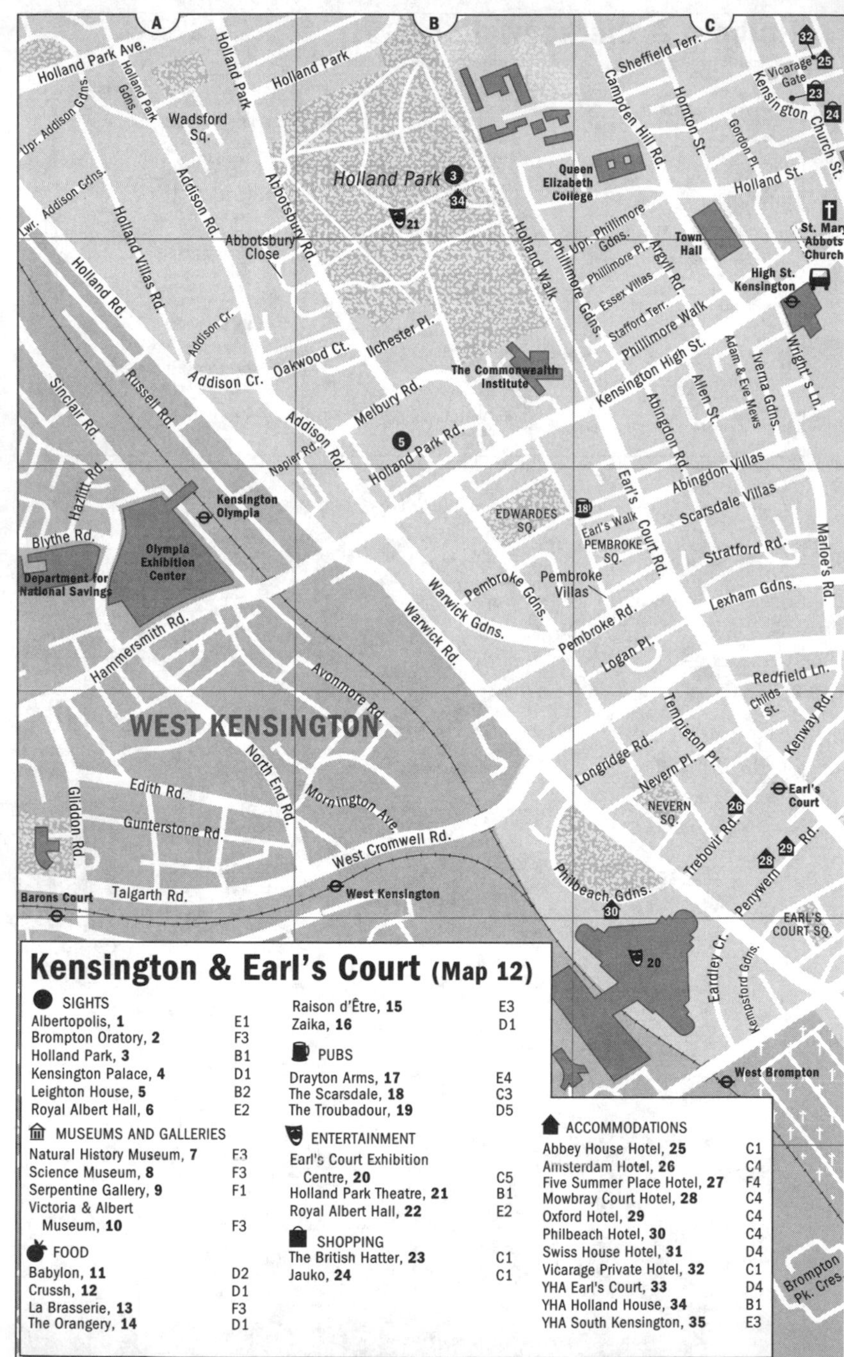
A
B
C
Kensington & Earl's Court (Map 12)
SIGHTS
Albertopolis, 1 E1
Brompton Oratory, 2 F3
Holland Park, 3 B1
Kensington Palace, 4 D1
Leighton House, 5 B2
Royal Albert Hall, 6 E2
MUSEUMS AND GALLERIES
Natural History Museum, 7 F3
Science Museum, 8 F3
Serpentine Gallery, 9 F1
Victoria & Albert Museum, 10 F3
FOOD
Babylon, 11 D2
Crussh, 12 D1
La Brasserie, 13 F3
The Orangery, 14 D1
Raison d'Être, 15 E3
Zaika, 16 D1
PUBS
Drayton Arms, 17 E4
The Scarsdale, 18 C3
The Troubadour, 19 D5
ENTERTAINMENT
Earl's Court Exhibition Centre, 20 C5
Holland Park Theatre, 21 B1
Royal Albert Hall, 22 E2
SHOPPING
The British Hatter, 23 C1
Jauko, 24 C1
ACCOMMODATIONS
Abbey House Hotel, 25 C1
Amsterdam Hotel, 26 C4
Five Summer Place Hotel, 27 F4
Mowbray Court Hotel, 28 C4
Oxford Hotel, 29 C4
Philbeach Hotel, 30 C4
Swiss House Hotel, 31 D4
Vicarage Private Hotel, 32 C1
YHA Earl's Court, 33 D4
YHA Holland House, 34 B1
YHA South Kensington, 35 E3
Holland Park Ave.
Holland Park Gdns.
Upr. Addison Gdns.
Wadsford Sq.
Holland Park
Lwr. Addison Gdns.
Addison Rd.
Holland Villas Rd.
Abbotsbury Rd.
Abbotsbury Close
Holland Rd.
Sheffield Terr.
Campden Hill Rd.
Hornton St.
Gordon Pl.
Vicarage Gate
Kensington Church St.
Queen Elizabeth College
Holland St.
Holland Walk
Phillimore Gdns.
Upr. Phillimore Gdns.
Phillimore Pl.
Essex Villas
Argyll Rd.
Stafford Terr.
Phillimore Walk
Town Hall
St. Mary Abbots Church
High St. Kensington
Kensington High St.
Adam & Eve Mews
Iverna Gdns.
Wright's Ln.
Allen St.
Abingdon Rd.
Addison Cr.
Oakwood Ct.
Ilchester Pl.
The Commonwealth Institute
Melbury Rd.
Holland Park Rd.
Napier Rd.
Sinclair Rd.
Russell Rd.
Hazlitt Rd.
Kensington Olympia
Blythe Rd.
Olympia Exhibition Center
Department for National Savings
Hammersmith Rd.
EDWARDES SQ.
Earl's Walk
PEMBROKE SQ.
Earl's Court Rd.
Abingdon Villas
Scarsdale Villas
Stratford Rd.
Marloe's Rd.
Lexham Gdns.
Pembroke Villas
Pembroke Gdns.
Warwick Gdns.
Warwick Rd.
Pembroke Rd.
Logan Pl.
Redfield Ln.
Childs St.
Kenway Rd.
Avonmore Rd.
WEST KENSINGTON
North End Rd.
Templeton Pl.
Longridge Rd.
Nevern Pl.
NEVERN SQ.
Earl's Court
Trebovir Rd.
Penywern Rd.
Edith Rd.
Gunterstone Rd.
Mornington Ave.
Gliddon Rd.
West Cromwell Rd.
Philbeach Gdns.
EARL'S COURT SQ.
Barons Court
Talgarth Rd.
West Kensington
Eardley Cr.
Kempsford Gdns.
West Brompton
Brompton Pk. Cres.

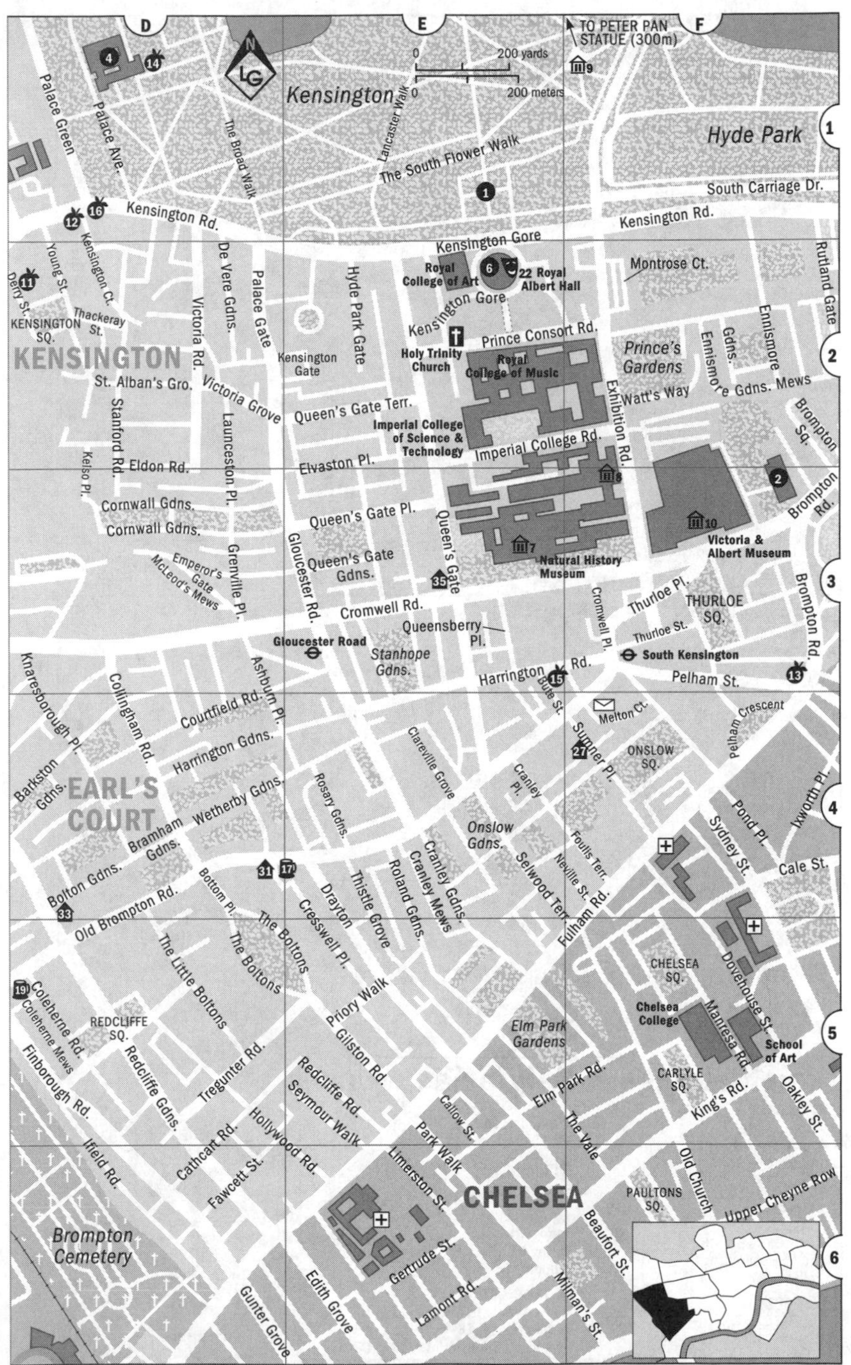
Kensington
Hyde Park
KENSINGTON
EARL'S COURT
CHELSEA
Royal College of Art
22 Royal Albert Hall
Holy Trinity Church
Royal College of Music
Imperial College of Science & Technology
Natural History Museum
Victoria & Albert Museum
Gloucester Road
South Kensington
Chelsea College
School of Art
Brompton Cemetery
TO PETER PAN STATUE (300m)
200 yards
200 meters

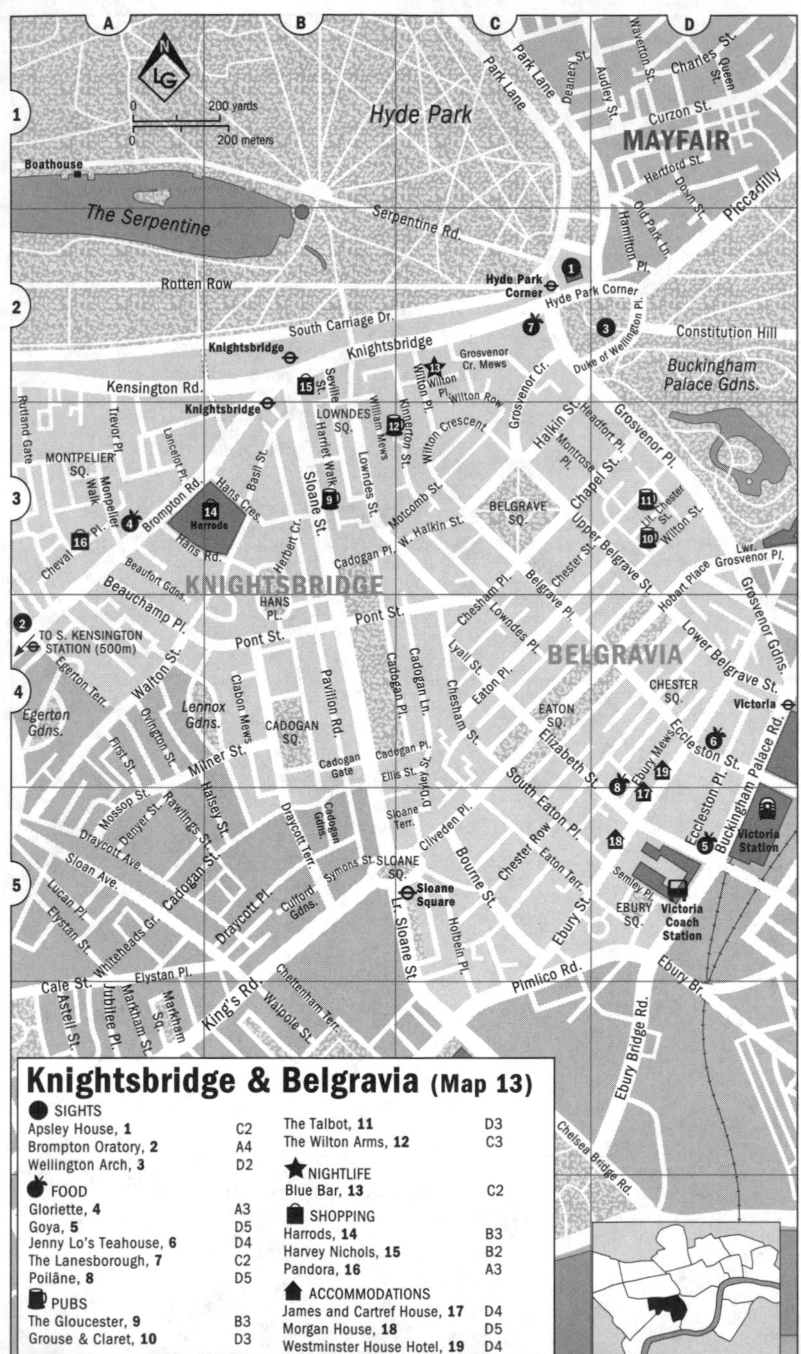

Knightsbridge & Belgravia (Map 13)

SIGHTS

Apsley House, **1**	C2
Brompton Oratory, **2**	A4
Wellington Arch, **3**	D2

FOOD

Gloriette, **4**	A3
Goya, **5**	D5
Jenny Lo's Teahouse, **6**	D4
The Lanesborough, **7**	C2
Poilâne, **8**	D5

PUBS

The Gloucester, **9**	B3
Grouse & Claret, **10**	D3
The Talbot, **11**	D3
The Wilton Arms, **12**	C3

NIGHTLIFE

Blue Bar, **13**	C2

SHOPPING

Harrods, **14**	B3
Harvey Nichols, **15**	B2
Pandora, **16**	A3

ACCOMMODATIONS

James and Cartref House, **17**	D4
Morgan House, **18**	D5
Westminster House Hotel, **19**	D4

Marylebone & Regent's Park (Map 14)

SIGHTS

All Souls Langham Place, **1**	D4
Baker Street, **2**	C4
Edgware Road, **3**	B5
The London Planetarium, **4**	C3
London Zoo, **5**	C1
Madame Tussaud's, **6**	C3
Portland Place, **7**	D3
Queen Mary's Gardens, **8**	C2
Regent's Park, **9**	C1
St. John's Lodge, **10**	C2

MUSEUMS AND GALLERIES

Sherlock Holmes Museum, **11**	B3
The Wallace Collection, **12**	C4

FOOD

Giraffe, **13**	C4
Mandalay, **14**	A4
Patogh, **15**	A4
Ranoush Juice, **16**	B5
Royal China, **17**	C4
Spighetta, **18**	C4

PUBS

The Golden Eagle, **19**	C4
O'Conor Don, **20**	D5
The William Wallace, **21**	C4

ENTERTAINMENT

Open-Air Theatre, **22**	C2
Wigmore Hall, **23**	D5

ACCOMMODATIONS

Edward Lear Hotel, **24**	B5
Lincoln House Hotel, **25**	C4
International Student House, **26**	D3
University of Westminster Halls, **27**	C3

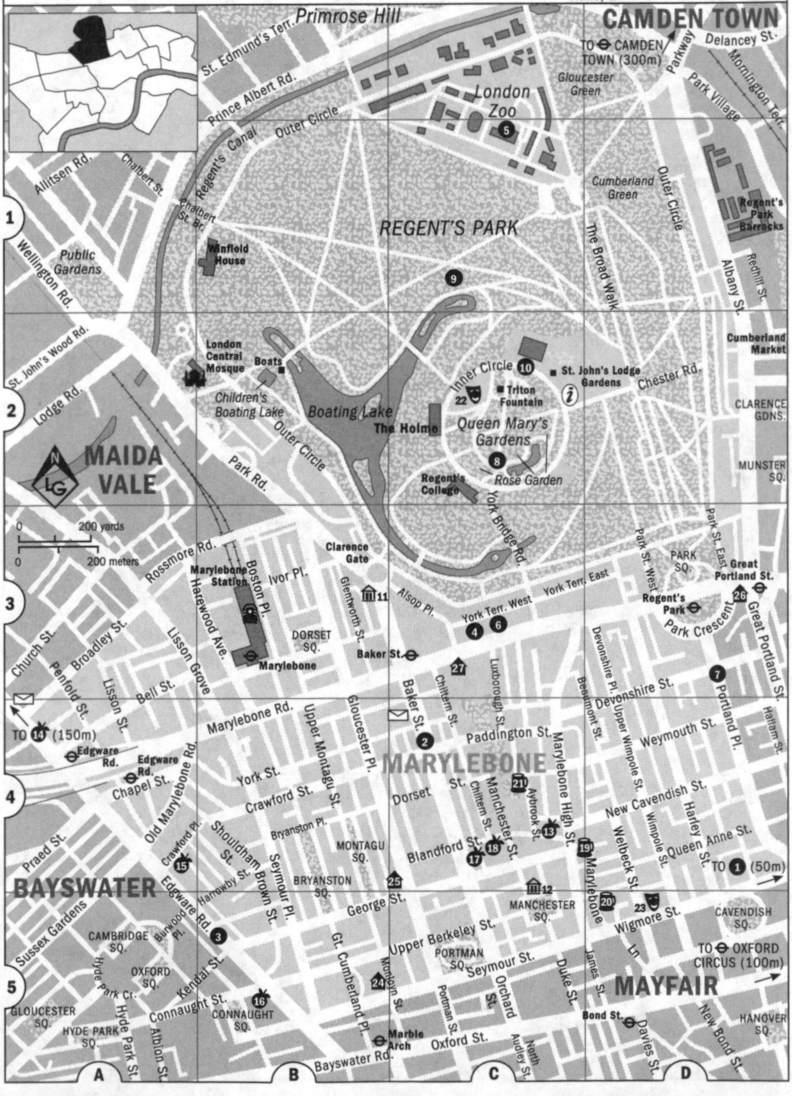

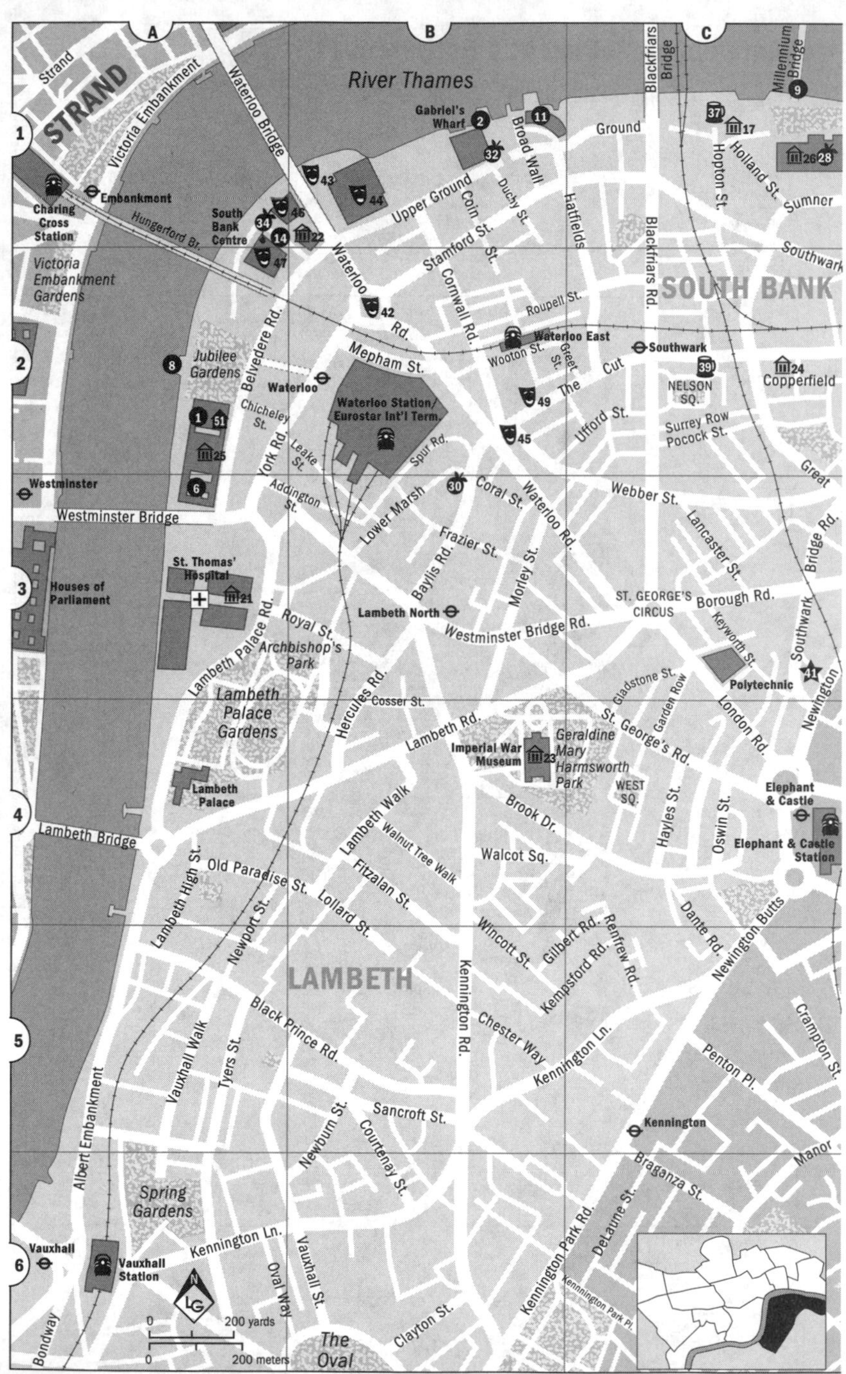
River Thames
STRAND
SOUTH BANK
LAMBETH
Charing Cross Station
Embankment
Victoria Embankment Gardens
Jubilee Gardens
Waterloo
Waterloo Station/ Eurostar Int'l Term.
Waterloo East
Southwark
Westminster
Westminster Bridge
Houses of Parliament
St. Thomas' Hospital
Archbishop's Park
Lambeth Palace Gardens
Lambeth Palace
Lambeth Bridge
Lambeth North
Imperial War Museum
Geraldine Mary Harmsworth Park
ST. GEORGE'S CIRCUS
Polytechnic
Elephant & Castle
Elephant & Castle Station
Kennington
Spring Gardens
Vauxhall
Vauxhall Station
The Oval
Gabriel's Wharf
South Bank Centre
NELSON SQ.
WEST SQ.
Copperfield
200 yards
200 meters

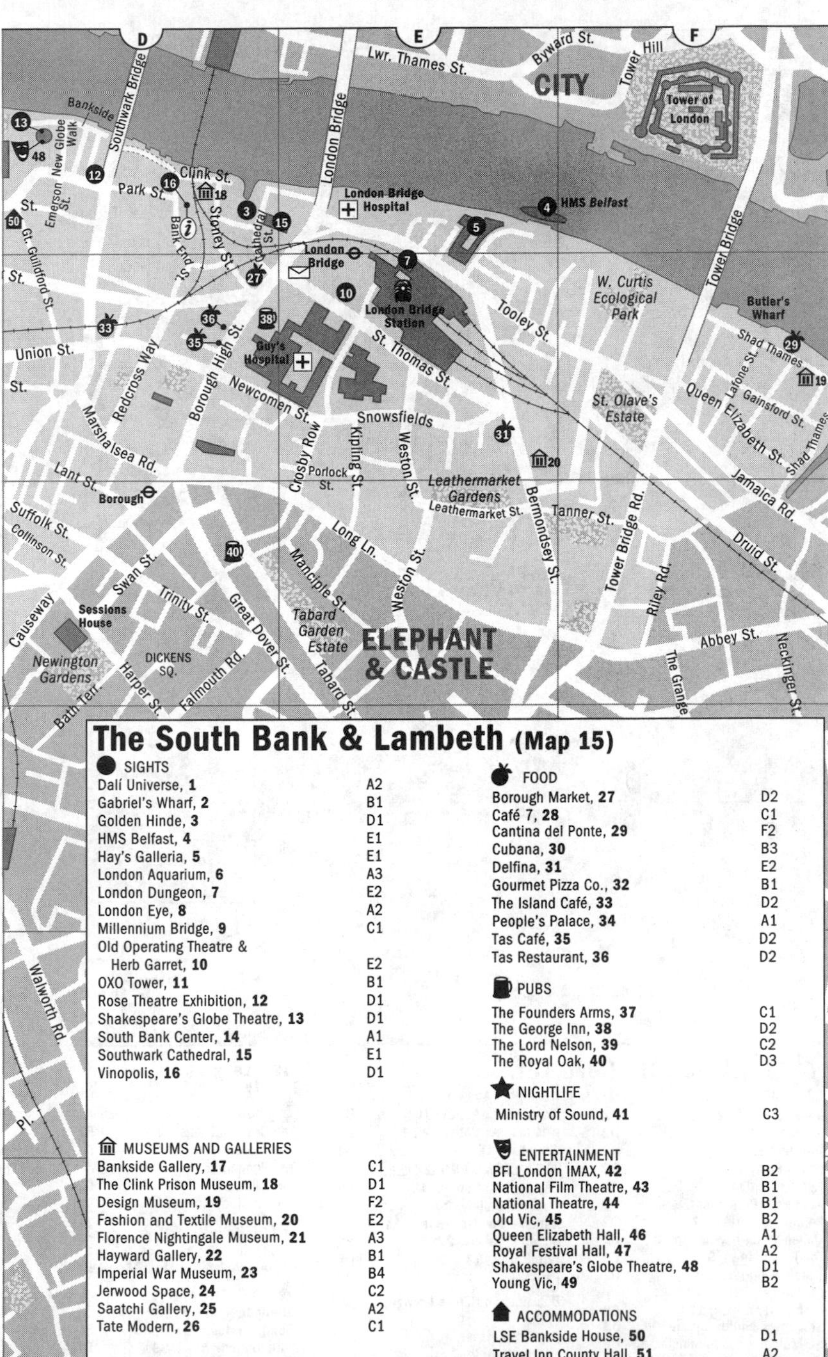

The South Bank & Lambeth (Map 15)

SIGHTS

Dalí Universe, **1** A2
Gabriel's Wharf, **2** B1
Golden Hinde, **3** D1
HMS Belfast, **4** E1
Hay's Galleria, **5** E1
London Aquarium, **6** A3
London Dungeon, **7** E2
London Eye, **8** A2
Millennium Bridge, **9** C1
Old Operating Theatre & Herb Garret, **10** E2
OXO Tower, **11** B1
Rose Theatre Exhibition, **12** D1
Shakespeare's Globe Theatre, **13** D1
South Bank Center, **14** A1
Southwark Cathedral, **15** E1
Vinopolis, **16** D1

MUSEUMS AND GALLERIES

Bankside Gallery, **17** C1
The Clink Prison Museum, **18** D1
Design Museum, **19** F2
Fashion and Textile Museum, **20** E2
Florence Nightingale Museum, **21** A3
Hayward Gallery, **22** B1
Imperial War Museum, **23** B4
Jerwood Space, **24** C2
Saatchi Gallery, **25** A2
Tate Modern, **26** C1

FOOD

Borough Market, **27** D2
Café 7, **28** C1
Cantina del Ponte, **29** F2
Cubana, **30** B3
Delfina, **31** E2
Gourmet Pizza Co., **32** B1
The Island Café, **33** D2
People's Palace, **34** A1
Tas Café, **35** D2
Tas Restaurant, **36** D2

PUBS

The Founders Arms, **37** C1
The George Inn, **38** D2
The Lord Nelson, **39** C2
The Royal Oak, **40** D3

NIGHTLIFE

Ministry of Sound, **41** C3

ENTERTAINMENT

BFI London IMAX, **42** B2
National Film Theatre, **43** B1
National Theatre, **44** B1
Old Vic, **45** B2
Queen Elizabeth Hall, **46** A1
Royal Festival Hall, **47** A2
Shakespeare's Globe Theatre, **48** D1
Young Vic, **49** B2

ACCOMMODATIONS

LSE Bankside House, **50** D1
Travel Inn County Hall, **51** A2

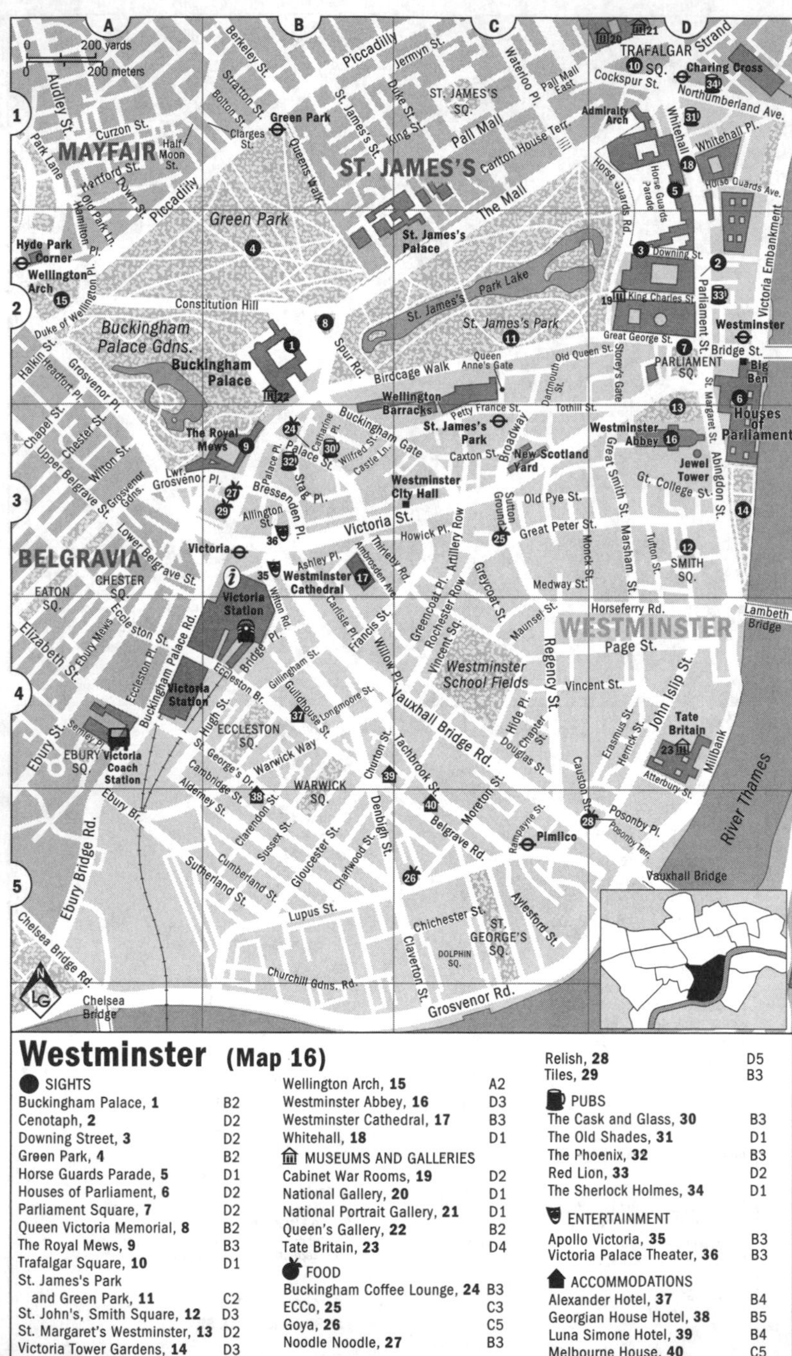

Westminster (Map 16)

SIGHTS

Buckingham Palace, **1**	B2
Cenotaph, **2**	D2
Downing Street, **3**	D2
Green Park, **4**	B2
Horse Guards Parade, **5**	D1
Houses of Parliament, **6**	D2
Parliament Square, **7**	D2
Queen Victoria Memorial, **8**	B2
The Royal Mews, **9**	B3
Trafalgar Square, **10**	D1
St. James's Park and Green Park, **11**	C2
St. John's, Smith Square, **12**	D3
St. Margaret's Westminster, **13**	D2
Victoria Tower Gardens, **14**	D3
Wellington Arch, **15**	A2
Westminster Abbey, **16**	D3
Westminster Cathedral, **17**	B3
Whitehall, **18**	D1

MUSEUMS AND GALLERIES

Cabinet War Rooms, **19**	D2
National Gallery, **20**	D1
National Portrait Gallery, **21**	D1
Queen's Gallery, **22**	B2
Tate Britain, **23**	D4

FOOD

Buckingham Coffee Lounge, **24**	B3
ECCo, **25**	C3
Goya, **26**	C5
Noodle Noodle, **27**	B3
Relish, **28**	D5
Tiles, **29**	B3

PUBS

The Cask and Glass, **30**	B3
The Old Shades, **31**	D1
The Phoenix, **32**	B3
Red Lion, **33**	D2
The Sherlock Holmes, **34**	D1

ENTERTAINMENT

Apollo Victoria, **35**	B3
Victoria Palace Theater, **36**	B3

ACCOMMODATIONS

Alexander Hotel, **37**	B4
Georgian House Hotel, **38**	B5
Luna Simone Hotel, **39**	B4
Melbourne House, **40**	C5

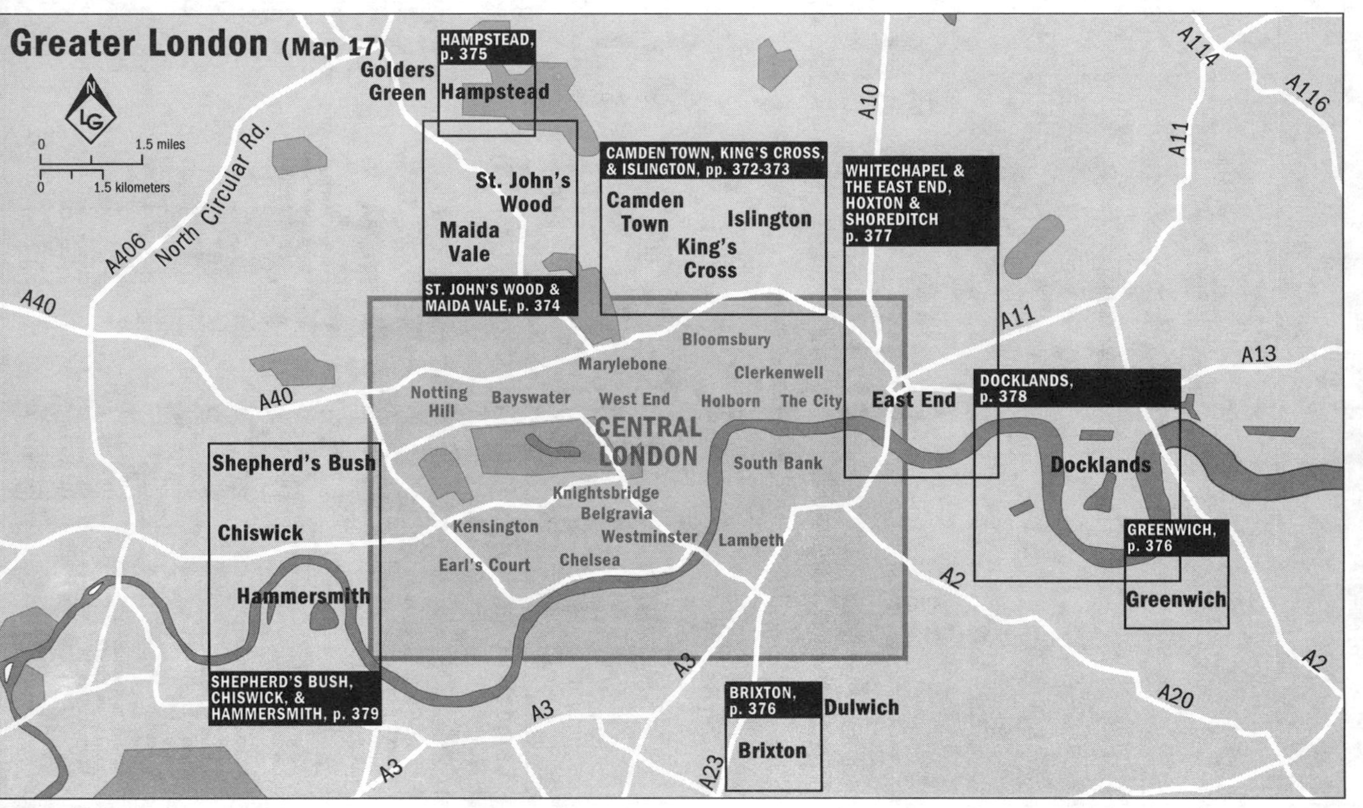

Greater London (Map 17)
N
LG
0
1.5 miles
0
1.5 kilometers
A406
North Circular Rd.
A40
A40
HAMPSTEAD,
p. 375
Golders
Green
Hampstead
St. John's
Wood
Maida
Vale
ST. JOHN'S WOOD &
MAIDA VALE, p. 374
CAMDEN TOWN, KING'S CROSS,
& ISLINGTON, pp. 372-373
Camden
Town
Islington
King's
Cross
A10
WHITECHAPEL &
THE EAST END,
HOXTON &
SHOREDITCH
p. 377
A114
A116
A11
A11
A13
Bloomsbury
Marylebone
Clerkenwell
Notting
Hill
Bayswater
West End
Holborn
The City
East End
DOCKLANDS,
p. 378
CENTRAL
LONDON
South Bank
Docklands
Shepherd's Bush
Knightsbridge
Belgravia
Kensington
Westminster
Lambeth
Chiswick
Earl's Court
Chelsea
GREENWICH,
p. 376
A2
Hammersmith
Greenwich
A3
A2
SHEPHERD'S BUSH,
CHISWICK, &
HAMMERSMITH, p. 379
BRIXTON,
p. 376
Dulwich
A3
A20
Brixton
A3
A23

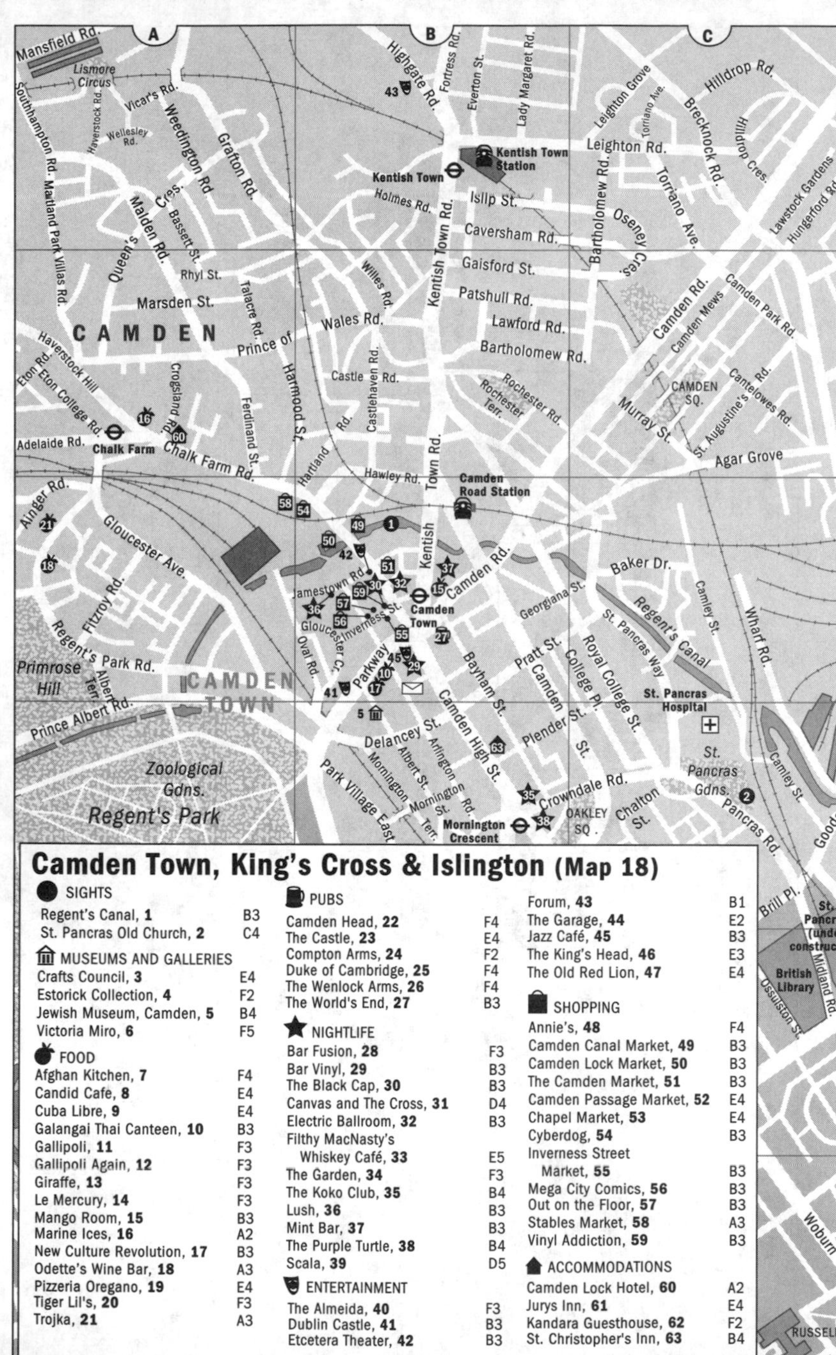
A
B
C
Mansfield Rd.
Lismore Circus
Southampton Rd.
Haverstock Rd.
Wellesley Rd.
Vicar's Rd.
Weedington Rd
Grafton Rd.
Highgate Rd.
Fortress Rd.
Everton St.
Lady Margaret Rd.
Leighton Grove
Torriano Ave.
Hilldrop Rd.
Breaknock Rd.
Hilldrop Cres.
Leighton Rd.
Kentish Town Station
Kentish Town
Holmes Rd.
Islip St.
Caversham Rd.
Bartholomew Rd.
Torriano Ave.
Oseney Cres.
Lawstock Gardens
Hungerford Rd.
Maitland Park Villas Rd.
Malden Rd.
Queen's Cres.
Bassett St.
Rhyl St.
Marsden St.
Talacre Rd.
Willes Rd.
Kentish Town Rd.
Gaisford St.
Patshull Rd.
Lawford Rd.
Bartholomew Rd.
Camden Rd.
Camden Mews
Camden Park Rd.
CAMDEN
Prince of Wales Rd.
Harmood St.
Castlehaven Rd.
Castle Rd.
Rochester Rd.
Rochester Terr.
CAMDEN SQ.
Murray St.
Cantelowes Rd.
St. Augustine's Rd.
Haverstock Hill
Eton Rd.
Eton College Rd.
Crogsland Rd.
Ferdinand St.
Hartland Rd.
Adelaide Rd.
Chalk Farm
Chalk Farm Rd.
Hawley Rd.
Camden Road Station
Agar Grove
Ainger Rd.
Gloucester Ave.
Baker Dr.
Jamestown Rd.
Camden Town
Georgiana St.
Regent's Canal
Camley St.
Wharf Rd.
St. Pancras Way
Fitzroy Rd.
Gloucester Cr.
Inverness St.
Oval Rd.
Parkway
Bayham St.
Pratt St.
Camden St.
Royal College St.
College Pl.
Regent's Park Rd.
Primrose Hill
Albert Terr.
CAMDEN TOWN
St. Pancras Hospital
Prince Albert Rd.
Delancey St.
Albert St.
Arlington Rd.
Camden High St.
Plender St.
Zoological Gdns.
Regent's Park
Park Village East
Mornington Terr.
Mornington St.
Crowndale Rd.
Mornington Crescent
OAKLEY SQ.
Chalton St.
St. Pancras Gdns.
Pancras Rd.
Camley St.
Goods
Brill Pl.
St. Pancras (under construction)
British Library
Midland Rd.
Ossulston St.
Woburn
RUSSELL

Camden Town, King's Cross & Islington (Map 18)

SIGHTS
Regent's Canal, 1 B3
St. Pancras Old Church, 2 C4

MUSEUMS AND GALLERIES
Crafts Council, 3 E4
Estorick Collection, 4 F2
Jewish Museum, Camden, 5 B4
Victoria Miro, 6 F5

FOOD
Afghan Kitchen, 7 F4
Candid Cafe, 8 E4
Cuba Libre, 9 E4
Galangai Thai Canteen, 10 B3
Gallipoli, 11 F3
Gallipoli Again, 12 F3
Giraffe, 13 F3
Le Mercury, 14 F3
Mango Room, 15 B3
Marine Ices, 16 A2
New Culture Revolution, 17 B3
Odette's Wine Bar, 18 A3
Pizzeria Oregano, 19 E4
Tiger Lil's, 20 F3
Trojka, 21 A3

PUBS
Camden Head, 22 F4
The Castle, 23 E4
Compton Arms, 24 F2
Duke of Cambridge, 25 F4
The Wenlock Arms, 26 F4
The World's End, 27 B3

NIGHTLIFE
Bar Fusion, 28 F3
Bar Vinyl, 29 B3
The Black Cap, 30 B3
Canvas and The Cross, 31 D4
Electric Ballroom, 32 B3
Filthy MacNasty's Whiskey Café, 33 E5
The Garden, 34 F3
The Koko Club, 35 B4
Lush, 36 B3
Mint Bar, 37 B3
The Purple Turtle, 38 B4
Scala, 39 D5

ENTERTAINMENT
The Almeida, 40 F3
Dublin Castle, 41 B3
Etcetera Theater, 42 B3
Forum, 43 B1
The Garage, 44 E2
Jazz Café, 45 B3
The King's Head, 46 E3
The Old Red Lion, 47 E4

SHOPPING
Annie's, 48 F4
Camden Canal Market, 49 B3
Camden Lock Market, 50 B3
The Camden Market, 51 B3
Camden Passage Market, 52 E4
Chapel Market, 53 E4
Cyberdog, 54 B3
Inverness Street Market, 55 B3
Mega City Comics, 56 B3
Out on the Floor, 57 B3
Stables Market, 58 A3
Vinyl Addiction, 59 B3

ACCOMMODATIONS
Camden Lock Hotel, 60 A2
Jurys Inn, 61 E4
Kandara Guesthouse, 62 F2
St. Christopher's Inn, 63 B4

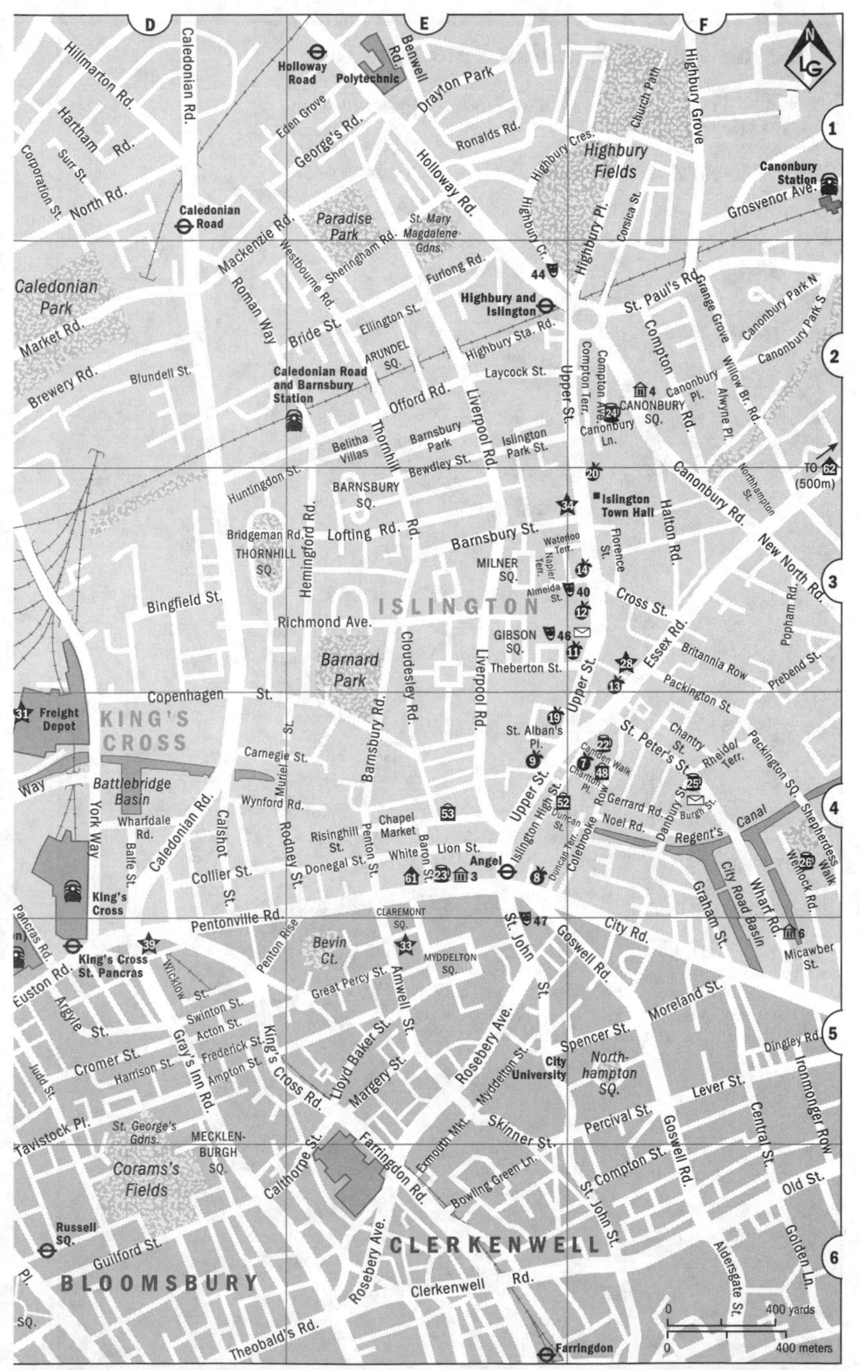
Holloway Road
Polytechnic
Caledonian Road
Highbury Fields
Canonbury Station
Paradise Park
St. Mary Magdalene Gdns.
Caledonian Park
Highbury and Islington
Caledonian Road and Barnsbury Station
CANONBURY SQ.
BARNSBURY SQ.
Islington Town Hall
THORNHILL SQ.
MILNER SQ.
ISLINGTON
GIBSON SQ.
Barnard Park
KING'S CROSS
Freight Depot
Battlebridge Basin
Chapel Market
Angel
King's Cross
King's Cross St. Pancras
CLAREMONT SQ.
Bevin Ct.
MYDDELTON SQ.
City University
Northampton SQ.
MECKLENBURGH SQ.
Corams's Fields
St. George's Gdns.
Russell SQ.
CLERKENWELL
BLOOMSBURY
Farringdon
Regent's Canal
City Road Basin
TO 62 (500m)
400 yards
400 meters

St. John's Wood & Maida Vale (Map 19)

SIGHTS
- Abbey Rd. Crossing, **5**
- Abbey Rd. Studios, **4**
- Lord's Cricket Ground, **6**

MUSEUMS AND GALLERIES
- Freud Museum, **1**

ENTERTAINMENT
- Canal Cafe Theatre, **8**
- Hampstead Theatre, **3**
- Puppet Theatre Barge, **7**
- Tricycle / Tricycle Cinema, **2**

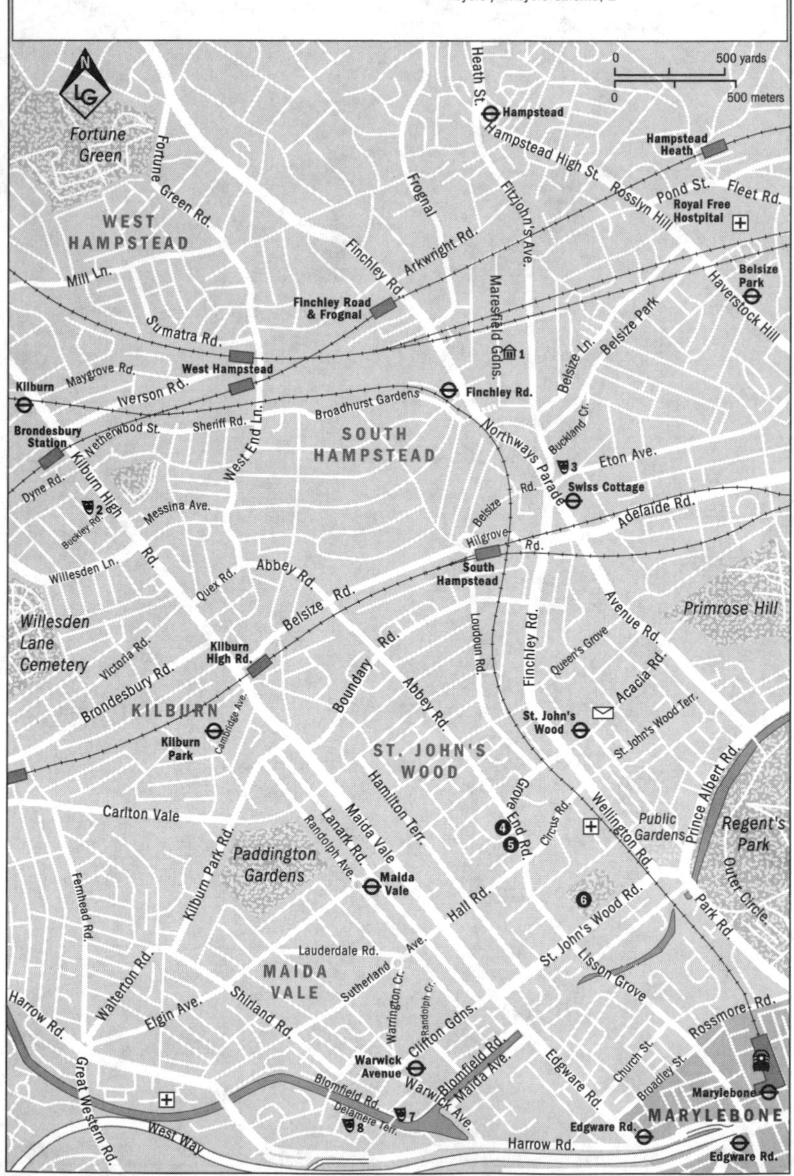

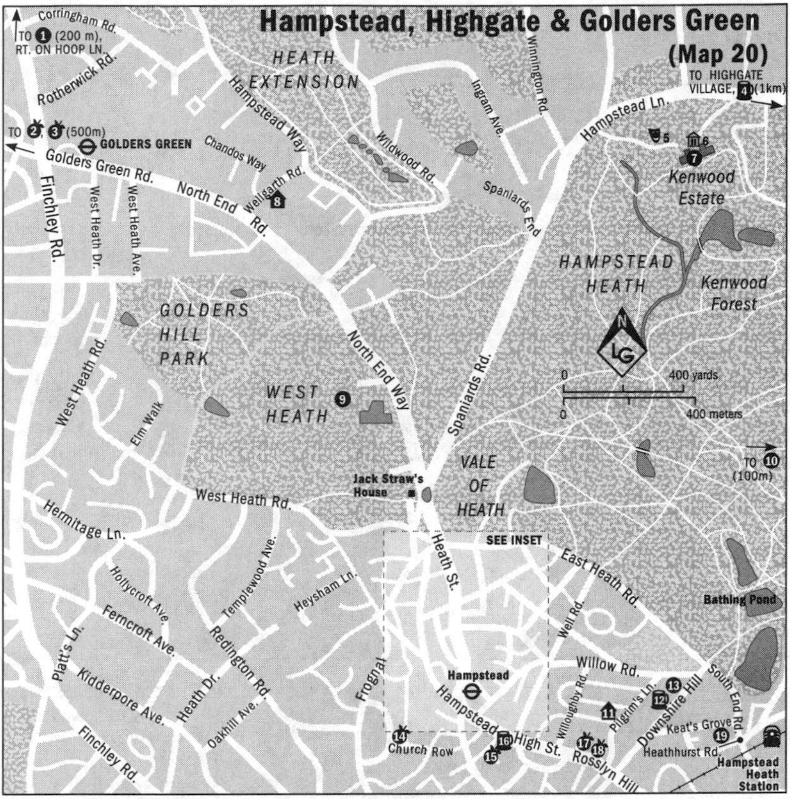

Hampstead, Highgate & Golders Green
(Map 20)
TO 1 (200 m), RT. ON HOOP LN.
Corringham Rd.
Rotherwick Rd.
HEATH EXTENSION
Hampstead Way
Winnington Rd.
Ingram Ave.
TO HIGHGATE VILLAGE, 4 (1km)
Hampstead Ln.
TO 2, 3 (500m)
GOLDERS GREEN
Chandos Way
Wildwood Rd.
5
6
7
Kenwood Estate
Golders Green Rd.
North End Rd.
Wellgarth Rd.
8
Spaniards End
Finchley Rd.
West Heath Dr.
West Heath Ave.
HAMPSTEAD HEATH
Kenwood Forest
GOLDERS HILL PARK
North End Way
Spaniards Rd.
0
400 yards
400 meters
West Heath Rd.
Elm Walk
WEST HEATH
9
VALE OF HEATH
TO 10 (100m)
Jack Straw's House
West Heath Rd.
Hermitage Ln.
SEE INSET
Heath St.
East Heath Rd.
Templewood Ave.
Hollycroft Ave.
Heysham Ln.
Bathing Pond
Ferncroft Ave.
Redington Rd.
Well Rd.
Platt's Ln.
Willow Rd.
Kidderpore Ave.
Heath Dr.
Frognal
Hampstead
Willoughby Rd.
13
South End Rd.
Oakhill Ave.
11
12
Pilgrim's Ln.
Downshire Hill
Keat's Grove
Finchley Rd.
14
Church Row
16
15
Hampstead High St.
17
18
Rosslyn Hill
Heathhurst Rd.
19
Hampstead Heath Station

0
100 yards
0
100 meters
East Heath Rd.
Hampstead Grove
Holford Rd.
Cannon Pl.
Lower Terr.
Christ Church Hill
The Mount
Heath St.
20
New End Sq.
Frognal Rise
21
Holly Hill
Flask Wk.
Holly Walk
Hampstead
22
Gayton Rd.
Holly Bush Vale
23
Hampstead High St.

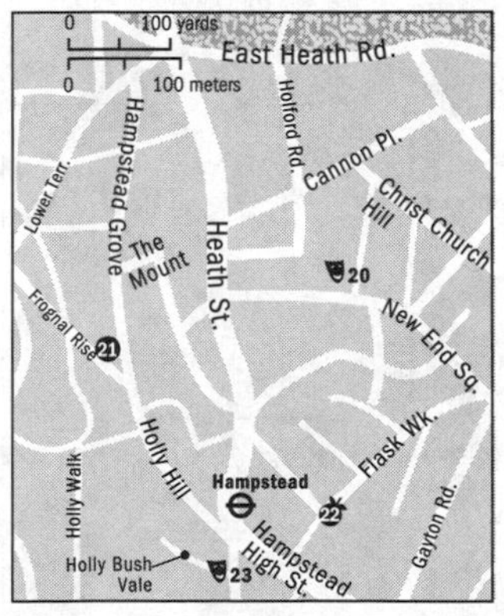

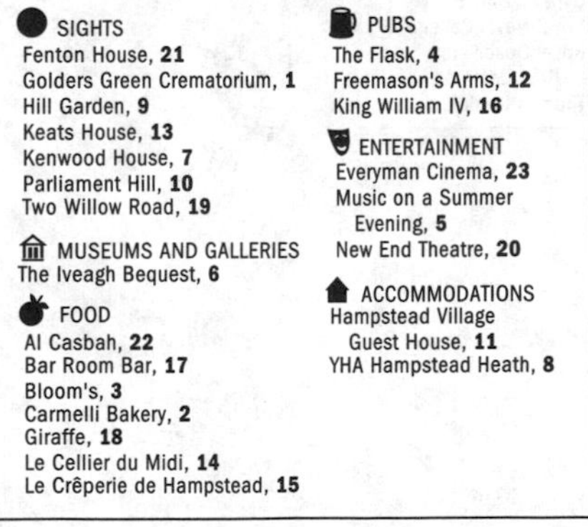

SIGHTS
- Fenton House, **21**
- Golders Green Crematorium, **1**
- Hill Garden, **9**
- Keats House, **13**
- Kenwood House, **7**
- Parliament Hill, **10**
- Two Willow Road, **19**

MUSEUMS AND GALLERIES
- The Iveagh Bequest, **6**

FOOD
- Al Casbah, **22**
- Bar Room Bar, **17**
- Bloom's, **3**
- Carmelli Bakery, **2**
- Giraffe, **18**
- Le Cellier du Midi, **14**
- Le Crêperie de Hampstead, **15**

PUBS
- The Flask, **4**
- Freemason's Arms, **12**
- King William IV, **16**

ENTERTAINMENT
- Everyman Cinema, **23**
- Music on a Summer Evening, **5**
- New End Theatre, **20**

ACCOMMODATIONS
- Hampstead Village Guest House, **11**
- YHA Hampstead Heath, **8**

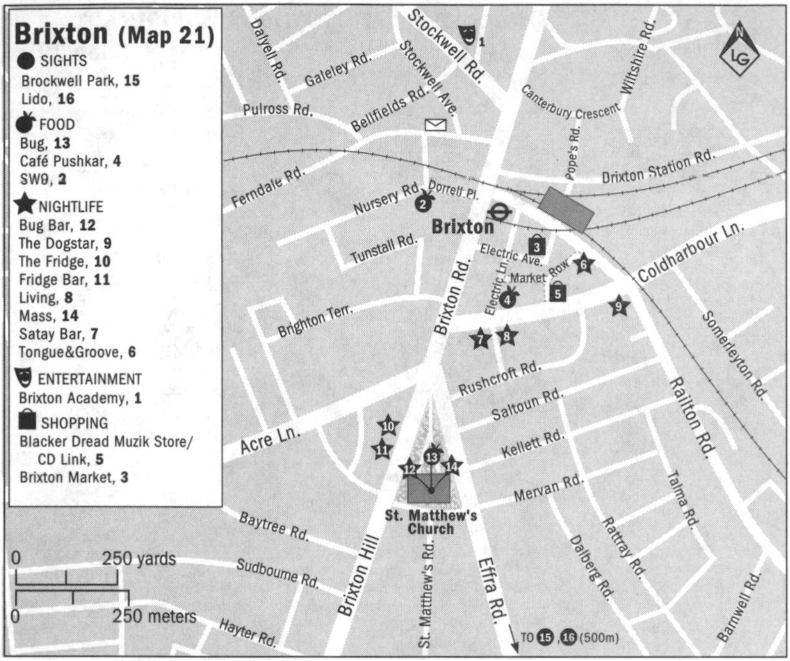

Brixton (Map 21)

SIGHTS
Brockwell Park, **15**
Lido, **16**

FOOD
Bug, **13**
Café Pushkar, **4**
SW9, **2**

NIGHTLIFE
Bug Bar, **12**
The Dogstar, **9**
The Fridge, **10**
Fridge Bar, **11**
Living, **8**
Mass, **14**
Satay Bar, **7**
Tongue&Groove, **6**

ENTERTAINMENT
Brixton Academy, **1**

SHOPPING
Blacker Dread Muzik Store/ CD Link, **5**
Brixton Market, **3**

0 250 yards
0 250 meters

Stockwell Rd.
Dalyell Rd.
Galeley Rd.
Stockwell Ave.
Pulross Rd.
Bellfields Rd.
Canterbury Crescent
Wiltshire Rd.
Pope's Rd.
Brixton Station Rd.
Ferndale Rd.
Nursery Rd.
Dorrell Pl.
Brixton
Tunstall Rd.
Electric Ave.
Electric Ln.
Market Row
Coldharbour Ln.
Brixton Rd.
Brighton Terr.
Somerleyton Rd.
Rushcroft Rd.
Saltoun Rd.
Railton Rd.
Acre Ln.
Kellett Rd.
Mervan Rd.
St. Matthew's Church
Baytree Rd.
Talma Rd.
Rattray Rd.
Dalberg Rd.
Sudbourne Rd.
Brixton Hill
St. Matthew's Rd.
Effra Rd.
Barnwell Rd.
Hayter Rd.
TO 15, 16 (500m)

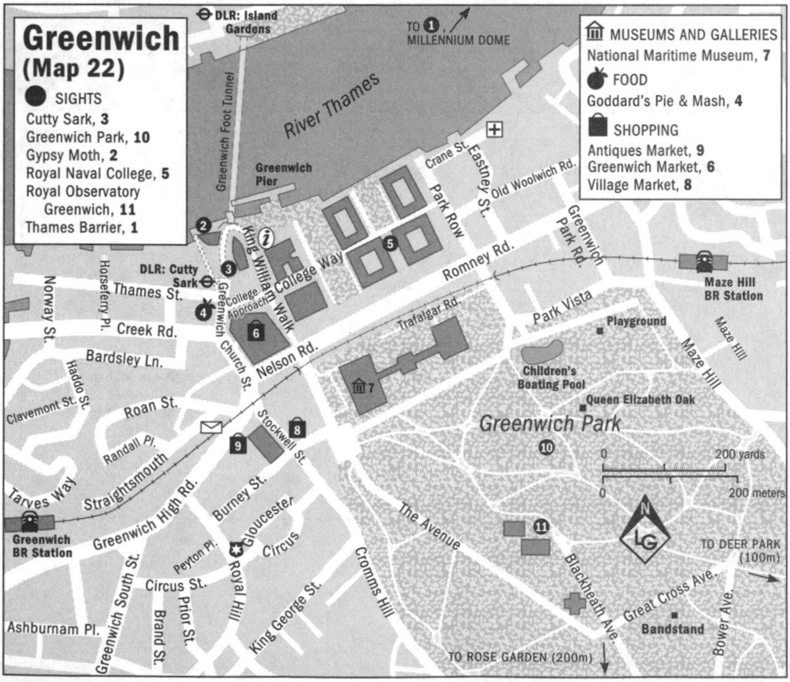

Greenwich (Map 22)

SIGHTS
Cutty Sark, **3**
Greenwich Park, **10**
Gypsy Moth, **2**
Royal Naval College, **5**
Royal Observatory Greenwich, **11**
Thames Barrier, **1**

MUSEUMS AND GALLERIES
National Maritime Museum, **7**

FOOD
Goddard's Pie & Mash, **4**

SHOPPING
Antiques Market, **9**
Greenwich Market, **6**
Village Market, **8**

DLR: Island Gardens
TO 1, MILLENNIUM DOME
River Thames
Greenwich Foot Tunnel
Greenwich Pier
Crane St.
Eastney St.
Old Woolwich Rd.
Park Row
Greenwich Park Rd.
King William Walk
College Way
Romney Rd.
Maze Hill BR Station
DLR: Cutty Sark
Thames St.
Horseferry Pl.
Norway St.
College Approach
Greenwich Church St.
Creek Rd.
Trafalgar Rd.
Park Vista
Playground
Maze Hill
Bardsley Ln.
Nelson Rd.
Children's Boating Pool
Queen Elizabeth Oak
Haddo St.
Clavemont St.
Roan St.
Greenwich Park
Stockwell St.
Randall Pl.
0 200 yards
0 200 meters
Tarves Way
Straightsmouth
Burney St.
Gloucester Circus
The Avenue
Greenwich BR Station
Greenwich High Rd.
Peyton Pl.
Royal Hill
Cromms Hill
TO DEER PARK (100m)
Circus St.
Great Cross Ave.
Blackheath Ave.
Greenwich South St.
Prior St.
King George St.
Bandstand
Ashburnam Pl.
Brand St.
Bower Ave.
TO ROSE GARDEN (200m)

Whitechapel & The East End; Hoxton & Shoreditch (Map 23)
(HS = HOXTON & SHOREDITCH DETAIL)
SIGHTS
Bevis Marks Synagogue, 1 A3
Brick Lane, 2 B3
Christ Church Spitalfields, 3 A3
East London Mosque, 4 B3
MUSEUMS AND GALLERIES
Geffrye Museum, 5 A5
Deluxe Gallery, 6 HS
Museum of Childhood, 7 C5
Victoria Miro, 8 HS
Whitechapel Art Gallery, 9 B3
White Cube², 10 HS
FOOD
Aladin, 11 B4
Beigel Bake, 12 B4
Café 1001, 13 B4
Grand Central, 14 HS
Shish, 15 HS
Yelo, 16 HS
PUBS
The Macbeth, 17 HS
NIGHTLIFE
333, 18 HS
93 Feet East, 19 B4
Cantaloupe, 20 HS
Cargo, 21 HS
Herbal, 22 HS
Hoxton Sq. Bar & Kitchen, 23 HS
Vibe Bar, 24 B4
ENTERTAINMENT
Comedy Cafe, 25 HS
Hackney Empire, 26 C5
Spitz, 27 A3
SHOPPING
The Beer Shop, 28 HS
Brick Lane Market, 29 B3
Hoxton Boutique, 30 HS
The Laden Showroom, 31 B4
Petticoat Lane Market, 32 A3
Spitalfields Market, 33 A3
0 450 yards
0 250 meters
TO 26 (1km)
SEE HOXTON & SHOREDITCH DETAIL
Cambridge Heath Station
Bethnal Green
Bethnal Green Station
Shoreditch
Whitechapel
Stepney Green
Liverpool St. Station
Liverpool St.
Aldgate East
Aldgate
Fenchurch St. Station
DLR: Tower Gateway
Tower Hill
Tower of London
Royal Mint
Royal London Hospital
Royal London Hospital Archives
Spitalfields Market
Lloyd's of London
London Bridge Station
Wapping
Weavers Fields
Burial Ground
Bethnal Green Park
Meath Gardens
Jewish Burial Ground
Stepney Green
Grand Union Canal
THE EAST END
WHITECHAPEL
CITY
SOUTH BANK
Hackney Rd.
Old Bethnal Green Rd.
Bethnal Green Rd.
Mile End Rd.
Whitechapel Rd.
Commercial Rd.
Commercial St.
Brick Lane
Cambridge Heath Rd.
The Highway
Wapping High St.
Wapping Lane
Cannon Street Rd.
Christian St.
St. Katharine's Way
Tooley St.
Hoxton & Shoreditch
(GRID REFERENCE = HS)
Pitfield St.
Hoxton St.
Kingsland Rd.
Hoxton Sq.
Old St.
Curtain Rd.
Charlotte Rd.
Rivington St.
Great Eastern St.
Shoreditch High St.
TO Old St. (200m) & 8 (750m)
Tabernacle St.
Leonard St.
Paul St.
Mark St.
Luke St.
Bateman's Row
New Inn Yard
A
B
C
D
1
2
3
4
5
6
7

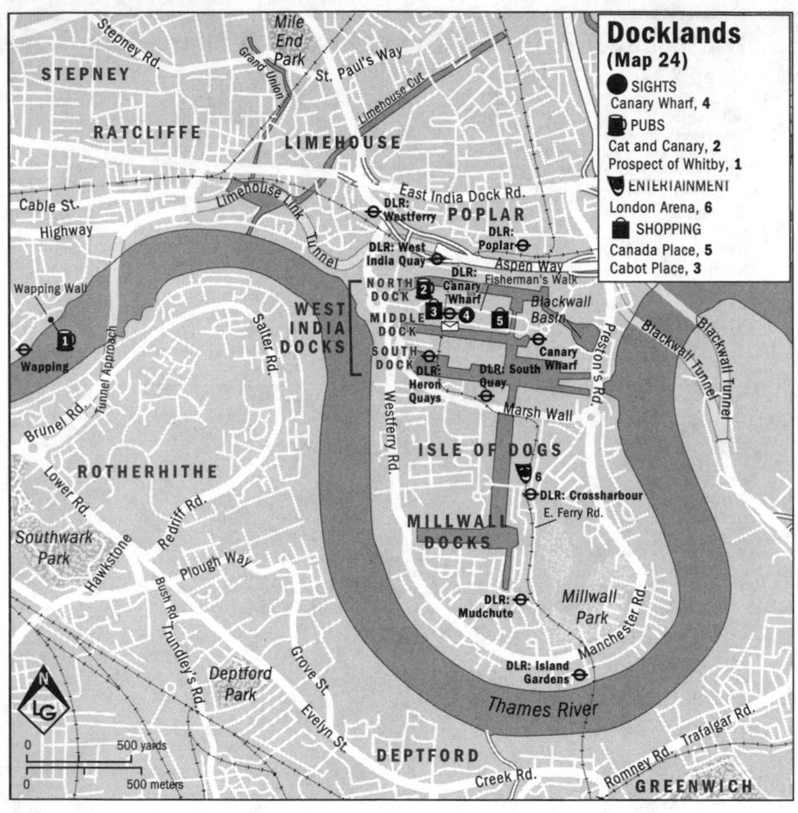
Docklands
(Map 24)
SIGHTS
Canary Wharf, 4
PUBS
Cat and Canary, 2
Prospect of Whitby, 1
ENTERTAINMENT
London Arena, 6
SHOPPING
Canada Place, 5
Cabot Place, 3
STEPNEY
Stepney Rd.
Mile End Park
Grand Union
St. Paul's Way
Limehouse Cut
RATCLIFFE
LIMEHOUSE
East India Dock Rd.
Limehouse Link Tunnel
Cable St.
Highway
DLR: Westferry
POPLAR
DLR: Poplar
DLR: West India Quay
Aspen Way
Fisherman's Walk
DLR: Canary Wharf
Wapping Wall
Wapping
NORTH DOCK
MIDDLE DOCK
SOUTH DOCK
WEST INDIA DOCKS
Blackwall Basin
Canary Wharf
Preston's Rd.
Blackwall Tunnel
Salter Rd.
Tunnel Approach
DLR: Heron Quays
DLR: South Quay
Marsh Wall
Westferry Rd.
Brunel Rd.
ISLE OF DOGS
ROTHERHITHE
Lower Rd.
DLR: Crossharbour
E. Ferry Rd.
Redriff Rd.
MILLWALL DOCKS
Southwark Park
Hawkstone
Plough Way
Bush Rd
Trundley's Rd.
DLR: Mudchute
Millwall Park
Manchester Rd.
Grove St.
Deptford Park
DLR: Island Gardens
Thames River
Evelyn St.
DEPTFORD
Creek Rd.
Romney Rd.
Trafalgar Rd.
GREENWICH
0 500 yards
0 500 meters

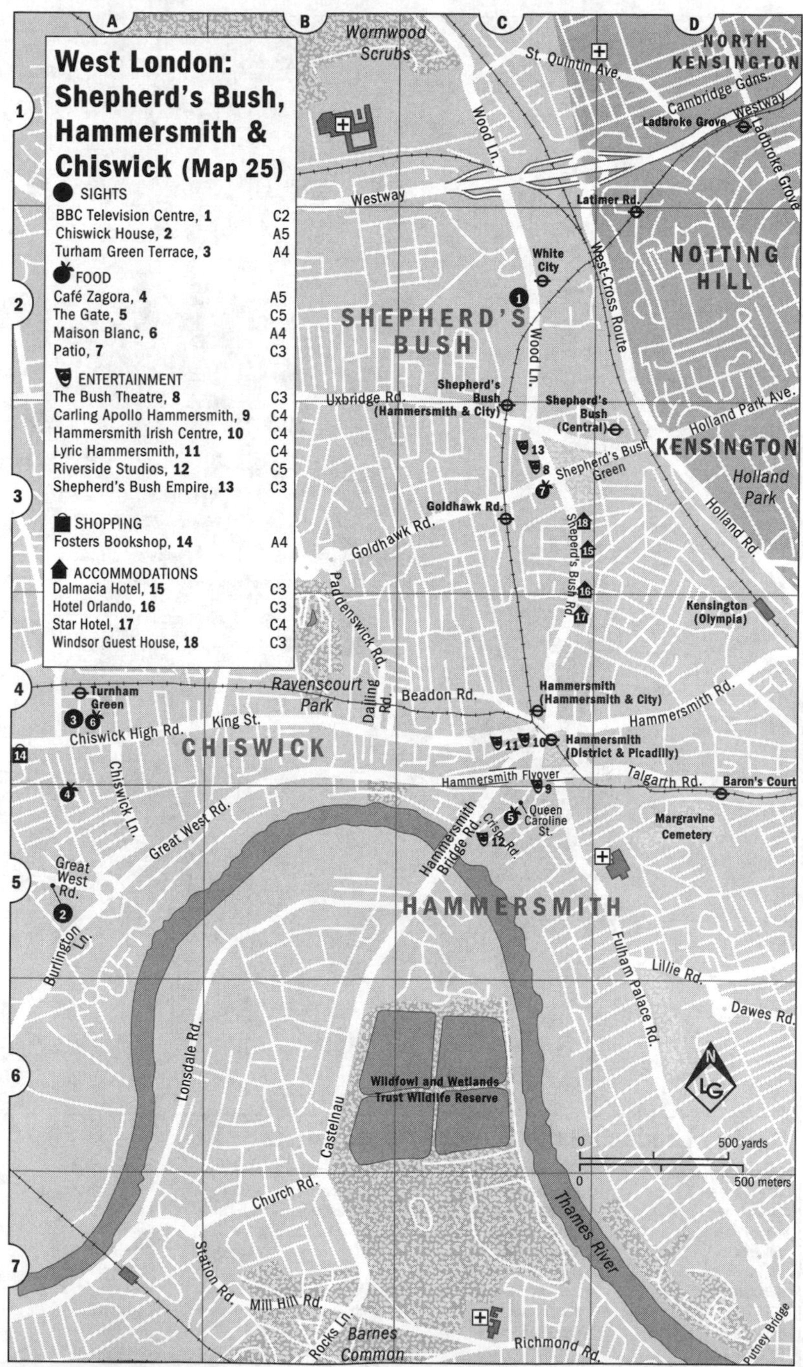
West London: Shepherd's Bush, Hammersmith & Chiswick (Map 25)
SIGHTS
BBC Television Centre, 1 C2
Chiswick House, 2 A5
Turham Green Terrace, 3 A4
FOOD
Café Zagora, 4 A5
The Gate, 5 C5
Maison Blanc, 6 A4
Patio, 7 C3
ENTERTAINMENT
The Bush Theatre, 8 C3
Carling Apollo Hammersmith, 9 C4
Hammersmith Irish Centre, 10 C4
Lyric Hammersmith, 11 C4
Riverside Studios, 12 C5
Shepherd's Bush Empire, 13 C3
SHOPPING
Fosters Bookshop, 14 A4
ACCOMMODATIONS
Dalmacia Hotel, 15 C3
Hotel Orlando, 16 C3
Star Hotel, 17 C4
Windsor Guest House, 18 C3
Wormwood Scrubs
St. Quintin Ave.
NORTH KENSINGTON
Cambridge Gdns.
Westway
Ladbroke Grove
Ladbroke Grove
Wood Ln.
Latimer Rd.
White City
NOTTING HILL
West-Cross Route
SHEPHERD'S BUSH
Wood Ln.
Uxbridge Rd.
Shepherd's Bush (Hammersmith & City)
Shepherd's Bush (Central)
Holland Park Ave.
KENSINGTON
Shepherd's Bush Green
Holland Park
Goldhawk Rd.
Goldhawk Rd.
Sheperd's Bush Rd.
Holland Rd.
Paddenswick Rd.
Kensington (Olympia)
Turnham Green
Ravenscourt Park
Dalling Rd.
Beadon Rd.
Hammersmith (Hammersmith & City)
Hammersmith Rd.
King St.
Chiswick High Rd.
CHISWICK
Hammersmith (District & Picadilly)
Hammersmith Flyover
Talgarth Rd.
Baron's Court
Chiswick Ln.
Great West Rd.
Queen Caroline St.
Hammersmith Bridge Rd.
Crisp Rd.
Margravine Cemetery
Great West Rd.
HAMMERSMITH
Burlington Ln.
Fulham Palace Rd.
Lillie Rd.
Dawes Rd.
Lonsdale Rd.
Wildfowl and Wetlands Trust Wildlife Reserve
Castelnau
0 500 yards
0 500 meters
Church Rd.
Thames River
Station Rd.
Mill Hill Rd.
Rocks Ln.
Barnes Common
Richmond Rd.
Putney Bridge
A B C D
1 2 3 4 5 6 7

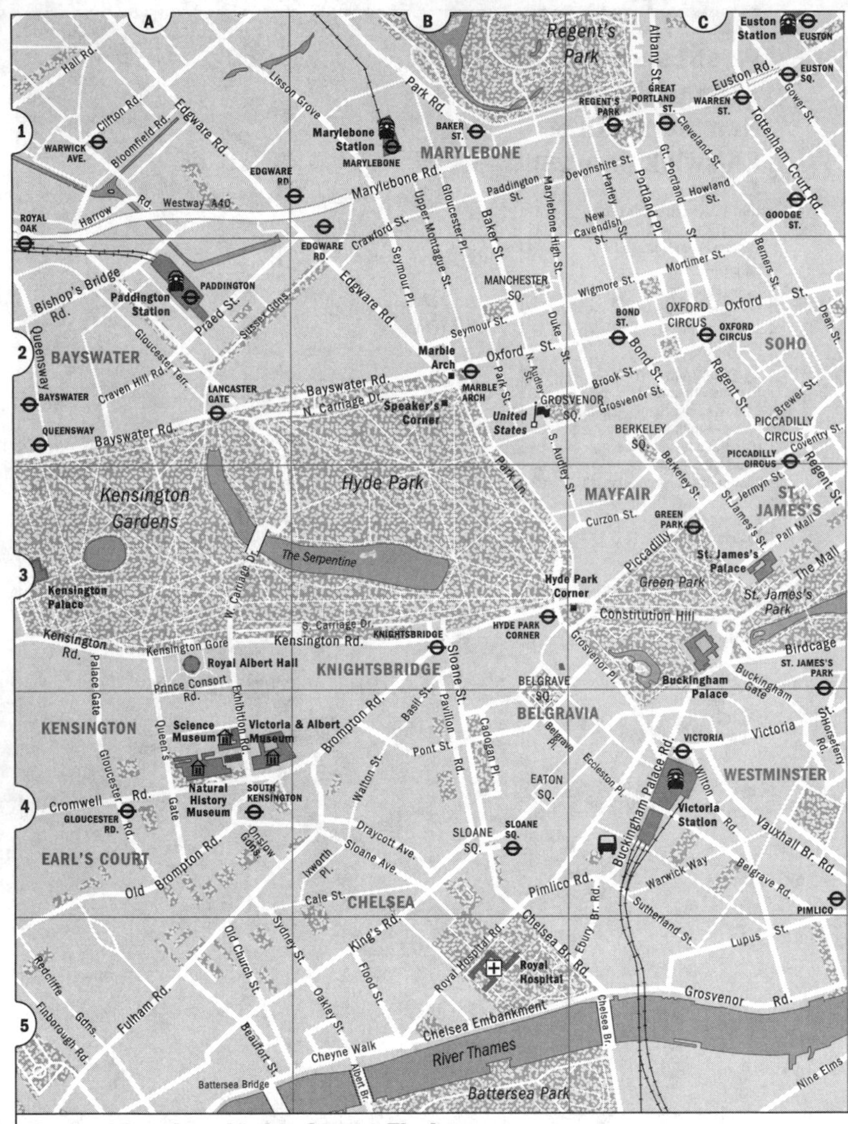

Central London: Major Street Finder (Map 26)

Albert Embankment **D4**
Aldersgate **E1**
Aldwych **D2**
Audley (N & S) **B2**
Baker St. **B1**
Bayswater Rd. **A2**
Beaufort St. **A5**
Beech St./Chiswell St. **E1**
Belgrave Pl. **B4**
Belgrave Rd. **C4**
Berkeley St. **C3**
Birdcage Walk **C3**
Bishop's Bridge Rd. **A2**
Bishopsgate **F2**
Blackfriars Rd. **E3**
Bloomsbury Way **D1**
Bond St. (New & Old) **C2**
Bow St. **D2**
Brompton Rd. **B4**
Buckingham Gate **C3**
Buckingham Palace Rd. **C4**
Cannon St. **F2**
Chancery Ln. **D2**
Charing Cross Rd. **D2**
Charterhouse St. **E1**
Cheapside **E2**
Chelsea Br. Rd. **B5**
Chelsea Embankment **B5**
Cheyne Walk **B5**
City Rd. **F1**
Clerkenwell Rd. **E1**
Constitution Hill **C3**
Cornhill **F2**
Coventry St. **C2**
Cranbourne St. **D2**
Craven Hill Rd. **A2**
Cromwell Rd. **A4**
Curzon St. **C3**
Drury Ln. **D2**
Eastcheap **F2**

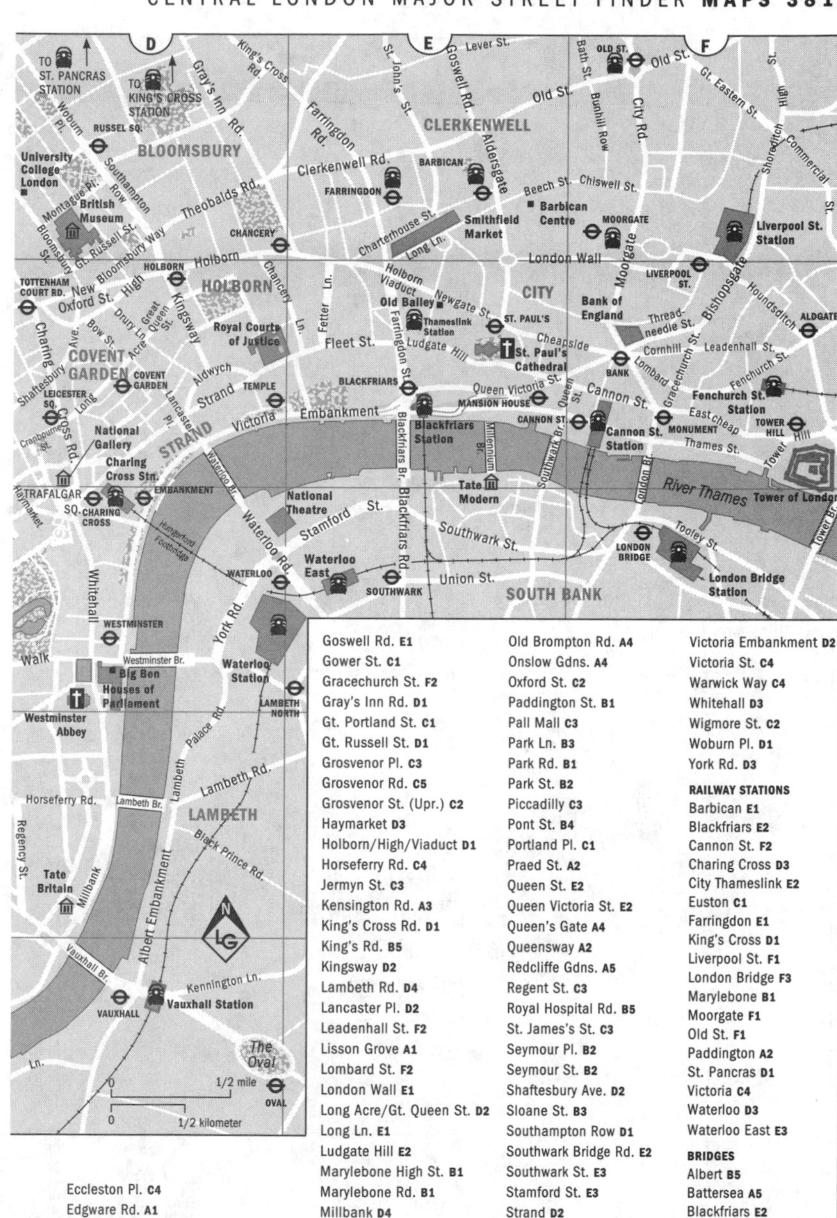

Eccleston Pl. **C4**
Edgware Rd. **A1**
Euston Rd. **C1**
Exhibition Rd. **A4**
Farringdon Rd. **E1**
Fenchurch St. **F2**
Fleet St. **E2**
Fulham Rd. **A5**
Gloucester Pl. **B1**
Gloucester Rd. **A4**
Goswell Rd. **E1**
Gower St. **C1**
Gracechurch St. **F2**
Gray's Inn Rd. **D1**
Gt. Portland St. **C1**
Gt. Russell St. **D1**
Grosvenor Pl. **C3**
Grosvenor Rd. **C5**
Grosvenor St. (Upr.) **C2**
Haymarket **D3**
Holborn/High/Viaduct **D1**
Horseferry Rd. **C4**
Jermyn St. **C3**
Kensington Rd. **A3**
King's Cross Rd. **D1**
King's Rd. **B5**
Kingsway **D2**
Lambeth Rd. **D4**
Lancaster Pl. **D2**
Leadenhall St. **F2**
Lisson Grove **A1**
Lombard St. **F2**
London Wall **E1**
Long Acre/Gt. Queen St. **D2**
Long Ln. **E1**
Ludgate Hill **E2**
Marylebone High St. **B1**
Marylebone Rd. **B1**
Millbank **D4**
Montague Pl. **D1**
Moorgate **F1**
Mortimer St. **C2**
New Cavendish St. **C1**
Newgate St. **E2**
Nine Elms Ln. **C5**
Oakley St. **B5**
Old St. **F1**
Old Brompton Rd. **A4**
Onslow Gdns. **A4**
Oxford St. **C2**
Paddington St. **B1**
Pall Mall **C3**
Park Ln. **B3**
Park Rd. **B1**
Park St. **B2**
Piccadilly **C3**
Pont St. **B4**
Portland Pl. **C1**
Praed St. **A2**
Queen St. **E2**
Queen Victoria St. **E2**
Queen's Gate **A4**
Queensway **A2**
Redcliffe Gdns. **A5**
Regent St. **C3**
Royal Hospital Rd. **B5**
St. James's St. **C3**
Seymour Pl. **B2**
Seymour St. **B2**
Shaftesbury Ave. **D2**
Sloane St. **B3**
Southampton Row **D1**
Southwark Bridge Rd. **E2**
Southwark St. **E3**
Stamford St. **E3**
Strand **D2**
Sydney St. **A5**
Thames St. **F2**
The Mall **C3**
Theobalds Rd. **D1**
Threadneedle St. **F2**
Tottenham Court Rd. **C1**
Tower Hill **F2**
Vauxhall Br. Rd. **C4**
Victoria Embankment **D2**
Victoria St. **C4**
Warwick Way **C4**
Whitehall **D3**
Wigmore St. **C2**
Woburn Pl. **D1**
York Rd. **D3**

RAILWAY STATIONS

Barbican **E1**
Blackfriars **E2**
Cannon St. **F2**
Charing Cross **D3**
City Thameslink **E2**
Euston **C1**
Farringdon **E1**
King's Cross **D1**
Liverpool St. **F1**
London Bridge **F3**
Marylebone **B1**
Moorgate **F1**
Old St. **F1**
Paddington **A2**
St. Pancras **D1**
Victoria **C4**
Waterloo **D3**
Waterloo East **E3**

BRIDGES

Albert **B5**
Battersea **A5**
Blackfriars **E2**
Chelsea **C5**
Hungerford Footbridge **D3**
Lambeth **D4**
London Bridge **F2**
Millennium **E2**
Southwark **E2**
Tower Bridge **F3**
Waterloo **D2**
Westminster **D3**

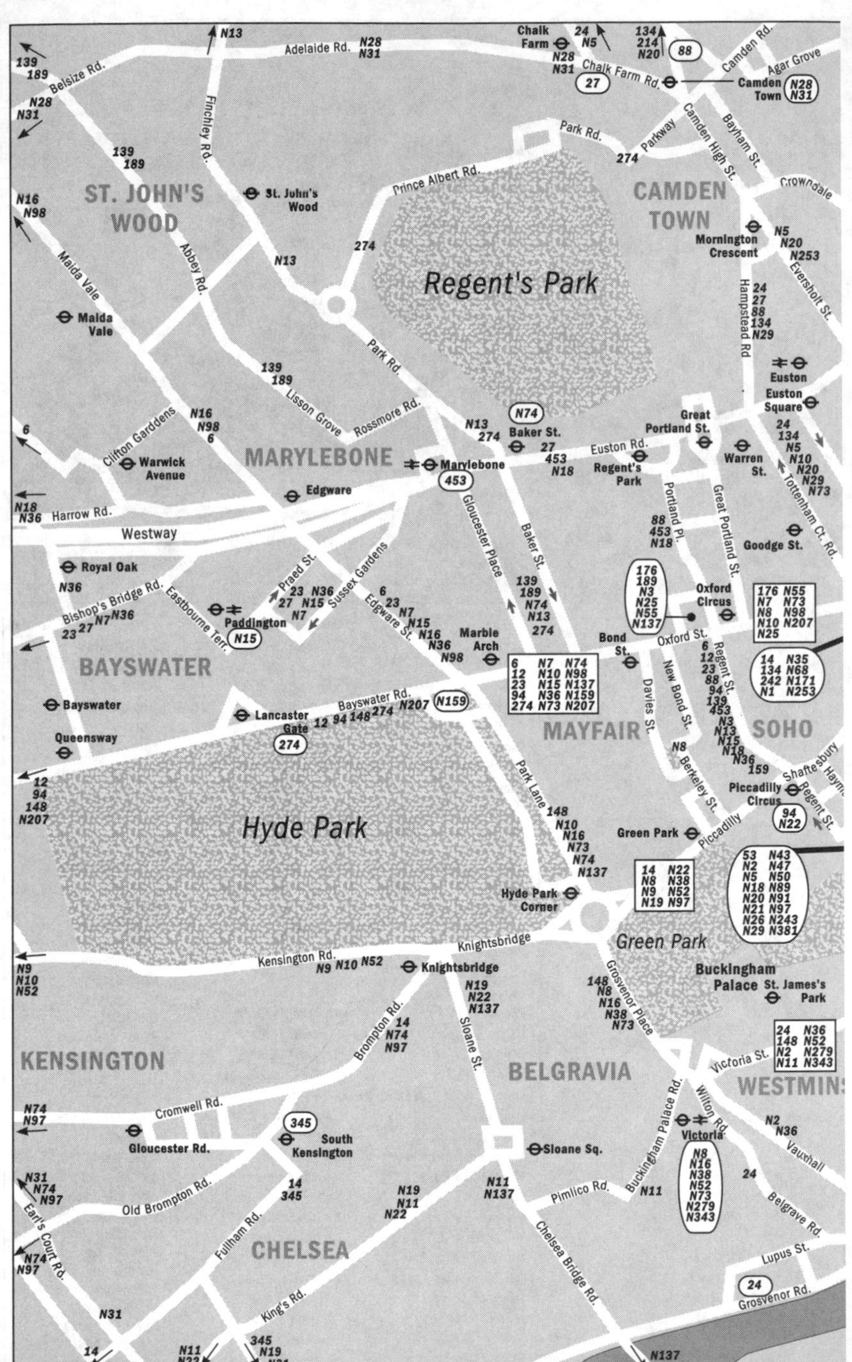

ST. JOHN'S WOOD
CAMDEN TOWN
Regent's Park
MARYLEBONE
BAYSWATER
MAYFAIR
SOHO
Hyde Park
Green Park
KENSINGTON
BELGRAVIA
WESTMINS
CHELSEA
Adelaide Rd.
Belsize Rd.
Finchley Rd.
Chalk Farm
Chalk Farm Rd.
Camden Rd.
Agar Grove
Camden Town
Park Rd.
Parkway
Camden High St.
Bayham St.
Prince Albert Rd.
Crowndale
St. John's Wood
Mornington Crescent
Abbey Rd.
Maida Vale
Hampstead Rd
Eversholt St.
Euston
Euston Square
Park Rd.
Lisson Grove
Rossmore Rd.
Great Portland St.
Baker St.
Euston Rd.
Regent's Park
Warren St.
Clifton Gardens
Warwick Avenue
Marylebone
Edgware
Harrow Rd.
Westway
Portland Pl.
Great Portland St.
Tottenham Ct. Rd.
Goodge St.
Gloucester Place
Royal Oak
Praed St.
Sussex Gardens
Bishop's Bridge Rd.
Eastbourne Terr.
Paddington
Edgware St.
Marble Arch
Oxford Circus
Oxford St.
Bond St.
Regent St.
Davies St.
New Bond St.
Bayswater
Bayswater Rd.
Lancaster Gate
Queensway
Park Lane
Berkeley St.
Piccadilly Circus
Shaftesbury
Piccadilly
Green Park
Hyde Park Corner
Knightsbridge
Kensington Rd.
Buckingham Palace
St. James's Park
Brompton Rd.
Sloane St.
Grosvenor Place
Victoria St.
Cromwell Rd.
Gloucester Rd.
South Kensington
Sloane Sq.
Buckingham Palace Rd.
Wilton Rd.
Victoria
Vauxhall
Old Brompton Rd.
Pimlico Rd.
Belgrave Rd.
Earl's Court Rd.
Fulham Rd.
Chelsea Bridge Rd.
Lupus St.
Grosvenor Rd.
King's Rd.

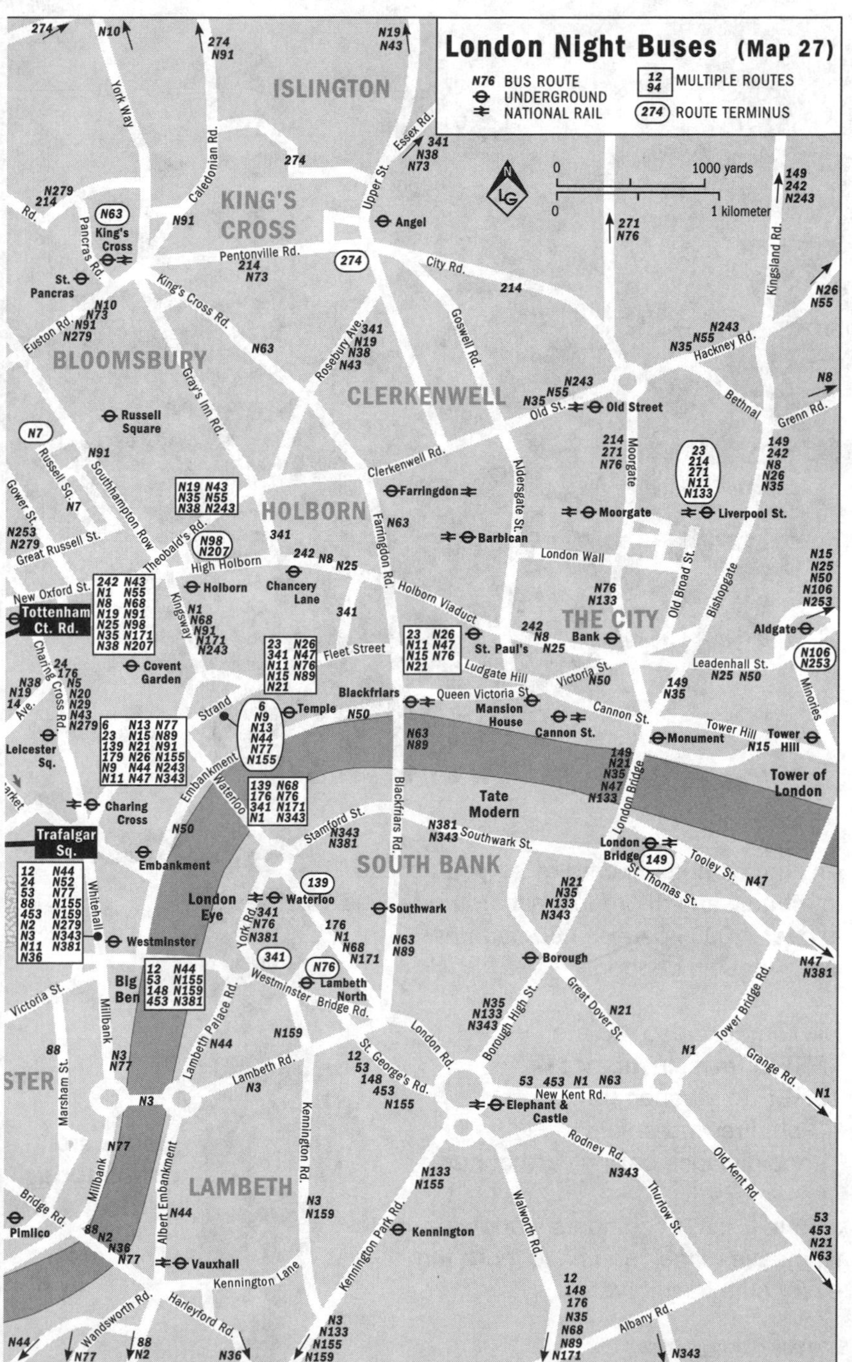
London Night Buses (Map 27)
N76 BUS ROUTE
UNDERGROUND
NATIONAL RAIL
12 94 MULTIPLE ROUTES
274 ROUTE TERMINUS
0 1000 yards
0 1 kilometer
LG
ISLINGTON
KING'S CROSS
BLOOMSBURY
CLERKENWELL
HOLBORN
THE CITY
SOUTH BANK
LAMBETH
STER
York Way
Caledonian Rd.
Essex Rd.
Upper St.
Pentonville Rd.
City Rd.
King's Cross Rd.
Pancras Rd.
Euston Rd.
Rosebury Ave.
Goswell Rd.
Gray's Inn Rd.
Old St.
Hackney Rd.
Kingsland Rd.
Bethnal Grenn Rd.
Clerkenwell Rd.
Aldersgate St.
Moorgate
Russell Sq.
Southampton Row
Gower St.
Great Russell St.
Theobald's Rd.
High Holborn
New Oxford St.
Kingsway
Farringdon Rd.
Holborn Viaduct
London Wall
Old Broad St.
Bishopsgate
Charing Cross Rd.
Fleet Street
Ludgate Hill
Victoria St.
Queen Victoria St.
Cannon St.
Leadenhall St.
Minories
Tower Hill
Strand
Embankment
Waterloo
Blackfriars Rd.
Stamford St.
Southwark St.
London Bridge
Tooley St.
St. Thomas St.
Whitehall
York Rd.
Westminster Bridge Rd.
Victoria St.
Millbank
Lambeth Palace Rd.
London Rd.
Borough High St.
Great Dover St.
Tower Bridge Rd.
Grange Rd.
St. George's Rd.
Lambeth Rd.
New Kent Rd.
Marsham St.
Kennington Rd.
Rodney Rd.
Old Kent Rd.
Thurlow St.
Albert Embankment
Kennington Park Rd.
Walworth Rd.
Bridge Rd.
Kennington Lane
Harleyford Rd.
Wandsworth Rd.
Albany Rd.
Ave.
Rd.
King's Cross
St. Pancras
Angel
Russell Square
Old Street
Farringdon
Moorgate
Liverpool St.
Barbican
Holborn
Chancery Lane
Tottenham Ct. Rd.
Covent Garden
St. Paul's
Bank
Aldgate
Blackfriars
Mansion House
Temple
Cannon St.
Monument
Tower Hill
Tower of London
Leicester Sq.
Charing Cross
Trafalgar Sq.
Embankment
Tate Modern
London Bridge
London Eye
Waterloo
Southwark
Westminster
Big Ben
Lambeth North
Borough
Elephant & Castle
Kennington
Pimlico
Vauxhall
274
N10
274 N91
N19 N43
341 N38 N73
274
149 242 N243
N279 214
N63
N91
271 N76
214 N73
274
214
N26 N55
N10 N73 N91 N279
341 N19 N38 N43
N63
N243 N55 N35
N8
N243 N55 N35
N7
214 271 N76
23 214 271 N11 N133
149 242 N8 N26 N35
N91
N19 N43 N35 N55 N38 N243
N63
N7
N253 N279
341
N98 N207
242 N8 N25
N15 N25 N50 N106 N253
242 N43 N1 N55 N8 N68 N19 N91 N25 N98 N35 N171 N38 N207
N1 N68 N91 N171 N243
341
N76 N133
242 N8 N25
23 N26 341 N47 N11 N76 N15 N89 N21
23 N26 N11 N47 N15 N76 N21
N106 N253
N25 N50
N50
149 N35
24 176 N5 N20 N29 N43 N279
N38 N19 14
6 N9 N13 N44 N77 N155
N50
6 N13 N77 23 N15 N89 139 N21 N91 179 N26 N155 N9 N44 N243 N11 N47 N343
N63 N89
N15
149 N21 N35 N47 N133
139 N68 176 N76 341 N171 N1 N343
N381 N343
N343 N381
N50
149
N47
12 N44 24 N52 53 N77 88 N155 453 N159 N2 N279 N3 N343 N11 N381 N36
139
N21 N35 N133 N343
341 N76 N381
176 N1 N68 N171
N63 N89
341
N76
N47 N381
12 N44 53 N155 148 N159 453 N381
N35 N133 N343
N21
N159
N44
88
N3 N77
12 53 148 453
N155
N1
53 453 N1 N63
N1
N3
N3
N77
N133 N155
N343
N3 N159
N44
53 453 N21 N63
88 N2 N36 N77
12 148 176 N35 N68 N89 N171
N44
N77
88 N2
N36
N3 N133 N155 N159
N343

go the
distance
with
HOSTELLING
INTERNATIONAL
An HI membership card gives you access to friendly and affordable accommodations at over 4,000 hostels in 60 countries, including 7 in London.
HI Members also recieve:
FREE Travel Insurance
FREE stay vouchers*
Global reward points*
Long distance calling card bonus
Join millions of members worldwide who save money and have more fun every time they travel.
Get your card online today!
HIUSA.ORG
*at participating hostels

CATCH YOUNG MONEY!

YOUNG MONEY is the premier lifestyle and money magazine for young adults. Each issue is packed with cutting-edge articles written by the nation's top college journalists.

Whether your goal is to save money, make more cash or get ahead in your career path, YOUNG MONEY will help you make smarter financial decisions. So subscribe now. It's one decision you will never regret.

Subscribe Online TODAY and Receive Your **FREE ISSUE**
www.youngmoney.com

LONG ON WEEKEND. SHORT ON CASH.

The fastest way to the best fare.

©2004 Orbitz, LLC.